THE NEW
BOOK OF KNOWLEDGE

B
volume
2

THE NEW
BOOK OF
KNOWLEDGE

Grolier
INCORPORATED
NEW YORK

ISBN 0-7172-0510-X
Library of Congress Catalog Card Number: 78-13814

The publishers wish to thank the following for permission to use copyrighted material:
Abington Press for excerpts from *The Bible Story for Boys and Girls, Old Testament,* and
The Bible Story for Boys and Girls, New Testament, by Walter Russell Bowie, copyrights 1952
and 1951 by Pierce & Smith.
Harold Ober Associates Incorporated, Pearl S. Buck, and Messrs. Methuen & Co. Ltd. for excerpt
from *The Big Wave* by Pearl S. Buck, copyright © 1947 by the Curtis Publishing Company, © 1948
by Pearl S. Buck.

Bb *Bb*

B, the second letter of the English alphabet, was also the second letter of the Phoenician, Hebrew, and Greek alphabets. The Phoenicians and Hebrews called it *beth*. The Greeks called it *beta*.

Many scholars believe that the Phoenician letters were pictures of objects. *Beth,* they say, was probably a simple picture of a house. It looked like this:

The Greeks borrowed this basic form for their *beta,* but they made a double-looped version. Since the Greeks wrote from left to right instead of from right to left like the Phoenicians, the *beta* was also reversed. By the 5th century B.C. it looked like this:

In adapting the Greek alphabet, the Romans kept the form of the *beta,* but changed its name to "be"—the name it still has today in most European alphabets.

In Roman times the writing material called parchment became popular. It was made from the stretched skin of a sheep or goat, and the Romans wrote on it with pen and ink. The writing could be applied smoothly, curves were easy to make, and the letters became smaller and often simpler. One way of writing the B was to start at the top, continue downward, then add the curves on the way up. Sometimes the top curve was omitted, and that gave us the small letter *b*.

We still find the *beta* in names of college fraternities such as Beta Theta Pi, and honorary societies such as Phi Beta Kappa.

B is the first consonant in the alphabet, just as A is the first vowel. The consonant, or closed sound, and the vowel, or open sound, are the two main kinds of sound. A closed sound is made when the teeth, tongue, or lips partly or completely block the air on its way out of the mouth.

The English B stands for many things. It has even been used in punishment. In Europe during the Middle Ages, and in the United States at the time of the Puritans, anyone who spoke against God was called a blasphemer. Sometimes a B was branded on the foreheads of the guilty ones as a sign of their sinfulness.

In chemistry B stands for the element boron. In a list of things, it labels the second item. In music B is the name of a note as well as an abbreviation for bass, the lowest part in a musical composition.

B occurs in abbreviations. The college degree bachelor of arts is shortened to B.A. When used in dates, B.C. means "before Christ," as in "48 B.C." The British Broadcasting Corporation is called the B.B.C. Some B abbreviations employ the small *b*. "Born," for instance, is indicated before dates by a small *b,* as in "Queen Elizabeth I, b. 1533."

Reviewed by MARIO PEI
Formerly, Columbia University

See also ALPHABET.

BABYLONIA. See ANCIENT CIVILIZATIONS.

BABY

A baby cat is called a kitten, and a baby dog is called a puppy. A human baby is often referred to as an infant. All of these babies are mammals.

Mammals are animals whose young, or offspring, are born alive after a period of development inside the mother. (Only two primitive types lay eggs.) After birth the offspring depend on their mothers' milk for survival. Mammals may be very large, like the elephant, or very small, like the mouse.

▶ **BEFORE THE BABY IS BORN**

By the time the human mammal, or baby, enters the world, it has undergone a complicated process of growth and development. This process begins when the **ovum**, or egg, of the mother unites with the **sperm**, or seed, of the father. For the next 9 months the fertilized egg grows inside the mother's uterus, or womb. In about 3 weeks various organs begin to form. The tiny fertilized egg is then known as an **embryo**. The embryo continues to develop. Later, it is called a **fetus**. When the fetus is 3 months old, it is about 8 centimeters (3 inches) long. By 4 months, it is about twice this length.

When the fetus is 4 or 5 months old, the mother may become aware of little movements within her body. These movements bring her great joy, for she knows she has begun to "feel life." At about the same time, the doctor may be able to hear a heartbeat by listening with a stethoscope through the mother's abdomen.

From these first slight movements, the mother and the doctor know that the fetus is developing and moving around in the bag, or sac, of fluid that surrounds and protects it. Inside the sac, the fetus is attached at the belly (abdomen) to the **placenta** by a cord containing blood vessels. The placenta is a pancake-shaped organ through which the mother's blood flows to give nourishment to the fetus until it is ready to be born.

If the fetus is born too soon, or prematurely, it may be difficult for it to survive. If it has not lived in the uterus for at least 7 months, the chances of survival are very poor indeed. After 8 months the risk is less. More than 90 percent of all babies are born at full term. This means that they have spent 9 months in the uterus of the mother and are now ready to come into the world.

▶ **AFTER THE BABY IS BORN**

At last the baby is born. If it is an average baby, its weight is around 3 to 3.5 kilograms (7 or 8 pounds). Boy babies usually weigh more than girl babies.

For many months, the baby's parents have been wondering what their infant would be like. Would it be a boy or a girl? What color hair and eyes would it have?

Hair and eye color are determined long before the baby's birth. The father's sperm and the mother's egg contain the ingredients that control these traits and many others. The sex of the baby is determined by ingredients in the father's sperm.

Most human mothers give birth to a single baby. In about 1 out of every 80 births twins are born. Some twins are **identical**. This means that they have developed from a single fertilized egg. Other twins are **fraternal**, which means that two eggs may have been fertilized at the same time. Identical twins are usually very much alike. Fraternal twins may be quite different from one another. Triplets are born about once in 6,400 births, quadruplets about once in 500,000. Quintuplets, five babies born at one time, are very rare indeed.

The healthy baby's first action after birth is to utter a sharp cry. With a good loud cry the baby's lungs expand and adapt to the outside world. The lungs enable the baby to breathe the air that now surrounds it. The cry also tells the doctor and the new mother that the baby is off to a good start.

Healthy newborns have a strong instinct to suck. For the first months of life, sucking enables babies to get the nourishment necessary for their growth.

During the 9 months of pregnancy, the mother's breasts have been getting ready to manufacture milk. If for some reason the mother cannot feed the baby with her own milk, the doctor will prescribe a mixture called a "formula." The formula is usually made of cow's milk mixed with a form of sugar and water. It is put into a bottle that has a nipple made to resemble the nipple of the mother's breast. When the baby's mouth is put to the nipple of the breast, or to the nipple of the bottle, the strong sucking instinct makes it possible for the infant to suck and swallow this first important food.

▶ CARE OF THE BABY

The newborn period in a baby's life is the first month after birth. This is a period of great change not only for the baby, but also for the rest of the family who have awaited the arrival for 9 months.

Newborn babies can do some things by themselves. They can breathe, cry, sleep, and move their arms and legs. They can suck and swallow food, and their bodies can take care of eliminating waste products. But since babies cannot control even these simple actions, they are completely dependent on others for their care.

Little babies must be carefully guarded against illness. People with colds or other infections should not handle the baby or get close to it, especially if the baby is premature or delicate. If the baby is bottle-fed, the formula must be carefully prepared. The bottle and nipple must be sterilized (made free of germs) according to the instructions of the doctor.

After the first few months the doctor will examine the baby and discuss its progress with the parents. The doctor will probably advise the parents to add vitamins and some foods such as cereal, fruits, and vegetables to the baby's diet. The doctor will also give the baby "shots," or vaccines. These will protect the baby from certain diseases, such as diphtheria, whooping cough, and polio.

Although babies vary a great deal, there is a general timetable for their growth and development, especially during the first year.

Very young babies sleep most of the time. When they are awake they are usually eating or crying. Their hearing is good, and they will react to loud noises. At birth babies' eyes do not focus well. But in about 2 weeks the eyes will follow light and fix on an object. At about the age of 2 months, much to the delight of their families, babies begin to smile.

Three- or four-month-old babies can hold their heads up. But babies cannot sit up alone until they are about 8 or 9 months old. Most learn to stand up at about 9 months. By this time babies are quite good at crawling around and exploring their world. At about the time of its first birthday, the baby can usually take a few steps.

When do babies learn to talk? Well, if you listen carefully, you'll notice that they begin to make sounds when they are still very young. We call these sounds "baby talk." Unfortunately, we don't understand baby talk very well, but we enjoy listening to it and talking back to the baby. Speech experts say that babies learn to speak by copying the sounds made by older people.

When babies are born they seem to have no teeth. But even at birth a baby's teeth are under the gums in the form of tooth buds. As the baby grows, the teeth begin to show through the gums. Most babies have a few teeth by the time they are 1 year old.

▶ ARE YOU A SIBLING?

Brothers and sisters in a family are called **siblings**. Siblings have an important role to play when a new baby arrives, just as parents do.

Parents sometimes worry that older siblings might be jealous of a new baby. Older children often feel that some of their parents' love and attention will have to be shared. Usually, however, siblings also welcome the arrival of a baby. They are proud of the newcomer and quickly discover the excitement of watching an infant grow.

Children who have the opportunity to live with a baby in the family gain valuable experience. If they are old enough, their parents will let them help take care of the new baby. They will learn to help feed the baby, change the diapers, and take the younger child for a walk in the carriage. All of this experience will help siblings to become good baby-sitters when they are old enough. It will also help them become good parents when they are adults.

In a family where love, tenderness, and respect for each member are important, babies and older siblings will thrive. Although no one really remembers what it was like to be a baby, what happened to all of us in our early years may have a great effect on us as we grow up.

JEAN PAKTER, M.D., M.P.H.
Director, Bureau of Maternity Services
and Family Planning
New York City Department of Health

BACH, JOHANN SEBASTIAN (1685–1750)

Johann Sebastian Bach was born on March 21, 1685, in Eisenach, Germany. He was the greatest member of a renowned musical family of more than 50 musicians who lived in central Germany between 1500 and the 1800's.

At the age of 10, Bach was left an orphan

Johann Sebastian Bach wrote several of his compositions for the purpose of teaching music to his large family.

and went to live with his older brother, who was a church organist at Ohrdruf. When he was 15, Bach went to Lüneburg, where a scholarship allowed him to continue his studies. There he sang in the choir and learned much of the best music of the time. He also studied with the great organist Georg Böhm (1661–1733).

In 1703 Bach became church organist at Arnstadt and immediately began to compose for the organ, the harpsichord, and voices. He went to Mühlhausen in 1707, and while he was an organist in that city he married his cousin, Maria Barbara Bach. The following year they moved to Weimar, where Bach remained in the service of the Duke of Weimar for 10 years.

Most of Bach's music at Weimar was composed for the organ and church choirs. When Bach wanted to change jobs again, the Duke put him in jail to try to make him stay. But Bach was determined to leave and journeyed to Cöthen, where he entered the service of Prince Leopold of Anhalt. During his 6 years at Cöthen, Bach composed many of his best-known instrumental works, such as the *Brandenburg* concertos, the English and the French suites for harpsichord, and much chamber music.

Bach's wife died in 1720. The following year he married Anna Magdalena Wilcken. Bach became the father of 20 children, and several of his talented sons became well-known composers.

Bach changed jobs for the last time in 1723 and became director of music at St. Thomas's Church and School in Leipzig. Though he was not happy with the post, he remained there for 27 years, until his death. Most of Bach's greatest religious works were composed during these years, including the *Magnificat,* the *St. John* Passion, the *St. Matthew* Passion, the B-minor Mass, and many cantatas. In Leipzig Bach also completed *The Well-Tempered Clavier,* a collection of 48 preludes and fugues in all the keys. Like most of Bach's music, it was not published until long after his death. Bach was well known as an organist, but during

his lifetime he never became a celebrated composer like his contemporary Handel.

In 1747 Bach journeyed to Potsdam to visit his son Karl Philipp Emanuel, who was a musician at the court of King Frederick II of Prussia. The King admired Bach and wanted to hear him play. To the King's delight Bach improvised on a melody that the King had given him. When Bach returned to Leipzig, he repaid the royal friendship by composing the *Musical Offering* based on the King's theme and dedicating it to the King.

Bach then turned to his last great work, *The Art of Fugue,* which remained unfinished at his death. It is the fruit of Bach's deep and lifelong study of counterpoint. As Bach grew older his eyesight became increasingly poor, until toward the end of his life, he was totally blind. He died on July 28, 1750. But it was not until almost 100 years later that the world recognized Bach as one of its greatest composers.

Reviewed by KARL GEIRINGER
Author, *The Bach Family*

BACKGAMMON

Backgammon is a game of luck and skill played with dice and checkers on a special board. It was probably introduced into Europe by the Crusaders. In the eastern Mediterranean area, it is still played with such enthusiasm that few other Europeans or Americans can match the skill of the better players there.

Each player has a set of 15 checkers. One set is dark and the other is light in color, or they can be of any two different colors. Each player also has two dice and a cup in which to shake them.

▶ **THE BOARD**

The backgammon board is a rectangle. It is divided into two halves by a bar that cuts across the board in a north-south direction. The player who sits to the south of the board has on his left-hand side the half called the **inner**, or **home**, **table**. The half on his right-hand side is called the **outer table**. Thus each player has his own inner and outer tables facing his opponent's inner and outer tables.

Going from the north and south edges of the board toward the center are two rows of triangular marks called **points**. There are twelve points on the north and twelve on the south side of the board. Each player has six on his inner and six on his outer table.

On some backgammon sets the points are numbered. From the south side of the board the points on both sides are numbered from 1 through 12, going from left to right. If the board is not numbered, the players have to keep the numbers of the points in their minds or pencil them in lightly on the board. Pencil markings help until the moves are learned.

▶ **PROCEDURE**

At the start of the game, the checkers are arranged as shown. The object is for each player to move all his checkers to his own inner table by advancing them according to the numbers he rolls on his dice and then to bear them off, or remove them, from his inner table. The checkers are advanced from the opponent's inner table around the board

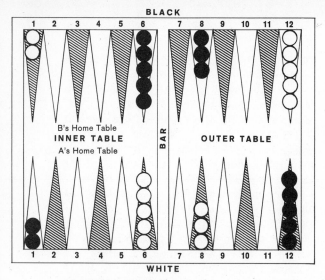

BLACK

1 2 3 4 5 6 | 7 8 9 10 11 12

B's Home Table
INNER TABLE
A's Home Table

BAR

OUTER TABLE

1 2 3 4 5 6 | 7 8 9 10 11 12

WHITE

The backgammon board.

by way of the two outer tables, until each player has all his checkers in his inner table.

To begin a game, each player rolls one die. The higher number plays first. If equal numbers are thrown, both players must roll again. The first player uses the numbers on the two dice for his first move. After this the players take turns rolling their dice and moving their checkers. The players shake the dice out of a cup onto the backgammon board. If a player throws a 3 and a 2, he moves his checkers three points and then two points, always in the direction of his own inner table. If he throws doubles (both dice the same), he may move twice as many times as shown on the faces of the dice. For example, a roll of 6-6 counts as four sixes instead of just two sixes. This makes a total of 24 instead of 12.

The numbers on the dice tell exactly how many points a player must advance his checkers. He can move one or two checkers on one roll of the dice. If he rolls a 2 and a 4, for example, he can move one checker two points and another four. If he throws doubles, each die is counted twice and he can move as many as four checkers.

▶ **MOVES**

A point (one of the triangular shapes on the board) is considered "open" when it is not occupied by two or more checkers of the same color. This means that a player may land on a point on which there is only one of his opponent's checkers. In this case he (A) has **hit** the opponent's (B's) checker, which

is put on the bar. B must return it to play, in A's home table, before playing any other checker. He returns it by throwing the dice and getting an open number. If two or more checkers of one color are on a point, that point is "closed." No checkers of the other color may stop, or land, on that point.

Each roll of the dice is thought of as two numbers rather than as a single total. If a player throws a 3 and a 5, for example, he might decide to advance three points and then five with a single checker. But if he advances three points and finds the last point closed, he may not even touch upon it before advancing his remaining five points. To get around this problem he will advance his checker five points first. If he finds that this point is free, he can then advance the checker the other three points. Sometimes all the points are closed. Then the player cannot move that particular checker at all. Checkers may skip over a closed point as long as they have open landing places.

A player may begin to bear his checkers off when they all lie in his own inner table. If one of his checkers is hit during the bearing off, it must be placed on the bar and moved around the board to its home table before bearing off can be started again. (A player need not bear off, but can move his checkers down to the points from which the bearing off is quicker.)

A checker is borne off a point that matches the number rolled on one die. For example, on a 4-2 roll, a checker may be removed from the 4 point and another from the 2 point. When a number on one die is higher than the highest point on which a player has checkers, the player takes the checker off his highest occupied point. That is, if the player throws a 5, and the 5 point is empty but there is a checker on the 4 point, the player bears off the checker from the 4 point. It is not permitted to bear off a checker from a point higher than the number on the die.

The player to bear off all his checkers first wins the game. If the loser has not borne off a single checker, he is **gammoned** and loses a double game. If he has a checker on the bar or in the opponent's home table, he is **backgammoned** and loses a triple game.

CHARLES H. GOREN
Author, *Goren's Hoyle*

BACON, FRANCIS (1561–1626)

Francis Bacon, English philosopher and essayist, was born in London on January 22, 1561. Both his parents were prominent in the intellectual world of Elizabethan England. His mother, daughter of Sir Anthony Cooke, Edward VI's tutor, was an extraordinarily learned woman and very religious. His father, Lord Keeper of the Great Seal, was a highly respected jurist and counselor to the Queen. He used to take Francis to court with him, and the boy soon became a favorite of Queen Elizabeth's. She was delighted with his wisdom in answering her questions.

Francis entered Cambridge University when he was 12. He finished his studies there in 2 years and began to study law at Gray's Inn. His father, however, wanted Francis to go into politics and a year later sent him to Paris with the British ambassador to France. His father died suddenly while Francis was still in Paris. Francis was forced to return to London to resume his law studies. He was admitted to the bar in 1582 when he was 21. In 1584 he was elected to Parliament, where he served until 1617. Then he took over his father's old office as Lord Keeper.

In 1621 Bacon was charged with accepting gifts from persons whose cases were waiting to be tried in the courts. Since the giving and receiving of gifts was common practice at that time, it was obvious that Bacon's political enemies were using the charge in order to rid the kingdom of his influence. Bacon insisted he had never let any gifts affect his judgment. Nevertheless, he was convicted, fined a large amount of money, and imprisoned in the Tower of London. After a few days he was released from the tower and the King remitted his fine.

Bacon devoted the rest of his life to philosophical writings and scientific experiments. An experiment in refrigeration led to his death. One day when there was snow on the ground, it occurred to Bacon that food could be preserved in snow as well as in salt. He went into a poor woman's house, bought a hen, and helped the woman to clean it out and stuff it with snow. Working in the snow, he caught cold. Bronchitis set in and he died a short time later, on April 9, 1626.

BACON, ROGER (1214?–1294?)

Roger Bacon, the 13th-century scientist, is a strange and shadowy figure. He is known for many discoveries—most of which he did not make. As for the discoveries he did make, most of them have since been proved worthless. In addition, almost nothing is known for certain about his life. (Scholars disagree about most of the facts in this article.) Even so, Bacon is a major figure in the history of science because of his insistence on the need for experiment.

So far as we know, Bacon was born about 1214, the son of a well-to-do family in Ilchester, England. It seems that he entered Oxford University at the age of 13—a common entrance age in those days. Around the year 1245 Bacon was teaching at the University of Paris.

The Europe of Bacon's day was having a revival of learning, based on the discovery of great written works from ancient Greece and Rome. Most scholars simply accepted and taught this knowledge from the ancient world. It seemed to them to be all that any man could know. Bacon, too, taught this knowledge. However, he also did something that most great men of his time failed to do. He learned from living men and from the world around him.

Bacon spent years studying how the eye works. He conducted his own experiments. He sprayed mouthfuls of water into the air to study the nature of rainbows. He tested superstitions of his day—would a diamond dissolve in goat's blood?—by performing experiments with the actual materials. His results no longer matter. What does matter is that Bacon dared to question the accepted beliefs of his day.

About 1250 Bacon returned to England, entered the Franciscan order of monks, and began to teach science at Oxford. In addition to the usual lectures, he gave simple demonstrations. These made his superiors angry.

They opposed anything that might cast doubt on the ideas of the ancients. In 1257 the Franciscans sent Bacon back to Paris. He was told to write and teach only what they approved.

However, Bacon was never one to keep his opinions to himself. He obtained a commission from Pope Clement IV to write a report on the importance of science. Then he proceeded to write not one, but three books. Their contents are of no value today. Their importance lies in Bacon's emphasis on the need to observe, test, and measure.

Then in 1278 Bacon was thrown into a prison for heretics—perhaps because of his scientific teachings, perhaps because of his religious views. He was not freed until 1290, when he started writing an encyclopedic work. He was a weakened old man, however, and he died, probably in 1294.

In his lifetime Bacon made many enemies.

He was quarrelsome and bad-tempered, and his ideas upset scholars. In time he became bitter, since no one took his scientific investigations seriously. Instead he was accused of being a magician. Later, people even said that he had been in league with the devil.

In the centuries that followed, Bacon the man became lost in myth. He turned up in plays and poems, where fiction was mixed with fact. Many inventions were wrongly credited to him—everything from spectacles to submarines. (One of the few things he does seem to have discovered on his own was an early form of gunpowder.) More recently students of science have begun to see Bacon in a new light and to call him the father of modern science. If he deserves this title, it is because he was perhaps the first man to recognize the need for experiments in science.

JOHN S. BOWMAN
Author and Science Editor

BACON'S REBELLION

In 1676 a group of Virginia farmers revolted against their government. This important event in American history was one of the earliest protests against English rule in the colonies. History calls this event Bacon's Rebellion because Nathaniel Bacon, a young planter, led the farmers' revolt.

In the 17th century Virginia was a colony made up of large tobacco plantations and small frontier farms. Life on the Virginia frontier was rugged, and most farmers were very poor.

In addition, the frontier farmers were treated unfairly by the English colonial government. The Governor, Sir William Berkeley, used his power to help the plantation owners, who were his friends, rather than the frontier farmers. Taxes were high, but the government did not use the tax money to benefit the majority of the people. Worst of all, Governor Berkeley did not protect the frontiersmen from attacks by the Susquehannock Indians and other neighboring warlike tribes.

Time after time the farmers begged Berkeley to send soldiers to fight the Indians. But the Governor did nothing. The farmers were terrified and very angry when in January,

1676, an Indian raiding party killed 36 frontiersmen. This time the frontiersmen demanded action. They felt that their lives were in danger. Since the government refused to help them, the farmers took matters into their own hands and turned to Nathaniel Bacon for leadership.

▶ NATHANIEL BACON (1647–76)

Bacon was born in England and came to Virginia in 1674. For a time he was a member of the Governor's council, but he was always sympathetic to the small farmers. He thought the Virginia government was unfair to them.

His chance came after the Indian raid. The frontiersmen decided to organize their own army and asked Bacon to lead them. He was a good leader, and his little force quickly defeated the Indians.

Governor Berkeley was furious. The frontiersmen had defied him. Berkeley called Bacon a rebel and refused to let Bacon's army fight again. But the angry frontiersmen came to Bacon's support.

What started out as self-defense turned into rebellion against the English governor.

Indians attack a pioneer family in the frontier country of western Virginia. Settlers in this vast wilderness had little defense if they were outnumbered.

The spirit of revolt spread quickly. In order to calm the angry citizens, Berkeley decided to hold a new election for representatives to the colonial assembly. This was the first such election in 15 years. Bacon himself was elected to the assembly, and as a result several new laws known as "Bacon's laws" were passed. These laws abolished many of the governor's privileges and gave every free man the right to vote.

Unfortunately Bacon died of a fever at the height of the rebellion. After his death the revolt collapsed. But the farmers had made their point. In time the government of Virginia provided protection against the Indians.

Bacon's Rebellion is an early example of the struggle for freedom in the colonies. The spirit that sparked Bacon's Rebellion in 1676 was the same spirit that started the American Revolution a century later.

BACTERIA

Bacteria are probably the most common form of life on earth. They are also among the simplest and smallest living things. They are micro-organisms, which mean they can be seen only under a microscope.

Some bacteria cause disease, but most do not. There are at least 2,000 species of bacteria. Most of them are harmless or helpful to other forms of life, including people.

How big are bacteria?

A bacterium consists of only one cell. ("Bacterium" is the singular of "bacteria.") The largest bacterium is about 200 times bigger than the smallest. A single drop of sour milk may contain 100,000,000 bacteria. A thousand of even the largest bacteria can sit side by side on the tip of a pencil.

Where do bacteria live?

Bacteria are everywhere. Some live in the mouths, noses, and intestines of animals and of people. Others live on fallen leaves or animal wastes; in water, milk, and most foods; and on dust and soil. Some bacteria can use hydrogen gas, ammonia, and iron compounds as their food. A few bacteria feed on gases and acids that are poisonous to us.

Most bacteria are killed by heat, yet there are a few kinds that live in hot springs. Freezing does not usually kill bacteria, but it checks their growth. Some kinds of bacteria resist drying, strong chemicals, or extreme temperatures by changing into tough-walled spores. The bacteria may last a very long time in this resting form. Under favorable conditions, the spore walls burst, and the bacteria become active again.

Are bacteria plants or animals?

Simple organisms like bacteria have some features of both plants and animals. Scientists have never entirely agreed on how to classify bacteria. Bacteria lack chlorophyll, the green

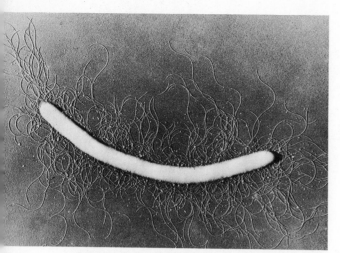

A long, rod-shaped bacterium with many little whiplike hairs, or flagella. It uses the hairs to swim about.

coloring matter that most plants need to make their own food. In their use of outside sources of food, bacteria seem like animals. But in their sizes, shapes, and general living habits most bacteria resemble lower plants such as fungi and algae. Many scientists classify bacteria and other micro-organisms that have characteristics of both plants and animals as protists, or "first things."

How do bacteria reproduce themselves?

Most bacteria reproduce themselves by fission—that is, the cell of a bacterium divides in two. Depending on the kind of bacterium, division may take place every 15 to 40 minutes. In theory this means that bacteria could multiply by the millions or billions within a few hours. But in actual practice there is not enough food or moisture in any one place to support such numbers. Competition for food keeps the bacteria population down; outside agents also kill many.

What shape are bacteria?

Bacteria have three basic shapes, which take their names from Latin words. A rod-shaped one is called a bacillus, meaning "little rod." The ball-shaped kind is the coccus, meaning "berry." And the one shaped like a corkscrew is the spirillum, meaning "spiral."

How are bacteria studied?

Because there are only three basic shapes, many different kinds of bacteria look alike. To tell one kind of bacteria from another, scientists study what each kind eats, where it lives, and what its special habits are. They observe the chemical changes produced by various bacteria.

For study, scientists grow bacteria in laboratories. They start with a mixture of many different bacteria from a source like spoiled food or the soil. The mixture is put into a flat glass dish—known as a petri dish—containing dissolved gelatin. The bacteria spread throughout the gelatin. When the gelatin cools and becomes solid, each bacterium is fixed in its own spot.

The bacteria feed on the gelatin and divide. Before long, colonies form, each con-

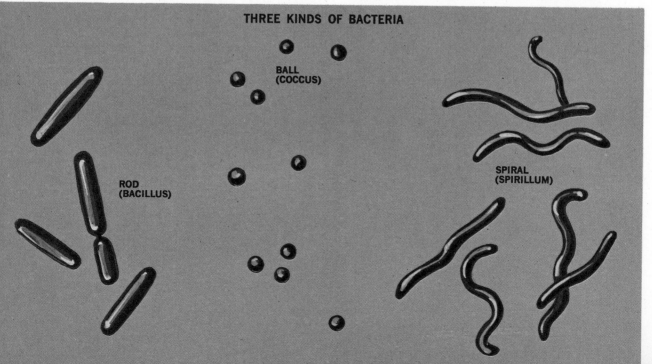

THREE KINDS OF BACTERIA

BALL (COCCUS)

ROD (BACILLUS)

SPIRAL (SPIRILLUM)

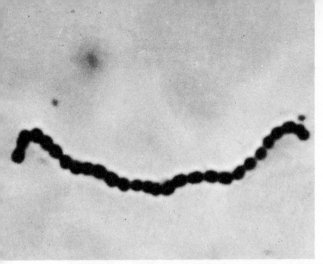

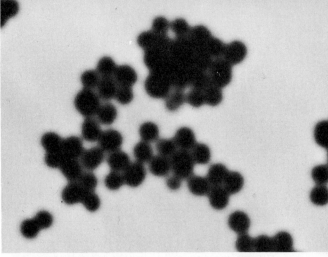

Some of the coccus bacteria look like curved chains. They are called streptococcus bacteria (*streptos* is the Greek word for "curved") and can cause many diseases, such as scarlet fever and "strep" throat.

Some of the coccus bacteria look like bunches of grapes. Called staphylococcus bacteria (*staphyle* is the Greek word for "bunch of grapes"), they cause skin infections and food poisoning.

sisting of only one kind of bacteria. Colonies can be seen to vary in shape, color, odor, and texture; such characteristics help in identifying the different kinds of bacteria.

The tip of a wire is then dipped into a particular colony. Thousands of one kind of bacteria are picked up and transferred into tubes. Each tube contains a different bacterial food, such as milk or the watery part of the blood. When one kind of bacteria grows on a particular food, scientists have what they call a pure culture. Experiments with pure cultures teach scientists about the bacteria.

Do bacteria need oxygen?

Like all living things bacteria need oxygen to burn up food materials for energy. (Bac-

Photo of bacteria colonies, each containing hundreds of thousands of bacteria.

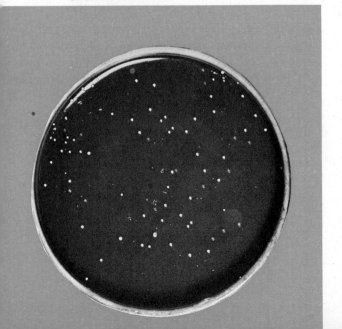

teria eat anywhere from 2 to 1,000 times their own weight in an hour.)

Most bacteria take oxygen from the air, but some get oxygen by breaking down chemical compounds in their food. For example, bacteria that ferment milk get oxygen from milk sugar. Some kinds cannot live in the presence of oxygen. These bacteria are called strict **anaerobes**, meaning "without air."

How are bacteria harmful to us?

Certain bacteria cause disease in people and animals. Some of the common human diseases caused by bacteria are cholera, diphtheria, pneumonia, tetanus, and tuberculosis.

Other bacteria produce disease in growing plants. Black rot in cabbage and fire blight in pears are caused by bacteria.

Food is spoiled by still other bacteria, such as those that cause meat to rot. Some bacteria damage food in unseen ways. For example, botulism, a dangerous disease, is caused by a poison-producing anaerobe in improperly canned foods. Another bacterium, Salmonella, found in contaminated meat and eggs, causes a severe digestive disease.

How are bacteria useful to people?

Most bacteria are useful. Some are necessary to life; others have been put to work.

Bacteria in the cycle of life. Bacteria cause the decay of dead plants and animals, both on land and in water. Without such bacteria the earth would be covered with dead matter.

Left: Nitrogen cycle on a farm. Soil bacteria decompose animal wastes and dead animals and plants, releasing nitrogen compounds. Plants use these compounds for proteins to build tissue. Animals eat plants. Animal wastes and dead bodies are decayed by bacteria, continuing the cycle. Above: Nodules on roots of a peanut plant. Nodules contain nitrogen-fixing bacteria, which add nitrogen to soil in the form of compounds that plants can use. Nitrogen can also be added artificially to soil by chemical fertilizers.

While eating, the bacteria break down these organisms' complicated substances into simpler ones. The simpler substances are then restored to the soil, water, and air in forms that can be used by living plants and animals.

Bacteria play an important part in the digestive processes of people and animals. There are a great many in the human intestine. As the bacteria eat, they break down foods. At the same time they make certain vitamins, which the body then uses. The bacteria inside the stomachs of grass-eating animals can break down cellulose, the stiff wall of green plant cells. By enabling cows to digest grasses, bacteria play a part in the production of milk.

Bacteria in Agriculture.　Bacteria are a vital link in the food chain that supports life. All living tissue—plant as well as animal—needs nitrogen, the gas that makes up almost 80 percent of the air. Some bacteria, called nitrogen-fixing bacteria, are the only organisms that can take nitrogen from the air. These bacteria live in the soil. They are able to change nitrogen into chemical compounds that plants can use. The nitrogen-fixing bacteria live in partnership with certain kinds of plants. Peas, beans, and alfalfa are among these. The bacteria grow in clumps or nodules around the roots of the plant. The plant supplies the bacteria with food in the form of sugar. The bacteria help to build plant tissue out of nitrogen.

Other bacteria preserve silage—crushed cornstalks and other crops eaten by cattle. This food would rot in storage if it were not "pickled" by bacteria. Bacteria are also responsible for the fermentation process by which such products as cheese, buttermilk, yogurt, and vinegar are made.

Bacteria in Industry.　The same process of fermentation is also used in industry to make substances essential for paints, plastics, cosmetics, candy, and certain drugs. Other industrial uses of bacteria include curing tobacco leaves, tanning hides, eating away the outer covering of coffee and cocoa seeds, and separating certain kinds of fibers for the textile industry. Mineral-eating bacteria help to "refine" metal and petroleum by eating away the unwanted impurities.

Bacteria in Research.　Scientists use bacteria in research on heredity. The biological and chemical processes of heredity are basically the same for people and bacteria. Because bacteria can produce a new generation about every half hour, many problems can be conveniently studied in a large number of generations.

Bacteria in the Community.　Another use for bacteria is in sewage disposal plants. Water carries impurities into the sewage tanks. The tanks are really "gardens" where large colonies of bacteria grow. While feeding on the sewage the bacteria break down the impurities into a gas and into solids. The solid material sinks to the bottom of the tanks, and the water is drained off. After further treatment the water may be safely released.

There is so much demand for bacteria in agriculture, industry, and research that special laboratories grow them.

▶ NEW AND FUTURE USES OF BACTERIA

Scientists are finding many ways of making bacteria work for the benefit of people. For example, they have developed a method for producing methane gas by processing the manure (solid wastes) of cattle. Methane is a valuable fuel. Like natural gas, it is used for heating homes and factories, and for other energy needs. In the same process, protein and minerals are extracted to be used for cattle feed. Protein-rich cattle feed has also been obtained by growing bacteria on wood, petroleum, and sewage wastes.

Some bacteria are used as living insecticides against certain insect pests. For example, *Bacillus thuringiensis* is a species of bacteria that kills Japanese beetles and certain other insect pests. Farmers and gardeners use sprays of these bacteria to protect their crops.

Scientists are experimenting to find answers to questions such as these: May bacteria be useful in fighting other bacteria that cause tooth decay? Are bacteria able to make cellulose, which can be used to make paper? Can bacteria that eat holes in underground deposits of limestone be used to make oil flow more easily? Can bacteria be used to generate electricity? While feeding on certain substances, some bacteria produce energy that can be converted to electricity. Scientists are trying to devise batteries that can use bacterial energy.

SARAH R. RIEDMAN
Author, science books for children
Reviewed by ARTHUR R. ENGLISH
Pfizer Inc.

See also DISEASES; FERMENTATION; FOOD SPOILAGE AND CONTAMINATION; MICROBIOLOGY.

BADMINTON

Badminton is a fast game played with rackets and a shuttlecock on a wood, dirt, or grass court. The court is somewhat like a tennis court, but smaller. The shuttlecock, often called simply the shuttle, or "bird," is hit back and forth over a net 5 feet high. It must be returned before it strikes the court. The game can be played by two persons (singles) or four persons (doubles). It is a very adaptable game and can be played both indoors and outdoors. Official tournaments are played indoors. The outdoor game is more suitable for family enjoyment at home.

Badminton developed from Battledore and Shuttlecock, an ancient game that was popular with children. There are several explanations of how the modern game began; one is that about the year 1870 English army officers brought a version of it to England from India, where it was called Poona. The new game took its name from the Duke of Beaufort's estate, Badminton, where the game was probably played indoors for the first time. Badminton became popular in England, and in the 1890's the Badminton Association was formed. In 1934 the International Badminton Federation was organized.

There are two international badminton championships: the Thomas Cup competition for men, which began in 1948, and the Uber Cup for women, which began in 1957. Malaysia and Indonesia have dominated the men's event, and the United States and Denmark the women's competition.

▶ PLAYING BADMINTON

The game starts with the player in the right service court serving to his opponent in the diagonally opposite right service court. He is allowed only one serve at the start of each point. The server continues serving to alternate courts as long as he or his side scores points. If a rally is lost, a point is not lost, only the serve. This is called side out. An opponent then takes a hand at serving.

Any of the following is called a fault, and results in side out if committed by the serving side or loss of a point if committed by a receiver:

Server

(1) Serving outside the service court.
(2) Contact with the serve anyplace above the waist.

Server or receiver

(1) Hitting the shuttle out of bounds, or twice in succession on the same side of the net, or under or through the net, or before it crosses the net.
(2) Carrying the shuttle with the racket.
(3) Touching the net or its supports during play.
(4) Serving or receiving the serve with the feet on the line, or with both feet not in contact with the floor until the shuttle is hit.

Any shuttle falling on a boundary line is good.

▶ SCORING

Points can be scored only while serving. A game is won by the first player or side to score 15 points, except in women's singles, in which game is 11 points. If a tie score of 13 all is reached (9 all in women's singles), the side that reached the tie score first may, if it chooses, set the game at 5 (or 3 in women's singles). This means that game will not be reached until either side has scored 5 (or 3) more points. Similarly, if the score becomes tied at 14 all (or 10 all in women's singles), game may be set at 3 (or 2) more points.

The side that wins a game serves first in the next game. The opposing sides change ends of the court after each game.

▶ THE BASIC STROKES

Overhead shots are played from above the head; underhand shots are those played from below waist level. Any stroke hit on the right-hand side of the body is a forehand; on the left-hand side of the body, a backhand.

The serve is the most important stroke because it puts the shuttle in play at the start of each point.

The smash, or kill shot, is the principal point-winning stroke in badminton. It is hit downward from an overhead position with as much speed as possible.

The clear is a shot that sends the shuttle high to the opponent's back boundary line.

The drop shot causes the shuttle to drop close to the net in the opponent's court. It may be hit either overhead or underhand.

The drive sends the shuttle skimming low over the net in a line parallel to the floor.

Several auxiliary shots are often useful in badminton. The hairpin and crosscourt net shots can be used to return a drop shot with a drop shot. They can be hit from one side of the court to the other (crosscourt), or directly back over the net (hairpin).

The round-the-head shot is an overhead backhand played as a forehand. It is protection against a weak backhand.

The half smash is used to angle the shuttle downward sharply. It takes less effort to hit but has less speed than the smash.

The driven clear has a flatter arc than the basic clear, and is used to put the shuttle to the back of the court quickly.

▶ GRIPS, FOOTWORK, AND STROKE PRODUCTION

There are different grips for holding the racket to make the various shots.

For the forehand and serve grip, hold the throat of the racket with your left hand. Keep the face of the racket perpendicular to the floor. Then place your right hand on the handle, as if shaking hands with it. Your fingers should be slightly spread.

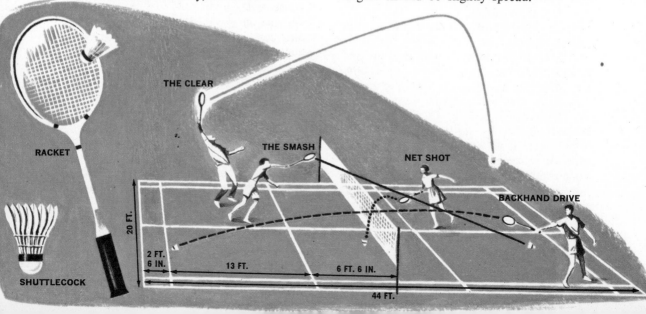

THE CLEAR

RACKET

THE SMASH

NET SHOT

BACKHAND DRIVE

SHUTTLECOCK

20 FT.

2 FT. 6 IN.

13 FT.

6 FT. 6 IN.

44 FT.

For backhand shots the hand is turned slightly to the left, the thumb placed flat along the back of the handle, not around it.

Keep your wrist firm and yet flexible, not stiff and tense. The wrist must be cocked back at the beginning of the backswing. As the arm comes forward the wrist snaps or whips the racket head to meet the shuttle.

Good footwork enables you to move quickly in any direction and to have your feet properly placed while stroking. The weight must be on the balls of the feet, and the knees should be kept mobile. For forehand strokes the left foot is advanced toward the net and the left side faces the net. On the backhand the right foot is advanced and the right side faces the net. These same principles apply to overhead forehands and backhands.

Stroking the overhead clear is similar to throwing a ball. The racket starts behind the back, with the wrist cocked. Then the arm swings forward and upward and straightens overhead. The idea is to meet the shuttle high and soon. As in throwing, the wrist, arm, shoulder, and body weight go into making the clear a power stroke.

The smash and the overhead drop shot are hit much like the clear. These strokes should appear exactly the same until racket and shuttle meet. Your opponent will be unable to tell which stroke you are going to use, therefore his return will be more hurried. This tactic is called deception, a very important factor in badminton. In making the smash, the shuttle should be directed downward with great speed, whereas the drop shot has little speed.

The stroke for the drive is similar to the arm motion in the sidearm baseball throw. The racket starts behind the upper back, with the wrist cocked. It is swung forward and parallel to the floor. Meet the shuttle about shoulder height and opposite the foot closer to the net. Transfer your weight from the back foot to the forward foot as your wrist whips the racket head toward the shuttle. The follow-through is forward and to the left side.

The service stroke must be made underhand. It is somewhat like a bowling swing. To make this stroke, the shuttle is held in front and away from the body. At the same time, the racket is taken straight back. Then the shuttle is dropped about an arm's length in front of the body. The racket swings forward to meet the shuttle at this point and follows through, forward and up.

A "must" in making any stroke is to keep your eyes on the shuttle.

▶ TACTICS AND STRATEGY

The object of the game is to win the required number of points by forcing your opponent to make errors. If your opponent does not make an outright error, he can be forced to make a weak return that can be put away —that is, placed beyond his reach.

The basic strategy in singles is to outmaneuver your opponent so that he is forced to "set up" the shuttle high in the forecourt, where it can be put away with a smash. Use the clear and the drop shot to run him to the corners of the court. If he is in the backcourt, drop-shot. If he is in the forecourt, clear. To give him less time, drive the shuttle.

Generally the singles serve is hit high and deep to the back boundary line. In doubles it should skim over the net and drop near the short service line. The value of a good low serve in doubles cannot be overestimated.

In doubles, attack by hitting the shuttle downward whenever possible. The shuttle is placed strategically to force the opponents to hit upward, or defensive, shots. In mixed doubles the woman usually plays the shots in the front half of the court. The man stands behind her and plays the shots coming to the backcourt.

▶ WHAT MAKES A CHAMPION?

The outstanding characteristic of a champion at badminton is his ability to react in split-second time with his eyes, his mind, his feet, and his hand. Becoming a champion takes combined physical and mental effort at all times. Constant practice, physical fitness, reading instructional books, and observing expert players help make a winner. Habits of concentration, confidence, and self-determination are necessary. The great players of the game have often been great sportsmen. This is apparent in their conduct and dignity on and off the court.

MARGARET VARNER
Former World Badminton Champion

BAGPIPE. See FOLK MUSIC INSTRUMENTS.

BAHAMAS

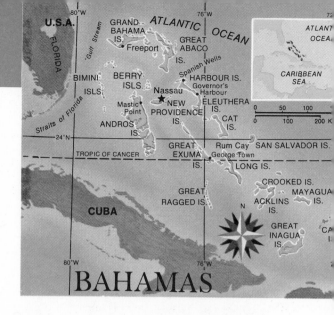

The Commonwealth of the Bahamas is made up of a group of small islands that extend like stepping-stones between Florida and the West Indies. Columbus may have first landed in the New World on one of the islands of the Bahamas, San Salvador (Watling Island). In the past the country's many isolated harbors and narrow channels proved to be excellent hiding spots for pirates and blockade runners. A warm climate and white beaches now make several of the islands popular tourist resorts.

▶ THE PEOPLE

Most of the people of the Bahamas are blacks whose ancestors were brought to the islands as slaves. Over half of the people live on New Providence Island. Nassau, the capital city of the Bahamas, is on New Providence. The city's permanent population of about 102,000 grows considerably during the tourist season. Nassau has many fine tourist accommodations. The quaint streets and houses and the great variety of shops selling goods from all parts of the world at low prices are important attractions for visitors. The

Eleuthera has some of the loveliest beaches in the Bahamas.

only other city of any size is Freeport on Grand Bahama, the second most populous island.

The country has an extensive primary and secondary school system, which contributes to its high literacy rate. School is free and compulsory for all children between the ages of 5 and 14. Students seeking higher education generally attend the College of the Bahamas on New Providence or the University of the West Indies in Jamaica or study in the United States, Canada, or Britain.

▶ THE LAND

There are about 700 islands and 2,000 tiny sand cays (keys) and exposed bits of coral reef in the Bahamas. The islands extend in an arc for some 1,200 kilometers (750 miles) to the northern edge of the Caribbean Sea. They are formed largely of coral and are mostly low-lying. The highest elevation is almost 120 meters (400 feet). Only a relatively small number of the islands are permanently inhabited.

The climate of the Bahamas is semitropical. Temperatures vary little with the seasons and are moderate in both winter and summer. Rainfall averages about 1,270 millimeters (50 inches) a year, which is enough for most types of farming. On the smaller islands there is less rainfall, and often there are shortages of fresh drinking water. The islands are subject to hurricanes in the fall. The heavy rains and strong winds that accompany these violent storms occasionally cause severe damage.

THE ECONOMY

The mainstay of the economy is the tourist industry. Well over 1,000,000 visitors a year are attracted by the climate, beautiful beaches, and clear water. Nassau and Freeport are the most popular tourist spots. But the waters near the Bimini Islands off the coast of Florida are famous for big game fishing. In the spring anglers gather there for annual fishing tournaments.

Nassau is also a center of finance because the tax laws of the Bahamas have encouraged the growth of international banking there. Nassau's importance to the Bahamas is so great that the islands other than New Providence are called Out Islands and their people are called Out Islanders.

Petroleum refining has become an important source of income for the Bahamas. Petroleum and petroleum products now rank as one of the country's leading exports. The islands are also a transfer point for petroleum being shipped to the United States.

Manufacturing and agriculture play a relatively small role in the economy. There is light manufacturing on Grand Bahama Island, where a deepwater port has been dredged at Freeport. Alcoholic beverages, tobacco, textiles, chemicals, paper, rubber goods, and plastics are produced.

Only about 1 percent of the land is cultivated, and this is used mostly for growing crops for domestic use. Eleuthera Island, one of the first islands to be settled, is an important farming area. Vegetables, pineapples, and dairy and poultry products are shipped from Eleuthera to Nassau. At Rock Sound, a prosperous farming community on Eleuthera, beef cattle are raised and shipped to New Providence.

Although the waters of the islands teem with fish, only crayfish (spiny lobster) are caught commercially. The country has little in the way of mineral resources except for salt, which is produced on the southernmost island, Great Inagua. There seawater is channeled into shallow basins. When the sun evaporates the water, the salt is left behind. Straw handicrafts provide additional income for the islanders. New ways to expand the economy and provide more jobs are constantly being sought. An influx of Haitian refugees has added to unemployment problems.

HISTORY AND GOVERNMENT

The Spanish explored the islands in the 1500's but made no serious efforts to colonize them. The few Indians who lived there were shipped to the West Indies to work in mines and on plantations. In the 17th century the British gained control of the Bahamas and began to settle some of the larger islands. During the United States Civil War, Nassau was a meeting place for blockade runners from the Confederate states and ships from England. There cotton from the South was traded for English goods.

The Bahamas became self-governing in 1964, although Britain still handled foreign affairs, defense, and internal security. When complete independence came in 1973, the Bahamian Government took over the management of these affairs.

The government of the Bahamas is headed by a prime minister, while a governor-general represents the British monarch, who is head of state. Parliament has two houses—the elected House of Assembly and the Senate, to which members are appointed.

JOHN F. LOUNSBURY
Arizona State University

BAHRAIN

Bahrain is a country made up of a group of islands lying in the Persian Gulf off the coast of Saudi Arabia. It is the smallest in area of all the states of the Arabian Peninsula. Indeed, it ranks among the smallest of the world's nations. In spite of its size, however, Bahrain has for centuries been one of the more flourishing states of the region and one of the most economically advanced. Its location made it important as a port and a center of trade for the countries bordering the gulf. It was famed for its pearls and for the skill of its boatbuilders. The discovery of oil brought further prosperity to Bahrain, although its reserves of oil are not nearly so large as those of some of its neighbors. Over the years Bahrain has used its income from oil to establish an extensive social welfare program for its citizens and to continue its economic development toward the day when its oil will be completely gone.

▶ THE PEOPLE

Bahrain is by far the most densely populated country of the Arabian Peninsula. Most of the people are Arabs, some of whom have immigrated to Bahrain from neighboring countries. There are sizable numbers of Pakistanis, Iranians, and Indians, some of whom work as merchants in the cities. It is estimated that about 20 percent of the people are non-Bahraini. Many came to Bahrain because of the relatively high standard of living and to work in the oil industry. The foreign communities include Europeans (mainly British) and Americans. The Arabs are Muslims, about equally divided between the Sunni and Shi'a sects, the two main branches of Islam.

About half the population is concentrated in the two leading cities of Manama and Muharraq. Manama is the largest city, the capital, and chief port. It is connected with Muharraq, which is on another island, by a 2.5-kilometer (1½-mile) causeway. The two cities present interesting contrasts. Manama, a commercial city, has been modernized, while Muharraq, with its old houses and narrow streets, retains a traditional look. The port of Muharraq is the center of Bahrain's boat-building industry. The boats are dhows, rather small vessels with triangular sails once common throughout the Arab world.

Traditional ways of life in the Arab states of the Persian Gulf began to change when oil was discovered. Bahrain was the first of the gulf states in which oil was found, and the effects of modernization are most evident here. The country has a growing middle class and a skilled work force. This is largely a result of Bahrain's emphasis on education. Schooling is free and compulsory for all children between the ages of 6 and 16. There are teacher-training colleges and a technical school. Bahrain has no university, but students are sent abroad to study.

Social welfare programs include free medical and hospital care and low-cost housing. One of the most striking examples of Bahrain's social planning is Isa Town, located a few kilometers from Manama. When fully completed, it will provide modern housing for some 35,000 people, with shopping centers, a library, schools, playgrounds, and a sports stadium.

▶ THE LAND

Bahrain is made up of about 33 islands, islets, and sandbars, most of them uninhabited. The largest island is Bahrain, from which the country takes its name. Other important islands include Muharraq, Sitra, Umm Nasan (Umm Na'san), and Hawar, which lies near Qatar. The land is mainly flat desert, with the only fertile area in the north. The highest elevation, 137 meters (450 feet), is at Jabal Dukhan on Bahrain

Island. Dukhan is the site of Bahrain's oil deposits. Plans for a causeway linking Manama with Saudi Arabia have been approved.

Summers are extremely hot and humid. Rainfall is slight, but springs and wells provide some fresh water for cultivation and for drinking. The chief crops are dates, vegetables, and alfalfa. The waters of the surrounding Persian Gulf are one of the world's richest sources of natural pearls, which were formerly one of Bahrain's most important products.

▶ THE ECONOMY

Most of Bahrain's income is derived from oil. It has the second largest oil refinery in the Middle East and refines not only its own crude oil but also oil from nearby Saudi Arabia. Before oil was discovered in 1932, Bahrain depended on commerce and trade, agriculture, fishing, pearling, and boat building. The development in Japan of cultured, or artificially induced, pearls led to the decline of Bahrain's industry. Shrimp abound in the gulf. Harvesting and freezing them for export is an important part of the fishing industry.

Oil experts predict that Bahrain's deposits of oil, never very large to begin with, will be exhausted before the end of the 20th century. To help diversify the economy, the government has encouraged foreign investment.

Bahrain is becoming a major transportation and commercial center for the Persian Gulf.

FACTS AND FIGURES

STATE OF BAHRAIN is the official name of the country.

CAPITAL: Manama.

LOCATION: Persian Gulf near Saudi Arabia.

AREA: 622 km² (240 sq mi).

POPULATION: 260,000 (estimate).

LANGUAGE: Arabic.

RELIGION: Islam.

GOVERNMENT: Emirate. **Head of state**—emir. **Head of government**—prime minister. **International cooperation**—United Nations, Arab League.

ECONOMY: Agricultural products—dates, vegetables, alfalfa. **Industries and products**—oil, fish, aluminum, boatbuilding. **Chief exports**—oil and oil products, shrimp, aluminum. **Chief imports**—machinery and transportation equipment, manufactured goods, food, chemicals. **Monetary unit**—dinar.

A new aluminum smelting plant and other industrial plants have been constructed. Port and storage facilities and ship repair yards are being enlarged at Mina Sulman, southeast of Manama. The Bahrain airport handles the largest planes. Engineering and international banking are developing rapidly.

▶ HISTORY AND GOVERNMENT

Bahrain's history goes back to very ancient times. In the northern part of Bahrain Island are many thousands of burial mounds, some extremely large, which indicate that people lived here perhaps as long ago as 3000 B.C. The Sumerians, who belonged to one of the world's oldest civilizations, had contacts with ancient Bahrain, which even then was known as an important port. Later the Greeks and Romans visited the islands.

Bahrain was colonized by the Portuguese in the 16th century and then fell under the rule of the Persians. In the 18th century the al-Khalifa family, who came from the Arabian mainland, became the ruling sheikhs of Bahrain and for a time exercised control over neighboring Qatar. Their descendants rule as emirs, or princes, in Bahrain today.

Early in the 19th century Bahrain came under British influence. A series of treaties was negotiated with Britain similar to the treaties with Britain signed by other gulf states. In return for British protection, Bahrain agreed, among other things, not to engage in slavery or piracy. Bahrain remained a British protectorate until 1971, when it declared itself completely independent. An attempt was made to form a federation of the gulf states—Bahrain, Qatar, Oman, and the United Arab Emirates—but it proved fruitless.

The emir, who is the chief of state of Bahrain, appoints the prime minister and the council of ministers. Bahrain's first constitution was approved in 1973. It established a parliament for the country consisting of elected members plus some members of the council of ministers. But in 1975 the emir dissolved parliament, and it has not reconvened.

Reviewed by Majid Khadduri
School of Advanced International Studies
Johns Hopkins University

BAKING. See Bread and Baking.

Statue of Balboa in Panama City, Panama.

BALBOA, VASCO NÚÑEZ DE (1475–1517)

Vasco Núñez de Balboa, a Spanish explorer and adventurer, was the first European to see the Pacific Ocean.

Balboa was born at Jerez de los Caballeros, Spain, in 1475. Little is known about his early life until about 1500, when he joined an expedition to seek his fortune in America. Finding no gold, he settled as a farmer on the island of Hispaniola (now Haiti and the Dominican Republic). Balboa soon found himself deeply in debt. To escape his creditors, he hid in a large barrel and was carried on board a ship bound for the settlement of San Sebastián, in Colombia.

When the ship was safely at sea, Balboa came out of hiding. The commander of the expedition, Martín Fernández de Enciso, was furious at the stowaway and threatened to abandon him on a desert island. However, Enciso allowed him to remain after Balboa convinced the crew that he would be valuable to them as a soldier.

This proved to be true, for when the expedition reached San Sebastián, they found it in ruins. Balboa took charge and led the survivors to Panama. There they started a new colony, which he called Darien.

But soon a quarrel broke out between Balboa and Enciso over who should be in command. Enciso was overthrown and sent back to Spain, and Balboa became governor of the new colony.

Balboa then set out to explore the surrounding country, hoping to find gold. His generosity won him the friendship of the Indians, who ordinarily distrusted and fought the Spaniards. The Indians had little use for gold. But seeing that Balboa prized it so highly, they told him of a marvelous land to the south where people ate from golden plates and drank from golden cups. They also said that just beyond the mountains lay a great sea. Balboa did not know that only a narrow strip of land (the Isthmus of Panama) lay between the Atlantic and Pacific oceans. He thought that this sea might be the route to Cathay (China), which Columbus had sought in vain.

Meanwhile, Enciso had returned to Spain and angrily complained about Balboa to King Ferdinand. Anxious to regain the King's favor, Balboa set out to discover the great sea the Indians had described. With 190 Spaniards and 1,000 Indians he cut his way across the jungle-covered mountains of Panama. On September 25, 1513, Balboa left his companions and climbed the last mountain peak by himself. From its summit he saw the gleaming Pacific Ocean stretching as far as the eye could see. He named it the South Sea and claimed it and all the land it touched for the King of Spain.

Balboa then planned to explore Peru—the land of gold. Before he could carry out his plans, a new governor, Pedrarias Dávila, arrived from Spain. Pedrarias, jealous of Balboa, had him arrested on a false charge of treason. And in 1517, not far from the colony he had founded and the ocean he had discovered, Balboa was executed.

Reviewed by KENNETH S. COOPER
George Peabody College

BALKANS

The Balkan Peninsula is in southeastern Europe, bordered by five seas—the Black Sea, the Aegean Sea, the Mediterranean Sea, the Ionian Sea, and the Adriatic Sea. For hundreds of years the Balkan Peninsula was a part of the Turkish Empire, and Balkan people were ruled by the Turks.

History

During the 19th century the people of the Balkans revolted against their Turkish masters. In 1830 the ancient country of Greece was the first of the Balkans to win its independence from Turkey. Then four other new and independent states were created—Serbia, Bulgaria, Rumania, and Montenegro.

The development of independent countries in this important region brought new political problems. Each country was different in language and customs and culture. The leaders of the Balkan countries distrusted one another, and the new states quarreled constantly among themselves.

The countries on the Balkan Peninsula agreed on only one thing: They all hated their former rulers, the Turks. Despite all the revolutions, Turkey still ruled much land bordering on the Adriatic Sea, and Macedonia, today a part of Greece. The continued presence of the Turks on the Balkan Peninsula angered the Balkan nations.

In 1912 the Balkan states agreed that Turkey must be banished from the Balkan Peninsula. In October, 1912, Greece, Serbia, Bulgaria, and Montenegro declared war on Turkey. This was called the First Balkan War. Everyone was surprised when the tiny Balkan states won a series of quick, impressive victories. Within 2 months the little Balkans defeated Turkey and forced her to give up most of Macedonia.

Soon, however, the Balkan states began quarreling among themselves over the division of liberated Macedonia. Each state claimed large portions of the region, so no agreement was possible. Another war broke out in July, 1913. Bulgaria had got a bigger piece of Macedonia than her neighbors, and they were determined to take it away. This time Greece, Serbia, and Rumania joined their old enemy Turkey and waged war on Bulgaria. The Second Balkan War lasted only a month, and Bulgaria was easily beaten. Bulgaria had to give most of its Macedonian territory to the victors.

Nevertheless, the Balkan wars represented a great victory for the Balkan states. Turkey lost about 142,000 square kilometers (55,000 square miles) of territory. This was divided up among the five Balkan states, and a sixth state—Albania—was created.

Balkan affairs were made more complicated by the interference of other European countries. Austria and Russia both were neighbors of the Balkan Peninsula and naturally were very concerned with what happened next door. Unfortunately Austria and Russia disagreed violently about Balkan affairs. As a result, trouble in the Balkans always created the danger of a European war. In fact, the Balkan Peninsula was called the powder keg of Europe. International tension increased during this time, and a year later, in 1914, World War I actually began in the Balkans.

During the war the only Balkan countries to side with Germany and Austria-Hungary were Bulgaria and Turkey. At the Paris Peace Conference in 1919, the borders of the modern Balkan nations were established. Yugoslavia, Rumania, Bulgaria, Albania, and Greece were said to be Balkan countries.

Between World War I and World War II other European countries continued to interfere in the internal affairs of the Balkan countries. This was one of the factors that caused unstable governments in the Balkans during this time.

Therefore it is not surprising that most of the Balkan Peninsula was occupied by Germany and Italy during World War II. Bulgaria and Rumania were on the side of the Axis powers (Germany, Italy and Japan).

At the end of World War II, the Soviet Union (then allied with the United States) freed the Balkans from the German and Italian occupation. However, almost at the same time, Communist governments were set up in all the Balkan countries except Greece. Today those countries still have Communist governments, although they do have varying degrees of independence from the Soviet Union.

Reviewed by KENNETH S. COOPER
George Peabody College

BALL

All over the world, people play ball and have done so since prehistoric times. The ball is mentioned in the earliest writings. Every people, from primitive times to the present nuclear age, has played a game using some kind of ball.

Some early people wove reeds into rounded shapes. Others used leather stuffed with feathers for ball playing. Later, generations of Greeks and Romans added a new idea—air; and a blown-up leather ball called a *follis* was used in games of catch. They also inflated balls of larger sizes, with which they played a kind of football and other kicking games.

Balls have been made from many materials, depending upon what was available in the country. North American Indians used balls made of deer hide, while across the world from them, Japanese children played with balls of tightly wadded tissue paper wrapped with string. It is said that Columbus found the Indians of Central America playing with solid, black balls made of vegetable gum and took some of these first bouncy rubber balls back to Europe with him.

We learn from the history of peoples and their folklore that many of our modern ball games started as religious and magical ceremonies. Ball games, like many present-day children's pastimes, were once the serious activities of older people. Often they retold in play the old beliefs about war, gods and devils, life and death. These ancient contests are the basis of many of the team and individual sports that we play today.

The Egyptians seem to have been among the first people to have ceremonial ball games. Each spring two large groups of peo-

Most popular games are played with a ball.

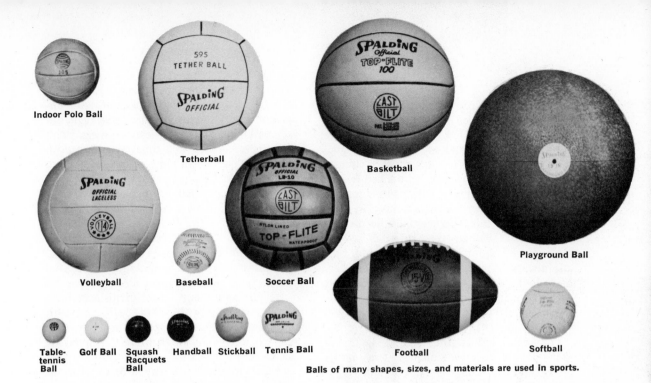

Indoor Polo Ball

Tetherball

Basketball

Playground Ball

Volleyball

Baseball

Soccer Ball

Table-tennis Ball

Golf Ball

Squash Racquets Ball

Handball

Stickball

Tennis Ball

Football

Softball

Balls of many shapes, sizes, and materials are used in sports.

ple acted out a contest between two of their gods. A round, wooden ball and crooked sticks were used. The object was to drive the ball through the opposing goal. The side that was able to knock the ball past the defenders won a victory for the god their team represented. The side playing for the god Osiris hoped that, by winning, it would gain favor with him and coax him into giving good crops. The other side, playing for Set, the brother and enemy of Osiris, hoped to persuade Set not to send famine or pestilence to the land.

Today a ball and crooked stick are used in playing such games as field hockey and lacrosse. Each team tries to score, as the Egyptians did, while keeping the other side from scoring goals. Polo is another ball-and-stick game, played on horseback.

Very few ball games are modern inventions. Only the organized skill with which they are played is recent. Baseball and tennis, as we now play them, were developed during the 19th century from earlier forms of these games.

At first games were played mainly to develop skill in tossing and catching. Later, when all the different sticks, bats, and rackets with which to strike or otherwise control the motion of the ball were added, many special games were invented.

Ball games range from simple, elementary child's play to very complicated adult games requiring great skill.

Today there are over 30 major sports in which a ball is the key object used in the game.

The ball has played a part in many other customs unrelated to sports. The phrase "to blackball," meaning to reject for membership in a club or fraternal organization, goes back to the Greeks' use of white and black pebbles in voting. They used an urn or vase to represent the candidate. The voter tossed a white pebble into the urn if he was in favor of the candidate, a black one if he was voting against him. Today a single blackball can still keep a person out of a club or lodge. It is also interesting to note that the ballot, used in voting, is named after the Italian *ballotta,* meaning "little ball."

A fast-disappearing sight, once seen in every city, is three golden balls swinging over a pawnbroker's shop. A pawnbroker lends money on silver, jewelry, and other valuables left with him as security. In Italy this trade of moneylending was an occupation of the Medici family. Part of their family coat of arms was three golden balls, which became the sign of the pawnbroker's trade.

The ball belongs to all mankind, so it is difficult to find out from what country it first started to roll to the four corners of the world.

BALLADS

The ballad is a form of folk song that tells a story. It developed in Europe during the Middle Ages. A ballad tells its story simply and directly, often by means of dialogue, always concentrating on the story's climax. Ballads may or may not be danced. They may or may not have instrumental accompaniment. But they are always sung in such a way that the words rather than the melody are stressed. Unlike the lyric, in which melody and emotion are most important, ballads always emphasize the story. However, the melodies used in ballads are beautiful and varied, ranging from those based on Gregorian chants in western Europe to Slavic types in the east.

The ballad differs from land to land and goes under a variety of names. It is known as *ballade* in France, *ballata* in Italy, *romance* in Spain, *vise* in Denmark, *duma* in the Ukraine, *bylina* in the U.S.S.R. Ballad scholars such as Francis Barton Gummere believed ballads dated from primitive times and were jointly composed by groups of people. This was known as the communal theory of ballad origins. Anthropologists and ballad scholars have since come to recognize that the ballad is a far more modern, sophisticated art form. An individual with some artistic education composed a particular ballad. Then the people took it over from the composer, who was soon forgotten. Finally it was varied, shaped, and re-created as it traveled by word of mouth from singer to singer. Possibly ballads originated with the country custom of composing narrative poems to be recited or sung at funerals. Then these story-poems were taken over by wandering medieval singers. At any rate, we know that the ballad does not date back to primitive times. Rather it has thrived from the late Middle Ages down to the present.

Ballads as known in America can be divided conveniently, if not completely accurately, into three groups: the traditional British ballads, the later products of the British city presses, and the native American narrative songs.

Traditional ballads are songs whose origins go back 6 or 7 centuries in British history. Passed on by word of mouth through many folk generations, they have developed a large number of versions and variants. Their plots are frequently confused, with many important details lost. Yet the best versions are strikingly beautiful and moving, with their sparse action, objective style, and deep insights. These traditional ballads are often called Child ballads. Professor Francis James Child collected 305 of them, with their variants, in his classic five-volume book, *The English and Scottish Popular Ballads* (1882–98). "Lord Randal," "Sir Patrick Spens," "Mary Hamilton," and "The Twa Corbies" are four Child ballads acclaimed over the years.

Ballads that came from British presses, particularly during the 17th, 18th, and 19th centuries, are loosely referred to as broadside ballads. Many of them were printed on the backs of newssheets, or broadsides, that sold for a penny in the city streets of Britain and her colonies. Others were printed in small books called chapbooks. These songs, like the movies and television shows of today, followed set plot patterns. They told moral tales of mistaken identity, disguised lovers, and cruel crimes. Professional singers sold these broadside ballads, which often used the music and text of traditional ballads as models. This city tradition created thousands of new songs. It also helped keep alive certain Child ballads that were printed on broadsides and in chapbooks and given wide distribution.

The British took their ballads to their colonies, where many of them survived long after dying out in the homeland. With British songs as models, the United States developed ballads about bandits like Jesse James and Billy the Kid, strong men like John Henry, and unfortunate girls like Young Charlotte and Naomi Wise. Most of these songs closely resemble their British ancestors. They are often set to old British tunes, sometimes using Americanized plots of British events.

Of course, there are nations other than the English-speaking lands with highly developed ballad traditions. The study of the ballad in Europe is a complex study indeed. For instance, Scandinavia has a large and varied stock of ballads that have been sung and danced for hundreds of years. Many of these songs are variants of well-known British and

American ballads that have crossed language barriers in one direction or the other. In Yugoslavia the ballad is one of the more important forms of literature, tracing back to the Middle Ages and preserving many national ideals and patriotic legends of the people. The ballads of Bulgaria and the Ukraine are also outstanding.

Ballads stress story, or narrative. Some countries prefer lyrics, which stress emotion and melody instead. The ballads of France and Italy are generally reworked from lyrics or imported from abroad. In Germany and the Low Countries, other lands partial to lyrics, balladry is less common than in Britain and the north. Germany, however, has many ballad-like pieces on political and religious themes.

Spain has a strong semi-historical narrative-song tradition. Her *romances* follow a set pattern and stress personality over fact. There are many *romance* cycles, or groups of songs about a single theme.

The Russian *byliny* differ greatly from the ballad types mentioned so far. *Byliny* are narrative, but they do not rhyme and are not divided into stanzas like the British ballads. Short and dramatic, *byliny* deal with the exploits of heroes. Many critics believe them to be related to the epic lay, a kind of heroic literature known to Europeans for over 1,000 years. The emphasis in such epic matter is on fantastic adventures of fabulous characters.

If one allows for differences in history and culture from area to area, one sees that the pattern of ballad development in English-speaking lands is generally the pattern of development for ballads elsewhere. Traditional ballads survive from ages past. They are reworked in the cities, where newer songs are modeled from them. They are carried to colonial areas when colonial areas exist. But a true understanding of the different forms and uses of the ballad from area to area calls for extensive study. Excellent guides are available. Perhaps the best general introduction to the subject is MacEdward Leach's *The Ballad Book* (1955). William J. Entwistle's *European Balladry* (1939), though somewhat out of date, is still the classic handbook of the European ballad. These books will lead interested readers to most of the scholarship and bibliography needed for an understanding of the ballad.

TRISTRAM P. COFFIN
American Folklore Society, Inc.
See also FOLK MUSIC.

BALLET

A ballet is theatrical entertainment combining the arts of dancing, stage design, and music. It may either tell a story or merely depict an idea or mood. Ballet is a French word that comes from the Italian *ballo,* "a dance."

The exercises, or technique, of ballet are designed to display the human body in the most elegant and harmonious way possible. Although ballet technique is strict and the training is strenuous, the result on stage is natural and beautiful. It makes all the hard work that goes into learning ballet seem worthwhile.

Ballet is nearly 500 years old—yet it is very young compared with dance itself, which is as old as man. Ballet began in Italy about the time Columbus discovered America. It was quite different then from what it is today. At that time ballet was a court entertainment with which Italian noblemen amused themselves and their guests during lavish balls and banquets. Dancing, music, pantomime, poetry, and drama were combined. The first ballet dancers were the royalty and nobles of the court, since there were no professional dancers. The steps were modeled on the elegant and rather simple court dances of the day, and the dancers did not wear the toe slippers worn by present-day ballerinas. However, dancing of this kind was not called ballet until almost 100 years later at the court of King Henry III of France.

▶ BALLET IN FRANCE

In 1581 Queen Catherine de Médicis ordered a grand entertainment to celebrate a royal wedding. The result was perhaps the

Daily practice at the barre is a part of every dancer's training.

most spectacular ballet ever seen. Thousands of people witnessed the lavish exhibition, a blending of dance, dramatic scenes, music, and splendid scenery. Hundreds of dancers, singers, and actors took part in portraying the goddess Circe and all of her friends and enemies. Huge machines and stage effects were moved about the room so that the audience, seated on three sides, could see them.

All this was the work of an Italian musician best known by his French name, Balthazar de Beaujoyeulx. He was probably the first choreographer, or maker of dances, as we know the word today. He called his work *Le Ballet Comique de la Reine* ("The Queen's Comic Ballet"), and ever since then performances of this kind have been called ballets.

King Louis XIV loved to dance. At the age of 13 he danced in the *Ballet de Cassandre,* and he continued to dance until 1669 when he made his last appearance in *Flore.*

All of the ballets in King Louis' time were elaborate and formal. They dealt usually with gods and goddesses. For a while only members of the court danced in them, but the King soon tired of their lack of skill. He brought together professional writers like Molière, Quinault, and Benserade; the composer Jean-Baptiste Lully; and the choreographer Charles Beauchamp. To improve the dancing, he organized a Royal Academy of Dance in 1661. This was

the beginning of today's Paris Opera Ballet School.

By 1681 France had her first prima ballerina, the leading lady in a ballet company. She was Mademoiselle Lafontaine. Paintings show her to be lovely and very dignified in her long gown, her high-heeled slippers, and plumed headdress. She danced the leading role that year in *Le Triomphe de l'Amour* ("The Triumph of Love") with music by Lully.

Mademoiselle Lafontaine was the first of a series of virtuoso dancers, each of whom brought something new to ballet. Marie Camargo (1710–70) boldly shortened the ballet costume from ankle length to calf length, which allowed her to move about more freely. She removed the heels from her slippers so that she could perform intricate steps like the *entrechat,* a quick crossing of the feet in the air. Gaetan Vestris (1729–1808) was the first male dancer to show in his leaps and swift turns that certain steps were better suited for men than for women. But dancers, no matter how clever they are, depend upon choreographers.

The great choreographer Jean Georges Noverre (1727–1810) looked at the dancers around him and became angry. Ballet had become merely an opportunity for dancers to show off their technique. Noverre believed that ballet should express strong emotions and tell a story. His ballets showed great dramatic movement and a wide range of expression. Since Noverre's reforms, ballet has become more like the drama and less like a display of dancing tricks.

Marie Taglioni (1804–84)

All of us have at some time wished to fly. The dancers of the early 19th century felt that way too. The ballerinas portrayed water sprites, tree sprites, and spirits of dead maidens. They wore soft, filmy dresses and often tiny wings on their shoulders. Sometimes they were actually attached to wires so that they could soar above the treetops or cast their shadow upon a lake. More often they gave the illusion of lightness by rising to the very tips of their toes. Pictures of Marie Taglioni always show her this way.

In 1832 Taglioni's father, Filippo, created a ballet especially for her, called *La Sylphide*. It was about a mysterious forest creature—a sylphide—so playful and so sad that she lured the young Scotsman, James, away from his fiancée. Poets and musicians of this period, called the romantic age, loved sadness. So in *La Sylphide,* as in most romantic ballets, the end was tragic and the sylphide died.

Carlotta Grisi (1819–99)

While Taglioni was touring in Russia, an Italian girl, Carlotta Grisi, arrived at the Paris Opera. Jules Perrot (1810–92), the finest male dancer of the day, fell in love with Carlotta. So did the famous poet Théophile Gautier.

Gautier wrote the ideal ballet for Grisi. It was *Giselle,* the story of a gentle peasant girl who fell in love with Albrecht, a count in disguise. The count was engaged to somebody else, and when Giselle found out, she went insane and died. Later she rose from her tomb to dance with Albrecht. Perrot designed all of Grisi's solos in *Giselle,* and Gautier saw her dance it for the first time in 1841.

▶ RUSSIAN BALLET

Many of the most popular ballets are the work of dancers and choreographers from Russia. If you were to ask a friend to name his favorite ballets, he might say *Swan Lake* and *The Sleeping Beauty,* or *Scheherazade* and *Petrouchka.* These—and many more—came from Marius Petipa and Michel Fokine.

Marius Petipa (1822–1910)

Petipa, born in France, won his fame as a choreographer in St. Petersburg in 1862 with a three-act spectacle, *The Pharaoh's Daughter.* In all of Petipa's ballets there were special display pieces called variations. These were performed by the leading virtuoso dancers and usually had nothing to do with the story.

Petipa's ballets were long, had much panto-

Dame Margot Fonteyn and Rudolf Nureyev in the Royal Ballet's *Swan Lake.*

mime (acting without words) and had complicated stories. But the costumes, settings, and music did not always fit the period in which the story took place. Nobody seemed to mind except Michel Fokine.

Michel Fokine (1880–1942)

Fokine was a student at the Imperial School of Ballet when Petipa was director of its company. Unlike many of the students, who were satisfied merely to learn technique, Fokine had a lively, curious mind. He spent hours in museums, read a great deal, and painted well.

One day Fokine wrote a letter to the director of the school saying that he would like to make a new kind of ballet. All of the parts would fit the period in which the story was set, and the dramatic action would not be interrupted by special variations. He was not allowed to go ahead, but in the meantime he began to make dances for his friends. His smallest dance, *The Dying Swan,* became his best known. His classmate Anna Pavlova first performed it in 1905 for a charity performance, and to this day *The Dying Swan* is associated with her.

Sergei Diaghilev (1872–1929)

In St. Petersburg, the home of the Russian Imperial Ballet, a group of young men—authors, painters, musicians—often met in the evenings to talk about their work. They decided to start a magazine called *The World of Art,* and they made Sergei Diaghilev the editor.

Diaghilev was a good organizer, and he was eager to show the French what the Russian arts were really like. In 1906 he took an exhibit of Russian paintings to Paris. In 1908 he gave the Parisians a performance of Moussorgsky's opera *Boris Godunov.* By 1911 he had put together his own ballet company, which combined Russian dancers, choreographers, scene designers, and composers. At the beginning Michel Fokine was its leading choreographer, and some of its best dancers were Anna Pavlova, Mikhail Mordkin, Tamara Karsavina, Vaslav Nijinsky, and Adolph Bolm.

Diaghilev was restless. He needed new faces around him, and so he encouraged three young men—Vaslav Nijinsky, Léonide Massine, and George Balanchine—to make ballets. He chose daring designers like Picasso, Léon Bakst, Alexandre Benois, Matisse, Rouault, Utrillo, Derain, Braque, and Laurencin; and composers like Igor Stravinsky, Manuel de Falla, Maurice Ravel, Debussy, Auric, and Milhaud.

The ballets we know best from the 20 years that the Diaghilev Company toured Europe are Fokine's *Les Sylphides, Scheherazade, The Firebird, Carnaval, Petrouchka,* and *The Spectre of the Rose;* Massine's *La Boutique Fantasque, The Rite of Spring,* and *The Three-Cornered Hat;* and Balanchine's *Apollo, The Prodigal Son,* and *Rossignol,* in which 12-year-old Alicia Markova danced the nightingale.

Diaghilev's company disbanded when he died in 1929. But artists like Massine, Balanchine, and Serge Lifar influenced dance in the United States, England, and France.

▶ BALLET IN ENGLAND

Ninette de Valois and Marie Rambert, formerly of the Diaghilev Company, taught and founded companies of their own in England.

Marie Rambert looked for new and experimental ballets. She discovered talented young dancers and choreographers like Frederick Ashton, who became leading choreographer for Britain's Royal Ballet, and Antony Tudor, who became leading choreographer for the American Ballet Theatre.

Ninette de Valois had always wanted a national ballet company. She took her first step in 1933 when she became head of the Vic-Wells Ballet. Alicia Markova was its leading dancer. The company grew and soon became known as the Sadler's Wells Ballet. In 1935 De Valois allowed a 16-year-old girl with large, dark eyes and a serious face to make her debut as the Swan Queen. This was Margot Fonteyn, who was to become one of the world's best-loved ballerinas. In 1957 De Valois saw her dream come true. As Dame Ninette, she was head of the Royal Ballet.

More than any other choreographer, Frederick Ashton transformed the style of the Royal Ballet. Whether witty (*A Wedding Bouquet, Façade*) or serious (*Ondine, Enigma Variations*), his ballets have delicacy, charm, and respect for the classical tradition. He retired as artistic director of the company in 1970.

Snow scene from *The Nutcracker*, performed by the New York City Ballet.

Melissa Hayden and Jacques d'Amboise in *Figure in the Carpet*.

Maria Tallchief in Balanchine's version of *The Firebird*.

DANISH BALLET

Just as Petipa had been the strongest influence in Russia, Auguste Bournonville was the father of Danish ballet. He taught his dancers to act with emotion, training his men to move strongly and his women to move delicately.

The Danish version of *La Sylphide,* staged by Bournonville, combines the best qualities of Danish dancing. And 20th-century works like Ashton's *Romeo and Juliet,* Roland Petit's *Carmen,* and Birgit Cullberg's *Moon Reindeer* have introduced audiences to outstanding Danish artists like Erik Bruhn, Henning Kronstam, Mona Vangsaa, Niels Bjorn Larsen, Toni Lander, and Peter Martins.

BALLET IN AMERICA

While the Diaghilev Ballet made a great impression on Europe, it was Anna Pavlova and her company who conquered American audiences. They first toured the United States in 1910, and to this day many people think first of Pavlova when they think of ballet.

In 1933 a group arrived in the United States with dancers whose names were strange and hard to pronounce. They included Alexandra Danilova, Natalie Krassovska, Milada

George Balanchine directs his dancers at a rehearsal.

Mladova, Mia Slavenska, Tamara Toumanova, Igor Youskevitch, and George Zoritch. They belonged to the Ballet Russe de Monte Carlo. American audiences loved this company. Its leading dancer, Alexandra Danilova, was the idol of many young people all over the country.

At first the Ballet Russe performed mostly Russian ballets by Russian choreographers. But after a while it turned to American themes like the cowboys and ranchers in Agnes de Mille's *Rodeo* (1942).

American dancers and choreographers began to form companies of their own. Catherine Littlefield started the company named after her; Willam Christensen started the San Francisco Ballet; and Chicago dancers Ruth Page and Bentley Stone organized their own company.

In 1933 George Balanchine made his home in New York City. He was eventually to become director and principal choreographer of the New York City Ballet. It is America's classical company, while the American Ballet Theatre (originally Ballet Theatre) is America's company of many styles.

While the New York City Ballet has centered around Balanchine's personality and style, the American Ballet Theatre has blended its Russian, English, and American heritages into dancing and choreographic styles that are very rich.

Typically American is Jerome Robbins, whose first ballets were for Ballet Theatre. The beginning was *Fancy Free* (1944), about three sailors on shore leave. It marked his style, which is witty, human, sometimes brash, and has a sense of rhythm that could only come from someone raised in a big city (New York) and exposed to jazz.

While Robbins is an American, Balanchine has a feeling for Americans. Since becoming artistic director of the New York City Ballet in 1948, he not only has made very musical ballets but has trained dancers with a long, slim, "American" line.

In his ballets *Serenade, The Four Temperaments,* and *Symphony in C,* Balanchine tested their technique. In *La Valse, Donizetti Variations,* and *Liebeslieder Walser,* he created a special atmosphere. In *Agon, Ivesiana,* and *Monumentum Pro Gesualdo* he challenged their intelligence. In all his works Balanchine

1

2

3

4

5

Ruth Ann King of the New York City Ballet demonstrates the five basic positions in ballet. Every dancer has learned them since Charles Beauchamp first named them at the end of the 17th century.

had fine dancers like Maria Tallchief, Edward Villella, Melissa Hayden, Jacques d'Amboise, and Violette Verdy.

Other professional companies have come into the picture, including the City Center-Joffrey Ballet, directed by Robert Joffrey; the National Ballet of Washington, directed by Frederick Franklin; and the Boston Ballet, directed by E. Virginia Williams.

And all over the country companies of younger dancers (ages 13 to 18) have been contributing a special flavor and quality to American dance. Some of these will become professional companies and others will not, but all of them are giving a great vitality to ballet in America.

As further proof of the strength of American dance, there are two national organizations—the National Association for Regional Ballet and the Association of American Dance Companies—dedicated to its welfare. And, if government funds continue to be channeled toward the arts, the future of American dance looks bright.

DORIS HERING
Associate Editor and Critic, *Dance Magazine*
Reviewed by GEORGE BALANCHINE

See also DANCE.

BALLOONS AND BALLOONING

A big balloon soars up into the sky for a very simple reason: It is filled with a gas that is lighter than air.

Air itself is made up of gases, the chief ones being oxygen and nitrogen. Certain other gases are lighter than air. One of these is helium, and that is why a balloon filled with helium rises. Hot air will also make a balloon rise because it is lighter than cold air.

You have probably heard people say that hot air rises. And so it does. In a room the air is usually hotter near the ceiling than near the floor. Hot air rises because its gas particles are less dense. That is, they have spread out; there are fewer of them in a cubic foot of space than there would be if the air were cold. This means that hot air is lighter than cold air.

You can demonstrate with this simple experiment that warming air expands. Snap the open end of a small balloon over the top of an empty soda-pop bottle. Since the air in the bottle is cold, the balloon hangs limp. Now set the pop bottle in a pan of hot water. The hot water heats the bottle, which warms the cold air inside the bottle. Gradually the hot air in the bottle pushes its way into the balloon. The balloon slowly fills with air and begins to inflate.

▶THE FIRST BIG BALLOONS

The first big balloon was built by two French brothers: Joseph-Michel and Jacques-Etienne Montgolfier. Made of paper and cloth, the balloon was many feet high. On June 5, 1783, they launched their balloon by building a fire under it. When hot air from the fire filled the balloon, the brothers released it and watched it float hundreds of feet into the air.

Since their first balloon had carried no passengers, the Montgolfier brothers decided to build one that could. When they announced their plan, people laughed, but the brothers went ahead. Watched by a big crowd, they built a fire under a huge balloon to which they had tied a basket carrier. Hot air from the fire filled the balloon, which was held down by ropes. In the basket the brothers put a rooster, a duck, and a young sheep. The balloon was released, and the basket, with its animal passengers, floated upward.

High above the earth the warm air inside the balloon cooled off, and the balloon slowly floated to earth. No longer laughing, the watchers cheered. Live passengers had been carried into the air and returned safely to earth for the first time in history.

▶MAN'S FIRST FLIGHT

The wonderful feat inspired two brave men to risk their lives by being the first humans to leave the ground and fly in the air. One man was the Marquis d'Arlandes; the other man was Jean François Pilâtre de Rozier, a French doctor. In a Paris park they tied a basket to the bottom of their beautifully decorated balloon. A roaring fire filled the balloon with hot air. The two men jumped into the basket and released the ropes. The balloon rose above the heads of the people on the ground for the first human flight. The year was still 1783.

The danger of fire was always present at these balloon launchings. One spark could have sent a balloon up in flames. That same year, 1783, a French scientist, Professor Jacques A. C. Charles, thought of a way around the problem: Why not inflate a balloon with hydrogen, a gas lighter than air? He tested the idea by filling a balloon with hydrogen and tying the balloon's nozzle to keep the gas from escaping. His hydrogen-filled balloon rose into the air.

After this success a friend, Jean Robert, joined Professor Charles in another balloon project. The two men built a balloon with a valve in the top; to the valve they tied a rope that led down into a basket under the balloon. Inflating the balloon with hydrogen, they climbed into the basket, which was weighted with sandbags. When Professor Charles tossed out a few sandbags, he and his friend rose to float high above Paris. After being in the air for 2 hours, they decided to come down. To descend they used their amazing new invention—the valve at the top of the balloon.

Professor Charles pulled on the rope and so opened the valve. The open valve allowed hydrogen to escape from inside the balloon. Little by little the hydrogen was allowed to escape, and slowly the balloon deflated (grew smaller). The weight of the men, sandbags, and basket pulled it toward the earth. The professor continued to open and close the valve, allowing more hydrogen to escape. (This action is called valving down.) The men landed safely.

From 1783 to 1785 many men went up in balloons in France, England, and Germany. Ballooning had become a sport. But, as always, someone wanted to do a daring thing that no one had ever done before. A Frenchman named Jean Pierre Blanchard wanted to cross the English Channel from England to France in a gondola, as the basket tied to a balloon is called. He was sure he could do it but didn't have the money to build the balloon. An American friend, Dr. John Jeffries, from Boston, Massachusetts, paid for the balloon. On January 7, 1785, Blanchard and Jeffries inflated their balloon on the cliffs of Dover, in England. They climbed aboard the gondola, released the balloon, and after a number of hair-raising experiences, floated across the English Channel to land in France. They were the first men to cross a body of water in a balloon.

SCIENTIFIC RESEARCH IN A BALLOON

Eight years later, in January, 1793, Blanchard was in Philadelphia, Pennsylvania, then the capital of the United States. He was there to make the first balloon flight in America. Many famous people came to watch, among them George and Martha Washington, Vice-President John Adams, and Secretary of State Thomas Jefferson. The French ambassador to the United States stood beside George Washington. At ten o'clock on the morning of January 9, Blanchard jumped into his gondola and took off. His balloon floated to a height of more than 5,000 feet. At that height he performed a few scientific experiments—the first ever made by a human being high above the earth.

An American scientist, Dr. Caspar Wistar, had wanted to know if the air at that height was different than air at ground level. So Blanchard let the air fill six bottles and then sealed them. Dr. Wistar later studied the air and learned that air 5,000 feet up has less oxygen than the air at sea level.

Dr. Benjamin Rush, a famous Philadelphia physician, had wanted to know what happens to a person's body at an altitude of 5,000 feet. He wondered whether the heart beats faster or slower. Blanchard counted his own heartbeats. High above the earth his heart beat 92 times a minute; on the ground it beat only 84 times a minute.

That was the first new scientific knowledge to come out of ballooning.

Years passed, and people performed amazing feats with balloons. A French balloonist, André Garnerin, announced that he would jump from a balloon and float to earth. In secret he invented a parachute. Then, in 1797, Garnerin floated up to 2,000 feet and jumped from the balloon's gondola. His body fell toward earth. Suddenly a silk parachute opened, and Garnerin floated down in safety.

FURTHER RESEARCH AND TRAGIC RESULTS

Scientists wanted to know many things about the upper atmosphere. Did the air get colder and colder? How high could man go

First manned balloon crossing of English Channel, 1785.

before there was so little oxygen that he would die of suffocation? As the years passed, daring balloonists attempted to find out.

On April 15, 1875, three Frenchmen floated up in a balloon named *Zenith,* carrying bottles of oxygen with them. At an altitude of 8,000 feet, they took their first breaths of oxygen from the bottles. At 15,000 feet they were shivering with cold but went on up to 25,000 feet—a world record for the time. But at that height the lack of oxygen in the air suddenly affected them. They lost consciousness so quickly that they could not lift the oxygen bottles to their faces. One of them pulled the valve rope before they all fainted. When *Zenith* landed, two men were dead. The third was unconscious, but he recovered to tell what had happened. Despite the loss of life, the attempt to explore the upper atmosphere was a success, for the instruments had recorded many scientific facts.

In 1927 an American military balloonist, Captain Hawthorne Gray, ascended in an open-gondola balloon. He made notes about what he did in flight and how he felt. At 12,000 feet he put on his oxygen mask. At 19,000 feet he took the air temperature—0 degrees Fahrenheit. At 31,000 feet the temperature was -32 degrees. At 40,000 feet the temperature had risen; it was only -28 degrees. This was an important discovery. (Many years later other scientists learned that above the warmer region at 40,000 feet the temperature drops again. Once more, the greater the height, the colder it is.)

Unfortunately Captain Gray also gave his life for science. He lost consciousness at 44,000 feet, after pulling his valve cord.

▶ HIGHER AND HIGHER

Scientists realized the importance of balloons in scientific research, and they wanted to go higher and higher, to explore the upper atmosphere—and outer space.

How could that be done safely? Auguste Piccard, a professor at the University of Brussels, decided to create a world within a world, and he did. He built an aluminum gondola that was round, like a ball. Inside it he put oxygen and pressure tanks as well as many other things to create a little world of his own. Hanging beneath a mammoth balloon, the gondola carried Professor Piccard and an assistant up more than 51,000 feet, in 1931. The men intended to go higher, but they ran into serious trouble and had to come back to earth.

Again, in 1932, Professor Piccard made an ascent in his round, metal gondola and reached a height of more than 54,000 feet. He made many tests, which added much to the knowledge of the upper atmosphere. Piccard also studied cosmic rays and gave us our first true knowledge of them. On both flights he and his assistants were the first men to see outer space without the aid of a telescope. They looked out into space, where they saw nothing but deep purple and black, with the rim of the earth like a halo.

In the United States two army captains, Albert W. Stevens and Orvil A. Anderson, experimented with balloons. Sponsored by the U. S. Army Air Corps and the National Geographic Society, they built a gondola that was a true laboratory in the sky. Stevens and Anderson put more than 70 pieces of scientific research equipment into the gondola and floated up to 72,395 feet—more than 13 miles above the earth. One of the many things they discovered on this flight is that spores of bacteria and fungi are carried by the air into the upper atmosphere and thus around the world. Their flight was made on November 11, 1935.

▶ NEW PLASTIC BALLOONS

World War II stopped balloon research. But during the war plastics were perfected, among them polyethylene plastic. This material is light, strong, and tough. It makes good balloons. So, soon after the war, balloon scientists went back to studies that opened the way for actual flights into outer space. Malcolm D. Ross and M. Lee Lewis were among the first men to explore again with balloons. Those two U. S. Navy officers went to 40,000 feet in an open basket, in 1954. In 1960 Ross and Victor Prather, Jr., ascended to 113,740 feet in an open gondola, a record altitude for both open and closed gondolas. The purpose of the flight was to test the pressurized space suits designed for astronauts.

On August 19, 1957, Air Force Major David G. Simons stepped into a capsule 8

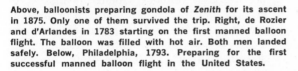

Above, balloonists preparing gondola of *Zenith* for its ascent in 1875. Only one of them survived the trip. Right, de Rozier and d'Arlandes in 1783 starting on the first manned balloon flight. The balloon was filled with hot air. Both men landed safely. Below, Philadelphia, 1793. Preparing for the first successful manned balloon flight in the United States.

Auguste Piccard in his aluminum gondola, 1932.

feet high and 3 feet wide. Alone in the capsule he rose to 102,000 feet and hung for 24 hours on the very edge of space. Almost 100 per cent of the atmosphere was below him. Above him was space.

▶ EXPLORING WITH UNMANNED BALLOONS

In the late 1950's scientists sent aloft hundreds of unmanned balloons to study the upper atmosphere. Instruments in the balloons sent back countless new facts. Several times telescope-cameras were sent to 85,000 feet to take photos of the sun, the moon, and other celestial bodies. From the earth we look skyward through the dense atmosphere and cannot get a clear, unobstructed view of the universe. But at 85,000 feet the air is clear. Dust and other particles that make our atmosphere murky have been left behind. Telescopes in unmanned balloons get a clear look at the universe.

However, scientists were not content to rely on complicated mechanisms operated by remote control. They wanted to go up with their telescopes. But they needed a special telescope that could stay on target and not be affected by the motion of the balloon. The first to design and build such a telescope was Dr. John Strong, professor of astrophysics at The Johns Hopkins University. When his instrument was mounted on top of the gondola, the scientists inside could operate it themselves. The first men to test the new equipment were Commander Malcolm D. Ross and astronomer Charles Moore. They ascended to 80,000 feet, in 1959. With the telescope they studied Venus and for the first time proved that there is water vapor in that planet's atmosphere.

▶ PRELUDE TO SPACE

During the 1950's balloons paved the way for men to enter outer space. Balloons as tall as 50-story buildings rose to gather information about cosmic rays and other radiations from outer space. Monkeys were sent aloft in balloons as a test of what happens to the body at high altitudes. Guided missiles were carried aloft by balloons and then fired from the edge of space out into space. The balloon was a workhorse, constantly providing space scientists with information needed before man himself could enter space.

On August 12, 1960, a rocket was launched carrying a satellite in the form of a balloon. When the rocket reached space and went into orbit, the balloon was ejected. The balloon-satellite, Echo I, began its continual orbit of the earth. Painted with aluminum so that it reflected the rays of the sun at night, Echo I was clearly visible in its nightly orbit. You may have seen it yourself. Much information of scientific value came from its orbiting.

Every day of the year weathermen send up hundreds of small balloons to gather information about the weather. As you read this several balloon-satellites are orbiting the earth. Scientists plan to launch more and more balloons carrying instruments to study the upper atmosphere.

The slow, lazily floating balloon is still vitally important to scientists engaged in weather and space research work.

LYNN and GRAY POOLE
Authors, *Balloons Fly High,*
Ballooning in the Space Age

BALLOT. See ELECTIONS.
BALTIC SEA. See OCEANS AND SEAS.

BALTIMORE

Baltimore, Maryland's leading city, is on the banks of the Patapsco River near Chesapeake Bay. The city's location between North and South has given Baltimore the flavor of an old southern city mixed with that of a modern industrial community. Rows of handsome red brick houses stand not far from huge factories and bustling highways.

Baltimore is one of the leading ports of the United States and a center of industry, culture, education, and transportation. The city's main industries are steel and other primary metals, shipbuilding, food processing, electronics, machinery, chemicals, copper refining, and the production of a variety of goods ranging from detergents to clothing.

Among the city's best-known colleges and universities are Johns Hopkins University, which has a world-famous school of medicine; the University of Maryland Baltimore Professional Schools; Loyola College; St. Mary's Seminary and University; the University of Baltimore; and Morgan State University. The Enoch Pratt Free Library is known for its excellent book collection. Outstanding art collections are housed in the Walters Art Gallery and the Baltimore Museum of Art. The city's symphony orchestra is considered one of the finest in the United States. To sports lovers, Baltimore is known as the home of the Orioles baseball team, the Colts football team, and Pimlico Racetrack, where horses run in the Preakness each spring.

Baltimore, which was first settled in the 17th century, takes its name from Lord Baltimore, the founder of the Maryland colony. Many monuments and landmarks reflect the city's long and colorful history. One of the United States Navy's first ships, the frigate *Constellation* (1797), is anchored in the inner harbor. It is believed to be the oldest ship still afloat in the world. During the War of 1812, Baltimore's Fort McHenry was heavily bombarded by the British fleet. This event inspired Francis Scott Key to write "The Star-Spangled Banner" (1814). One of the nation's greatest writers, Edgar Allan Poe (1809–49), is buried in Westminster Churchyard. Baltimore also contains such landmarks as the nation's first Roman Catholic cathedral, the country's oldest museum building, and the first railroad station in the United States.

The Cumberland Road had brought prosperity to Baltimore in the early years of the 19th century. When the Erie Canal was opened in 1825, Baltimore was threatened by a loss of trade. The city met this threat by building the first railroad in the United States—the Baltimore and Ohio.

Baltimore has also played an important part in the country's political history. It was the meeting place of the Continental Congress during the Revolutionary War. Later the city was the site of many national political conventions. About ten of the country's presidential candidates won their party's nomination in Baltimore.

Reviewed by GEORGE BEISHLAG
Formerly, Towson State University

See also MARYLAND.

The skyline of downtown Baltimore.

BALZAC, HONORÉ DE (1799–1850)

Honoré de Balzac, French novelist, was born May 20, 1799, in Tours. His father was a civil servant there and important in local politics. At the age of 8 Honoré was sent to one of the best schools—the Collège de Vendôme—but he spent most of his time day-dreaming and reading. He returned to Tours in 1813 and moved with his family to Paris in 1814. He studied law from 1816 to 1819, but when his father retired to the country Honoré announced he would never be a lawyer. He wished to try writing instead. His parents reluctantly agreed.

His first work, a verse tragedy, *Cromwell*, was a failure. Balzac then turned out, either alone or in collaboration with other writers, a number of inferior popular novels. He used pseudonyms for these and never considered them part of his true work.

Balzac observed in detail the life around him in Paris and later described it in his novels. He fell in love with Madame de Berny, an older woman who became his counselor and "conscience" for nearly 15 years. The heroine of his novel *Le Lys dans la vallée* is a portrait of her.

Discouraged by his lack of literary success, Balzac sought his fortune as a publisher, printer, and type manufacturer, but he earned only heavy debts. He returned to writing and for the first time, in 1829, published a novel under his own name. It was an immediate success and gained him entrance into high society.

His first masterpiece was *Eugénie Grandet* (1833), about the daughter of a miser. A plan now began to take shape in Balzac's mind. He would portray the whole of society. He wrote novels depicting private life, provincial life, Parisian life, political life, country life, and even military life. He gave these novels the over-all title *La Comédie humaine* (*The Human Comedy*), in contrast to Dante's *Divine Comedy,* for he wished to show in detail the earthly activities of men. He was not able to complete his plan before he died on August 18, 1850, but he left a vivid history of the society of his time.

BAMBOO. See GRASSES.

BANANA

Bananas were used as a food for men even before history began to be written. The armies of Alexander the Great found the banana growing in India in 327 B.C. No doubt it was growing there long before that time. Because of an old story that the sages of India rested in the shade of the plant and ate its fruit, the banana is often called the "fruit of the wise men."

Plant scientists believe that roots of banana plants were carried to the east coast of Africa by a people who moved there in ancient times. From there the banana plant was carried across the African continent to the Guinea Coast by early Arab traders.

When Portuguese explorers discovered the Guinea Coast of Africa in 1482, they found bananas growing there. These explorers took roots of the plant, and its African name, banana, to the Portuguese colonies in the Canary Islands. The next step in the journey of the banana plant was across the Atlantic Ocean to the New World. In 1516, only a few years after Columbus' famous voyages of discovery, a Spanish missionary brought this useful plant to the Caribbean island of Hispaniola. Other missionaries followed his example and planted bananas on the other islands of the Caribbean and on the tropical mainland. Thus, the banana plant had to go more than halfway around the world to reach Central America, where so many of the world's bananas are grown today.

There is a story that the fruit of the banana plant was first brought from the Caribbean islands to New England about 1690. It is said that the Puritans boiled the strange fruit and didn't like it at all.

Not until the latter part of the 19th century were bananas brought into the United States in quantities for sale in the stores. Before that time very few people except those who had traveled in tropical countries had ever seen or tasted a banana. Even after banana schooners began coming into New Orleans, Boston, and other ports, only those who lived in or near the seacoast cities were able to eat bananas. The banana is perishable. It cannot be stored, like some other fruits. Within a period of 10 to 20 days bananas must be harvested, shipped several thousand miles, ripened, and sent out to the stores where they are sold. Today's modern transportation—fast ships, trains, and trucks —makes it possible for families in Chicago or in Calgary to have bananas to eat every day.

▶ **THE BANANA PLANT AND ITS GROWTH**

The banana plant is often called a tree. However, it is not a real tree because there is no wood in the stem rising above the ground. The stem is made up of leaves growing very close together, one inside the other. The leaves spreading out at the top of this stem usually are from 8 to 12 feet long and about 2 feet wide. These leaves spread out and rise in the air, making the banana plant look like a palm tree. When the plant is old enough to bear fruit, it is from 15 to 30 feet high and its stem is from 9 to 16 inches thick.

Bananas grow in bunches. Each bunch is made up of 9 to 16 clusters of fruit, called "hands," and each hand contains from 12 to 20 separate bananas, called "fingers." A bunch of bananas usually weighs from 60 to 100 pounds.

The size of the plant and the size of the bunch of fruit depend on the climate and the kind of soil in the place where the plant grows. Bananas grow best where the soil is deep and rich and the climate is warm and moist. Bananas cannot be grown satisfactorily in any place where the temperature goes below 55 degrees Fahrenheit. For good fruit the temperature should not go below 70 degrees for any length of time. Bananas grow in all the moist, tropical areas of the world. Most of the bananas grown for sale in North America and Europe are grown in the lowlands of Central America, northern South America, tropical Africa, and in the Caribbean islands. In other tropical areas bananas are grown mainly for local use.

To grow bananas, pieces of rootstock (bits cut from the base of growing plants) are planted in holes about 1 foot deep and 11 to 18 feet apart. Each piece of rootstock must have one or more sprouts, or "eyes," like the eyes of a potato. Green shoots appear above

Bananas grow well in tropical Costa Rica. This bunch will be cut while still green and sent to far-off markets.

the ground 3 or 4 weeks later. Only the strongest shoot is allowed to become a plant. This plant forms its own rootstock, from which other plants later grow up beside the first one.

Banana plants need care and attention in order to produce fruit of good quality. They must be provided with water by irrigation if the normal rainfall does not supply enough water. The leaves must be sprayed to prevent damage by insects or plant diseases. The area around the plants must be kept free of weeds and grass. On a large plantation many workers are required to care for the plants and harvest the fruit.

About 9 or 10 months after planting, a flower appears on the banana plant. This flower is at the end of a long stalk, which grows from the base up through the center of the stem and turns downward when it emerges from the top. Small bananas form on this flower stalk as it grows downward. Bananas really grow upside down. As the small bananas form on the stalk, they point downward, but as they grow they turn and point upward. In three months they are plump and ready to harvest. Bananas are harvested while they are still green. Even when they are to be eaten where they are grown, they are not allowed to ripen on the plant. A banana that turns yellow on the plant loses its flavor. Also, the peel bursts open and insects get into the fruit. The finest flavor develops only when the fruit is cut while green and ripened afterward. The bananas sold in stores in the United States, Canada, and Europe are shipped there under refrigeration (53 to 56 degrees) while still green and then ripened in special rooms where cool temperatures (60 to 70 degrees) and moist air combine to allow the best-tasting fruit to be developed.

Each banana plant bears only one bunch of fruit. When the bunch is harvested, the plant is cut down. But as the plant has been growing to maturity and producing fruit, another plant has been growing beside it from the same rootstock. Soon this plant's fruit will be ready to harvest. This cycle of production will continue for years, if the plants are not destroyed by diseases, high winds, or floods.

NORWOOD C. THORNTON
United Fruit Company

BANDS AND BAND MUSIC

Everyone loves a band. No football game, parade, circus, or Fourth of July celebration would be quite complete without a rousing march. Not only does everyone love to hear a band, but almost everyone loves to play in one. In the United States alone there are millions of people who play in bands now or who have played in school, college, or town bands.

The word **band** is a broad term that describes a group of musicians performing on wind and percussion instruments. One thinks immediately of a brightly uniformed marching band, perhaps part of an army or navy unit or the band of a college or high school.

Aside from marching bands and bands that entertain at fairs, public ceremonies, and informal social gatherings, there are other bands that exist only to perform music in a concert, just as an orchestra does. Such bands are known as concert or symphonic bands, or wind ensembles. What all bands have in common is that they are composed of wind and percussion instruments in various combinations. Bands usually have at least 50 players.

Since bands often perform out-of-doors, they require instruments whose sounds carry easily. Trumpets, trombones, tubas, horns, drums—all are instruments capable of making plenty of noise with little effort on the part of the player. The large family of woodwinds, including clarinets, oboes, bassoons, and flutes (and their relatives, bass clarinets, English horns, saxophones, and piccolos), also has this advantage.

A second requirement is that the instruments be easy to carry. It is impossible to march while playing a cello or a double bass; even the violin is not easy to play while one is walking. But one can easily play brass and woodwind instruments while marching. And of course the band has always required instruments that create the proper military excitement. For this the brass and percussion instruments are perfect.

There is a special type of band called a brass band. As its name implies, it uses only brass instruments and no woodwinds. Many excellent Salvation Army bands are of this type. They usually have 24 players and produce a good, well-blended sound despite their limits of tone quality and range.

A fife and drum band from Newport, Rhode Island.

EARLY HISTORY

Bands of some sort have existed almost from biblical times. Armies have always marched to the beat of drums, and soldiers have always taken their signals from the sounds of a trumpet or bugle of some sort. Little groups of wind-instrument players have sounded the hours of the day. (In 16th-century Germany the players assembled on the tower of the town's tallest building for this.) Bands have added to the beauty and impressiveness of church services and accompanied all kinds of outdoor public ceremonies.

Until the middle of the 18th century, however, there were practically no regularly organized bands. The combination of instruments used for any occasion was determined by whatever instruments were available in the town and whatever players were free at the moment and could be assembled for the occasion. New instruments were being invented (the clarinet, for instance, appeared around 1700) and old ones improved. Great excitement was created in Europe when, around 1750, a whole family of new percussion instruments was introduced by traveling bands from Turkey. Composers were soon busy writing "Turkish music," with parts for tambourines, cymbals, triangles, bass drums, and other clanging and beating instruments.

In 1763 King Frederick the Great of Prussia was the first to regulate the kinds and number of instruments used in his bands. He ordered that all of his military bands have at least two oboes, two clarinets, two horns, and two bassoons. To this basic group other instruments, including flute, trumpet, and drum, were gradually added. By the end of the 18th century, the bands were playing regularly not only for military parades but also for special court functions and popular outdoor concerts.

BEGINNINGS OF THE MODERN BAND

The modern band was born in the year 1789 as a result of the French Revolution. In that year Bernard Sarrette (1765–1858) founded the Band of the National Guard in Paris. This group of 45 players was immediately in demand for the popular demonstrations and numerous public ceremonies of the new government. By 1790 this band had 70 players and led to the formation of many military and town bands throughout Europe.

Many of the leading composers of the time served as bandmasters and wrote pieces for their bands. François Joseph Gossec (1734–1829) served for a time as bandmaster of the National Guard Band, with Charles Simon Catel (1773–1830) as his assistant. Their symphonies and overtures are still played by bands today. Others who composed for band included Luigi Cherubini (1760–1842), Ferdinando Paër (1771–1839), Etienne Mehul (1763–1817), and even the great composer Ludwig van Beethoven (1770–1827). The French band tradition reached its highest point in the great *Funeral and Triumphal Symphony* of Hector Berlioz (1803–69). It was written for a band of 208 players for the dedication of the Bastille Column in 1840.

WILHELM WIEPRECHT (1802–72)

Wilhelm Wieprecht was chiefly responsible for organizing the band as we know it today. A forward-looking musician, he experimented with mechanical improvements for the instruments. It was through his example that the use of horns and trumpets with valves, or keys, became universally accepted. It was then possible to play these instruments in more difficult kinds of music, and a greater variety of sound in band music resulted. This and the work of Adolphe Sax (inventor of the saxophone) and Theobald Boehm (who developed the modern flute) contributed to the development of the modern band and its music.

Wieprecht was responsible for the first of the massed-band festivals and band contests, forerunners of today's school and college band festivals. In 1838 he organized a grand festival in which over 1,000 players plus 200 extra side drummers performed. The occasion was the visit of the Russian Emperor Nicholas to the King of Prussia. What a royal welcome it must have been!

By the middle of the 19th century, bands in Europe had become an important part of every country's musical as well as military life. Among the most famous bands in England were the band of the Royal Horse Guards and the band of the Grenadier Guards led by Sir Daniel Godfrey (1831–1903). Godfrey was probably the best-known bandmaster of his time. His many arrangements for band are still performed in England and America.

BANDS IN THE UNITED STATES

The development of bands and band music in the United States is one of the most colorful stories in American history. The earliest American bands were based on British models, and even before the American Revolution there is record of a band led by Josiah Flagg, of Boston. He was one of the first organizers of concerts in the American colonies. It is an interesting fact that Flagg's *Collection of the Best Psalm Tunes* was engraved by Paul Revere.

Although there is little historical record of bands in America before 1800, we know there was a wealth of band music composed in Revolutionary times and shortly thereafter. People, then, must have enjoyed band concerts and employed small bands for military purposes and public celebrations. Every American schoolchild knows the famous painting *The Spirit of '76*.

Marches were composed to celebrate patriotic occasions. The *Federal March* of Alexander Reinagle, performed in 1788, was written for the Fourth of July procession in Philadelphia celebrating the ratification of the United States Constitution. There were also many marches written in honor of the country's leading citizens and military heroes, such as *General Washington's Grand March* and *Jefferson's March*. During this period almost every town had its local band, attached to the town's militia.

PATRICK SARSFIELD GILMORE (1829–92)

Patrick S. Gilmore, born in County Galway, Ireland, in 1829, arrived in the United States at the age of 19. He was a man of enormous energy and vivid imagination and a born showman. In 1859 he took over the Boston Brigade Band, clad the players in bright new uniforms, rehearsed them over and over, and began an enormous schedule of performances. His band played for concerts, parades, and public ceremonies of all kinds. Also, as was the custom then, he provided dance music for balls and other events.

During the Civil War Gilmore conceived the idea of a huge band festival. With the help of the Army, he organized a Grand National Band consisting of 500 Army bandsmen plus a number of additional drum and bugle players. They were accompanied by a chorus of 5,000 schoolchildren. As a crowning touch Gilmore added 36 cannons, firing them by pushing hidden electric buttons. The great event took place in New Orleans on March 4, 1864.

Spectacular as this event was, it was only a hint of greater things to come. Returning to Boston after the war, Gilmore began to work on his next celebration, the National Peace Jubilee, given in 1869. This time he used an orchestra of 500, a band of 1,000, a chorus of 10,000, two batteries of cannons, and 100 firemen with hammers and anvils. The Jubilee lasted 5 days.

But Gilmore had even grander ideas. For 10 days, in 1872, he presented a World Peace Jubilee. His performers included an orchestra of 1,000, a band of 2,000, a chorus of 20,000, cannons, anvils, organ, and bells.

In 1873 Gilmore moved to New York, where he became leader of the 22nd Regiment Band. This became known as Gilmore's Band. He made several tours with the band in the United States, Canada, and Europe. He died in 1892.

JOHN PHILIP SOUSA (1854–1932)

John Philip Sousa was perhaps the greatest bandsman who ever lived. Trained as a violinist, he was only 24 years old when he was asked to take over the United States Marine Band. During Sousa's 12 years as director of the Marine Band, it achieved a national reputation for brilliance of performance that it retains to this day.

In 1892 Sousa left the Marine Band and formed a band of his own. He then toured extensively throughout the United States, Canada, and Europe. Sousa's band was probably the greatest band in the history of America. Its members included the leading virtuoso players of the day. His band had something that no band before him had and that every band since his has depended upon: Sousa's own marches. Brilliant in sound, rousing in spirit, and absolutely perfect for a band, they still form the backbone of band music everywhere. In fact, when most people think of band music, it is the sound of a Sousa march that they usually have in mind. Sousa wrote about 140 marches, including the famous *Stars and Stripes Forever, The Washington Post,* and *El Capitan*.

The United States Marine Band at Washington, D.C.

▶ EDWIN FRANKO GOLDMAN (1878–1956)

In the 20th century the nature of the band changed. The great touring bands of Sousa's time disappeared. Movies, television, and radio took the place of the old-time touring band that gave concerts wherever it went.

There is, however, no lack of popularity for the concert band, the kind that does not go on tours. The leading band of this type in the United States is the Goldman Band, founded in 1911 by Edwin Franko Goldman. Trained as a trumpet player, Goldman was for 10 years a member of the Metropolitan Opera Orchestra, in New York City. While he was playing there, he conceived the idea of forming a permanent concert band. By 1918 he was giving a regular series of outdoor summer band concerts; his players were among the leading musicians of the day. The summer concerts he started have become a tradition in the musical life of New York. They are now given under the direction of his son, Richard Franko Goldman.

Edwin Franko Goldman was the first bandmaster to encourage leading composers of the day to compose original works for band. It is through his efforts that today we are able to hear a large variety of music composed especially for bands.

RICHARD FRANKO GOLDMAN

See also PERCUSSION INSTRUMENTS; WIND INSTRUMENTS.

The Band of the Canadian Guards at Ottawa, Ontario.

Tourists relax at scenic Lake Louise.

A survey team visits a remote park area by helicopter.

Deer are protected in the park.

Moraine, one of Banff's lakes.

BANFF NATIONAL PARK

Banff National Park in Alberta is the oldest and one of the largest of Canada's national parks. Engineers were surveying a route for the Canadian Pacific Railway in the 1880's when they discovered hot springs on the eastern slopes of the Rocky Mountains, at the spot where the town of Banff now stands. When the discovery of these springs amid the beautiful, snow-capped peaks became known, the Canadian Government decided to preserve the mountain scenery and wildlife of the area as a public park. In 1885 an area around Banff was set aside as Rocky Mountains National Park. Later it was renamed Banff National Park. The area has been expanded until now it covers more than 6,500 square kilometers (2,500 square miles).

Through the deep valleys of Banff National Park, between such famous mountains as Eisenhower, Rundle, and Temple, glacier-fed streams flow into crystal-clear lakes. The main river is the Bow, which runs southward through most of the park. The most famous lake is Louise, renowned for its magnificent natural setting. The towns of Banff and Lake Louise are two world-famous resorts located in this park. People come long distances to enjoy such sports as skiing and tobogganing in winter and hiking, golf, and mountain climbing in summer. Banff's popular swimming pools use water from the hot springs at the foot of Sulphur Mountain. Wild animals are protected from hunters so that tourists may see moose, elk, mountain goats, and bears close by the highways.

Lake Louise is on the main Canadian Pacific Railway line at the east end of Kicking Horse Pass. Banff is also on the Canadian Pacific Railway and on the Trans-Canada Highway as well.

The Banff School of Fine Arts, now a part of the University of Calgary, was established at Banff in 1933 as a summer school to teach subjects connected with the theater. Since then it has grown tremendously. It offers courses in drama, ballet, opera, creative writing, and fine arts. Every summer students come from many countries to attend this unusual school.

JOHN S. MOIR
University of Toronto

The resort of Banff is popular in both summer and winter.

BANGLADESH

Born out of the ashes of what was once East Pakistan, Bangladesh is one of the newest nations of the world. With an estimated 75,000,000 people, it ranks eighth in population among the world's nations. It lies in the northeastern corner of the Indian subcontinent, at the head of the Bay of Bengal, and is bordered by India on the west, the north, and the northeast and by Burma on the southeast.

▶ THE PEOPLE

The people of Bangladesh are a mixture of Indo-Aryan, Mongoloid, and Dravidian elements. The two major divisions among the people are the Bengalis of the plains and the hill tribes who live in the Chittagong Hills in the east. Most of the people are Muslims. Hindus form the largest minority group, about 10 percent, and there are smaller numbers of Buddhists, Christians, and animists.

The Bengalis. The average Bengali is short and dark, with sharp features and a slender build. He has a vibrant personality. He is dreamy, emotional, changeable, and alert. He is poetical in his choice of words and articulate in his speech. He delights in argument, in the subtlety of ideas, and in ceaseless conversation. By nature he is tolerant, but he can be aroused to frenzied action when seized by indignation or passionate loyalty to an ideal. He is gentle and easygoing but is capable of hard and sustained work when called upon to do so.

Village life. The basic unit of life in Bangladesh is the village. It is usually located along the course of a river or canal with rice fields nearby. Communication between villages is chiefly by boat. There are thousands of these, of all sizes and shapes, and they travel up and down the rivers carrying people and goods. One of the most enchanting sights is a riverboat tossed on the gentle ripples of the water and framed in the rising or setting sun.

The people are poor; the average per capita income is estimated to be only between $70 and $75 a year. But they are by no means gloomy, and a smile comes readily to their lips. The everyday diet consists of rice and fish with some vegetables. The typical house is a slight structure, generally built of reeds, bamboo, and mats and plastered with clay or mud.

The usual dress for men is the lungi, a length of colored cotton cloth worn wrapped around the waist and stretching to the ankles. At work the men wear it tucked up to the knees. Women wear the sari, a long, often very colorful garment, which is draped around the body from the shoulders to the ankles. With their slim figures, graceful walk, and dark wistful eyes, the Bengali women are attractive in their own way. Traditionally, Muslim women cover their faces, especially when strangers are around.

▶ THE LAND

Bangladesh has an area of 55,126 square miles. It is a land of low plains crisscrossed by rivers, of which the most important are the Ganges and the Brahmaputra and their

---

FACTS AND FIGURES

PEOPLE'S REPUBLIC OF BANGLADESH is the official name of the country. Bangladesh means Bengal Nation.

CAPITAL: Dacca.

LOCATION: South Asia. **Latitude**—26° 38' N to 20° 46' N. **Longitude**—92° 41' E to 88° 02' E. **Area**—55,126 sq. mi.

PHYSICAL FEATURES: Highest point—Keokradong (4,034 ft.). **Lowest point**—sea level. **Chief rivers**—Ganges, Brahmaputra.

POPULATION: 75,000,000 (estimate).

LANGUAGE: Bengali, English.

RELIGION: Islam (predominant).

GOVERNMENT: Republic. Independent since 1971. **Head of state**—president. **Head of government**—prime minister. **International co-operation**—Commonwealth of Nations.

NATIONAL ANTHEM: "My Golden Bengal."

ECONOMY: Agricultural products—rice, jute, tea, mangoes, pineapples, coconuts, bananas, oilseeds. **Industries and products**—jute manufacturing, handicrafts, various light industries. **Chief exports**—jute and jute manufactures, fish, tea, tobacco, timber. **Chief imports**—metals, petroleum, coal, machinery, textiles. **Monetary unit**—taka.

A Bengali selling red peppers in a marketplace.

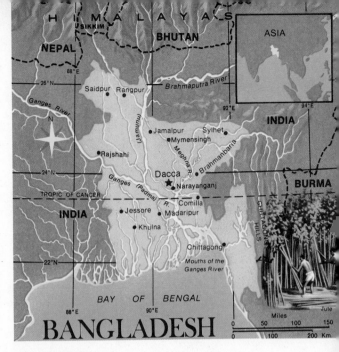

BANGLADESH

tributaries. It is a tropical land where there is no real winter, for the average mean temperatures range from over 60 degrees to over 90 degrees Fahrenheit. It is also a land of torrential monsoon rains—which fall from June to September—and violent winds called cyclones. These often bring heavy flooding and death and devastation to wide areas. (The cyclone of 1970 is reported to have killed 500,000 people.) In its gentler aspects, it is a pleasant, rather lazy land of many small villages. There are fewer than a dozen major urban centers. Of these, the most important are Dacca, the capital, with a population of about 1,250,000 (counting suburbs and surrounding towns), and Chittagong, which is the chief port.

▶ THE ECONOMY

Bangladesh is an agricultural country. The main food crop is rice. Jute and tea are the major commercial crops. Bangladesh is the world's leading exporter of jute, a fiber used to make sacks, burlap, and twine. Jute forms the basis of the country's foreign earnings. Mangoes, pineapples, coconuts, and bananas are also grown. Linseed and mustard seed provide much of the oil used for cooking. What industry there is consists mainly of jute mills and processing and consumer industries.

Bangladesh is not rich in minerals, and the lack of large-scale deposits of coal, petroleum, or natural gas makes firewood the major source of fuel. The country's hydroelectric

A farmer watering his rice fields. Rice is the staple food in Bangladesh.

Left: Riverboats are a common form of transportation.
Above: A typical small Bangladesh village.

potential is considerable but much of it still awaits development.

The size of the average farm is small and the farming methods used are old-fashioned. Bangladesh is one of the most densely populated areas in the world and the population is rising at a rate of 2.5 percent a year. At this rate, unless agriculture is modernized and effective means of population control are adopted, the country will not be able to feed its people adequately.

The many rivers and canals are both a blessing and a problem. They provide the chief means of transportation of people and goods. But to be used efficiently they require effective methods of flood-control and mechanization. The great hydroelectric potential of the country can be utilized for industrial growth only if the rivers are harnessed. This would enable Bangladesh to provide power for industrialization. But such projects require vast amounts of money, which the new nation, poor as it is, cannot easily supply.

▶ **HISTORY**

The history of Bangladesh can be told briefly. Originally it was part of the larger Bengal region of eastern India and its historical roots are deep in the ancient past. Successive groups of invaders ruled over the land—Turks, Moguls, and lastly the British. In 1947, when India gained its independence from Great Britain, East Bengal became part of the new nation of Pakistan. The creation

Bicycles and pedicabs crowd the busy city of Dacca, the capital of Bangladesh.

44b

of Pakistan was a result of the demands of the Muslim League for an independent and separate nation for those parts of the former British Indian Empire where the Muslims were a majority.

The new nation of Pakistan was born with a built-in flaw. It was composed of two parts, East Pakistan and West Pakistan, separated by some 1,600 kilometers, or about 1,000 miles, of Indian territory. Other problems also undermined the new state. The two parts of Pakistan were completely different in their peoples and their cultures. All aspects of Pakistani national life came to be dominated by groups from West Pakistan. East Pakistan turned out to be a fertile field for commercial investments, but the Bengalis charged that most of the profits were drained off to West Pakistan. The West Pakistan leadership was accused of neglecting the interests of the Eastern region and treating it as a colony. The East Pakistanis also complained that they were not receiving their fair share of political power, which they claimed on the basis of having over 55 percent of the total population of the nation.

Other issues led to frustration and discontent among the Bengalis of Pakistan. The government at first refused to accept Bengali as one of the national languages. Popularly elected local governments in the East were dismissed on charges of wanting to secede from Pakistan. Bengali leaders were imprisoned as traitors. There were frequent riots, and a long period of military rule (from 1958 to 1971) created dangerous tensions in the East.

The climax came in the elections of 1971. The Awami League, led by Sheikh Mujibur Rahman, won most of the seats in the East Pakistan provincial legislature and a majority of the seats in the national legislature. This would have given Sheikh Mujib a decisive role in Pakistani politics. It was a situation unacceptable to General Yahya Khan, the leader of the national government, and Zulfikar Ali Bhutto, who had emerged as the leader of the Pakistan People's Party, the majority party in West Pakistan. Particularly objectionable to them was the Awami League's Six Point Program, which included self-government for the Eastern region. West Pakistani leaders believed this would lead to the dismemberment of Pakistan.

The Birth of Bangladesh. Negotiations for the establishment of civilian rule and the drafting of a new constitution proved fruitless, setting off widespread riots in the East. The West Pakistan army retaliated with brutal suppression during which, it is charged, millions of people lost their lives and hundreds of villages were destroyed. Some 10,000,000 Bengalis, mostly Hindus, are believed to have fled to India as refugees, placing an intolerable burden on the Indian economy. As a result India became involved in what was essentially a civil war between East and West Pakistan.

The Bengalis, helped in part by India, had organized their own guerrilla forces, called the Muktibahini. The guerrillas cut communications and ambushed West Pakistani troops in widespread areas of East Pakistan. Incidents mounted until, in December 1971, India and Pakistan went to war in both the Eastern and Western regions. The war was swift. In less than 2 weeks the Indian Army, with the aid of the Bengali guerrillas, had compelled the Pakistani forces to surrender. The Bangladesh provisional government, which had been formed earlier in India, arrived in Dacca and took over control of the new nation.

Sheikh Mujibur Rahman, who had been arrested and imprisoned in West Pakistan, was released by Zulfikar Ali Bhutto, who became president of Pakistan, following the downfall of General Yahya Khan. On January 10, 1972, Sheikh Mujib arrived in Dacca and became prime minister of Bangladesh. After some 10 months of bloodshed and destruction, the new nation of Bangladesh ("Bengal Nation") had come into existence.

But great problems faced the new nation. Ravaged by war, Bangladesh was hard put to it to feed its people, and political problems beset the new government. In 1975, Sheikh Mujib, who had become president, was assassinated in a military coup. The leaders of the coup were themselves overthrown and a martial law government was formed.

BALKRISHNA G. GOKHALE
Director, Asian Studies Program
Wake Forest University

BANJO. See FOLK MUSIC INSTRUMENTS.

Banks today have an attractive and friendly appearance. Bars and locked cubicles have been replaced by glass walls and open counters.

BANKS AND BANKING

When someone has money that he wants to put in a safe place, he naturally takes it to a bank. Until recently the very appearance of the bank building was designed to assure people that their money would be safe. There were thick, solid walls and barred windows. All the windows and doors were wired to set off the burglar alarms if anyone tried to force his way in. The vaults where the money was kept had huge, steel doors with complicated locks. Uniformed guards with pistols in their holsters were always on duty in the bank. The tellers' cages—the cubicles where the bank clerks, or tellers, worked—actually resembled cages. They had gratings across the front, high sides and back, and a door that could be opened only by pushing a release button.

The new style of bank design retains some of these protective features, but the idea now is to make the bank seem like a friendly place rather than a forbidding fortress. The modern bank buildings are open and light, with large glass windows and doors. The tellers' cages have been replaced by flat, unobstructed counters. The guards and burglar alarms are still there, but they are less noticeable than they used to be.

Besides the strong doors and vaults, burglar alarms, and guards, there are other protections for the customer. The money deposited in the bank is insured, so that even if the bank had

to go out of business, the customer would get his money back. The bank is very careful with the money the customer has deposited, because the bank's reputation depends on its being absolutely trustworthy.

If he is depositing his money in a savings account, the customer receives a savings passbook that shows the amount of money he has in the bank. Only with the passbook can the money be withdrawn from the bank, and only the owner of the passbook—or a person authorized by him—can take out the money.

Long ago it was not easy for people to find such a safe place for their money. They had to hide it in their houses—perhaps in an old sock under the floorboards, or in a sugar bowl—or lock it up in a strongbox. A theft or fire that could deprive people of all their savings was a constant danger. Rich people could have strong vaults or safes built in their houses to protect their money, and there were some banks for merchants. But the average person simply had to take care of his money as best he could.

This situation changed in the early 19th century. Mutual savings societies were set up to provide a safe place for people's money. From such societies the savings bank eventually developed.

An early form of banking was the money-lending carried on in Florence, Venice, and other northern Italian cities during the Middle Ages. In fact, the word "bank" comes from the Italian word *banca,* meaning the "bench" or "counter" on which the money was displayed.

The flourishing trade going on in the Italian cities and throughout Europe put more and more money into the hands of many people. Money became so important that ways to protect it and handle it wisely had to be found. In the 17th and 18th centuries commercial banks were set up to help people do these things.

The early European commercial banks were privately owned. Their chief business was to assist merchants to finance their trading activities. These banks accepted deposits of money, collected bills for sellers, acted as exchange houses for converting the money of one country into the money of another, and extended loans to their depositors to help them pay for shipping and storing their wares.

Some of these private banking establishments were owned by individual families. The famous Medici family, which ruled Florence for 3 centuries, got its power and influence through the banks founded by Giovanni de' Medici in the 14th century.

One of the most interesting and successful of the family banking enterprises was the House of Rothschild. The founder of the business was Meyer Amschel Rothschild, who started as a moneylender in Frankfurt, Germany, in the second half of the 18th century. Rothschild's shrewdness and good financial sense made the firm a solid success. Its power and influence began to spread over Europe. Besides the Frankfurt office, branch offices were opened in London, Vienna, Paris, and Naples. Each of these offices was directed by one of Rothschild's five sons, who carried on and expanded the business. Close co-operation among the five branches, plus shrewd but honest business dealings, soon made the Rothschilds extremely wealthy. As early as 1803 Meyer Amschel Rothschild was able to lend a large sum of money to the king of Denmark. During the 19th century the Rothschilds became famous as moneylenders to European governments. For example, when the British Government needed £4,000,000 on very short notice in order to buy control of the Suez Canal, they borrowed it from the English branch of the House of Rothschild. This sum would be equal to about $30,000,000 today. It was often said jokingly that the House of Rothschild was one of the great powers of Europe.

This all-glass building represents the modern style in bank architecture.

A large portion of the business of early commercial banks involved foreign trade. The banks naturally came to be located in important seaport cities, where goods arrived from foreign countries and home products were shipped out. These cities, such as London and Amsterdam, and later New York, became the first financial centers. They have continued to be banking centers.

▶ BANKING TODAY

Although time has brought many changes in banking methods, the American commercial bank still offers the services originally provided by the first commercial banks in London and Amsterdam. However, there are many more commercial banks today than there were in the past, and they offer their services to private citizens as well as to business and government.

Although the ordinary full service **commercial bank** accepts savings deposits, there are also banks called **savings banks** that specialize in individual savings accounts.

A service available only at commercial banks is the **checking account**. It allows customers to deposit, withdraw, and transfer their money whenever they want to do so. When a person puts his money into a checking account, he receives blank forms called checks.

If he wants to withdraw some of his money or transfer it to someone else, he fills out the check. He gives the check to the person to whom the money is to go (the payee). The payee can cash the check to get the money, or he can deposit the check in his own bank account. The money is deducted from the account of the person who wrote the check and is added to the account of the payee.

A check is not money in itself. It is simply an order to the bank to pay money.

Because a person can withdraw or transfer his money from the bank without previous notice, by presenting a demand in the form of a check, money in checking accounts is sometimes called **demand deposits.**

National and State Banks

In the United States at the beginning of 1970 there were more than 33,800 bank offices, managed by 13,660 different banking organizations. Their total assets (money and property) came to $531,800,000,000. This was equal to over $2,500 for each man, woman, and child in the United States.

Commercial banks in the United States are of two types: national and state banks. Before a bank can carry on business, it must have a charter, or license to operate. If the bank is chartered by the federal government, it is

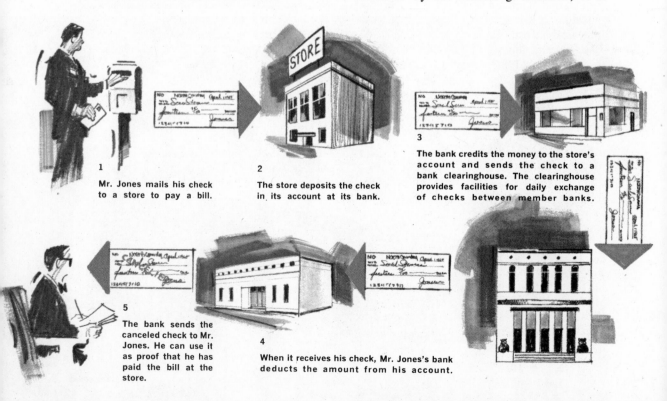

1 Mr. Jones mails his check to a store to pay a bill.

2 The store deposits the check in its account at its bank.

3 The bank credits the money to the store's account and sends the check to a bank clearinghouse. The clearinghouse provides facilities for daily exchange of checks between member banks.

5 The bank sends the canceled check to Mr. Jones. He can use it as proof that he has paid the bill at the store.

4 When it receives his check, Mr. Jones's bank deducts the amount from his account.

called a national bank. State banks must be chartered by the state in which they are located. With one major exception, the Bank of California, commercial banks are permitted to operate in only one state. In many states banks are also strictly limited in the number of branches they can establish. When a bank receives its charter, it agrees to obey the banking rules and regulations of the state or federal government.

▶ EARLY AMERICAN BANKS

When the United States gained its independence, banking services were provided by merchants and private lenders. The center of finance at that time was the Bank of England, called the Old Lady of Threadneedle Street because of its age and location.

The first banks established in the United States were state banks. In 1781 the Bank of North America, the first bank to receive a charter, was organized in Philadelphia. Other states soon issued charters to banks of their own. The first national bank, called the Bank of the United States, was opened in 1791. This bank, whose charter was to expire in 20 years, had branch offices in the major cities of the United States.

Banks Could Issue Their Own Money. Until the Civil War, both state and national banks could issue **bank notes** (paper money). At that time, a federal tax on bank notes issued by state banks resulted in the disappearance of state bank notes. In 1936 national banks were prohibited by law from issuing bank notes. Today all bank notes are issued by 12 government banks. They are called Federal Reserve Banks and, together with their 24 branches and the Federal Reserve Board in Washington, D.C., make up the nation's central bank system.

There were good reasons for placing restrictions on the issuing of bank notes. In the early years of the 19th century the notes of many banks quickly lost their value. This was because the banks did not have enough gold or silver coin (called **specie**) to back the notes up. If someone brought paper money to the bank that issued it, the bank might not be able to give him gold or silver in return. Some banks, called wildcat banks because they were located in out-of-the-way places, issued paper money knowing that they

could not back it up with gold or silver. Even regular city banks often would not accept each other's money at face value, but only at a discount. Thus, a $10 bill issued by a bank in Boston might be worth only $9 at a bank in Philadelphia.

Opposition to a Central Bank. The situation became worse after the Bank of the United States went out of business. Some people disliked the idea of a central federal bank and preferred that the banking system be based on the state banks. When the charter of the Bank of the United States expired in 1811, it was not renewed. The Bank of the United States had had the authority to control the amount of paper money issued by the state banks. After it went out of business there was no longer any control. A great deal of paper money was issued without the specie to back it up. There was a large amount of paper money in circulation, but much of it was valueless. As the value of the paper money went down, it took more and more of it to buy necessities like food and clothing.

This dangerous financial situation was stopped for a time when the second Bank of the United States was established in 1816. But in 1832 President Andrew Jackson, an opponent of the central bank idea, vetoed a bill that would have renewed the bank's charter.

Financial Panic. With the closing of the second Bank of the United States, the financial situation became bad again. President Jackson distributed the federal money, which had been in the Bank of the United States, to state banks. The state banks began to issue paper money in large quantities once more, and the amount of paper money again quickly exceeded the amount of gold and silver they had to back up their paper money. Rich areas of the West were being opened up and settled at that time. Financial speculation, especially in land buying, was at its height. President Jackson attempted to halt the speculation. In 1836 he ordered that only specie (which was also called "hard money") was to be accepted for the purchase of public lands in the West. This action stopped the speculators from buying up land with worthless paper money, but the economy was already damaged. When President Van Buren took office in 1837, he was faced with a severe depression.

Between 1840 and 1843 a fourth of all the

commercial banks failed. When a bank failed, there was no way for the people who had their money in the bank to get it back. Many people lost their life savings.

Crash and Depression Bring Changes. This problem continued into the next century. The situation was particularly bad after the stock-market crash of 1929. In 1930 more than 1,300 banks failed. There were 2,300 failures in 1931 and a little over 1,400 in 1932. In 1933 the number of failures reached 4,000.

On March 6, 1933, the President of the United States, Franklin D. Roosevelt, acting under his emergency powers, closed every commercial bank in the country for 4 days. This action helped the banks by preventing panicky depositors from withdrawing all their money.

▶ SAFEGUARDS FOR DEPOSITORS

In order to strengthen the banking system and to help prevent failures, a new federal banking act was passed in 1933. This act, which covered more ground than any banking legislation passed before, established the Federal Deposit Insurance Corporation (FDIC), strengthened the Federal Reserve Board (a government body established in 1913 to regulate banks' operations), restricted bank loans for speculation in stocks and bonds, and encouraged branch banking. The Banking Act of 1933, together with additional laws passed in 1935, took the risks out of banking for the average depositor.

Many of the controls and regulations that govern commercial banks are intended to protect the depositor from loss due to fraud, and to protect the economy from damage because of bad bank management. Today commercial banks are subject to rules, regulations, and inspection by at least one of three different national agencies: the Federal Deposit Insurance Corporation, a Federal Reserve bank, and the Comptroller of the Currency, who is an official of the U.S. Treasury. If the commercial bank is chartered by a state, it is subject to supervision and inspection by the state's banking department.

The banks of the District of Columbia and all commercial banks that have "National" in their names are chartered by the Comptroller of the Currency. They must, by law, be member banks of the Federal Reserve System.

Most of the larger state banks are members of the Federal Reserve System, although they are not required to belong.

Although there are about twice as many state banks as there are national banks, the total value of deposits in each kind is about equal. This is because national banks are usually much larger than state banks.

The FDIC guarantees all deposits up to $20,000 in member banks. Almost all the commercial banks in the United States have this deposit insurance. In return they must meet the FDIC's requirements for good banking practices. The FDIC is the only national agency responsible for examining state banks that are not members of the Federal Reserve System.

▶ VARIED SERVICES OF COMMERCIAL BANKS

Commercial banks are accurately described as "department stores of finance." They provide many services in addition to the traditional banking services discussed earlier. An important service provided by commercial banks is lending money. People borrow from banks to buy automobiles, household appliances, and similar goods. Banks also lend large amounts of money for long terms to persons wishing to purchase or build a home. (When the bank makes this type of loan, it holds a **mortgage**, or claim, on the property, until the loan is repaid.) In addition, banks operate trust departments and provide safe-deposit vaults. Most banks also have savings account departments and an international division.

Sources of Money for Loans

The money with which banks make loans comes from two sources. Some of it is money invested in the bank by stockholders and accumulated from profits from the bank's operations. The rest comes from deposits in the bank. These deposits are made by business concerns, private individuals, and the government. About 40 per cent of all the commercial bank deposits are demand deposits. The remaining 60 per cent are savings or time deposits. One type of time deposit, the certificate of deposit (largely funds of business firms), has increased rather rapidly. Savings accounts of individuals, the other major type of time deposits, have grown less rapidly. Interest is paid on time deposits but not on demand deposits.

Since the banking legislation of the 1930's, commercial banks have not been permitted to pay interest on demand deposits. Banks are allowed to pay interest to their depositors for the use of their money in time and savings accounts. The interest rates are regulated by the Federal Reserve Board.

Interest is a fee paid by the borrower to the lender for the use of the money he borrows. It is like a rental charge for the use of the money. If $100 is loaned for 1 year and the borrower pays a fee of $6 for the use of this money, the interest rate amounts to 6 per cent a year.

Types of Loans

Commercial banks make most of their income from interest earned on loans and investments in stocks and bonds. The types of loans made by banks have changed considerably since World War II. In 1947 nearly three times as much money was loaned for business purposes as for private uses, like buying a house or car. In 1971 loans for private consumer goods were equal to about two thirds the amount of business loans.

Commercial banks are much more interested in the financial needs of families and individuals than they were 20 or 30 years ago. Big-city banks have established branches in the suburbs for the convenience of their customers. They have also begun making a large number of small loans and dealing with customers of limited business experience.

Each month commercial banks must prepare statements for customers who have checking accounts. The statement shows how much money has come into and gone out of the checking account during the month. The preparation of these statements adds up to a large portion of the nation's bookkeeping. Deducting the amount of each check from the proper account and adding it to the account of the payee requires an enormous amount of paper work. The number of checks being written has reached a total of 20,000,000,000 (billion) a year. In the early 1970's much of the paper handled arose from credit cards. In order to handle this heavy load of paper work, commercial banks have turned to computers and other automated equipment.

A new convenience is sidewalk bank deposit windows.

The Trust Department

The trust department of a commercial bank provides a number of important services. As its name implies, this department manages money and property that have been entrusted to its care. Financial experts in the trust department perform such services for the bank's customers as investing money in stocks and bonds, buying and selling securities, managing real estate and collecting rents, and giving advice on drawing up wills so as to gain the most advantage from tax exemptions. The bank charges a fee for these services. The trust department serves businesses as well as private individuals. Many company pension plans and health-insurance plans are handled by the trust department of a bank. Money left to charities, too, is often administered by a bank's trust department.

▶ OTHER TYPES OF BANKS

There are a variety of banks that serve special purposes.

Investment banks perform an important job in the world of finance. When a company needs to raise money, instead of borrowing from a bank it often sells stock (shares in the company). In return the investors, or purchasers of the stock, receive a share of the profits the company makes. The investment bank pays the company a guaranteed amount for its stock issue. The investment bank hopes to resell the stock to the public at a high enough price to make a profit on the transaction. Meanwhile the company has got the money it needed without having to wait for the public to buy up the stock.

Mutual savings banks, the descendants of the 19th-century savings societies, are owned by the depositors. Their money is usually invested on a long-term basis. Mutual savings banks are nonprofit organizations. There are also savings banks, owned by stockholders, that are in business to make profits.

Savings and loan associations are also mostly mutually owned, profit-making businesses. These associations make loans, chiefly for home building. By the early 1970's they had expanded into general consumer lending.

The Federal Reserve System

The Federal Reserve System, which was established in 1913, consists of a board of governors in Washington and 12 banks and 24 branch offices distributed around the country. Because they make loans to member

A bank vault protects the depositors' money from fires and burglaries.

banks, the federal reserve banks are often called bankers' banks. They provide many important services to other banks.

The Federal Reserve authorities have the task of administering laws that deal with operations of the monetary system and the banking system. In addition, the Federal Reserve System acts as the government's financial agent. The government raises some of the money it needs by selling bonds. The Federal Reserve System must either find buyers for these bonds or be prepared to purchase them itself.

Other Government Banks

A number of special-purpose banks to help farmers have been established by the federal government. The oldest of these banks were the land banks and their lending agencies, the federal land bank associations. These banks make loans chiefly to purchase farms. Loans for cattle feeding and similar operations are made by the intermediate credit banks and their lending agencies, the production credit corporations and associations. Banks for co-operatives lend money to farmers' co-operatives. They get most of their money from the Central Bank for Co-operatives, which sells its securities to the public. In the United States the federal government has been drawn into the banking field through its regulation of the private banking system. The government itself has also tended to provide banking services in areas that the private banks have not covered. As a result, in the United States a decentralized, privately owned banking system exists side by side with government banking institutions. This dual system of private and government banking is one of the unique features of American banking.

▶ INTERNATIONAL BANKS

The increase in international trade in recent years has made it necessary to have co-operation in monetary matters among the various nations. There must be some agreement on whose money is worth how much, and on a fair rate of exchange from one currency to another. To help promote such co-operation, the International Monetary Fund was established in 1944 at the Bretton Woods Conference in New Hampshire. Representatives of 44 nations were present.

At the time of the Bretton Woods conference, World War II was nearing its end. The governments that took part in the conference realized that some provision had to be made for rebuilding devastated areas after the war. Such reconstruction would require large amounts of money. To help provide the money, the nations established the International Bank for Reconstruction and Development, which is often called the World Bank.

Besides helping to rebuild areas damaged by the war, the World Bank assists in the economic growth of underdeveloped countries by providing long-term loans. The bank's loans are made only to governments that are members of the organization, or to private businesses that have the backing of a member government.

In 1956 the World Bank established the International Finance Corporation (IFC), whose purpose is to stimulate private investments in underdeveloped countries. While the World Bank lends money only for public or publicly sponsored projects, the IFC helps to finance private-enterprise projects.

A third international lending agency, the International Development Association (IDA), was set up in 1960. The IDA's lend-

The Calcutta, India, branch of a New York bank.

ing policy is less strict than that of either the World Bank or the IFC. The IDA makes loans on easy terms to either public or private organizations for projects in underdeveloped countries.

RICHARD W. LINDHOLM
University of Oregon

See also ECONOMICS; INFLATION AND DEFLATION; MONEY.

BANNISTER, SIR ROGER GILBERT (1929–   )

Because he was the first man to run the mile in less than 4 minutes, Roger Bannister will always be known as the Miracle Miler.

Before Bannister's historic race at Oxford, England, on May 6, 1954, many people believed that there was an invisible barrier that would prevent any man from ever running a mile in less than 4 minutes. In spite of chilling winds and mud on the Iffley Road track, Bannister shattered both the record and the myth as he crossed the finish line in 3 minutes 59.4 seconds. In an amazing burst of speed, Bannister had covered the final ¼ mile in 58.9 seconds.

Later that summer, at Vancouver, British Columbia, Bannister again broke "the 4-minute barrier" when he finished 5 yards ahead of John Landy of Australia. This time he broke his previous record by 0.8 seconds.

Roger Gilbert Bannister was born at Harrow, England, on March 23, 1929. He showed early promise of his track ability by winning his first race when he was 13 years old. He was educated at Oxford University, where he studied medicine and was captain of the Oxford-Cambridge track team. Competing at Franklin Field, Philadelphia, in 1951, Bannister ran the mile in 4 minutes 8.3 seconds. This broke the mile record set by Glen Cunningham in 1934.

After 1954 Bannister gave up international athletics to practice medicine.

Roger Bannister has received many honors, including the Silver Pears trophy for "outstanding British achievement in any field." He is a Knight Commander, Order of the British Empire (K.B.E.). He has written an autobiography, *The Four Minute Mile*.

BANTING, SIR FREDERICK GRANT (1891–1941)

Frederick Grant Banting, Canadian doctor and scientist, was born on November 14, 1891, near Alliston, Ontario. His parents were pioneers in what was then a frontier region. Banting grew up to work on the frontiers of medical research; his greatest advance was against the disease of diabetes.

Doctors had long known that a person suffering from diabetes could not make use of the sugar in his body. For this reason victims of the disease were certain to die. By the early 1900's medical scientists had traced the cause of diabetes to the pancreas gland. They knew that a normal pancreas produced a chemical, which we call insulin. Insulin helped the body make use of sugar. In a diabetic the pancreas produced little or no insulin.

The problem was how to provide diabetics with insulin. Scientists thought they knew the answer: Give a diabetic insulin taken from the pancreas of a healthy animal. But no one had been able to extract insulin. This was to be Banting's achievement.

Banting had not set out to do research but had trained to be a surgeon. By the time he earned a medical degree at the University of Toronto, World War I had started. Banting volunteered for the Canadian Army Medical Corps. He was wounded in France but continued to take care of other injured men. Banting was awarded the Military Cross for his courage.

After the war Banting returned to his medical studies and to teaching in London, Ontario. One evening he was preparing a lecture on the pancreas. As he worked he suddenly realized how he might extract insulin. Banting knew that he would need a good laboratory. So he went to the University of Toronto and asked Professor John J. R. Macleod for help. Macleod was director of a large laboratory.

Macleod did not think Banting's idea would work. But he finally agreed to let Banting use the laboratory for a few weeks.

In May, 1921, Banting set to work. He was assisted by Charles H. Best, a young graduate student. They were so anxious to get results that they worked day and night. Within several weeks they obtained the first insulin from the pancreas of a dog. By January, 1922, after many tests, they were able to give insulin to a diabetic, a young boy near death. He showed immediate improvement. When insulin was given to other patients, they, too, improved.

There was still much work to be done. Another researcher, James B. Collip, perfected the method of preparing insulin. Indeed, the story of insulin illustrates the teamwork that is necessary in modern science. Because of the efforts of many men working before, with, and after Banting, most diabetics can now live almost normal lives.

Following Banting's breakthrough, honors were awarded to the four men who had helped. In 1923 Banting and Macleod were awarded the Nobel prize, which they chose to share with Best and Collip. The University of Toronto set up a new medical research institute named after Frederick Banting. During his years there Banting did important work in many fields of medicine.

Banting was knighted in 1934, but he never changed his quiet ways. He continued to enjoy wood carving and painting. He also had a great interest in his country and its past; he traveled to many parts of Canada, collected historical documents, and read all he could about the early explorers.

When Canada entered World War II, Banting again volunteered for the medical corps. On February 21, 1941, he was flying to Britain to report on Canadian medical research. The plane crashed in Newfoundland, and Banting was killed.

JOHN S. BOWMAN
Author and Science Editor

Frederick Banting found a way to extract insulin from animals. Insulin is used in treating people with diabetes.

BARBADOS

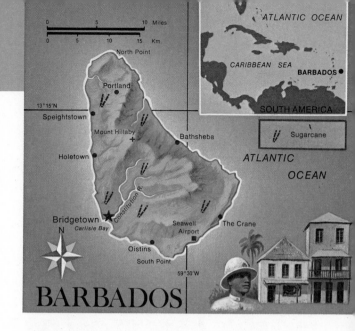

BARBADOS

The island of Barbados became independent in 1966. But there are many reminders of more than 300 years of British rule. People play cricket and take afternoon tea. Cars use the left-hand side of the road, and green, rolling fields are dotted with tiny cottages.

▶ THE PEOPLE

More than 90 percent of the people of Barbados are black. The rest are white, chiefly of British origin. The people are known as Barbadians, or "Bajas." The Barbadians are soft-spoken people whose literacy rate is one of the world's highest.

▶ THE LAND

Barbados, a coral island, is the easternmost of the Lesser Antilles in the West Indies. From its highest point—Mount Hillaby, 336 meters (1,104 feet)—the island slopes gently to the sea. Along the Atlantic side the coast is rugged, and the surf is high. On the Caribbean side, smooth, wide beaches lead gradually to calm, blue water. Bridgetown, the capital, is on the Caribbean coast.

The climate of Barbados is moderately tropical. The weather is pleasant all year round. The cool trade winds have a moderating effect on the temperature. Rainfall is abundant, especially in the north.

▶ THE ECONOMY

The standard of living is high in comparison with other underdeveloped countries, but over-population is a major problem in Barbados. The sugar crops and related industries, which until recently have maintained the island, no longer employ the entire labor force. Light industry is being encouraged, to create jobs and lessen the dependency on sugar. The fine beaches and pleasant climate have made tourism the chief source of income.

▶ HISTORY AND GOVERNMENT

The original inhabitants were Arawak Indians from South America. They had already died out when the Portuguese mariner Pedro a Campos landed on the island in the early 16th century. He named it Barbados, which means "bearded," probably for the beardlike vines or moss that hung from the trees.

The island remained uninhabited until 1627, when the English established the first permanent settlement. During the 1630's slaves were brought from Africa to work on plantations. At first tobacco and cotton were the chief crops, but sugarcane soon was introduced and remains the principal crop.

Barbados recognizes the British monarch, represented by a governor-general, as the head of state. But real political authority rests with the Barbadian Parliament. It is made up of the House of Assembly, elected by popular vote, and the Senate, whose members are appointed by the governor-general. The prime minister is chosen from the majority party in the House.

BRANFORD M. TAITT
Former Consul General of Barbados, New York

FACTS AND FIGURES

BARBADOS is the official name of the country.

CAPITAL: Bridgetown.

LOCATION: Easternmost of the Caribbean islands. **Latitude**—13° 4′ N. **Longitude**—59° 37′ W.

AREA: 430 km² (166 sq mi).

POPULATION: 250,000 (estimate).

LANGUAGE: English.

GOVERNMENT: Constitutional monarchy. **Head of state**—British monarch, represented by governor-general. **Head of government**—prime minister. **International co-operation**—United Nations, Commonwealth of Nations, Caribbean Community (CARICOM), Organization of American States (OAS).

ECONOMY: Agricultural products—sugarcane, cotton, onions. **Industries and products**—tourism, molasses, rum, fishing. **Chief exports**—sugarcane, food, beverages. **Chief imports**—machinery, petroleum, foodstuffs. **Monetary unit**—Barbados dollar.

BAROMETER

The air around you is heavy. It has weight. There is a ton of air over each square foot of the earth's surface. There is a name for the air's weight pressing down on the surface of the earth. The name is air pressure. A **barometer** is an instrument that can measure this air pressure.

You may have seen a barometer hanging on a wall. Inside it there is a small box, or chamber, with thin metal walls. Most of the air has been drawn out of this chamber. The thin walls move in or out slightly when there is an increase or decrease in the air pressure outside. A pointer on the front of the barometer is connected by a lever to the chamber walls and shows these small changes. The pointer moves in front of a dial that is marked off in units of air pressure. The units are usually inches or centimeters.

Air pressure is important in weather forecasting. A change in air pressure usually means a change in weather. A drop in pressure often means that bad weather is coming. A rise in pressure usually means that clear weather is on the way. Ships and airplanes carry barometers. Weathermen use barometers in making their forecasts.

Air pressure also changes when you move from sea level to higher altitudes. When you climb a mountain, you find that the air grows thinner. It weighs less, and so it presses down less strongly. Airplane pilots often use barometers called **altimeters** to tell them how high they are above the ground.

The barometers you have read about so far are called aneroid barometers. Aneroid means "without liquid." There are other barometers that do use liquids. The very first barometer was of this type. An Italian scientist named Evangelista Torricelli (1608–47) designed it in 1643. He took a long glass tube that was closed at one end and filled it with mercury. He turned this tube upside down in a pan that contained more mercury. The mercury in the tube started running out, of course. Soon the mercury stopped running out. The weight of the mercury in the tube was balanced by the pressure of air on the mercury outside.

Mercury barometers are still used today. Scientists read a mercury barometer by seeing how high the column of mercury in the tube is. When air pressure increases, the mercury column goes up. When the pressure decreases, the column goes down.

Mercury barometers are very accurate. But they are clumsy to move around, and they have to be kept upright, so that the liquid stays level. That is why ordinary barometers in homes or on ships and airplanes are aneroid barometers. Mercury barometers are used mainly in scientific laboratories.

Reviewed by SERGE A. KORFF
New York University

See also WEATHER AND CLIMATE.

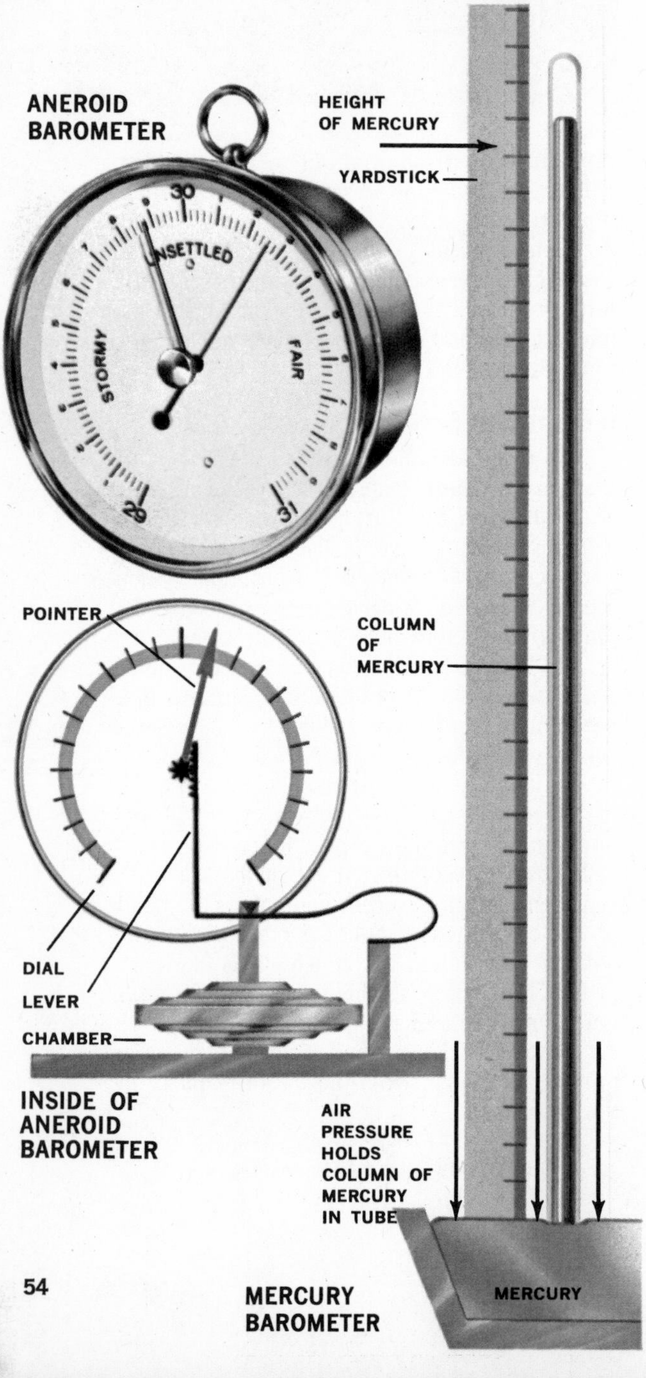

ANEROID BAROMETER

HEIGHT OF MERCURY

YARDSTICK

30
UNSETTLED
STORMY
FAIR
29
31

POINTER

COLUMN OF MERCURY

DIAL
LEVER
CHAMBER

INSIDE OF ANEROID BAROMETER

AIR PRESSURE HOLDS COLUMN OF MERCURY IN TUBE

MERCURY BAROMETER

MERCURY

Church of Santa Maria della Salute, in Venice, Italy, by Baldassare Longhena (1604-82).

BAROQUE ART AND ARCHITECTURE

Baroque is the name given to the art of the 17th century. But the baroque style, like all other styles in the history of art, began gradually. It started in the latter part of the 16th century and continued to be used well into the 18th century.

The 17th century was a period of great change. Some Europeans were exploring and settling new lands. Others were exploring the whole universe, from the distant heavens to the tiniest drop of water, by using the newly invented telescope and microscope. Whether they stayed at home or whether they traveled, the people of the 17th century looked at their own world with lively, inquiring eyes and minds. Their artists depicted what they saw in such a way that we are led to look and feel with them.

Describing their art as "baroque" is curious. The word itself has a strange sound, and this is the very reason why the term was first used. A large, irregularly shaped pearl is called a baroque pearl. It differs from the smooth, perfectly round pearls that we usually see. In the 18th century, architects who thought that all buildings should have smooth, simple shapes disliked the more complicated, elaborate buildings of the 17th century. They therefore angrily called them absurd, fantastic, and baroque. While the word has continued to be used ever since, this first meaning has now largely been forgotten. Today we simply use the term to describe the special qualities of 17th-century art.

The painters of the 17th century, for example, wanted to draw the viewer into the picture. Instead of using horizontal and vertical lines, they tended to use curves and diagonal lines that pull the viewer into the action on the canvas. The paintings are full of movement and dramatic lights and colors. Often baroque painters tried to give the illusion of unending space.

The architecture of this period also gives a feeling of excitement, motion, and drama.

Vision of Saint Theresa, (1645–52), by Giovanni Lorenzo Bernini. Church of Santa Maria della Vittoria, Rome.

The façades, or fronts, of buildings were ornamented and the interiors richly decorated. Curving shapes were frequently used —the dome was the most typical architectural form. Another common feature of baroque buildings was great sweeping staircases.

Architects became interested in the surroundings of their buildings. They placed elaborate gardens around palaces. They set off important buildings in the cities by open squares decorated with fountains or colonnades. Roads leading from the squares give a dramatic view of stairways, sculpture, or other buildings far in the distance.

▶ BAROQUE ART IN ITALY

Rome was the birthplace of baroque art, and from that artistic center the style spread all over Europe and to the European colonies in North and South America. One of the pioneers of baroque art was Michelangelo Merisi (1573–1610), always known as Caravaggio. In Caravaggio's painting *The Conversion of Saint Paul,* we see nothing but two men and a large work horse, yet we are made to feel that this is a scene of very special importance. Caravaggio gives us this feeling by placing the scene as if we were a part of it. He has used a very strong, almost blinding light and has left out any details that might be distracting.

Caravaggio thought of the people of the New Testament as if they were people living in his own time, and painted them to look real. This may appear to us a reasonable way to paint but it seemed startling and new in his day. Some people objected violently to this new style, but many of the younger artists, both in his day and the years that followed, were so struck by what he did that they painted in his way. They too made figures look like real human beings, moving near us as though they were in the same space as ourselves. These figures are painted as though there were no separation between ourselves and the work of art. The followers of Caravaggio also used light to make their figures seem like solid objects with empty space between them. Light was used for dramatic effects. By illuminating certain figures, Caravaggio indicated the important ones, making the picture clear and memorable.

Malle Bobbe (date unknown), by Frans Hals.
Metropolitan Museum of Art, New York City.

The Conversion of Saint Paul (1601?), by Caravaggio. Church of Santa Maria del Popolo, Rome.

Caravaggio painted at the beginning of the 17th century, and his work seems much more simple than later baroque art. In many ways Caravaggio laid the foundations for the complex works of sculpture and architecture—as well as painting—that followed.

Bernini

Giovanni Lorenzo Bernini (1598–1680) was one of the most brilliant and energetic of all the 17th-century artists. A painter, sculptor, and architect, Bernini is said to have written music, composed operas, and even designed stage sets. All these interests are shown in his work as a sculptor and architect.

The *Vision of Saint Theresa* shows an angel appearing to the saint. The sculpture is presented as a scene on the high altar of a chapel.

This chapel is built to resemble a theater so that if we enter it we are part of the audience. A stage is suggested by a great, gilt-bronze frame that curves forward in our direction. A beam of light shines down on the two carved figures, whose gestures lead us into the action on stage. But we are not all of the audience. Carved on the walls of the chapel are figures seated in theater boxes. They too are aware of the miracle being enacted before their eyes and ours.

As an architect Bernini makes us actually become the actors on a stage he builds for us. One of the largest and most splendid churches in the world, St. Peter's in Rome, gives us a sense of acting in an important occasion. Bernini was responsible for much of what we see and feel in this church. Many of the

Landscape with the Flight into Egypt (1647) by Claude Lorrain. Royal Gallery, Dresden.

Head of a Young Girl (1665?) by Jan Vermeer. Royal Picture Gallery, The Hague.

Peasant Dance (1636–40) by Peter Paul Rubens. Prado Museum, Madrid.

colored marbles, paintings, gilt-bronze ornaments, and sculpture were made by him or his assistants and followers.

Bernini also designed the large square in front of St. Peter's. Two fountains with sparkling jets of water are placed as accents in the wide, open space before the entrance. As an approach to the church, he built a great curving colonnade on either side of the square. The colonnade was made low in height and simple in shape to set off the façade of the church, which seems to rise as steeply as a mountain.

Another place where we can see the combination of different arts is on the painted ceiling of the church of Sant' Ignazio in Rome. The vision of glittering splendor that we see there was painted by Andrea Pozzo (1642–1709). Looking up at the ceiling, we get even more of a sense of distant spaces and the vast expanse of heaven than we could by looking through the telescopes used at that time. Columns and arches appear to tower far above our heads, but these columns, which seem to reach far into the sky, are not real but painted ones.

The four continents Asia, Africa, Europe, and America are shown as human beings. These large figures dominate what seems to be hundreds of figures swirling and rising higher and higher into the painted sky. In the distance is the small figure of Saint Ignatius being received into heaven. Everything leads to this one crucial point, so that the scene is clear even though it includes many forms and many rich and gay colors: icy pinks, light greens and blues, silver, plum, chocolate-brown, and gold.

▶ FRENCH ARTISTS IN ITALY

Nicolas Poussin (1594–1665), a Frenchman, was one of the greatest of the many foreign artists who traveled to Rome in the 17th century. Many artists were attracted to Italy and especially to Rome. Some made rather short journeys; others, like Poussin, stayed the rest of their lives. These foreign artists helped to spread all over Europe a feeling for the new kinds of art produced by such men as Caravaggio and Bernini.

Poussin is typical of a large and important group of artists. These men looked very carefully both at the new art of their time and also at the works of earlier men, as far back as the ancient Romans. Poussin loved Rome and the Roman countryside, the river valleys, and the nearby mountains. He studied and sketched the ruins of ancient buildings and drew copies of ancient statues. He thought of the gods and goddesses of Greece, the heroes of Roman legends, the figures of the Bible as having lived in just this kind of setting. He painted them as they might have been, wearing Roman costumes and living in Roman buildings in the city or country.

Bernini once spoke of Poussin as a great storyteller who always worked with his mind. Poussin read and thought about the real meaning of stories and then worked steadily to find the very best way of telling his story as a painter. He felt that tragic or sad stories should be painted in a sober, severe way. Gay and happy subjects he painted in a more cheerful, lively manner, with glowing lights and colors and flowers sprinkled about as graceful ornaments.

Whatever the subject he chose, Poussin always organized his paintings very carefully, building them as firmly as a carpenter. In the *Holy Family on the Steps,* each figure is very clearly formed and is part of a group that is as stable and solid as a pyramid. The pyramid is balanced by the flat, horizontal steps and by the high, vertical columns above. The whole painting seems exactly right, so perfectly balanced that no single part could be changed even a fraction of an inch without destroying the effect of the whole work.

However, Poussin was a man of the 17th century who shared many ideas with the artists of his own day. Like other baroque painters he often used strong lights and deep shadows. His colors are deeper, richer, and more glowing than Raphael's. Poussin's paintings show a feeling for space and atmosphere—looking at his paintings we feel a part of them. In the *Holy Family on the Steps,* he has placed a group of objects so near our eyes that we can almost reach out and touch them. A strong light shines from somewhere on our left—it seems to fall on ourselves as well as on the painted scene before us. In short, we feel as close a connection with this work as we do with Caravaggio's *Saint Paul;* Poussin has simply used other means for the same end.

Another French artist, who spent most of

his working life in Rome, was Claude Lorrain (1600–82), called Claude. His interest was entirely in landscapes or scenes with rivers or seaports and harbors.

Claude, an orphan, went to Rome to work as a pastry cook, but he became an apprentice landscape painter instead. His love of nature and his eye for composition gave his paintings an agreeable sweetness. His *Landscape with the Flight into Egypt* is pleasant to look at. The peaceful countryside has a little river winding its way back into the distance, and trees and bushes placed at just the right points lead our eyes back toward the horizon, where land and sky meet. A longer look at such paintings shows us the quiet seriousness beneath their surface sweetness.

▶ SPANISH ART

Diego Velázquez (1599–1660), court painter to King Philip IV of Spain, is best known for his many royal portraits, but he treated every subject with equal interest and respect. His pictures of beggars or soldiers, dwarfs or tiny children have just as much dignity as those of the King himself. In every case Velázquez painted with a great concern for the actual way we see. He painted exactly what he saw; he never lets us know how he felt or suggests how we should feel.

Velázquez used his paintbrush very freely. Thin, broad strokes or long, tapering ribbons of paint are laid easily on the canvas. Almost magically these strokes fuse together. When we look at one of Velázquez' portraits, such as the one of Pope Innocent X, we feel that we are in the same room with the person at the very moment he was painted. The result of Velázquez' sensitivity to what he saw and his way of painting is that we believe what he shows us. We feel that we know as much as can be known of his people from the way they look at a given moment.

Two other famous Spanish painters of the 17th century were José Ribera (1591–1652) and Francisco de Zurbarán (1598–1664). These artists painted religious pictures with strong dramatic lighting and realistic details that are similar to Caravaggio's.

▶ NORTHERN BAROQUE ART

The northern counterpart of Bernini in Italy was Peter Paul Rubens (1577–1640) in Flanders. He was equally brilliant. Rubens produced a vast number of works by training many younger artists who learned from him by working with and assisting him.

All Rubens' drawings, oil sketches, and paintings reveal his great sense of pleasure and enjoyment of everything he saw. In his *Peasant Dance* we can almost feel the ground shake as the great circle of dancing people wheels forward and away from us in the golden light spreading all over the land.

One of Rubens' most gifted younger artists was Anthony Van Dyck. Like Velázquez he is best known for his portraits of royalty. Van Dyck painted King Charles I of England and his court with such grace, elegance, and distinction that they are always remembered as he saw and recorded them.

▶ DUTCH ART

The cackling laugh we seem to hear in the vigorous painting of an old fishwife, *Malle Bobbe*, by Frans Hals (1580–1666) is a far cry from the quiet, gentle, rather sad figures by Van Dyck. Frans Hals and all the Dutch took pride in their independence. The people of the tiny Dutch Republic had fought long and bravely for their freedom and had earned all the good things of life they knew in this period. One of the things they valued most was painting. And hundreds of artists provided many different kinds of paintings for them. Some painters specialized in landscapes, some in seascapes. Some painted flowers or fruits and flowers; others, animals. Some painters recorded buildings, while still others presented scenes from everyday life.

No matter what the subject matter is, almost every Dutch painting is really a portrait —a record of the people, places, or objects that were part of Dutch life.

In Frans Hals's portraits we feel the same interest and closeness to the subject as in Caravaggio's paintings or Bernini's sculpture. But all the noise, fun, and gaiety of Hals's portraits are absent in the paintings of Jan Vermeer (1632–75). Vermeer's paintings are as quiet and orderly as those of Nicolas Poussin. Vermeer's subjects are very different from Poussin's large historical paintings but they have the same feeling of seriousness. In the *Head of a Young Girl,* the sphere of the girl's pearl earring echoes the perfect shape

Six's Bridge (1645), an etching by Rembrandt. The Pierpont Morgan Library, New York.

of her whole head and her dark eyes. Vermeer repeats the same shape in different kinds of objects to show the basic order of all things.

Vermeer studied with great care the effect of light on different textures—on crusty bread or creamy milk. He shows the number of colors reflected on a bare plaster wall and the brightness of colors even in shadows. But Vermeer never let these careful observations clutter his paintings. Everything in his paintings is controlled to make a thoughtfully arranged scene. The perfection of Vermeer's paintings makes the few examples of them that remain with us today both rare and precious.

Rembrandt

Fortunately, hundreds of drawings, prints, and paintings exist to show the astonishing genius of Rembrandt van Rijn (1606–69).

Rembrandt seems to have been interested in everything in his world—from pigs and elephants to a side of beef, from quiet, sunny landscapes to stormy scenes on rainy days. He drew, painted, or prepared prints of these

subjects and countless others, but his constant interest was always in human beings. Rembrandt studied and recorded human beings of all sorts and kinds, of all ages and types, in every kind of situation: a tiny child tottering unsteadily in its first steps or an old, worn, blind man. Some of these records are merely swift pen sketches; others are formal paintings of single persons or groups of people.

Rembrandt made studies of his own appearance from the time he was a gay and lively young artist until he was a very tired and ill old man. In these self-portraits Rembrandt never made himself look handsome or brave. He was always honest and used these many studies to train his hand in recording what he saw and to increase his understanding of himself and other people.

Rembrandt was deeply religious. The scenes and figures of the Bible were profoundly important to him. Most of his countrymen in Holland were Protestants who felt that religious figures and scenes should not be represented in art. But Rembrandt interpreted what he read and believed in the Bible in his own way, as an artist.

His way of presenting religious scenes changed as he grew older and wiser. Some of his paintings done as a young man are like a splendid theatrical performance, with the figures in colorful, rich clothes. In 1631 Rembrandt painted a picture of Christ appearing before his disciples after the Crucifixion. The disciples are shocked and frightened. Their gestures are dramatic— Rembrandt painted them as though they were actors recreating the scene under powerful spotlights. But in his later works Rembrandt told stories in simpler and more human terms. He painted the same scene again in 1648. This time, however, the disciples sit quietly, and the face of Christ reflects his great suffering.

▶ FRANCE

The young King Louis XIV was determined to make his country, France, the strongest country in all Europe. From the very beginning of his long reign, Louis XIV thought of the arts as an important part of his campaign. He encouraged painting, sculpture, and architecture to provide an appropriate setting for himself as the new monarch.

In the late 17th century, France became the new center of artistic interest. French art became known, admired, and copied all over Europe. Louis XIV appointed a very able man, Charles Le Brun (1619–90), his superintendent of the arts. Le Brun acted for the King in supervising everything from a new factory for tapestries to the training of young artists in the Academy of Fine Arts in Paris and the French Academy in Rome.

The Chateau of Versailles is evidence of Le Brun's energetic activity for the King. An army of workmen and the talents of dozens of artists were organized to create this new palace. What was once a small hunting lodge was enormously enlarged and transformed into a city-palace. Dozens and dozens of rooms and hundreds of acres of gardens are all connected with one another in a design that is as clear and orderly as it is huge and ambitious. Gardens with terraces, pools, and fountains seem to stretch for miles in the distance. The paths of the gardens and the three highways that lead to the palace are all directed toward the royal apartments.

▶ LATER BAROQUE ART

In the 17th and 18th centuries, the Portuguese and the Spaniards brought the baroque style to their colonies in South America. The cathedrals built during this time combined the native artistic tradition with the baroque. The abundance of the carved and gilded ornaments that decorate these churches was especially influenced by the old native crafts.

In Europe itself the baroque style did not die with the closing years of the 17th century. It was carried forward and flourished especially in Germany and Austria, and then became the basis for the new style that developed in the course of the early 18th century. This style was called rococo, a lighter, more fragile, and decorative form of art than the baroque art of the 17th century.

ELEANOR D. BARTON
Chairman, Department of Art
Sweet Briar College

See also ARCHITECTURE; DECORATIVE ARTS; PAINTING; SCULPTURE.

BAROQUE MUSIC

"Baroque" is a term used to describe the music of the period extending roughly from 1600 to 1750. The word originally was used to describe the architecture of the 17th century, which was heavy and elaborate in style and full of decoration and ornamental details. Musical compositions during this period were often huge and elaborate, and often required a great number of singers and players to perform

them. The melodies were complicated and had highly ornamented passages. The way in which voices and instruments were combined often resulted in complex musical patterns. The characteristics of this music seemed to resemble those of baroque architecture. Musical scholars decided, therefore, that the word baroque could also be used to identify the music of that time.

The baroque era includes all the music from the time of Claudio Monteverdi in the late 16th century to Johann Sebastian Bach and George Frederick Handel in the 18th. Many of the most important musical forms were developed during this period. These forms include the sonata, symphony, concerto, suite, opera, oratorio, and many others.

The composers of baroque music struggled to express intense human emotions such as rage, passionate love, fear, exaltation, awe, wonder, joy, and despair. As a result, music became much more dramatic than it had ever been before. Furthermore, secular music came to be regarded as equally important as—if not more than—religious music. While most of the best music of earlier times was composed for the church, a great quantity of baroque music was composed for other purposes.

▶ THE NEW MUSIC

The new music of the baroque era started in Florence, Italy, near the end of the 16th century. There a group of amateur poets, musicians, and painters met to discuss art, music, and the drama. This little group, known as the Florentine Camerata, wanted to revive ancient classical Greek drama. They knew that Greek drama had been accompanied by music, but they were not sure what kind of music it was or how it was used in the drama. In imitation of the Greeks, they decided to write plays based on classical subjects and to set the plays to music. Polyphony, the musical style of that day, was poorly suited for this purpose. Polyphony is a Greek word meaning the sounding together of many different sounds. In polyphonic music several melodies in combination are sung together at the same time. In polyphonic music it was difficult to hear the words clearly. Can you imagine a musical play in which all the singers sing their parts to different melodies at the same time? Of course the words would not be clearly understood and no one would be able to follow the story.

A new kind of music, then, was needed and it was soon invented. It was called **recitative.** It consisted of a single melodic line for a solo voice with a simple instrumental accompaniment. Through the recitative, words could be clearly expressed and the story could be easily followed.

The composers of the Florentine Camerata began writing this new kind of music for classical dramas. But instead of reproducing the drama of ancient Greece as they had hoped, they produced something entirely new—the opera.

▶ VOCAL MUSIC

The world's first opera was *Dafne*. It was the work of two members of the Florentine Camerata. The poet Ottavio Rinuccini wrote the play. Jacopo Peri (1561–1633) composed the music. *Dafne* was first performed in 1597. Unfortunately it has been lost, but Peri's second opera, *Euridice* (1600), still exists. The success of both *Dafne* and *Euridice* removed any doubt that opera was to become an important form of music.

Opera now needed the imagination of a musical genius. Such a genius soon appeared in Claudio Monteverdi (1567–1643). Monteverdi was the most daring composer of his time. Only a decade after the first performance of Peri's *Dafne,* Monteverdi composed an opera that is still performed. That opera is *Orfeo,* which was first performed in Mantua, Italy, on February 22, 1607. Monteverdi was the first to write ensemble numbers such as duets and trios, and to give an important role to the orchestra. With orchestral interludes Monteverdi created the mood of a whole scene. He made expressive use of colorful orchestral effects. He enlarged the orchestra and developed new techniques of performance. For this reason many people consider Monteverdi the father of the symphony orchestra.

Monteverdi's music possessed a human element not found in Peri's operas. He expressed human emotions through his music so well that audiences were said to burst into tears sometimes at a performance of one of his operas. Monteverdi showed the same power of expression in his wonderful madrigals, for which he is equally famous.

The opera developed rapidly. In Naples Alessandro Scarlatti (1660–1725) established many of the traditions of Italian opera that later composers followed. In France Jean Baptiste Lully (1632–87) laid the foundations of French opera. Lully emphasized the drama in his operas and gave the orchestra a more important part. He also established the ballet in French opera. In England Henry Purcell (1659–95) composed *Dido and Aeneas* (1689), which has remained the most important English opera.

While baroque musicians created opera, they also enriched church music. They developed large new forms such as the oratorio and the Passion. These required choruses, recitatives, solo and ensemble numbers, and orchestral interludes and accompaniment. Both the oratorio and the Passion were dramatizations of Bible stories. They were meant to be performed usually without scenery or costumes.

The Oratorio

The oratorio got its name from the place where some of the earliest oratorios were first performed. The place was the oratory of St. Philip Neri's Church in Rome. Here in the late 16th century, composers began to write music for dramatized stories from the Bible. The early oratorios were very simple in design. The first composer to write a fully developed oratorio was Giacomo Carissimi (1605–74).

A favorite solo instrument of the baroque age was the harpsichord. It also played an important part in the performance of chamber music and orchestral works.

Carissimi's oratorio *Jephtha* (about 1660) established some of the traditions that later oratorio composers followed. Carissimi was one of the first to leave out scenery and costumes (oratorios given at St. Philip Neri's Church had been staged). He was also one of the first to use the narrator, who kept the story moving. Finally, he was one of the first to write dramatic and expressive choruses. For these reasons Carissimi's *Jephtha* is considered the first modern oratorio.

The Passion

The Passion was a musical setting of Christ's Passion according to the Gospels. It had been used occasionally by the Renaissance composers but it underwent great change in the baroque era. The Passion of the Renaissance was a composition for an unaccompanied chorus. The baroque Passion, however, added solo voices and orchestra. A new kind of episode was also introduced—the chorale. The church congregation was supposed to join in the singing of the chorales. Heinrich Schütz (1585–1672) was the first important composer of Passions. Schütz studied in Italy, and was strongly influenced by the Italian composers, especially Monteverdi. Besides Passions and many other works, he wrote music for all the psalms in the Bible.

The Cantata

The cantata was another important musical form that developed in the baroque era. It began as a secular form of music. Carissimi realized that many churches did not have enough musicians to perform large works like the oratorio. He therefore introduced the cantata into the church. The cantata was a small composition that required only a few musicians to perform. They were composed for one or two solo voices accompanied by a small instrumental group. These pieces usually began with an introduction for instruments alone. Contrasting sections consisting of recitatives and arias followed. Church cantatas were based on biblical texts.

The cantata became very popular in 17th- and 18th-century church music. Its form was perfected by Dietrich Buxtehude (1637–1707). Many of Buxtehude's cantatas use chorale melodies of the Lutheran Church. Next to Heinrich Schütz, Buxtehude is Germany's finest composer of church music before Bach. The most famous Italian composer of cantatas was Alessandro Scarlatti, who is better known for his operas. Scarlatti wrote 600 or more cantatas in addition to over 100 operas and about 150 oratorios.

The Aria

Arias were usually in A-B-A form; that is, the first part was repeated after the end of the contrasting second, or middle, part. These are called *da capo* arias, a form that became very common in baroque opera, cantata, and other vocal music. *Da capo* means to repeat from the beginning of a piece. In the *da capo* aria singers often had an opportunity to show off their skill in singing high notes and difficult florid passages called coloraturas.

▶ INSTRUMENTAL MUSIC

In the baroque era instrumental and vocal music became equally important for the first time. Probably nothing else in this period has had more far-reaching effects than the development of instrumental music. As in vocal music, all the baroque instrumental forms began in Italy. Baroque composers developed music with only one melody and a supporting accompaniment. This style of music allowed composers to give more attention to inventing new and interesting harmonies.

The Figured Bass

The importance of harmony in the baroque era is shown in a new kind of harmonic notation called the figured bass. It was so widely used that the baroque era in music is sometimes called the figured-bass period. It was used in both instrumental and vocal music. Figured bass is a kind of musical shorthand. The composer indicated the harmony by writing figures (numbers and letters) under the bass part below the staff. Only the melody and bass needed to be written out in the musical score. The keyboard player, who played the bass part with the left hand, filled in the harmony according to the figures. As the system of notation became more complicated so did the harmony. In baroque music, therefore, we can see the beginnings and early development of modern harmony.

Renaissance composers like Giovanni Gabrieli (1557–1612) and Jan Pieters Sweelinck

Often several kinds of instruments were used in the performance of baroque church music.

(1562–1621) wrote many pieces for the organ. But they wrote them in the polyphonic vocal style, as though the organ were a combination of human voices rather than an instrument. Beginning with Girolamo Frescobaldi (1583–1643), however, composers of organ music began to develop a distinctly instrumental style of writing. They emphasized the tonal qualities for which the organ was best suited. In doing this Frescobaldi perfected some of the chief forms of organ music. These included the organ toccata, fugue, and partita.

Frescobaldi's most important successor was Buxtehude. With Buxtehude, organ music reached a stage of development that remained unsurpassed until Johann Sebastian Bach. Music for instruments other than the organ also had to develop a non-vocal style before it became independent from vocal music.

Instrumental music developed rapidly because brilliant new stringed instruments were being made by the famous violin-making families of Cremona, Italy. First the Amati family and later the Guarnieri and Stradivari families made wonderful new violins, violas, and cellos. These instruments have never been surpassed for their beautiful tone and perfect craftsmanship. The most renowned of all violin makers is Antonio Stradivari (1644–1737). One of his violins is worth several thousands of dollars today.

The Sonata and the Concerto

Early in the baroque era a new musical idea emerged for which a new term was invented —sonata. A sonata was a composition that could be performed only on an instrument, just as the cantata was a piece of music that was meant only to be sung. Once composers started making this distinction, they began to develop a strictly instrumental style completely different from vocal music.

The first master to do so was Arcangelo Corelli (1653–1713). Corelli was the foremost violin virtuoso of his time and the first important composer of violin music. He produced two epoch-making works. One of these consisted of 12 sonatas for violin and keyboard accompaniment. In these sonatas a new style of violin performance was demonstrated fully for the first time. His second great contribution was a set of 12 *concerti grossi* (grand concertos) for a combination of instruments. Corelli's violin sonatas and concertos were the ancestors of the later solo sonata and the classical concerto.

The practice of contrasting the tone color of instruments with each other, singly or in groups, was a baroque invention. For the first time on a large scale the special tone quality of individual instruments was fully used. This formed the basis upon which modern orchestral writing was built. Baroque composers wrote many concertos for violin, flute, cello, and keyboard. Later in the period, concertos for other instruments such as the horn and the oboe also became popular.

The sonata and the concerto developed rapidly. The leading composers were Antonio Vivaldi (1675?–1741), Giuseppe Tartini (1692–1770), and Domenico Scarlatti (1685–1757), the son of Alessandro. Scarlatti was the first important composer in Italy to write sonatas for a keyboard instrument. He also created a brilliant new style of keyboard writing and perfected a new technique of performing on the harpsichord.

The Dance Suite

Outside of Italy, too, great advances were being made in instrumental music. Composers were creating a treasury of smaller pieces for keyboard instruments. These pieces were often based on dances. Composers began to arrange them in groups called suites. The dance suite consisted of several dance movements contrasting in mood, tempo, and rhythm. The basic arrangement consisted of four dances: an allemande in moderate tempo; a courante, or running dance; a slow and stately saraband; and a quick and lively gigue, or jig. Composers often added dances between the saraband and gigue, such as the minuet, gavotte, bourrée, or passepied. Outstanding composers of dance suites and other beautiful keyboard pieces were Johann Froberger (1617–67) in Germany, Henry Purcell in England, and François Couperin (1668–1733) and Jean Philippe Rameau (1683–1764) in France.

▶ HANDEL AND BACH

Baroque music reached a climax with two of the greatest composers who have ever lived: George Frederick Handel (1685–1759) and Johann Sebastian Bach (1685–1750). With these giant creators, baroque music came to its final fulfillment. With Handel, opera in the old Italian tradition reached its highest development. Henceforth opera would develop in completely new directions. With Handel, too, the oratorio—and with Bach the Passion—reached a stage of perfection upon which it was not possible to improve.

Few composers before Bach and Handel wrote instrumental music with such expressiveness, emotion, and beauty. Both these masters composed sonatas, concertos, suites, and solo instrumental music that fully achieved all the possibilities of the baroque style. They also pointed the way for the future. Bach and Handel not only represent the end of the baroque era, they anticipate the beginnings of the classical period that followed.

DAVID EWEN
Music Historian

BARRIE, SIR JAMES MATTHEW (1860–1937)

James Matthew Barrie was born in the Scottish village of Kirriemuir on May 9, 1860. His father was a weaver, and his mother was the daughter of a stonemason. James was the ninth of their ten children.

Very early in his life James Barrie knew he wanted to become a writer. While he was still a young boy he wrote a school play and also a novel that he later destroyed. After his graduation from Edinburgh University in 1882 he went to work for a small Scottish newspaper.

In 1885 Barrie moved to London and began to write the novels and plays that were to make him famous. His early works dealt with Scotland and the people of his village, which he called Thrums in his stories. Barrie's first novel, *Better Dead,* appeared in 1887. *The Little Minister* and *Sentimental Tommy* are among his later novels.

Barrie is best known as a writer for the stage. He dramatized *The Little Minister* in 1897, and afterward had great success with *What Every Woman Knows, Dear Brutus,* and *The Admirable Crichton.* In 1904 London audiences first saw Barrie's most famous work, *Peter Pan.* The American actress Maude Adams played the title role in this delightful fantasy about a boy who refuses to grow up.

Through the theater, motion pictures, and television, millions the world over have shared the adventures of Peter Pan, Wendy, Tinker Bell, and the Lost Boys of Never-Never Land. The play has been given in London every year since the author's death. Performances take place during the Christmas holidays, and the proceeds go to charity.

Barrie never had children of his own, and his marriage to the actress Mary Ansall ended unhappily. However, he did have a godchild and a ward—children he provided for.

During the early 20th century, Barrie was a great literary figure who counted among his intimate friends Thomas Hardy and George Bernard Shaw. King George V gave Barrie the rank of baronet, which allowed him to use the title Sir. In 1922 he received the special honor of the Order of Merit. Fifteen years later—June 19, 1937—Sir James Barrie died.

See also PETER PAN.

BARRYMORE FAMILY

Ethel Barrymore (1879–1959) said of herself and her brothers, Lionel (1878–1954) and John (1882–1942): "We became actors not because we wanted to go on the stage but because it was the thing we could do best."

Born into a family connected with the theater for many generations, the three Barrymores were leading actors on the stage and in motion pictures. Only twice did all three appear together: when as children they put on *Camille* in an old barn on Staten Island, and in 1933 in the talking picture *Rasputin and the Empress.*

Ethel's first starring role was Madame Trentoni in *Captain Jinks of the Horse Marines* in 1901. She went on to a variety of roles—in drawing-room comedy, Shakespeare, Ibsen, Barrie, even blackface—and became the nation's romantic idol. She is best remembered as the schoolmistress in Emlyn Williams' *The Corn Is Green.*

Lionel preferred painting, etching, and composing music to acting. He studied painting for 3 years in Paris but returned to earn his living in the theater. He detested romantic roles and played only character parts. His first hit was as an Italian organ grinder in *The Mummy and the Humming Bird* in 1902. In 1918 he was a great success as Milt Shanks in *The Copperhead,* followed by *The Jest* (in 1919 with his brother), *Macbeth* (1921), and *The Claw* (1921). After that he devoted most of his time to motion pictures. *A Free Soul* in 1931 won him an Academy Award. When a broken hip confined him to a wheelchair, he was cast as the semi-invalid Dr. Gillespie in the Dr. Kildare series. Millions heard him each Christmas as Scrooge in the radio dramatization of Dickens' *Christmas Carol.*

John's interpretation of *Hamlet* in 1922 established him as one of the leading actors of the English-speaking stage. He broke

Edwin Booth's record of 100 consecutive performances in New York and repeated his success in London. He tired quickly of his parts, however, and turned to motion pictures in preference to long stage runs. A chronic drinker since boyhood, he was extremely unstable yet possessed spirit, wit, and a great sense of self-criticism. He was continually haunted by the fear that he would collapse mentally as his father had.

BARTÓK, BÉLA (1881–1945)

Béla Bartók, the great modern Hungarian composer, was born in Transylvania (now part of Rumania) on March 25, 1881. His mother, a schoolteacher and amateur musician, gave him his first piano lessons.

Bartók continued his musical studies at the Royal Academy of Music, in Budapest, and became an instructor there after he graduated. By then he was a brilliant pianist. But most of the pieces he played at his recitals were his own compositions.

He thought of himself as a composer rather than a performer. He was especially fond of the old folk music of Hungary. He listened as peasants sang and danced, and he wrote down the melodies and rhythms in a notebook. Then he used these in his compositions, often accompanying the simple old tunes with a kind of harsh but pleasing harmony that was all his own.

Bartók's fame soon spread throughout Europe and America. He made a concert tour of the United States in 1927–28. After another period of teaching and composing at Budapest, he moved to America permanently in 1940. He died in New York on September 26, 1945.

Bartók's music has influenced many 20th-century composers. His works include an opera, several concertos, and many piano pieces for children to play. Among his best-known works are the *Concerto for Orchestra*, six string quartets, and *Music for Strings, Percussion, and Celesta*.

BARTON, CLARA (1821–1912)

Clara Barton devoted most of her life to helping people. Her greatest accomplishment was the founding of the American Red Cross.

Clarissa Harlowe Barton was born on December 25, 1821, at Oxford, Massachusetts. The youngest of five children, she received her early education from her brothers and sisters. At the age of 17 Clara became a teacher.

After 18 years of teaching, Clara Barton moved to Washington, D. C., where she worked in the United States Patent Office. She was in Washington when the Civil War broke out. Reports of suffering wounded soldiers troubled her. She urged people to contribute medicines and bandages. And to make sure the supplies arrived promptly, she sometimes took them to the battlefield herself. She was often under fire, and her clothes were torn by bullets several times.

When the war was over, Clara Barton headed a group that searched for missing soldiers and identified the graves of unknown soldiers. After 4 years of this work she became ill and went to Switzerland to recuperate. There she first learned of the Red Cross, an organization for the relief of suffering caused by war. When the Franco-Prussian War began in 1870, she remained in Europe to work with the Red Cross.

In 1873 Clara Barton returned to the United States. Although she was not well, she devoted all her energy to establishing an American branch of the Red Cross. In 1881 she succeeded, and became its first president, serving for over 20 years. As a result of her efforts, the work of the Red Cross was enlarged to include help in peacetime disasters such as earthquakes, fires, and floods. In 1904, at the age of 83, Clara Barton retired. She died 8 years later, on April 12, 1912, at Glen Echo, Maryland.

See also RED CROSS.

BASEBALL

Baseball is called the great American game. Hardly a boy in the United States has grown up without playing it. The game has also become popular in Canada, Mexico and other parts of Latin America, and Japan.

This game is so much a part of American life that its terms have been adopted into the everyday speech of the people. "Pinch hit," "going to bat," and scores of other baseball terms are used by people who have never seen a game.

During World War II Germans dressed in American uniforms turned up behind the American lines. Many of them spoke English very well and could pass as American soldiers. However, the United States Army found a way to tell which were false and which were real Americans. They halted strange soldiers at checkpoints and asked them questions about baseball and some of its star players. Genuine Americans could answer the questions easily. But the Germans, who couldn't, were promptly made prisoners of war.

▶ WHERE DID BASEBALL BEGIN?

It has been claimed that Abner Doubleday of Cooperstown, New York, invented baseball in 1839. But a game with bases, and sometimes called "base ball," was played before then.

Stick and ball games were played long ago, as part of the religious rites of ancient Egyptians. A game more like baseball, called prison ball, was once enjoyed in France. And English boys played rounders, in which posts were used as bases. Boys in New England called the game "town ball," and it was played in the United States into the 1800's. When there weren't enough boys for two big teams, they played "one old cat" or "two old cat," depending on the number of bases used.

Young men began to take up the game and improve the rules. Flat bases took the place of stakes, and runners were put out by being tagged instead of "plugged" (hit) with the ball.

Baseball as we know it began in 1845, when Alexander J. Cartwright drew up some rules for the game. These set the bases about

90 feet apart, as they are today. They also established the foul lines, the strikeout, three-out innings, and nine-man teams. However, the ball had to be pitched underhand, and 21 (or more) runs, rather than nine innings, made a game.

Cartwright helped to organize the first regular baseball club, the New York Knickerbockers. In 1846 the Knickerbockers lost the first recorded game to the rival New York Nine, 23 to 1, in four innings. After that, amateur baseball spread to other eastern cities. The new game attracted wide interest during the Civil War (1861–65), when the soldiers played baseball behind the lines. Then it was well on its way to becoming the "great American game."

▶ HOW BASEBALL IS PLAYED

Baseball is a game played by two teams of nine players each. The equipment consists of a ball, a bat, and gloves that the players wear to soften the impact of the ball on their hands. The object of the game is to score more runs than the opposing team. A run is scored each time a player can run safely around four bases, starting from and returning to home base (or home plate).

The field on which baseball is played has two parts: an infield and an outfield. Although the infield is popularly called the diamond the bases are laid out to form a square. The outfield reaches to the fence or grandstand, if any, that closes in the playing area.

An official baseball has a cork and rubber core. This core is wound with yarn and has a bleached white horsehide cover stitched on. The ball weighs between 5 and 5¼ ounces and is between 9 and 9¼ inches in circumference. A bat must be a round piece of wood (solid or laminated), not more than 2¾ inches in diameter at the thickest part. It must be no longer than 42 inches, but there is no limit to its weight.

The visiting team takes the first turn at bat. It remains at bat until the home team, fielding, has put out three of the visiting players. The home team then bats until three of its men have been put out. When each team has had a turn at bat and a turn in the field, an inning is completed.

Nine innings are normally a complete game. However, if the home team is ahead after 8½ innings, or if it goes ahead in the last half of the ninth inning before three outs, it is automatically the winner and the game

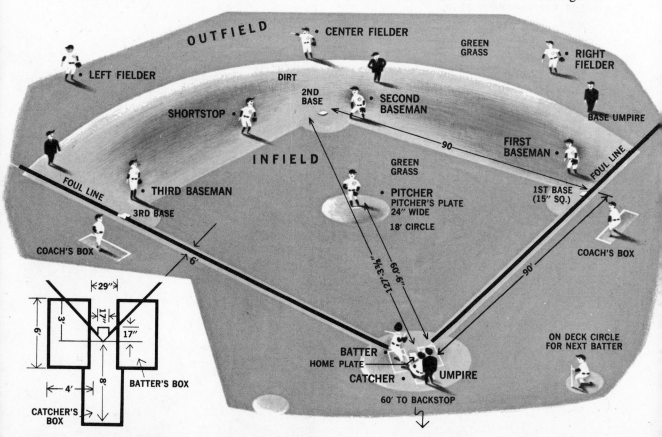

The strike zone. To be in the strike zone the ball must be pitched over home plate between the batter's armpits and the top of his knees, when he assumes his normal stance.

is over. A game stopped, or "called," because of rain or any other reason, after at least five innings have been played (4½ if the home team is ahead), is a complete game. If the score is tied at the end of nine innings, the game goes on until the tie is broken or the game is called. The Brooklyn and Boston National League clubs played a 26-inning 1–1 tie in 1920, a major league record.

Batting and Base Running

The members of a team bat in any order submitted by their manager or coach before a game starts. Each must then always bat in the same order. If a substitute comes into the lineup, he bats in the same order as the man he replaces.

A batter must stand in one of the boxes on either side of home plate, depending on whether he bats right-handed or left-handed. From there he attempts to hit the ball when it is thrown by the pitcher, if the throw is to his liking. A **strike** is called if he swings at a pitched ball and misses, or if he hits the ball foul (outside the foul lines) and it is not caught for an out. A strike is also called if a pitch at which the batter does not swing goes through the strike zone. Any pitch that does not pass through the strike zone and at which the batter does not swing is a **ball**. An umpire who stands behind the catcher decides whether a pitch is a strike or a ball.

The batter may get on base in various ways. If he hits the ball into fair territory (that is, between the two foul lines) and

neither he nor any runner is put out before he reaches first base, he has made a one-base hit, or **single**. If he can reach second base safely on the same hit, it is a **double**; third base, a **triple**. A fair ball hit into the stands or over the fence is a **home run**. It is also a homer if the batter hits the ball so far into the outfield that he can run around all the bases and beat the ball back to home plate.

The batter may also get on first base if he is "walked" on four balls, or bad pitches; if he is hit by a pitched ball; if the catcher interferes with him; or if the catcher drops a third strike and fails to throw the ball to first base before the batter reaches it.

A base runner may advance to the next base anytime he thinks he can do so safely. If he advances without the aid of a batted ball or a fielder's misplay, he is said to "steal" a base. He may also advance if the ball is hit into fair territory by a teammate. However, after a fly ball is caught, he must "tag up" at the last base he held before he can run to the next base.

It is said that when John McGraw was playing third base, he would sometimes hook his finger into the belt of a runner there when a fly ball was hit. This would delay the runner's takeoff for home plate once the fly was caught. One day a base runner in this situation unbuckled his belt. And when he ran for home he left the belt dangling in McGraw's hand—visible proof of the crime. Of course umpires today are too watchful to allow such a trick as McGraw's to happen.

Every ballplayer has his own way of standing, of gripping his bat, and of swinging. In the split second it takes a pitched ball to reach home plate, the hitter must decide whether or not to swing. All good hitters have level swings, but they hold their bats differently. A bat held at the end in a free-swinging grip is hardest to control but produces the most power. A batter who chokes up on his bat has less power but more control.

The batter waits for the ball, tenses as it is pitched, and begins to level his bat.

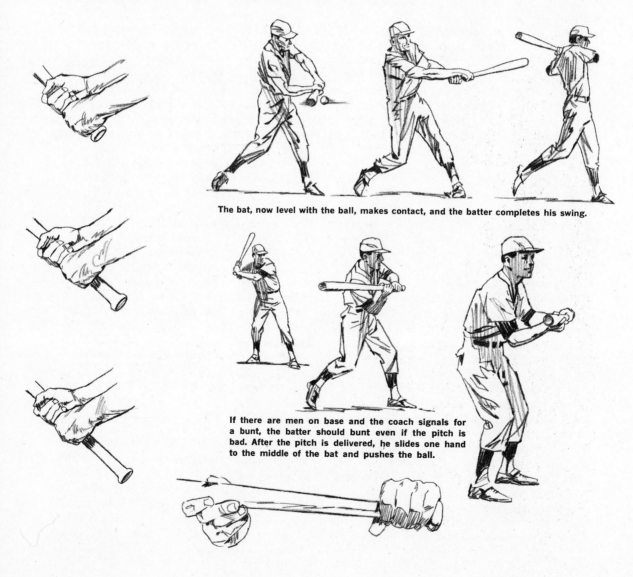

The bat, now level with the ball, makes contact, and the batter completes his swing.

If there are men on base and the coach signals for a bunt, the batter should bunt even if the pitch is bad. After the pitch is delivered, he slides one hand to the middle of the bat and pushes the ball.

The Players Fielding

A team in its turn in the field attempts to keep the team at bat from scoring. Each of the nine players has a key role in defense.

The Pitcher. From his position on a mound near the middle of the diamond, the pitcher throws the ball to the batter. He may use a variety of overarm or sidearm pitches—fast and slow balls, curves and sliders—in an effort to keep the batters from hitting. He also fields batted balls that fall near him, keeps a watchful eye on base runners so they won't advance, and covers first base when necessary.

On the pitcher's shoulders rests much of the responsibility for seeing that the team at bat does not score. If he loses control of the game and lets too many opposing players

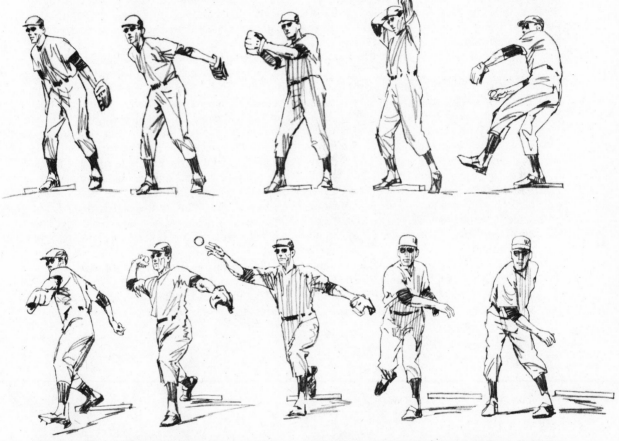

Many experts think that the pitcher is the most important man in a game. A team with good hitters will not win the pennant unless its pitchers prevent the opposition from getting too many runs. The catcher signals the pitcher, telling him the sort of pitch that is likely to fool the batter.

If he agrees, the pitcher nods and winds up. He throws the ball, then completes his motion, and waits for the batter's—or umpire's—decision. If there are men on base, the pitcher cannot use a full wind-up, for if he does, the runners may steal.

To keep the hitters guessing, pitchers use several kinds of pitches. The slow, change-of-pace ball is gripped loosely (A). The knuckle ball (B) is hard to hit because it dips and wiggles. A good fast ball (C) is in the catcher's glove while the batter is swinging. A curve ball is held off-center (D) and released from the middle finger (E).

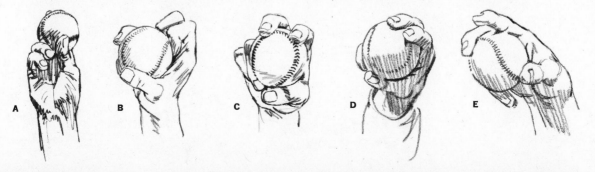

A   B   C   D   E

get on base and score runs, he is taken out of the game and a relief pitcher takes over.

The Catcher. The catcher stands in a box behind home plate. His job is to catch all the pitcher's throws that are not hit by the batter. He is expected to guard home plate against base runners who try to reach home from third base. He is also expected to field such batted balls as fall within his territory, and to keep runners from stealing bases. The catcher wears a face mask, a heavy body pad, and leg guards for protection against balls tipped by the bat. He also wears a mitt that is much thicker than the leather gloves worn by other fielders.

The catcher must play in close harmony with the pitcher. He studies opposing batters and gives signals to the pitcher telling him what type of balls to throw.

The Infielders. Four members of the team are infielders. The first baseman guards first base and the area around it. The second baseman plays on the side of second base toward first, while the shortstop plays on the other side; together they defend second base. The third baseman guards third base and the area around it.

The Outfielders. The three outfielders guard the territory in back of the infielders. They are the left fielder (on the third-base side), the center fielder, and the right fielder.

Putting a Player Out

There are several ways in which a batter can be put out. He is struck out if three strikes are called against him. (A foul ball is not called strike three unless it is a foul tip caught by the catcher before it touches the ground.) A batter is also out if he hits a fly ball or line drive (fair or foul) that is caught before it touches the ground. If he hits a fair ground ball and it is caught by a fielder and thrown to first base before the batter reaches that base, he is said to be "thrown out."

A base runner is out if a fielder tags him with the ball when he is off base; if he goes outside the marked base lines to avoid being tagged; or if, after a fly ball is caught, he fails to touch the base he held before the ball is thrown to a fielder touching that base.

A base runner can also be forced out. For example, if he is on first base and his teammate hits a ground ball, he must advance to second base so that first base will be left open for the hitter. If the ball is fielded and thrown to a fielder at second base before the runner arrives, he is out. If a runner on first base is forced out at second and the batter is thrown out at first on the same play, it is called a double play.

The umpires decide whether batters and runners are safe or out.

Baseball is a game of inches. A winning single may be a speedy ground ball hit through the infield: an inch or two in either direction could make it an out. A good infielder watches the ball from the second it is pitched. At the crack of the bat he knows where to move. His eyes still on the ball, he gathers it in and throws the runner out.

The fielder must tag the runner before the runner touches the base if the play is not a force play.

PROFESSIONAL BASEBALL

By the 1860's some players were receiving a share of the money paid by fans to watch baseball games. But the first professional team that paid its players was the Cincinnati Red Stockings of 1869.

Modern professional baseball got its true start in 1876, when the National League was founded. A rival American Association was formed in 1881 but disbanded after 10 years. The present American League had its first season in 1901. The National and American leagues are known as the major leagues.

In 1903 the champion teams of the two leagues met in the first World Series. For the following 50 years each league had the same eight teams it had then.

The National League, or senior circuit, as it is sometimes called, included, until 1953, the Boston Braves, Brooklyn Dodgers, Chicago Cubs, Cincinnati Reds (now Redlegs), New York Giants, Philadelphia Phillies, Pittsburgh Pirates, and St. Louis Cardinals. The Braves moved to Milwaukee (1953) and then to Atlanta (1966). The Dodgers opened the 1958 season in Los Angeles, the Giants in San Francisco. The league expanded to 10 teams in 1962, when the Houston Astros and the New York Mets joined it. The San Diego Padres and the Montreal Expos were added in 1969, the year the Mets became the first expansion team to win the World Series.

In the American League, or junior circuit, founded in 1903, were the Boston Red Sox, Chicago White Sox, Cleveland Indians, Detroit Tigers, New York Yankees, Philadelphia Athletics, St. Louis Browns, and Washington Senators.

The St. Louis Browns became the Baltimore Orioles in 1954. The Athletics moved to Kansas City (1955) and then to Oakland (1967). The league expanded to 10 clubs in 1961 with the creation of the Los Angeles (now California) Angels and a new Washington Senators

---

BASEBALL TERMS

Assist—a play by one fielder that makes it possible for another to make a put-out.

Balk—an illegal motion by the pitcher, entitling base runners to advance one base each.

Battery—a team's pitcher and catcher.

Batting average—number of hits divided by times at bat (as: $18 \div 60 = .300$). If a batter reaches base safely on an error or fielder's choice, he does not get credit for a hit. If he hits a sacrifice or gets a base on balls or is hit by a pitched ball, he is not charged with a time at bat.

Bunt—a batted ball tapped with the bat rather than hit with force.

Designated pinch hitter—a player who takes the pitcher's place when it is the pitcher's turn at bat.

Double play (DP)—a play in which the batter and a runner, or two runners, are put out in one continuous action.

Earned run—any run scored except one that results from a fielding misplay.

Earned run average (ERA)—number of earned runs charged against a pitcher divided by total innings pitched times 9 (as: $10 \div 50 \times 9 = 1.80$).

Error—any play on which a fielder misses a reasonable opportunity to put out a batter or runner, or a misplay that allows a runner to advance.

Fielder's choice—an attempt by the fielder of a fair ground ball to put out a runner instead of the batter who hit the ball.

Fielding average—total put-outs and assists divided by total chances (put-outs, assists, and errors) (as: $\dfrac{66 + 33}{66 + 33 + 1} = \dfrac{99}{100} = .990$).

Force play—a play in which a runner must try to advance to the next base to make room for the batter or runner behind him.

Infield fly—a fair fly ball hit above the infield when there are runners on first and second or on all three bases and there is not more than one out. The umpire declares "infield fly," and the batter is automatically out.

Passed ball—a failure of the catcher to hold a pitched ball (other than a wild pitch), permitting a runner to advance; not scored as an error.

Percentage (team or pitcher)—number of games won divided by total games won and lost (as: $\dfrac{15}{15 + 9} = \dfrac{15}{24} = .625$).

Pinch hitter—a substitute for another player in his turn at bat.

Run batted in (RBI)—a run that scores and is credited to a batter as a result of his safe hit, sacrifice, or infield out; or his reaching first base on a fielder's choice; or his getting a base on balls or being hit by a pitched ball with the bases full, forcing in a run.

Sacrifice—a successful attempt by the batter (before two are out) to advance a runner or runners by means of a bunt or a long fly out.

Shutout—a game in which a team fails to score.

Squeeze play—an attempt to bring home a runner from third base by means of a bunt.

Stolen base—the act of a runner in advancing one base without the aid of the batter or any misplay by the defending team.

Twi-night doubleheader—two games played under floodlights, one after the other, with the first starting in early evening. Night baseball was first played under arc lights back in the 1880's. But it did not become common until 1930, when it was adopted in the Western Association. The first major league use of floodlights for night games came in 1935 at Crosley Field in Cincinnati.

Walk—a base on balls, also called a free pass.

HANK AARON

JOE DI MAGGIO

MAURY WILLS

WILLIE MAYS

MICKEY MANTLE

SANDY KOUFAX

club. The original Washington team moved to Minneapolis-St. Paul as the Minnesota Twins. In 1969 the Seattle Pilots and the Kansas City Royals were added to the league. The Pilots moved to Milwaukee in 1970 as the Brewers. In 1972 the Washington Senators moved to Texas as the Texas Rangers. In 1977, two teams were added, the Toronto Blue Jays and the Seattle Mariners.

Both leagues are divided into eastern and western divisions. The division winners play each other in a best-of-five-game series for the league title, or pennant. The two pennant-winners then meet in the World Series, in which a team must win four games to become world champion.

The Minor Leagues

The major league clubs get most of their players from the minor leagues and the winter leagues in Latin America. Each major league club provides financial support to minor league teams. These farm clubs give training and experience to promising athletes.

The Limited-Reserve and Draft Systems

For many years major league clubs operated under the reserve system, which required a player to sign a contract with a club and remain with it until traded, sold, or released. Under changes made in 1976, a player may become a free agent after six years of service.

Each year the major league clubs draft players from the minor leagues for a certain price. When several major league clubs want the same player, he is awarded to the team that stood lowest in the league standings that year. In the same way minor league clubs can draft players from leagues of lower classes.

Baseball as Big Business

Professional baseball is very definitely big business. Any one of the big-league clubs is worth several million dollars.

The business office is usually headed by the club secretary. The office takes care of the sale of tickets, the upkeep of the home park, and the payment of salaries.

The man in direct charge of the players is the manager. He is almost always an old-time player. Many have had experience as coaches or minor league managers. The manager is responsible for his team's success and is in personal charge of each game. Some managers direct just about every play on the diamond. The manager also develops young players collected by his scouts from the minor leagues, colleges, high schools, and even sand-lot teams. He has one or more coaches, who help him train members of the team and coach them in the strategy of the game.

A Player's Life

The regular major league playing season is from April to October. Half the games are played at home and half away, so a team travels much of the time. There are day and night games. On many days two games—doubleheaders—are played.

The long, tiring season means that players must be in top condition. They are whipped into shape in spring training in southern and

---

SOME IMPORTANT MAJOR LEAGUE RECORDS ESTABLISHED SINCE 1900

Highest lifetime batting average: .367, Ty Cobb.

Highest season batting average: .424, Rogers Hornsby, Cardinals, 1924.

Most hits, lifetime: 4,191, Ty Cobb.

Most hits, season: 257, George Sisler, Browns, 1920.

Longest consecutive-game hitting streak: 56 games, Joe DiMaggio, Yankees, 1941.

Most runs batted in, lifetime: 2,297, Hank Aaron, Braves, 1954–74, 1977, Brewers, 1975–76.

Most runs batted in, season: 190, Hack Wilson, Cubs, 1930.

Most home runs, lifetime: 755, Hank Aaron. Other leaders: Babe Ruth, 714; Willie Mays, 660; Frank Robinson, 586; Harmon Killebrew, 573; Mickey Mantle, 536; Jimmy Foxx, 534; Ted Williams, 521.

Most home runs, season: 61, Roger Maris, Yankees, 1961 (162-game season schedule); 60, Babe Ruth, Yankees, 1927 (154-game schedule). Other leaders: Hank Greenberg, 58; Jimmy Foxx, 58; Hack Wilson, 56.

Most stolen bases, lifetime: 900, Lou Brock.

Most stolen bases, season: 118, Lou Brock, Cardinals, 1974.

Most consecutive games played: 2,130, Lou Gehrig, Yankees, 1925–39.

Most games won by a pitcher, lifetime: 511, Cy Young, 1890–1911. Other leaders: Walter Johnson, 414; Grover Alexander, 373; Christy Mathewson, 373; Warren Spahn, 363.

Most games won by a pitcher, season: 41, Jack Chesbro, Yankees, 1904.

Longest winning streak by a pitcher: 24 games, Carl Hubbell, Giants, 1936–37.

Most strikeouts, lifetime: 3,497, Walter Johnson, Senators, 1907–27.

Most strikeouts, season: 383, N. Ryan, Angels, 1973.

southwestern states, especially Florida and Arizona. Major and some minor league teams meet in exhibition games that give fans and managers a preview of the coming season.

A professional baseball player generally has a limited major league playing life. Some stars play 10 or 12 years, but most players retire soon after they are 30. Leroy ("Satchel") Paige, the great black ballplayer, is a notable exception. Paige did not get his chance to become a big leaguer until he was about 40. That was because blacks were not accepted in the major leagues until 1947, when Jackie Robinson joined the Brooklyn Dodgers. The first black to manage a major league team was star player Frank Robinson, who was named manager of the Cleveland Indians in 1974.

Near the middle of each season an all-star game is played, from which 75 per cent of the proceeds goes to a players' pension fund. The rival American and National all-star teams are chosen by the fans, who vote for the players they think best at each position, except pitcher. The pitchers are chosen by the managers. This annual event was started in 1933.

Babe Ruth

A story is told of how in one game Babe Ruth, the famous "Sultan of Swat," pointed to a place in the distant stands. He then waited calmly for the pitch and drove the ball into that very spot for a home run.

The Babe had great, hulking shoulders, which gave him his power as a hitter. His legs were thin and too small for the rest of his body, and he would break into a funny little trot when he circled the bases after hitting a home run. He hit a record 714 home runs in his major league career. This record stood for many years until it was broken by Hank Aaron in the spring of 1974.

Hank Aaron

At 9:07 P.M. on Monday, April 8, 1974, in Atlanta Stadium, Hank Aaron of the Atlanta Braves hit a fast ball pitched by Al Downing of the Los Angeles Dodgers. The ball went over the fence and Aaron chalked up his 715th home run, thus becoming the leading home run hitter in major league history. Henry Louis Aaron, known to baseball as Hank Aaron, was born in Mobile, Alabama, in 1934. He began his major league career with the Milwaukee Braves, the team that later became the Atlanta Braves.

▶ GROWING UP IN BASEBALL

All across the United States and Canada, in Mexico, and in many places overseas, boys 8 years and over begin to play in organized baseball under adult leaders. Boys 12 and under can play in the Little Leagues. For boys over 12 there are opportunities to play in Babe Ruth, Pony, Connie Mack, and other leagues; in the Veterans of Foreign Wars' Teener championships; and in American Legion junior baseball. Many schools also have baseball teams.

For young men there are opportunities to play in various amateur, semiprofessional, or industrial leagues.

Baseball has become an organized sport in many colleges since 1859, when Amherst defeated Williams 66–32. The National Collegiate Athletic Association holds a tournament each year for the champions of the various college leagues.

In the early days professional players were generally a hard-living group of men who thought that amateur and college players were sissies. This idea was changed by one of the greatest baseball managers of all time, Connie Mack of the Philadelphia Athletics. He developed Eddie Collins of Columbia University into one of the top second basemen of his generation. Other famous college-graduate pioneers in the game were Christy Mathewson, Frankie Frisch, Lou Gehrig, and Gordon ("Mickey") Cochrane.

Not all boys can become professional baseball players when they grow up. But the experience of playing baseball gives them a lifelong feeling that they are experts in the game. That is why baseball fans will discuss by the hour the mistakes and triumphs of their favorite teams and players.

STEPHEN C. FLANDERS
Commentator, Columbia Broadcasting System
Reviewed by JIM BROSNAN
Former National and American League Pitcher
Author, *Pennant Race*
See also LITTLE LEAGUE BASEBALL; ROBINSON, JACK ROOSEVELT ("JACKIE"); RUTH, GEORGE HERMAN ("BABE"); SOFTBALL.

THE WORLD SERIES

Baseball's most dramatic event of the year is the World Series. This is a series of games between the champion teams of the National and American leagues. The first team that wins four games is called the world champion.

The World Series has produced many thrills and heroes. The first series was played in 1903 between the Boston Puritans (now the Red Sox) and the Pittsburgh Pirates. This series was decided on a best-of-nine basis —the winner was the first team to win five games. (The series of 1919–21 were also played on a best-of-nine basis.) The Puritans won the 1903 series, 5 games to 3.

The New York Giants, National League champions in 1904, refused to meet Boston, again winner of the American League pennant. But baseball fans, backed up by the

WORLD SERIES — YEAR-BY-YEAR RECORD
The winning team is indicated by an asterisk (*).

Year	American League	National League	Games Won–Lost		Year	American League	National League	Games Won–Lost	
					1940	Detroit	*Cincinnati	4	3
					1941	*New York	Brooklyn	4	1
					1942	New York	*St. Louis	4	1
1903	*Boston	Pittsburgh	5	3	1943	*New York	St. Louis	4	1
1905	Philadelphia	*New York	4	1	1944	St. Louis	*St. Louis	4	2
1906	*Chicago	Chicago	4	2	1945	*Detroit	Chicago	4	3
1907	Detroit	*Chicago	4	0	1946	Boston	*St. Louis	4	3
1908	Detroit	*Chicago	4	1	1947	*New York	Brooklyn	4	3
1909	Detroit	*Pittsburgh	4	3	1948	*Cleveland	Boston	4	2
1910	*Philadelphia	Chicago	4	1	1949	*New York	Brooklyn	4	1
1911	*Philadelphia	New York	4	2	1950	*New York	Philadelphia	4	0
1912	*Boston	New York	4	3	1951	*New York	New York	4	2
1913	*Philadelphia	New York	4	1	1952	*New York	Brooklyn	4	3
1914	Philadelphia	*Boston	4	0	1953	*New York	Brooklyn	4	2
1915	*Boston	Philadelphia	4	1	1954	Cleveland	*New York	4	0
1916	*Boston	Brooklyn	4	1	1955	New York	*Brooklyn	4	3
1917	*Chicago	New York	4	2	1956	*New York	Brooklyn	4	3
1918	*Boston	Chicago	4	2	1957	New York	*Milwaukee	4	3
1919	Chicago	*Cincinnati	5	3	1958	*New York	Milwaukee	4	3
1920	*Cleveland	Brooklyn	5	2	1959	Chicago	*Los Angeles	4	2
1921	New York	*New York	5	3	1960	New York	*Pittsburgh	4	3
1922	New York	*New York	4	0	1961	*New York	Cincinnati	4	1
1923	*New York	New York	4	2	1962	*New York	San Francisco	4	3
1924	*Washington	New York	4	3	1963	New York	*Los Angeles	4	0
1925	Washington	*Pittsburgh	4	3	1964	New York	*St. Louis	4	3
1926	New York	*St. Louis	4	3	1965	Minnesota	*Los Angeles	4	3
1927	*New York	Pittsburgh	4	0	1966	*Baltimore	Los Angeles	4	0
1928	*New York	St. Louis	4	0	1967	Boston	*St. Louis	4	3
1929	*Philadelphia	Chicago	4	1	1968	*Detroit	St. Louis	4	3
1930	*Philadelphia	St. Louis	4	2	1969	Baltimore	*New York	4	1
1931	Philadelphia	*St. Louis	4	3	1970	*Baltimore	Cincinnati	4	1
1932	*New York	Chicago	4	0	1971	Baltimore	*Pittsburgh	4	3
1933	Washington	*New York	4	1	1972	*Oakland	Cincinnati	4	3
1934	Detroit	*St. Louis	4	3	1973	*Oakland	New York	4	3
1935	*Detroit	Chicago	4	2	1974	*Oakland	Los Angeles	4	1
1936	*New York	New York	4	2	1975	Boston	*Cincinnati	4	3
1937	*New York	New York	4	1	1976	New York	*Cincinnati	4	0
1938	*New York	Chicago	4	0	1977	*New York	Los Angeles	4	2
1939	*New York	Cincinnati	4	0	1978	*New York	Los Angeles	4	2

newspapers, made officials of the game realize how popular the interleague contest could be. Rules were then set up for the series to be held every year. Starting in 1905, they have been held continuously. The Giants won the 1905 series, when Christy Mathewson became a national idol by pitching three shutouts.

Chicago had the series to itself in 1906, when the White Sox team of "hitless wonders" beat the Cubs. But with good hitting and pitching, and the famous combination of "Tinker to Evers to Chance" for making double plays, the Cubs played in four series in 5 years, winning two of them.

From 1910 through 1914 the Philadelphia Athletics, managed by Connie Mack, were in four of the five series, winning three. The Boston Braves, who were in last place in the middle of the 1914 regular season, won the National League pennant and went on to beat the Athletics in four straight games. It was the first time that a team had swept a series.

Babe Ruth saw series action for the first time in 1915, pinch-hitting for the Red Sox. In the 1916 series he was the victor in a 14-inning game against Brooklyn. He also began a pitching streak of 29⅔ scoreless innings. This record stood until Whitey Ford of the Yankees bettered it, reaching 33 innings before the Giants scored off him in the 1962 series.

The series of 1919 will be remembered forever as the one in which the Reds defeated the vastly superior White Sox. There were rumors that several White Sox players had accepted bribes from gamblers to lose the series. The suspected players were barred from the game for life.

An unassisted triple play by Bill Wambsganss was a feature of the 1920 victory of Cleveland over the Brooklyn Dodgers. From then until 1964 the New York Yankees made the series a personal playground, playing in and winning a great number of them. Miller Huggins lost to his rival New York manager, John J. McGraw of the Giants, in 1921 and 1922, but turned the tables the next year. Huggins' team swept the 1927 and 1928 series from the Pirates and the Cardinals. Later Joe McCarthy, manager of the Yankees, took the series of 1932; then four straight (1936–39); and finally two more in 1941 and 1943. But Casey Stengel's achievement stands above all others. He managed the Yankees into 10 series and won seven, including five straight (1949–53).

In the fifth game of the 1956 series Yankee pitcher Don Larsen retired all 27 Dodger batters who faced him. It was a perfect no-run, no-hit game—the only one in World Series history.

DONALD SCHIFFER
Author, *Baseball: How to Play It and Understand It*

BASEBALL'S NATIONAL HALL OF FAME AND MUSEUM

The National Baseball Hall of Fame and Museum, at Cooperstown, New York, was dedicated on June 12, 1939, to the pioneers and great players of the game.

In 1908 a commission of the outstanding baseball executives of the day was organized to investigate a claim that Cooperstown was the "Home of Baseball." In the late 1800's Abner Graves, a native of the town, had claimed that the game of baseball was invented at Cooperstown by Abner Doubleday, who taught him to play the new game. The commission produced proof that Abner Doubleday had indeed marked out a diamond on the turf at a Cooperstown military academy,

and had explained the rules of a new game he had invented, which he called "baseball."

In 1935 a descendant of Abner Graves' opened an old trunk that had been stored in his attic for generations. Among the contents of the trunk, which had belonged to his grandfather, was a baseball unlike any seen today. It was small, out of shape, and obviously homemade. Instead of the wool and cotton yarn stuffing of the modern ball, cloth was used to stuff this antique ball. That same year, Stephen C. Clark of Cooperstown bought the old baseball. He decided to exhibit the ball, and any other obtainable baseball objects, in a room in the village club.

The first five modern baseball players selected for the Baseball Hall of Fame were (a) Ty Cobb, (b) Honus Wagner, (c) Walter Johnson, (d) Christy Mathewson, (e) Babe Ruth.

Clark's exhibit interested Ford C. Frick, president of the National League; Kenesaw Mountain Landis, baseball's first commissioner; and William Harridge, president of the American League. Soon contributions and valuable baseball relics poured in from everywhere to join the antique baseball.

It was Frick who suggested that a National Baseball Hall of Fame and Museum be built. Plans were immediately approved to erect a building that would house a museum and a hall of fame where the great players of baseball would be honored.

Members of the Hall of Fame are elected by the Baseball Writers' Association of America and by the Committee on Veterans.

The Baseball Writers' Association holds a yearly election. To be eligible, a player must have played in the major leagues at least 10 seasons during a period that began 20 years before and ended 5 years before the election. While he must have been retired as an active player during the 5 years preceding the election, he may be otherwise connected with professional baseball. This 5-year rule was waived for Lou Gehrig in 1939 when he was desperately ill and for Roberto Clemente in 1973 after a fatal air crash while he was on a mercy mission. Clemente was the first Latin American to be inducted into the Baseball Hall of Fame.

The Committee on Veterans is appointed by the board of directors of the Hall of Fame and holds a yearly election. To be eligible, players must have played at least 10 seasons. They must have been retired from the major leagues as players for at least 20 years, which disqualifies them for the Baseball Writers' elections. Managers, umpires, and executives who have been retired from organized baseball for at least 5 years prior to the election are also eligible.

Because black players were excluded from the major leagues before 1947, many failed to qualify for the Hall of Fame. To honor outstanding players of Negro leagues before 1947, the Hall of Fame changed its admission requirements in 1971 so these players could be admitted. Each year a special committee elects one player who has had at least 10 years experience in the Negro leagues. Satchel Paige was the first to be named.

JUMP BALL

BASKETBALL

Basketball is one sport that can be called truly American. The man who invented it, Dr. James A. Naismith, was born in Canada. But he developed the game in the United States, and it is there that basketball has become the most popular indoor sport through the winter months.

Two teams of five players each play the game on a court. At each end of the court is a basket attached to a backboard. The bright orange metal ring of the basket is 18 inches in diameter and placed 10 feet above the floor. From it hangs a white cord net. The object of each team in a game is to score goals by throwing the ball into one of the baskets.

The basketball is a rubber bladder inflated with air and covered with leather or a composition material. It is 29 to 30 inches in circumference and weighs between 20 and 22 ounces.

In 1891, when he invented basketball, Dr. Naismith was an instructor at the International Training School of the Young Men's Christian Association (YMCA) in Springfield, Massachusetts. It was winter, and he noticed a lack of interest in formal gymnasium exercises among some of his students. What they needed, he thought, was a fast-action game that could be played indoors when the football season ended. He decided that some kind of game in which players would have to throw a ball into baskets would be interesting. So he attached a couple of old peach baskets to the ends of the gym balcony.

In the early days a soccer ball was used. Every time a goal was made, someone had to climb a ladder to get the ball out of the basket. After a while wire mesh baskets were used. In 1906 the metal hoop similar to that of today was used for the first time. At first when a basket was missed, the ball would go into the crowd. This caused much delay. Then backboards were put up so the ball would bounce back into the playing court.

When the game was first played, nine men formed a team. Later it was changed to permit nine, seven, or five to play. Today five men make up a team. Then, as now, running with the ball, pushing, and tripping were not allowed. The early scoring rules allowed 3 points for each basket. The center jump was used to start play after every goal. And when a ball went out of bounds, the first player to get it would put it back into play.

Basketball has come a long way since Dr. Naismith hung those two peach baskets in the Springfield YMCA gymnasium.

Today it is a major winter sport in schools, colleges, YMCA's, and clubs throughout the United States and Canada. It is played outdoors and indoors by boys and girls, men and women. Thousands of people crowd into gyms and sports arenas to watch tournaments and championship games. On a makeshift court in the back yard or the polished hardwood floor of an arena, basketball is a great game whether you play it or merely watch.

Several Canadians were among Dr. Naismith's pupils, and through them basketball was introduced in Canada. Other YMCA leaders and American armed forces abroad helped to spread the popularity of the game in Latin America, Europe, the Philippines, China, and Japan.

In 1961, on the 100th anniversary of the birth of the inventor of basketball, the cornerstone was laid for the Naismith Memorial Basketball Hall of Fame in Springfield.

▶HOW THE GAME IS PLAYED

Each team has five men on the court. They are the center, two forwards, and two guards. Substitutes may come into the game when the ball is dead (out of play). The officials are two referees. They are assisted by one or more scorers and timers.

A high school basketball game is played in four 8-minute quarters, while younger teams play 6-minute quarters. There is a 10-minute rest period at half time. College games are divided into 20-minute halves, professional games into 12-minute quarters. In case of a tie score at the end of the last period, overtime periods are played—3 minutes in high school games, 5 minutes in college and professional games.

To start each period, the referee tosses the ball up between the opposing centers in the center circle. Each of these players jumps up and tries to tap the ball to one of his teammates. The two forwards are in front of and to the right and left of their own center, but outside a restraining circle. The two guards are in similar positions in back of their center, on the end of the court toward the goal they are defending.

As soon as a player gains possession of the ball, his team goes on the offense. The object is to advance the ball toward the team's own basket (the opponent's basket, under international rules) and score a goal. A shot for the basket may be made from anywhere on the court. It is best, however, to move the ball as close to the goal as possible before shooting.

Players may pass the ball back and forth or from side to side in an effort to confuse the defensive players. If this happens, one of the offensive team can get under the basket for a clear shot. Passes do not have to stay in the air; the bounce pass is often used. The only requirement is that the ball stay on the playing court.

The only other legal way a player can move the ball is by bouncing it along the floor with one hand. This is called dribbling. Once a player stops dribbling and holds the ball with both hands, he must either pass it or shoot for a basket. If he dribbles again or if he walks or runs while holding the ball (traveling), the ball is awarded to a player of the opposing team, who, standing out of bounds, may toss it to a teammate.

When the ball goes out of bounds, the referee decides which player touched it last. He then awards the ball to a player of the opposing team to throw in. If two opposing players hold the ball firmly at the same time, the official calls for a jump ball and tosses it up between them.

Field Goals

A team scores a field goal when a player (except on a free throw) throws or taps the

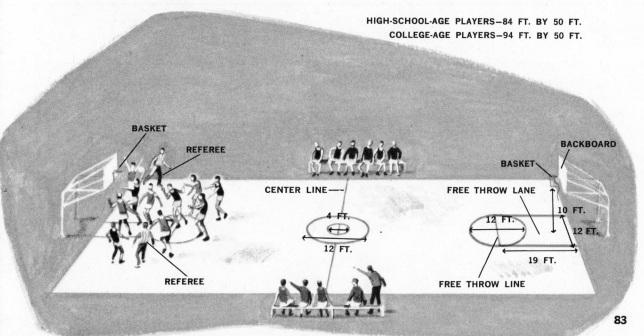

HIGH-SCHOOL-AGE PLAYERS—84 FT. BY 50 FT.
COLLEGE-AGE PLAYERS—94 FT. BY 50 FT.

BASKET
REFEREE
BACKBOARD
BASKET
CENTER LINE
FREE THROW LANE
10 FT.
4 FT.
12 FT.
12 FT.
12 FT.
19 FT.
REFEREE
FREE THROW LINE

ball in such a way that it goes over the rim of the hoop and down through the team's own basket. A field goal counts 2 points. After each goal is made, the ball is thrown back into play by the team scored on, from out of bounds behind the end line. This rule, made in the 1930's, replaced the center jump after every goal. It is partly responsible for the high-scoring, fast-breaking game we know today.

Fouls and Free Throws

The only other scoring opportunity is the free throw. A free throw is made from a line 15 feet from the backboard, when the opposing team has committed a foul. Other players must stay outside the free-throw lane while the thrower is shooting, and opponents may not hinder his attempt. Each successful free throw at the basket counts 1 point.

There are two types of fouls, personal and technical. Pushing, charging, holding, tripping, roughing, or impeding the progress of an opponent is a personal foul. A player who commits five personal fouls (six in professional basketball) must leave the game. A technical foul occurs when a team takes more

time-outs than allowed, delays the game, has too many men on the court, or breaks a similar rule. Unsportsmanlike acts, such as disrespect to an official, are also technical fouls.

For a minor violation of the rules, the ball is awarded to an opponent to throw in from out of bounds. If an official decides that a foul was slight or unintentional, the opposing team is allowed one free throw. Two free throws are allowed for a more serious foul, such as a personal foul that causes a player to fail in the act of trying to shoot a field goal. (If the goal is made, it counts 2 points, and the fouled player gets one free throw.) In some situations a one-and-one free throw is allowed; that is, if his first free throw is good, the thrower gets another try. An offended player gets two free throws in case of a multiple foul—when he is fouled by two or more opponents at almost the same time. If two opponents commit personal fouls against each other, a double foul is called, and no free throws are awarded.

▶HINTS ON PLAYING BASKETBALL

Good footwork is one of the most important things a basketball player must have.

ONE-HAND PUSH
SHOT FREE THROW

UNDERHAND FREE THROW

You have a better chance to score if you can get away from the man who is guarding you. When a teammate has the ball, you must try to get free and in position where you can take a pass and have an open shot at the goal.

To be in a position to move fast, stand with one foot slightly forward. Your knees should be bent slightly, your shoulders a bit forward. Hold your arms out a little, with the fingers spread. When you start to run down court, use your rear foot as a spring. Take short steps. To move to the side or rear, pivot on the rear foot. Use the front foot to guide you in whatever direction you want to go.

It is equally important to know how to stop suddenly. There are two reasons for this: to avoid a personal foul for running into an opponent, and to get in the best possible position to take a pass.

How to Dribble

You dribble the ball when you want to move in close to the basket for a shot, or when you wait for a teammate to get in position to take a pass. When you are unguarded and trying to move the ball down court, use the high, or normal, type of dribble. Lean forward a little and bend your knees slightly as if running. The hand that controls the ball should have fingers spread wide. Your other hand should be at your side for balance. Always look straight ahead while dribbling.

While dribbling always keep alert for a teammate you can pass to. At the same time try to keep an opponent from getting too near the ball.

To keep your opponent from getting possession of the ball, use the low dribble. The stance is the same as for the high dribble except that you bend your knees more. When you are crouching, keep the ball close to the floor, bouncing it easily as you move around. If you are dribbling with your right hand and an opponent moves in on your right, switch to your left hand. To do this, just tap the ball easily toward your left toe and pick up the rebound with your left hand.

The change-of-direction dribble starts as a fake. You make a move as if to dribble in one direction. As the man guarding you starts in that direction, you cross your foot to go another way. Use the low dribble.

DRIBBLING

How to Pass

The quickest way to get the ball down court is by passing. It is also the riskiest way because an opponent may intercept the pass.

The **two-hand chest pass** is the most widely used for short, quick throws. Hold the ball chest high with both hands, fingers forward, thumbs in back of the ball. As you get ready to pass bring the ball back toward your chest, turning it so that your thumbs are now under the ball. Then step out with your forward foot while pushing your arms straight ahead. With your wrists snap the ball to the receiver.

When the man guarding you is close with arms high, use the **two-hand under pass**. Hold the ball close and waist high, with your knees bent in a half crouch. With your wrists snap the ball under the arms of the man guarding you.

When you are guarded by a player using his hands waist- or chest-high, use the **two-hand bounce pass**. With both knees bent hold the ball waist high. Look straight ahead and fake left, then right. When your receiver is clear, bend your rear knee almost to a kneeling position. Straighten your arms and flip the ball downward on a bounce toward your receiver.

To throw high to a teammate, use the **two-hand overhead pass**. Hold the ball as for a chest pass, but with your fingers a little more behind the ball. Your feet should be just slightly apart and knees bent slightly. Lift your hands above and a little in front of your head. Take a forward step as you bend your wrists back then push the ball forward with a quick wrist action.

When all of your teammates are behind you and you are being closely guarded from the rear, you have to use the **hook pass**. As you turn one foot toward the man to whom you intend to pass, raise the ball in a semi-circle high over your head with the opposite hand and pass it.

Still another way of passing the ball is the **hand-off**. As a teammate runs in front of you, hand him the ball. The receiver must immediately dribble the ball. The hand-off calls for perfect timing.

When you become expert enough, you can even pass backward.

It is also important to learn how to fake. Look high, pass low. Look low, pass high.

TWO-HAND
CHEST PASS

HOOK PASS

HOOK SHOT　　　**LAY-UP SHOT**

How to Shoot

Everybody on a basketball team likes to shoot for the basket. Shooting is one of the most important parts of the game.

Behind the foul line the **two-hand set shot** is the most common shot for younger players. Your feet should be close together, knees bent. Hold the ball near your chin, with the fingers spread and thumbs back. Bend your knees just a bit more and at the same time bring your wrists back so that the ball is cupped in your hands. Straighten your knees and arms, pushing the ball toward the basket with a snap of the wrists.

The **one-hand set shot** is used when you are close to the basket. Come to a complete stop. Put the weight of the ball on one hand

and use your other hand to guide the ball as you raise it toward the basket.

You can make the **lay-up shot** when you dribble in from the side, close to the basket. Just before shooting, push off the floor on the foot opposite your shooting hand. If the ball is in your right hand, push off with your left foot and then shoot.

The **one-hand jump shot** is made from a complete stop, as in the one-hand set shot. However, you bend your knees and jump, snapping the ball toward the basket with the bent wrist of your shooting hand.

The **hook shot** is most used by the pivot man, who is usually the tallest player on the team. He will try to move into the foul circle with his back to the basket.

**ONE-HAND
SET SHOT**

**TWO-HAND
SET SHOT**

From there he will take a high pass, spin around, and throw the ball into the basket with a one-hand circular motion above his head.

How to Guard

It is as important to keep an opponent from scoring as it is to score yourself. When the other team has the ball, all five players on the defensive team must guard. There are two types of defense. One is man-to-man, in which each player is assigned to guard a certain opposing player when the other team has the ball. The other type of defense is called zone defense. For this the players are assigned certain areas of the court. Each man guards any opponent who enters his area.

To guard an opponent properly, you must know his ability and playing habits. Does he usually pass overhand or does he use the bounce pass? Can he make a basket with a long shot? The more you know about him, the better your chances are of stopping him from passing, dribbling, and shooting to score.

Stay as close to your opponent as possible if he is in scoring territory. But be careful not to touch or foul him. When he is out in the middle of the court or beyond, you can stay about 5 feet away. However, if he is noted for his ability to score from way out, you may have to guard him a little closer.

In guarding, spread your feet with one slightly in front. If your left foot is forward, hold your left arm head high with fingers spread. Hold out your right arm to the side, between knee and hip. When your opponent has the ball, stand in front of him and move your arms constantly. Your object is to block any pass and keep him from taking a shot. The hand on the side is for blocking a pass. The raised hand is for blocking a goal shot or high pass. If he tries to get away from you by dribbling to the side, move in the same direction with a shuffle, or side step.

An excellent player must be used to guard a good pivot man. When the pivot man's right shoulder is toward the basket, it is best to stand a bit behind him in a straddle position with your left hand raised to a point near the back of his left shoulder. When his left shoulder is toward the basket, he should be guarded from the left. When he has his back to the basket, stand in back of him.

The most difficult shots to block are the jump shot and the lay-up. When your opponent with the ball jumps, jump with him and try to touch the ball as it leaves his hand. However, you must not risk a two-shot penalty for a foul by touching your opponent.

Girls' Basketball

Some teams of girls or women play under the same rules as boys and men. Most of them, however, play the game as laid out by the National Women's Basketball Committee. In this game there are six players on a team. The three forwards of each team play against the three guards of the opposing team at one end of the court. Only one roving forward and one roving guard of each team may cross over the center, or division, line of the court. Therefore, there can be four players of each team at either end of the court at any time. When the guards recover the ball, they attempt to advance it to their own forwards in the other half of the court. The guards must stay in the back half and are not allowed to throw for the basket.

One of the most famous girls' teams of all time was the Edmonton Grads, formed in 1915. For 2 decades these graduates of McDougall Commercial High School in Edmonton, Alberta, played in Canada, the United States, and abroad, winning nearly all of the games they played.

GUARDING A DRIBBLER

GUARDING IN SCORING TERRITORY

AMATEUR BASKETBALL

Most boys and girls learn to play basketball when they are in grade school. In high schools, prep schools, and colleges, especially in the United States, basketball is the major sport during the winter months. It is also a popular game in YMCA's, Boys' Clubs, and similar organizations. There are many leagues of teams sponsored locally by churches, synagogues, clubs, business firms, and industrial plants.

Biddy basketball is organized like Little League baseball for boys 12 years old and younger and girls 13 or under. The courts and equipment are smaller than those used in regulation basketball. There are local and regional play-offs, and a yearly national tournament is held with teams from other countries taking part. Headquarters of Biddy basketball are in Scranton, Pennsylvania.

American college basketball began in the East and spread westward. The players in early days were of average height. Even the centers, the tallest players, were shorter than their modern counterparts. Low-scoring games were much more common then.

As the years went by, the game began to change. Teams in the East concentrated on speed and dribbling. In the Midwest they used a blocker who would get between a teammate who had the ball and the man guarding him. Farther west they began trying the one-hand set shot.

During the 1930's basketball had a boom. Rules were adopted to speed up the game. State high school tournaments were held before big crowds, and college gyms were overcrowded. Major tournaments were held in big arenas like New York's Madison Square Garden. Newspapers gave more and more space to the sport. And basketball players became as well known as the stars in other amateur sports. The National Basketball Committee of the United States and Canada makes the rules for high school and collegiate athletic associations, the YMCA, and other amateur organizations.

In 1936 basketball became a regular event in the Olympic Games. As athletes in more and more countries have shown interest in the sport, the competition has become stronger. Since 1950 the strongest bid against American teams, which have dominated Olympic basketball, has come from Russia. Rules of the International Amateur Basketball Federation (FIBA) differ only in minor details from those of college play.

PROFESSIONAL BASKETBALL

There were professional basketball teams as early as 1898. In the 1920's the New York Celtics became famous, with such stars as Nat Holman, Henry "Dutch" Dehnert, and Joe Lapchick. The professional game was organized permanently in 1949, when the National Basketball Association (NBA) was formed. A second league, the American Basketball Association (ABA), began play in 1967. The two leagues planned to merge in 1976, with the NBA absorbing four (of the six) ABA teams.

Under the merger the NBA would be organized into two conferences—the Eastern and Western. The Eastern Conference would comprise the Atlantic and Central divisions; the Western Conference the Midwest and Pacific divisions. The Atlantic Division would comprise the Boston Celtics, Buffalo Braves, New York Knickerbockers, New York Nets, and the Philadelphia 76ers. In the Central Division would be the Atlanta Hawks, Cleveland Cavaliers, Houston Rockets, New Orleans Jazz, San Antonio Spurs, and the Washington Bullets. The Midwest Division would have the Chicago Bulls, Denver Nuggets, Detroit Pistons, Indiana Pacers, Kansas City Kings, and the Milwaukee Bucks. The Pacific Division would have the Golden State Warriors, Los Angeles Lakers, Phoenix Suns, Portland Trail Blazers, and the Seattle Supersonics.

In professional basketball a team cannot keep the ball more than 24 seconds without shooting for the basket. This is one of the reasons why professional scores are higher than those in schools and colleges.

An independent professional team known as the Harlem Globetrotters is one of the best-known teams in basketball history. Made up entirely of black players, the team was started in 1927. Their unusual style of play, combining expert ball handling with a bagful of tricks, made them famous.

DONALD SCHIFFER
Author, *The First Book of Basketball*

BASTILLE. See FRENCH REVOLUTION.

BASUTOLAND. See LESOTHO.

BATHS AND BATHING

Since earliest times, baths have had different purposes and meanings among different people. During many periods in history, the main purpose of bathing was not to become clean, for little was understood about the connection between cleanliness and health. Some people bathed for relaxation and a sense of well-being. For others, bathing and washing were religious rites. Still others sought cures from diseases by bathing in waters from natural mineral springs. The custom of "taking a cure" at a spa (mineral springs) is still popular.

History of Bathing. Built-in bathtubs with drainage systems and hot and cold running water were found in the homes of the wealthy in Greece, Rome, and India thousands of years ago. But the luxury of home bathtubs and hot water from a faucet did not begin to become widespread until well into the 19th century.

Public baths played an important part in the social life of the ancient Greeks and Romans. The luxury-loving Romans built magnificent public baths that could serve thousands of bathers at a time. The baths contained gymnasiums, libraries, gardens, and shops in addition to the bathing facilities.

Soap was unknown to the ancients. (It was first manufactured commercially in the 12th century in Europe.) To clean themselves, the Romans applied to the skin a mixture of sand and oil, which they then scraped off with a curved metal tool called a strigil.

By the 12th century in Europe there were many public baths, where large numbers of people bathed together. These communal baths were called "stews." But there was no way of disinfecting the bath water. The stews contributed to the spread of disease, and a frightened public stayed away. By the end of the 16th century the stews had disappeared.

Over the next few centuries there was little improvement in bathing facilities. Water for baths was heated in cauldrons. Portable bathtubs were filled by hand. Since drawing and heating enough water for individual baths was difficult, it was not unusual for whole families and their guests to bathe together in a common tub. In Japan and some of the Scandinavian countries families still bathe together.

From the middle of the 19th century, Britain, Germany, and America tried to deal with the problem of cleanliness, but progress was slow. A survey taken in the 1880's showed that five out of six people in American cities had no bathtubs. There was no bathtub in Buckingham Palace when Queen Victoria came to the throne in 1837. Nor did the White House have a real bathroom until 1851.

In the late 1800's, crowding in the rapidly growing cities and the lack of home plumbing brought back public bath houses. Although most bathrooms in private homes had been converted from bedrooms, the new homes were being designed with bathrooms.

Daily Baths. Today's knowledge of prevention of disease places great emphasis on hygiene and personal cleanliness. A daily bath with soap and warm water is recommended for everyone except those people with unusual medical conditions. Soaping, lathering, and scrubbing perform two important functions. Dirt is dislodged, and blood circulation to the skin is increased. Some people find a tub bath more relaxing than a shower bath. But the shower, with its soapy scrub followed by a rinse with clean water, is more effective for cleansing purposes. The combination of soap and warm (or hot) water removes from the skin the oil that holds the dirt.

Steam Baths. The Finnish saunas and the Russian steam baths are believed to have had their beginnings in the Scythian baths. The Scythians were a tribe of nomads living in southern Russia thousands of years ago. They produced steam by throwing water on red-hot stones. The North American Indians used a similar kind of steam bath.

The modern Finns produce steam just as the Scythians did. Most Finnish families have their saunas in a separate building or in the basement of the house. The steam bath is used in addition to the regular soaping and scrubbing. As part of the sauna, the bathers beat themselves with a bundle of birch twigs to cleanse the skin and stimulate circulation. They complete the bath by rolling in the snow or plunging into a stream of ice-cold water.

The Russian bath includes a steam room, a hot room, a scrubbing administered by a bath attendant, and a cold shower. The Turkish bath is similar to the Russian bath.

Reviewed by ALEXANDER KIRA
Author, *The Bathroom*

BATS

In the animal kingdom bats are classed as mammals, a large group that includes men, mice, lions, and dogs. Like all mammals, bats nurse their young on milk. Like most mammals, they have hair and bear living young. But in one way bats are different from all other mammals: Bats can fly.

There are mammals known as flying squirrels and flying lemurs, but they do not truly fly. Rather they glide from tree to tree. Bats are the only mammals that move through the air with wings.

A bat's wing is not like a bird's wing. The bird's wing is formed chiefly of feathers; these grow out from bones that make the front edge of the wing. The bat's wing is a double layer of skin stretched over the thin bones of its arm and fingers. A bat's wing is something like a kite.

A bat's skeleton is the framework for a living flying machine. The arm extends from a shoulder socket, bends at the elbow, and ends with long, slender fingers. The fingers are almost as long as the rest of the body. They support the main part of the wing and are webbed. These webbed fingers account for the bat's scientific name, Chiroptera, meaning "wing-handed."

The wing covers all fingers except a short thumb, which is left free. A sharp claw on the end of the thumb forms a hook at the top of the wing. When its wings are folded, the bat uses its hooks to climb tree trunks, rocky walls, and other rough surfaces.

The skin connecting the webbed fingers is also attached to the bat's clawed feet. This makes the back part of the wings. Most bats have an extra flap of skin connecting their feet. While flying, many can fold this flap into a pocket for catching insects.

Since its leg bones and leg muscles are included in its wings, a bat can fly more easily than it can walk. But the feet are far from useless. Like human hands, a bat's feet can turn inward, which enables them to grasp objects like twigs and branches. Sharp claws hook securely into cracks or around bumps in the wall or ceiling of a cave. These claws are so strong that they support the bat's whole weight, even during sleep.

When resting, a bat can use its claws to cling to a wall or tree trunk—or it may hang upside down, suspended by its feet. Bats hang upside down because it is easier for them than perching upright. Their small legs are attached to the body in a way that makes perching awkward.

▶ HOW BATS LIVE

There are nearly a thousand different species, or kinds, of bats. They live in almost every part of the world except the polar regions. Each kind of bat has different habits, depending on where it lives. Yet with all their differences the various species have many things in common.

Bat Colonies

Bats are usually social animals. That is, they live in groups. Unlike other social ani-

Brown bat's wing. Skin fills space from tip of long arm to tail. Small hook at top of wing is thumb.

Skeleton of a bat. Fingers are almost as long as rest of body. They support main part of wing.

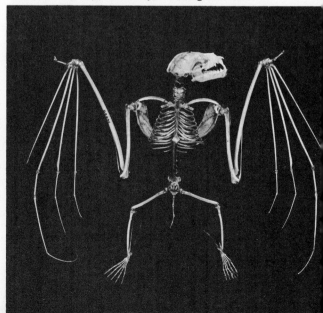

FINGERS (PHALANGES)

THUMB (POLLEX)

FOREARM

HIND FOOT

CALCAR

TAIL

WING STRUCTURE OF THE BROWN BAT

A flittermouse in flight. This bat is helpful to man because it eats insects.

mals such as bees and prairie dogs, bats do not make their own dwellings. They usually live in caves.

If you see one bat flying into a cave, you can be reasonably sure there are other bats inside. In some caves thousands of bats crowd together on walls or ceilings. In such large colonies scientists often find bats of one kind sharing a cave with a few bats of a different species. Smaller bat colonies numbering only 10 or 12 bats may live in a hollow tree.

Where Bats Roost

Caves and hollow trees are not the only places where bats live. Some bats simply roost in trees, hanging like leaves from twigs and branches. Two kinds of tropical bats make little tents from palm leaves. Such a bat slits the leaf with its teeth, then hangs inside the folds.

There are bats living in the pyramids of Egypt and in the fruit trees of Australia. In North America and Europe human beings sometimes share a house or a barn with a whole colony of bats and never know the animals are there. A bat can squeeze through narrow cracks and roost between layers of wall and ceiling.

Night Creatures

Most bats are nocturnal. This means that they are active only at night. They sleep in the daytime and come out at night to find food. Only a few kinds of bats venture out in bright sunlight. Bats are probably night creatures for the same reasons that most small mammals are. A small animal is in less danger at night. In the daytime there is the constant danger of being eaten by larger animals that sleep at night. Also, at night bats can catch insects with less competition from birds.

The Search for Food

Most bats live on insects alone. Some eat only fruit. Some eat both insects and fruit. A few kinds of bats eat other things—meat, fish, and even flower nectar.

In Canada and the United States the most familiar bats are insect eaters, though there are nectar-feeding bats in Arizona and California. Probably the best-known fruit bats are the huge flying foxes. In Australia these giant bats have become a serious nuisance to fruit growers. They swarm over the orchards, devouring fruit at night and roosting in the trees by day.

In India one kind of bat has been seen eating mice, birds, and lizards. When captured, the large spear-nosed bats of tropical America will eat almost anything. They have been fed bananas, horsemeat, liver, and hamburger. They will even eat smaller bats.

The bats with the most unusual diets are found in the tropics. *Noctilio* bats of South and Middle America eat fishes. They skim over

Red bat holding baby. Mother forms cradle by hanging from a branch. Soon baby will hang onto her fur.

a pond or lake, dragging their sharp claws through the water to catch small fishes swimming near the surface. Another group of jungle bats, the tiny hummingbird bats, eat chiefly the pollen and nectar of flowers.

Probably the most famous tropical bats are the vampires, found only in South and Middle America. The vampire bat has inspired legends, superstitions, and horror tales—all of them false. A vampire bat does bite other animals and drinks their blood. But, contrary to the legends, it does not drain its victims. A vampire bat may bite a sleeping horse, cow, or goat—or even a man—without being noticed. Its sharp teeth make a shallow cut. Then the bat simply laps up a small amount of blood and flies away. The chief danger to the victim is infection. Vampire bats—as well as several other species—are known carriers of rabies.

Migration and Hibernation

Bats cannot survive in extremely cold weather. So some fly to warmer climates for the winter. When spring comes, these bats return to a favorite roost as accurately as homing pigeons. To find out where they go, how far they travel, and whether or not they return to the same roost, scientists have attached identification bands to the wings of migrating bats. Some banded bats have been found as far as 800 miles away from the place where they were released.

Instead of migrating, other bats hibernate deep in caves, where the temperature changes very little from season to season. For many weeks hibernating bats hang head downward, sometimes packed together in thick clusters. At such times the bat's body temperature drops very low. Hibernating bats have built up an extra layer of fat by eating more food before retiring for the winter. This provides the fuel they need to keep alive until spring.

Mothers and Babies

Bats mate in the fall, before hibernating or flying away for the winter. When the weather begins to warm up, female bats gather in the roosts that will become nurseries. In late spring or early summer the baby bats are born. Most mother bats have just one baby at a time. (Some have up to four, but this is as rare as twins in human families.)

When a baby bat is born, the mother forms a living cradle by hanging belly-up from the ceiling or a branch. She may hang by the hooks at the top of her wings as well as by her feet. The newborn bat rests in this cradle. Within minutes the mother bat is nursing her baby and a cradle is no longer needed. The baby bat is able to hang on to its mother's fur, using its own sharp teeth and claws. Little bats cling so tightly that at first mother bats carry them when flying in search of food.

However, young bats grow so rapidly that a 10-day-old bat can be too heavy for its mother to carry. Then the babies stay in the roost at night when the mothers go hunting for food. At dawn the mothers return to nurse their babies. A mother bat can find her own child even in a crowded cave. Some scientists think that mother and baby bats call to each other in high squeaks and recognize each other's voices.

Within a month after birth, the baby bat has grown to its full size. A bat born in June is flying on its own nightly hunting trips by August. It may live as long as 10 to 14 years, a remarkably long lifetime for a small mammal.

▶ANCESTORS

Ancestors of today's bats were flying about the earth at least 50,000,000 years ago. Since that time some bats have changed very little. One 40,000,000-year-old bat fossil found in Europe looks very much like the skeleton of a modern bat.

Pocketed free-tail bat.

East African fruit bat.

Noctule.

Mexican vampire bat.

Leaf-nosed bat.

Lump-nosed bat.

Bats hanging from wall of main bat room in cave.

There are many different kinds of bats. They live in almost every part of the world except in polar regions. Above are some of the more common kinds.

Bat hanging upside down on a twig. It is suspended by its feet.

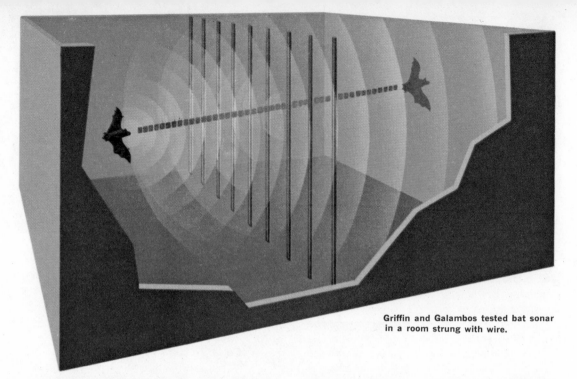

Griffin and Galambos tested bat sonar in a room strung with wire.

Some scientists think that the first bats may have evolved from a tree-climbing mammal that could leap and glide after insects. Over millions of years the limbs of some gliding animals may have developed into wings. These winged animals would have been the first bats.

Scientists have not been able to prove this theory. They are still looking for fossils of gliding animals to provide the missing link between flying and non-flying mammals. There is one animal living today in the jungles of Malaya and the Philippines that may resemble an ancestor of the bat. Known as the flying lemur, it has layers of skin stretched between hands and feet. But since its limbs do not form true wings, it is a glider, not a flier.

▶ HOW DO BATS FIND THEIR WAY IN THE DARK?

For centuries men who studied bats wondered how they found their way in the dark. How could a bat with no light to see by find a flying insect and catch it in flight? Many people used to think that bats had unusually keen eyesight and could see by light too faint for human eyes to detect. Scientists now know that a bat's ability to navigate depends not on its eyes but on its ears and vocal organs.

Early Experiments

The first steps toward understanding how bats navigate were taken in the 1780's. An Italian zoologist named Spallanzani suspected that bats could not see in the dark. To find out, he blinded some bats and released them into a room crisscrossed with silk threads. The bats flew through the maze without touching the threads. Then he tried plugging their ears with wax. The animals blundered about, flapping their wings helplessly and becoming entangled in the threads.

Spallanzani wrote about his experiments with bats. He hinted that bats used their ears rather than their eyes to find their way in the dark. But he died before his experiments were completed, and few scientists took his ideas seriously.

Spallanzani's work was almost forgotten until 1920. That year, at Cambridge University in England, Professor H. Hartridge suggested that bats sent out signals that were beyond the range of human hearing. (Such sounds are called **ultrasonic.**) He thought bats might use the echoes of these signals to navigate in the dark. But Hartridge couldn't prove his theory. He had no way of listening to ultrasonic sounds.

Proof Is Found

In 1941 two scientists in the United States proved that Spallanzani and Hartridge had been on the right track. Donald R. Griffin and Robert Galambos of Harvard University were experimenting with bats. They decided to use a new electronic instrument that detected ultrasonic signals.

Griffin and Galambos placed bats in front of the microphone of this instrument. The men could hear no sounds, but patterns on a screen showed that the bats were uttering high-pitched cries. A special attachment changed these cries into lower-pitched sounds that could be heard by the scientists.

Griffin and Galambos strung a room with a network of wire and repeated some of Spallanzani's experiments. They added their own modern equipment—microphones and recording devices. Patterns on the electronic screen showed that the bats were constantly squeaking as they flew successfully through the maze of wires.

The two Harvard experimenters proved that a bat's vocal organs are as important as its ears in navigating. When they taped the bats' mouths shut, the animals blundered as badly as deaf bats.

A bat sends out signals—high-pitched squeaks that bounce off anything in its path. A sound that is bounced back, or reflected, is called an echo. The bat uses echoes to locate things in the dark. So scientists call this system **echolocation.** It is often compared to man-made radar and sonar systems, which also use reflected signals to locate objects. But radar and sonar are newcomers. Bats have been using echolocation for millions of years.

Future Research

There is still a great deal to be learned about echolocation. Scientists in many countries are studying the process in bats and in other animals such as shrews and dolphins. They hope to gain information that may be helpful to man. For example, blind people may someday learn from this research how to use reflected signals. Also, the designers of radar and sonar know that they will benefit from research on echolocation in animals.

BARBARA LAND
Columbia Graduate School of Journalism
Reviewed by KARL F. KOOPMAN
The American Museum of Natural History

See also DOLPHINS AND PORPOISES; ECHO; HIBERNATION; HOMING AND MIGRATION; MAMMALS; RADAR, SONAR, LORAN, AND SHORAN; SOUND AND ULTRASONICS.

BATTERIES

A battery is a source of electric current. There are several kinds of batteries, and they come in many sizes. But they all work on the same principle: A battery changes chemical energy directly into electrical energy.

A battery is made up of two or more units called cells. Sometimes a number of cells are packaged together, as in the battery of a portable television set. Sometimes each cell is separate, as in the ordinary flashlight. That is, what most people call a two-battery flashlight is really a two-cell flashlight. There is no battery until two or more cells are connected. A single cell can produce electric current, but it is more practical to use several cells and get more current.

▶ DRY CELLS

A flashlight battery is made of so-called dry cells. But as you may know, they are not really dry. If you cut one apart with a saw, you will find it is filled with a slightly damp paste of chemicals. In the middle there is a rod of carbon. The zinc casing itself is an important part of the cell. Zinc and carbon are also chemical substances.

How Dry Cells Work

In a dry cell electricity is produced by the reactions among the chemicals. But electric current cannot flow unless there is a closed circuit—a continuous path starting and ending at the cell. So long as there is no complete metal path between the carbon rod and the zinc casing, the cell's circuit is open. (In a flashlight a switch moves a piece of metal into position to bridge the gap in the circuit.)

In the dry cell shown on the next page, the circuit is closed the instant a wire connects the rod to the casing. In a flashlight the circuit goes from the zinc casing to the metal flashlight container and switch, through the bulb, down into the carbon rod, and back through the damp paste to the zinc.

SOME TYPES OF BATTERIES

DRY CELL

Dry cell cut away to show the inside. Chemical action of the zinc, damp paste, and electrolyte causes an electric current to flow when the circuit is closed. The carbon rod acts as the positive electrode. The zinc casing is the negative electrode.

FLASHLIGHT

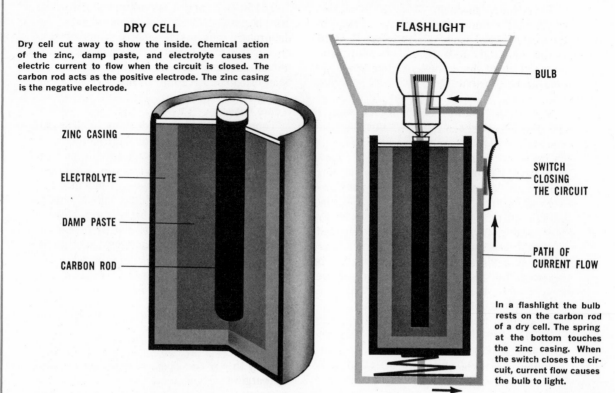

ZINC CASING

ELECTROLYTE

DAMP PASTE

CARBON ROD

BULB

SWITCH CLOSING THE CIRCUIT

PATH OF CURRENT FLOW

In a flashlight the bulb rests on the carbon rod of a dry cell. The spring at the bottom touches the zinc casing. When the switch closes the circuit, current flow causes the bulb to light.

STORAGE BATTERY

Lead-acid storage battery used in an automobile. Lead plates are set in a container filled with sulfuric acid. Separators keep the plates apart to prevent a short circuit. Below right, side view of set of plates. Negative lead plates are joined to the negative post. Positive lead-dioxide plates are joined to the positive post.

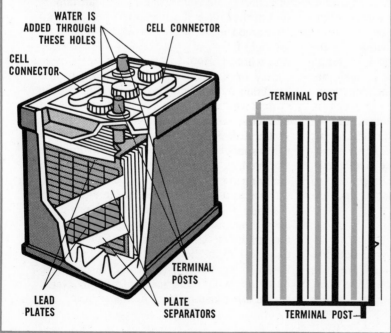

WATER IS ADDED THROUGH THESE HOLES

CELL CONNECTOR

CELL CONNECTOR

TERMINAL POST

TERMINAL POSTS

LEAD PLATES

PLATE SEPARATORS

TERMINAL POST

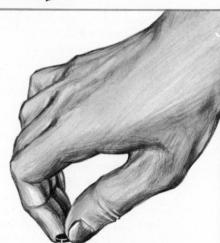

MERCURY BATTERY

Above, a tiny mercury battery has important uses. It supplies power to hearing aids and to certain wristwatches. It is also used for power in a device inserted in the body to keep a weak heart beating steadily.

Every time a flashlight is used, a small part of each cell's zinc container is eaten away by the electrical and chemical action taking place. Waste materials form and slow down the action. Finally there comes a time when the current becomes weak and the light grows dim.

Sometimes a dry cell runs down even though it has not been used very often. This is caused by "local action"; it occurs because the casing is not pure zinc, which would be too expensive. There are impurities in the zinc, which serve to close a circuit within the cell even when the cell is not in use. That is, tiny electric currents flow in small paths all the time, and this gradually wears down the cell. Once a dry cell wears down, it is not used over again. A cell's chemical materials could be renewed, but the process is too expensive.

THE STORAGE CELL

However, there is a kind of cell that can easily be recharged, or renewed. This is the storage cell used, for example, in automobile batteries. An automobile battery usually consists of three **wet cells** connected together inside one container. The wet cell is so named because it has a liquid chemical instead of a damp paste.

The basic process in a storage cell is the same as in a dry cell. When the ignition switch of an automobile is on, the circuit running between the battery and the engine is closed. A chemical reaction then starts within the battery, releasing electric current.

The advantage of a liquid chemical is the ease with which reactions can take place in either direction. After a storage battery has been used for some time, the liquid has given up all its electric charges to other materials in the cells. If the storage battery is connected to an outside source of electricity, the charges are forced back into the liquid.

That is what happens when a storage battery is recharged. A storage battery is so called because energy is stored in it in the process of recharging.

USES OF BATTERIES

Batteries provided the first continuous electric current. Early batteries were called voltaic piles; they were named for Alessandro Volta, the Italian scientist who made the first one over 150 years ago. These early batteries were too large to be of much use outside the laboratory, but in time smaller batteries were made. For many years batteries provided the electric current for running all small devices such as doorbells and railroad signals. Electricity from other sources has done away with many of these uses. But batteries are still widely used to power portable lights and radios, and to start motor vehicles.

Today tiny batteries are used to power some camera exposure meters. Batteries smaller than a dime are being used in wristwatches and hearing aids. A device placed inside the body can keep a weak heart beating steadily by sending out electric impulses; it is powered by a tiny battery. These small, long-lasting batteries have come about through the use of new materials such as mercury and cadmium.

NEW KINDS OF BATTERIES

All the batteries described wear out eventually. Scientists have long hoped to make a battery that would have unlimited life without recharging. The problem was to get a chemical reaction that would produce electricity as long as there was a continuous supply of chemicals. Such batteries—called **fuel cells**—now exist. The chemicals are fed into the cell, where they react and generate electricity. Since no part of the cell's container is involved in the reaction, electricity is given off as long as fresh chemicals are supplied.

Large fuel cells may someday use gas or oil straight from the ground to provide electricity for whole cities. Most small fuel cells in use today operate on hydrogen and oxygen. In addition to producing electricity, the reaction forms water. Such fuel cells are used in space vehicles, where they also provide drinking water for the men aboard.

A special kind of fuel cell is the biological fuel cell, or **biocell.** It uses bacteria or enzymes to bring about chemical reactions that produce electricity. A biocell using sea water may provide a continuous electric current. Scientists hope to find bacteria that can release electricity while feeding on garbage and sewage.

Reviewed by IRA M. FREEMAN
Rutgers—The State University
See also CHEMISTRY, HISTORY OF; ELECTRICITY.

BATTLES IMPORTANT IN WORLD HISTORY

Over a century ago an Englishman named Edward Creasy made a list of 15 battles that changed the course of history. The following list includes Creasy's choices plus several decisive battles that occurred after his book was published in 1851.

Marathon, 490 B.C. The Persians invaded Greece, and the Athenian army marched out to meet them. For 8 days the two armies glared at each other across the plain at Marathon. On the 9th day the Athenians marched onto the plain, fanned out into battle line, and attacked. The Persians panicked, ran for their ships, and were slaughtered. Some historians believe that the Greek victory saved Western civilization from being absorbed by the Orient.

Syracuse, 413 B.C. When the Athenian fleet sailed for Syracuse in Sicily, Athens was at the peak of her power. But now she tried to do too much. Far from home, cut off from supplies, the Athenians were trapped in the Great Harbor at Syracuse. In a desperate attempt to break free, the Athenian fleet was largely destroyed. The Athenian Empire, shaken by this disaster, began to fall apart.

Arbela, 331 B.C. Alexander the Great dreamed of a world empire. The conquest of Persia was part of that dream. The two armies met at Arbela. The huge Persian force included 15 elephants and 200 chariots. But it was no match for Alexander's experienced Macedonians. The Persians were totally defeated. Persia's losses were so great that she never again was able to threaten Western civilization.

Metaurus, 207 B.C. For 11 years the Romans and the Carthaginians had been fighting for control of the western Mediterranean lands. Carthage had invaded Italy in 218 B.C. and was still trying to conquer the country. At Metaurus the Romans turned the tide. In a furious battle Hasdrubal's army was destroyed when a Roman legion crept up behind him and made a surprise attack. The power of Carthage was broken.

Teutoburg Forest, A.D. 9. In A.D. 9 a German tribe revolted against its Roman rulers. Led by young Arminius, the Germans swooped down from hiding places and slaughtered the Romans. Roman prestige received a fatal blow. The Germans had shown that Rome could be beaten. The limits of the Roman Empire in Europe were fixed.

Châlons, 451. In the 5th century Europe faced a dangerous invasion. Out of the East came Attila the Hun, the "Scourge of God," and one of the most savage figures in history. Riding on their fast little ponies, Attila's barbaric hordes destroyed everything they touched. Finally, at Châlons, they met the Goths and the Romans in a brutal hand-to-hand struggle. Attila was completely beaten and Europe was saved.

Tours, 732. In the 8th century Europe again faced a grave threat to her civilization. The Muslims had invaded France. The Franks, led by Charles Martel, met the oncoming Arabs at Tours. Time and time again the Muslim cavalry charged the unbreakable French lines. When at last the invaders were exhausted, the Franks attacked. The Muslims were routed and thrown out of France. Some historians think Tours saved western Europe from Arab rule.

Hastings, 1066. William the Conqueror, of Normandy, claimed the English throne. With about 7,000 men he sailed to England to win his crown. At Hastings he met and defeated

GETTYSBURG, 1863

NORMANDY, 1944

the army of King Harold. Harold was killed, and William became king of England. He unified the country and strengthened the monarchy. William drew England closer to western Europe by blending two different cultures, the Norman French and the Saxon of England.

Orléans, 1429. In 1422 the King of England claimed to be the king of France as well. The French did not accept him, but they had been beaten. England occupied much of the country. France needed a leader. Suddenly one appeared—a 17-year-old peasant girl named Joan of Arc. Joan said that voices from heaven told her that she was chosen by God to lead France to victory. Carrying the flag, Joan led the French into battle. Inspired by her courage and piety, the French drove the English out of Orléans. In a few years the English were swept out of France. The modern French state was born because of the great victory at Orléans.

Spanish Armada, 1588. The English coast was lighted with bonfires to warn the people that the Spanish Armada was coming. The Armada was a huge fleet that Philip II had gathered to conquer England. The English set sail at once to meet the Spaniards. Led by Sir Francis Drake, the faster, lighter Eng-

lish ships outsailed the massive Spanish galleons. Spain lost 63 ships, England not even one. Spain's plans for a world empire went down with her fleet.

Blenheim, 1704. The battle of Blenheim broke the power of Louis XIV's France. For years Louis had dreamed of dominating Europe, sending his armies far and wide with much success. Finally, at Blenheim, the great French army met its match in the combined forces of England and the Holy Roman Empire, commanded by the Duke of Marlborough. Marlborough's brilliant tactics completely fooled the French. Louis' army was swept off the field. This victory prevented Louis from controlling the Holy Roman Empire and shattered the prestige of the French army.

Poltava, 1709. At the end of the 17th century the huge Russian Empire began to stir. It was being modernized by Czar Peter the Great. Peter was determined to take his place among the powers of Europe. Poltava helped him reach that goal. By defeating Charles XII of Sweden, Peter gained control of northern Europe and the Ukraine. This victory gave Peter enough power to unite his sprawling country and create the modern state of Russia.

Saratoga, 1777. The battle of Saratoga,

BLENHEIM, 1704

ARBELA, 331 B.C.

JOAN OF ARC AT ORLEANS, 1429

New York, was the turning point in America's struggle for independence. The Americans, led by Horatio Gates and Benedict Arnold, beat the British in a fierce battle that lasted over 5 hours. Even more important than the British defeat was the fact that Saratoga won France over to the American cause. Saratoga gave the American Revolution a tremendous push forward, with incalculable effects on the history of the Western world.

Valmy, 1792. Valmy was the deathbed of the French monarchy. With its passing, a stormy new period of revolution and change began. Despite its historic importance, the actual battle of Valmy was only a minor skirmish. The army of the French Revolution defeated the Prussians, who had come to support the French king. In the entire battle less than 500 lives were lost. The French Revolution had triumphed and was now strong enough to carry its doctrine of "liberty, equality, and fraternity" to the rest of Europe.

Waterloo, 1815. For Napoleon Bonaparte, Waterloo was the end of a glorious career. Here he faced the wrath of a united Europe, led by the English soldier-statesman the Duke of Wellington. For an entire day the French cavalry charged Wellington's defensive positions. Then, as night closed in, Wellington's Prussian reinforcements arrived. Thus strengthened, the Duke gave the signal to attack. Forty thousand soldiers poured down on the French. The French army fled, and the Napoleonic era was brought to a close. Napoleon was sent into exile, and peace was restored.

Gettysburg, 1863. The battle at Gettysburg, Pennsylvania, was the turning point in the American Civil War. The fate of the Union depended on its outcome. For 2 days the bloody battle raged. Still the result remained in doubt. On the 3rd day the South launched a tremendous attack, known as Pickett's Charge. Fifteen thousand men rushed toward the Union positions on Cemetery Ridge. After a violent hand-to-hand struggle, the Confederates were thrown back. Lee lost one third of his army and had to withdraw. His hope for victory in the North was shattered.

Sedan, 1870. The battle of Sedan marked a fateful moment in history. The French Army was trapped by the Prussians. Napoleon III, seeing the hopeless condition of his men, surrendered his entire army. French military power was crushed, and Napoleon III was overthrown. Even more important, the victory completed the unification of Germany. The creation of a unified and powerful German Empire dramatically altered the European balance of power. After Sedan, France and Germany remained mortal enemies. This helped push the world into World War I.

First Marne, 1914. When World War I began, the Germans seemed unbeatable. They over-ran Belgium and sliced through France. Within thirty days they threatened Paris. The French had to counterattack quickly. So great was the emergency that ordinary Paris taxicabs were used to take some of the troops to the front lines. The German advance was stopped, and Paris was saved.

Stalingrad, 1942–43. Stalingrad (now Volgograd) was the turning point in World War II. Here the advance of the Germans into Russia was stopped and turned back. The battle itself lasted almost six months. The fighting was brutal, but the Russians grimly held on to their ruined city until more Russian troops came and trapped what was left of the German army. Then the Allies began to push the Germans back.

Normandy, 1944. In 1944 Europe was under the rule of Nazi Germany. The world eagerly awaited the Allied invasion that would free these nations. In the early hours of June 6, a huge armada—the largest military force ever assembled—sailed from England to France. In the morning the Allies hit the Normandy beaches. Wave after wave of soldiers scrambled ashore under heavy fire. After a day of bloody battle, the Allies established a beachhead. The invasion was a success.

Inchon, 1950. The successful amphibious landing by U.S. forces at Inchon marked a turning point in the Korean War. With air and sea support from U.N. forces, which were pinned down in the south by Communist North Koreans, the U.S. Army attacked the North Koreans from front and rear. This victory enabled the U.N. forces to regain control in South Korea.

Reviewed by KENNETH S. COOPER
George Peabody College

BAUHAUS

A year after the end of World War I a new and unusual art school was founded in Germany by the famous architect Walter Gropius. He named it the Bauhaus, which means "house for building."

Although it was in existence for only 14 years, the Bauhaus changed the look of the modern world. Students and teachers there redesigned anything that they thought could be made more beautiful. They gave new shapes to skyscrapers and steam irons, chairs and containers, textiles and toys. Photography was treated as a serious art. The printed page was made more attractive because of Bauhaus experiments with printing methods. The Bauhaus helped to create what we today are so used to: everyday beauty.

▶THE BIRTH OF THE BAUHAUS

In April, 1919, Walter Gropius was asked to become director of the School of Arts and Crafts at Weimar, Germany. He agreed, on the condition that the Weimar Academy of Fine Arts, another public institute, be put under his direction as well. The local leaders consented to combine the two schools, and the Bauhaus was born.

Gropius' idea for his new school was unusual. In addition to learning to paint and sculpt and to design buildings, students would be trained to create ordinary products for everyday use. If artists designed these prod-

ucts, our surroundings would become more beautiful.

But artists then knew little about the problems of manufacturing. An artist might design, for example, a handsome teapot, but it certainly wouldn't work as well as one made by a manufacturer. Gropius planned to change this. In each class he placed two teachers, one an artist and the other a fine craftsman. Students learned everything about teapots because they designed and made teapots. The Bauhaus was about to create the profession of industrial design.

▶A NEW SCHOOL WITH NEW IDEAS

Excellent instructors were hired. Among them were the famous painters Paul Klee and Wassily Kandinsky.

New courses of every type were given. There were regular art courses in which the many aspects of beauty and construction were studied. And there were some unique courses too. In one taught by Paul Klee, the entire term was devoted to the study of the circle.

The idea that form follows function was emphasized in all classes. This means that the shape, or form, of a product must contribute to its usefulness, or function. In other words, a design is not good if it makes the product look better without making it work better, too. A modern iron, for example, is more attractive than an old one, and it is also more useful. Its shape makes it easier to push, it irons a larger area, and its handle is molded to fit the hand. Our appliances today are both pleasing to the eye and more efficient mainly because of Bauhaus teaching.

Education did not end when classes were over. Bauhaus students used their spare time in artistic projects. They created a theater and built scenery. They designed and made costumes for their ballets and Saturday-night masquerade parties. On "Kite Day" they flew homemade kites. Evening picnics in the park were lighted by the colorful lanterns they had constructed. The activities of the students made Weimar a brighter city.

But the Bauhaus was not popular in Weimar. The growing National Socialist (Nazi) Party was opposed to modern art and design. As the party grew stronger in Weimar, the attacks on the Bauhaus increased. Gropius had to defend himself in court. By 1924, however, the Nazis had gained a great deal of influence in the local government. The allowance the school received from the city was cut. Since the Bauhaus was a public school and had no income except that which the government provided, Gropius was unable to pay the school's expenses. Most of the students were poor and could not help. Therefore Gropius closed the school.

▶ THE DESSAU BAUHAUS

The little industrial city of Dessau in eastern Germany invited the Bauhaus to re-open there. Gropius was given money to design and build a new school. The structure was a spacious glass and concrete building with large classrooms, dormitories with balconies, and even a theater. The latest equipment was installed. Students and teachers were much happier in their new quarters.

Since Dessau was an industrial city, the students could go to work for short periods in the factories. There they learned about the difficult problems of manufacturing. Their designs were improving and their reputation was growing. Manufacturing companies all over Europe wrote to the Bauhaus offering to buy designs for products.

In 1928 Gropius resigned in order to return to his own work. He was replaced by the Swiss architect Hannes Meyer.

But the influence of the National Socialists eventually reached Dessau. In 1928 funds were cut again. Several Bauhaus instructors, upset and afraid that the school would have to close again, spoke out against the party. The Bauhaus became a center of political arguments.

▶ THE LAST YEARS

Hannes Meyer was now director of the Bauhaus. But after 2 years the city of Dessau asked Gropius to return. Because he could see more trouble coming in the future, Gropius refused. However, he did suggest that the architect Ludwig Mies van der Rohe be appointed director to replace Meyer.

Under Mies van der Rohe the Bauhaus prospered again. Although the government funds were all but cut off, the school was able to support itself. The sale of Bauhaus designs

The studio workshops of the Dessau Bauhaus were spacious and well equipped.

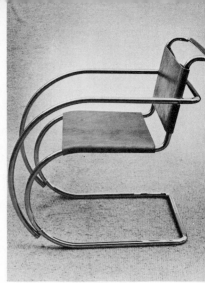

Wooden chess set by Josef Hartwig.

Table lamp by K. J. Tucker and W. Wagenfeld.

Steel and leather chair by Ludwig Mies van der Rohe.

PRODUCTS DESIGNED BY BAUHAUS ARTISTS

Toy boats of wood by Alma Buscher.

Teapot by Marianne Brandt.

for manufactured products brought in enough money to support the school.

The Nazi threat continued to grow. In 1932, just before Adolf Hitler became chancellor, Mies van der Rohe moved the Bauhaus to Berlin and made it a private school. He hoped that the Nazis would not care about a private institution. Unfortunately they did care. Hitler became chancellor. The National Socialists seized control of Germany. The Bauhaus closed.

▶ THE IDEAS SURVIVE

Although the Bauhaus never reopened, its ideas continued to be taught. Most of the instructors left Germany, and many began to teach again. Gropius, Mies van der Rohe, and the painter Josef Albers went to America to train young artists and architects. L. Moholy-Nagy, a painter, photographer, designer, and writer who had taught at the Bauhaus,

started the New Bauhaus (which later became the excellent Institute of Design) in Chicago. He died in 1946, but his books on Bauhaus ideas have greatly influenced North American teachers and designers.

The new glass, steel, and concrete buildings we see everywhere today are spacious and uncluttered. But notice that no space is wasted. Look at your toaster, iron, and refrigerator. Each serves a purpose, but each is attractive too. Look at the tools in your house. Pick them up. Most likely they are easy to look at and to handle. The artists who designed them were trained to improve the product and to make it handsome. Designers today want to bring beauty into everything man creates so that his life will be more pleasant. This was a Bauhaus idea. The school closed, but the ideas survive.

Reviewed by WALTER GROPIUS
Founder of the Bauhaus

BEARS

A shaggy giant wades into a stream. Ducking its head, it lunges forward. Then it comes up, a big salmon flopping between its jaws. Triumphant, the huge beast clambers ashore to eat its meal in comfort. This expert catcher of fish is the Alaskan brown bear—the world's largest land-dwelling flesh eater. It may be nearly 3 meters (about 9 feet) long.

Alaskan brown bears feed almost entirely on fish when salmon are running upstream to spawn. At other times the bears make a meal of whatever is in season and available. They may dig for roots and bulbs and eat berries, fruits, eggs, and insects. They burrow after squirrels and other small mammals. Sometimes they even eat grass.

▶ "BEASTS THAT WALK LIKE PEOPLE"

Although they eat many different kinds of food (and much of it vegetable), bears make up one family of the Carnivora, or meat-eating mammals. Raccoons and pandas are their close relatives, but bears also share a common ancestry with dogs. All bears have bulky bodies and stubby tails. Their legs are thick and powerful. When they walk, their heels touch the ground, just as ours do. The prints of their hind feet are remarkably like those of a huge, flat-footed human being. Indeed, the American Indians called grizzly bears "the beasts that walk like people." Bears ordinarily move at a lumbering walk, but they can run at nearly 50 kilometers (30 miles) an hour when necessary. Many of them are skilled tree climbers. Generally amiable in captivity, bears are favorite exhibits in zoos, where they sometimes live 20 or 30 years.

In the wild, bears are found throughout the Northern Hemisphere, ranging from Arctic wastes to tropical forests. There are no bears in Australia, and only one species lives south of the equator. This is the South American spectacled bear. Four main types—big brown bears, grizzly bears, polar bears, and American black bears—inhabit North America.

▶ THE BLACK BEAR APPEARS IN MANY COLORS

The American black bear, which weighs up to 225 kilograms (500 pounds), is the smallest of the North American bears. A wide-ranging species, it is found from Alaska and northern Canada to central Mexico. In spite of its name, the black bear appears in a number of different colors. In the East most of these bears grow shiny black fur. In the West many have brown or cinnamon-colored coats. Brown cubs are often born in the same litter with black ones. A race with grayish blue fur—the glacier, or blue, bear—lives in southern Alaska. The creamy white Kermode's bear appears on islands off British Columbia.

Like bears everywhere, the American black fills up on many different kinds of food during the summer and fall. By the time cold weather comes, the bear is very fat and ready for a long winter's nap. Curling up in a den under a ledge or under the roots of a tree, it goes to sleep. Eating nothing and living off its fat, the bear stays in this snug retreat until spring. Once in a while it wakes up and grumbles, but soon it is snoozing again.

This winter-long sleep is not true hibernation. The bear's temperature remains almost normal, and it breathes regularly four or five times a minute. (In true hibernation a mammal's body temperature may drop close to freezing, while its heartbeat and breathing are very slow and faint. To all appearances the animal seems to be dead. Woodchucks and many ground squirrels hibernate in this way, but bears do not.)

Cubs are born in late January or early February while the mother is in her den. Usually she has two cubs, but sometimes three or four are born. Their eyes are closed, and they are almost naked. Each one is less than 25 centimeters (10 inches) long and weighs under 0.5 kilograms (1 pound). They remain in the den with the mother until late March or early April. By then covered with thick coats of woolly hair, they come out and wander through the spring woods with her. The mother keeps a constant and careful watch over the cubs. She teaches them how to hunt for food. If danger threatens, she sends them up a tree. If they disobey, she cuffs them soundly. The cubs usually stay with the mother until they are 1½ years old.

▶ THE GRIZZLY, A VANISHING MONARCH

The grizzly bear, weighing up to 450 kilograms (1,000 pounds), is much larger than the black bear. Its smaller cousin has a straight

Above, polar bears in northern Canada. They roam ice packs and coasts of the Arctic Ocean. Right, Alaska grizzly. Notice its shoulder hump. These bears have almost disappeared south of Canada.

Left, black bears climbing a tree. They are the smallest North American bears. Below, Alaskan brown bear with salmon. When full-grown, these bears are the world's largest land-dwelling flesh-eaters.

profile, but the grizzly's face has a concave (curved-in) appearance. The grizzly also has a shoulder hump and very long, straight claws. In color it ranges from a yellowish shade to almost black. Some individuals have light-tipped hair and are called "silvertips."

This mighty bear once ranged from Kansas and the Dakotas to California, and from Alaska to northern Mexico. Now grizzlies have almost disappeared south of the Canadian border. Probably no more than 500 of them still roam wilderness areas of Montana and Wyoming, while a few dozen more live in the mountains of Idaho and Colorado. The most likely place to see a grizzly bear is Yellowstone National Park or a zoo.

Grizzlies are closely related to the great brown bears of the Alaskan coastal areas and islands. Some experts consider that the two are merely different races of the same species. Larger than grizzlies, Alaskan brown bears may weigh more than 450 kilograms.

Left: The Malayan sun bear displays a crescent marking on its chest. It is a skillful tree climber and has a long tongue that helps it obtain honey from bees' nests. Right: The Himalayan bear is a hunter of livestock. Black in color, it has a light crescent marking.

▶ THE GREAT WHITE SEA BEAR

The polar bear is sometimes almost as big as the Alaskan brown. This great white bear roams the ice packs and coasts of the Arctic Ocean, all the way around the earth. A powerful swimmer, the polar bear is sometimes found far at sea, traveling from one iceberg to another. Equipped with keen eyes and an extra-sharp sense of smell, it is an expert hunter. It stalks seals, walrus pups, and whatever other prey it can find. When it is hungry enough, it will attack people.

The only polar bear to den up during the winter is a female who is expecting cubs. Before Arctic winter descends, the expectant mother travels inland and digs out a snug den in deep snow. There she sleeps through the cold, months-long night. And there her cubs, each about 25 centimeters (10 inches) long, are born. Like black bear cubs, they sometimes remain with their mother until they are 1½ years old.

▶ OTHER KINDS OF BEARS

A number of different kinds of bears are found in other parts of the world. The spectacled bear, with whitish rings around its eyes, lives in the Andes Mountains of South America. Many varieties of brown bears inhabit lonely mountainous areas of Europe and Asia. Asia also has such interesting species as the Himalayan black bear, which has a sort of mane; the insect-eating sloth bear of India and Sri Lanka; and the small, short-haired Malayan sun bear. All three have white or yellowish crescents on their chests.

ROBERT M. McCLUNG
Author, science books for children

BEAUMONT, WILLIAM (1785–1853)

William Beaumont was a frontier surgeon who discovered how the human stomach works. He made his discoveries in a remarkable way: by acquiring a patient with a hole in his stomach. His work ranks as a landmark in medicine. Yet compared with modern doctors, Beaumont had almost no training.

Born on November 21, 1785, in Lebanon, Connecticut, he was one of nine children. His father was a veteran of the Revolutionary War. Young William received some schooling, but no one knows how much. In 1806 he moved to upstate New York, where he taught school. Here he began to read many books about medicine. Four years later he became an apprentice to a doctor and did everything from sweeping floors to assisting in surgery. That was his first medical training. In 1812 he entered the army as a surgeon's assistant.

When the War of 1812 ended, Beaumont practiced medicine in Vermont for a few years. Then he re-enlisted in the Army and was assigned to Fort Mackinac, an outpost in northern Michigan. Before going west in 1821, he married. In time he and his wife had three children.

Beaumont was post surgeon at the fort. One day in 1822 he was called to treat a wounded French-Canadian Indian named Alexis St. Martin. St. Martin, who was 18, had been accidentally shot. The bullet had both exposed his stomach and made a hole in it the size of a man's finger.

Beaumont placed him in the post hospital. There, for almost a year, Beaumont treated the wound and kept St. Martin alive. Later Beaumont took St. Martin into his own home and fed and clothed him.

By 1825 St. Martin was well enough to chop wood, but he still had a hole in his stomach. A small flap had grown over the hole, but it could be easily pushed aside. This meant Beaumont could study a human stomach at work and see how it digested food —if St. Martin would let him. Beaumont made an offer. If St. Martin would serve as a human laboratory, Beaumont would give him food, drink, and lodging.

St. Martin agreed, and Beaumont began 10 years of experiments that were to make

William Beaumont, as he appeared around 1821.

him famous. He tied bits of food to string and held them in the opening. This way he learned which foods were most easily digested. Sometimes he actually watched the food being digested. He saw how the stomach muscles moved to tear the food apart. He discovered that the stomach produces gastric juice, the fluid that dissolves food. He collected this juice in bottles and noted that it continued to dissolve foods there. Beaumont's studies still stand as the greatest single contribution to understanding digestion.

During the years that Beaumont was making his study, the army assigned him to various posts. But wherever he went, Beaumont took St. Martin along. St. Martin often tired of being a human laboratory; twice he left and went back to Canada.

Beaumont received some help from other scientists and some support from the U. S. Government. But for the most part he carried on the work on his own. He paid St. Martin's expenses even after St. Martin married and had children. When Beaumont finished writing his classic book about his work, he had to pay for publishing it.

In 1834 St. Martin left for the third time, and Beaumont could not persuade him to return. Still, the important discoveries had been made. Beaumont retired from the Army in 1840 and settled in St. Louis as a private doctor. He died on April 25, 1853.

JOHN S. BOWMAN
Author and Science Editor

BEAUTY CULTURE

Everything that people do to improve the appearance of their bodies can be considered beauty culture. However, through the centuries the chief concern of beauty culture has been to make the female face and hair more beautiful.

The excitement of using cosmetics and trying different hairstyles is not new. Queen Jezebel painted her eyes and decorated her hair in the 9th century B.C. Professional barbers started working in Rome more than 2,000 years ago.

The carving in an Egyptian tomb thousands of years old shows us that beauty culture is an ancient art.

▶ BEAUTY AIDS

The use of cosmetics has continued since ancient times. The origins of make-up may have been religious. Bright colors were painted on the body to please the gods. Gradually make-up was used to beautify the body. People have placed more emphasis on beauty culture at some periods in history than at others. It received little attention during the Middle Ages but became more important during the 16th and 17th centuries.

Eye Make-up. Different kinds of beauty aids have been emphasized at various times. To the Egyptians the eyes were all-important. Cleopatra, Queen of Egypt 2,000 years ago, is said to have painted her eyebrows and eyelashes black, her upper eyelids blue-black, and her lower eyelids green. In Egypt even the men's eyes were circled with color. This may have been done partly to protect their eyes from the dazzling rays of the sun.

Both Roman women and Italian women of the 16th century used black eye make-up to set off their blonde hair and fair skin.

Skin Lotions. It was common in the ancient world to use mineral as well as animal and vegetable products in making cosmetics. The Egyptians, for example, used copper in making green eye shadow and lead in making black. But often the minerals were harmful to the skin and caused blemishes. Soothing masks containing honey, milk, or various oils were put on the face at night. Roman women used a mucilage made of certain birds' nests as a remedy for common skin blemishes. Lotions to whiten the skin were also used.

Beauty Spots. Beauty spots, which are tiny patches of black cloth pasted on the cheek, chin, or forehead, were known in Egypt. They looked pretty and hid blemishes at the same time. Many years later, in 17th-century France, it became fashionable to wear beauty spots or patches of black taffeta or velvet cut into circles, crescents, or star shapes to emphasize the milky whiteness of the skin.

Rouge and Lipstick. Egyptian women knew about rouge and lipstick but concentrated on eye make-up. Greek and Roman women used rouge. They admired the pink-and-white look of the fair-skinned blonde.

In 16th-century England, during the reign of Queen Elizabeth, women were heavily powdered. But the greatest use of powder and rouge occurred in 18th-century France, before the Revolution. Women's faces were thickly coated with powder, often made of starch. Brilliant circles of rouge were painted on the cheeks, and the lips were also painted.

Poisonous chemicals were sometimes used to give rouge and lipstick their red coloring. Only since 1938 have the ingredients used in the manufacture of cosmetics been controlled by law in the United States.

Nail Care. Care of the hands and nails has been another important part of beauty culture. About 700 B.C. the women of Assyria tinted their palms and nails red with a dye made from the leaves of the henna plant. Egyptian women colored their nails with henna, and the pharaohs dyed their palms and the soles of their feet with it as well.

Both fingernails and toenails were cut and polished in Rome, but remained their natural color. In 16th-century Italy women polished their nails with fragrant sandalwood.

Perfume. Fragrance has always gone with

cosmetics. Early peoples used sweet-smelling plants, oils, and spices in making beauty products. As a result of the Crusades, musk and ambergris, two important products used in making perfume, came to the Western world, and many different fragrances were created. Musk comes from the male musk deer. Ambergris is a grayish, sticky substance believed to come from the sperm whale.

▶ FROM MUD CURLS TO PERMANENT WAVES

Curling, dyeing, and dressing the hair have been a major part of beauty culture through the ages.

Curling the Hair. Making straight hair hold a curl is an undertaking that has kept beauticians busy for 2,500 years. In Egypt women wet their hair, wound it around smooth sticks, and packed the curls in mud. Then they stayed in the sun until the mud baked dry. This was the crudest of permanent waves, but its results were looked upon as beautiful.

Since the mud curls of Egypt, great progress has been made in methods of curling the hair. An important contribution was made in France in 1872 by a barber named Marcel Grateau, who was unknown at the time. He was dissatisfied with the frizzy sausage-curl effects of the curling irons then in use. So he changed their design and the method of using them. He copied the soft side-to-side swinging movement of waves in naturally wavy hair. The result was known as the Marcel wave.

In 1905 Charles Nessler, a German hairdresser in London, gave the first really permanent wave. The Marcel wave and others like it washed out when the hair was shampooed. But Nessler's method actually changed the hair structure. A solution containing borax, called an alkaline solution, softened the hair while it was wrapped around curling coils. Heated gas irons dried it into permanent "bends" or waves. These came out only when the hair had grown several inches.

The early permanent waves took all day, as only a few curls at a time could be processed on the huge machines used. Each curl cost at least $1, so permanent waves were considered a luxury. Around 1928 beauty-shop competition and permanent-waving techniques had advanced to the stage where an entire permanent wave could be given for $1. "Dollar shops" introduced millions of people to professional beauty services that they might not otherwise have tried.

Dyeing and Bleaching. The Egyptians used henna, a reddish powder made from the leaves of the henna, or mignonette, tree, to dye their hair. Roman women bleached their hair blonde. In 16th-century Italy blonde hair was the ideal, so hair was again bleached. In the 17th century white wine and rhubarb were boiled together and used as a hair brightener.

Dressing the Hair. The taste for wigs and powdered hair has been important at various times in history. Elaborately curled wigs were used in Egypt. Roman women also wore wigs. After the fall of the Roman Empire, the women of the Byzantine Empire, with its center in Constantinople, carried on the Roman custom of wearing wigs. (They used cosmetics as the Romans had, too.) Wigs were again popular in Elizabethan England.

In 17th- and 18th-century France, hair was powdered. Before the French Revolution the fashion for powdered hair and towering hairdos reached an extreme. Once, Queen Marie Antoinette's hair was sculptured into waves to resemble the ocean, and a small model of a French warship was perched on top.

▶ NOT FOR WOMEN ONLY

Beauty culture has not always been the exclusive pleasure of women. Pliny the Elder (A.D. 23–79) reported the import from Gaul of liquid soap that Roman men used to turn their hair bright red. Cold cream was invented by Galen, the Greek physician (2nd century A.D.), who is said to have used it himself with excellent results.

Fine gentlemen of the Elizabethan period curled their hair and beards by using hot irons. In both England and France in the 16th century, the gentlemen of the court used powder and painted their faces.

▶ BEAUTY TODAY

Today beauty culture starts with absolute cleanliness of face, body, and hair. A fresh, healthy look is the ideal. Many beauty authorities agree with the Roman poet Propertius (50–15? B.C.), who wrote, "The face is ever best as nature made it."

GEORGINA C. WILLISCROFT
Former Group Advertising Manager, Revlon, Inc.

See also COSMETICS; PERFUMES.

BEAVERS

Beavers inhabit ponds and streams in wooded areas from Alaska to northern Mexico. Their bodies are ideally constructed for their varied activities on land and in the water. A beaver's large hind feet are webbed for swimming. His broad, flat tail is scaly and naked, except for a few bristles. It serves as a prop when he stands up to gnaw on trees; it becomes an alarm signal when slapped against the water; it is a rudder and an oar when he is swimming.

Though air breathers, beavers are thoroughly at home in the water. They can remain submerged for 15 minutes at a time. When a beaver dives, flap-like valves in his ears and nostrils close, shutting out the water. Except for his tail, the beaver is clothed in a shiny coat of soft, thick underfur; this is overlaid with longer, coarser guard hairs. Glands on either side of the tail supply oil, which keeps the coat waterproofed and glistening. The two inner claws of the beaver's hind feet are grooved; they make efficient combs for grooming the coat and spreading the oil through it.

▶CHAMPION HEWERS OF WOOD

Beavers live in family groups, or colonies. The family usually consists of the parents and their young of the past 2 years. Together they cut trees, build and repair their dams and lodges, and store branches for the winter food supply. This work makes them the most remarkable engineers among the Rodentia, the order of gnawing mammals to which they belong. And among mammals, only men are better engineers than beavers.

For felling trees, a beaver uses his four front teeth—the orange-colored, chisel-edged gnawing teeth (incisors). With these sharp tools he takes only a few minutes to cut down a small willow tree. Occasionally he tackles and fells trees as big as 2 feet in diameter. Favorite beaver trees are softwoods like aspen, poplar, and willow. But the beaver also cuts birch, sugar maple, wild cherry, and alder. Once in a while he fells hemlock and pine.

Selecting a tree to cut, the beaver gouges out first one chip, and then another, 2 or 3 inches below. Next he tears out the middle chip of wood. Working in this way, he girdles

Left, tree felled by a beaver to make a dam. Below, beaver uses its four chisel-edged front teeth on a tree branch.

Below, a beaver dam. The dam keeps the pond level constant during spring rains and summer droughts.

Chinks in this beaver lodge are plastered with mud and debris. Note beaver's tail.

the tree, then cuts deeper and deeper until the tree falls. The beaver cannot control the direction in which the tree will fall. As it begins to totter he dashes for safety.

When all is quiet, he returns to work. But first he may make a meal of tender green bark, buds, and twigs. Holding a section of wood in his hand-like front paws, the beaver nibbles away like a person eating corn on the cob. Stomach full, he starts cutting the tree into convenient lengths for moving to the pond.

▶BUILDING DAMS AND LODGES

In deep streams with high banks, beavers sometimes make underground dens in the bank instead of building lodges. Digging the entrance underwater, they tunnel upward beyond the water level. There they hollow out a living chamber in the bank. In such a den the beaver family is safe from most enemies. Even in shallow streams beavers often build bank dens when they first settle in an area. Then they start to dam the stream.

The dam blocks the flow of water and creates a pond where the beavers will live. The dam keeps the pond level constant during spring rains and summer droughts. It is deep enough not to freeze solid in winter.

To build a dam, the beavers drag branches to the place they have selected in the stream. The branches are laid side by side, parallel to the current. Their butts are often thrust into the bottom mud to anchor them. Mud and debris are piled on top. Layer upon layer, the dam is built up. To prevent leaks, the beavers plaster the upstream face with mud, leaves, and stones. Diving to the bottom, they gather such material by scooping it up in their arms.

Ordinary dams vary in length from a few feet to a hundred or more. Their height ranges from 1 to 4 feet. Exceptional structures may be as much as 8 or 10 feet high.

In the pond that forms behind their dam the beavers usually build an island lodge. Pulling boughs and branches into the water, they build up a broad foundation of sticks and wood—sometimes as much as 30 feet or more across. Making the huge pile slope inward, they construct mounds that may stand 5 to 8 feet above the pond's surface. When the outer structure is complete, the beavers plaster the chinks and holes with mud and debris. A section of the roof is left unchinked, as an air hole. Underwater entrances lead to the main living space, which is hollowed out above water level. This chamber may be as big as 8 feet across and 4 or 5 feet high.

As time goes by, the beavers have to travel farther and farther from the pond to find suitable trees. Dragging branches and logs, they wear smooth paths, or "tote roads," through the woods. To make the going even easier, they often dig canals outward from the pond. Then they connect the tote roads with the canals. A beaver canal may be a few feet wide and a foot or more deep.

Sometimes the job of bringing wood in from constantly increasing distances finally be-

Oil keeps the beaver's thick fur shiny and waterproof.

comes too difficult, even with the handy tote roads and canals. Then the beavers leave the area. Traveling on to a new location, they start to work all over again.

▶FAMILY LIFE OF THE COLONY

From early spring until late fall, all the members of the beaver colony are busy. They repair their dams after the spring floods. They build or enlarge their lodge. They stock food for winter eating. By the time ice and snow arrive, the beavers have a huge quantity of branches stored in the bottom of the pond, close to the lodge. These are thrust into the pond bottom, where they stay fresh.

When the surface of the pond freezes over, the beavers retire to their lodge. Whenever they are hungry, they simply swim out under the ice, cut a fresh branch from the food supply, and carry it into the lodge. Stripped of its tender bark, the branch is finally thrown out. It may be used the next spring for repairing the dam or lodge.

As spring approaches, the expectant mother beaver prepares a soft nest of wood and bark shavings on the floor of the lodge. Here her young, usually three or four in number, are born during April or May, nearly 4 months after mating. When the female is expecting, the father beaver moves out for the time being. The year-old youngsters may move out with him. The 2-year-olds leave home for good at this time; they search for mates with whom they will live for the rest of their lives.

The baby beavers, called kits, weigh about a pound at birth. They are born with coats of fine hair; their eyes are open; and they can move about. They grow rapidly and may weigh 20 to 25 pounds in a year's time.

▶THE BEAVER AND AMERICAN HISTORY

In the exploration and settlement of North America, the beaver played an important part. Highly valued for its thick, warm coat, the beaver was widely trapped and hunted during pioneer days. Mountain men, trapping for beaver, led the way for the settlement of the Far West. Over the years the fur-coated animals were hunted so much that by 1880 they had disappeared in many areas.

Today the beaver has made a comeback because of protective laws and wise conservation efforts. It is again seen in much of its old territory. To hasten the spread, some states trap beavers alive and then release them in areas where they haven't lived for many years.

▶THE BEAVER AND CONSERVATION

In a few areas beavers may become nuisances when their dams flood roads, croplands, or timber areas. But the beaver's good points far offset such problems. Beaver ponds act as fire guards in the forests. They provide homes and breeding places for fish, water birds, and other wildlife. Beaver dams help to control floods and conserve water. They keep soil from washing away. Rich silt backs up behind the dams year after year. When the beavers finally move on, the ponds gradually fill in. They become part of wide, gentle valleys covered with fertile soil.

ROBERT M. MCCLUNG
Author, science books for children

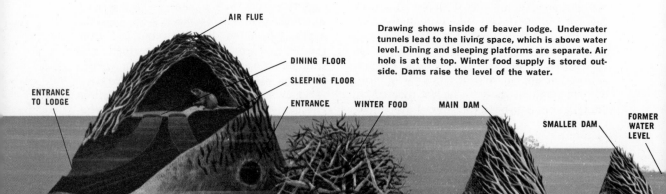

Drawing shows inside of beaver lodge. Underwater tunnels lead to the living space, which is above water level. Dining and sleeping platforms are separate. Air hole is at the top. Winter food supply is stored outside. Dams raise the level of the water.

AIR FLUE

DINING FLOOR

SLEEPING FLOOR

ENTRANCE TO LODGE

ENTRANCE   WINTER FOOD   MAIN DAM

SMALLER DAM

FORMER WATER LEVEL

BECHUANALAND. See Botswana.

BECKET, THOMAS À (1118?–1170)

Thomas à Becket was archbishop of Canterbury during the reign of Henry II of England. As archbishop he clashed with the king over the rights of the church against the rights of the crown. The conflict led to Thomas' death and made him one of the most famous of English martyrs.

Thomas was born in London, probably on December 21, 1118. His father, a merchant, came from Normandy. While in his 20's Thomas entered the service of Theobald, who was then archbishop of Canterbury. In 1154 Thomas was appointed archdeacon of Canterbury. That same year 21-year-old Henry of Anjou came to the English throne as King Henry II. He made Thomas his chancellor, or chief official. Thomas served the king faithfully and ably, and a warm friendship grew up between the two men. In 1162, after the death of Theobald, Henry offered Thomas the office of archbishop. He accepted reluctantly, fearing that the policies of the strong-willed king would conflict with his own views.

In 1164 the king had a document prepared known as the Constitutions of Clarendon. Its purpose was to restore some of the power of the crown, which had been weakened during the chaotic period before Henry came to the throne. Among other things, it provided that clergymen convicted of crimes by church courts were to be punished by civil courts. Previously, the church had both tried and punished its own members. Thomas' refusal to sign the document infuriated the king, who had expected his old friend's help. Thomas fled to France. He continued to condemn the Constitutions as a violation of the rights of the church, and he excommunicated two bishops who supported Henry. Finally, in 1170, Thomas and the king were partly reconciled, and Thomas returned to England. But his refusal to lift the ban against the bishops angered the king again. On December 29, 1170, four of Henry's knights murdered Thomas in the cathedral at Canterbury.

Henry denied having ordered or wished Thomas' death. However, he did penance at Thomas' burial place in the cathedral, which at once became a shrine for pilgrims. In 1172 Thomas was made a saint.

BEECHER, HENRY WARD (1813–1887)

Henry Ward Beecher was an American clergyman and one of the most famous preachers of his time. He was born on June 24, 1813, in Litchfield, Connecticut. His father, Lyman Beecher, was a distinguished Presbyterian minister, and four of Henry's brothers also became clergymen. His sister Harriet later won fame (as Mrs. Harriet Beecher Stowe) for her novel *Uncle Tom's Cabin*.

In 1834 Beecher graduated from Amherst College in Massachusetts. He was not a very good student, mainly because he disliked studying. But he was popular for his friendliness and good nature, traits that remained with him all his life. After graduating from Amherst, he studied at Lane Theological Seminary in Cincinnati, Ohio, of which his father was then president. His first appointment, in 1837, was to a small church in Lawrenceburg, Indiana. That same year he married Eunice White Bullard, who bore him 10 children. From 1839 to 1847 he was pastor of a church in Indianapolis, Indiana. Then he accepted an invitation to become minister of Plymouth Church in Brooklyn, New York.

For almost 40 years, until his death on March 8, 1887, Beecher was minister of Plymouth Church. As his fame grew, so did his congregation. Between 2,000 and 3,000 people came each week to hear him speak on the social and political issues of the day, as well as on religion. He spoke out strongly against slavery and championed the right of women to vote. He defended Darwin's theory of evolution, something few other clergymen would then do. His religious views were liberal, and it was said that he preached a religion of the heart. Beecher's appearance was striking. He was strongly built, with a lionlike head and hair that reached to his coat collar. He was a brilliant orator with a fine voice and a poetic command of language.

BEER AND BREWING

Beer is a mild alcoholic beverage that man has made and used for thousands of years. Ancient Sumerian and Egyptian writings refer to the beverage as "the joy bringer." Shakespeare described a quart of ale (a type of beer) as "a dish for a king."

Exactly when men first started making, or brewing, beer is unknown. But brewing appears to have begun very early and to have been carried on by people in all parts of the world. Historians have found evidence that a beer-like beverage was made in Mesopotamia as early as 6000 B.C. It is known that in the ancient world beer was brewed by Assyrians, Egyptians, Greeks, and Romans.

During the Middle Ages most beer was brewed by monks, who also engaged in many other trades and crafts. Almost every monastery had a brewhouse. Eventually non-churchmen took over this task. As brewing grew into an industry, craft guilds, or organizations of brewers, were formed.

In medieval England ale was often the chief drink at festivals and celebrations. Ale was such an important part of their revels that Englishmen occasionally used the word "ale" to mean a festival. Lamb-ales were celebrations held at lamb-shearing time. At church-ales and clerk-ales, the drink was sold to help raise money for the church or parish. College-ales were parties at which students drank the ale they had brewed. Our word "bridal" comes from "bride-ale," which was the wedding feast.

Beer in the Middle Ages was a thick, heavy beverage, almost as much food as drink. It also had a much higher alcohol content than today's beer. For hundreds of years this thick, nourishing beer was an important item in the daily diet of Europeans. Water supplies were usually polluted in that era, and beer was a much safer drink.

The knowledge of brewing was brought to the New World by the colonists. The Pilgrims brought beer with them on the Mayflower. Their journals tell us that the supply of beer was running low when they landed at Plymouth Rock.

As the colonies became settled, brewing was established as an industry. William Penn built one of the first breweries in 1683 at Pennsbury, Pennsylvania. By the time of the American Revolution the industry was an important part of the nation's economic life. Thomas Jefferson, Samuel Adams, and Patrick Henry were interested in the brewing industry.

Brewing was also carried on as a home craft. Owners of large farms and plantations often had their own small breweries. George Washington's own formula for the beer that was made on his plantation at Mount Vernon is still in existence.

▶ HOW BEER IS MADE

The brewing of beer starts with grain. The chief grain for brewing is barley, though corn or rice is sometimes used as well. The grain is mixed with water and kept in a warm room until it begins to germinate, or sprout. After a week of germination, the grain is roasted in a furnace and the germination stops. This partly-sprouted grain is known as **malt.** Part of the starch in the grain has been changed into **maltose,** or malt sugar.

The malt is mixed with water and boiled to form a sweet-tasting liquid called **wort.** Then the dried seed cones of a plant called the hop vine are added to the wort and the mixture is boiled again. The seed cones, called **hops,** which have a slightly bitter taste, give beer its characteristic tangy flavor.

All the solid matter is then filtered out of the brew. Next **yeast** is added. Yeast is composed of very tiny one-celled living organisms that feed on sugars and starches. As these microscopic organisms feed on the sugars of the wort they give off alcohol as a waste product. This change from sugar to alcohol is called fermentation. Fermentation is the most important step in the brewing process. During fermentation carbon dioxide gas is also given off. It is this gas that gives beer its bubbles.

The beer is pumped into closed storage tanks where it ages for about 6 weeks. Then it is filtered again before it is put into barrels, bottles, or cans. From start to finish, the brewing process may take as long as 3 months.

Since bottled and canned beer is often stored for long periods, it is pasteurized to keep it from turning sour.

The most popular kind of beer in the United States is **lager beer.** This beer originated in Germany. It gets its name from the German word for "storage" (*Lager*) because it is stored away for some period of time before it is used. Lager beer makes up about 90 per cent of the beer produced in the United States. It is usually pale in color and has an alcoholic content of about 3 to 4 per cent. **Bock beer,** a type of lager, is darker and sweeter than regular lager.

Ale, porter, and stout are favorite types of beer in Great Britain. **Ale** has a paler color and sharper taste than lager beer. Its alcoholic content is about 4 or 5 per cent. **Porter** is a dark brown beverage with a slightly sweet taste. **Stout** is the darkest, heaviest, and strongest of the beers mentioned. Its alcoholic content is also higher—about 5 to 6.5 per cent.

In most parts of the world, including the United States, people prefer to have their beer chilled. The English, however, are different. They serve their beer when it is either at room temperature or slightly warmed. (The chilliness of the English climate may have something to do with this.)

Brewing was formerly done by traditional rule-of-thumb methods learned from experience. Yet, with all their skill, the old-time brewers could never be certain that each batch would turn out exactly the same. Today brewing is a highly scientific process, with each step closely controlled. All the ingredients—even the water—are carefully tested. The beer made today is as uniform in quality as any other manufactured product.

Not only the methods of production but also the volume of production has changed. In the past people brewed beer for their personal use or professional brewers made the beverage in small quantities. Today the brewing industry is a mass-production enterprise.

EDWARD V. LAHEY
Chairman and President
United States Brewers Association, Inc.

BEES

There are probably 15,000 to 20,000 different kinds of bees living today. Ninety-five per cent of these various kinds are **solitary bees** that live alone. Five per cent are **social bees** that live together in colonies containing hundreds, and in some cases, thousands of members. The most social bee of all is the honeybee. It has developed a most efficient social system. Thousands of honeybees live co-operatively in hives and divide the labor of the colony.

▶HONEYBEES

An average honeybee colony has about 30,000 bees, but there may be up to 80,000 in one hive. There are three different kinds of bees in the hive: a queen, several hundred drones, and thousands of worker bees.

The colony is headed by the **queen bee.** She is a big female who lays all the eggs in the colony. She starts to lay them during the first warm days of spring and continues to lay them every day till the end of the summer. At first

THE THREE KINDS OF HONEYBEES

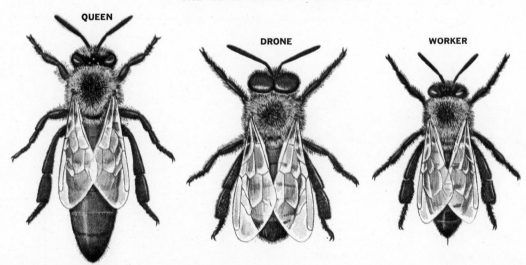

QUEEN   DRONE   WORKER

the number of eggs runs into dozens a day; then it becomes hundreds and keeps increasing as the season goes on. At the height of the season, the queen may lay as many as 1,000 to 2,000 eggs a day. Since she lives about 5 years, she may lay up to 1,000,000 eggs in her lifetime. The queen is the mother of the entire colony, and the whole hive is one big family of bees.

The **drones** are the males of the colony. They take no part in the work of the hive. They have only one function—to fertilize the eggs of the queen.

The **worker bees** are females smaller in size than the queen. They cannot lay eggs, but they do all the labor in the hive necessary for the maintenance and growth of the colony. The beehive is a smoothly running, organized society with an efficient division of labor.

Division of Labor

If you watch the entrance of a beehive, you will see a busy traffic of bees coming and going. One after the other, bees take off and launch themselves into the air. Other bees, heavily loaded with pollen and nectar, land and enter the hive. These are workers, called **forager bees,** who fly out to the flowers and bring back the food needed to supply the colony. Pollen is the fine powdery dust in flowers that is necessary for the formation of their seeds. For bees it is a source of protein food. Nectar is the sweet sugary liquid that collects in flowers; it is 40 to 80 per cent water.

While a bee is flying homeward the sugar in its honey stomach undergoes a chemical change. In the hive the nectar is handed over to worker bees who store it in open cells to dry. When the nectar dries out, it is called **honey** and is a great source of energy food for the bees.

For studies of what is going on inside, hives with transparent walls have been built. They are called **observation hives.** Through the glass walls of such a hive, scientists have watched the hustle and bustle inside. Patient observation shows that the worker bees are doing different jobs.

Some worker bees are building the honeycomb (sheets of six-sided wax cells). Some are feeding and nursing the growing young. Some others are cleaning out empty cells and preparing them for the eggs that the queen will deposit there. Guard bees stand at the entrance to the hive and repel all enemies. Fanning bees ventilate the hive.

Still other worker bees are taking care of the nectar and pollen the forager bees bring to the nest. The forager bees open their mouths; the receiving bees suck up droplets of nectar from the tongues of the foraging bees. The foraging bees that have collected pollen deposit it in special cells; worker bees in the hive rush up and ram the pollen hard into the cells.

No bee issues orders to the rest. Yet all the work of the colony is co-ordinated and everything seems to be done for the good of the community as a whole.

PARTS OF WORKER BEE'S BODY

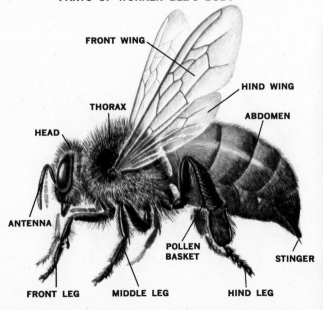

FRONT WING

HIND WING

ABDOMEN

THORAX

HEAD

ANTENNA

POLLEN BASKET

STINGER

FRONT LEG

MIDDLE LEG

HIND LEG

Bees, attracted to sugar water, are having colored dots painted on backs. In this way, investigator will be able to keep track of individual bees in an experiment.

How the Labor Is Divided

For hundreds of years men have wondered about these perfect honeybee societies. How does each newly hatched bee "know" what to do? Is it possible that each bee hatches out as a particular kind of bee specialized to do only building or nursing or foraging? By using observation hives and by marking bees with spots of colored paint or numbers to distinguish one from another, scientists have tried to find the answers to these questions. Most of the research has been done in recent years.

From the experiments of G. A. Rösch in Germany, we know now that each worker bee follows a schedule of duties according to her age. A worker bee lives for only 5 or 6 weeks of summer. During that time her job changes as she grows older. At first she cleans out brood cells for new eggs. After 3 days at this job, she becomes a nurse bee and feeds pollen and honey to the older larvae (wormlike grubs that hatch from the eggs). From the 6th to the 12th day she feeds the younger larvae and the queen on royal jelly secreted by special nursing glands in her head. At 12 days the same bee becomes a builder of wax cells. From the 16th day she begins to receive the nectar and pollen brought to the hive. Around the 20th day she stands guard at the entrance to the nest. From the 3rd week until the end of her life, she shifts to her last and longest job—foraging, the collecting of nectar and pollen.

The schedule is not rigid. It can be changed to suit the needs of the colony, as Rösch showed. If only forager bees were left in a hive, some of these older bees grew new nursing glands and started to nurse the young brood again, even though they were far past the normal nursing age. A colony left without foraging bees responded to the emergency, too. Even though there were only young bees of nursing age left in the colony, some of these began to fly out and bring back pollen and nectar after a few days.

How does this happen? How does a bee "find out" what jobs have to be done to guarantee the continued life of the colony? Martin Lindauer, a scientist from the University of Munich, Germany, has given us part of the answer to this question. He and his research team watched one bee continuously, from the first day of its life to its last. And he found out that every bee gathers on its own

Karl von Frisch, pioneer in bee studies, watches bees through transparent wall of an observation hive.

One of the marvels of the honeybees' labors is the honeycomb, with its almost perfect six-sided cells.

the information about the needs of the hive. In any one day it spends about a third of its time patrolling the hive: it inspects cells and larvae, and it looks over the building areas and the stores of food. From such inspection tours new forms of activity start—nursing or building or cleaning, as the need arises.

For foraging work, worker bees are recruited by a special system of "dances."

Bee "Dances"

The experiments of Karl von Frisch, an Austrian zoologist, revealed that bees could get other bees from their hive to gather nectar and pollen from good flower sources. Foragers return to the hive and do dances on the vertical (up-and-down) surfaces of the combs. The bees around the dancing bees become excited and start to follow behind a dancer and imitate her movements. Then they leave the hive and—without the dancing bee to lead them—fly directly to the food source. The dancing bees communicate to their hive mates the direction and the location of the food. Although the dances are normally done in complete darkness inside the hive, the bees following and imitating the dancing bees correctly interpret the signals.

If the returning foragers do a **round dance,** then the bees that follow the dance fly out to find food in the immediate neighborhood of the hive. The round dance communicates that there is food available near the hive. The odor of the nectar on the dancer identifies the flowers from which the nectar was collected. The antennae (feelers) of bees have organs of smell on them. Through their antennae the bees surrounding the dancing bees pick up the scent message; when they leave the hive, they search for flowers with this particular scent.

If the returning bees do a **wagging dance** (see diagram), it means that the food is more than 100 yards away. But the wagging dance also tells direction and distance.

Von Frisch watched the wagging dances for a long time when the feeding place stayed the same. He noticed that the direction of the straight part of the dance gradually shifted from morning to afternoon as the sun changed its position in the sky. He found out that the bee dance signaled the direction of the food source. If the straight run pointed directly upward, the feeding place was toward the sun. If the straight run pointed downward, the feeding place was opposite the sun's position. If the straight part of the dance was 60 degrees to the left of vertical, the feeding place was 60 degrees to the left of the sun, and so on.

The speed of the dance showed the distance to the feeding place. If the dance was done very quickly—about 10 times every 15 seconds—then the distance between the hive and the feeding place was about 100 yards. When the feeding place was about 10,000 yards away, the dance was carried through only once every 15 seconds. The greater the distance was the slower the dance was.

When the source of the food is plentiful and rich, the bees recruited by the first foragers also dance on returning to the hive. When the amount of food is reduced, the incoming bees simply deliver the nectar and pollen and do not dance. In this way many bees appear at a good source of food. When the supply wanes, fewer and fewer bees visit those flowers. And so the bees form groups just large enough to collect the available food.

Other Kinds of Communication

The food collected is rapidly shared by all members of the hive. In one experiment, 6

Foragers inform bees in hive of food's location by dance patterns. Round dance (A) means food is nearby. Wagging dances signal both greater distance and direction. If straight run is upward (B), direction is toward sun. Straight run downward (C) means food is away from sun.

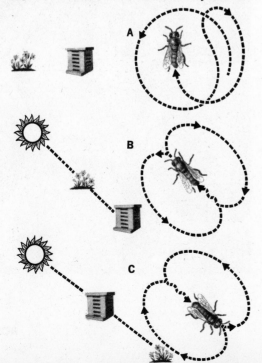

Nectar is passed through "tongues" in food-sharing that goes on continually in hives.

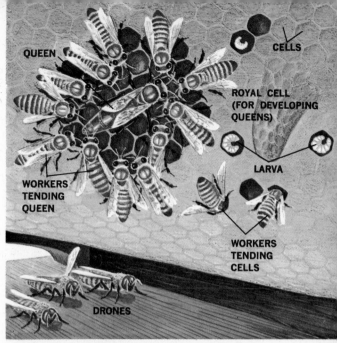

In the hive the workers, drones, and the queen all do their special jobs for the bee community.

bees from a colony of 25,000 were fed a bit of sugar syrup containing radioactive phosphorus. (Radioactive phosphorus can be traced easily because it gives off radiations that can be picked up by a Geiger counter). Within 4 hours more than half of the foraging bees and about one fifth of the home bees were radioactive. In a few days most of the bees in the hive were radioactive.

This kind of food-sharing binds the members of the colony together. Scientists are conducting many experiments to find out how bees change their food-gathering activities so that the right kinds and quantities of food are available for a colony. For example, if there is a surplus or lack of pollen in the hive, this information is communicated to forager bees, and the number of pollen gatherers changes. We still do not know exactly how this happens.

Bees also communicate information by the secretions from their bodies. It has been shown that the bees who attend the queen constantly lick a substance from her body and share it with other members of the colony. If for some reason the hive loses its queen, the other bees of the colony become aware of her absence in a few hours. They look for her, and if she can't be found, they immediately set about replacing her with a new queen.

By sharing of food and body secretions and by the recruiting dances, the members of the bee community become sensitive to the needs of the hive. They respond to those needs in a way that benefits the entire community.

Swarming

When beehives get overcrowded, new types of cells appear in the hive. They are much bigger than the other wax cells and are shaped somewhat like a peanut. Inside these special cells queen bees develop. When these cells appear, the old queen, surrounded by mostly older worker bees, leaves the hive to found a new colony. This act of collecting in a group and departing from the hive to start a new colony is called swarming.

After swarming from old hive, these bees have settled on avocado tree until they find place for new colony.

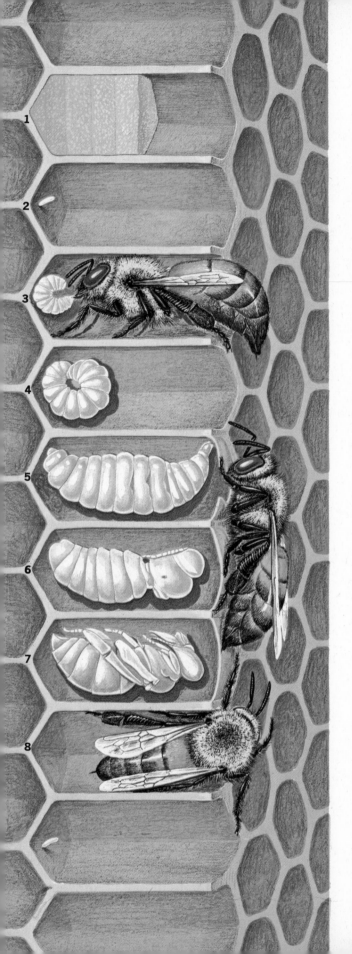

The Marriage Flight

Left behind in the hive are many of the younger workers, drones, and several virgin queens ripening in their peanut-shaped cells. The first queen to emerge destroys those developing in other queen cells. When the queen is about a week old, she moves toward the entrance of the hive. The drones (males) move toward the entrance, too. Then the queen flies into the air followed by the drones. One drone reaches the queen and mates with her in midair. In this process he transfers enough sperm (male sex cells) into her body to fertilize all the eggs she will lay for the rest of her life. The male dies after mating. The queen returns to the hive and a few days later starts to move over the combs, looking for empty cells in which to lay her eggs. The other drones return to the hive.

From Egg to Adult Bee

The queen has stored within her the sperm transferred to her by the drone. She can expose some of her eggs to sperm just before they are laid, or she can lay the eggs unfertilized by sperm. All the unfertilized eggs become males (drones). All the fertilized eggs become females. But there are two kinds of females, the egg-laying queens and the female workers that cannot lay eggs. How does this come about?

All eggs change into larvae (little wormlike grubs) after 3 days. All larvae receive the same food for the first 3 days. This is a substance called **royal jelly.** It is a protein-rich food secreted by special nursing glands in the heads of young worker bees. Queen larvae get this food all the time they are developing. The other larvae get this food for only 3 days; then they are shifted to a food containing more honey. These larvae become the worker bees. If scientists transfer a larva in a worker cell to a queen cell before the 3rd day so that it is fed royal jelly the rest of the time, it still can develop into a queen. Thus, food determines whether a fertilized egg will become queen or worker bee.

Nurse bees visit each larva with food nearly 1,300 times a day. The larva grows. On the

Food is stored (1) to support hive while egg (2) hatches into larva that worker feeds (3). Larva grows (4) until it matures and is sealed in with wax by worker (5). Larva enters pupal, or resting, stage (6) as body develops (7). Fully formed young adult then breaks out (8) to begin activities of worker bee.

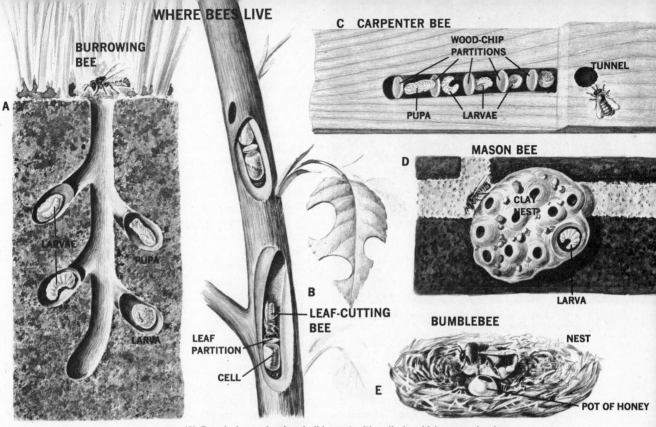

WHERE BEES LIVE

BURROWING BEE

A

LARVAE

PUPA

LARVA

B

LEAF-CUTTING BEE

LEAF PARTITION

CELL

C CARPENTER BEE

WOOD-CHIP PARTITIONS

TUNNEL

PUPA

LARVAE

MASON BEE

D

CLAY NEST

LARVA

BUMBLEBEE

NEST

E

POT OF HONEY

(A) Female burrowing bee builds nest with cells in which young develop.
(B) Leaf-cutting bees burrow in wood, stems, or ground and line nest with leaves.
(C) Carpenter bees bore tunnels in wood or plant stems and divide nest into cells.
(D) Mason bee builds nest with cells of moist clay, sometimes fastened to stone wall.
(E) Bumblebee colony lives in nest made by queen in hole where she laid first eggs.

6th day it starts to spin a cocoon, a shell of silk, inside its wax cell. Outside, attendant nurse bees cap the cell with wax. Meanwhile the larva changes into a pupa—a stage during which the wormlike body of the larva changes into the form of an adult bee. A full-sized queen bee emerges from the cell after 16 days. A perfect, full-sized worker bee makes its way out of its wax cell 21 days after the egg was laid.

Unfertilized eggs go through the same stages as fertilized eggs. They change into larvae then become pupae. Full-sized drones emerge from the cells in 24 days.

With a queen laying 1,500 eggs a day, a new bee probably emerges every minute to take its place in bee society.

▶FROM SOLITARY BEES TO BEE "CITIES"

It is hard to understand how the honeybee's complicated society developed in the history of life on the earth. But we can get some hints if we look at a few of the solitary bees.

Many of these solitary bees have curious habits. **Carpenter bees** bite tunnels through solid wood. In the tunnels they make a series of cells, one on top of the other and separated by walls of tiny wood chips. **Mason bees** cement pieces of stone together, forming groups of cells that are attached to cliffs or stone walls. **Leaf-cutter bees** use their jaws like scissors and snip out pieces of leaves or flowers to line their nests and make partitions between the cells. **Burrowing bees** tunnel into the ground.

The solitary bees get their name from the fact that most of them live alone. The female solitary bee puts pollen and nectar in the cells of the nest. She lays an egg on each lump of food, seals the cells, and flies away. She usually dies at the end of the summer. When the eggs hatch the following spring, the developing young feed on the food left for them. They are completely on their own, having no contact with the mother. When they are adults, male and female mate.

A bumblebee hovers before a lily of the valley and prepares to suck its nectar.

But even among the solitary bees, there are kinds that show the beginnings of social co-operation. Burrowing bees are particularly interesting for this reason. A few females dig a main tunnel in the ground together. Then each female digs her own small side tunnel that runs off the main one. Some of the members of the colony even guard the entrance to the main tunnel.

Other burrowing bees show another step toward social co-operation. In this case females manage to live through the winter and lay eggs in the spring. Some of the eggs hatch out into worker bees that never mate like the other females; they spend their days caring for the other eggs and the young that hatch from them. Here are two advances: The females continue to have contact with the eggs and young. And there is the beginning of division of labor. There are two kinds of females that look alike but have different duties. One kind of female just lays eggs. The other kind, the worker female, does the work.

▶BUMBLEBEES

Bumblebees go a step further than the solitary burrowing bees whose females live through the winter. The bumblebee colony not only has division of labor, but also has worker bees that look different from the egg-laying female queens.

In the spring a queen bumblebee selects a nest, which is usually some abandoned hole in the ground. Then she builds two cells of wax and collects pollen and nectar. In one cell she stores the food; in the other she lays eggs. Twenty-two days later adult worker bumblebees emerge.

The only way the worker bees look different from the queen is in their size. They are much smaller. The queen now does nothing except lay eggs. The rest of the work is done by the worker bees; they collect the food, build more cells, and feed the young that develop from the eggs laid by the queen. At the height of the season, the queen may be surrounded with a few hundred bee "children" all working for the good of the colony. Late in the season queens and drones appear among the brood. The drones mate with the queens and then the queen bumblebees hibernate in the ground during the winter. All the other bumblebees die, but the queens are there to emerge in the spring to form new colonies.

The solitary bees and the bumblebees show us some possible steps by which honeybees may have developed their complicated societies.

MILLICENT E. SELSAM
Author, science books for children
See also FLOWERS AND SEEDS; HONEY; INSECTS.

BEETHOVEN, LUDWIG VAN (1770–1827)

Ludwig van Beethoven was born in Bonn, Germany, on December 16 or 17, 1770, and was baptized on December 17. His father, Johann, and his grandfather Ludwig van Beethoven were both musicians.

Beethoven revealed his own musical talents when he was very young. His father, an irresponsible drunkard, hoped the boy would be a profitable child prodigy like Mozart. Beethoven was often dragged out of bed in the middle of the night and forced to practice the piano. At the age of 7 he was playing in public. When Beethoven was 13, the elector of Cologne made him assistant organist at his chapel in Bonn.

In 1787 Beethoven traveled to Vienna and

met his idol, Mozart. When Beethoven improvised on a melody that Mozart had given him, the great master was astounded. It is said that Mozart remarked, "This young man will leave his mark in the world some day."

But Beethoven could not stay in Vienna. His mother fell ill, and he rushed back to Bonn. The death of his mother left Beethoven and his brothers at the mercy of their drunken father. At the age of 18 Beethoven had to assume full responsibility for the family.

In 1792 Beethoven returned to Vienna, where he spent the rest of his life. He became a pupil of Haydn. But he was dissatisfied with Haydn's method of teaching, which he considered not thorough enough. To avoid offending the famous master, he took lessons in secret from another composer, Johann Schenk.

Beethoven presented a strange appearance to the people of Vienna. He was a short, stocky man, untidily dressed, with dark, piercing eyes and a wild shock of black hair. Knowing himself to be a genius, he lived by his own rules. He refused to bow down to the nobility. He was a man of violent temper and was often rude, even to his closest friends. Goethe, the great German poet, called him an "utterly untamed personality."

Nevertheless, he quickly became famous. Several princes became his patrons, and for a few years he was happy. Then tragedy struck. He discovered that he was slowly becoming deaf. This was the great crisis of his life. In an anguished letter to his brothers, in 1802, Beethoven described his growing deafness and his life of loneliness. "I must live like an exile," he wrote. "I almost put an end to my life—it was only my art that withheld me."

After this, Beethoven's music became more profound. He developed a completely original style of composing. It reflected his violent emotions, his sufferings and joys. At this time Beethoven composed the most popular of all symphonies, his fifth. Other famous works of this period are the *Eroica* and *Pastoral* symphonies, the *Appassionata* Sonata, the *Emperor* Concerto, his only opera, *Fidelio,* and the *Rasumovsky* string quartets.

In 1815 Beethoven became the guardian of his nephew Karl. Beethoven adored the

Beethoven with the score of his great *Missa Solemnis.*

boy, who gave his uncle nothing but trouble. Beethoven's hearing problems steadily increased; by 1820 he was almost totally deaf and had to carry on all conversation in writing.

Despite his deafness Beethoven now composed his greatest works. These include the five last piano sonatas, the *Missa Solemnis,* the Ninth Symphony, with its choral finale, and the last five string quartets, which many people consider the finest of all his works.

In 1826 Beethoven became seriously ill. It is said that as he lay unconscious on his deathbed, on March 26, 1827, there was a loud clap of thunder. In response Beethoven sat straight up, shook his fist at the heavens, and fell back dead.

Beethoven is perhaps the most popular and revered of composers. He was a man of profound vision and his music has deeply moved its listeners for generations.

In 1970, the 200th anniversary of his birth was celebrated all over the world with a great many performances of his music.

Reviewed by KARL GEIRINGER
University of California—Santa Barbara

BELGIAN ART. See DUTCH AND FLEMISH ART.

BELGIUM

Belgium is a constitutional monarchy in northwestern Europe. Its importance is much greater than its small size suggests. It is one of the world's most prosperous countries, and it plays an important role in European and world affairs. Belgium is a leading industrial country. Its people give the world fine manufactured products ranging from steel and cut diamonds to woolens and delicate lace. Because so many Belgians work in mines and factories, the country is often called the Workshop of Europe.

▶ **THE PEOPLE**

About 10,000,000 Belgians live in an area not much larger than the state of Maryland in the United States. This means that the country is densely populated.

The Belgian people are divided into two large groups—the Flemings and the Walloons. The Flemings, who make up about 55 percent of the population, live in the northern part of Belgium, mainly in a region called Flanders. The Flemings are descended from ancient German tribes. They speak Dutch, locally called Flemish. The majority of the Flemings are country people and devout Roman Catholics.

French-speaking Belgians are called Walloons. Most of the Walloons live south of an official linguistic line running from Courtrai through Waterloo to a point north of Liège. The Walloons are descended from ancient Gallic tribes and the Romans who conquered the Gauls in the 1st century B.C. Most Walloons live in cities and work in industry or business.

Language. When Belgium first became independent in 1830, French was the official language in government and schools. Toward the end of the 19th century the Flemish people protested against the exclusive use of French. In 1898 the Dutch language won legal equality. Besides the two major language groups, some people in the eastern part of Belgium speak German.

Belgium is a country with two official names. In Dutch it is called the Koninkrijk België. In French it is the Royaume de Belgique. Many places in Belgium are known by a French and a Dutch name. For example, the great seaport city of Antwerp is called Anvers by the Walloons and Antwerpen by the Flemings. Books, newspapers, advertisements, and official documents are published in French and in Dutch. Both languages are taught in the schools, but considerable friction has developed over the status and use of the two languages.

Religion. Although the Belgians are divided by their languages, they are united in their religion. Roman Catholicism is the leading religion. Complete religious freedom is guaranteed by the Belgian Constitution. Although the state may not interfere in religious matters,

---

FACTS AND FIGURES

KINGDOM OF BELGIUM is the official name of the country. Belgium was named after the Belgae, the Gallic tribe that lived in the region in Julius Caesar's time. In French it is Royaume de Belgique, and in Dutch, Koninkrijk België.

CAPITAL: Brussels.

LOCATION: Northwest Europe. **Latitude**—49° 30′ N to 51° 30′ N. **Longitude**—2° 35′ E to 6° 25′ E.

PHYSICAL FEATURES: Area—30,513 km² (11,781 sq mi). **Highest point**—Botrange, 696 m (2,283 ft). **Lowest point**—sea level. **Chief rivers**—Lys, Scheldt, Sambre, Meuse, Ourthe.

POPULATION: 10,000,000 (estimate).

LANGUAGES: French, Dutch, German.

RELIGION: Mostly Roman Catholic.

GOVERNMENT: Hereditary, constitutional monarchy.

Head of state—king. **International co-operation**—United Nations; North Atlantic Treaty Organization (NATO), Council of Europe, Organization for Economic Cooperation and Development (OECD), European Communities, Benelux.

NATIONAL ANTHEM: *La Brabançonne.* The anthem begins with the words *Après dès siecles d'esclavage* ("After centuries of bondage").

ECONOMY: Agricultural products—sugar beets, potatoes, wheat, oats, barley, livestock. **Industries and products**—steel, cement, textiles, chemicals, foods, glass, brick, tobacco goods, timber, paper, cut diamonds, railroad equipment. **Chief mineral**—coal. **Chief exports**—metals, textiles, machinery and electrical equipment, chemical and pharmaceutical products, ores, precious stones, and minerals. **Chief imports**—ores and minerals, base metals and products, textiles, clothing and accessories, machinery and electrical equipment, motor vehicles. **Monetary unit**—Belgian franc.

it does pay part of the salaries of recognized ministers of all faiths.

Education. All Belgian children between the ages of 6 and 14 must go to school. There are public and private primary and secondary schools. Most private schools in Belgium are run by religious groups. Private as well as public schools may receive financial support from the government, which also pays most teachers' salaries. Higher education in Belgium is provided by several excellent universities. Belgium's largest university, Louvain, is also one of the oldest in Europe. It was founded in 1426.

Way of Life

The Belgians live much the way people of other modern industrial nations do. Because Belgium has a high standard of living, many homes have modern appliances such as television sets, refrigerators, and washing machines. More and more Belgians are able to afford an automobile, and traffic problems are serious in the winding streets of the old towns. But superhighways have been built to span the countryside and ease traffic congestion.

Belgians enjoy their modern way of life,

but many old buildings remain to beautify the towns and villages. Although Belgians put great emphasis on the new, they think of these old landmarks as valuable relics of their past. Belgians are proud of the fact that more than 90 per cent of Belgian homes have electricity. They are also proud that housing is generally far above average—even for prosperous northwestern Europe.

Food. The Belgians enjoy good food and

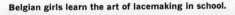

One of the canals in the city of Bruges.

Belgian girls learn the art of lacemaking in school.

In the begonia festival held every August, displays are made entirely of flowers.

Steelworkers ride motor bicycles to foundries in Athus, an area of heavy industry.

Flax, the source of linen, drying near Courtrai.

pleasant dining. Like their neighbors the French, the Belgians are expert cooks. Every region of Belgium has its own specialties, but certain dishes are popular all over the country. A typical Belgian meal might begin with a kind of chicken soup called *waterzooï de poulet.* The main course might be *carbonnade à la flamande,* which is a beef stew made with beer. For dessert there might be sweet tarts or tiny, paper-thin, jelly-filled pancakes called *crêpes.*

Recreation. Movies, theaters, radio, and television are very popular in Belgium. Spectator sports such as soccer attract large audiences. Bicycling, bowling, and basketball are favorite sports, and ice skating on the frozen waterways is special winter fun for children in Belgium. Visitors from all over the world flock to the many richly filled art galleries.

The Arts. Belgium has been the home of many famous composers, writers, and painters. Among the 15th- and 16th-century musicians who won great fame were Guillaume Dufay, Josquin des Prez, and Roland de Lassus. The best-known modern Belgian composer, César Franck, lived in the 19th century.

Belgium's artists have been world famous for many centuries. Many famous Flemish artists lived between the 15th and 18th centuries. They include Jan van Eyck, Hieronymus Bosch, Pieter Brueghel the Elder and his son Jan, Peter Paul Rubens, Sir Anthony Van Dyck, and David Teniers the Younger. In modern times two Belgians, Paul Delvaux and René Magritte, have won fame for their surrealistic paintings.

Belgians have also made important contributions to world literature. Three of the outstanding Belgian authors who wrote in Dutch are the novelist Hendrik Conscience and the poets Guido Gezelle and Karel van de Woestijne. Among the most noted Belgians who wrote in French are the poet Emile Verhaeren; Charles de Coster, who wrote about the legendary prankster named Till Eulenspiegel; and Maurice Maeterlinck, who won the Nobel prize for literature in 1911. Georges Simenon, the popular modern mystery story writer, was born in Liège.

▶ THE LAND

Belgium is shaped almost like a triangle. There is also a tiny 18-square-kilometer (7-square-mile) fragment of Belgium, called Baarle-Hertog, that is entirely surrounded by the territory of the Netherlands. The Netherlands borders Belgium on the north and northeast. Germany and Luxembourg are on the east. France is on the south and west. Belgium's northwestern boundary is formed by the North Sea.

Belgium can be divided into three equal sections. They are the lowlands in the north and west, a low plateau in the center, and the uplands in the south and southeast.

The lowland north is generally level, and in some sections it is practically flat. Parts of the northwestern lowlands were reclaimed from the sea and marshes during the Middle Ages. Picturesque windmills, which once pumped away excess water from the earth, used to dot the lowlands. Now engine-driven pumps do the work of the old windmills. The Kempen (Campine) is the name given to the sandy, gravelly, and in places marshy northeastern lowlands. The short, straight Belgian coastline has many wide beaches that are popular resorts in summer. Much of the coast is bordered by sand dunes, and dikes have been built to protect the coast against sea flooding.

The southern two thirds of Belgium is more elevated. Central Belgium is on a low and rolling plain. Belgium's highest point is the Botrange, in the rugged Ardennes Plateau in the east.

Major Rivers. From northwest to southeast the principal Belgian rivers are the Lys, Scheldt, Sambre, Meuse, and Ourthe. Most Belgian rivers are tributaries of the Scheldt or Meuse. Northern and central Belgium are crisscrossed by many waterways. Some of the waterways are artificial ones used for drainage and navigation.

Climate. Belgium's climate is of the type known as marine west coast, which is typical of northwestern Europe. This kind of climate has changeable and cloudy weather with frequent rains and moderate temperatures. Winters are generally mild except in the interior uplands. Summers are usually cool rather than warm. Daytime temperatures are rarely higher than 27°C (80°F).

About 750 millimeters (30 inches) of precipitation—mostly in the form of rain—fall on northern Belgium in an average year. The uplands receive even more precipitation.

Natural Resources. Belgium has become a great industrial nation even though it is quite poor in natural resources. Only coal and phosphates (which are used in fertilizers) are found in large quantities. Coal, which has been taken from pits in Belgium since Roman times, is found in the Sambre and Meuse river valleys. Newer fields are being worked in the eastern Kempen. Earth, sand, and clay, used in the manufacture of glass, brick, and cement, are also found.

Belgium's agricultural resources are important. About 50 percent of the land is cultivated. Some of this is land that has been reclaimed from the sea and marshes. Centuries of skillful farming have also made the soil fertile in many other sections that once had no value.

▶ THE ECONOMY

Industry. Belgium is able to keep its high standard of living because it is a highly industrialized nation. About half of all Belgian workers are engaged in mining and industry. Many Belgian cities have industrial specialties. The capital, Brussels, is the general center of manufacture and commerce. Textiles and lace come from the cities of Ghent, Tournai, and Courtrai. Liège produces firearms. Mechlin is a furniture-making center. Woolens are made in Verviers. Charleroi, Mons, and Namur are the center of iron and steel processing.

Belgian industries depend to a large extent on imported raw materials. For example, Belgian steel is made from iron ores imported from France and Luxembourg. Belgium produces over 11,000,000 metric tons (over 12,000,000 tons) of steel a year, making it one of the world's important steel-producing countries. Other leading industries include the manufacture of railroad equipment and armaments and the processing of such metals as zinc, copper, and lead. The manufacture of woolens and other textiles has been important in Belgium since the Middle Ages. Today hundreds of thousands of metric tons of cloth goods are made in Belgian mills. "Made in Belgium" also is found stamped on such products as glassware, foods, tobacco goods, timber, and paper products.

The products of Belgium's industries are sold all over the world. Foreign trade is very important to the Belgian economy, which has widespread commercial interests, particularly in Europe. Belgium is a member of the European Communities and also has trading connections with the United States.

Agriculture. Although industry is dominant, many Belgians earn their living from farming. The average Belgian farm is small, covering only about 6.5 hectares (16 acres). But the farms are intensively cultivated. Many farmers combine farming with some other occupation such as factory work.

The major crops produced by Belgian farmers are wheat, oats, barley, potatoes, sugar beets, and rye. Flax, used for linen making, and tobacco are also grown. Truck gardening of vegetables and fruits is a leading occupation in Flanders. Bulbs for flowers are also grown in Flanders.

Belgium's climate is good for grass growth, and as a result the country has a flourishing livestock industry. Livestock feed crops are widely grown and occupy about one half of the cultivated acreage. Dairy cattle, beef cattle, and hogs are the most important livestock. Belgian horses were once widely used as draft animals. Today they have largely been replaced by farm machines in Belgium, as elsewhere.

Transportation and Communication. Belgium's farms and industries are served by an excellent transportation system. Roads reach every corner of the country. Belgium has one of the world's densest networks of railroad facilities, and an extensive system of navigable rivers and canals.

Belgium has a small merchant navy and an airline, Sabena, which is partly owned by the government. Antwerp, Belgium's most important port, on the Scheldt, competes with Rotterdam in the Netherlands and Hamburg in Germany as northwestern Europe's leading port.

▶ **GOVERNMENT**

Belgium is a hereditary, constitutional monarchy. The king is the head of the state and commander of the army. The king must approve all laws passed by Parliament. When a king dies, he is succeeded by his son. Daughters may not succeed to the throne. If a king has no sons, he may nominate his successor. But his choice must be approved by Parliament.

Although the Belgian king seems to have great powers, the actual government is headed by a prime minister, who is helped by other ministers. The Belgian Parliament is divided into two houses—the Senate and the Chamber of Representatives. The minimum voting age is 18. All qualified voters are required by law to vote.

▶ **HISTORY**

Julius Caesar wrote, "Of all the tribes of Gaul, the Belgae are the bravest." These words of the man who conquered the Belgic tribes in the 1st century B.C. have been echoed by others who tried to conquer Belgium during its long history. But the Belgians sought independence during centuries of foreign rule and finally won it in 1830.

Roman rule over Gallia Belgica lasted about 500 years. During the early Middle Ages, Belgium's history was very complicated and closely interwoven with that of its neighbors. By the end of the Middle Ages, however, northern Belgium, under the rule of the counts of Flanders, had grown strong and prosperous. Commerce, manufacture, and the arts grew. Towns slowly grew up, and guilds and other trade organizations were established. A powerful, wealthy, and well-educated middle class developed. Even so, Belgium was often involved in the military adventures of her larger neighbors.

After being tied to the Austrian Empire for over two centuries, Belgium passed to Spanish control in 1519. Then, in 1598, Belgium began a brief period of independence. This ended in 1621, when the Spanish once again took over the area they called the Spanish Netherlands. In 1713 Belgium was again made a part of the Austrian kingdom, but in 1797 France annexed the country. After the final defeat of the French emperor, Napoleon, at Waterloo, near Brussels, in 1815, Belgium and the Netherlands were set up as a united kingdom. The Belgians were unhappy about this union and on October 4, 1830, declared their independence.

The first king of the newly independent nation was a German prince, Leopold of Saxe-Coburg-Gotha. During the rule of Leopold, Belgium became one of the pioneer leaders of the industrial revolution in Europe.

The late 19th century was a period of active European colonization, but Belgium did not participate directly. However, King Leopold II, acting more or less as a private individual, claimed a huge expanse of land in Africa's Congo River basin. In 1908 the Belgian Congo colony was placed under the direct control of the Belgian Parliament.

In 1909 Albert I became king. The early years of his reign were prosperous and happy ones for Belgium. But at the outbreak of World War I in 1914, German armies invaded and quickly occupied most of Belgium. Some of the bloodiest battles of the war were fought in Belgium at Ypres, Antwerp, Namur, and Mons.

At the end of the war, the Belgians began restoring their war-torn country. Acting with their usual vigor, they quickly re-equipped and modernized their industries. Then in May, 1940, shortly after the beginning of World War II, Belgium again became a European battleground. Belgian soldiers, aided by British and French allies, were unable to resist a German invasion. After 18 days of combat, Belgium came under German occupation for the second time in a generation.

Allied armies succeeded in driving the Germans out of Belgium in September, 1944, but in December of that year German armies re-entered the country. The savage Battle of the Bulge was fought in the Ardennes region during the winter of 1944–45. It was a desperate counteroffensive, which was doomed to fail. At last in February, 1945, Belgium regained its freedom.

The Belgians once again set about re-

The City Hall on the Grand' Place in Brussels is a baroque building completed in the 17th century.

building their country. Prosperity and high employment marked the postwar years. But there were also serious problems. The conflict between the Flemings and the Walloons became more bitter. King Leopold III abdicated because many Belgians disapproved of his wartime behavior, and in 1951 his son, Baudouin, became king.

Early in the 1960's, Belgium granted independence to the Belgian Congo (now the country of Zaïre) and to the Trusteeship Territory of Rwanda-Urundi (now the countries of Rwanda and Burundi). At home there were increasing disorders connected with the language problem. In 1978, agreement was reached on a plan to transform Belgium into a federated state by the mid-1980's.

The headquarters of many international organizations, including the European Communities and the North Atlantic Treaty Organization (NATO), are in Brussels.

KENNETH THOMPSON
University of California—Davis

Reviewed by J.-A. GORIS
Former Commissioner of Information
Belgium Information Service

BELIZE

Belize is a small self-governing British dependency on the east coast of Central America facing the Caribbean Sea. It is bounded on the north and west by Mexico and on the west and south by Guatemala. Once known as British Honduras, the dependency was renamed Belize in 1973.

▶ THE PEOPLE

Belize is the home of many different peoples. The largest group is made up of Creoles. They are the descendants of African slaves who were brought to the area to cut the valuable trees in the forests. There is also a large group of mestizos, people of mixed European and Indian descent. The rest are Maya and Carib Indians, East Indians, Chinese, Europeans, and others. All these various peoples generally get along well together.

English is the official language. It is spoken as a local dialect containing many Creole words, and so is difficult for other English-speaking people to understand. Spanish is spoken as a mother tongue or a second language by many. Schooling is free and compulsory for children from age 6 to 14. The great majority of people can read and write.

Most of the people live along the coast. About a third live in Belize City, the chief port and former capital. Belmopan, the official capital since 1972, was built in the jungle in the central part of the country.

▶ THE LAND

Belize has a long, swampy, and irregular coastline, fringed by small islands known as cays. The low coastal plain rises gradually toward the interior. In the south are the Maya Mountains and the Cockscomb Mountains. Victoria Peak, in the Cockscombs, rises to 1,122 meters (3,681 feet) and is the highest point in Belize.

The hot and humid climate is cooled along the coast by northeast trade winds. In the south there can be over 4,300 millimeters (170 inches) of rainfall a year. The country lies within the Caribbean hurricane belt, and storms have caused great damage in the past. The new capital, Belmopan, was established inland because the former capital, Belize City, had been devastated twice by hurricanes.

There are many rivers, most of them shallow and none very long. The Belize River is the most important. Much of the country's timber is floated downriver to the coast. A large part of the country is forest land, and for two centuries lumbering was the major

Royal Welsh Fusiliers parade in Belize City, the country's chief port and largest city.

industry. Mahogany, cedar, rosewood, and other woods were the chief exports, but now sugar is the leading export. It is followed by citrus fruits (chiefly oranges and grapefruit). Corn, rice, and beans are grown, mostly for local use. Fish are abundant and lobsters are a valuable export.

► HISTORY AND GOVERNMENT

Belize was once part of the Maya Empire. In 1638 British sailors who were shipwrecked off the coast became the first European settlers. Other British settlers followed.

Spain, which governed the neighboring territories (now Mexico and Guatemala), tried in vain to drive the British out. When Guatemala became independent in 1821, it claimed Spain's right to the land. Guatemala and Britain have tried over the years to settle the dispute, but they have never agreed on the boundary between the two countries.

Belize, then known as British Honduras, became self-governing in 1964. It has a prime minister, an elected House of Representatives, and an appointed Senate. The governor, chosen by the British monarch, oversees foreign affairs.

Many Belizeans want independence. But to be self-supporting, Belize must raise the level of its economy. With its entrance into the Caribbean Community (CARICOM),

it is hoping to sell more of its products. It is increasing agricultural production and hopes to expand its tourist industry.

Britain supports Belize's wish for independence. But it will not guarantee military support against Guatemala if Belize is no longer a British dependency. In 1978, Barbados, Guyana, and Jamaica agreed to an alliance to protect Belize after it gains independence. But before independence is granted, Guatemala's claim must be settled.

Reviewed by SIR PETER STALLARD
Former Governor, Belize

Village produce is carried to market in dugout canoes.

FACTS AND FIGURES

BELIZE is the official name of the dependency.

CAPITAL: Belmopan.

LOCATION: East coast of Central America. **Latitude**— 15° 54′ N to 18° 30′ N. **Longitude**—88° 11′ W to 89° 13′ W.

AREA: 22,965 km² (8,867 sq mi).

POPULATION: 140,000 (estimate).

LANGUAGES: English, Spanish, Indian dialects.

RELIGION: Roman Catholic, Protestant.

GOVERNMENT: Self-governing British dependency. **Head of state**—British monarch, represented by governor. **Head of government**—prime minister. **International cooperation**—Commonwealth of Nations, Caribbean Community (CARICOM).

ECONOMY: Chief agricultural products—sugar, citrus fruits, rice, corn, beans. **Industries and products**— hardwoods and wood for pulp, citrus fruits (canned, juice, and concentrates), sugar refining. **Chief exports**— sugar, citrus fruits, mahogany, cedar, and pine. **Chief imports**—foodstuffs, machinery and transport equipment, petroleum, manufactured goods. **Monetary unit**—Belize dollar.

The first telephone call. Bell's command was carried by wire from speaking tube to receiver in another room. Startled assistant Thomas A. Watson rushed in.

BELL, ALEXANDER GRAHAM (1847–1922)

The date was March 10, 1876. The place was a small laboratory in a Boston boarding-house. A young man was working with an electrical instrument that was wired to one in another room. Suddenly the instrument spoke: "Mr. Watson, come here. I want you." Watson rushed into the other room, where his employer, Mr. Bell, had spilled some acid. Both men forgot the acid in their excitement over Watson's report: Bell's words, spoken near one instrument, had issued clearly from the other. These words had become the first spoken telephone message.

Alexander Graham Bell is so famous for his invention of the telephone that some people think it was his life's work. Yet this is far from true. Bell was still a young man when he invented the telephone. He went on to make important contributions in many fields of science. Throughout his life he also worked as a teacher of the deaf, a family interest that had a good deal to do with his invention of the telephone.

Alexander Graham Bell was born on March 3, 1847, in Edinburgh, Scotland. He was born into a family with an interest in speech and hearing. Both his grandfather and his father were teachers of correct speech. His father had developed "visible speech," a method of helping the deaf to learn how to speak. From his mother, young Graham, as he was known, inherited a talent for music.

Bell's schooling was far from regular. In his early years he was taught at home along with his two brothers. At the age of 13 he spent a year in London with his grandfather. In his grandfather's library he read all he could about sound and speech—about the vibrations set up by the voice. (Place your fingers on your throat while you speak. You will feel these vibrations.) He later recalled this year as the turning point of his life.

By the age of 16 Graham Bell was teaching music and speech at a boys' school. Within a few years he was teaching his father's visible speech to deaf children. Though he did study at the universities of Edinburgh and London, Bell probably learned most on his own.

While studying how the human voice works, for example, Bell came upon the writings of

Helmholtz. Helmholtz was a German scientist who had used electric vibrations to make vowel sounds. Interested, Bell at once began to study electricity so that he could repeat Helmholtz's experiments.

Bell's family had moved to London, and he joined them there in 1868. But by 1870 both of Bell's brothers had died of tuberculosis, and his own life was in danger. Seeking a more healthful climate, the Bells left Britain and moved to Brantford, Ontario.

Resting in his new home, Bell had time to carry on his studies of Helmholtz's electrical experiments. By 1871 his health had improved, and he went to Boston, Massachusetts. There he again took up his life's work of teaching the deaf.

Bell also continued his experiments. By now his work with electricity had led him to think about inventing a harmonic telegraph. This was a system that could carry several messages over one wire at the same time.

Bell began to work on two basic problems. He needed a way of sending a continuous electric current that could be made to vary in strength. And he had to find some material that would vibrate while sending or receiving such a current. (Though he did not realize it at the time, he was also facing the two basic problems of the telephone.)

Bell needed money to carry on his experiments. It was given to him by two wealthy men, Gardiner Hubbard and Thomas Sanders. Hubbard had a deaf daughter, and Sanders a deaf son, both of whom were receiving instruction from Bell. It was arranged that the two fathers would share in any profits from Bell's work. Bell was now able to hire a skilled assistant, Thomas A. Watson.

It was during the summer of 1874 that Bell's thinking first went beyond his plan for a harmonic telegraph. What if an electric current could be made to vary, just as the air varies with sound waves? Then any sound—including human speech—could be carried by electricity. This was the idea of the telephone.

The next year was a busy one for Bell. Now that he had the idea of a telephone, he wanted to develop it. But he felt he should concentrate on the telegraph. As things turned out, he never did perfect the harmonic telegraph. His experiments with it kept taking him closer to the telephone.

On June 2, 1875, Bell and Watson were experimenting with their telegraph, which made use of thin steel reeds. One of the reeds was stuck, and Watson plucked it with his finger. In another room Bell heard a reed in his instrument vibrate as if he himself had plucked it. The electric current had reproduced in this second reed the vibrations of the first.

If the current had done this, then surely it should also reproduce vibrations caused by the human voice. Bell now knew that the telephone was a practical idea. It was only a matter of time before he could perfect an instrument that would send words clearly. Success came on March 10, 1876, with the famous words, "Mr. Watson, come here. I want you."

There was still much work to be done on the telephone. But by the end of 1877 the Bell Telephone Company had been formed, and many phones were in use. Bell himself did not take part in the telephone business that developed. Rather, he leased the right to build a company around his invention.

In the meantime Bell had married Mabel Hubbard, the deaf girl whom he had taught. They had two daughters. In 1882 Bell became a citizen of the United States. He divided his time between Washington, D. C., and his summer home, Beinn Bhreagh, on Cape Breton Island, Nova Scotia. (In 1956 a museum for his many inventions was opened near there.)

Bell had invented the telephone before he was 30. In the remaining 45 years of his life he applied his talents to many questions. He experimented with sending sound by light waves. He was interested in heredity and carried on breeding experiments with sheep. He was one of the first to foresee the future of the airplane. As early as the 1890's, Bell was experimenting with the problems of flight. Throughout his life Bell continued working for the deaf and dumb. Bell's work in all these fields won him many honors, but he remained a kindly, modest, and generous man. Bell died on August 2, 1922. He was so greatly admired that during the funeral the telephones of North America were silent in his honor.

JOHN S. BOWMAN
Author and Science Editor

See also ELECTRICITY; TELEPHONE.

BELLINI FAMILY

During the 15th century Jacopo Bellini, a Venetian painter, owned one of the busiest workshops in Italy. When he was not traveling, Jacopo spent his time in the Venice shop, painting portraits for the rich and altars for the Church and teaching the young artists who came to study with him. Two of his best students were his own sons, Gentile and Giovanni.

Jacopo was born around 1400, and his sons sometime between 1429 and 1432—we do not know the exact dates. The three artists worked in the shop for years, experimenting with a new medium, oil paint. After the father died, about 1470, the brothers continued to paint. In 1474 they began a series of historical paintings for the ducal palace in Venice, a project that lasted many years.

The sultan of Turkey asked the rulers of Venice to lend him one of their best painters. Gentile Bellini received the honor and was sent to Turkey in 1479. Giovanni remained in Venice, working at the palace, teaching, and painting religious pictures. Today Giovanni is regarded as the greatest of the Bellinis. Gentile returned to Venice in 1480, and the brothers worked together again.

Gentile died in 1507, and Giovanni in 1516. In 1577 a tragic fire burned through the palace. Afterward, it was discovered that countless canvases by the Bellinis—among the first masterpieces of oil painting—had been completely destroyed.

BELLS AND CARILLONS

For centuries bells have rung to mark the passing hours, but they have often been used for quite different purposes—for magic and superstition. African witch doctors shook sticks of bells to drive off evil spirits. The Egyptians wore bells on their ankles as a protection against lightning. In old England bells were attached to costumes and jingled by folk dancers to awaken the spirit of spring from a long winter's sleep.

In ancient Rome, bells announced public assemblies and church services. Bells were rung to frighten off witches, fiends, devils, and demons. In the Middle Ages, bells were used for a variety of reasons. At daybreak bells woke up the medieval city, calling the people to morning prayers; through the day bells solemnly counted the hours, the half hours, and the quarters. They pealed for weddings and tolled for funerals and were heard at Easter and Christmas.

▶ THE FIRST BELL MUSIC

The earliest attempts to make music with bells occurred in the Middle Ages, with the *cymbala,* or bell chime. This was a small set of bells hung from a rack.

The clock bell originated in the monastery. The bells rang from a tower and regulated not only life in the abbey but the life of the surrounding town as well. The tower with its bells became so necessary to a town that the bells were considered civic property.

Since the first clock bells could not ring by themselves, a man was hired for the job of striking them at the proper times of the day. He was sometimes called Jack of the Market, for he was also paid to sweep the marketplace between the times he rang the hour bell. The human bell ringer was soon replaced by clock machinery. With machinery it was possible to ring many bells, and it became customary to ring a short tune as a warning that the hour bell was about to strike. This is known as a clock chime tune.

▶ FROM BELLS TO CARILLONS

In Flanders the clock tune was called the *voorslag,* or "forestroke." It was from the *voorslag* that the carillon evolved. At first the tunes played were very simple, but gradually more and more bells were added. They were rung automatically by a **tambour**, a device constructed on the music box principle. Later a clavier, or keyboard, operated by a **carillonneur**, was added.

In France a carillon may be a group of four or more bells. Elsewhere, however, a carillon is an instrument with at least 23 bells, capable of producing harmony.

Gog and Magog adorn the front of a jewelry store in Greenfield Village, Michigan.

The carillon keyboard consists of levers and pedals. The levers resemble small broomstick handles. The carillonneur sits at a bench and strikes the levers with his clenched hand and plays the pedals with his feet. Unlike the Jack of the Market, a carillonneur must be a musician.

The oldest carillon in the world is in the Rijksmuseum in Amsterdam. It has 24 bells cast in 1554. The most famous carillon is at Saint Rombold's Cathedral in Mechelen, Belgium. It has 49 bells.

The first carillon in North America was installed at Notre Dame University in South Bend, Indiana, in 1856. In 1922 the first modern cast-bell carillons were installed at the Church of Our Lady of Good Voyage in Gloucester, Massachusetts, and at the Metropolitan Church in Toronto. In 1927 the government of Canada installed one in the Peace Tower of the Houses of Parliament in Ottawa. The largest carillon in the world is at the Riverside Church in New York City. This instrument contains six octaves of bells, of which the **bourdon**, or bass bell, weighs over 18 metric tons and is the largest and heaviest tuned carillon bell in the world.

In the United States there are many instruments called carillons, but they are different from traditional carillons. They are electronic carillons and are similar to electronic organs in that they imitate the sound of bells through the use of electronic equipment. Their source of tone is a set of rods that are struck by tiny hammers. Their vibrations are amplified electronically and broadcast through loudspeakers. Electronic carillons may be played from a piano or organ keyboard, or sounded automatically.

▶ **HOW BELLS ARE MADE**

A bell is a hollow, cup-shaped vessel made of metal. Suspended inside the bell is a metal ball called a clapper. When the clapper strikes the bell, the bell rings, or makes a musical sound.

Bells are made from bronze, an alloy of copper and tin. In bell casting, two molds of baked clay are constructed. One forms the interior of the bell, and the other forms the curved shape of the outside surface. Molten bronze is poured between the two molds. When the metal has cooled and hardened, the molds are removed. Bells are tuned by filing or shaving strips of metal from their inside surfaces.

JAMES R. LAWSON
Carillonneur, Riverside Church (New York City)

BELORUSSIA

Belorussia, or White Russia, is one of the 15 republics that make up the Union of Soviet Socialist Republics. It lies in the western part of the Soviet Union, just east of Poland, and has an area of about 207,000 square kilometers (80,000 square miles). Belorussia is independently represented in the United Nations.

Belorussia is a country of low hills sloping northwest and south from the central ridge on which Minsk, the capital city, is built. Belorussia's forests contain valuable pine, spruce, oak, and maple trees, which are used in industry. For centuries the Pripet Marshes in the south were almost untouched, but vast areas have been drained and are now used for crop growing.

Industry has grown greatly since the end of World War II. Fertilizers, trucks, textiles, glass, radios, television sets, watches, and clocks are produced. Because of abundant timber resources, the production of prefabricated homes is of great importance.

More than 9,000,000 people live in Belorussia. They speak Belorussian, but Russian is taught as a second language. There are over 25 schools of higher education and more than 125 technical schools. The V.I. Lenin State University is located in Minsk.

Many families work together on collective farms, sharing farm machinery and the products of the farm. Old traditions live on in Belorussia, and folk songs, dances, and legends are still enjoyed by the people.

For hundreds of years, Belorussia was part of the Lithuanian, and then the Polish-Lithuanian, kingdom. The Russians first took over Belorussia at the end of the 18th century. Poland reoccupied western Belorussia in 1918. Eastern Belorussia formally became a Soviet republic in 1922. Western Belorussia was added to the republic in 1939, at the start of World War II. During that war the invading Germans devastated Belorussia. But the nation's story since 1945 has been one of rebuilding and dramatic growth.

ALOYS A. MICHEL
University of Rhode Island

BEN-GURION, DAVID (1886-1973)

David Ben-Gurion became the first prime minister of Israel after the country became independent in 1948. He served as prime minister and minister of defense from 1949 to 1953 and from 1955 to 1963.

Ben-Gurion was born David Gryn on October 16, 1886, in Plonsk, Poland. His father, Avigdor Gryn, was a Zionist. The father inspired young David with the hope of some day going to Palestine.

In 1906 David decided that the time had come for him to go to Palestine, then a part of the Turkish Empire. The new land was strange to someone who had always lived in Poland, but he soon found work as a farm laborer. In 1910 David became editor of the Palestine Labor Party's magazine. He signed one of his articles "Ben-Gurion," Hebrew for "son of the young lion." From then on he was known as David Ben-Gurion.

When World War I broke out in 1914, Ben-Gurion was arrested by the Turks and expelled from Palestine. First he fled to Egypt and later to the United States. In America he encouraged young people to emigrate to Palestine. One of these Americans was a nurse named Paula Munweis, who eventually became Ben-Gurion's wife. In 1917 Ben-Gurion helped organize the Jewish Legion to fight with the British Army against the Turks. In 1918 he returned to Palestine.

For the next 20 years Ben-Gurion devoted himself to Zionism and politics. He helped organize Histadrut (the General Federation of Jewish Labor). In 1935 he became chairman of the Jewish Agency for Palestine, an organization that assisted Jewish immigrants who wanted to settle in Palestine.

Israel declared its independence on May 14, 1948. Under Ben-Gurion's leadership the new nation became a modern democracy as well as a home for Jews seeking refuge. Ben-Gurion died in 1973, a national hero.

Reviewed by HOWARD M. SACHAR
George Washington University

See also ISRAEL; ZIONISM.

BENIN

Benin, formerly called Dahomey, is a small country on the west coast of Africa. It traces its history back to the powerful 17th-century kingdom of Dahomey. Later the territory came under the rule of France, from which it gained its independence in 1960. Since then its leaders have tried to bring a measure of prosperity to a country poor in natural resources.

▶ THE PEOPLE

Most of the people of Benin live in the southern part of the country, which has the richest soil. The northern region is more sparsely populated.

The majority of the people are of black African stock. The Fon, farmers who live in the south, are the major ethnic group. Next are the Adja, who dwell along the Mono River. The Bariba and Fulani live in the north, and the Yoruba in the southeast.

Most of the people are farmers who produce food chiefly for their own use. The main food crops are cassava, maize (corn), beans, millet, sweet potatoes, and rice. Cassava is used in making bread and tapioca (*gari*). The farmers also keep cattle, sheep, and goats. Fish are plentiful in the rivers and lagoons. They are an important source of food and are also one of the country's exports.

The improvement of education is essential to the country's development. Most schools are in the south, but the government is trying to provide schools for the scattered population in the north. In 1975, the government took over the maintenance of all elementary schools in Benin. There are a number of high schools, vocational schools, teacher-training schools, and a university. Most of the schools of higher education are located in Porto-Novo, the capital, and Cotonou, the largest city.

Government-operated public health services combat such common tropical diseases as malaria, yellow fever, sleeping sickness, dysentery, and leprosy. Cotonou has a modern hospital. Rural clinics are scattered throughout the countryside. In addition, mobile health units visit the most remote areas.

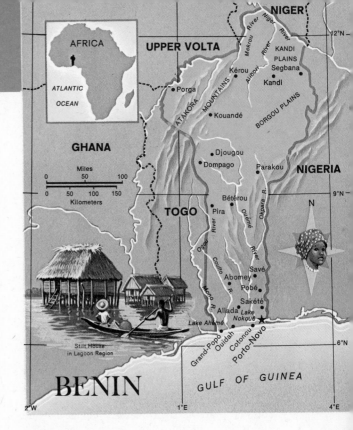

Stilt House in Lagoon Region

BENIN

▶ THE LAND

Benin occupies a long, narrow strip of land that includes both lowlands and highlands. It has a short coastline on the Gulf of Guinea, a part of the Atlantic Ocean.

The country has four geographical regions. In the south there is a flat coastal area along the Gulf of Guinea. Next is a region of lagoons and lakes that meet the sea at Grand-Popo and Cotonou. Farther north the land rises to a broad plateau that reaches as high as 460 meters (1,500 feet). In the far north the land is divided between the Atakora Mountains and the broad, fertile plains of

Modern bank and wide paved streets in Cotonou.

Borgou and Kandi. The major rivers are the Ouémé (the country's longest), the Mono, and the Couffo. Ships can travel up the Ouémé for about half its length in the rainy season.

The northern and southern parts of the country have different climates. The south is hot and humid, with two dry and two rainy seasons. The north has one dry and one rainy season.

▶ THE ECONOMY

Benin is a relatively poor and underdeveloped country. Its economy is largely agricultural. The major industries are those that process the chief export crops—palm oil, palm kernels, and nuts. Palm products supply about three quarters of the country's exports. Palm oil is used in making soap and margarine. Copra (dried coconut meat), shea butter (the fat of shea tree nuts), peanuts, and castor oil are among the other important agricultural exports.

Providing transportation is one of the country's greatest problems. There is one major railroad line, the Benin-Niger, which operates from Cotonou northward to Parakou. Two smaller lines run along the coast and for a short distance inland. Only a few of the roads can be used during the rainy season. Cotonou has a major international airport, and there are several smaller airports in the north. The coastline has no natural harbors, but a deepwater port has been built at Cotonou.

▶ HISTORY AND GOVERNMENT

The three great kingdoms of Ardra, Jakin (Porto-Novo), and Dahomey flourished in the early 17th century. During the 18th century the strong kings of Dahomey seized control of Ardra and Jakin in the south in order to sell slaves to the European traders.

In 1738 the Yoruba from Nigeria seized Abomey, the capital of the kingdom of Dahomey, and forced the Dahomean rulers to pay tribute for nearly 100 years. In the late 19th century, the great Dahomean king Gezo reorganized the Dahomean army, which included a famous band of female warriors. He succeeded in shaking off the yoke of the Yoruba.

During this time the French were extending their influence along the Gulf of Guinea. Gezo

signed the first trade agreement with the French in 1851, but the kings who came after him did not respect the agreement. In 1894 France forcibly deposed the last of the Dahomean kings, Béhanzin, and annexed the territory to French West Africa.

For the next 50 years France ruled Dahomey. In 1946 France began to give Dahomey and other French African territories more control over their own affairs. Dahomey elected its own legislature in 1952. In 1960 it proclaimed its independence. To advance its economic development, it formed the Council of the Entente with Upper Volta, the Ivory Coast, Niger, and Togo.

Since gaining its independence, Benin has experienced a number of changes of government. Personal and regional rivalries were the major causes of at least four coups d'etat in the 1960's. In 1970 the Government of National Unity was formed. Under this system a three-member presidential council governed the country. Each member of the council in turn was to serve a 2-year term as president. In 1972, however, the country again came under military rule following a coup d'état. The name of the country was changed from Dahomey to Benin in 1975.

L. GRAY COWAN
Columbia University

BEOWULF

Beowulf is the longest and greatest of the poems that have come down to us in Old English. It is a hero's story made into a poem, so that all the pleasures of poetry are added to the lively events of a hero's life. *Beowulf* had to be exciting and easy to understand, because when it was composed, literature was not read quietly out of books but was recited after feasts in the halls of kings and nobles. The *scop* or *gleeman*—early words for "poet"—spoke *Beowulf* and other poems aloud, probably striking a small harp to mark the rhythm. Such poems often inspired warriors before battle or celebrated a victory.

Though *Beowulf* was composed by a *scop* who called England his native land, the scene of the story is not England. Beowulf was a Geat, which means that he came from the south of Sweden. Hrothgar, the king he came to help, was a Dane, and most of the story happens in Denmark. Though the poem could not have been written down before A.D. 700, the events in it probably happened in the 6th century. Like writers of historical novels today, the *scop* went back in time and far away in space to find his story.

The only copy of *Beowulf* that we have was written down about A.D. 1000 in the West Saxon dialect. This manuscript looks to us now as if it were in some strange language. These are the opening lines:

> Hwaet! we Gar-Dena in geardagum,
> þeodcyninga þrym gefrunon,
> hu þa aeþelingas ellen fremedon!
> Oft Scyld Scefing sceaþena þreatum
> monegum maegþum meodosetla ofteah,
> egsode eorlas, syððan aerest wearð
> feasceaft funden;

The unfamiliar þ and ð are only ways of showing the sounds we write as *th*. Some words in *Beowulf* are still in our language.

Many things about the poem must have stirred the listening warriors. Old English is very powerful, with harsh consonant sounds like K, D, G, KH, and GH. The Old English *scops* used alliteration, the repetition of one consonant sound, instead of rhyme. "*G*reat was the *g*rief of the *g*old-friend of Scyldings" shows how the *scop* tied his line together with the sound of G.

The rhythm is as strong as the beat of marching feet. Each line has two parts and is divided by a pause. Each of the two parts has two strong beats. So there are four strong beats in each line, two on one side of the pause and two on the other:

> *Great* was the *grief*//of the *gold*-friend
> of *Scyld*ings . . .

If we say the line aloud, accenting the words in italics and pausing at the double line, we will feel the rhythm that could make warriors wish to grasp their spears and march.

Old English poems are rich in images—words that make pictures. That is because the *scops* used *kennings,* colorful ways of saying ordinary things. The *scop* who composed *Beowulf* calls the sea a whale-path; a traveler an earth-stepper; a battle, spear-play. Since his England was misty, craggy, and gloomy, with many empty wildernesses, his images are often mysterious and frightening.

The Story

The main story of *Beowulf* runs as follows: Hrothgar, King of the Danes, built a great house called Heorot. Here his warriors gathered to drink mead and listen to the *scop* sing his songs. Their revelry enraged an evil monster named Grendel, who lived in the marshes. He began attacking the mead-hall at night, killing the men while they were sleeping. Finally Hrothgar was forced to abandon Heorot.

Beowulf, a young hero, heard in Geatland of Hrothgar's grief and determined to help. He crossed the icy sea with 14 companions-at-arms, told Hrothgar his good intentions, and got permission to try his might. After

At night the monster Grendel attacks the Danish warriors in their mead hall.

the Danes had feasted the visiting Geats in Heorot, Hrothgar and his warriors went elsewhere, and Beowulf and his companions stayed in the hall. Grendel came, opened the iron-bolted door at a touch, fell upon one of Beowulf's sleeping friends, and killed him. But before Grendel could carry the body off to the marsh, Beowulf caught the beast's hairy arm and dragged on it until he wrenched it out of its shoulder socket. Grendel fled, leaving his arm and a trail of blood behind. The next morning Geats and Danes followed the trail to a pool that was boiling with the blood of the dead monster. They returned happy. That night the Geats lodged elsewhere, and the Danes went back to sleep—safely, they thought—in Heorot. But Grendel's mother, a monster-hag, came to the hall seeking vengeance and killed a Danish warrior. Again Beowulf took Hrothgar's troubles upon himself. He followed the trail of Grendel's blood to the pool in the wasteland and leaped in. Under the water, in a vaulted room, he found and killed the hag. He also found the dead body of Grendel and cut off the head and carried it back to the king.

Beowulf contains other stories telling how the hero became king of the Geats and killed a dragon, but the best part of the poem is his visit to Hrothgar.

Beowulf is a strange mixture. It refers to pagan rites and Christian beliefs. It tells about real things, such as lordly feasts and sea journeys, and imaginary things, such as monsters and dragons. It contains at least one event that we know happened in history, and many events that could happen only in fairy tales. Although it is not so great an epic as Homer's *Iliad,* it is a noble and exciting poem that shows us much about the earliest heroes—their courage, generosity, and faithfulness and their love of glory and danger. Like a rich barbaric bracelet found by excavators, no one knows who made it or exactly when it was made. It is rough and dark, but strongly beautiful. It speaks to us of old times, old customs, and men and women who would be quite forgotten if the *scop* had not told of them in the king's hall.

GLADYS SCHMITT
Author, *David the King,*
The Heroic Deeds of Beowulf

BERING, VITUS (1680–1741)

In the early years of the 18th century, many people still believed that a bridge of land connected Asia and North America. Vitus Bering, a Danish sailor working for the Czar of Russia, proved that this land bridge did not exist. Bering was born at Horsens, Denmark, in 1680 or 1681, and joined the Russian Navy when he was 23. In 1724 Czar Peter the Great appointed him to lead an expedition across Russia and Siberia to the peninsula of Kamchatka, north of Japan. Here Bering was to build a ship in which to seek the land bridge.

The long journey across snow-covered Siberia was filled with terrible hardships for the members of the expedition. After more than three years they reached a little village at Kamchatka. Bering built a ship and in 1728 set sail across the uncharted sea. West of Alaska he discovered an island, which he named St. Lawrence Island. Then he sailed north through the strait (now called Bering

Strait) separating Asia and North America. The discovery of this strait proved that the two continents were not linked. But heavy fog prevented Bering from seeing the coast of Alaska, 63 kilometers (39 miles) away.

Bering returned to Russia in 1730 to plan a second expedition. In 1741 he sailed from Kamchatka with two ships, the *St. Peter* and the *St. Paul.* On July 16, while he was gazing at the horizon from the deck of the *St. Peter,* Bering saw a jagged coastline and a lofty mountain range. He had discovered Alaska. He named the highest mountain peak Mount Saint Elias. However, bad weather made further exploration difficult, and Bering and many of his men were ill. Violent storms drove the *St. Peter* back toward Asia and wrecked the ship on a desert island off the coast of Kamchatka. Here, on December 8, 1741, Bering died and was buried. The island and the sea he had explored were named after him.

BERLIN

A heavily guarded wall is the symbol of Berlin, a divided city that was once the capital of Germany. The wall, built in 1961, separates East Berlin—the capital of the Communist German Democratic Republic—from West Berlin. West Berlin, a political enclave of the Federal Republic of Germany, is separated from it by 160 kilometers (100 miles) of East German territory.

▶ HISTORY

Seven centuries ago merchants and tradespeople settled near the Spree River. The settlement grew slowly until the 13th century, when it gained importance as a market for herring, grain, and wood. By the 17th century the growing town was encircled by strong walls at the order of Frederick William of Brandenburg. His wife, Dorothea, planted the first linden tree on the now famous Unter den Linden ("Under the Lindens") Avenue. Frederick William forbade his citizens to let their pigs roam the streets, lest they should ruin his trees.

From 1701 to 1945 Berlin was a capital city. It served first as the capital of the Kingdom of Prussia, then of the German Empire, and during the last century of the Weimar Republic and National Socialist Germany. At the end of World War II in 1945, Germany was divided into an eastern and a western zone. Berlin, in East Germany, was divided into four sectors. These sectors were occupied and governed by the Soviet Union, France, Britain, and the United States.

The new Kaiser William Memorial Church rises beside the war-damaged old church.

On June 24, 1948, the Russians attempted to force the three Western powers out of the city by suddenly cutting off all land transportation and communication between West Germany and West Berlin. The blockade of the city lasted until May 12, 1949. During that time the United States and Great Britain saved the people of West Berlin from starvation and sickness by delivering food and medicines by airplane.

In the summer of 1961 another cruel blow hit the war-scarred city. In order to stop the steady flow of refugees fleeing to West Berlin, the East German police built a high wall along the 42.6-kilometer (26.5-mile) border between the east and west sectors. Whole families were divided, and busy streets were barred. Parks, gardens, and even graveyards were cut in two. West Berliners call the barrier of concrete and barbed wire the Wall of Shame.

▶ DAILY LIFE IN THE TWO BERLINS

West Berlin. *Berlin bleibt doch Berlin* ("Berlin is still Berlin") are the words of an old song that summarizes the remarkable rebirth of West Berlin since the war. Insulaner, a huge landscaped hill made of rubble and debris from wartime ruins, is a reminder of

Modern buildings in the two Berlins. Above: The Hansa Quarter, a residential district of West Berlin. Below: Alexandra Platz, one of the central squares of East Berlin.

this rebirth. The busy streets are crowded with yellow double-decker buses, an elevated train, and cars from many nations. Thousands of West Berliners and tourists crowd the Kurfürstendamm—the city's most fashionable avenue—which is famous for its elegant shops, theaters, movie houses, charming sidewalk cafés, and old-fashioned tearooms.

West Berliners enjoy all that their "island" in East Germany has to offer. They walk along the Havel River, sit on benches along the Spree, and swim and sunbathe on the beaches of the Wannsee. They may stroll by the Hansa Viertel ("Hansa Quarter"), the unique residential district designed and built by internationally famous architects. They may stop at the fairgrounds to look at an industrial or agricultural exhibition. Another landmark is the Congress Hall—a gift of the United States—which has won the nickname The Baby Scales because of its unusual shape.

Visitors and Berliners throng the historical museum in Charlottenburg Castle and visit the art museums in the Dahlem section of the city. The beautiful Opera House, a museum, several concert halls, and many theaters have been built in West Berlin since the war. The city's Philharmonic Orchestra is world famous.

Few cities offer so much to young people as Berlin. Soon after the war ended, new ultramodern schools were built. West Berlin's Free University was established in 1948. Today its handsome buildings welcome students from all parts of the world. Young Berliners can enjoy their free time in many different ways. There are numerous playgrounds, swimming pools, recreation centers, and athletic fields. There are also many youth organizations.

East Berlin. Life in East Berlin is dominated by the Communist Party. Even department stores are government controlled. East Berlin is not only the capital of East Germany but the center of its flourishing electronics industry. There is little unemployment, although individual prosperity has not greatly increased since the war. The wartime ruins near the wall remain deserted. But to the east, on the site of medieval Berlin, are many new government buildings, hotels, shops, restaurants, and modern apartments. Industrial plants and housing developments have been built along the outer edge of the city.

DOROTHEA SPADA
Journalist, *Die Stuttgarter Zeitung*

Reviewed by PRESS AND INFORMATION OFFICE
West Berlin

BERLIOZ, HECTOR (1803–1869)

Louis Hector Berlioz, one of the most original of all composers, was born near Grenoble, France, on December 11, 1803. His father, a country doctor, insisted that his son follow in his footsteps. In 1822 Hector was sent to the Medical School of Paris.

Berlioz hated medical school. Defying his father, he resigned and entered the Paris Conservatory to study music instead. As a boy he had played the flute and guitar for pleasure, but he had never studied music seriously before. He worked hard at the conservatory, but because he was a difficult and undisciplined young man, he often quarreled with his professors and did not learn as much as he might have.

After leaving the conservatory, Berlioz studied for a time in Italy. Then he returned to Paris and married an Irish actress. Though he was composing continuously, few of his works received public performances. They were too new for people to understand.

Berlioz earned almost nothing from his composing. To support his family, he wrote essays and musical criticism for the newspapers.

Finally he began to win fame. In 1843 he made a triumphant tour of Germany, conducting his own compositions. This was followed by equally successful trips to Austria, Russia, and England.

But in Paris Berlioz continued to be misunderstood. In 1863 his opera *The Trojans at Carthage,* meant to be his masterpiece, was a failure. Heartbroken, he stopped composing. He died in Paris on March 8, 1869. Since then his reputation has steadily grown. He is now regarded as one of the world's foremost composers and one of the first great conductors.

BERMUDA

Bermuda is a sunny group of islands in the vast Atlantic Ocean. The nearest land is Cape Hatteras, North Carolina, about 1,075 kilometers (670 miles) to the northwest.

The islands are a British colony known officially as the Bermudas or Somers Islands. The total land area is about 54 square kilometers (21 square miles), and the length of the island chain is 35 kilometers (22 miles). The land is shaped like a giant fishhook.

Nature was symbolic when it shaped Bermuda this way, for the islands are noted as a superb fishing area. Anglers have caught bonefish, wahoo, and tuna of record size in Bermuda waters. Over 600 species of fish have been found along the reefs and in the open sea around Bermuda. The Bermuda Government Aquarium has one of the world's finest collections of tropical marine fish.

THE PEOPLE

The population of Bermuda is about 57,000. About two thirds of the people are of African or mixed descent. The remainder are mostly of British origin. Some 10,000 American service personnel also live on the islands.

Bermuda is famous as a vacation and resort center. People come to relax in the pleasant climate and enjoy the scenic beauty. Because of its relative nearness to New York,

Bermuda is a favorite port for cruise ships. Planes carrying tourists fly daily between New York and the islands.

In a way Bermuda is of a different day and a different age. There are no large cities and no humming factories. The tempo of life is not hurried, as it is in much of the industrial world. The sound of a railroad train is never heard, for there are no railroads. Until 1946 automobiles were not permitted. Horse-drawn carriages and bicycles were used instead. Automobiles are now used, but their size and ownership are strictly limited. Many people ride bicycles and motorbikes.

THE LAND

Bermuda's islands are the most northerly coral islands in the world. There are no natural lakes or streams in all Bermuda. People depend on rainfall for drinking water. The rain that falls on rooftops is channeled into cisterns, or tanks. In 1930 Sir Henry W. Watlington drilled into the hillsides and found a way of using the rainwater that lay trapped in the rock. Today this water is piped into Hamilton and some other communities.

The Gulf Stream makes Bermuda's climate unusually mild for a region so far north of the equator. Tropical palms flourish on the islands. But Bermuda rarely has excessive heat in the summer. Ocean breezes sweep in off the water and cool the islands.

The seven largest islands are connected by bridges and causeways. This group is generally considered to be the "mainland" of Bermuda. Hamilton is the capital of Bermuda. This community of some 3,000 inhabitants contains most of Bermuda's shops and public buildings. Though it is a small port, Hamilton handles a large quantity of shipping.

THE ECONOMY

Bermuda has no heavy industries. Almost 70 percent of its income is from the tourist trade. There are a few small boat-building yards, a perfume factory, and a growing business in resort fashions. The government is encouraging light industry to settle on the far western end of the islands.

Bermuda's only important export is Easter lilies. Lily heads and cut lily stems are exported to the United States, Canada, and Britain. The Bermuda Easter lily is popular

BERMUDA

Hamilton, Bermuda's capital, is the island's main port. Although a British Colony for centuries, Bermuda is named after a Spanish navigator, Juan de Bermúdez, who discovered the uninhabited islands in 1503.

Because of its pleasant climate and scenic beauty, Bermuda is a land of leisure and holiday. Tourists enjoy swimming, sunbathing, and bicycle-riding.

because it blooms early and has a particularly sturdy stalk.

Almost all food and manufactured goods must be imported.

▶ HISTORY AND GOVERNMENT

A Spanish navigator, Juan de Bermúdez, entered the area some time in 1503. The islands were named after Bermúdez. However, no Spaniards ever settled there, nor was any claim made by Spain.

In 1609 a party of English settlers bound for Virginia was shipwrecked in Bermuda. Their ship, the *Sea Venture,* was beached on a reef. Passengers and crew came ashore on July 28, 1609. The *Sea Venture* was under the command of Sir George Somers. To this day July 28 is celebrated as Somers Day, the national holiday of Bermuda.

The first permanent settlement of Bermuda was made in 1612. In 1684 the islands were given the status of a self-governing colony. In 1815 the capital of the islands was moved from St. George to Hamilton. The British government granted a 99-year lease to the United States in 1941 for naval and air bases.

Bermuda is the oldest self-governing colony in the Commonwealth of Nations. The chief executive is the governor, who is the official representative of the Crown. The Bermuda parliament has two houses, the Legislative Council (the upper house) and the House of Assembly. The members of the Legislative Council are appointed by the British Crown, and the members of the House of Assembly are elected.

The first election in which all adults were allowed to vote was held in 1968. Women had been given the vote in 1944. But until 1968 only property owners could vote, and no political parties took part. Since that time Bermuda has moved toward greater equality between its black citizens and its white citizens, and labor unions have gained strength.

Reviewed by BERMUDA TRADE
DEVELOPMENT BOARD

BERNINI, GIOVANNI LORENZO (1598–1680)

Rome in the 17th century was filled with elegant statues, chapels, fountains, and palaces. Many of them were designed by Giovanni Lorenzo Bernini, the Italian sculptor, painter, and architect who ruled the artistic life of Rome for over 50 years.

Bernini was born on December 7, 1598, in Naples. His father, a sculptor, received a

Terra-cotta study for the equestrian statue of Louis XIV (1669?) by Giovanni Bernini. Galleria Borghese (Rome).

commission from the Pope and moved his family to Rome about 1605. Except for a short trip to Paris in 1665, Bernini spent his entire life in Rome. In 1639 he married Caterina Tezio; they had 11 children.

At 17 Bernini received his first commission: a series of statues for the villa of Cardinal Borghese. Among them is the famous *David,* whose tense figure, portrayed with great feeling, shows the taste of the baroque period. Another of his works is a study for a statue of King Louis XIV of France on horseback. Its curving, graceful lines show both Bernini's technical skill and his ability to produce dramatic effects.

Bernini died on November 28, 1680. He had been a painter, scenic designer, and decorator. But he was most famous for his sculpture and architecture. One of his most powerful works is the square outside of St. Peter's Church. There are 162 statues on top of the 200 columns. It is difficult to realize Bernini's importance without visiting Rome, the city to which he gave the fruits of his life.

BERRIES. See GRAPES AND BERRIES.

BESSEMER, SIR HENRY (1813–1898)

The thriving industrial city of Bessemer, Alabama, is named in honor of Sir Henry Bessemer, the English inventor who made the steel industry possible. In 1855 and 1856 he patented a method of purifying iron so that it could be made into steel cheaply and easily. This method, called the Bessemer process, and a machine called the Bessemer converter are still used in steel manufacturing.

Henry Bessemer was born January 19, 1813, in the village of Charlton in southern England. His father, also an inventor, had a factory there for casting type. Young Henry spent his spare time in his father's workshop, learning to make use of his natural mechanical ingenuity.

When he was 17 years old, Bessemer went to London, where he cast metal into artistic figures that were exhibited by the Royal Academy. Then he turned to embossing designs on cards and cloth, and in 1833 he invented a method of canceling tax stamps so that they could not be used again, illegally.

During his busy life Bessemer worked out and patented 114 inventions. One of the most profitable was a method of making gold paint. The money from this invention enabled him to experiment and develop his steelmaking process, the most important of all his inventions.

The Bessemer process practically created the modern steel industry. Before the invention of this process, steel could only be made in small batches and as a result was very expensive. Bessemer's discovery made possible large-scale production of steel. It has been ranked with printing, the magnetic compass, and the steam engine as an invention that changed the world.

In 1879 Bessemer was knighted in reward for his tax-stamp canceling process. He died on March 15, 1898.

See also IRON AND STEEL.

BETHUNE, MARY MC LEOD (1875–1955)

Mary McLeod Bethune was born twelve years after Lincoln issued the Emancipation Proclamation freeing black slaves. She helped bring about many changes that gave blacks more opportunities for jobs and education and for better living conditions.

Mary McLeod was born on July 10, 1875, near the small town of Mayesville, South Carolina. She was the 15th of 17 children born to Sam and Patsy McLeod, recently freed slaves who had become farmers.

Even after the Civil War ended, there were not many schools for black children in the South. Mary was 11 years old before a mission school was opened in Mayesville. She completed her education at the Moody Bible Institute in Chicago and went home to the South to teach. After her marriage to a teacher, Albertus Bethune, she moved to Florida and in 1904 opened a school for black girls in Daytona Beach.

The Daytona Normal and Industrial Institute for Negro Girls was only a shack, but its goals were high. The school's motto, "Enter to learn, depart to serve," described the aim of its founder, which was to educate black girls to become teachers.

The early years of the school were difficult. Few of the students were able to pay tuition. Mary Bethune raised the money to keep the school going by selling ice cream and sweet potato pies to winter visitors in Daytona Beach. Before long the school received donations that made it possible to add a high school, a small hospital, and then a college. Later the institute merged with a boys' college and became Bethune Cookman College.

As a leader of southern and national black women's organizations, Mary Bethune attracted the attention of officials in Washington. During the depression years of the 1930's, she served on the National Youth Advisory Board, which had been set up to help train young people for jobs. During World War II she worked as a special civilian assistant to the War Department to help end discrimination in the armed services.

The last years of Mary Bethune's life brought her many honors and rewards. She died on May 18, 1955.

High in the Himalayas of south central Asia lies the tiny kingdom of Bhutan. For most of its history this mountainous country has been a forgotten and seldom-visited part of the world. Even today it remains largely undeveloped and remote from modern life and technology.

▶ THE LAND

Snowy Himalayan peaks and bleak mountain uplands tower only a few kilometers from dense jungles and valleys rich with rice fields. There are three land regions—the High Himalayan region in the north, the Inner Himalayan region in central Bhutan, and the Duars plain in the south.

The High Himalayan region borders China. Many peaks in this part of Bhutan are part of the Great Himalayan range. They tower as high as 7,300 meters (24,000 feet). Even the lowest part of the region is more than half that height above sea level. Except for a few scattered Buddhist monasteries, the Great Himalayas are uninhabited.

Most Bhutanese live in the valleys of the Inner Himalayan region. These valleys are as high as 2,400 meters (8,000 feet) above sea level. Rainfall is moderate, and the valleys are broad, fertile, and healthful. Paro, the former capital, and Thimbu, the new and still-developing capital, are both found here.

South of the Inner Himalayan region is a narrow strip of the Duars plain. The plain must be crossed to reach the narrow valleys that lead through the jungle-covered Himalayan foothills into the valleys of central Bhutan. The southern part of the Duars plain is covered with tall grass and bamboo. The north is rugged and heavily forested. There are many wild animals. Few people live on the Duars plain because of the heavy rainfall, dense vegetation, and malaria-ridden swamps.

The climate of Bhutan is as varied as the land. The high elevation gives the northern interior bitterly cold winters. But the lowlands of southern Bhutan have a humid, tropical climate throughout the year.

▶ LIFE IN BHUTAN

Life in Bhutan is extremely isolated. Most Bhutanese are farmers; many are skilled artisans. Settlements often cluster around a *dzong* (a fortress or castle-monastery). Thimbu, where Indian engineers are helping to build the new capital, has none of the conveniences of a modern city. Bhutan discourages visitors and tourists.

Travel is very difficult in all parts of Bhutan. There are no railroads and few good roads. A gravel road connects Paro with Phunchholing, on the India-Bhutan border. A branch of this road goes to Thimbu. The road was built for military defense, with Indian aid. Indians are also helping to build hydroelectric power plants on Bhutan's rushing rivers.

The Bhutanese speak a Tibetan dialect, and most practice a form of religion known as Lamaism, or Tibetan Buddhism. A few people still cling to the old ways of Bon—the worship of things in nature—that was common in Tibet before the days of the Buddha.

Most houses are two stories high. In southern Bhutan they are usually built of mud brick and thatch. In the mountains they are built of stone. The family lives in one room on the upper floor, and the yaks and other farm animals are kept in the room below. The family sleeps on beds made of loose rice straw spread on the ground and covered with thick blankets of yak wool. Because there are no chimneys, the houses are often dark and smoky inside.

Before 1960 fewer than one person in a hun-

FACTS AND FIGURES

KINGDOM OF BHUTAN is the official name of the country. The Bhutanese call it Druk-Yul, which means "Land of the Dragon."

CAPITAL: Thimbu.

LOCATION: South central Asia. **Latitude**—26° 45′ N to 28° N. **Longitude**—89° E to 92°E.

AREA: 47,000 km² (18,147 sq mi).

POPULATION: 1,200,000 (estimate).

LANGUAGE: Dzongkha (official), Nepalese, dialects.

GOVERNMENT: Monarchy. **Head of state**—king. **International co-operation**—Colombo Plan, United Nations.

ECONOMY: Principal products—rice, yak wool, handicrafts. **Chief exports**—rice, timber, coal, fruit. **Chief imports**—fabrics, light machinery, gasoline. **Monetary unit**—ngultrum.

dred in Bhutan could read and write. Now there are many elementary schools, and the government is planning to build more in the near future. In the new schools, teachers from India teach the children to read and write, using the Bhutanese and Hindi alphabets. The children of well-to-do Bhutanese families are sent away to schools in India.

▶ THE ECONOMY

Bhutan's economy is based on farming. Most farms are in the fertile valleys of the Inner Himalayas. The land is cultivated in a series of terraces, each terrace bordered by a stone embankment. Rice and buckwheat are grown in the valleys and on the lower slopes. Rice is the country's leading export. Vast forests make timber an important resource.

Yaks, sheep, and goats are raised in all parts of Bhutan. These animals are used as beasts of burden as well as for their meat, milk, and hides. Yak milk is also used to make a creamy, yoghurt-like cheese.

▶ HISTORY AND GOVERNMENT

Old Tibetan manuscripts preserved in Buddhist monasteries tell us that about 300 years ago an influential Tibetan priest called Sheptoon La-Pha became the first man to proclaim himself king of Bhutan. His successors ruled

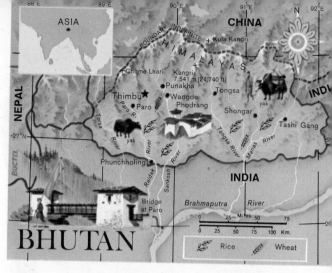

BHUTAN

Bhutan until 1907. In that year the British helped Sir Ugyen Wangchuk, the governor (*penlop*) of Tongsa, to become the king. Sir Ugyen Wangchuk was the most powerful of all the *penlops*. Jigme Dorji Wangchuk, the grandson of Sir Ugyen Wangchuk, ruled Bhutan until his death in 1972. He was succeeded by his son, Jigme Singye Wangchuk. There is a national assembly, the Tsongdu.

Bhutan's foreign affairs have been guided by India. Although Bhutan now maintains its own diplomatic corps, India still assists in its development efforts. Bhutan was admitted to the United Nations in 1971.

P. P. KARAN
University of Kentucky

Bhutanese come down from the hills to buy supplies in Phunchholing, a town near the foothills of the mighty Himalaya mountains.

BIBLE

The Bible, a collection of diverse books written in ancient times, is one of the world's most famous pieces of literature. The English word "Bible" comes from the Greek word *biblia,* meaning "books," and aptly describes this library of religious writings. The books form the sacred scripture of Jews, Christians, and, to some extent, Muslims. The Bible has had more influence on art, drama, language, and other literature than any other single collection of books. It has been translated into more languages and published in more editions than any other single collection, and it has remained a best seller up to modern times.

The Bible may be divided into three major sections: the Old Testament, the New Testament, and the Apocrypha. "Testament" comes from the Latin word *testamentum,* meaning "will," "covenant," or "agreement," and described for ancient Israelites and early Christians the type of relationship that they had with their God.

The Old Testament, composed of 39 books, makes up the sacred literature of Judaism. In addition, Christianity also accepts the 27 books of the New Testament. The remaining 14 books, called the Apocrypha, are sometimes referred to as the Inter-Testament, since they fall chronologically between the Old Testament and the New Testament. Acceptance of this part of the Bible has varied from time to time among Christian groups.

Transmission and Translation

How did these collections come down to us from ancient times? This handing down of Biblical materials is properly called transmission. Since the Old Testament is the earliest part of the Bible, its transmission must be considered first. Ancient Hebrews, whose literature this was, began to tell of their God and his relation to them long before they began to write. As a result, the material that finally became the Bible began in oral form. Around the campfires, at the village gates, and in religious services, this sacred history had its beginning. After a while some of the material was put into written form, and other material was written and added. The collections grew and were reworked through the centuries as men felt they had new insights from God or about God. Eventually "books" were put together and became fixed in written form. These were finally accepted as authoritative for religious use. The list of such accepted books is called canon (from a word meaning "rule"). The making of such a list is called canonization and took place at various times for various books or collections of books. Since the apocryphal books were never accepted by Judaism, they did not form part of the official canon in the Hebrew Bible.

Transmission of the New Testament was considerably different. The reason is that by the time Christianity began, the civilized world was using written language as a means of communication. As a result, the stories about the life and ministry of Jesus, the missionary work of the Apostles, letters to churches, and similar material soon spread all over the Roman Empire in written form. In the course of time, individual collections of these materials were made, books were formed, and eventually the whole collection known as the New Testament came into being and was accepted as canonical by the early Christian Church. There is also a New Testament Apocrypha, but it has never been widely used by Christians because of the high esteem in which the canonical books were held.

Hebrew, except for some Aramaic in Ezra and Daniel, was the language in which the

Old Testament was written. The New Testament books were recorded in Greek ("everyday," or *koinē,* Greek). How did the Bible get into English, then, along with so many other languages? This, of course, came about through translations, called versions, from the original Hebrew and Greek. Thus there are as many versions of the Bible as there are translations of it. Some of these have become very famous. They were either very early, in a language that had a wide use, or became the Bible for a particular group.

Earliest translations were obviously of the Old Testament. Probably the most important of these was the Greek translation called the Septuagint. The name of this translation, meaning "seventy," was derived from the tradition that it had been done by 70 scholars (actually 72—6 from each tribe of Israel) at the request of one of the Ptolemies of Egypt in the 3rd century B.C. About a century earlier the Samaritans, who also followed Jewish law, had made a translation of the first five books of the Hebrew Bible (the Pentateuch). In the early Christian period, another important translation, called the *Peshitta,* was made from the Hebrew Bible by Syriac-speaking Christians. Jewish scholars likewise made translations for popular use (more properly a paraphrase with commentary) called the *Targumim,* in Aramaic.

Early Christians had adopted the Greek version of the Old Testament because it could be understood by most of them. After a while, however, a need was felt to have both the Old Testament and the New Testament in the language that was becoming more widely used—Latin. One very early Latin translation was made (using the Greek Old Testament for that part of the Bible), called the Old Latin, or Itala. The most famous early Christian translation, however, was that made by Saint Jerome in the early 4th century A.D. Since this was in the common ("vulgar") language of the day, the version is still called the Vulgate. Jerome used both the Hebrew and Greek versions for his translation. The Church accepted Jerome's translation, and it became the official version of the Bible, although the older Latin translation of certain books continued in use. The most famous edition of this version is the Sixtine edition, done at the order of Pope Sixtus V in 1590.

Christian missionaries had also gone to all parts of the ancient world and carried the Bible with them. In many places the Hebrew, Greek, and Latin versions were translated into the language of the people among whom they worked. As a result, translations appeared in Arabic, Gothic, Coptic, Ethiopic, Armenian, and a myriad of other languages.

All these translations were written by hand. When the printing press was invented about 1450, the production of individual translations of the Bible, as well as editions in the original languages, was tremendously advanced. In the 16th century the Christian Church was divided into Roman Catholic and Protestant branches by the Church dispute called the Reformation. From that time both Catholics and Protestants began to make their own translations independently.

Many printed editions of the Bible appeared. Of them, the German translation (1522–32) of Martin Luther set the pattern for many others. Just about the same time, an English printed edition was issued by William Tyndale but was quickly suppressed by the authorities in England. About 1535, however, Myles Coverdale published an English translation, probably in Zurich. This time the Church was less opposed to a "popular" version, and Coverdale's Bible became widely read. A whole series of English Bibles then began to appear, with the names of translators (Matthew's Bible, Taverner's Bible) or of the cities of publication (the Geneva Bible) or even with descriptive titles (the Great Bible, because of its size) to identify them. Finally an approved Bible called the Bishops' Bible (a revision of the Geneva Bible) was published in England in 1568.

In France a group of English-speaking Roman Catholics also felt the need for a translation of the official Latin version of the Bible. As a result, an English translation of the Vulgate was completed between 1582 and 1610 and is still known as the Rheims-Douai Version, in honor of the two cities in which it was done.

King James I called a conference at Hampton Court in 1604 in an effort to reconcile the religious parties of England. Out of this conference came the King James Version of the Bible, published in 1611. This is perhaps the best-known English Bible and has continued in use up to the present time. It was supposed to be only a revision of the Bishops' Bible, but other editions and newly discovered manuscripts in the original languages were also used.

As English changed and more new copies of ancient Biblical manuscripts (texts) were found, revisions of the King James Version were made from time to time. The English Revised Edition was completed in 1881; the American Revised Edition (or American Standard Version) appeared in 1901; and the Revised Standard Version was published between 1946 and 1952. At the same time a great number of independent translations were made of all, or part, of the Bible. These include many translations into modern speech as well as many versions for special use.

OLD TESTAMENT

In Hebrew the Old Testament is divided into three parts: the Law, the Prophets, and the Writings. These divisions are not followed exactly in the English Bible but make the contents of the Old Testament easier to summarize. Traditionally attributed to Moses, the first five books of the Old Testament make up the Law, or Pentateuch. In Hebrew they are named after the first word of each book, but in English the names are derived from the Greek Bible: Genesis, Exodus, Leviticus, Numbers, and Deuteronomy. These books trace the relationship of man to God, in a series of agreements, beginning with creation, through the division of people into nations, to the days of Abraham. Then the record of the special relation of the Hebrews to God is told, from the time of Abraham's call by God into the land of Canaan.

Abraham and his descendants, the patriarchs, traveled through Canaan until the family of Joseph finally entered Egypt. There they were ultimately enslaved, made their escape under Moses (the Exodus), and fled to the Sinai Peninsula, between the Mediterranean Sea and the Red Sea. At Mount Sinai the people, now properly called Israelites, received the Law from God and prepared to enter the Promised Land. Because of arguments among some of the people, they were all forced to wander for 40 years in the desert wilderness. At the end of that time the Israelites were permitted to enter Palestine under the leadership of Joshua.

This group of five books contains a great variety of literary styles and types. Some of the stories illustrate great religious truths: the creation, the fall of man, the flood, the Tower of Babel, the Passover and Exodus, the giving of the tablets of the Law, and other short narratives. Certain of the books contain great poetry: the Song of Lamech, the Blessings of the Patriarchs, the Song of Moses, and the Blessing of Moses. Others tell about specific people: Noah and his scoffing neighbors, Abraham's faith, Lot's inquisitive wife, the cunning of Jacob, and the frustration of Balaam when all his curses against Israel became blessings. The land, the nations, and the local customs are also described: the wilderness experience, the fire and smoke at Mount Sinai, the varied inhabitants of Canaan, the building of the Ark of the Covenant, the casting of metals and weaving of cloth, the marriage of Rebecca and Isaac, and other details of everyday living. In addition, long lists of ancestors and descendants, codes of law, rules for festivals and sacred ceremonies, are also presented. Yet with all this diversity, the entire Pentateuch is held together by the religious faith that the God of Israel cared for his people, from the first man to the birth of the Israelite nation, and that He had made a covenant, or agreement, with that people. Obedience to the covenant brought Israel to the promised land, but disobedience to its terms brought disaster.

Next in the Hebrew Bible is the group of books called the Prophets because it contains those books that the Jews considered to be the work of men speaking for God. The word "prophet" comes from the Greek word *prophetes,* "one who speaks forth." This division of the Bible is composed of the Former Prophets—Joshua, Judges, I and II Samuel, I and II Kings; and the Latter Prophets—Isaiah, Jeremiah, Ezekiel, and the Book of the Twelve. This last "book" contains the books of Hosea, Joel, Amos, Obadiah, Jonah, Micah, Nahum, Habakkuk, Zephaniah, Haggai, Zechariah, and Malachi. Some books that are generally found among the prophetical books in the English Bible are not included in the Hebrew Bible under that title but are placed among the Writings. Certain of the prophetic books also have slightly different names in the Hebrew and Greek Bibles and in the versions used by Roman Catholics and Protestants.

The Former Prophets are books that consider the history of Israel from the conquest of Canaan under Joshua down to the release from prison of Jehoiachin, Israel's last king, by the Babylonian king, Evilmerodach, in about 561 B.C. Here, then, is the great story of the wars fought, the settlement of the land, the rise of the monarchy under Saul, the history of King David, Solomon's reign and the building of the first Temple, the split of the united monarchy into the kingdoms of Israel in the north and Judah in the south, the fall of Jerusalem, and the Babylonian exile.

This part of the Bible is probably the most interesting to read as literature because it is a connective history and contains stirring tales of battles, stories of great people, the life of David, and tales of court intrigues and plots. It also tells of the sad downfall of the two kingdoms of Judah and Israel. Also, since Hebrew literature was in its classical period at this time, one can find some of the best examples of both poetry and prose.

The Latter Prophets are less easy to summarize, since each has its own specific message. Isaiah, Jeremiah, and Ezekiel make up the Major, or Greater, books because they are the longer ones in this section of the Bible. Historically these prophets span the period from King Uzziah in the 8th century B.C., to the time of the exile during the 6th century B.C. Isaiah is concerned with the religious and political problems of Judah in his day as relations with Assyria became more and more difficult for the people. A great promise of new hope for Israel has been added to Isaiah's words (Deutero-Isaiah) as a fitting climax to his book. Isaiah's "call" to prophecy (Chapter 6) is one of the most impressive accounts in ancient Hebrew literature.

Jeremiah lived at the end of the monarchial period, during the trying days of the destruction of the city of Jerusalem. He, too, speaks against the religious and social decay of his own day, but gives to the people going into exile the promise of a new covenant. God, says Jeremiah, has now made a covenant with Israel that shall not be kept on tablets of stone, but shall be in the heart of every man, no matter where he goes. This was a message of great hope to a people saddened by the loss of their great city and forced to live in a strange land.

Ezekiel might be called the planner of Judaism because he gave to the Israelites in exile a plan whereby they could keep their faith alive in times of strife and struggle. With the writings of Ezekiel, the religion of Israel became known as Judaism and was closely linked with the Law and the Temple. The God of Israel became known as the Holy One in Israel, and Jews tried to honor this holiness by strict observance of the proper religious ritual and duties.

Not less important, however, are the Minor, or Lesser, Prophets. Their books are just "smaller in size," the meaning of the Latin word *minor* used to describe them. In the Hebrew Bible the Book of the Twelve just fills one scroll of writing material, so these prophetical books have been put together for that reason. Here, again, each prophet has his own particular message, and each is a separate book in itself. Amos is really the oldest of the prophetic writers and is the first literary, or written, prophet. Amos, Hosea, and Micah all preach against the social, political, and religious abuses of their individual periods, and each one declares that God will punish His people for their evil. Nahum, Zephaniah, and Habakkuk give their attention to specific foes of Israel—the Assyrians, the Scythians, and the Neo-Babylonians—and use those threats to the nation to stress the need for the people to trust and obey God. A little later, in the 6th century B.C., the prophet Obadiah uses the example of the fall of Edom, one of Israel's neighbors, to illustrate the action of God in the world and to stress hope for the future of his own people. Jonah, with the famous story of the great fish, urges the Jews, now restored to their homeland, to reform themselves. In the same way, the prophets Haggai, Zechariah, and Malachi speak to the new generation. In Haggai religious duty is centered upon the rebuilding of the Temple, and in Zechariah there is hope offered of a better age to come. In Joel, the last book among the prophets in terms of date, hope is again given to the people during a new time of national disaster.

Thus, the prophetical books of the Old Testament furnish a great array of religious ideas, individual styles and approaches, and relate to many historical situations. From these books have come many of the religious beliefs of Judaism and Christianity as well as many influences upon other literature through the ages. In English, for example, there are many expressions in common use today that have their origin in the Old Testament: "the fat of the land," "a man after his own heart," "the skin of my teeth," "one among a thousand," "angels' food," "eat, drink, and be merry," "see eye to eye," "holier than thou," "no new thing under the sun," "to every thing there is a season."

The final division of the Old Testament in the Hebrew Bible might be called Miscellaneous. In the section known as the Writings are those books that the Jewish leaders considered to be of religious worth but not of the same type as those of the other two divisions. Therefore, in this category are found Psalms, a collection of hymns or religious poems said to be composed by David; Proverbs, which gives helpful advice on everyday living; Job,

in which the whole meaning of human suffering is considered; The Song of Solomon, a love song, once seen to have religious application; Ruth, a story of deep personal devotion as well as a protest against racial bigotry; Lamentations, a series of sorrowful reflections concerning the exile and the sad plight of the people; Ecclesiastes, a book of "wisdom," or religious philosophy; Esther, which explains the festival of Purim; Daniel, a book of stories of heroes, which urges religious faithfulness in a time of oppression; I and II Chronicles, Ezra, and Nehemiah, which summarize Israel's history up to the exile and then give an account of the events that followed.

Here, again, the individual books of this part of the Bible are all different and each one has its own special characteristics. Likewise, each of these books has had its own influence upon religious thought and upon the literature of the world. Psalms, for example, has furnished the basis for many hymns still sung in places of worship; Job has provided much material for modern literature; Ruth and Esther have given the world two great heroines; while Daniel and his friends have found their place in folk songs, art, and in such popular quotations as "the handwriting on the wall" or "into the lions' den."

PHILIP C. HAMMOND
Princeton Theological Seminary

APOCRYPHA

The Apocrypha were written between the 3rd and 1st centuries B.C. Although they have come down to us in Greek, Latin, and other translations, including the English of the King James Bible that was published in 1611, fragments of the Apocrypha in the original Hebrew and Aramaic have been found among the Dead Sea Scrolls from the caves around Qumran, in northwest Jordan.

For Catholics most of the Apocryphal books are sacred. For Protestants and Jews the Apocrypha are respected as instructive writings, but not as divinely inspired.

Judaism between the 3rd century B.C. and the 1st century A.D. was split into many sects. The rabbis felt it necessary to put an end to the developments that were dividing the peo-

ple. They chose a simple way out. By excluding all books written after the fall of the Persian Empire in the 4th century B.C., the rabbis removed the authority of all the later writings that were splitting the community. This is why the Old Testament does not include any books that were thought to come from the period after Alexander's conquest in the 4th century B.C.

The Apocrypha begin with the First Book of Esdras. This book has to do with the return of the Jews from their Babylonian exile to Palestine in the days of the Old Testament leaders Ezra and Nehemiah. The most famous passage from this book is the tale of the Three Guardsmen (3:1—5:6), showing that truth is the most powerful force in the world.

The Second Book of Esdras justifies God's ways through divinely inspired visions.

The Book of Tobit is a story about virtue and love. It has enough magic to make the tale doubly interesting. The dog appears as man's pet and companion in Tobit for the first time in Jewish literature.

The Book of Judith is about the trials of the Hebrew people. The heroine Judith saves her people by cutting off the head of the enemy general, Holofernes.

There are six additions to the Book of Esther. These additions, examples of how reverent the Apocryphal books are, add religious tone to the Old Testament Book of Esther, which never even mentions the name of God.

The most important literary books in the Apocrypha are known as Wisdom Literature. This type of writing has as its aim the improvement of men through virtuous and sensible living so that they may be respected in society and successful in their careers. The first of these Apocryphal books is The Wisdom of

An 11th-century Psalter (Book of Psalms) in Greek.

An illuminated page, in Latin, from the Gutenberg Bible. Johann Gutenberg invented printing from movable type.

This page from a Hebrew Bible begins the history of the Israelites in Egypt.

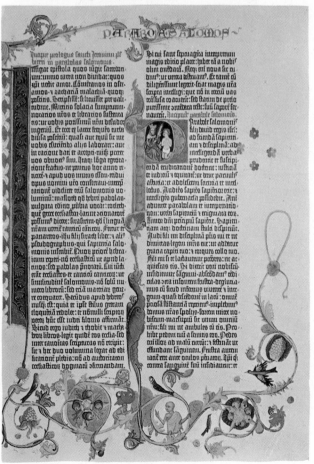

Jeremiah

Jonah

Paintings of famous prophets are a part of Michelangelo's work in the Sistine Chapel, St. Peter's, Rome.

Zechariah

Isaiah

Ezekiel

Solomon, which praises "Lady Wisdom," not a woman of flesh and blood, but wisdom treated as a divine person. The author of The Wisdom of Solomon is not only interested in teaching wise principles. He wants, in addition, to save the people from uncivilized heathenism.

The other book of Wisdom Literature is in many ways the finest composition in the Apocrypha. It is called Ecclesiasticus or The Wisdom of Jesus, Son of Sirach ("Jesus" is simply the Greek form of the old Hebrew name "Joshua"). Ecclesiasticus is a practical as well as a reverent teacher. While he advises us to turn to God with piety and prayer to save us from misfortune and illness, he reminds us that physicians and medicines have been created by God for our benefit (38: 1–15). He praises the practice of justice and reminds us that good character brings rich rewards. Life is short but a good name endures forever. Ecclesiasticus ends his book by telling us, "Work your work betimes, and in his time he will give you your reward."

The Book of Baruch is supposed to come from the pen of Baruch, the secretary of the Prophet Jeremiah. Among the books of the Apocrypha, this one comes closest to Old Testament prophecy. It ends with an appendix, The Letter of Jeremiah, in which the prophet tells the Jewish exiles in Babylonia to avoid worshiping idols.

There are three additions to the Old Testament Book of Daniel. (1) The story of Susanna tells how Daniel saved Susanna from the false accusations of two evil elders. (2) The story of the Three Children tells about Shadrach, Meshach, and Abednego, who according to the Book of Daniel were thrown into the fiery furnace. It is typical of Apocryphal literature to fill gaps in the "authoritative books." Since the Book of Daniel does not tell us what happened to the three men after they were thrown into the fiery furnace, a later author took advantage of the opportunity to write this story. (3) The story of Baal and the Dragon tells how Daniel proved to the king of Babylon that idols are false and God is true.

The Prayer of Manasseh is supposed to be the prayer recited, according to the Biblical II Chronicles 33:18, by the repentant King Manasseh of Judah. This composition is of high religious and literary quality.

The Apocrypha end with First and Second Maccabees. First Maccabees, covering the years 167–134 B.C., is a reliable historic account of the Jewish war against Antiochus Epiphanes and the developments that followed. Antiochus, whose empire included Palestine, tried to force the Jews to conform to Greek culture at the expense of their ancestral religion. The Jews rebelled under the leadership of the Maccabean brothers. Their victory is still celebrated by the Jews during the feast of Hanukkah.

Second Maccabees is more emotional than First Maccabees and is concerned with its special kind of Jewish viewpoint. Second Maccabees covers the period 175–160 B.C. It is not a continuation of First Maccabees but another account covering some of the same years.

CYRUS H. GORDON
Brandeis University

NEW TESTAMENT

The New Testament is that part of the Bible that is the heritage of Christians. It states a new relation between man and the God of Israel, in the person of Jesus of Nazareth. He is seen by the writers of the New Testament as the long-awaited Messiah of Israel and of the whole world, and is known by the Greek word for "Messiah," or "Saviour," which is "Christ."

The New Testament was written mainly in the days of the Roman Empire and covers the historical period from the last part of the reign of King Herod (37–4 B.C.) to just after the destruction of Jerusalem in A.D. 70. Often this period is referred to in Christian writings as "the fullness of time," because of the religious significance of the coming of Jesus. But it was a "full time" historically as well. Roman government had brought peace to most of the civilized world; Greek language had made international communication easy; and the weakening of the hold of old pagan gods on

For a Bible published in 1866 Paul Gustave Doré did this illustration of the miracle of the loaves and fishes.

the people had provided an atmosphere that welcomed a new faith.

Followers of Jesus, called the Apostles, began to spread the story of the risen Lord to all the world. The Apostles themselves went from town to town, preaching and teaching. From that activity the New Testament was born. First came collections of Jesus' own words; then the stories about his life and work, as well as letters to various individuals or groups explaining Christianity. Since writing had now become more common, these materials were written down very quickly or even appeared in written form originally (for example, the letters). As a result, the New Testament evolved into written form, then into collections of written books, and finally into the collection of canonical books, much more rapidly than the Old Testament did. Very soon these writings were considered to be equal in importance, in the religious sense, to the Old Testament, which Christians shared with their Jewish neighbors. Thus the New Testament was also regarded as holy, or sacred, literature for Christians.

When we examine the New Testament, we again see a collection of diverse books under one cover. Again divisions can be made in the material, just as the earliest Christians made them. In the New Testament the two main divisions consist of Gospels and Epistles, plus a single book called Revelation.

The Gospels are books that tell the story of Jesus—what he did, what he said, how he acted in relation to people. These books are four in number and bear the names of their writers, Matthew, Mark, Luke, and John. The early Church considered these to be the four best books of the many written about Jesus. Thus, they attributed them to Apostles or to close associates of the Apostles. They are called Gospels because that word means "good news"—the good news of Jesus' message and life for the world.

The Gospel of Mark stresses the human side of Jesus and explains many of the Jewish customs and words for Gentile readers. It is therefore referred to as the "human" Gospel or the "Roman" Gospel (to explain that it was written for non-Jewish readers). It begins the story of Jesus with his baptism in the river Jordan and ends with his appearances to the Apostles after his Crucifixion.

The Gospel of Matthew, on the other hand, is sometimes called the "Jewish" Gospel because of the arrangement of its material. In this book Jesus' teachings are carefully set down into categories for easy reference, just as the Jewish teachers in that period classified their teachings. There are really five such divisions in Matthew: Jesus' ancestry and birth, which introduces his baptism and temptation, leading up to his first "sermon"; stories of healing, with instructions to the disciples; Jesus' relation to John the Baptist and to other religious leaders, with a series of parables, or teaching stories; more healing stories, the feeding of the multitude, and the story of the Transfiguration; the Judaean ministry of Jesus, the triumphal entry into Jerusalem, parables, other teachings, and a conclusion that tells of his death and resurrection.

The Gospel of Luke is really a letter and should be read with Luke's other book, The Acts of the Apostles. Both books form what is called an apologia, or defense, of Christianity to the non-Christian world. Luke begins his Gospel with the birth of Jesus and a brief narrative of his boyhood, his ancestry, and his work. Since Luke tells so many stories about

Jesus' ministry to the common people, this Gospel is often spoken of as the "social" Gospel. In the Book of Acts the "history" of Jesus' message is continued, as it was carried out into the Gentile world by the Apostles and other missionaries. Again Luke is concerned with the effect of this message on people and their lives. The book therefore tells about the early Christian Church as it developed and grew from Jerusalem and other early centers of the ancient world.

The Gospel of John is quite a different book. It is not so much a story about Jesus as it is an interpretation of who and what he was. The language is more philosophical and is therefore harder to read. In early Christian art John was depicted as an eagle because his writings soared to such great height. John likes to contrast light and darkness, for example, in speaking about Jesus' relation to the world, and he likes to use many similes and metaphors. He begins his Gospel "In the beginning . . ." and shows how God entered the world because of his love for man. This view of Jesus is called the Incarnation (that is, God becoming man and living among men), and John stresses the reality and meaning of it for the world.

These four Gospels were written down to preserve the sayings and works of Jesus for future generations. They were all written relatively soon after his death, probably all before A.D. 100. At the same time that the Gospels were being put into writing, so were the Epistles, or Letters, which form the second main division of the New Testament. As people began to join the Christian sect questions were asked, problems came up, communications were sent, and disputes arose. Thus, letters began to be written by important Church leaders such as Paul, James, John, and others. They were carefully preserved by those who received them, often recopied, and were gradually collected. Since they dealt with important matters, they were finally joined with the Gospels and became part of the official literature of Christianity.

Traditionally the Epistles are classified into Pauline Epistles, attributed to the Apostle Paul, and General, or Catholic (in the sense of worldwide), Epistles, which were not addressed to any one particular church. To these are added the Epistle to the Hebrews, whose author is unknown, and the Book of Revelation.

The Pauline Epistles include the letters to individual churches: Romans, Galatians, I and II Thessalonians, I and II Corinthians, Philippians, Colossians, and Ephesians; along with letters to two young Church leaders named Timothy and Titus. Most of these letters are concerned with specific problems Paul wished to discuss with particular churches or groups, as well as answers to questions that they had asked him. One additional letter, however, known as Philemon, concerns a runaway slave.

In the letter to the Romans, Paul presented a system of Christian belief as he saw it, in order to instruct the people. To the Galatians, Paul wrote about the independence of Christians from some aspects of the Jewish law and gave warnings about falling away from the teachings that he, himself, had given them. Moral and theological problems arose in Thessalonika and Corinth, and Paul's letters to those people consider those issues, as well as matters of Church discipline and his own authority to deal with them. The letters to the Philippians, Colossians, and Ephesians stress the need for loyalty to Jesus' teachings and for loyalty within the Church itself. By this time

The German artist Albrecht Dürer created this engraving called *The Holy Family*.

some teachers had arisen in the Church who wished to modify or change the teachings of the original disciples of Jesus. As a result, Paul was often called upon to decide issues of faith and warn the people against false ideas. The letters to Timothy and Titus reflect somewhat the same problems. They are called pastoral letters, since Paul was giving advice to young men in charge of churches in regard to meeting theological problems, to conducting themselves, and to settling problems within their churches. The letter of Philemon stands by itself in the Pauline collection because it did not result from any question asked Paul, but from his own interest in a runaway slave, Onesimus, whom he had met. Paul sent Onesimus back to his master, Philemon, with a message stressing Christian brotherhood and freedom in Christ.

The anonymous letter to the Hebrews is unusual not only because it is unsigned, but the name of its author never seems to have been known in the early Church. Like the Gospel of John it is a more philosophical letter. Its purpose was to urge faithfulness to Christianity in a time of great persecution. It accomplishes its purpose by using much of the Old Testament to trace the history of faith down to the writer's own time, with Jesus seen as the fulfillment of the ancient promises of God.

Seven letters, the General Epistles, are known by their writers' names but were not addressed to any particular groups. These letters also arose from specific problems or from theological disputes in the Church, just as did the letters of Paul. The letter of James thus stresses good works along with faith, in order to keep Christians active as well as faithful. The two letters of Peter try to answer questions about suffering (I Peter) and to stress morality as an important Christian virtue (II Peter). John's first two letters meet problems arising out of false teachings by insisting on the "reality" of Jesus as human, as well as asserting his divine aspect. These letters thus mirror a controversy in the early Church concerning the nature of Jesus. Such controversies are termed Christological because they were about interpretations of Christ. The third letter of John is administrative and considers matters of Church government and authority. Jude returns to the matter of false teachings and again insists on the Christian interpretation of the life and ministry of Jesus. Many of the General Epistles relate to matters of interpretation, both of theological and administrative affairs. The early Church was growing rapidly, and many new converts had no background in the Old Testament viewpoints from which much of the thinking of Christianity had come. In addition, groups began to arise within the Church who wished to modify or change the words of Jesus, or to offer new interpretations. As these issues arose they had to be settled, reconciled, or denied by the leaders of the early Church.

The book called The Revelation of John is an apocalypse. That is a particular type of writing, full of hidden symbols and word pictures and often oriented toward some indefinite "end of time" sometime in the future. The symbols used by the writer of Revelation were such that they were familiar to Christians but hidden from non-Christians. When this book was written, Christians were undergoing persecution. The author therefore urged them to remain faithful, for Christianity would finally triumph over evil through Jesus, the Christ. The word pictures also helped to make the author's ideas alive—people could "see" what the author was trying to say in words. Since the Rome authorities could not understand the symbols and word pictures in the book, Christians could read it publicly and not be in danger of arrest. This book is very rich in beautiful allusions and has had a great effect on other Christian literature through the ages.

The Bible is a book of variety: the Old Testament gives us the record of ancient promise, while the the New Testament discusses its fulfillment for Christians in the person and message of Jesus. The period between the two is spanned in both history and ideas by the Apocrypha.

PHILIP C. HAMMOND
Princeton Theological Seminary

Entire article reviewed by JAMES I. MCCORD
President, Princeton Theological Seminary

A. L. SACHAR
President, Brandeis University

MSGR. JOHN J. VOIGHT
Secretary of Education, Archdiocese of New York

See also BIBLE STORIES.

BIBLE STORIES

The Bible is great literature. Many writers have retold its stories for boys and girls. The following selections from the Old and New Testaments were adapted by Walter Russell Bowie.

▶ NOAH'S ARK

From the years far back, before the Bible was written, there had been handed down the tale that one time the earth had grown so wicked that there seemed nothing for God to do but to wash it clean and to start again.

God had to find someone fit to make the new start, and the one he found was Noah. God told Noah that there was going to be such a flood as had never been seen before. The waters would be so wide and deep that they would cover all the earth. God said that Noah must build a boat that would be big enough to take in all his family and also two of every sort of bird and animal he could find in the whole world. The boat was to be like a floating house, and it should be called the ark. It needed to be big, considering all that was going to be in it!

So Noah began to build the ark. It was a hard job to build such a tremendous boat, and it must have been all the harder when the neighbors stood around and laughed. "Who ever heard of building a boat in a dry meadow?" they asked. There the sun was shining down, and there was not enough water to float a stick, much less a thing like this huge ark. Noah must be crazy! But Noah kept on working.

Then one day it began to rain. Noah and his family went into the ark and took with them a male and female of every kind of living thing that came walking and running and creeping and flying from the face of the earth. As the water came up higher, the ark was lifted up and floated above the meadows.

When it started to rain, Noah, his family, and a male and female of every kind of animal went into the ark.

Goliath, armed with a sword, a spear, and a shield, came toward David. David drew back his arm and whirled his sling with deadly aim.

It kept on raining, and it rained harder. Day after day the water poured out of the sky as if the earth had been turned upside down and the ocean put on top. Forty days and forty nights it rained.

All the other people and creatures had climbed up to the tops of the hills to try to be out of the reach of the flood. But at last every spot of earth was covered, and nothing was left alive except Noah and his family and what they had with them in the ark.

At last the rain stopped and the sun came out, but for a hundred and fifty days the ark floated on the waters, above the empty earth. Then, little by little, the flood began to go down. One day Noah felt the bottom of the ark jolt on something, and there it was, scraping the top of the highest mountain that had been in all that part of the earth—Mount Ararat. No other land could be seen around it, but Noah knew that before long the rest of the earth would begin to be uncovered.

Noah went into the part of the ark where the birds were. He took a dove and opened a window and let the dove fly away. But presently the bird came fluttering back in the window again, because it had not found a single dry spot anywhere to rest.

A week longer Noah waited. Then he sent the dove out again. This time when the dove came back it carried in its bill a green olive leaf. Noah knew by this that somewhere the earth and the trees were rising above the water. Once more he sent the dove out. This time the dove did not

come back at all, and Noah knew that it had found a place to build its nest.

Then at last the ark itself settled down on solid ground. Noah opened the doors, and he and his family and all the beasts and birds and everything else came flying and running and scrambling out, glad to be back on the earth again.

Noah thanked God, and when he looked up he saw a rainbow in the sky. The rainbow was God's sign—the sign of his promise that "while the earth remaineth, seedtime and harvest and cold and heat and summer and winter and day and night shall not cease."

▶ DAVID AND GOLIATH

About that time the Philistines collected an army again and marched up into a valley in the land of Israel. They had with them a man who was as huge as a giant. His name was Goliath. On his head he wore a helmet of brass, and he had armor on his body and on his legs. His spear was as thick as a wooden beam, and his armor-bearer went before him with his great shield.

Every day Goliath came out into the valley between the camp of the Philistines and the camp of Israel and dared any man to come and fight him. But nobody dared, not even Saul. So Goliath shouted and strutted and shook his spear. "I defy the armies of Israel," he cried. "Give me a man that we may fight together!"

Now the three elder sons of Jesse, the brothers of David, were in Saul's army. David had gone back to Bethlehem for a while to take care of his father's sheep. One day, while the armies of Israel and of the Philistines were watching each other, Jesse decided to send his soldier sons some food—parched corn and bread and cheese. He told David to carry the food to the camp and give it to his brothers, and to find out how they were.

Early the next morning David left the sheep in charge of another shepherd, and started off. When he reached the camp of Israel there was a great stir in both armies, and a noise of shouting as of a battle about to begin.

David ran ahead until he found his three brothers. As he stood there talking with them, out came Goliath. He was shouting, as he always did, "What are you here for? I am a Philistine, and you are servants of Saul. Choose a man on your side, and let him come out and fight me. If he can kill me, we will be your slaves; but if I kill him, you shall be slaves to us. I defy you!"

The men around David drew back. None of them had any idea of going out to fight Goliath. They said to David, "You see that man? Whoever kills him will be rich. And Saul will give him his daughter to marry, and will make his family great in Israel."

As David looked at Goliath, he was filled with anger and contempt. "Who is this Philistine," he said, "that he should defy the armies of the living God?"

Eliab, his oldest brother, heard David say that, and was annoyed. "Why did you come down here?" he demanded. "And who have you left to keep those few sheep in the wilderness? I know your pride, and I know that you have come down here just to watch us fight."

David asked Eliab what he had done to make him speak like that. There was reason for his being there, and he would show it, too. He was not going to be frightened by Goliath, or by anyone else.

Presently the army began to talk of this young man, David, who had turned up in the camp, and word about him came to Saul. Saul sent for him. Here was the same lad who had been his armor-bearer and had played for him on the harp!

"Nobody need be troubled about Goliath," David said to Saul. "I will fight with this Philistine."

"You cannot fight with this Philistine," said Saul. "You are only a boy, and this man has been a fighter ever since he grew up."

But David had a different idea. "I have kept my father's sheep," he said, "and once there came a lion, and another time a bear, and took a lamb out of the flock. I went out after those beasts and killed them, and saved the lambs. Both the lion and the bear I killed, and this heathen Philistine shall be like them, since he has defied the armies of the living God. The Lord God who saved me from the paw of the lion and from the paw of the bear will save me from this Philistine."

Saul looked at David and thought for a moment. Then he said, "Go, and the Lord be with you." He put his own armor on David, helmet and breastplate and all, and he gave David his own sword. But David said he could not do anything in that heavy armor. He had never worn armor before, and he did not know how to handle a sword. He took them off, and gave them back to the king. Then David went down to a brook that ran through the valley. There he chose five smooth stones. He put these into the shepherd's bag which he wore at his waist. In one hand was his shepherd's staff, and in the other, his sling. With these David went out to meet the giant Philistine.

On came Goliath, with the man who carried his shield walking in front. When Goliath caught sight of David, he laughed. "Am I a dog," he shouted, "that you come to me with a stick?" And he cursed David by all his gods. "Come on," he said, "and I will give your flesh to the birds and beasts!"

But David answered: "You come to me with a sword, and with a spear, and with a shield; but I come to you in the name of the Lord of Hosts, the God of the armies of Israel, whom you have defied. This day the God of Israel will deliver you into my hands. I will kill you, and take your head from your body. The carcasses of the army of the Philistines I will give this day to the birds and the beasts, that all the earth may know that there is a God in Israel. Yes, all these people shall know that the Lord does not save with the sword and spear. The battle is the Lord's, and he will give you today into our hands."

The Philistine came on with heavy steps. David ran toward him. Putting his hand into his bag, David took out a stone and fitted it into his sling. His arm drew back and whirled with deadly aim. Out from the sling the smooth stone shot, and whistled through the air. It caught Goliath between the eyes and sank into his forehead. Goliath, the giant, pitched forward on his face.

As he fell, David ran and stood over him. He drew Goliath's own sword out of its sheath and cut off his head.

When the Philistines saw that, they fled in panic. The Israelites, shouting, poured after them along the valley and down across the country as far as the gates of Ekron. Then the army of Saul came back and took everything that was in the tents of the Philistines. But all David wanted was the armor of Goliath.

The sailors threw Jonah overboard. He had hardly touched the water when a whale came up and swallowed him.

▶ JONAH

Jonah was commanded by God to go and preach to the great and wicked city of Nineveh. This was the very city from which armies had often come to make war against the people of Israel.

Jonah did not want to go to Nineveh. Instead, he went down to the city of Joppa on the sea. There he found a ship that was going in the opposite direction from Nineveh. He paid his fare, went on board, and sailed away.

The ship had not gone far before a tremendous storm arose. The sailors were frightened and they began to pray. They threw overboard much of the cargo to lighten the ship and give it a better chance to keep afloat when the great waves broke over it. In spite of all the commotion, Jonah was asleep down below the decks. The captain went down and awoke him, and asked him to pray to God that they all might be saved.

But the sailors thought that this storm had come because there was an especially wicked person on the ship. They drew lots to see who it might be. The lot fell upon Jonah. Then the sailors asked him who he was, and what he had done, and why he was on the ship.

Jonah admitted that he was running away from God and from what God had told him to do.

The sailors tried to bring the ship to land. When they could not do this, they took Jonah and threw him overboard.

Hardly had Jonah touched the water, when up came a huge fish, like a whale, and swallowed him. Inside the fish, Jonah had plenty of time to think about God and to change his mind.

After three days, the fish came close to shore and cast up Jonah, unhurt, on the dry land. Now again Jonah heard the voice of God speaking in his heart. Once more it told him to go to Nineveh and preach there. This time he went. He preached that Nineveh and all its people would be destroyed unless they repented of their wickedness.

To Jonah's surprise, the people of Nineveh listened and repented. They fasted and put on sackcloth in sorrow for their sins. Even the king took off his royal robes, dressed himself in sackcloth, and sat down in ashes as a sign of being ashamed for the city's sins. And he gave a command that all the people should pray to God, and that everyone should turn away from whatever wickedness he had been doing.

But instead of being glad that his preaching had had such a great and wonderful result, Jonah was annoyed. He did not like Nineveh. He had not wanted to go there in the first place, and he did not want any good to come to Nineveh because of him. He began to complain to God. He said he had known that God was merciful and slow to anger and full of love and kindness, but he had not wanted God or anyone else to feel that way toward Nineveh. So far as he was concerned, he would rather die than see Nineveh blessed by God. So Jonah went outside the city. He made himself a little shelter and sat there alone and pouted, waiting to see what would happen.

It was very hot in the sun where Jonah sat. When God made a gourd vine to grow and cover Jonah's thin shelter with its cool green leaves, Jonah was pleased. But the next morning worms began to eat the gourd vine, and it withered.

When the sun rose there came a sultry east wind. The sun beat down so hot on Jonah's head that he fainted, and again he wished that he were dead.

At last God spoke to Jonah in a way to bring him to his senses. "You are angry because your gourd vine is withered," he said.

Jonah blurted out, "Yes, I am angry. I do well to be angry."

Then said the voice of God: "You did not make this gourd vine in the first place, and you did not make it grow. It was a thing that came up overnight and lasted only a day. And you are angry because it is gone. Yet here is Nineveh, the great city with more than a hundred thousand people in it and all the cattle upon which they depend, and you want to have it all destroyed."

So the Book of Jonah ends, and at least some men among the people of Israel began to appreciate its meaning: that God has pity upon all peoples, and that men must have pity too.

▶DANIEL IN THE LIONS' DEN

Belshazzar was slain, and Darius, the king of Media, took his throne.

At first Daniel was honored by the new king even more than he had been honored before. Darius appointed a hundred and twenty princes as governors in the kingdom. Three of these he put in authority over all the others, and among these three Daniel stood first, so that he was next to the king.

That made the princes jealous. They did not want Daniel to be greater than they were. So they began to whisper among themselves, and to try to plan a way to get rid of Daniel. They knew that they could not find Daniel doing wrong. Everything that he did for the king was done well. But suppose they could persuade the king, without his thinking much about it, to make some law that Daniel would think was wrong. They knew that Daniel would not obey such a law. Then, if the king had solemnly declared that anyone who disobeyed it should be punished, they would have Daniel in a trap.

So the princes went to the king. They said to him that it was a dangerous thing to have people of other religions in his kingdom. Why could not everyone think as the king thought and believe what he believed? They suggested that the king give an order that for the next thirty days no one in the kingdom should pray to any god, or act as though even in heaven there could be anyone more important than the king.

The king, without stopping to understand just what might happen, gave the order and signed it with his royal seal. Then the princes who had persuaded him to do that persuaded him also to say that a law, signed and sealed in that fashion, would always be the law, and never could be changed.

Now they were ready to have their revenge on Daniel. When the law had been proclaimed, they watched to see what he would do. Daniel did just what they thought he would do. Law or no law, he went into his house at his regular times to pray. With the windows wide open, he knelt down, with his face turned toward Jerusalem, the Holy City, and prayed to God, just as he had always done.

The men who were trying to trap Daniel went off to tell the king. Had not the king made a law that for thirty days no one in his kingdom

Daniel was thrown into a den of lions, but the lions did not hurt him.

should pray to any god or make any petition to anyone except the king himself? And had it not been declared that any person who dared to disobey that law should be thrown into a den of lions? Well, there was one man who had paid no attention; one man who had gone right on praying as though what the king ordered did not matter.

"Who has done this?" the king wanted to know. And the princes told him it was Daniel.

Now the king was exceedingly sorry and distressed. All day long he thought and tried to find some way by which he could save Daniel. But he had made the law. Besides that, he had been persuaded into declaring that it should be one of the laws of the Medes and Persians that never could be changed. There was nothing left for him to do but to give the order that Daniel should be brought and thrown into a den of lions.

And so Daniel was put into the den where the lions were. The gate was fastened, and sealed with the king's own seal, so that no friend of Daniel could come and let him out.

The king grew more and more distressed. That night in his palace he would not eat, and he would not let any musicians play. When he lay down on his bed he could not sleep. Early the next morning he got up and went to the mouth of the den. In a miserable voice, hardly hoping for anything, he called, "Daniel, servant of the living God, has your God been able to save you from the lions?"

To his amazement and joy, he heard the voice of Daniel from the den, saying, "God has sent his angel and shut the lions' mouths so that they have not hurt me."

The king was filled with great joy. He ordered that Daniel should be taken out of the lions' den immediately. And there he was, safe and sound, not even scratched.

When the king thought of the men who had planned to have Daniel thrown into the den of lions, he ordered that they and everybody connected with them should be thrown in there themselves.

▶ **THE BOY JESUS**

When Jesus was twelve years old, he went with Joseph and Mary to Jerusalem to celebrate the Feast of the Passover. This was the greatest festival of the Jewish year. It had begun far back in the time of Moses, when the people of Israel were slaves in the land of Egypt. They had worked there making bricks for the temples and for the great monuments which Pharaoh, king of Egypt, commanded to be built. The story of all that happened then is written in the Old Testa-

ment Book of Exodus. The Feast of the Passover was the glad reminder of the way in which Moses helped the people of Israel to escape from Egypt and led them across the Red Sea to Palestine, the Promised Land. Everyone was happy when this festival came. It made men proud to remember God's help long ago, and it filled them with belief that God was with them still.

Jewish families always wanted to celebrate the Passover in Jerusalem, where the Temple was. Thousands and thousands of people, beyond anybody's counting, went up to the Holy City at Passover time. All of them were happy at the thought that they were going to see Jerusalem, the Holy City. They sang the beautiful old songs called the "pilgrim songs," which had first been written hundreds of years before.

One of them began:

"I was glad when they said unto me,
Let us go into the house of the Lord.
Our feet shall stand within thy gates,
    O Jerusalem."

And another song began:

"As the mountains are round about Jerusalem,
So the Lord is round about his people from
    henceforth even for ever."

Hardly anything could have been so exciting to Jesus as this first journey to Jerusalem. Joseph's family and their friends walked together in the midst of the growing crowds. The neighbors went too, and people from other towns along the way joined them. They stopped now and then by the roadside to eat the food they had brought with them. It was much more than one day's journey from Nazareth to Jerusalem. So at night they made a place to sleep on the ground and lay down under the open skies and the stars.

The Passover was in the spring, when the fruit trees were blossoming and the fields were bright with flowers. The road from Nazareth to Jerusalem led across the wide Plain of Esdraelon. Jesus knew the stories of the heroes who had walked on that same ground. Gideon had been there with his three hundred men; and David, and Jonathan, and Saul. Many armies had marched across it. Here and there in the earth one might come upon a broken sword blade or a piece of rusty iron from a chariot that had lain there for hundreds of years, left from some battle with the Philistines or the Egyptians or the terrible armies of the Assyrians.

After the pilgrims to Jerusalem had crossed the Plain of Esdraelon, they did not keep straight on. Instead, they crossed the Jordan River and

The young Jesus talked with the oldest and wisest teachers in the Temple court.

went through the country on the east side of the river. Jesus knew that this was because the people of Israel despised the Samaritans, who lived in the country just beyond the Plain of Esdraelon, and did not want to go into the Samaritans' land.

Along the valley of the Jordan River the roads ran south as far as the fords opposite the old city of Jericho. Here the travelers went back across the river. Then they began to climb up through the steep hills that led toward Jerusalem. Up and up they went, until at last they came to where they could see the Holy City. The first sight of it made them stand still in happy wonder.

Outside the walls of Jerusalem, and also within the walls, were green gardens that belonged to rich men's houses. On the highest hill was the splendid palace which Herod the king had built. A great tower of it rose against the sky. But the most glorious thing was the Temple. It was even more magnificent than the Temple of Solomon which had stood on the same ground long before. The walls and columns were of colored marble, and great gates opened from each court to the court beyond. At the end of the farthest court there stood the holiest part of the Temple, so beautiful that hardly any other building in the world could be compared to it. Its marble walls were richly carved, and its roof was of shining gold.

Now that Joseph and Mary and Jesus had reached Jerusalem, they made ready for the Passover. Each family ate the Passover supper by itself. As the evening grew dark, a lamp was lighted, and the old, old prayers were said. Then the family ate a roasted lamb, and bread that had no yeast in it. They ate with their belts tightened and their sandals tied, because they were remembering the night when Moses had told the Hebrew people to be ready to leave Egypt the instant he should give the word. The people of Israel were no longer in Egypt, but again they were not free. Rome ruled over them. Roman soldiers were there in the castle on the hill, next to the Temple. Many men who kept the Passover were hating the Roman rule and wishing to get rid of it.

Jesus may have been thinking that what they needed more was to get rid of their hatred and bitterness. Certainly he was thinking much about God and asking himself how he could know surely what God wanted for his people.

When the days of the Passover were finished, the people from Nazareth started for home. Again there was the great throng of friends and neighbors journeying along together. Joseph and Mary thought that Jesus was walking with some of the other groups. But when evening came and they stopped to camp for the night, they could not find Jesus anywhere. Then they were frightened. They went straight back to Jerusalem, looking for him. At last they came to the Temple. In one of the Temple courts some of the wisest teachers—teachers who knew most about the sacred books and the law of God— used to sit and let people ask them questions. There, in the midst of them, Mary and Joseph found Jesus. They were glad, and yet a little annoyed. Why had Jesus stayed there and let them be so worried?

"Son," said Mary, "why did you treat us so?"

Jesus was surprised. He thought they should have understood where he would be. "Did you not know," he answered, "that I must be in my Father's house?"

BIBLIOGRAPHY

A bibliography at the end of a composition is a list of publications arranged so a reader can find them in a library. It deals with a particular topic and shows the writer's sources of information. The sources are usually listed alphabetically by author, and the title, the name and address of the publisher, and the date of publication follow. Each of these items is included for a particular reason.

The name of the author gives credit to the source of one's information and shows that there is good authority for statements made in a paper. This is particularly important when you are writing a paper on a technical subject, such as mathematics, chemistry, or aviation. When you give a source, the author's full name should be listed: for example, Lindbergh, Charles Augustus. (Unsigned articles, such as some of those in encyclopedias, are listed under the name of the publication.)

The title of the book or article should be listed next. Since an author may have used several similar titles, the full title is important.

The name and address of the publisher help identify the material. Many books, especially those no longer copyrighted, are issued by several publishers. Louisa May Alcott's *Little Women* is an example. Since editions vary in size of print and size of page, page 60 in one edition may differ from page 60 in another edition of the same book.

The date of publication should always be given. It not only helps identify the book but often indicates the value of the information. An article written in 1900 about space travel might be amusing or interesting, but it could not give information about modern developments. When a periodical is used, the year, month, and day, if that is given, should be included: *The New York Times,* January 23, 1944; *The Atlantic Monthly,* May, 1880. Magazines and newspapers may be identified also by volume, thus, 20:148–52, August, 1964. This means that the periodical, if it was bound only once a year, was in its 20th year. The page numbers are 148–52.

If only part of a book is needed, list the pages that have been read or are to be read. A book about presidents of the United States would have information on Theodore Roosevelt, but only a few pages would tell about this one man.

There are several different methods of punctuating a bibliography. The example uses one good pattern. It is usual to put quotation marks around the name of an article and to underscore the name of a book or magazine.

This encyclopedia has a bibliography, entitled HOME AND SCHOOL STUDY AND READING GUIDES. It comes in a separate volume and includes a list of suggested readings for every major subject in the set.

LOU LaBRANT
Dillard University

See also REFERENCE BOOKS; REPORTS.

My South Seas Adventures

Bibliography

(1) Hall, James Norman. The Far Lands. Boston, Little, Brown and Co., 1950.

(2) Hall, James Norman. My Island Home; an Autobiography. Boston, Little, Brown and Co., 1952.

(3) Heyerdahl, Thor. Kon-Tiki. Chicago, Rand McNally, 1950.

(4) Marden, Luis. "Huzza for Otaheite." The National Geographic, 121:435–59, April, 1962.

(5) Nordhoff, Charles Bernard, and James Norman Hall. Mutiny on the Bounty. Boston, Little, Brown and Co., 1932.

Note: For school reports, the name and address of the publisher are usually omitted. Number (1) would then read:

Hall, James Norman. The Far Lands. 1950.

In many European cities, thousands of people ride bicycles to work.

BICYCLING

A bicycle is your ticket to fun, adventure, and good health. It is also a thrifty means of transportation. All this two-wheeled machine needs to start you down the road is the power of your own two legs.

Millions of boys and girls ride bicycles to and from school. School leaders and parents alike have found that the use of bicycles offers helpful exercise, where safety and distance allow.

Riding a bike is fun. Going through town or open countryside at your own pace, seeing the sights, smelling the smells, hearing the sounds, and feeling the wind in your face and the sun on your back—these are some of the pleasures of cycling. There are times when it feels good to ride alone. And there are times when it is more pleasant to cycle with one's family or friends. Bike picnics, overnight bike hikes, and longer bike trips by families and club groups grow more popular year by year. Youth hostels have taken the lead in arranging bicycle trips for fun and health.

In many countries bicycles are used for both work and pleasure, by grownups as well as children. In European cities such as Copenhagen, Denmark, and in many cities of the Far East, there are more bicycles than motor vehicles on the streets. Some countries provide special paved roads for cyclists.

▶ BICYCLE RACING

Bicycle racing, too, finds favor with young people. The Amateur Bicycle League of America holds road and track races all over the United States. Young athletes from more than 40 American colleges take part in meets held by the Intercollegiate Cycling Association. One object of these races is to help select men for the cycling events that are an important part of the Olympic Games.

Races of the Union Cycliste Internationale (U.C.I.) are most popular in Western Europe. There are sprint races and pursuit races, and there are races for tandems (two-seated bikes). A motor-paced race is one in which the cyclist follows close behind a motorcycle that cuts down the air resistance for him.

Road races are also important. The best-known of these is the yearly Tour de France, which lasts about 25 days and covers about 3,000 miles.

▶ THE HISTORY OF BICYCLES

The velocipede (swift walker) of the early 1800's was a granddaddy of the bicycle. It had a wooden frame with two wheels. The rider sat on its seat and pushed it along with his toes. There were probably such machines earlier, but the first practical one was a kind of large-wheeled hobbyhorse called a draisine. It

THE CARE OF THE BICYCLE

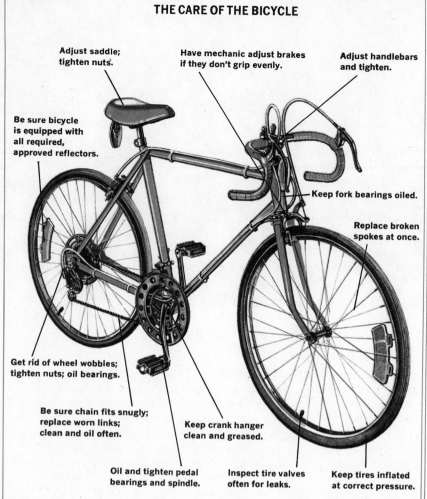

Adjust saddle; tighten nuts.

Have mechanic adjust brakes if they don't grip evenly.

Adjust handlebars and tighten.

Be sure bicycle is equipped with all required, approved reflectors.

Keep fork bearings oiled.

Replace broken spokes at once.

Get rid of wheel wobbles; tighten nuts; oil bearings.

Be sure chain fits snugly; replace worn links; clean and oil often.

Keep crank hanger clean and greased.

Oil and tighten pedal bearings and spindle.

Inspect tire valves often for leaks.

Keep tires inflated at correct pressure.

HAND SIGNALS

RIGHT TURN
Left arm pointed up

LEFT TURN
Left arm straight out.

STOP OR SLOW
Left arm pointed down.

BIKE SAFETY

DOS

Obey all stop signs and traffic signals. Always dismount and walk your bicycle across busy streets.

Ride only on the right side of the street, as near the curb as possible. But be alert for suddenly opened doors when passing parked cars, for drain grates, loose gravel, and other hazards.

Ride single file on busy or narrow streets.

Stop and make sure sidewalks and streets are clear when coming out of driveways and alleys. Be sure your bicycle has good brakes; a sounding device; front, rear, side, and pedal reflectors; and a light.

DON'TS

Don't weave in and out of traffic.

Don't make sudden turns or stops.

Never ride more than two abreast and never stunt or race in traffic, or hitch onto trucks or cars.

Don't carry another person on your bicycle. This obstructs your vision and makes steering and balancing more difficult.

was built in 1818 by Baron Karl von Drais, of Germany. Velocipedes were also called dandy horses because they were very popular among the dandies, or fancily dressed young men of the time.

In 1839 Kirkpatrick Macmillan, a Scottish blacksmith, added back-and-forth pedals with connecting rods to drive the rear wheel of a velocipede. The next important step came about the year 1862, when Ernest Michaux of France made a velocipede with a front wheel larger than the rear one. It was like the present-day tricycle in this way. Pierre Lallement patented such a machine in the United States in 1866. These iron-rimmed two-wheelers were called boneshakers because they jarred their riders so.

In 1877 Colonel Albert Pope of Boston made the first American bicycle. It was an ordinary high-wheeler, much like one made earlier in England by James Starley. It had a front wheel about 56 inches tall and a much smaller rear wheel. By this time wire-spoked wheels with solid rubber tires had come into use. The large front wheel of the ordinary bike gave the rider extra speed, but made it hard and risky to ride.

At about the same time, in the 1870's, the first safety bicycle was made by another Englishman, Harry J. Lawson. This was a machine more like the bike of today, having a chain drive from pedals to rear wheel. However, the safety bicycle did not begin to take the place of the high-wheeler until after 1885. That was when the Rover, a model with wheels of equal size, was produced. Soon afterward air-filled tires, ball bearings, coasting hubs, and two-speed gears were added; brakes were improved.

From 1877 until about 1902, the popularity of the bicycle grew quickly—not with youngsters, but with adults. It was the height of fashion to ride a bicycle—the first step forward from the horse and buggy. Mrs. Amelia Bloomer thought up the Turkish-style pants that made it easier for women to ride. Indeed, the change in women's sports clothes from bloomers to slacks, culottes, pedal pushers, and shorts has been brought about largely by the bicycle.

Bicycle racing was a leading sport, and the champion bike racer was as widely known as a baseball star is today. The first of the once

The rubber-tired high-wheeler of 1877 was an improvement over the earlier "boneshaker" with its iron-rimmed wheels.

popular 6-day bicycle races was held in New York's old Madison Square Garden in 1891. One well-known racer was Charles "Mile-a-Minute" Murphy. He got his nickname in 1899 by riding his bicycle a mile in $57\frac{4}{5}$ seconds on a board track behind a train.

All America was excited about the wonders of "the wheel." The men who were to play important roles in building automobiles and airplanes were once bicycle makers, too. Among such men were Henry Ford, Glen Olds, the Wright brothers, and Glenn Curtiss.

▶TRAFFIC RULES

The bicycle is subject to the same rules of street traffic applying to automobiles and other vehicles. As a bike rider you have to obey all local traffic laws. You are expected to give persons on foot the right of way and to follow all rules of courtesy and good sense.

JOHN AUERBACH
Bicycle Institute of America

See also HOSTELS AND HOSTELING; TRANSPORTATION.

BILLIARDS

There are many variations of billiards. However, the basic skills and equipment are much the same in all. A white cue ball is struck with a stick, or cue, so as to roll across a level table top and strike other balls. The two most popular versions are pocket billiards and three-cushion billiards.

Few sports have the blue-blooded lines of billiards. There is evidence that the game developed as an indoor version of lawn bowling in England, about 600 years ago. Shakespeare mentioned the sport, and Mary Queen of Scots was a noted wielder of the cue. The word "billiards" comes from the Old French *billart,* meaning "playing stick," or "cue."

Spaniards are said to have brought a billiard table to St. Augustine, Florida, in 1565. The game matured in America, where championship matches became popular during the late 1800's. Billiards lost some of its popularity with the coming of motion pictures and other attractions in the 20th century. Today, however, it has found its way back into the hearts of hundreds of thousands. Much of this new rise in popularity can be attributed to the introduction of the home billiard table.

Another factor is the bowling alley that includes billiards in an ultramodern setting with games for all the family to enjoy.

▶ HOW TO PLAY BILLIARDS

A good billiard player is relaxed when he makes a stroke. There is a smooth rhythm to the swinging back and forth of his arm. His shoulder, elbow, and wrist join in free and easy action. This can be seen especially in his "warm-up" strokes as he prepares to shoot the ball. As in golf, tennis, and bowling, follow-through is very important. Without it control is lost. The warm-up is preparation not only for the shot but also for the follow-through.

A good stroke and follow-through are achieved with practice. Remember that the stroke is not a rigid poke at the ball. Instead it is a springy action that results from gripping the cue lightly and achieving whiplike action with the free and easy motion of wrist, elbow, and shoulder joint.

Pocket Billiards

Various games of pocket billiards are played with a white cue ball and 15 colored object balls, numbered 1 through 15. The order in which the object balls are sought is

ROTATION POCKET BILLIARDS: RERACK POSITION

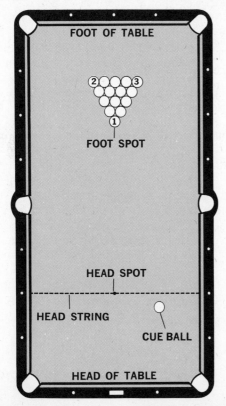

FOOT OF TABLE

② ③

①

FOOT SPOT

HEAD SPOT

HEAD STRING

CUE BALL

HEAD OF TABLE

THE CAROM TABLE

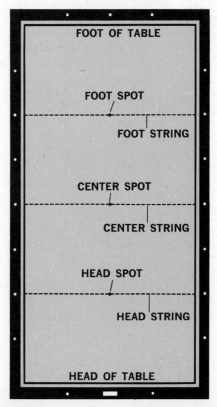

FOOT OF TABLE

FOOT SPOT

FOOT STRING

CENTER SPOT

CENTER STRING

HEAD SPOT

HEAD STRING

HEAD OF TABLE

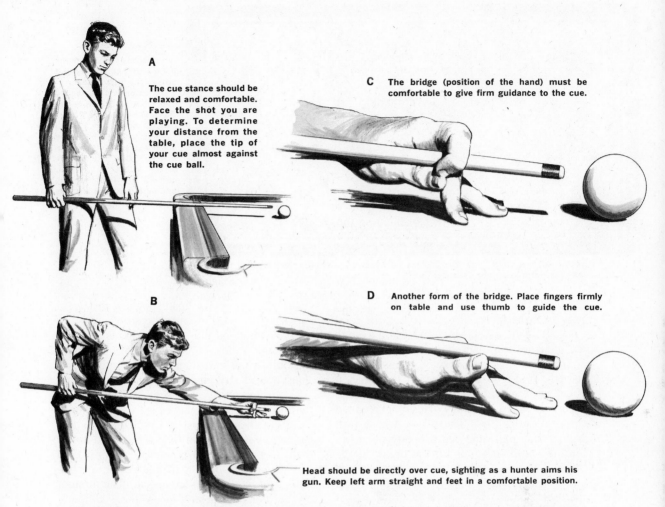

A The cue stance should be relaxed and comfortable. Face the shot you are playing. To determine your distance from the table, place the tip of your cue almost against the cue ball.

C The bridge (position of the hand) must be comfortable to give firm guidance to the cue.

D Another form of the bridge. Place fingers firmly on table and use thumb to guide the cue.

B Head should be directly over cue, sighting as a hunter aims his gun. Keep left arm straight and feet in a comfortable position.

the basis for different games. In the simplest version the player (or side) who first pockets any 8 of the 15 balls is the winner.

In the most popular form of pocket billiards, called rotation, the balls must be pocketed in order, from 1 to 15. For the start, or break, the object balls are racked in a triangle with the 1-ball on the foot spot. The 2-ball is placed at the farthest left point of the triangle, the 3-ball at the farthest right point.

The players draw lots or lag to see who will play first. In lagging, each player places a ball behind the head string (that is, between the head string and the head of the table, where he is standing). He shoots the ball so that it will rebound from the foot cushion. The player whose ball comes to rest nearest the head cushion has the choice of either playing or not playing first.

In making the break shot, the opening player may place the cue ball anywhere he chooses behind the head string. After that the cue ball is played from wherever it lies after a stroke.

The 1-ball is the first object ball. When it is pocketed, the 2-ball becomes the legal object ball, and so on. The cue ball must always strike the legal object ball before touching another ball. In case of a miss, any other balls pocketed on the same shot are spotted. That is, the lowest-numbered ball of those returned to the table is placed on the foot spot; any others are lined up in order of value in a string behind the first ball. Any object ball that is knocked off the table is spotted in the same way.

If a player hits the legal object ball first with the cue ball, he is entitled to all object balls pocketed on that stroke. This is so whether or not the legal object ball goes into

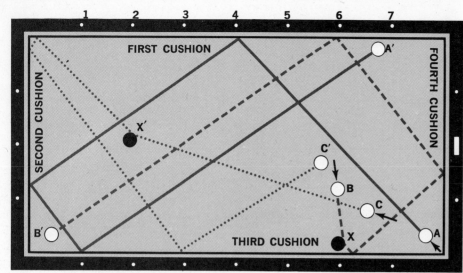

A follow shot (A) from the lower right hand corner that strikes the first cushion at 4 will carom off the second and third cushions and hit the first ball (A') at 7. Cue ball (B) hits object ball (X) ¼ left, caroms off three cushions, and hits second ball (B'). Cue ball (C) hits object ball (X') ⅓ right, caroms off first, second, and third cushions, and hits second ball (C').

The white dots on the rail of a billiard table make up the diamond system, which allows players to figure angles easily.

a pocket, and even if another object ball jumps off the table. The player has the right to shoot again, and his inning goes on as long as he scores on each shot.

If the cue ball is pocketed, it is called a scratch. And if it is knocked off the table, it is called an error. In either case the player's inning is ended, and any balls pocketed on the shot are spotted. The player whose turn is next may place the cue ball anywhere behind the head string, as for the break. If the object ball is on the same side of the head string, it (the object ball) must be placed on the foot spot.

The total value of the numbered balls is 120. The player or side first scoring 61 points is the winner.

Three-Cushion Billiards

Only three balls are used in this game. Two are white cue balls, one of which has two dots on it so you can tell it from the other. The third ball is red. The game is played on a carom table—one without pockets.

Players lag for the opening shot. The winner of the lag has a choice of cue balls. After the selection of cue balls has been made, each player must continue to use the same cue ball throughout the game. His opponent's cue ball and the red ball are always his object balls.

At the start the red ball is placed on the foot spot. The opening player must place his cue ball within 6 inches of his opponent's cue

ball, which is on the head spot. On the opening shot the red ball must be struck first.

Each three-cushion carom counts 1 point. A count is valid when the cue ball (1) strikes an object ball and then three or more cushions before striking the second object ball, (2) strikes three or more cushions before hitting the two object balls, (3) strikes a cushion, then the first object ball, then two or more cushions, and then the second object ball, (4) strikes two or more cushions, then the first object ball, then one or more cushions, and finally the second ball. The number of cushions does not mean three different ones.

When the cue ball is frozen to (touching) an object ball, the player must shoot away from that object ball, not counting it as a hit. Or he may choose to have the balls spotted as for the opening shot.

Points are subtracted from a player's score for fouls, such as causing the cue ball to jump off the table or shooting the wrong cue ball. Any ball that leaves the table is spotted as for the start of the game. A player's turn continues as long as he continues to score points. Usually 50 points make a game.

Straight-rail billiards is a simpler game for beginners than three-cushion billiards. Contact must be made with both of the object balls, but not necessarily with any cushions. Each carom is scored as a point.

LOU VRANA
Brunswick Corporation

BILL OF RIGHTS

The American Bill of Rights guarantees to every person in the United States the rights and liberties that are the basis of democracy. It is one of the most important and respected documents in America.

The American Bill of Rights is made up of the first 10 amendments to the Constitution of the United States. When the Constitution was written, its authors believed it protected the rights of the people. However, there were many who thought the Constitution was not definite enough. The Constitution explained what the national government could and could not do. But it did not list most of the important rights of the people. The people wanted their rights and liberties guaranteed in black and white. As a result several states refused to sign the new Constitution unless it included a list of the people's rights. George Washington promised that such a bill of rights would be added to the Constitution by amendment when the first Congress met.

At that first meeting of Congress in 1789 James Madison, then an influential young congressman, proposed 17 amendments. After much discussion and rewriting Madison's amendments were cut to 12 by Congress. Of these 12 amendments, 10 were ratified by the states. The remaining 10 form what we now call the Bill of Rights.

▶ WHY AMERICANS WANTED A BILL OF RIGHTS

After the American Revolution most people were afraid of a strong central government. They had learned from bitter experience that a very powerful central government could be unfair to the people. The British Parliament had taxed the American colonists without their consent. Colonists who criticized the British Government were pun-

James Madison stands to argue in favor of the Bill of Rights at the first session of the United States Congress.

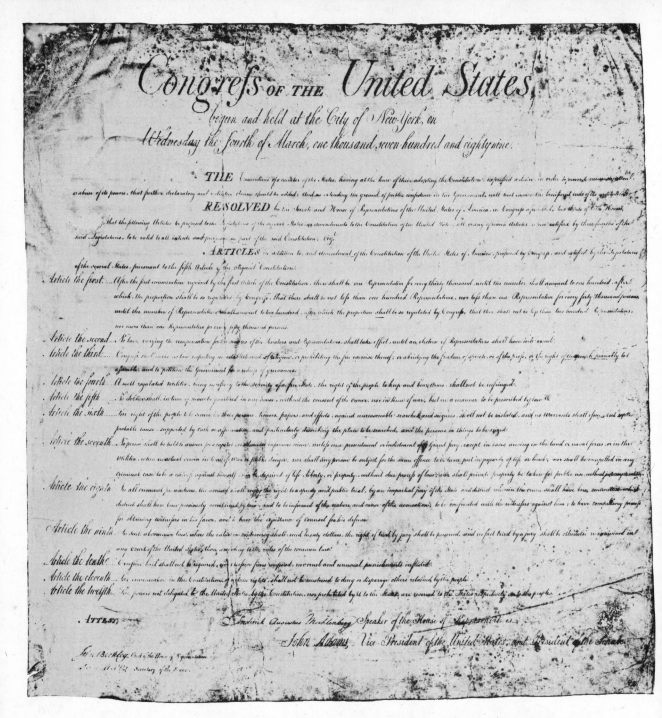

ished. British officers could search the home of any colonist at any time with a general search warrant. British soldiers were stationed in the homes of colonists without their consent.

Americans thought that they were entitled to better treatment from their government. The Declaration of Independence said that "all men are created equal" and have "certain un-

alienable rights." Unalienable rights are rights that a man is born with, rights that cannot be taken away from him. In order to preserve these unalienable rights, the American people wanted a written bill of rights.

▶ WHAT THE BILL OF RIGHTS SAYS

The Bill of Rights is a fundamental part of the American system of law. It covers a wide variety of subjects. It protects the basic civil liberties of free speech, free press, and choice of religion. It is especially concerned with the rights of people accused of crimes. In the American legal system a man is innocent until proven guilty. The Bill of Rights preserves this principle by providing very strong legal protection for accused persons. The Bill of Rights also upholds the old idea that "a man's home is his castle."

The 10 amendments that make up the Bill of Rights grant the following rights and privileges.

First Amendment. Guarantees freedom of religion, speech, press, assembly, and petition.

Second Amendment. Gives the people the right to keep and bear arms. (This amendment was originally intended to give the people the right to resist tyrannical governments by force. However, today Congress and many states forbid the carrying of hidden weapons. All firearms must be registered with the proper authorities.)

Third Amendment. Restricts the right of the government to quarter troops on the people. (In colonial times British soldiers often lived in the homes of private citizens. These citizens were forced, whether they wanted to or not, to give the soldiers food and shelter. This is called quartering of soldiers.)

Fourth Amendment. Guarantees freedom from unreasonable searches and seizures. (This amendment protects the privacy of a man's home.)

Fifth Amendment. States (1) that no person may be deprived of life, liberty, or property without "due process of law" (this means that everyone is entitled to a legal trial or hearing); (2) that no person may be placed in double jeopardy (this means that no one may be tried twice for the same crime); (3) that no person on trial may be forced to incriminate himself (this means that no one may be forced to testify against himself).

Sixth Amendment. Guarantees trial by jury, the right to confront hostile witnesses, and the right to a defense lawyer in criminal cases.

Seventh Amendment. Guarantees the right to trial by jury in civil suits of more than $20.

Eighth Amendment. Prohibits excessive bail or fines and "cruel and unusual" punishment (torture).

Ninth Amendment. Makes it clear that other rights, though not listed in the Constitution, will be retained by the people.

Tenth Amendment. States that all powers not granted to the United States or prohibited to the individual states will be kept by the states and the people. Many of the powers of the states grow out of this amendment.

▶ **THE RESPONSIBILITIES OF FREEDOM**

The founding fathers believed that freedom carried with it certain responsibilities. They felt a man was free to do as he pleased as long as his actions did not hurt anyone else. The Bill of Rights assumed men were reasonable. One of the greatest things about the Bill of Rights is that it trusts the people. It is based on the belief that every individual is responsible and can behave properly and is therefore entitled to fair treatment from the government.

Although the Bill of Rights gives broad, general guarantees, the Supreme Court, which is the final umpire, or referee, on questions of constitutional law, has ruled that these rights have some limits. For example, a man who causes a panic by yelling "Fire!" when there is no fire abuses his privilege of free speech. The Supreme Court has also ruled that the government may limit freedom of speech when an opinion or action represents a "clear and present" danger to the general welfare. This might be the case in time of war.

▶ **STATE BILLS OF RIGHTS**

Even before the official adoption of the Bill of Rights, a few states already had similar provisions in their state constitutions. Virginia enacted the first state bill of rights in 1776.

Today each state constitution contains a bill of rights or a declaration of rights. Some of these are even more detailed than the national Bill of Rights.

At one time the American Bill of Rights applied only to the national government. It did not protect people from their state governments. However, after the Civil War the Fourteenth Amendment to the Constitution made certain rights in the Bill of Rights applicable to the states as well as to the national government. The Supreme Court has ruled that neither the national government nor any state can deprive a person of the First Amendment rights: freedom of speech, press, religion, petition, and assembly.

Today the people are actually protected by two bills of rights—the first 10 amendments to the Constitution and the bill of rights of the individual state.

▶ ENGLISH BILL OF RIGHTS

The idea of a bill of rights did not originate in the United States. American colonists looked to British history for their examples. The first bill of rights was the Magna Carta, which King John of England was forced to sign in 1215. This historic document limited the power of the King.

The actual phrase "bill of rights" comes from an English law passed by Parliament in 1689. This law listed the "true, ancient, and indubitable rights and liberties of the people."

The English Bill of the Rights limits the power of the King and upholds the power of Parliament. It entitles the people to due process of law, free elections, and freedom to petition the King without fear of punishment. In fact, several amendments in the American Bill of Rights are based on articles in this English document.

▶ FRENCH BILL OF RIGHTS

In 1789, at the beginning of the French Revolution, France adopted the Declaration of the Rights of Man and of the Citizen. This document defined the revolutionary slogan, "Liberty, Equality, Fraternity." It guaranteed religious freedom, freedom of speech and the press, and personal security. It declared that all men were born equal. It has been a part of the constitutions of all French republics since the Revolution.

▶ UNIVERSAL DECLARATION OF HUMAN RIGHTS

Most national constitutions written after 1789 have included a section that can be called a bill of rights. But the most general statement of fundamental rights is the Universal Declaration of Human Rights, adopted by the United Nations General Assembly on December 10, 1948.

This document attempts to establish a "common standard of achievement for all peoples and all nations." It states that all persons everywhere are equal in dignity and rights. It grants the five freedoms of the First Amendment to the United States Constitution. In addition it upholds certain social and cultural rights like the right to education and free choice of employment, the right to form trade unions, and the right to a decent standard of living. It also outlaws slavery and supports the principles of democratic government. However, the Universal Declaration of Human Rights does not have the protective power of other constitutional bills of rights. The United Nations, which adopted this document, does not have power to act on individual citizens of member nations.

▶ CANADIAN BILL OF RIGHTS

Canada's Bill of Rights, known officially as An Act for the Recognition and Protection of Human Rights and Fundamental Freedoms, was passed in 1960.

The Canadian Bill of Rights guarantees the same rights and freedoms as the American bill—freedom of speech, press, and religion; equality before the law; the right to due process; and enjoyment of property and security of person. The Canadian bill also states that a person is innocent until proven guilty.

The passage of the Bill of Rights was the result of untiring effort by civil liberties groups in Canada. The purpose of the Act was to protect these civil rights from abuse by the national government.

▶ BILL OF RIGHTS DAY

The American Bill of Rights became a part of the Constitution on December 15, 1791. On the 150th anniversary of this event, in 1941, President Franklin D. Roosevelt proclaimed December 15th Bill of Rights Day, and it has been observed nationally ever since.

The purpose of the day is to make Americans aware of their rights and duties as citizens and to encourage them to think about the meaning of the Bill of Rights. Some states set aside an entire week as Bill of Rights Week.

Reviewed by ISIDORE STARR
Queens College (New York)

See also UNITED STATES (History and Government of the United States).

BIOCHEMISTRY

Biochemistry forms the meeting ground of two great sciences: biology and chemistry.

There is a Greek word, *bios,* which means "life." For that reason **biology** is the name given to the study of living things—animals, plants, and microscopic forms of life. Biology takes in the description of living things. It takes in their ways of living and growing and reproducing.

Chemistry is the name given to the study of the composition of various substances. It includes the manner in which the composition changes or can be changed. Chemists are interested in all substances: those in rocks, in sea water, and even in distant stars.

Now suppose you combine biology and chemistry. You have the study of the substances that make up living things, their composition and the changes they undergo. This is **biochemistry**.

▶ THE ORIGINS OF BIOCHEMISTRY

Biochemistry is a fairly new science, but many of its processes are as old as life. The means by which green plants make their food is a biochemical process. So is digestion in human beings and in other animals. Long before people knew anything about science, they stumbled upon biochemical processes. Cooking is one. Some substances in food are changed when the food is cooked. The food is made tastier and easier to digest. Primitive people also found that if fruit juice was allowed to remain in a warm, dark place, certain changes took place in it. The juice fermented and changed to wine.

Such discoveries were accidental. People did not understand what happened during cooking or fermentation. They understood only that by certain methods they could change various substances. Then in the late 1700's modern chemistry was developed.

How Chemistry Led to Biochemistry

The early chemists were concerned with what we call inorganic chemistry, or the chemistry of nonliving things. For example, they were interested in minerals. Yet they could not ignore living things altogether. Certain substances existed both in living organisms and in the nonliving world. For instance, all creatures are made up mostly of water; this is the same water that we find all about us.

However, chemists also knew that many substances of living organisms are not at all like those of the nonliving world. One important difference has to do with what happens when they are heated.

When inorganic substances are heated, no basic change takes place in them. Iron that is melted is still iron. Water that is boiled is still water. If a copper bowl is broken up and melted down, a second bowl can be made of the material.

With organic substances the basic form is easily changed by heat. They char, smoke, or burn. And then they are no longer what they were to begin with. There is no way that a cooked or burned egg can be made back into a raw egg.

Because organic substances are easily changed, the chemists who studied them had to work more carefully and slowly than the chemists who studied rocks and minerals. Even so, between 1750 and 1850 chemists learned much about the nature of these substances. Organic chemistry, or the chemistry of living things, became the first approach to biochemistry.

Among the early discoveries were the three main kinds of organic substances that make up all living matter. Chemists called them carbohydrates, fats, and proteins. Examples of carbohydrates are starch and sugar; wood is mostly cellulose, which is another kind of carbohydrate. Butter and olive oil are examples of fats. Gelatin and egg white are examples of protein.

The human body uses carbohydrates and fats for energy. It uses protein to form new tissue.

Both fats and carbohydrates are made up of three elements. They are carbon, hydrogen, and oxygen. In the body these combine with oxygen from the air to supply energy. Before long, chemists discovered that proteins were far more complicated than either fats or carbohydrates. Protein contains not only carbon, hydrogen, and oxygen, but also nitrogen. The body uses nitrogen in building new tissue.

In spite of these discoveries, scientists still thought that organic matter had no connec-

Friedrich Wöhler (1800–82) proved that it was possible to make an organic substance from inorganic chemicals.

tion with inorganic chemicals. They believed it was impossible to change inorganic substances into organic substances.

Then in 1828 a German chemist named Friedrich Wöhler accidentally proved that false. While heating some inorganic chemicals he happened to make an organic substance, urea. Up to that time scientists believed that only a living body could make an organic substance.

Wöhler's discovery was the first real breakthrough into biochemistry. Scientists then realized there could be no clear dividing line between chemical processes and life processes. Chemists and biologists found that their work was overlapping more and more.

▶ WHAT BIOCHEMISTS STUDY

Biochemists today explore a great range of subjects. These fall into several main areas.

Pharmacology

One of the oldest branches of biochemistry is called **pharmacology.** It is the study of how chemicals affect living tissue. Everyone who orders drugs or a prescription from the pharmacist comes in touch with this branch of biochemistry.

The fact that certain plants could be used to cure various diseases had long been known. In the 1800's scientists began to learn about the chemical basis of these cures. They also learned to make new substances that resembled natural chemicals in many ways but were not found in living tissues. Some of these substances that they made had powerful effects on living tissue.

Among the great discoveries of the 1800's were the antiseptics, chemicals that could kill germs. Scientists also discovered chemicals that could deaden pain. These are the anesthetics.

Chemotherapy

Chemotherapy, a special branch of pharmacology, is the treatment of diseases with chemicals. In the 20th century laboratories made new chemicals that could destroy germs without hurting human beings. Other chemicals, called antibiotics, were obtained from microbes. They were even more deadly to germs. By the 1970's chemotherapy had brought many ancient diseases under control. Other diseases, such as cancer, were under constant attack by researchers.

Dietetics

Toward the end of the 1800's the science of **dietetics** became very important. This is the study of how the body makes use of foods. Biochemists began by using animals in experiments. They fed special diets to rats or guinea pigs and studied the effects on the animals.

By 1900 biochemists realized that it was not enough just to eat food. People had to have the proper foods. Certain substances were important to health and to life, even though these substances were present in the body only in tiny quantities. Many of these substances could not be made by the body, so they had to be present in the diet. Some of these substances were inorganic. Others were organic. They were given the name "vitamins."

If vitamins are missing from the diet, a person can develop a deficiency disease such as anemia or scurvy. The most common form of anemia is caused by a lack of iron in the blood. Scurvy was once common among sailors on long ocean voyages. It was caused by a lack of vitamin C.

To fight such deficiency diseases, biochemists have learned what foods are necessary to good health. They have also learned how to make vitamins in the laboratory.

Endocrinology

Shortly after 1900 the biochemists discovered that certain organs in the body produce substances that keep the body in proper working order. These chemical substances are called hormones. The study of hormones is called **endocrinology.**

If the body's organs do not produce the proper amount of hormones, serious disorders can result. The most common disease of this sort is diabetes; it is caused by a lack of the hormone called insulin. Biochemists have learned how to take hormones such as insulin from the glands of animals. People with diabetes can use insulin that has been obtained from cattle. Diabetics can now lead almost normal lives if they use insulin carefully. And biochemists are learning how to make other hormones in the laboratory.

The Body's Chemistry

Since 1900 biochemists have concentrated more and more on the chemical changes that go on in people. The changes that can occur are so many and so complicated that it takes long, hard work for the biochemist to untangle all the threads.

The most complicated organic substances are the proteins. They are made of long

Modern techniques have made possible important advances in biochemistry. Left, radioactive phosphorus in the leaf shows how different parts of the leaf take up different amounts of phosphorus as food. Below, biochemist studies an experimental antibiotic. He is comparing its effect on a bacteria culture with the effect of a known antibiotic on a culture of the same kind of bacteria.

Below: cells of a green leaf as seen through an electron microscope, showing chloroplasts.

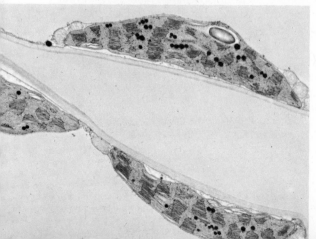

chains of organic chemicals called amino acids. Although there are only about two dozen different kinds of amino acids, the body can put them together in millions of different ways. Each different protein has its own special purpose in the human body.

For example, there are special kinds of proteins called enzymes. Each of the millions of changes that take place in the body depends on one particular kind of enzyme. If this particular enzyme is missing from the body, then the body cannot change one substance into another. There are special enzymes, for example, that make it possible for food to be digested. Biochemists have also discovered that enzymes are responsible for the fermentation of bread dough and fruit juice.

▶ FUTURE DEVELOPMENTS

The most exciting future developments in biochemistry lie in two directions.

Photosynthesis

For many years scientists wanted to work out the exact changes that go on in green plants when they combine the carbon dioxide of the air with water and form starch. The green plant uses the energy of sunlight to bring about this change, and the process is called **photosynthesis.**

It is photosynthesis that creates the world's food supply. And when plants form starch, oxygen is given off to the air. It is photosynthesis, therefore, that keeps the air breathable and prevents us from ever using up the world's oxygen supply.

Until 1945 practically nothing was known about photosynthesis. Now the details are being revealed at a fast rate. If biochemists can learn enough about photosynthesis, they may be able to bring about the same chemical reactions. Then they may be able to learn ways of making food out of air, water, and sunlight so that we will depend less on rainfall and good harvests.

Genetics

The other exciting development involves the study of the way in which the pattern of chemical change in a body is inherited. Children inherit far more than outward appearance from their parents. Many of the internal substances and processes that make us what we are—the diseases we may have or how long we live—are determined by our inherited chemical patterns. The study of these patterns is called **genetics**.

This science takes its name from the genes, tiny elements in certain body cells that determine heredity. Biochemists have discovered that the genes are made up of special proteins called nucleic acids. Each nucleic acid brings about the formation of a particular enzyme by what is called the "genetic code." In the 1950's and 1960's biochemists began to work out the genetic code.

Once the code is fully understood, scientists may be able to correct many human conditions that cannot now be helped. It may become possible to assure health and long life from the beginning.

Biochemistry as a New Science

Many of the important advances in biochemistry have been made possible only by modern tools and techniques for investigation. More has been learned since 1945 about chemical changes in the body than in all history before that time. As biochemists learn more and more about the workings of the body they come closer to understanding such disorders as hardening of the arteries and high blood pressure. Some biochemists are working hard to learn how cancer attacks the body. Others are studying the virus —the smallest form of living matter. Viruses are responsible for many serious illnesses like polio and diphtheria, as well as for the common cold.

In reading about biochemistry you may have noticed that almost everything biochemists discover is put to use by doctors to help them fight disease. Today, in fact, medicine can hardly be separated from biochemistry. And in biochemistry itself it is hard to say where chemistry stops and biology begins. But it is important to realize that the name "biochemistry" represents far more than a convenient label for certain scientific activities. It indicates a completely new view of the nature of life.

ISAAC ASIMOV
Boston University School of Medicine

See also BIOLOGY; BODY CHEMISTRY; CHEMISTRY, HISTORY OF; GENETICS; PHOTOSYNTHESIS.

BIOGRAPHY, AUTOBIOGRAPHY, AND BIOGRAPHICAL NOVEL

Biography is both a craft and an art. As a craftsman the biographer begins with research, gathering all the available information about a person's life. There are first the surface facts about a chosen subject. Then the biographer looks beneath the surface for evidence of inner truths—what the man or woman thought, felt, desired, suffered.

The biographer as an artist sets down the meaning of a person's life. With his research at hand, the writer chooses the facts he will use. Sometimes it is the bulk of detail; sometimes it is the essence, or pith. With this task of selection comes the task of writing the story in a clear, convincing way. The artist must so construct his book that every portion of the person's life fits into an understandable, moving whole. The writing must have style; the structure must have architectural form. That is the meaning of art.

▶ BIOGRAPHY OLD AND NEW

Modern biography, as an independent and popular literary form, is fairly new. Writing about individual lives, however, is an old practice. The Bible is full of stories about the prophets and saints. The earliest Greek biographical writing was done by Xenophon, who wrote about Socrates in the 4th century B.C. Plutarch's *Parallel Lives* (about A.D. 100) is still famous. The best-known Latin biographer is Suetonius, author of *Lives of the Caesars* in A.D. 120. Tacitus set down an account of the life of his father-in-law, Agricola, in A.D. 97–98. The purposes of these early Greek and Roman biographers were mixed. Some tried to tell the history of a dynasty or of a war. Others attempted to justify a moral or philosophical system. As a result the human story was sometimes lost.

Modern biographers' aims are varied. Some wish to tell an exciting, dramatic, and often inspirational human story. Others study the life of a person so that we can profit by another's experience and better understand ourselves and the world about us. Still others wish to make the past more alive. Instead of writing about the impersonal forces of history, the biographer tells of the impact of an individual on the life of his times. There is Lytton Strachey's *Eminent Victorians,* which describes an interesting age in England. Douglas S. Freeman's *George Washington* portrays the beginning of the American nation. Hendrik Willem van Loon's *R.v.R.,* a biography of Rembrandt, serves as an introduction to art. René Jules Dubos' *Louis Pasteur* gives us a picture of the scientist at work.

Biography may be written out of love or hate but never out of indifference. It may take years to write. It may require thousands of hours of study in libraries, law courts, halls of records, city halls, museums, family archives. Frequently many miles must be traveled to visit the places where the subject lived and worked, to interview men still alive who can add to the body of knowledge. This concentrated effort can be achieved only by people who love deeply—such as the biographers of Jefferson or Michelangelo or Edison—or by those who hate deeply, such as the biographers of Torquemada or Hitler or Mussolini.

Often the search is frustrating. For a conscientious biographer the easily available material won't be half enough. A researcher is a detective. He hunts down clues, pursues scraps of evidence, never gives up looking for material he senses must exist. In his hero's life there are always blank spaces that must be filled in if the biography is to be complete and true. To a good biographer everything is findable. When he comes up empty-handed, he must return to the quest with fresh ideas and renewed courage. For it is not enough to know everything a man did. It is also important to know why he did what he did—his reasoning, his fears, his failures before he achieved something important.

Once all his material is collected, the biographer faces a new challenge. The reader must feel that he is in the hands of a thorough and honest workman. Therefore, the biographer has to be objective. He has to tell the complete truth, based on his findings. He must not conceal his hero's faults, omit his shortcomings, bury his failures. He must not allow his own prejudices to take over. What is known as his "principle of selection," that is, his choice of materials to use, must be strictly ethical. Otherwise the reader will sense that something is wrong. He will feel that he is being deceived.

But when he reads an honest, well-balanced biography, such as Benjamin Thomas' *Abraham Lincoln* or Muriel Rukeyser's *Willard Gibbs* or Carl Van Doren's *Benjamin Franklin,* he will know that the strands of each story are accurately woven.

Biography is one of the most enjoyable forms of reading and learning. While reading biographies, one can sit at home yet roam the realms of time and space with *Genghis Khan* (Harold Lamb), *Napoleon* (Emil Ludwig), *Aristotle* (W. D. Ross), and *Madame Curie* (Eve Curie). A good biographer will become as one with the person he is writing about. This union enables the reader, in turn, to live another's life in his imagination.

▶ **AUTOBIOGRAPHY**

Autobiography is a very different medium. "Auto" comes from the Greek for "self," "one's own." An autobiography is the story of a person's life written by himself. Sometimes an autobiography is ghostwritten, that is, written by someone else, frequently with journalistic experience. Sometimes the real writer is completely unknown. Sometimes there is an "as told to . . ." approach.

Autobiography is a difficult art form, yet it looks easy. Perhaps that is what tempts so many thousands to try it.

A man sometimes writes his own story because he has experienced some kind of self-discovery. The discovery may be about his relationship to life, to his fellow man, or to God. Others write about their struggles against great odds and their eventual success. The autobiographies of Alfred E. Smith and Helen Keller show a refusal to be held down or defeated. Some autobiographies, like those of Booker T. Washington and Jane Addams, glow with an individual's dedication to a life of serving mankind. Greatness of character, which seems to spring from selflessness and courage, often reveals itself in an autobiography. The best of these life stories raise the stature of the human race. They inspire the reader and deepen his understanding.

Not all autobiographies are written for noble purposes. Many are written for selfish reasons—to get money, attention, sympathy, or revenge. Yet all too often the writer of autobiography conveys the exact opposite of the impression he had hoped to impart.

Every kind of American has written an autobiography. As a group, clergymen are more interested in writing about themselves than any other single category. Authors and politicians follow close behind. Industrialists, scientists, and engineers tend to remain silent. In between come the educators, the reformers, the military and the professional men. It has become fashionable for actors and athletes to have their stories ghostwritten.

▶ **THE BIOGRAPHICAL NOVEL**

In recent years a third biographical form has become increasingly popular and important. It is called the biographical novel. This is biography presented in the form of a novel, with dialogue, suspense, and plot structure. The biographical novelist can use his creative imagination to develop these aspects of the novel. But he must do so only within the framework of truth. The novelist will have found the truth in documents—diaries, letters, journals, notes, recorded deeds.

The biographical novel is thus the fruit of a marriage between the research of biography and the fictional devices of the novelist. Books like *I, Claudius* (Robert Graves) and *The Romance of Leonardo da Vinci* (Dimitri Sergeevich Merezhkovski) are fine examples of the biographical novel. It offers a more emotional approach to life, with more personal interpretation by the author. Facts can be forgotten, but rarely an emotional experience. The biographical novelist tries to catch up his readers in the emotions of his hero. Emotions felt while reading a biographical novel can be almost as unforgettable as the emotions one experiences in real life.

Not every life will fit into the form of the biographical novel. Dramatic elements must be present, along with an overall pattern into which the parts can be fitted. Many lives, important in their achievement, do not lend themselves to the nature of the novel. Other lives seem to have been lived as though the subject were constantly aware that he was creating a dramatic structure.

Biography, autobiography, and the biographical novel are personal books. They tell the story of men's lives, in order to help us understand mankind.

IRVING STONE
Author, *Lust for Life, The Agony and the Ecstasy*

The science of biology is the study of all living things.

BIOLOGY

Since the very beginning of human history, men have taken an interest in what they saw, particularly in everything that moves or grows and can be called alive. **Biology** is the name given to this study of living things. Much of the study has been, and still is, simply a process of looking at what can be seen and thinking about it. This activity may be broadened by carefully dissecting (taking apart) living things so that more internal (inside) structure can be seen. The study may also be broadened by use of a lens or a microscope. And since all living things are active in some ways, the action may be interfered with; that is, the action may be experimented with, just as one can experiment with any piece of working machinery to discover what stops it or changes the manner in which it works.

▶ GREAT BIOLOGISTS OF THE ANCIENT WORLD

All we know of ancient efforts to study the nature of living things comes from the records made by the early biologists. Unfortunately, only some of those records survived to later times. What is now known is mainly the work of Aristotle, who lived in Greece about 2,300 years ago. Aristotle observed the world

of nature, thought about it, taught about it, and left records. And he was undoubtedly one of the best naturalists of all time. He described in a remarkably accurate manner the animal life that was familiar to him and attracted his attention—particularly the habits of fishes, the breeding habits of octopuses, the behavior of bees, and the nature of whales, dolphins, and porpoises. All are still being studied by biologists today. Aristotle also attempted to analyze the nature of reproduction, heredity, and sex, with which biologists are still deeply concerned. Aristotle, in fact, represents the climax of the great intellectual adventure of the ancient Greeks. For nearly 2,000 years afterward no one really tried to improve on his ideas concerning the nature of life.

We have a record of only one other important biologist of ancient times. This is Galen, a Greek who spent most of his active life in Rome during the 2nd century A.D. Aristotle was an observer, who saw things as they were and thought about their nature. Galen was outstanding for his skill and inventiveness in making experiments. He paid much attention to the flow of blood in the

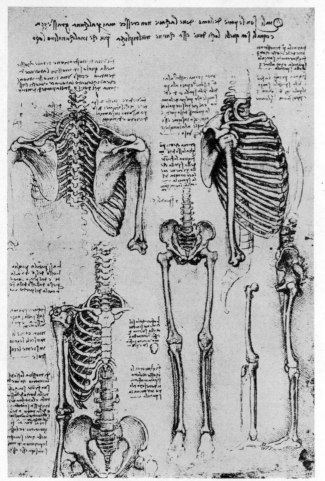

These drawings of the human skeleton were made by Leonardo da Vinci, who lived from 1452 to 1519.

were greatly interested in the exact portrayal of animal and plant forms, as well as the structure of the human body. These artists needed also to be scientists because they were intensely curious about the real nature of what they were attempting to portray on canvas or in stone. For the first time in ages men began to look at plants and animals as they really were, rather than studying old drawings and descriptions.

At the same time the discovery of the New World and of the Far East took place. Explorers brought home accounts of an exciting variety of strange forms of life.

All of this happened at the same time as the invention of printing and of reproducing drawings by means of wood engravings. So it became an easy step for other students of nature to produce the first biological textbooks of this new period of biology. In Germany the first books of this sort dealt with plants. In Italy, at the University of Padua, great advances in the study of the human body were made by Vesalius and Fabricius. And somewhat later another great advance was made by William Harvey, an Englishman who had been a student under Fabricius at a time when Galileo was also present at Padua. In 1628 Harvey published his demonstration that blood circulates through the body, a fact previously unknown.

Harvey and the Founding of Physiology

Proof that the blood must circulate through the body depended in part on observations. It also depended on measurement, of a kind proposed by Galileo. The procedure is familiar to us but was new at the time. Harvey first showed that blood can leave the ventricle (chamber) of the heart only in one direction because of the valves in the heart. He then measured the capacity of this chamber. Since the normal heart beats 72 times a minute, it was possible to calculate the amount of blood that passes through it. (If the capacity of the chamber is 2 ounces, then in 1 hour the heart pumps $60 \times 72 \times 2$ ounces, a total of 8,640 ounces, or 540 pounds, of blood into the blood vessels.) This amount is about three times the weight of the body. Where did it all come from? Where did it go? The answer was that the same blood must be going round and round. This knowledge that

body. He was also much concerned with the effect of injuries to the spinal nerve cord with regard to paralysis and death. Galen stands for the second period of biology.

After Galen biology ceased to be an active science. It made no progress throughout the Dark Ages and most of the Middle Ages. It came to life again only as part of the general reawakening of scientific interest during the Renaissance.

▶ BIOLOGY DURING THE RENAISSANCE

The Renaissance, which means "rebirth," was the great surge of intellectual activity that came into full force during the 1500's. It showed itself in art, science, and exploration. Biological science has its roots in all three of these activities.

This was a time of great painters and sculptors, such as Botticelli, Leonardo da Vinci, Dürer, and Michelangelo. All of them

Above, the University of Padua in Italy. Many discoveries were made here. For 1,300 years, since the days of Galen, medical scholars had merely read about the body. Around the 1500's they began to study how it actually worked. One of these new scholars was Andreas Vesalius, a professor at Padua. His book on the workings of the human body led him to be called the father of modern anatomy. The book's Latin title was *De humani corporis fabrica*. One of its woodcuts is shown at the right.

CIRCULATION OF BLOOD

Also trained at Padua was the Englishman William Harvey (*below*). He discovered that blood travels in a complete path through the body, as shown in the diagram at left. Blood goes from the arteries to the capillaries in the body tissues, where gases are exchanged. Then the blood goes into the veins and so back to the heart. Until the 17th century, men believed blood ebbed and flowed out of the heart, like a tide.

HEAD

ARTERIES

VEINS

LUNGS

BLOOD LOSES CARBON DIOXIDE AND PICKS UP OXYGEN IN THE LUNGS

BLOOD RETURNS TO THE HEART IN THE VEINS

BLOOD LEAVES THE HEART IN THE ARTERIES

TRUNK

HEART

LIVER

CAPILLARY BED: HERE BLOOD GIVES NOURISHMENT TO CELLS AND PICKS UP WASTE MATERIAL

LEGS

Leeuwenhoek, Dutch lens maker, holds one of his tiny early microscopes. They showed an unknown world.

of physiology since Harvey's time has been the answering of questions such as these. Gradually a clearer picture of the animal body as a working mechanical model has been obtained.

Advances with the Microscope

Although he was not concerned with biology, Galileo worked out and described the construction of the compound microscope; in it a system of two or more lenses was employed. It gave biologists a means of seeing what had previously been invisible.

During the second half of the 1600's the great pioneers in the use of the microscope were at work. The most important of these men were Robert Hooke in England, Anton van Leeuwenhoek and Jan Swammerdam in Holland, and Marcello Malpighi in Italy. All contributed to the growth of the new biology, each in his own way. Malpighi, for instance, saw and described the circulation of the blood in the fine capillary vessels in the lung of a frog. Swammerdam's magnificent book called the *Bible of Nature* is probably the finest collection of microscopic observations ever published and is still used. Leeuwenhoek drew attention to the complexity and beauty of microscopic structure in plant and animal tissues. Hooke showed that plant material is made up of small units enclosed by cell walls. Thus began **microscopy**, which is the name given to the use of microscopes generally; **histology**, which is the study of tissues; and **cytology**, which is the study of cells. However, little headway was made in those fields for another 150 years. Then, in the early 1800's, important improvements in microscopes made more rapid advances possible. Meanwhile, biology had been divided into **botany** (the study of

blood circulates has formed the foundation of the science of **physiology** (how living organisms work). It raised many questions: What does the blood carry on its rounds, and why? How and where does it pick up its loads? How, where, and why does it give them up? And what does it bring back? The main task

A model of one of Leeuwenhoek's microscopes. The scale shows size. Object was placed on the needle point, and viewed through a lens set in the center hole of the flat stage at left.

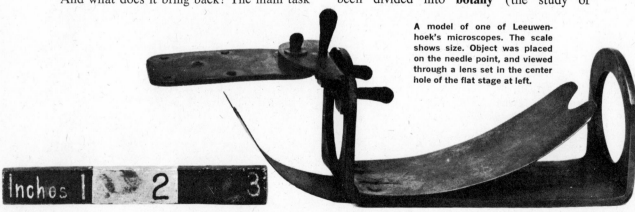

Inches 1 2 3

plants) and **zoology** (the study of animals). And it had made progress in various ways.

▶ BIOLOGY AFTER THE RENAISSANCE

The 1600's and 1700's were periods of worldwide exploration. And so the need arose for cataloging and describing in an orderly way the great variety of animals and plants that were being collected. This was early undertaken by John Ray, an English naturalist; he paved the way for the great work of Carolus Linnaeus of Sweden.

Linnaeus and Classification

Linnaeus' scheme for classifying and describing living things was adopted by naturalists in all countries. He described the parts of an animal or a plant in a regular and sensible way, according to definite rules; he also drew up a scheme in which all kinds of plants and animals had their place. Thus, plants were divided into classes, and classes into orders, according to the number and arrangement of the parts in the flower. Animals were grouped as the classes of Mammals, Birds, Reptiles, Fish, Insects, and Vermes, the last name meaning "worms." Linnaeus also developed the system of giving every living thing two Latin names, first of the genus and second of the species, as in *Homo sapiens* for man.

However, Linnaeus chiefly observed, described, and classified the external (outside) characteristics of plants and animals. It was the French anatomist Georges Cuvier who showed the importance of the structure and relations of the inner parts of the animal body.

Cuvier and the Correlation of Parts

Cuvier was actually more concerned with structure than function—that is, with **morphology** rather than physiology. But his great contribution was his principle of the correlation of parts—if one knows the structure of a particular organ or part of an animal, he can reconstruct the whole. For example, if one has a feather, or perhaps a bone of a certain kind, he can be sure that it belonged to a bird and only to a bird. If one finds a certain kind of tooth, he can safely say that it belonged to a mammal and to no other kind of animal. This principle has been extremely useful in the study of fossils, or **paleontology**. Here one usually has only fragments of some

Cuvier in his laboratory. On his left is a microscope of the early 1800's. In the background is a fossil elephant's skeleton. Cuvier excelled in rebuilding extinct animals from a few bones.

animal. Yet from the fragments it is usually possible to work out the structure of the whole animal.

This process of comparing and contrasting the structures of living things is known as **taxonomy**. It occupied many biologists during the first half of the 1800's. Other biological advances took place during the same time. And this period saw the slow coming together of various separate approaches into what we now regard as modern biology. These approaches were principally: the development of the general theory of evolution; the devel-

RED-FOOTED BOOBY

FUR SEAL

GALÁPAGOS PENGUIN

GALÁPAGOS TORTOISE

PELICAN

FLAMINGO

LAND IGUANA

By studying the animals of the lonely Galápagos Islands, "a little world in itself," Charles Darwin got important ideas for his world-shaking book *The Origin of Species.*

opment of the cell theory; and a deepening understanding of the living organism as a functioning mechanism.

▶THE THEORY OF EVOLUTION

Animals and plants have slowly changed, one way or another, throughout the ages. That is, they have undergone **evolution**, and simpler kinds have given rise to more complex kinds. That idea grew slowly. It was based in part on this realization: Living things can be arranged in some order from simple to complex. Aristotle long ago drew up his "ladder of nature," with simple forms of life at the bottom and man at the top. The vast information acquired during the early 1800's about animal and plant structures unmistakably pointed to an orderly and evolutionary pattern of relationships.

The Forerunners: Lamarck and Lyell

The Chevalier de Lamarck, a French zoologist, was among the first to propose such an idea. He suggested that animals had not always been as they are today. Rather, the various kinds had undergone progressive change; the cause had been changing external circumstances. During the same period the Scottish geologist Charles Lyell added im-

portant evidence. Lyell was an expert on rocks and fossils. He showed that each layer of rocks contained its own distinctive fossil remains of animals and plants. And the nature of the fossils showed a gradual change within succeeding layers. The idea of evolution and the evidence of progressive change were therefore being discussed by scientists in 1830. This was just before young Charles Darwin set out on his famous voyage aboard the *Beagle.* That 5-year voyage led to Darwin's theory of evolution.

Darwin's Theory of Evolution

Darwin himself later wrote that three things above all influenced him in favor of the idea of evolution. These were:

(1) The discovery of fossil remains of giant armored animals clearly related to the small living South American armadillos.

(2) The way in which species of animals gave way to close relatives as Darwin went south.

(3) His experience in the Galápagos Islands. These are young, volcanic islands in the equatorial Pacific Ocean. They are far removed from continental land. On them live peculiar kinds of giant tortoises and lizards, and various birds, including some flightless

sea birds. The significant fact was this: The tortoises and certain birds were common to all the islands but were in small ways different on each particular island. It became clear that since the group of islands had first acquired its animals and plants, those on each separate island had undergone change.

So the principle of evolution was firmly established in Darwin's mind. He spent the 20 years after his voyage building up an immense quantity of evidence in support of the theory. He published it in 1859 in his book *The Origin of Species*.

Darwin finally showed that:

(1) The offspring of every kind of living thing vary among themselves.

(2) Every kind breeds to excess, and the numbers are continually cut down through the struggle for survival.

(3) The result is a process of natural selection of some varieties rather than others. This causes a race or species to adapt to its external conditions.

The general theory of evolution stated that all living things are related to one another and that the animal and plant kingdoms have each had an immensely long and changing past. The theory rapidly became one of the most influential ideas in the history of human thought.

The general theory of evolution was the outcome of a broad, far-reaching study of living things. Other biological advances came about in very different ways. One of these depended on improvements in the microscope. And it led to the development and acceptance of the **cell theory**.

▶ THE CELL THEORY

The microscopists of the 1600's had studied infusions—liquids made by boiling hay or dead leaves in water. When the infusions were allowed to stand awhile, a large variety of microscopic organisms could be seen swimming about in them; these organisms were called infusorians.

In the 1800's, through the use of better microscopes, microscopists slowly came to an important conclusion: Almost all organisms that can be seen without a microscope are aggregates (collections) of cells, while the infusorian organisms consist of single cells. Biologists gradually recognized that organisms consist of one cell or of many cells. In living things the cell is the unit of construction.

Also, during the first part of the 1800's, it was seen that each cell has a central nucleus; this was regarded as the controller of the cell. It was seen that living matter is a sticky, slimy substance with very definite optical, chemical, and physical qualities; this substance was given the name protoplasm. And it was recognized by Theodor Schwann that all eggs are cells, whatever their size may be.

Schwann, a German, concluded that an entire animal or plant is composed either of cells or of cells and substances thrown off by cells; that cells have a life that is to some extent their own; and that this individual life of all the cells is under the control of the organism as a whole. Those are three of the widest general conclusions reached in biology. We must add to them the conclusion of Rudolf Virchow, a German: Every cell originates from a cell. Together these constitute the cell theory.

▶ DEEPER UNDERSTANDING OF LIVING FORMS

One other major development in biological science took place during the first half of the 1800's. It lay in applying chemistry to investigations into the nature of living processes.

Liebig's Work

Baron Justus von Liebig in Germany classified foods in relation to their use in the animal body—that is, as fats, carbohydrates, and proteins. He taught that plants obtain carbon dioxide and ammonia in the atmosphere and from ammonia and nitrates absorbed through their root systems. He taught that these substances are eventually returned to the atmosphere and soil through the process of decay. He claimed that carbon dioxide,

Plant cells (much enlarged) contain chloroplasts (dark spots) that make starch out of carbon dioxide and water.

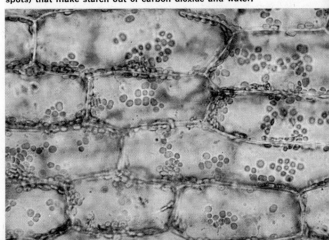

ammonia, and water contained all the necessary elements for the production of vegetable matter. And, he said, these substances were used over and over again through death and decay. Liebig adopted the term "chlorophyll," which is Greek for "green leaf," and used the term as a name for the green pigment of plants. Somewhat later Julius von Sachs, another student of plant nutrition, showed that chlorophyll is not spread all through the plant cell; it is confined within small bodies called chloroplasts. He also showed that sunlight is needed for chloroplasts to absorb carbon dioxide.

Pasteur's Work

In the middle 1800's Louis Pasteur in Paris discovered the cause of fermentation and decay. The changes were caused by the activity of microscopic organisms. He then turned to the question of the origin of these organisms. By 1859 Pasteur was engaged in a scientific argument concerning the origin of such living things. In a beautifully simple experiment he put some fermentable fluid in a flask; he heated the neck of the flask and drew it out into a long, narrow S with an open

Louis Pasteur sealed boiled fluid in a flask to show that life does not start up by itself.

end. Next, he boiled the fluid repeatedly to kill anything alive. Finally, he left it to stand for several months. Nothing happened. Pasteur broke the neck of the flask, thus exposing the fluid to the fall of atmospheric dust. Within a few hours fermentation started, and organisms were discovered swimming about in the liquid; they arose from spores (seed-like cells) drifting about in the atmosphere. The old belief that such life sprang into being without a cause could be held no longer.

▶ **THE START OF MODERN BIOLOGY**

The modern period of biology begins about 1860. It begins with the launching, almost at the same time, of Darwin's theory of organic evolution and Pasteur's theory of **biogenesis** (that is, living matter always arises through already existing living matter). In that same period, in an Austrian monastery garden, the Abbé Mendel was performing his famous breeding experiments concerning hereditary features of pea and bean plants. However, his experiments did not become generally known until 1900; so, in effect, they belong to a later period.

Within 20 years following 1860 the whole outlook of biology underwent a complete change. The causes were:

(1) The discovery that plants and animals reproduce in basically the same way—by means of sex cells.

(2) The discovery that living substance, or protoplasm, is similar in both plants and animals.

(3) The discovery that processes of nutrition and respiration (breathing) are practically the same in all living things.

(4) The recognition that plants use the chlorophyll apparatus to make their food and so, indirectly, the food of animals.

(5) The realization that the cell is the unit of life in all organisms.

(6) The evolutionary view of life.

(7) The realization that all living organisms come from living organisms; life, therefore, has been continuous throughout the ages.

During this later part of the 1800's biologists gave great attention to the evolutionary relationships of animals and plants, both living and extinct. They studied the development of eggs and embryos, and whole life histories in the hope that more light would be thrown on evolutionary history. And they turned to the working of the animal body. The studies of the French physiologist Claude Bernard were outstanding here.

Bernard discovered, for instance, that the liver builds up substances obtained from the blood, stores them, and breaks down substances for distribution to the body. Bernard also introduced an extremely important idea: The various forms of body activity are closely related and respond to the body's general needs. He emphasized the importance of what is called "the internal environment of the body." It consists of (1) neighboring cells and their products, (2) substances contributed by the blood, (3) substances thrown off by the cells and removed by the blood, and (4) the messages, or impulses, brought by nerves. Modern physiological research is mainly the continuing investigation of those four areas.

▶ BIOLOGY IN OUR CENTURY

Twentieth-century biology has developed along several major lines. All are related to the work that went on before.

In physiology the greatest advance has been in our understanding of the nervous system. Today we view nerve cells as systems capable of transmitting electrical and chemical signals in a number of ways. We see the patterns of pathways and centers in the brain and spinal cord. And we can relate all this and also the nature of sense organs to the behavior of animals.

This physiology of the nervous system is known as **neurophysiology**. It is now one of the most active fields of biological research. In it elaborate electronic equipment is used to record the passage of nerve impulses within the brain and spinal cord; such equipment is also used in connection with sense organs and muscles. Simple reflex actions, such as scratching an itching place, had been shown to work through simple nerve connections. Early in the century the Russian physiologist Ivan Pavlov and his school attempted to explain all unconscious forms of behavior in terms of reflex actions. But this was an overly simple way of thinking of the activity of the nervous system. It has been replaced by a much more complex and satisfactory viewpoint, known as **nervous integration**. This was

Machine that "feels" brain impulses through the scalp.

developed chiefly by the English neurophysiologist Charles Sherrington.

The nervous system is now known to be in direct or indirect control of all that goes on in the body: for example, the action of sweat glands in the skin, the nutrition of muscles, the mechanism of childbirth, and so on. Brain and body are now seen to be so closely interrelated that neither can be understood by itself. How do mental states influence the body? How does body chemistry influence the mind? These questions are among the most important being investigated. Great efforts are also being made to analyze and understand the working of the brain itself: How is the brain related to sensation, action, thought, memory, feeling, and both consciousness and sleep?

Progress in any branch of biology depends to a great extent on advances in methods and instruments. This has been true of **biochemistry**. This science deals with the chemical analysis of the processes occurring in the living cell and in the organism as a whole. Knowledge of microscopic cell structure has grown continually as microscopes have improved or changed. Some of the most important advances in cytology (the study of cells) were made toward the end of the 1800's. They were made through improvements in

Linus Pauling, Nobel prizewinner in chemistry, has studied the structure of giant molecules (model at left).

various techniques of staining and in the use of the microscope. As a result, the fine detail of the mechanism of cell division was observed. It was observed both of the cell as a whole and of the nucleus with its chromosomes. Division of the nucleus was seen to be so exact that each resulting nucleus was the image of the parent nucleus.

Studies of this kind were extended to the reproductive cells of both sexes. This information, combined with that from Mendel's breeding experiments, laid the foundation for the rise of **genetics**, the science of heredity. The chromosomes of the cell nucleus were recognized as the bearers of the hereditary agents.

During the first half of our century, geneticists carried out extensive breeding experiments with plants and with the fruit fly *Drosophila*. At the same time they investigated the nucleus of the sex cells of these organisms. The result has been an elaborate and enlightening theory of heredity. Recent progress in this field comes from the study of bacteria and viruses. Bacteria have now been discovered to reproduce by a process basically

like that of plants and animals. Viruses are half-living particles close to the limits of microscopic vision; they can reproduce only when inside bacterial cells or the cells of plant or animal tissues. They are now known to be capable of transferring hereditary qualities from one cell to another. The study of bacteria and viruses has become the new and promising approach to the study of the mechanisms of heredity.

Two outstanding biological research methods have now become joined.

One of these methods is the use of the electron microscope, which can produce a photograph of an object magnified 200,000 times. It shows cellular parts not visible with the best magnification (2,000 times) of the ordinary (light) microscope. The result is that the internal structure of cells has become known in very great detail. And it has become possible to analyze these structures in terms of the chemical substances that compose them.

The other approach is the study of the chemistry, physics, and general organization of macromolecules. (These are the giant molecules formed by the linking of other molecules.) This new **molecular biology** includes the study of: the way that protein molecules join to form the fibers that make up muscle and the supporting structures of the body; the way in which the molecular structure of the cell membrane relates to the life of the cell; the way in which the molecular structure of chloroplasts relates to photosynthesis; the chemical changes that take place in the protoplasm of a developing egg; and, above all, the way in which the nucleus controls the cell.

Biology has now reached a critical stage in its own development. Rapid advance is being made along many separate approaches that appear to be coming together. As the various lines merge, our understanding of the nature of life and our capacity to control life will take a great leap forward.

N. J. BERRILL
McGill University

See also BIOCHEMISTRY; CELL; DARWIN, CHARLES ROBERT; EVOLUTION; FERMENTATION; FOSSILS; GENETICS; HARVEY, WILLIAM; MEDICINE, HISTORY OF; MICROBIOLOGY; PASTEUR, LOUIS; PHOTOSYNTHESIS; TAXONOMY.

BIOLUMINESCENCE

Light from fireflies and other living things is called **bioluminescence**. There are many bioluminescent things in nature—plants, animals, and bacteria.

The glowing plants include only a few kinds, such as certain toadstools and molds. But animals that light up are more numerous; they range from tiny one-celled sea creatures to sponges, clams, worms, and insects. The most numerous glowing forms of life are found in the salt water of oceans. The most familiar forms are found on land—fireflies, glowworms, and fox fire fungus.

Bioluminescence is called "cold" light to distinguish it from incandescence, or heat-giving light. (For example, electric light bulbs, oil lamps, and candles give off "hot" light.) Living plants and animals could not produce incandescent light without being burned up. Their light is caused by chemicals combining in such a way that little or no measurable heat is given off.

The substance that gives off the light in living things is called luciferin. This "glowing" chemical was named in 1887 by one of the earliest scientists to study living light, Raphaël Dubois of France, who took a glowing fluid from a clam. The fluid continued to glow in a test tube for a few minutes, then went out. Dubois found that he could make the fluid glow again by adding an extract from another clam. Clearly, something in the extract was needed to produce light. Dubois named this unknown "luciferin," meaning "light bearer."

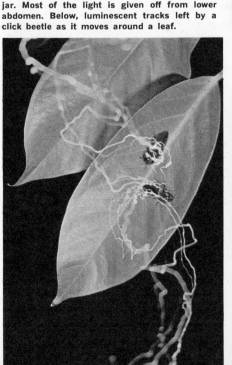

Familiar sources of bioluminescence on land are fireflies and click beetles. Above is abdomen of firefly photographed through bottom of glass jar. Most of the light is given off from lower abdomen. Below, luminescent tracks left by a click beetle as it moves around a leaf.

Above, *Mycena* toadstools photographed in daylight. Below, same toadstools photographed in dark by their own light. Most of the light comes from the gills under the cap.

Above: Tiny luminous sea creatures called siphonophores. The photograph shows the creatures magnified many times. Below: *Chauliodus*, a deep-sea luminous fish.

Bioluminescence is a complicated chemical process, but it can be summed up in a simple way: Living light is produced when luciferin and oxygen combine in the presence of luciferase. In addition, in fireflies a compound called adenosine triphosphate (ATP) is needed to produce light. ATP is a source of energy in living things for such work as muscle contraction.

Scientists who study the cells of living things need a way to measure the tiny amounts of ATP in the cells. To do this, they use an extract, or liquid preparation, made from fireflies. The extract gives off light that soon disappears. But the light can be brought back by adding ATP to the extract. As more ATP is added, the light glows brighter. By measuring the brightness of the restored light, a scientist can tell how much ATP there is in a cell sample.

Why do so many kinds of life light up? Scientists who study bioluminescence think the answer goes back to the time when there was no oxygen in the earth's atmosphere. If there were living things on the earth at that time, they had to depend on other elements for life. The oxygen that gradually formed in the atmosphere was poisonous to these living things. They had to be able to use it up, or die.

How could the oxygen be used up? One theory states that living things did it by producing light. In those early days all life glowed or flashed to survive. As millions of years passed, living things became used to oxygen and finally came to depend on it. They no longer needed to light up to stay alive. Some primitive bacteria and fungi went on glowing, and they still do.

Some higher forms of life also continued to glow, but they used the light in a new way. Fireflies, for example, use flashes as mating signals, and some fishes seem to use the light to attract prey. A squid releases a glowing liquid into the water that seems to protect it from large fish.

Much remains to be learned about the chemistry of bioluminescence. Perhaps some day enough will be known to produce this cold light for everyday use instead of the energy-wasting electric light we use now.

W. D. McElroy
University of California—San Diego

Further experiments convinced Dubois that the light was caused not by one chemical but by a team of chemicals working together. Luciferin would not light up except in the presence of a second unknown chemical, which Dubois called "luciferase."

Dubois' work was carried forward many years later by E. Newton Harvey of the United States. In Japan, Harvey collected and studied a tiny sea creature, *Cypridina*. After years of trial and error Harvey found that the luciferin contained carbon, hydrogen, and oxygen—the same elements found in all living cells. Scientists have since learned that all luciferins are not the same. All luciferases are not the same, either. Luciferins and luciferases vary with the sea animals, insects, and bacteria they come from.

BIRDS

Birds are flying animals. That is the single most important fact about them. Birds are not the only animals with the power of flight—insects and bats fly; so did certain ancient reptiles. But birds are the only really numerous flying animals that have backbones. There are about 8,600 species of birds, but fewer than 1,000 of bats. The flying reptiles have long been extinct. And insects do not have backbones.

Flight is a very difficult activity for a living thing. The strains and stresses on the bones and muscles of a flying animal are tremendous. Its senses, such as those of balance and sight, must be of a special sort. Flying demands a much greater supply of energy than do most forms of getting about. Therefore birds have very special features and abilities.

For instance, only a very light animal can fly, but its supporting framework must be very strong. A bird's skeleton is a simple, stiff framework that is both light and strong. It is light because most of the bones are thin plates or hollow, air-filled tubes and struts.

It is strong because many of these bones have special shapes; the shapes give the bones their strength, rather than the weight or thickness of the bones.

A flying animal also needs strong but flexible surfaces for wings. Feathers fit this need perfectly. Overlapped like shingles, they also serve as the warmest yet lightest of insulators for these warm-blooded, flying animals. Feathers are found only in the group of animals we call birds—the class Aves.

The forelimbs (or arms) of birds serve as wings. This means that they are of little use for anything except flying. So birds must walk on two legs. They must have very flexible necks and strong beaks to handle food, to care for feathers, and to build nests. Birds must also use their beaks to care for young, as weapons of defense, and for many other jobs that non-flying animals do with the paws, claws, or hands on their forelimbs.

▶ FEATHERS

Examine the next feather you find. This marvel feels almost weightless—yet how strong and flexible it is when you run your

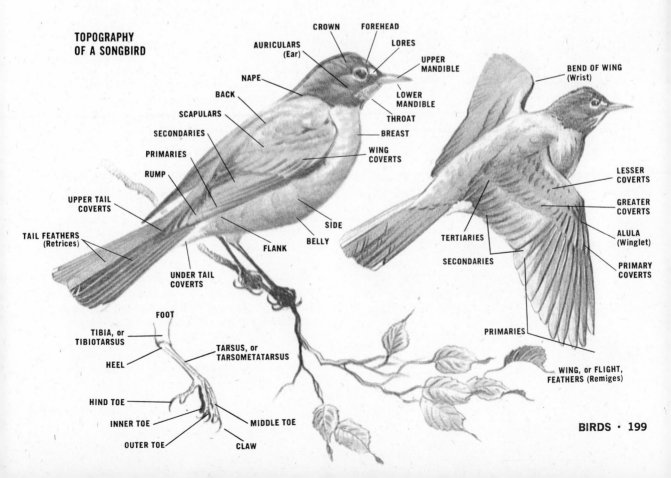

TOPOGRAPHY OF A SONGBIRD

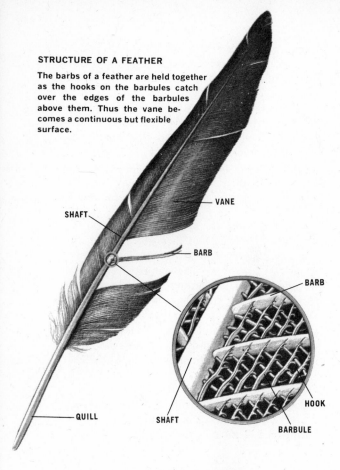

STRUCTURE OF A FEATHER

The barbs of a feather are held together as the hooks on the barbules catch over the edges of the barbules above them. Thus the vane becomes a continuous but flexible surface.

VANE

SHAFT

BARB

BARB

HOOK

QUILL

SHAFT

BARBULE

MALE MALLARD DUCK

IN BREEDING PLUMAGE

IN THE POST-BREEDING MOLT, OR ECLIPSE

finger along its vane! Feathers are very special outgrowths of the skin (as are the scales of reptiles and the hoofs, horns, claws or nails, and hair of mammals).

A bird grows a series of feather coats during its lifetime. A baby bird is covered with down feathers either when it hatches or shortly afterward. The down is followed by one or more sets of juvenile feathers, which push out the down as they grow. Last comes the plumage typical of the adult members of the species.

Adult birds change this plumage from time to time as old worn feathers molt (drop out) and new ones grow in their place. If a feather is pulled out, it begins to replace itself at once. In addition, some birds take on their breeding plumage by molting and growing bright, new feathers. So most birds molt twice a year, once before and once after the breeding season.

Since most birds do not shed many of their flight feathers at the same time, they are able to fly all through the molting period. Also, flight feathers are often shed in pairs, one from the right and one from the left wing, and flying balance is not upset.

Ducks, swans, and geese are an exception to this. They lose all their flight feathers at the same time and become flightless. But these are water birds and do not have to fly if threatened; they can take to the water in times of danger. The brightly colored males often take on a drab-colored set of feathers during this molt. This gives the protection of camouflage and makes it easier for them to hide during such a dangerous time.

▶ SKELETON AND MUSCLES

The skeleton of a bird is a light, strong airframe that has become greatly simplified as compared to that of a ground-living animal. Many of the parts have disappeared in the course of bird evolution. Other parts have become fused (united), giving the stiffness needed for flight.

A bird skull is notable for its huge eye sockets, which hold the large bird eyeballs; for a large rounded braincase; and for the complete absence of teeth, a weight-saving feature. Like many bird bones the bones of the skull are exceptionally light in weight.

While the bird's neck vertebrae (bones)

are shaped so that the neck is extremely flexible, most of the rest of the skeleton has become stiffened. The vertebrae of the back and hip sections are fused with only one or two slightly flexible joints. Thus the bird's backbone amounts to a strong, rigid girder for the support of the bird in the air.

The bird's breastbone is a thin flattened plate, reinforced down its center by the keel; in cross section it has the strong T shape. The keel also gives extra area and mechanical advantage for the attachment of the great muscles of flight.

The heaviest, strongest bone in the bird's skeleton is the coracoid. It and the ribs serve as struts between the breastbone and the rigid backbone, holding them apart when the flight muscles contract and tend to pull them together. The coracoid and the wishbone also form a strong tripod (three-legged frame) at the top of which are the upper-wing bone sockets. This tripod is anchored to the bird's back and rib cage by the shoulder blade, embedded in muscle.

The muscles that pull the wings down are called the major pectoral (breast) muscles; those that pull them up are the minor pectorals. The pectoral muscles may account for as much as one fifth of the weight of the entire bird. These muscles are the familiar "white meat" of chickens and turkeys. In stronger fliers, such as ducks, these muscles are a dark, rich red. This is due to the huge supply of blood that furnishes the energy needed in the muscles of these better fliers.

▶ INTERIOR ORGANS

Like all other bird features, the inside workings of birds are greatly adapted for flight. This strenuous activity requires large

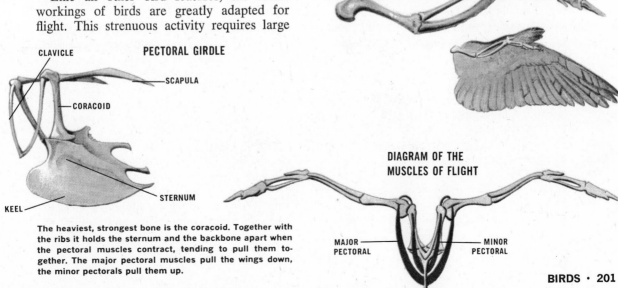

SKELETON OF A PIGEON

ORBIT

THUMB

WRIST

FINGERS

RADIUS

ULNA

CERVICAL VERTEBRAE (Neck bone)

HUMERUS

ELBOW

VERTEBRAE OF THORAX, HIP AND TAIL (Largely fused)

RIBS

CORACOID

SCAPULA (Shoulder blade)

CLAVICLE (Wish bone)

STERNUM (Breastbone)

FEMUR (Thigh)

KEEL

TIBIOTARSUS (Shin)

HEEL

TOES

TARSOMETATARSUS (Foot bone)

ARM OF MAN AND BIRD COMPARED

PECTORAL GIRDLE

CLAVICLE

SCAPULA

CORACOID

STERNUM

KEEL

DIAGRAM OF THE MUSCLES OF FLIGHT

MAJOR PECTORAL

MINOR PECTORAL

The heaviest, strongest bone is the coracoid. Together with the ribs it holds the sternum and the backbone apart when the pectoral muscles contract, tending to pull them together. The major pectoral muscles pull the wings down, the minor pectorals pull them up.

BIRDS · 201

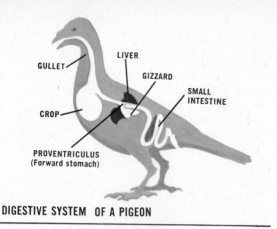

DIGESTIVE SYSTEM OF A PIGEON

GULLET
LIVER
GIZZARD
SMALL INTESTINE
CROP
PROVENTRICULUS (Forward stomach)

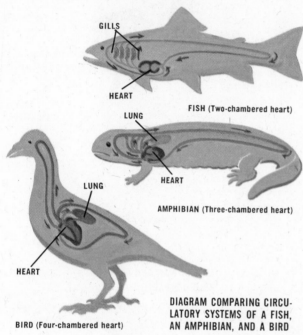

GILLS
HEART
FISH (Two-chambered heart)

LUNG
HEART
AMPHIBIAN (Three-chambered heart)

LUNG
HEART
BIRD (Four-chambered heart)

DIAGRAM COMPARING CIRCULATORY SYSTEMS OF A FISH, AN AMPHIBIAN, AND A BIRD

pointing points, or papillae. The tongue also is hard and has papillae. The papillae help in swallowing food—especially the wriggly kind.

The gullet is a thin-walled tube through which food moves from the mouth to the stomach. In many birds, especially grain eaters, it expands into the crop, a large, balloon-like storage chamber at the base of the neck. Here food is moistened and softened, as well as stored, before it moves on to the stomach.

The bird's stomach has two parts: the forward part, where food is treated with digestive juices, and the second part, the gizzard, in which the "teeth" of the bird are found. The gizzard has strong muscular walls and a hard, ridged lining. With the grinding action of its muscles and the help of the small stones that most birds swallow, this living mill can grind the hardest food.

After the food is prepared in the mouth, crop, and stomach, it moves into the long tube called the small intestine. The digested part is absorbed through the thin walls of the intestine into the blood. The blood carries it all over the body to every living cell by way of the circulatory system.

Birds and mammals are the only animals whose temperature is controlled from within; in popular language these animals are "warm blooded." Birds and mammals are also the only animals covered with a material that keeps in the body's heat—feathers in birds and hair in mammals. A third feature shared by birds and mammals also has much to do both with temperature control and with good circulation. This is the four-chambered heart.

In this type of heart, used blood comes from the body with a load of waste carbon dioxide and enters one side of the heart; it is pumped to the lungs. In the lungs the blood exchanges carbon dioxide for fresh oxygen and flows back to the heart. The heart then pumps the blood to the body by way of its other side.

In birds and mammals each side of the heart, with its two chambers, is completely separate from the other. The used blood being pumped into the lungs never mixes with fresh blood being pumped into the body. In fishes, amphibians, and reptiles, the

amounts of energy. Bird metabolism (the living processes that produce and use this energy) is rapid. Bird temperatures are high, usually between 40 and 44°C (104 and 112°F). Their pulse (heartbeat) and breathing rates are very fast. For example, a sparrow's heart beats more than 500 times a minute and a hummingbird breathes 250 times a minute when at rest.

An extra-good digestive system is also necessary, to supply the large quantities of food needed as fuel for this rapid metabolism. Because birds have no teeth, most of them swallow their food much as they find it, although many do crack seeds, crush fruits, or tear large prey into pieces small enough to swallow. The inside of the mouth is hard and horny; in places it has small, backward-

two sides of the heart are not completely separate and the used blood does mix with the fresh to some degree.

When you breathe, the action of your ribs and diaphragm expands your chest cavity. The air pressure within the chest cavity is lowered, causing outside air to rush into the lungs. The greatly branched air passages in the lungs have a huge total area—over 90 square meters (about 1,000 square feet) in human lungs—through which oxygen may be absorbed. Because the lungs are inside the body, this surface is continually moist; oxygen can pass through the walls of the lung's blood vessels and combine with the hemoglobin in the red blood cells. These cells then transport the oxygen to all the living cells of the body, where it is used in metabolism.

Birds must have very efficient breathing. Their lungs are small and light in keeping with the need for weight saving. But in addition to the lungs, there are a number of delicate, bubble-like, almost weightless air sacs located in various parts of the bird's body. These connect with the lungs and with many of the hollow bird bones. When a bird breathes in, some of the air goes directly into the air passages of the lungs, where its oxygen is absorbed. But much of it passes through the lungs to the air sacs, where it is stored for a moment. When the bird breathes out, this stored air then enters the lungs and is used. In this way fresh air passes through a bird's lungs both when it breathes in and when it breathes out. In a sense a bird receives two breaths for every one taken. Birds thus have small, light lungs in keeping with the need to save weight. But they have very efficient breathing equipment in keeping with the need of a flying animal for tremendous energy.

NERVES AND SENSES

The bird's brain is very large in comparison with that of the average backboned animal. However, it has developed in a way quite different from that of the mammal. In the evolution of both birds and mammals, the cerebral hemispheres of the brain have become greatly enlarged. In birds the enlargement is mostly in the part called the corpus striatum; in mammals it is the cerebral cortex that has enlarged the most.

If we compare the way birds and mammals go about their affairs, we can see what this difference in size of these parts means.

Most of the habits of birds are the inherited abilities we call instincts. Birds are born knowing how to do almost everything needed to carry out their normal lives. They have no need to learn very much. Well-developed instinctive behavior can probably be connected with the large corpus striatum of birds.

The behavior of mammals is controlled to a much larger extent by their ability to profit from experience and to learn new habits and new ways of doing things. Thus learning and intelligence are probably connected with the large cortex in mammals.

A large part of the brain and nervous system of birds is also connected with senses such as sight and balance, which are important in flight. Fine eyesight is vital for a flying animal. It is one of the most important features of birds. In proportion to the size of the animal, bird eyes are much larger than those of most other backboned animals. The eye of the ostrich is about 65 millimeters (2½ inches) in diameter—the largest eye of any living land animal regardless of its size.

Birds such as sparrows and warblers hunt for food among grasses and brush or in shrubs

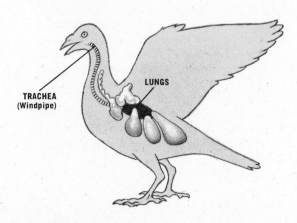

DIAGRAM OF AIR SACS

TRACHEA
(Windpipe)

LUNGS

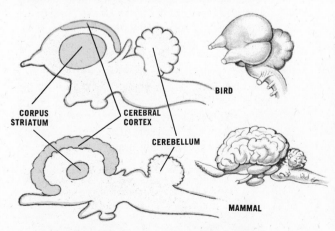

CORPUS
STRIATUM

CEREBRAL
CORTEX

CEREBELLUM

BIRD

MAMMAL

DIAGRAM COMPARING BIRD AND MAMMAL BRAIN

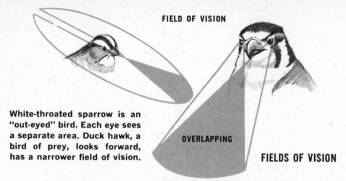

FIELD OF VISION

White-throated sparrow is an "out-eyed" bird. Each eye sees a separate area. Duck hawk, a bird of prey, looks forward, has a narrower field of vision.

OVERLAPPING

FIELDS OF VISION

BIRD PROPELLER

ENTIRE WING

SINGLE PRIMARY FEATHER

In flight, the outermost primaries are often turned forward, each acting as small propeller.

and trees; they usually have a wide angle of vision. They are also "out eyed"; each eye looks out at right angles to the bird and sees a completely separate area. As a result, such birds can cover a very wide area of vision in their search for food and in their constant watch for the animals that prey upon them.

In birds of prey the eyes are set to look more forward, as yours do. The area each eye sees overlaps with the other's, and the angle of vision is narrower. But these birds have the "telescopic" ability to see very small objects and great detail at long distances.

The ability of birds to see color is more or less like that of a human, as far as we can tell. In the retina of the eye, the cells that are sensitive to light are of two types. Those that are most sensitive to color and able to distinguish fine detail are called cones; those most sensitive to dim light are called rods. Daytime-living birds have a greater number of cones in the retina. Birds of the night have retinas with a greater number of rods. Also, the lenses in the eyes of night birds, like owls, are relatively larger. This type of eye is able to gather and concentrate dim light.

The sense of hearing is excellent in birds. So are the senses of balance and of place in and movement through space. All these senses are centered in the ears. In spite of the hard, horny character of the beak and mouth, many birds also have a good sense of taste; they can select their proper food instantly. However, the sense of smell seems to be almost or entirely missing in most birds.

▶ FLIGHT

The principles of flight are the same for the bird as for the airplane. If you look at the cross section of a plane wing, you will notice its similarity to the cross section of the bird wing. Both the bird and the plane overcome the downward pull of gravity by means of

lift; lift is caused by the forces of air as it moves past such wings. To move forward, both must overcome the resistance of air as well. Again the bird and the plane are similar; both overcome this resistance by means of a propeller.

The propeller of a bird cannot revolve. Also, instead of being separate it is part of the wing. Nevertheless the bird propeller works on the same principles as the plane propeller.

A bird does not fly by simply flapping its wings up and down. The downstroke is the most important in flight; it moves downward and *forward*. The upstroke moves upward and *backward*.

On the downstroke the wing has its leading edge held lower than the rear edge. As the wing cuts downward and forward through the air, the angle and shape of the wing is similar to that of the blade of a propeller when it is cutting downward during its rotation. In addition, each primary feather is under muscular control and may be rotated. Often several of the outermost primaries are also turned forward so that the leading edge of each is low and each acts as a small, individual propeller.

When a wing is held at too great an angle to the direction of flight or when the speed of flight is too slow, the smooth flow of air over the top surface of the wing is disturbed and lift is destroyed. This condition is known as stalling. Again birds and planes are similar in the devices they use to help correct the condition. If any small wing is held in front of the leading edge of a large wing, a slot is formed through which air flows. This air is speeded up; it smooths out the flow of air over the top surface of the wing, and to a degree prevents stalling. In birds the winglet (little wing) forms such a slot when it is extended. The tips of the primaries are also

Downstroke is more important than upstroke in flight. In downstroke, wings move downward and forward. In upstroke, they move upward and backward.

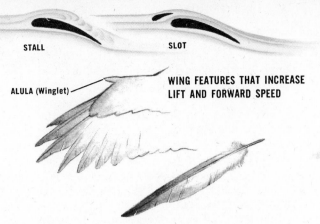

STALL

SLOT

ALULA (Winglet)

WING FEATURES THAT INCREASE LIFT AND FORWARD SPEED

Air (represented by shading) flows over two wing surfaces (shown in black cross section). Along rear edge of wing, air flow is disturbed, creating stall. When alula is raised, slot in upper surface results in smooth air flow. Below, wing feathers slotted, or spread out, reducing air disturbance at tips of wings. Some primary feathers have special narrow tips, which allow better slotting.

SOARING

Several birds soaring on currents of air rising from earth.

WING SHAPES

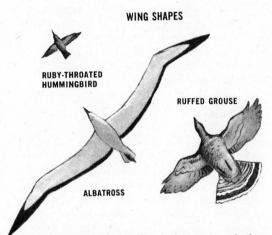

RUBY-THROATED HUMMINGBIRD

RUFFED GROUSE

ALBATROSS

often spread, as you would spread your fingers, to form slots.

There are almost as many shapes of wings as there are kinds of birds. The wings of the pheasant or partridge are short, broad, and rounded. They are well suited for short bursts of rapid flight in wooded or brushy country. The wing of the albatross is long, narrow, and pointed. It is well suited for almost effortless flight in strong ocean winds for days on end.

The hummingbird has a small, triangular wing that is almost all propeller. Its rate of wingbeat is very fast—up to 4,800 strokes a minute in one South American species. A hummingbird can rotate its upper arm almost 180 degrees. Therefore it can reverse the angle of its small wing on the upstroke and get lift. The hummingbird can hover in place, and fly up, down, and even backward.

The wings of the condor are very different. This large bird soars for hours on end high over mountains, hills, and valleys with hardly a movement of its wings. The condor and other soaring birds take advantage of currents in the air.

The wind blows parallel to the ground; buildings, mountains, and steep shorelines make it swerve upward. Also, the land reflects heat, sending columns of heated air upward. The amount of heat depends upon the land's surface; a plowed field or a sandy beach of white sand reflects more heat than a wood or a brushy pasture.

A soaring bird takes advantage of these currents. It does so by gliding downward in a column of air that is rising as fast, or faster, than the bird is dropping. The wings of soaring birds are broad and quite large in proportion to the size and weight of the bird. Also, they may be greatly slotted; thus the bird can maintain lift at slow speeds in very uneven air.

A bird doubtless uses its tail to keep itself steady in flight. The tail also serves as a flap to slow air speed without stalling, just as an airplane's wing flaps are used in landing. If you watch a bird closely, you can see countless other ways in which they use their flexible wings, tails, and bodies. These animals of the air really use almost every nerve, muscle, and feather; even the extended feet or twisted body or head can aid in their marvelously agile flight.

LOUIS DARLING
Author, *Bird*

See also AERODYNAMICS; MAMMALS.

HISTORY AND EVOLUTION OF BIRDS

Every living thing is descended from the first simple forms of life that appeared on the earth 2,000,000,000 or 3,000,000,000 (billion) years ago. So every living thing is the end product (result) of a long and complicated history. To understand a present-day plant or animal, it is necessary to know something about the great host of ancestors that have lived before it.

About 400,000,000 to 450,000,000 years ago, the first vertebrates (animals with backbones) appeared on the earth. These were fishlike water animals. They were the beginning of the great stream of vertebrate life that has resulted in all the backboned animals we know today: the fishes, amphibians, reptiles, birds, and mammals.

▶ ARCHAEOPTERYX: THE FIRST BIRD

Birds first appear in the "family tree" of the vertebrates about 150,000,000 years ago, when they branched off from the reptile line. (The first mammals evolved at about the same time, although they were descended from a different group of reptiles.) There are no known fossils of these near ancestors of birds. Most likely they were small, lightly built, agile, tree-living reptiles. For them the ability to glide a bit, and eventually to fly, would have been a tremendous advantage.

This simplified family tree shows the relationships of birds to the other major groups of vertebrates.

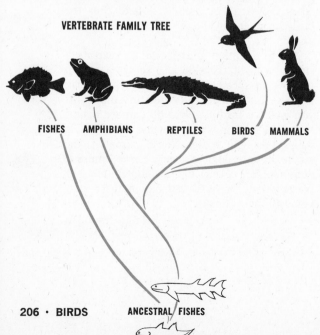

VERTEBRATE FAMILY TREE

FISHES   AMPHIBIANS   REPTILES   BIRDS   MAMMALS

ANCESTRAL FISHES

Flight helped in moving about freely to find food. But its most important advantage was probably the safety that it brought to small animals.

(Note, however, that birds did not descend from the flying reptiles, the pterosaurs. These reptiles lived at the same time as ancient birds. But they differed from birds in their anatomy and method of flying.)

The fossil record of birds and their near ancestors is far from complete. Light animals of the trees and air do not often die in places where mud or cave-ins preserve their remains. There is much guesswork in our ideas about ancient birds. But we do have two very old fossil specimens of birds. An almost complete specimen was found in Bavaria in 1861. Then, in 1877, another one was found not far from the first. Some 150,000,000 years before, this part of the world had been a warm sea studded with coral islands. The first specimen was named *Archaeopteryx*, meaning "ancient winged one." (Another name was given to the other specimen, but the birds were so similar that it is possible to group both under the name *Archaeopteryx*.)

These two birds must have fluttered to their deaths in the shallows of that long-ago sea. Here they became embedded in the limy mud. More mud in the form of silt was deposited upon them before they decomposed or were destroyed in some other way. Then through long ages the mud hardened and was compressed into fine-grained limestone. The shallow seas vanished, and great forces raised and tilted the earth's crust, forming the mountains of Bavaria. Millions of years went by. Primitive people evolved and appeared on earth for the first time. Civilizations like those of ancient Sumer, Egypt, Greece, and Rome developed, prospered, and faded away. Then some modern stonecutters, while at work, happened on the remains of old birds, the ancient winged ones. The story of any fossil is exciting. But the story of these ancient bird bones is especially dramatic. The two specimens are very rare—rarer and more valuable than priceless jewels.

The fossils, particularly the first one found, are among the most beautiful and delicate known. They clearly show the impression of wing and tail feathers as well as good detail of the skeleton. *Archaeopteryx* was so much like its reptile ancestors that it must have looked like a befeathered lizard. It was about the size of a pheasant and had a reptilelike head with sharp teeth. The three "fingers" on its wing had claws, which were probably used in climbing. Its tail was long and jointed, with about 19 vertebrae (bones). There was no trace of a keel on its small breastbone, and the wings were short and rounded—the birds must have been poor fliers. Fewer hip vertebrae were fused (united) than in modern birds. And unlike a modern bird's, bones were not hollow and air-filled.

However, these ancient creatures had feathers and were almost certainly warm-blooded. Feathers and warm-bloodedness are the two main features that distinguish birds from their reptile ancestors. So *Archaeopteryx* was undoubtedly a bird, although what we call it is not really important. The important thing is that here are the remains of an ancient animal that was almost exactly halfway between modern birds and ancient reptiles. We might think of *Archaeopteryx* as a connecting link in that slow, almost miraculous, flow of life called evolution; a link between the gray, cold, scaly creatures of the distant past and the gay feathered beings we see in our gardens, fields, and woods today.

▶ HESPERORNIS AND ICHTHYORNIS

The next clear glimpse into the history of birds comes some 30,000,000 years later. It is given by fossil specimens of two kinds of ancient birds, *Hesperornis* and *Ichthyornis*. These birds lived during the Cretaceous period, which is famous as the time of dinosaurs. Numerous fossils of both birds were found in chalk deposits in Kansas.

Hesperornis was a large swimming and diving bird that seems to have lived chiefly in the water. Its legs were located far back on its body and they also pointed backward. Its feet were large, paddlelike, and completely adapted for swimming. *Hesperornis* probably could not walk very well on dry land. It may only have come out of the water to lay and brood its eggs. Also, the single known wing bone is so small that this water bird must have lost the power of flight.

Ichthyornis was different; it was more like a modern bird. It was about the size of a tern or a small seagull. It had a deep keel

ARCHAEOPTERYX

HESPERORNIS

THREE EARLY BIRDS

From the remains of ancient feathered animals, scientists have reconstructed these three birds.

ICHTHYORNIS

FLICKER. This big woodpecker has a barbed tongue. It can drive the tongue deep into the holes it drills for insects. The bird's tail feathers are heavy and stiff. Two of the four toes on each foot point backward. Both feathers and toes help brace the bird as it climbs.

SCREECH OWL. This hunting bird of the night has huge eye lenses and its retinas are especially adapted for seeing in dim light. The owl's keen hearing enables it to find the source of a sound. The soft, fluffy feathers make for silent flight. Like many birds of prey, the owl has sharp, curved, grasping talons.

RED CROSSBILL. Like the grosbeak, this finch has a heavy seed-eating beak. However, the upper and lower mandibles are "crossed." This special adaptation enables the bird to pry the seeds from evergreen cones.

EVENING GROSBEAK. Like most finches, this one eats seeds. Its heavy, strong, sharp-edged bill can crack tough seed shells with the greatest of ease.

RUBY-THROATED HUMMINGBIRD. With its long tongue and bill this small bird finds its food in the blossoms of flowers. Its narrow, pointed wings beat with tremendous speed. This bird can hover in place, fly straight up or down, and even backward.

RUFFED GROUSE. This heavy woodland bird has short, broad, rounded wings, well adapted for rocketing bursts almost straight upward, useful for quick escape.

GREAT BLUE HERON. Long legs and large toes allow this wader to fish in deep water, even on soft muddy bottoms. Its long, curved neck can straighten and strike with flashing speed. The mandibles are spearlike with backward pointing slits.

and was a strong flier. The brain, judging from the shape of skull, was much like that of today's birds.

Both *Hesperornis* and *Ichthyornis* were long thought to have had teeth. Because of this, it was also supposed that *all* birds of the Cretaceous period and earlier had teeth. But recent study has shown that the toothed jaws involved may not have belonged to *Ichthyornis* at all. The jaws may have belonged to a small swimming reptile of the same period whose remains got mixed up with those of the bird. So now it is no longer certain that all birds of the Cretaceous had teeth.

The really important thing that the fossils of *Hesperornis* and *Ichthyornis* show is that the evolution of birds was well advanced by the time of the Cretaceous period. And there must have been many kinds of birds, since the two we know were strikingly different from one another. *Hesperornis* had changed so greatly as it became a specialist at swimming that it had lost the power of flight, as have the penguins of today. *Ichthyornis* had become much more like modern birds than was *Archaeopteryx*. In the days of the dinosaurs, there must have been a plentiful variety of bird life.

▶ BIRDS EVOLVE INTO MODERN FORMS

The end of the Cretaceous period marked the end of the great Age of Reptiles. The horde of dinosaurs and many of their relations slowly became extinct; among them were the flying reptiles. But the birds were more successful than ever; they went on evolving steadily to become more and more like the birds of today.

Fossils that date from about 60,000,000 years ago are recognizable as the ancestors of hawks, eagles, herons, ducks and geese, and the chicken family. During the Pliocene epoch, 10,000,000 years ago, there were groups of birds whose very close relations are alive today. Most of the species that lived during the Pleistocene ice ages still live today.

Birds are probably now past their greatest peak of numbers and of variety. During the Miocene and Pliocene epochs, most of the world had a warm, even, humid climate. The wonderful plenty of today's tropical bird life suggests the wealth of bird life that must have thrived over most of the world in those warm, balmy times long ago, before the cold of the ice ages crept over the land.

▶ ADAPTIVE RADIATION

No two beings are born exactly alike. Some of the differences that appear in living things are of no importance in life. Other differences may be harmful or fatal to the creatures in which they originate. But once in a while some helpful new feature appears. The animals or plants that possess it are able to live a little better than others of their kind. Such animals or plants are likely to have more offspring than those that do not have the favorable new feature. Thus they multiply and pass the advantage on to a greater number of descendents. Eventually whole populations of species come to have the new feature. Our name for this favorable difference is an **adaptation.** It is by such adaptations, which appear by accident, that living things slowly change, or evolve, through millions of years.

Most of the features of any living thing are adaptive. For example, the heron has long legs that enable it to wade through fairly deep water in search of food. Its bill is long and the inside edges have backward-pointing slits that keep slippery fish from escaping. These and other adaptations make the heron's way of life possible.

The owl has the sharp, curved, grasping talons of a bird of prey. It also has eyes that are sensitive to dim light, an extra-good sense of hearing, and feathers with soft fluffy edges that permit almost silent flight. These adaptations and many others enable the owl to live as a nighttime bird of prey.

The crossbill is a member of the finch family. Like other finches it has a strong bill highly adapted for eating seeds. However, the crossbill's bill is even more specialized than this. It is adapted for eating the seeds of pines and other cone-bearing trees. The bird can extract seeds from between the scales of the cones because of the remarkable "crossing" of its bill. In a way, the crossbill has a special adaptation on top of a special adaptation.

So far adaptations have been referred to as if they were separate features tacked on to an animal like gadgets on an automobile. Actually, a living thing is a bundle of adapta-

HUMMINGBIRD

SPARROW

HERON

OWL

SWIFT

ARCHAEOPTERYX

EAGLE

OSTRICH

DUCK

PENGUIN

Once flight had become well developed in Archaeopteryx, many adaptations to special ways of life appeared. Birds of prey developed sharp talons and beaks; shore birds developed webbed feet and sieve-like bills. How many such special adaptations can you see in these birds?

tions—it is made up of adaptations. Life itself is an adaptation that makes it possible for non-living materials to combine into collections of chemicals that can grow and reproduce. There are other such important adaptations, which we will call basic adaptations. The development of the stiff backbone in ancient fishes was a basic feature that made all later vertebrate life possible. Another basic adaptation slowly changed the swim bladder of fishes into air-breathing lungs and so opened the world of air for backboned animals. The adaptation we call legs evolved from the fins of certain ancient lobe-finned fishes; this adaptation made it possible for air-breathing vertebrates to walk and live on land.

The basic adaptations of birds are those that make flight possible. These were well developed in *Archaeopteryx*. But once some basic adaptation has appeared and creatures develop that are capable of a completely new way of living, the stage is set for many lesser, special adaptations.

Once flight had developed in birds, there came to be water birds adapted to swim as well as fly; long-legged wading and shore birds; birds of prey armed with sharp talons and beaks; seed-eating birds, fruit-eating birds, and insect-eating birds; birds of the deep woods and birds of the grassland or desert; birds of the north that turn white in winter; birds of the night; slow fliers; fast fliers; and even non-fliers—birds that lost the power of flight when it was no longer of any special advantage.

There is a name for this kind of change, or evolution, that takes place in groups of living things after some important and basic new feature of life has appeared. It is called **adaptive radiation.** Living things radiate out to take advantage of every possible way of making a living for their kind. Every possible way and place in which life can exist is filled with life.

Birds have not provided much material for the study of evolution through the fosssil record. But the living birds of the world do give a wealth of material with which to study the wonder and the beauty of adaptive radiation.

LOUIS DARLING
Author, *Bird*

See also DINOSAURS; EVOLUTION; FOSSILS.

THROUGH THE YEAR WITH BIRDS

The earth is home to many thousands of different species of birds. In size, habits, range, and even the ability to fly, they vary greatly. Yet for all of them the basic pattern of life is set by the rhythm of the seasons.

In general, spring and summer are the busy seasons for birds. Then mates are chosen, nests built, eggs laid and hatched, and the young reared. (Many birds raise several families during these seasons.)

Many birds migrate to a winter home. Preparation for the long trip begins in fall, when migrating birds stuff themselves with food. Soon they are off for their winter homes, often flying in dense flocks that darken a patch of sky. After a winter in a warmer climate, the birds return with spring to begin again the cycles of mating and nesting. Birds that spend the whole year in the same area, instead of migrating, also begin to mate and nest in spring.

▶ **SPRING MIGRATION**

In parts of the United States and Canada, some robins may appear during the first mild spell of winter. But the coming of spring is really announced by the large flights of migrant birds such as grackles, red-winged blackbirds, and cedar waxwings. Geese, ducks, and other birds heading for northern nesting grounds are also seen overhead; their flights mark the final withdrawal of winter, for they move north only as ice and snow melt. They follow the melting so closely that their northward flight stalls whenever cold weather lingers in one area. Spectacular "logjams" of birds may then occur. For example, not long ago several hundred thousand ducks and geese were seen grounded on a marsh in southwestern Iowa.

Smaller birds arrive as the weather becomes warmer. Wave after wave of colorful warblers arrive as leaves are unfolding from buds. By the time nighthawks are seen skimming over city rooftops and the wood thrush's melodious voice is heard in the woods, most of the spring birds have arrived.

▶ **SELECTION OF TERRITORY**

Many adult birds always return to the same region, and some even return to the same nest. (How birds navigate so surely is not yet well understood.) Generally the males arrive first at the nesting ground, and each chooses a territory where there will be enough food for a nest full of young. A male claims his territory

Tule Lake Waterfowl Refuge in northern California. Millions of waterfowl flock to this refuge every autumn on their way south. They stop over to feed and rest in the marshlands.

Peacock spreads his fanlike train in courtship ceremony.

by singing from a prominent perch in it. Thereafter he guards his claim against all other males of the same species.

The size of the territory varies with the species. Birds such as gannets, which nest in colonies, guard an area no wider than their wingspan or the reach of their stabbing beak. A kingfisher may protect a mile-long stretch of brook where he feeds, even though his nest is hundreds of yards away.

▶ COURTSHIP AND MATING

The bird songs and calls heard in spring are part of the courtship that precedes mating. The male uses his song to lay claim to a territory. He also sings to attract a mate. When male and female have found each other, the male woos the female by more singing. In some species the females respond with songs of their own.

However, not all males carry on courtship by singing. Some impress females by displaying their bright colors, for in many species the males are more brightly colored than the females. Since birds have good color vision, the female can see this bright display and is attracted. Males may also engage in some other kind of courtship ceremony. The ruby-crowned kinglet raises his tiny crown of feathers. The peacock spreads his fanlike train. Birds of paradise somersault, swing upside down, and leap around. Some species perform what look to us like dances (in which the females may take part). In still other courtship displays, males drum on logs or puff their feathers.

In cities the courtship displays of pigeons can be observed in parks and on sidewalks. With throat puffed out and tail spread wide near the ground, the male coos to attract a female. If she is attracted, she touches his bill with her own.

When a female is attracted by the male's wooing, the birds pair off and mate. But in many species there does not seem to be a strong attachment. Some kinds of birds mate two or three times a year with different partners. Some males have more than one mate at a time; a male pheasant may have a "harem" of five or more females. In most cases mates probably separate soon after their young are able to feed themselves. However, some birds do seem to mate with the same partners year after year, although no one is sure whether the birds are attached to each other or to a particular nest. There have also been reports of swans and of Canada geese that have never remated after the death of a partner.

▶ NEST BUILDING

After the birds have paired off, they begin their search for a place to build a nest. Some species nest high in trees; others build their nests on the ground. The nesting site is usually picked because it is secure from the birds' enemies and from bad weather.

Usually the female picks out the nest site in the territory defended by the male. However, male and female doves search together, and no one knows which makes the final choice. And among house wrens the male seems to select the site. It is also the female who usually takes the chief role in building the nest, although the male may help with the work. In a few species the male builds one or more nests in his territory even before the females arrive.

Nests are built out of the materials that a region offers. For example, on barren antarctic shores Adélie penguins build their nests out of pebbles and the bones of their ancestors, the only materials available. However, in most parts of the world, birds build nests of grass, twigs, and other plant materials. They may pick up and use animal hair. Some nests contain shiny cellophane, tissue paper, and colored yarns that have caught the bird's eye. Birds carry their nest materials in their beaks or talons.

NEST OF ADELIE PENGUIN   NEST OF BALTIMORE ORIOLE   TAILORBIRD'S NEST   JACKDAW'S NEST

Four different bird nests. The jackdaw's nest is built of twigs, sticks, and bark.

The form of nest may vary from a scooped-out hollow in the ground to the complicated bags of the Baltimore orioles. Tailorbirds in Asia and Africa sew a leaf together with their bills to form a sack in which to nest and lay eggs. They puncture holes in each edge of the leaf and then sew it with plant threads or spider silk, even tying knots.

Some nests are used year after year. The Adélies build up old nests with new supplies of stones. One bald eagle used the same nest for 35 years, adding a bit each year until a storm blew down the tree holding its nest.

The bald eagle builds the largest nest in North America. One nest found in Florida was about 3 meters (9½ feet) wide and twice that deep. Hummingbird nests are the smallest —a soda-bottle cap might cover one of these.

Most small birds can build a nest in less than a week. However, if bad weather interferes, the same bird may take up to 20 days to finish the job. Woodpeckers can peck and hollow out a home in a week.

▶ EGGS

Egg laying begins soon after the nest is completed. In some species it starts the day after the nest is finished. Morning seems to be the time when most eggs are laid, usually at a rate of one a day. The number of eggs laid in a single nesting period is known as a set, or clutch. With small birds an average set may consist of 4 eggs, but among birds as a whole a set may range from 1 egg to 20 or more. Some species lay only one set of eggs a year, but others lay as many as four.

Bird eggs may be various shades of white, green, blue, brown, and even black. The eggs are often marked by several colors. Since nests are found by the sea, in trees, and on the ground, the coloration often blends with the background color, helping to conceal the eggs from the birds' enemies. (Similarly, the often drab coloring of the mother and young helps to camouflage them.) Most eggs are oval in shape, but there are always exceptions. Owls, for example, have rounded eggs. The eggs of the auk family, seabirds, are usually

Murre (auk family) lays a single, pear-shaped egg (lower left). Egg's shape helps keep it from rolling off ledge.

The hooded warbler is an altricial bird. Here the male is bringing food to the young birds in the nest.

so shaped that they can roll only in a circle. This proves a great advantage because these birds lay their eggs on some steep ledge above the ocean surf. Since they do not build a nest, an egg that rolls in a circle is less likely to fall off the ledge and break.

Ostriches lay the largest eggs—up to 20 centimeters (8 inches) in length. More than one dozen chicken eggs could fit inside an ostrich egg. Hummingbirds lay the smallest eggs—about 7 millimeters (¼ inch) long.

▶ INCUBATION

Once the eggs are laid, the next job is to sit on them and keep them warm until they hatch; this procedure is called incubation. In most species the female does the incubating. But in some species the male does it, and in others male and female share the job. Again

The young of geese and chickens are precocial. Soon after hatching they can run about and get their own food. Above, Canada goose is leading young in the water. Below, chickens hatching from eggs. Note various stages of breaking out of egg.

Chicken breaking out of shell. The baby chick inside the shell taps with its egg-tooth to break a hole.

depending on the kind of bird, it takes any-where from 10 to 80 days to hatch the eggs.

The incubating parent tucks the eggs under its stomach feathers, close to a bare spot called the incubation patch, or brood patch. Here a network of blood vessels lies close to the surface and the blood carries heat to the skin. The brood patch is the warmest surface of the parent's body and heat passes readily from it to the eggs. Probably to ensure proper development of the eggs, the parent usually turns them once in a while. It stands up, turns the eggs carefully with its bill, and sits down again.

During the incubation period most males will defend their nest and eggs against intrud-ers. Smaller birds can only scold and peck, but big birds can inflict painful injuries with their beaks, wings, and talons. The big Canada gander will even attack dogs and people to protect his nest and eggs. Females will also defend their eggs.

Some birds attempt to distract the enemy. For example, they may perform some distance away from the nest, pretending to be hurt, in an effort to draw attention from the nest.

As hatching time draws near, both parents are usually present. The instinct for protect-ing the eggs is so strong that they ignore what would frighten them at other times. For in-stance, normally shy wood thrushes have allowed people to touch them rather than leave their nests when the young were hatching.

Young birds can often be heard cheeping inside the eggs about 1 day before hatching. Interestingly enough, a cry of alarm by the parents will silence the unborn youngsters immediately.

The hatching process takes from several hours to a day. First a star-shaped crack appears in the shell. The crack gets larger as the young bird taps with its "egg tooth," a spike on its beak that helps it break through. Finally the shell cracks apart and the young bird emerges.

▶ THE NEWBORN BIRDS

Some young birds are born with a downy covering on their bodies, and their eyes wide open. They can run about—or even swim —after hatching. They are called **preco-cial**, which means that they mature early.

The adults of many precocial species never have to feed the young, although they may lead the chicks to food. Ducks, shorebirds, and pheasants are among the precocial species.

Other young birds are born blind and are usually naked and helpless as well. Parents must feed them and keep them warm as they mature. These birds are called **altricial**, from a Latin word meaning "nurse." The best-known altricial bird is probably the robin.

All newly hatched birds must be protected from bad weather and sharp changes in tem-perature. Young birds, especially those with-out down, become easily chilled. A parent protects its young by covering them with its body. This process is known as brooding, and it is really a continuation of incubation.

▶ CARING FOR THE YOUNG

Most precocial birds are ground-dwelling or water birds and their young are hatched knowing how to run or swim. Soon after hatching, young mallard ducklings will follow their mother to the water's edge and swim out into the pond.

However, the precocial young apparently must be taught what to eat and what not to eat. At first the young ones pick at everything. Parents help the young by dropping the right kind of food in front of the offspring.

Neither precocial nor altricial young seem to recognize their own parents at first. Pre-cocial ducklings have been happily adopted in the barnyard by a hen. Precocial geese hatched in a laboratory followed a research scientist around just as they would have followed a mother goose. Altricial birds are no better at recognizing their parents at first. They accept food from any bird that will substitute for their parents. Any movement near them sug-gests food, and as soon as they sense it, they open their mouths and beg.

Altricial young are hungry a good deal of the time, and the parents make many trips for food during the day. (A pair of phoebes was once observed to make 845 trips in 1 day to feed the young.) When a parent arrives at the nest with food, it must announce this fact, since the young are blind at first. Some species give a special cry. Among others, movement announces the food; for example, when a robin lands on the edge of the nest, the slight jar prompts the young to open their beaks. The inside of the open beak is usually brightly colored, which helps the parent place the food deep in the young bird's throat. That is where the strong muscles used for swallowing are located.

Most young birds cannot digest the same food as their parents. In some species the parent eats first and then brings up predigested food for the young to eat. In other species the parent may collect special food for its young. Parents know by instinct what their young need. One observer watched a family of cedar waxwings. During incubation the female stayed in the nest and the male brought her fruit to eat. As soon as the babies were hatched, the male began to collect insects for them.

Eating constantly, most altricial young grow very fast—their rate of growth is the fastest known of any animal with a backbone. A few birds may even double their weight within 1 day after hatching. Some young birds grow so fast that at one point they weigh a little more than their parents.

Female redwing blackbird shielding young from heat of the sun. Nest is built among reeds and cattails.

AS THE YOUNG GROW UP

Many precocial land birds try to fly when only 2 or 3 weeks old. Most water birds need 6 to 12 weeks before their feathers develop enough to support them in flight. Generally speaking, the larger the bird, the more time needed before the first solo flight.

The same thing is true of the altricial birds. A large bird like the California condor may spend more than 20 weeks in the nest, while a small perching bird like the ovenbird will leave its nest in 8 days. Birds that will be flying long distances in fall also remain in the nest for a longer time.

However, many young birds never live to fly away from the nest. Studies indicate that only about one third of the young birds hatched in a season will survive that year. Hawks, crows, cats, squirrels, snakes, and other animals kill some; diseases and bad weather kill many others.

Among the surviving precocial birds, family ties remain strong until brooding is unnecessary and the young can fly well. With some birds such family life may last into autumn. The young often pass their time fighting, chasing, or pecking one another.

Parents of altricial birds often feed the young even after they have learned to fly and left the nest. But as soon as the young birds grow up, this stops and the young may be driven from the feeding territory. The adults then take up their own lives again. Most pairs break up and go their separate ways.

At the end of the summer nesting season, adult North American birds shed their worn feathers and grow new ones. The shedding, known as **molting**, occurs gradually. Most birds lose only a few feathers at a time and can always fly. During this same period, after the nesting season, birds tend to scatter from the nest area. Many wander farther north— herons from the southern United States have been seen in New England in late summer and early autumn.

THE FALL MIGRATION

As autumn approaches, many birds begin to gather in huge flocks. Thousands of swallows are seen on telephone wires. Ducks begin to move from their northern nesting grounds. It is migration time again, and soon millions of birds are filling the air and heading south.

The birds travel definite routes, known as **flyways**. Some bird experts recognize seven major flyways across North America: Atlantic coast, Appalachian, Mississippi, Great Plains, Sierra Nevada, Pacific coast, and cross-country. Shorebirds throng down the Atlantic coast flyway, heading as far south as the Pampa of Argentina. Gliding hawks ride the air currents along the Appalachian flyway. Thousands of ducks fly down the Mississippi Valley to winter along the Gulf coast.

Some birds migrate only short distances. A chickadee nesting on mountain slopes in the Rockies merely drops down into a sheltered valley for the winter. Other birds go great distances. The arctic tern is famous for the distance it migrates. It travels over 35,000 kilometers (22,000 miles) each year to make the round trip between its nesting grounds in the Arctic and its second home in the Antarctic.

Few wild birds have long lives. Most are killed by enemies, diseases, or accidents. And a great many of the accidents occur during migration. Collisions with lighthouses, bridges, and monuments kill many birds. Storms kill still others. One of the worst such accidents occurred when 750,000 Lapland longspurs, sparrowlike birds that nest in the Arctic, died in a Minnesota snowstorm.

▶ MIGRATION MYSTERIES

In spite of many studies and experiments, no one yet understands how migrating birds find their way over long distances to a particular place. It seems probable that birds have some instinctive sense of direction. One theory suggests that they are guided by the sun and stars. Another suggests that birds have an internal "compass" that responds to the earth's magnetic field.

Nor is it fully understood why birds migrate as they do. In some cases a shortage of food in winter makes migration necessary, but this does not explain all migration. There are birds that migrate only if their food runs short, while other birds migrate even if food does not run short.

▶ BIRDS IN WINTER

Nonmigrating birds that winter in the cold, snowy sections of North America are kept busy just surviving. Their search for food is constant, and wherever people have put out

FLYWAYS OF
NORTH AMERICA

1. ATLANTIC COAST
2. APPALACHIAN
3. MISSISSIPPI
4. GREAT PLAINS
5. SIERRA NEVADA
6. PACIFIC COAST
7. CROSS-COUNTRY

food, the birds gather to compete for it. Since they no longer have families to raise, the birds often stay in large flocks.

Many kinds of birds look different in winter, regardless of whether or not they migrate. Their bright colors are hidden under a drab coat. A few birds look so different that people from the north might fail to recognize familiar kinds that are wintering in the southern United States and in South America. Eventually, however, the bright feathers are exposed again and the birds flock north to tell once more of the coming of spring.

VINCENT J. MARTEKA, JR.
Reviewed by RUTH T. and JAMES P. CHAPIN
The American Museum of Natural History

See also ANIMALS: COMMUNICATION AND SOCIAL ORGANIZATION; HOMING AND MIGRATION.

Left, ruby-throated hummingbird hovers beside a flower as it takes up nectar. Above, kingfisher returns to its burrow carrying a minnow.

European swift clings to a brick chimney in which its nest is built.

Above left, white-rumped sandpiper walks along the shoreline looking for food. It pecks in the water for insects and other small creatures. Above right, woodcock, which lives in swampy places with many bushes and small trees. It searches deep in the mud with its long bill looking for food.

Barn swallow returning to its nest with food for its young. The nest is built of mud. It is fastened to beams in farm buildings where it can be reached from outside.

WHERE BIRDS LIVE

Living birds are present at one time or another throughout the whole world, except perhaps on the solid caps of ice and snow near the poles. Birds are both venturesome and adaptable. Among the 9,000 known species of birds there are always a few ready to take advantage of every opportunity to find food. Although they do not live there, some birds fly over the summits of the highest mountains. And wherever there is open water, no matter how far from land, some birds occasionally fly over it. Only when the time comes to raise their young are birds restricted in their movements. All birds hatch from eggs, and these eggs must in some way be kept warm until a young bird has time to develop within the shell.

The different kinds of birds have various ways of surviving in the world. Only a few have lost the power of flight (among them the ostrich, rhea, emu, cassowary, kiwi, and penguin). Thus, most birds are able to move about freely over the land or water. Many land birds have made their way in the past from one continent to another. Each species of bird must seek an area where it can find food, shelter at unfavorable times, and a place for laying and hatching eggs. These basic needs differ according to the structure, size, diet, and instincts (inherited behavior) of any given kind of bird.

That is why a particular kind of bird finds it best to live in particular "haunts," as they are called. Oak woods, evergreen woods, thickets, fields of grass, plowed fields, marshes or ponds with fresh or salt water—each type of haunt is suited to certain kinds of birds.

▶SOME FAMILIAR BIRDS AND THEIR HAUNTS

One of the first birds observed by boys and girls in eastern North America is the house sparrow. It is often called the English sparrow, because its ancestors were brought over from Europe and set free. In the Old World this kind of sparrow had learned to live in company with men. The crumbs from man's table and the grains he grew guaranteed a supply of food for the house sparrow. Small holes in houses and barns or in trees near them provided safe places for nesting. Scattered feathers from barnyards made a soft lining for the nests. Brought to eastern North America, this European sparrow flourished in its new home and later spread westward.

The pigeon, or rock dove of the Old World, was also brought to North America as a domestic bird. Here it has become a city bird. Its instinct to nest on high, rocky places is satisfied by big buildings, while its inability to find food under snow prevents its spreading away from towns.

The European starling, a more recent introduction, has settled here successfully. It found the countryside and the climate much like those of its homeland. Larger than the house sparrow, and with a longer beak, the starling wears a glossy black plumage that is speckled with light brown in autumn and winter. Its diet is varied, consisting largely of insects and fruit, and it nests in tree hollows; thus it can range much farther out from villages and towns.

Native American birds also learned to live near man. The barn swallow took to building its mud nest on beams or rafters in farm buildings, easily reached from out-of-doors. The house wren found chinks in walls very suitable for setting up its home. The barn owl chose lofts where people were not apt to intrude.

Another of the birds most familiar to North Americans is the robin. It is often seen hopping about on some green lawn, turning its head as though cocking an ear, then seizing an earthworm with a quick peck. Besides its red breast the robin has further attraction in its pleasing song. If watched carefully, a robin may reveal its nest in the fork of a maple or other shade tree.

Another early acquaintance may be the chipping sparrow; it is much smaller than the house sparrow and the top of its head is brownish-red. The chipping sparrow feeds on small seeds and, in the proper season, tiny caterpillars. Its song is almost tuneless. Its little cup nest, lined with horsehairs, is found in some evergreen bush or tree planted not far from houses.

An observer also notices other wild birds, particularly those with brilliant colors or loud musical songs. In the eastern United States, for example, such a bird is the male Baltimore oriole; it is orange and black and sings most attractively. It hangs its baglike nest on a drooping bough of a tree. Another bird that attracts attention is the cardinal, a seedeater with a bright red breast and crest. Or there is the bluebird, with head and back mostly blue. Its preference is for insects. In the early spring a gathering of crows in the sky may attract attention by its noisy cawing; but the crows will go back to distant woods to nest.

Overhead too all through the summer are the chimney swifts, small, sooty-black birds. With long curved wings and stubby tail, the swift is shaped like a bow and arrow. While gathering their insect food they can never be seen to settle anywhere. But careful watching may be rewarded by the sight of one dropping into the top of an unused chimney. This is where the swifts fasten their nests. Shaped like half-saucers, the nests are built entirely of small, dry twigs, which the swifts have broken off while flying from tree to tree. The twigs are glued together on the inside of a chimney with the birds' saliva. Here is another example of a native bird adapting its ways to man's structures. Originally this swift must have nested in hollow trees.

The smallest and most amazing of the birds to be seen in a garden is the ruby-throated hummingbird. As it hovers in front of some flower with a deep cup and sweet nectar, its buzzing wings seem like shadows. Its slender bill enables it to reach the nectar and suck it up with the tongue. This bird's feet are tiny, but they do permit it to perch. Its small, cup-shaped nest is difficult to find, for it is saddled on some bough in a tree or shrub.

Toward sundown larger birds, the night-hawks, may be seen flying about overhead. They are not hawks but are related to the swifts; like the swifts they catch their insect food in the air. The nighthawks lay their eggs on isolated bare spots of earth or sometimes on the flat roofs of high buildings in towns.

▶ BIRDS OF WOODS AND FIELDS

Exploring the woods, a bird watcher will meet the blue jay, the chickadee, the scarlet tanager, the red-eyed vireo, the wood thrush, the wood pewee, and perhaps the downy woodpecker. All these are common species in woods of the middle eastern United States. Each has its own way of life, its own song or call, and its own way of building a nest. The diet of these woodland birds consists largely of insects. Such birds are not attracted by houses or open fields unless—in winter—food is laid out for them.

In an apple orchard nearby, a screech owl may be hiding during the day in a deep hollow of a tree. The owl is waiting to come out at dusk; then it will often betray its presence by its faint "shivery" voice—no screech at all, despite its common name.

Near a lake or pond, an observer may see a belted kingfisher keeping silent watch from a tree for an unsuspecting fish in the water below. The spotted sandpiper trips its way along the shore and pecks occasionally in the water to find insects and other small creatures. A phoebe may be perching on some low branch above the water and darting out to take insects in the air.

People who walk across pastures or hay-fields learn to watch and listen for a meadow-lark; perhaps they will see a father bobolink, all black, white, and gold, sitting on a wire fence or singing vigorously as he flies slowly across the field. There his dull-colored mate is probably crouching in a cup-nest made of grass in some hollow in the ground. A king-bird, a large flycatcher with white-tipped tail feathers, may perch on a small tree at the edge of the field or even fly up to pursue a passing crow or hawk. A quail, commonly known as a bobwhite, may attract attention by the loud, half-whistled notes that gave it its familiar name; when frightened, it may rise with a whir from the ground and go speeding away.

The bushes that grow near the edges of woods or in hedgerows near fields have other characteristic birds such as the song sparrow, indigo bunting, brown thrasher, Maryland yellowthroat, and the towhee, or chewink. Their common names are often derived from their coloration, but sometimes their voices account for these names. Towhee and chewink are both used for the same bird, a rather large relative of the American sparrows. Both names refer to its well-known call note. The thrasher and yellowthroat have slender bills and feed largely on insects; the sparrow, bunting, and towhee are mainly seedeaters with beaks suitable to that diet, but they may also eat a few insects or insect larvae. Each of these kinds of birds has its own way of building a nest, but all their nests are close to the ground.

If there is an open marsh nearby, it too is worth a visit; almost certainly it will harbor the showy red-winged blackbird. Swamp sparrows and marsh wrens are among the less noticeable inhabitants; rails and snipe, the most secretive. Woodcocks probe deep in the mud with their long bills and prefer swampy places with many bushes and low trees. Some of these birds build nests in the reeds or cattails above the water; others incubate their eggs in simpler nests on the damp ground.

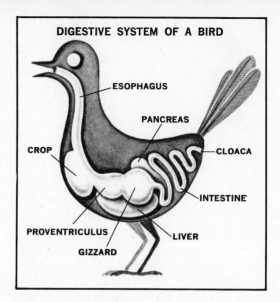

DIGESTIVE SYSTEM OF A BIRD

ESOPHAGUS
PANCREAS
CROP
CLOACA
INTESTINE
PROVENTRICULUS
LIVER
GIZZARD

▶ BIRDS OF THE OCEAN SHORE

Most boys and girls who live near the ocean will go to sandy bathing beaches in the summer. They may not see many birds there, except for gulls and terns flying out over the water. But if they follow the beaches to spots where few people stray, things will be different. The gulls will be alighting there; terns, as well as plovers and sandpipers, may be nesting. Sparrows and other small birds dart about among the grass or bushes.

In back of the beach, there is frequently a wide salt marsh inhabited by seaside sparrows and sharp-tailed sparrows, red-winged blackbirds, and long-billed marsh wrens. These wrens attract attention by their bubbling song; they build globe-shaped nests, easily found, in low bushes along the ditches. Out of sight, down in the grass, may be Virginia rails and clapper rails.

▶ ADAPTATION TO A HABITAT

Each species of bird has its own way of life, dependent on its particular form of body, digestive system, plumage, beak, and limbs.

For example, many birds eat insects. These are easily digested, and the birds' stomachs can readily handle such food. But birds that feed on dry seeds have a special adaptation. The gullet connects with a pouch called a crop. Food is held in the crop before passing on to the stomach, and here seeds are moistened and softened. The gizzard, or stomach, of such birds is likely to have exceptionally thick muscular walls, which help in grinding up the seeds. Many birds of prey also have a crop; it enables them to gorge themselves and move away quickly, digesting their food at a later time.

Some birds, like pheasants, quail, and grouse, have feet that are suited to running

about on the ground as the birds search for food. They have strong wings that enable them to fly up immediately if necessary. The numerous perching birds, which include most North American songbirds, have feet with three toes pointing forward and one longer and stronger toe directed backward. These birds are generally small in size, and such a foot enables them to perch with ease on small branches. Some of these birds come to the ground and walk there, but many others can only hop when they come down to earth. Still others, with much the same kind of feet, climb about in trees with ease and seek their food in the bark. Familiar examples are the nuthatches and creepers.

The wings of perching birds are usually rather short; when folded they reach only to the base of the tail. Swallows, however, have long, pointed wings that enable them to spend much of the day in the air, where they catch flying insects for food. Swallows have short bills and wide mouths, well suited to this method of feeding. Sparrows and finches, on the other hand, have thicker, more conical bills, which permit them to feed on seeds. With such bills they can remove any husk and even crack hard seeds.

Many insect-eating and fruit-eating birds, like thrushes and warblers, have bills of still different forms. The bill is broadened and flattened in the flycatchers, which dart out to capture passing insects. To seek food in crannies of bark requires a long, slender bill like that of a brown creeper. Shrikes have stout, hooked beaks, suited for seizing large, hard-bodied insects or even a young bird.

BROWN CREEPER

BILL FOR PICKING
INSECTS OUT OF BARK

FOOT DESIGNED
FOR CLIMBING
TREES AND LIMBS

RED OWL

HOOKED BILL
FOR TEARING

STRONG FOOT
FOR SEIZING PREY

GREAT HERON

BILL TO SEIZE
FISH AND EELS
IN THE WATER

FOOT FOR
WADING

CANVAS-BACK DUCK

WEBBED FOOT
FOR SWIMMING
IN WATER

BILL TO SCOOP UP
AND STRAIN WATER

SPECIAL ADAPTATIONS

The bill of the cuckoo is suitable for picking up caterpillars; that of the parrot is stronger and hooked for shelling large seeds and cutting up fruits. The woodpecker has a bill that is straight with a chisel-like tip. This is used with great skill in chopping insects out of deadwood and in excavating nesting holes.

The feet of the birds of prey, such as eagles, hawks, and owls, are very strong and have sharp, curved claws on all four toes. Feet like this are perfect for seizing a small animal and carrying it aloft. Birds of prey also have strong, hooked beaks for tearing the prey apart if it is too bulky to be swallowed whole. Birds of prey have become adapted to many kinds of hunting. Owls hunt by night and have the large eyes that see well in the dark. Many owls hunt rats and mice, but a few are specially adapted for fishing. These have feet with the undersurface of the toes roughened, which gives a much better grip.

The various day-hunting hawks, falcons, and eagles also have many methods of securing food. The hawks that hunt small birds in the woods usually have rather rounded wings and long feet and toes. Falcons fly in the open and have longer, pointed wings. Marsh hawks or harriers patrol open marshes; they have long wings for gliding and slender feet for pouncing upon mice and other small prey. The fish hawk, or osprey, feeds almost entirely on fish. It dives into the water, then grasps and holds the fish securely as it flies away. Its strong toes have spiny scales on the underside for this.

The wading birds that seek many kinds of food in shallow water belong to several widely different groups, such as sandpipers, rails, cranes, storks, and herons. Some of their food is obtained near the edges of marshes and streams, but their long legs enable them to venture out until the water touches the feathers of the lower body. The bill varies greatly from group to group. It is slender in the sandpipers and rails, stouter in cranes and storks, and spearlike in the large herons. It may even expand to a spoon-shaped form, with strainers at the sides for feeding on tiny aquatic plant life such as algae.

In the open water there are ducks and geese, with short, webbed feet and buoyant plumage, both of which enable them to swim easily. Their bills have built-in strainers on each side to sift tiny plants and insects from the water. Some ducks dive for food. But most ducks cannot dive as well as the grebes, which have broad flaps on each of their toes rather than webs connecting them.

Other web-footed birds like the petrels and albatrosses seek their food far and wide over the oceans. The wings of the albatrosses are unusually strong and long. Thus, these large birds can sail low over the water with scarcely a flap of the wings, since they are supported by steady winds or the eddies of air rising from the waves. Their hooked beaks enable them to snap their prey swiftly from the surface of the water.

The penguins of the Southern Hemisphere, which are also web-footed, feed beneath the surface and have lost the power of flight. Their wings have become paddles, with only tiny feathers. They remain close to ocean water and nest on islands or antarctic shores where they have few enemies.

The several ostrichlike birds are also flightless. But they roam about on the land without great risk; because of their large size and strong feet and beak, they can run rapidly and can fight off their enemies.

▶ **A WIDER VIEW**

The great variety in the bills, feet, and wings of birds has adapted them for all kinds of dwelling places. Their feathers may be thick and soft to retain body heat or water repellent to keep the skin dry. Digestive systems are designed to make use of many

PURPLE FINCH
SEEDS

HERMIT THRUSH
INSECTS AND FRUIT

LOGGERHEAD SHRIKE
LARGE INSECTS AND SMALL BIRDS

CAROLINA CUCKOO
CATERPILLARS

CAROLINA PARROT
LARGE SEEDS AND FRUIT

PILEATED WOODPECKER
INSECTS

kinds of foods. These wide variations in the makeup of birds have enabled them to spread over the whole world.

In general their distribution is related to the broad belts of climate and of food sources that encircle the earth.

The climate of Europe is much like that of North America, but the barrier of the ocean accounts in part for certain differences between their bird populations. The nightingales of Europe are not represented in the New World. The American robin is quite different from the true robin of Europe, although it is closely related to the European blackbird.

Other birds have close relatives on both continents. Some of the European titmice are closely related to the American chickadee. And the peregrine falcon is represented on both continents. Such relationships are explained by the birds' abilities to move out from the regions in which they originated.

Birds of the North

In the North Temperate Zone, there is a warm summer season and enough rainfall for a generous development of trees and other

The ptarmigan living in the north grows white plumage in winter. This helps to camouflage it from enemies.

Above: Touraco, a little larger than a robin, lives only in Africa. Right: Harpy eagle of South American forests preys on monkeys and other tree-dwelling animals. Below: Vegetation zones of the world. Birds live in all these zones.

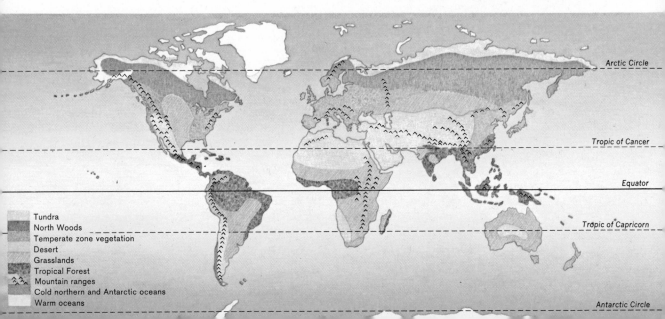

Tundra
North Woods
Temperate zone vegetation
Desert
Grasslands
Tropical Forest
Mountain ranges
Cold northern and Antarctic oceans
Warm oceans

Arctic Circle

Tropic of Cancer

Equator

Tropic of Capricorn

Antarctic Circle

plants. (This is the zone in which most of the United States lies and in which most of the people of the world live.) Here too is a wide variety of birds. However, many birds move southward each year to escape the cold and the snows of winter.

Farther north changes in the vegetation involve corresponding changes in bird life. The evergreen woods of Canada lack many of the birds found in the United States; but these forests have many other birds that do not nest in the milder climate and woodlands of the United States. Some of them spend the entire year in Canada's northern belt. The United States knows others as migrants—autumn travelers on the way to warmer lands; they return to Canada in spring to their preferred spots for nesting and rearing young.

Still farther north the vegetation becomes stunted; but even the arctic tundra has birds that are accustomed to a short summer and long months of existence in the snow. Some, like the ptarmigan—a bird of the grouse family—grow a white plumage, which helps to camouflage them against foxes and other enemies during the long winter. The feathers of the ptarmigan's feet then grow longer and thicker, thus serving as snowshoes.

Birds of the oceans have also become adapted to the northern climate. Puffins, murres, guillemots, and gannets find plenty of food in the cold northern waters; in summer they lay their eggs on rocks and cliffs. Snow geese breed on the barren shores of Greenland and Alaska.

The Equatorial Rain Forests

The equatorial belt is well heated by the sun throughout the year; right along the equator heavy rains fall during much of the year. Under such conditions great forests develop.

These equatorial forests are rich in different kinds of small birds, particularly those that eat insects and fruit. There are also many hawks and larger birds of prey, which feed on birds, squirrels, monkeys, and even snakes. There is a balance between predators and the creatures preyed upon, and the populations remain fairly stable.

To list even a fraction of the land birds that live near the equator would be impossible here. For example, because of the wide ocean barrier between South America and Africa, the birds of those two continents differ greatly. Australia, New Guinea, and neighboring islands also differ with regard to their birds.

The fowl-like birds in tropical America belong largely to the family of curassows and guans; they spend more time in trees than do the pheasants and francolins of tropical Asia and Africa. In the region of New Guinea and Australia both those groups are replaced by the megapodes, or mound builders. These last bury their eggs in warm ground or under huge heaps of decaying vegetation (which gives off heat), piled up by the birds themselves. The eggs are thus kept warm until they hatch, when the young make their own way to the surface.

Only Africa possesses touracos, often known as plantain eaters. These are birds about the size of crows, but they have weaker beaks, used for eating fruits. Many of them have lustrous plumage and crested heads. When the wings are extended they often show large areas of bright red.

Tropical South America has many kinds of parrots, while Africa has only a few. Yet the gray African parrot with red tail—a favorite cage bird—is at home only in the equatorial forests there. Australia and the islands of Southeast Asia have many parrots and parakeets, while the cockatoos and lories inhabit New Guinea, Australia, and neighboring islands.

There are many species of hummingbirds in tropical America, but the Old World does not have any. In Africa and Asia their place is taken by the family of sunbirds, which are not so small; nor do they have the same extraordinary buzzing flight. Like the hummingbirds, the sunbirds seek their food at flowers, usually perching on a twig as they probe the flowers with their long, thin bills. Farther to the east, near Australia, other small birds with similar bills—the honey eaters—feed at flowers in the same way.

New Guinea and neighboring islands are famous as the home of the birds of paradise. Probably these birds are related to crows and jays; but in plumage and often in the form of the beak they are totally different. The males have many kinds of ornamental plumes and display their charms in a great variety of ways.

In three different areas of heavy tropical

forest live large eagles that prey on monkeys and other tree-dwelling animals of similar size. In South America it is the harpy eagle; in Africa, the crowned eagle; and in the Philippines, the monkey-eating eagle.

The Dry Tropics

About 1,500 miles north and south of the equator are zones with far less rainfall. Deserts tend to develop in such areas around the globe. The best known of these is the Sahara. Quite a few birds have become adapted to desert life; the sand grouse of Africa and Asia is one notable example.

Closer to the equatorial forests are tropical belts where the rainfall is relatively light. In the dry lands and open grasslands of these regions live many other different kinds of birds.

For example, in the northern tropics between the Sahara Desert and the equatorial forests of Africa runs a broad belt of open country, largely covered with grasses. Many of the characteristic birds of Africa live there; among them are the ostrich, the secretary bird, bustards, larks, guinea fowl, and francolins. Many of the smaller birds are especially well adapted to life in great expanses of grass, where they find seeds for food, and where some also hang their nests.

The whole eastern part of Africa is largely open and grassy. A clear route thus exists for birds that live to the north and south of the equatorial belt. Many of the grass-loving birds range widely between both sides of the equator.

In South America, in the dry regions directly to the south of the Amazonian rain forests, different bird species have developed. Largest and best known are the rheas. The great condor lives mainly in mountainous areas; its behavior is like a vulture's but it is not in the same family as the true vultures of the Old World. The seriema, which looks somewhat like the secretary bird, belongs to a very distinct South American family. Tinamous are still another American family; they have habits like those of partridges.

The Australian region is very isolated. Thus the birds living in open lands there are very different from those to the north of the equator. The emu is only one of the outstanding examples.

Birds of the Warmer Oceans

The seabirds that live within the tropics are markedly different from those that fish in the colder waters of the temperate and polar seas. The tropical Pacific is richer in bird life than the same belt in the Atlantic; probably this is because the numerous groups of Pacific islands provide many nesting places. Also there are greater areas of shallow water in which fish can readily be caught.

Of the several groups of ocean birds that live around the world in tropical seas, the frigate birds are readily identified. They are large, blackish birds with extremely long, pointed wings and forked tails; their feet are somewhat webbed. Beneath the long, hooked beak the male has a red pouch that can be inflated at will to attract the females. Masters of sailing flight, frigate birds perch on trees but never alight on the water. They live largely by robbing other seabirds of the fish they have caught.

The real "fishermen" are the tropic birds and the boobies, both related to the gannets of colder waters. There are also numerous tropical species of petrels and certain kinds of terns, including the sooty terns, noddy terns, and the white terns. This last kind makes a home in trees without building any nest. Its single egg is simply deposited on some little hollow in a bough. Gulls are scarce in tropical waters.

The South Temperate Zone

The land masses south of the Tropic of Capricorn are small as compared with the neighboring oceans. Moreover, the southern extremities of these landmasses are separated by great bodies of water. As a result the southern lands have widely different birds. The birds in the neighboring seas have much more in common.

New Zealand, situated far to the south and separated from Australia, offers an extreme case. It has some remarkable birds that are found nowhere else. The outstanding examples are the kiwis, flightless owl-parrots, kea parrots, and wattlebirds.

Cold Southern Oceans and Antarctica

Many groups of seabirds are well represented in the oceans in this cooler southern region. It is the home of many petrels and albatrosses, as well as of penguins. Such cold-

Above, kiwi bird of New Zealand cannot fly. Its wings are so small they cannot be seen on the outside of the body. Right, secretary bird, which lives in open grasslands of Africa. It kills snakes and small animals.

Left, emu, second largest living bird. It is found only in the open grasslands of the interior of Australia. Below, frigate birds live around tropical seas. They perch on trees, but never alight on the water.

Albatross lives mostly around cold southern seas. It can go to sea for months, sleeping on the ocean surface and feeding on small sea creatures, such as cuttlefish.

water fishing birds are not particularly influenced by the amount of sunlight they get. To them, as to the fish on which they feed, what matters is the temperature of the water.

Currents of cool water flow out from the southernmost oceans and run northward along the southwest coast of Africa and the western side of South America. Such waters bring even a few kinds of penguins much farther northward than might be expected. One of the jackass penguins—so-called because of a braying voice—lives on islands along the western coast of South America from Tierra del Fuego to Peru; another very small species of the same group has developed in the Galápagos Islands, almost on the equator.

The albatrosses are most characteristic of the cold southern seas; but with their great powers of flight, they have one species nesting at the Galápagos Islands and three other species on islands in the North Pacific.

The birds of Antarctica are quite different from those of the Arctic, even though both live in cold, icy surroundings. Penguins are the best-known inhabitants of Antarctica. Emperor penguins and the snow petrel are two birds that travel far inland onto the snowcap around the South Pole.

▶ MOUNTAIN DISTRIBUTION

Just as currents enable seabirds from the cold south to invade the tropics, high ranges of mountains attract certain species of birds characteristic of colder belts. This is particularly true in the Northern Hemisphere. In a way it can be said that climbing a high mountain in the Rockies is like crossing belts of climate and vegetation between the base of that mountain and the arctic ice cap. With both one starts with rich evergreen woods, crosses an open tundralike zone, and finally reaches the level of perpetual snow and ice.

This effect on bird life is not confined to North America. High mountains in South America, Europe, Asia, and Africa all show marked zones of bird life. At each higher level new kinds of mountain-dwelling birds appear, while those of the lower levels tend to disappear. Within the tropics mountain birds are apt to be related to species living in the neighboring lowlands. Yet while adapting themselves to the colder mountain climate, they have become different.

▶ A SUMMING UP

Birds are present at least in some season from mountaintops to ocean levels and from the Arctic to the Antarctic. Yet they must find food and favorable places to hatch their eggs.

Among birds as a whole there are countless adaptations in the limbs, the beaks, the plumage; there are also many modifications in the digestive system. This diversity enables one or more kinds of birds to occupy haunts around the globe. And the many ways in which the species take advantage of what is offered can only fill man with wonderment.

JAMES P. CHAPIN
The American Museum of Natural History

BIRDBANDING

When John James Audubon was a young man, in the early 1800's, he wondered whether any of the birds that went away in autumn were the same ones that came back in the spring. Many other people had wondered the same thing. But Audubon decided to try to find out. Near his home in Pennsylvania he found several nests of phoebes. Before the young birds were able to fly, he fastened a silver wire around one leg of each. Going back to the same spot a year later, he found phoebes nesting once more. One of them had a silver wire around its leg.

That was the start of birdbanding in North America. Nowadays more than 1,000,000 wild birds are banded every year in the United States and Canada. The U.S. and Canadian governments co-operate in issuing standardized bands for all of North America. Most bands are made of aluminum. They come in 17 sizes to fit anything from a hummingbird to an eagle. Each is stamped with a serial number. Bands are given to licensed banders —persons at least 18 years old who can recognize birds and have been trained to handle them. A report of every bird banded goes into a large file in Laurel, Maryland. Only about one tenth of banded birds are recovered.

Anyone who finds a live banded bird should not try to remove the band. The person should write down the number on the band and then let the bird go. This number, with the place where the bird was found and the date, should be reported to the Bird Banding Laboratory, U.S. Fish and Wildlife Service, Laurel, Maryland 20811, U.S.A. This center collects reports from the United States and Canada.

Bands may be removed from dead birds. These should be sent to the same address with a report on where, when, and in what condition the bird was found. From such reports we have learned how far and how fast birds travel. For example, a banded pintail duck turned up in England just 21 days after it had been seen in Labrador—more than 3,500 kilometers (2,200 miles) across the Atlantic Ocean. In the same way we know that Arctic terns make a yearly trip of over 40,000 kilometers (25,000 miles). The flight extends from the Arctic Circle to their winter grounds near Antarctica.

From these records we also know that most wild songbirds live less than 5 years and that some larger birds such as Canada geese may live more than 20 years. Birds in captivity often live much longer than in the wild.

Besides aluminum bands, color markers are sometimes used so that birds can be recognized from a distance. These include plastic leg and neck bands, wing tags, paints, and dyes.

AMY CLAMPITT
Former Librarian, National Audubon Society

EXTINCT AND THREATENED SPECIES OF BIRDS

One of the most famous birds is the dodo. Yet nobody alive today has seen a living dodo —or ever will. The dodo belongs to an extinct species—a group that has completely died out. Fortunately, before it disappeared almost 300 years ago the dodo was seen and described by various people; it was painted by several artists; and museums have reconstructed the bird from bones that have been found. From all these sources the story of the dodo's extinction has been pieced together.

The dodos lived only on the island of Mauritius in the Indian Ocean. They were large birds, weighing as much as 22 kilograms (50 pounds). They could not fly but nested and lived on the ground.

The dodo has been extinct for almost 300 years.

Left: Whooping cranes, which began to die out when the prairie marshes where they nest were drained. Above: Trumpeter swan. Refuges set up for the trumpeter swan have brought an increase in its numbers.

Left: Ivory-billed woodpeckers are almost extinct because southern forests in which they lived were cut down. Above: Bald eagle—insecticides in its food are causing this bird to lay eggs that fail to hatch.

Below: Colony of flamingos. If they are disturbed in any way, they may produce no young. Strict protection has saved the American flamingo from extinction. Right: Audubon painting of passenger pigeons, the last of which died in 1914. Some were shot by farmers as pests. Hundreds of thousands were shot and shipped to cities as food.

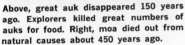
Above, great auk disappeared 150 years ago. Explorers killed great numbers of auks for food. Right, moa died out from natural causes about 450 years ago.

So far as is known, the first human beings to visit Mauritius were sailors from Portugal who stopped there in the early 1500's. By the end of that century settlers had come, bringing cats, dogs, pigs, and monkeys. All these animals turned out to be enemies of the dodos. The pigs trampled on the nests; the monkeys stole the eggs and ate them; dogs and cats caught the young birds. By 1700 no dodos were left. The arrival of people had caused a drastic change in habitat.

The same kind of change has affected other birds. On the lonely Pacific island of Midway there lived a small bird called a rail, which could not fly. During World War II Midway became a naval station and ships began to stop there regularly. Rats came ashore from the ships. By 1945 the rails of Midway were extinct. The rats had killed them all.

The Midway rails, the dodos, and many other birds became extinct because of a sudden change in their surroundings. Such changes are often brought about by human beings, but there may be other causes. Disease, a long rainy period, and volcanic eruptions probably explain what happened to the moas of New Zealand. These giant birds—they were even larger than ostriches—disappeared several hundred years ago. People may have killed the last of the moas. But

other factors had caused their numbers to decrease over a long period.

Some birds became extinct long before human life existed. During the millions of years that life was evolving on earth, such birds did not adapt to changing conditions.

▶ EXTINCT SPECIES OF NORTH AMERICA

More definite details are known about birds that have become extinct during the last 150 years. One was the great auk, which looked like a penguin and lived on rocky islands in the North Atlantic. A powerful swimmer, the great auk could not fly. Explorers who came in the 1500's found the birds so clumsy and tame that they were easy to kill. Since the great auks' meat was fat and tender, they were killed in large numbers. By 1844 there were no great auks left.

The Passenger Pigeon

However, not all extinct birds lived in limited numbers on isolated islands. The passenger pigeon may have once been the most numerous bird in North America. Certainly it was more common than its relative the mourning dove. Yet today the mourning dove is still a common bird, and the passenger pigeon is extinct.

The disappearance of the passenger pigeon

is partly explained by the birds' habits. They were sociable, nesting in great colonies and traveling in flocks so dense that they darkened the sky. They lived mainly on nuts, but sometimes they swooped down into fields and gardens and ate everything in sight. Farmers shot them as pests or caught them in nets, hundreds at a time.

The passenger pigeon also made good eating. For years market hunters did a profitable business in them. Hundreds of thousands of the birds were shot on their nesting grounds and shipped to cities. The last great nesting took place in the late 1800's near Petoskey, Michigan. By 1900 the passenger pigeon was already rare. The last one, a captive bird named Martha, died in a Cincinnati, Ohio, zoo in 1914.

The Carolina Parakeet

The last Carolina parakeet, also a captive bird, died in 1918. Its wild relatives were already gone. Because they traveled in flocks and sometimes did great damage to orchards, they were killed as pests. Some were sold as cage birds. Many were trapped for their feathers, which were used to trim women's hats. If there had been laws to protect these parakeets, some might still be alive.

▶ **THE FIGHT AGAINST EXTINCTION**

All over the world as people develop the land, more and more birds are threatened with extinction. Many countries have laws to protect birds. But laws are not enough. For example, no law was able to save the heath hen. Once it was common along the eastern coast of the United States. It seems to have declined mainly because people disturbed the lands that had been its nesting grounds. By the late 1800's the only flock left was on Martha's Vineyard, Massachusetts. The last heath hen was seen in 1932. It is important for people to remember that once a species of birds becomes extinct, those birds will never be seen again and can never be replaced.

▶ **THREATENED SPECIES OF NORTH AMERICA**

The prairie chicken of the western and midwestern United States is a close relative of the heath hen. Today it is believed to be in danger of becoming extinct. The birds are not hunted. But much of the grassland where they once gathered for their mating ceremonies has been plowed up to make way for towns or fields or turned into grazing lands for cattle. Unlike many small birds, prairie chickens need space in order to thrive.

For almost the same reason, the whooping crane is one of the rarest of North American birds. Probably there never were more than a few thousand. By the late 1930's, only 14 were left. Many had been shot. But their numbers grew so small mainly because the prairie marshes where they once nested had nearly all been drained. Whooping cranes now nest only in northern Canada. They spend winters on the Texas coast, where there is a refuge to protect them. By the late 1970's they numbered over 100, about 20 in captivity.

The California condor is another large bird that needs space. Only about 40 birds remain, high in the mountains of California.

The ivory-billed woodpecker, even rarer, fed on grubs from under the bark of dead trees in the forests of the southern United States. As the forests were cut, the birds disappeared. Reports of sightings do come in, but if any of these birds remain, they are very few indeed.

The bald eagle is far from extinct, but it may be in trouble. The main reason is the presence of poisons such as DDT, which accumulate in the fish the eagles eat. Some birds have been poisoned directly. In others, the poison seems to prevent them from laying eggs that will hatch. This has also happened to other fish-eating birds and to some hawks and falcons that feed on smaller birds. DDT has not been sold in the United States since 1972. But it remains in soil and water for a long time. This may be why no bald eagles are being hatched in places such as the Chesapeake Bay, where they were once common.

But fortunately, not all birds are in danger of extinction. Some farmers and gardeners try to attract certain kinds of birds to protect what they grow from insects. Many small birds, such as swallows and warblers, live almost entirely on insects. Thrushes live partly on insects, and sparrows and finches feed their young on insects. Knowing this, farmers and gardeners grow plants that will attract these birds as a way of controlling insects and caterpillars.

AMY CLAMPITT
Former Librarian, National Audubon Society

BIRD WATCHING

As a bird watcher, you will often see only a flash of color or hear a snatch of song, and then the bird will be gone. But if you know what to look for, even a brief glimpse will tell you a great deal about a bird.

▶ HOW TO IDENTIFY BIRDS

Begin with birds you see often. Learn to know them well, so that they become familiar friends and you can compare them with other birds. Notice their size, shape, color patterns, and what they are doing.

Three birds are useful in comparing sizes. The sparrow is about 15 centimeters (6 inches) long, the robin 25 centimeters (10 inches), and the crow 50 centimeters (20 inches). It is usually easy to say that a bird is smaller than a sparrow or bigger than a robin.

Learn to see quickly the shape of a bird. A starling looks chubby, with a short tail. A catbird is slender, with a long tail. If the bird is flying, notice the shape of its wings. The wing shape is related to its migratory and feeding habits. Birds that are at home in the woods or brushy places usually have short, rounded wings, so that they can dodge and turn

Birds of a particular species are not all the same size. The measurements shown with the following pictures are averages. Individual birds may be somewhat shorter or longer.

Baltimore oriole (19 cm; 7½ in).
Black-billed cuckoo (30 cm; 11¾ in).

Chickadees (13 cm; 5¼ in).

Bobolink (18 cm; 7 in).
Bobwhite (quail) (Male: 26 cm; 10¼ in. Female larger).

Cactus wren (20 cm; 8 in).

Bronzed grackle (blackbird) (28 cm; 11 in).

Cardinal (21 cm; 8½ in).

Cedar waxwing (18 cm; 7 in).

Catbird (22 cm; 8¾ in).

Cowbirds (Male: 19 cm; 7¼ in. Female smaller).

Crows (50 cm; 20 in).

Common tern (37 cm; 14½ in).

Eastern phoebe (17 cm; 6¾ in).

Eastern goldfinch (13 cm; 5¼ in).

Hermit thrush (18 cm; 7 in).
Herring gull (61 cm; 24 in).

Eastern towhee (20 cm; 8 in).

Loon (81 cm; 32 in).

Lark buntings (17 cm; 6¾ in).

quickly. Birds with long, narrow, pointed wings, like gulls and shorebirds, are more at home in wide-open spaces. Tail shapes can help in identifying, too; tails can be rounded, pointed, slightly notched, or deeply forked.

Notice what the bird is doing. If it is on the ground, does it walk or hop? If it is on a tree trunk, does it climb in a circle around the tree, hitch itself upward stiffly in short jerks, or does it scamper easily up, down, or sideways? Each kind of movement is typical of a different bird.

Flight patterns are useful clues, too. Some birds, like the crow, fly very straight, with a steady wingbeat. Others, like the woodpeckers, swoop up and down as if they were riding a roller coaster. Only a few birds can hover, so this can be a useful thing to notice. For example, if a bird much smaller than a sparrow hovers in front of a flower, it is a hummingbird. If the bird is larger than a robin, has a large head with a crest, and is hovering over water, it is a kingfisher. But if the head is small and the wings pointed, then it probably is a sparrow hawk.

Color is important in identifying birds, especially songbirds, but flash patterns are often more helpful. Flash patterns are patches of white on either wings or tail that show as the bird flies off. For example, few birds show a white rump patch as they fly. Two are larger than a robin, but smaller than a crow. These are the flicker and the marsh hawk. The flicker, a plump brown bird with rounded wings, shows its rump patch as it flies away from an anthill on a lawn. The marsh hawk, more slender with pointed wings, shows its patch as it courses low over marshes or wet meadows hunting for mice.

Get a good field guide and carry it with you. Size and shape, action and pattern can be checked quickly and the bird identified at once. If you wait until you get home to look it up, it will be harder to be sure. Look through the book often, so that you become familiar with the pictures, and you will be pleased to see how often you will be able to identify a new bird the first time you see it. As you become more familiar with birds you will find new ones easier and easier to identify, because you will be able to make more careful comparisons between the new birds and the birds you already know.

▶ LEARNING BIRDSONGS

Each kind of bird has a song all its own, but birds make other sounds, too. There are notes, signals from one bird to another of the same kind, and there are alarm calls, which all species of birds recognize as meaning danger. If a snake approaches a nest too closely, this alarm call will be used, and birds of many kinds in the area will arrive and try to help. Notes and calls are used throughout the year, but the songs are usually heard during the nesting season only.

Don't try to learn too many of the songs at once by listening to recordings. You will get very confused. Use records only for checking a song you are not sure about, after you have learned a number of them. Learn one song at a time by listening to the bird carefully as it sings, and comparing its song to the songs you know. For example, the robin's song is a familiar rollicking melody. The scarlet tanager's song is like the robin's in rhythm, but the quality is hoarse—it sounds like a robin with a sore throat. And a rose-breasted grosbeak sounds like a glorified robin and sings very fast. Birdsongs differ from each other in pitch, pattern, rhythm, and quality.

To help you remember birdsongs, it's fun to think of a word phrase that fits the song in rhythm and pitch. For example, the goldfinch's song sounds like "per-chick-o-ree," while a crested flycatcher shrieks "Thief! Thief!" Many birds, like the bobwhite and the chickadee, tell you their names clearly as they sing.

▶ HOW TO FIND BIRDS

Early morning and late afternoon are the times that birds are most lively. Because they live such active lives, they need a great deal of food, so they are particularly hungry after they wake up and before they go to sleep. Of course, during the nesting season they have baby birds to feed, so they are far busier in spring all through the daylight hours than they are the rest of the year.

Even though birds seem free to wander, each species needs its own kind of food, shelter, and nesting site, so it makes a habit of staying in the place where it can find them. This special place is called a habitat.

If you would like to know many kinds of birds, you must visit many habitats. City

WHERE BIRDS LIVE

PIGEON

ROBIN

EGRET

SPARROW

SCARLET TANAGER

WOODPECKER

GULL

Mallard (Male: 60 cm; 23½ in. Female smaller).

Mockingbird (25 cm; 10 in.)

Red-bellied woodpecker (25 cm; 10 in).

Mountain bluebirds (18 cm; 7 in).

Red-eyed vireo (15 cm; 6 in).

Redstart (13 cm; 5¼ in).

Red-winged blackbird (21 cm; 8½ in).

Robin (25 cm; 10 in).

Rose-breasted grosbeak (20 cm; 8 in).

Scissor-tailed flycatcher (34 cm; 13¼ in).

Scarlet tanager (18 cm; 7 in).

Skylark (18 cm; 7 in).

Slate-colored junco (16 cm; 6¼ in).

Screech owl (23 cm; 9 in).

Western meadowlark (23 cm; 9 in).

Tufted titmouse (15 cm; 6 in).

White-throated sparrow (18 cm; 7 in).

White-breasted nuthatch (14 cm; 5½ in).

Yellow-shafted flicker (32 cm; 12½ in).

Wood pewees (16 cm; 6¼ in).

streets are the habitat of English sparrows, pigeons, and starlings. Parks and gardens are home to robins and catbirds. In a marsh you will find herons and blackbirds. A field is the habitat of meadow larks and field sparrows. Go to the edge of a woodland and you will find chickadees and tanagers, while in the deep woods live woodpeckers and veeries (a kind of thrush probably so named in imitation of its song). Along the seashore, gulls, terns, and sandpipers feel at home. In each of these habitats there lives a special group of birds held there by the seeds, insects, or fish it eats and by the bare ground, bushes, or trees it needs for nesting.

▶ HOW TO ATTRACT BIRDS

Instead of going out into the field to hunt for birds, you may want to concentrate on bringing them to you. Set up a shelf feeding station and one or two hanging feeders near your windows. Be sure to place these feeders near shrubs or trees so the birds can find shelter quickly if something alarms them.

Seed mixtures will be the mainstay of most of your guests, and you will want to add suet and peanut butter in winter. Fruit is attractive to insect-eating birds, so try halves of oranges, sliced apples, or raisins. Better yet, try to plant shrubs or trees that produce berries. Dogwood, viburnum, and mulberry are especially good—98 species of birds eat dogwood berries.

Water, both for drinking and bathing, is very important, again near cover. Birds are attracted by dripping water, so you might try hanging a can with several small holes in it over a birdbath so the birdbath will fill slowly.

Birdhouses are fun to make, and they replace natural cavities in trees that are missing from many built-up areas. Remember that a bird will use a house with an opening large enough only for it to enter. This keeps out larger birds and animals and makes it a safer place to raise young.

In the spring you can try putting out short lengths of yarn or string to attract birds. Hang these lengths over a clothesline or put them in a bag made of string, such as the kind in which oranges are sold. Don't use pieces longer than 15 centimeters (6 inches). A bird's legs may get tangled in them.

SHELF FEEDING STATION

HANGING FEEDER

Nest of a red-shouldered hawk, high on the branches of a tree.

The American bittern's nest, hidden among long grasses.

Nest of a swallow beneath the eaves of a house.

▶NESTS AND FEATHERS

All songbirds build new nests each spring. They even build new nests if they have second broods in the same season. A nest is used only as a nursery, a place to raise babies. When the young fly from the nest, they do not return—a nest is not actually a home. From that first flight on, the young birds perch on branches to sleep at night, just as their parents do.

A word of caution about nests. If you should find a nest with eggs or baby birds, don't visit it too often or for too long a time. The path you make to the nest may lead danger to the family. And if you keep the parents away too long, the eggs or the nestling may chill.

You'll notice that each kind of bird always chooses the same kind of place for its nest. A robin always builds its nest on a fork of a branch, and an oriole's nest is always hung from the tips of thin twigs high up from the ground. Each kind of bird always uses the same materials. To identify a bird's nest you need to know where the nest was (near water or in a thicket), how high up from the ground it was built, its size, and the materials used.

Feather collections can be fascinating. Every bird grows a new set of feathers at least once a year, sometimes twice. The process of shedding the old worn-out feathers, usually a pair at a time, is called molting and occurs in late summer. If there is a sec-

ond molt, it takes place in very early spring, but August is the best time to look for discarded feathers.

▶KEEPING RECORDS

Part of the fun of watching birds is keeping records, and there are many ways this can be done. First, write down the date and place where you see each new bird. This will be your "life list." You can keep daily lists of birds you see and compare them from year to year. During spring and fall migration you might record the number of each kind of bird you see each day, and thereby learn when the peak day is for that kind of bird. If you like to get up early, keep a list of the order in which birds begin to sing and what time birdsong begins each day. Perhaps you are interested in how many trips a bird makes to a feeder in a day, or even in an hour. You may, by careful observation and records, contribute a new fact about bird behavior, for bird experts certainly don't yet know all of them.

As you become more advanced, you probably will, and should, acquire good binoculars, which will help to bring birds closer to you. But your increasing skill in knowing when and where to look for birds, and how really to see and hear them, must come first.

ELEANOR B. GILCHRIST
Assistant to the Curator of Education
Stamford (Conn.) Museum and Nature Center
See also BIRDS AS PETS.

This blue jay is tame enough to be fed by hand.

BIRDS AS PETS

Keeping pet birds is one of the most popular hobbies today, and it is one that has been enjoyed for many hundreds of years.

Pirates of old delighted in the company of parrots. And it is recorded that a governor of an African colony presented a pet parrot (one that could speak French) to Queen Marie Antoinette. Alexander Wilson, pioneer student of American bird life, kept a Louisiana parakeet as a companion. Wilson even took the bird on long journeys exploring the West. The parakeet rode in his pocket during the day. It seemed to enjoy the rhythm of the jogging horseback ride, and at night it perched beside his campfire.

Canaries were luxury pets about 500 years ago. When the Spaniards took over the Canary Islands, they discovered the lovely songsters there and sold them at high prices to the wealthiest families of Europe. It became fashionable for a lady to receive visitors with a canary perched on her forefinger. Through the years careful breeding has produced a variety of beautiful and talented canary pets.

What kind of bird makes the best pet? The answer is not easy, because some people enjoy a bird that sings, such as the canary. Others like a talking bird, such as the parrot, parakeet, or mynah. And many people like birds, such as pigeons, that are used in sport.

▶ PARAKEETS

A bird that is worth considering as a pet is the parakeet. It is among the most popular of all house pets, feathered or furred. It is called by several names. Budgerigar is one, for parakeets originally were native to Australia. In that country "budgeree" means "pleasant," and by some natives a bird is called "gah" or "gar." Thus the name was made by putting these two words together. It is now commonly shortened to "budgie." In the Orient the birds are known as shell parakeets.

Parakeets belong to the parrot group. There are certain marks by which to tell such birds. The feet have two toes in the front and two in the rear. The bill is thick, strong, and hooked. The body is short and compact, with a short neck, large head, and thick tongue. Parakeets are hardy birds and long-lived. They seem quite content in a confined life. These pets have wonderful ability to imitate a human voice and perhaps to learn to speak. Not only are they inclined to breed in captivity, but various color strains are quite easily crossbred, so that a variety of beautiful plumage has come about.

The best place to buy a parakeet (or other cage bird) is at a reliable pet store. There you can learn the age and the sex of the bird you are buying. You can also ask for advice on the correct size and type of cage.

These birds do well on prepared parakeet foods. Many of them have tastes for certain specialties. With some it is apples; others enjoy bits of such vegetables as celery (which should be carefully washed and dried). Drinking water must always be within reach. Ways to keep pet parakeets healthy and happy may be found in printed booklets given without charge by bird-food companies.

▶ CANARIES

Like parakeets, canaries also are mostly seedeaters. They are easily cared for with foods you find at pet shops or markets. Since their song is the feature for which they are

Macaws are often seen in Trinidad, as well as Central and South America. They are among the most colorful and long-lived of all birds. Some have lived for 64 years.

most noted, the smart canary hunter will look into this before buying a bird. There are many kinds of canaries, but all of them may be grouped into two main types of singers—the rollers and the choppers. The choppers are the kind most often found in pet shops. They may be sold when only 5 or 6 months old and without training in singing. However, the rollers are usually given careful schooling so that their song is heard to best advantage. The chopper sings loudly with high-pitched, short notes. The roller performs with soft, sweet, rolling trills. The male is always the singer.

▶ PARROTS AND MYNAHS

A parrot or a mynah bird does not have to say anything really funny to be amusing. The way these birds talk is funny enough. They seem to know what they are saying and why they are saying it. Of course this is not true. They merely imitate sounds they have heard. But it makes them seem almost human.

Like parakeets, they are hardy, long-lived, and seem completely content in captivity. But they must be given roomy living quarters and a well-balanced diet. They also need a great deal of attention. As with other cage birds, proper seed foods for them will be found at pet shops. But parrots have a definite need for more than seeds. Hard-boiled eggs, nuts, fruits, and greens are all important for a parrot. People often feed these friendly birds table foods. They give them bits of meat, cake, and pastry, for they are apt to eat anything; but such unnatural fare is not good for them.

The Amazon parrot, with blue markings on its face, and the African gray are very popular as cage birds. Both can be taught to speak clearly and often to sing and whistle. One way to teach a parrot is to hide from its view and slowly repeat several words over and over, always using the same tone. If you are buying a parrot, you will find a wide range in price. Some are young and completely untrained, while others are older and used to talking and living with people.

The mynah bird is quick to imitate human talk. It is also likely to startle its owner with a piercing squawk or scream. Though members of the starling family, mynahs are native to Southeast Asia and the islands of Indonesia. There are several kinds, some as small as robins, some as large as crows, but all bright and perky. Again proper food (mynah birds like a soft mixture) is to be found at pet shops. Once a day they should be given fruit, such as cut up bananas, apples, and grapes.

▶ PIGEONS

Keeping pigeons is one of the oldest hobbies. Records show that these birds were tamed in Egypt nearly 5,000 years ago. They are popular today for several reasons: They can be used for racing and also for producing the squabs or young pigeons people use as a luxury food. There are three main classes of pigeons—flyers, fancy, and utility.

The **racing homers** (flyers), developed by interbreeding the best flyers of several breeds, and **tumblers** are two kinds most often used for racing. The **pouter** pigeons, which strut around looking for attention, are outstanding in the fancy variety and are bred only for color and beauty. The **king** is favored in the utility class because it may produce as many as 11 squabs a year.

Surprisingly, pigeons are kept in many city areas as well as in the country. Houses for their use may be built on an apartment-house roof (if the house owner and city rules approve). From the rooftop the pigeon fancier may release his birds for exercise flights. Pigeons are hardy, but they do need air and light and protection from drafts and mice.

The colorful parakeet is able to imitate the human voice. Like the macaw, it belongs to the parrot group.

Starling (left) and blue jay quarrel over a feeding tray.

The soft, sweet trills of the roller canary make it one of the most popular of all pet birds.

Seed mix that can be bought from a pet shop is their chief food. If you feed them by hand, they become very tame and friendly. A pair of pigeons may be purchased for $2 or $3, while a single champion racing bird may cost several hundred dollars.

It should be mentioned here that parrot fever (psittacosis) can be passed along to humans from sick parrots, parakeets, pigeons, and similar birds. This disease is a virus infection something like pneumonia. The best way to avoid it is to buy these birds from a reliable dealer, keep their cages clean, and never handle sick birds. If the bird gets sick, have a veterinarian take care of it and tell you how to disinfect its cage. It is wise never to touch any pigeons you see on the streets or in the parks. Each year there are several hundred cases of psittacosis in the United States. Most of them could have been prevented by following this advice.

▶ FARM BIRDS

Chickens, ducks, and geese are birds that need to live in the country. These birds are usually thought of as utility birds, but any one of them may be tamed and kept as a pet.

A chicken is interesting to watch and to hear (it has a varied and unmistakable "language" all its own). Ducks and geese too make interesting and unusual pets. Ducks and geese resemble each other, but there are many differences. Geese usually have longer necks than ducks. The beak of a goose is harder and not as flat as that of a duck. Its legs are not so far back on the body, and it can walk and run more freely than a duck can. Male and female geese are alike in color. But the male and female ducks have different coloring.

▶ BIRDHOUSES ATTRACT WILD BIRDS

The best way to enjoy wild birds is to attract them close to your home without taking away their freedom. Bird feeders, baths, and shelters are helpful. Constructing birdhouses can be an interesting hobby. There is endless variety in the project because different kinds of birds need and are attracted to different types of houses.

DOROTHY E. SHUTTLESWORTH
Author, *Exploring Nature With Your Child*
Founder, *Junior Natural History Magazine*

HOW TO BUILD A BIRDHOUSE

One of the most important measurements to check in building a birdhouse is the size of the entrance opening. Careful study has been given to this feature. As a result, certain sizes are known to be best for certain types of birds. Red-headed and hairy woodpeckers and house finches need a diameter of 2 inches for comfortable entrance; tree swallows and bluebirds need only $1\frac{1}{2}$ inches. The little chickadee requires only $1\frac{1}{8}$ inches, while house wrens need no more than 1 inch. All these are minimum requirements. The hole, in each case, should be high enough on the front of the house so that the mother bird will not be seen when she is sitting on the nest. On large houses a perch below the entrance is worthwhile. On smaller houses it is best to leave off the perch, as it provides a landing place for unwelcome birds after the nest is occupied.

▶ SOME DOS AND DON'TS

Do use wood for making birdhouses. Tin and other metal become extremely hot under the sun, and young birds are likely to die as a result. **Do** have a house well ventilated and drained. For the sake of the young, it must be cool and dry at all times. Ventilation is created by drilling small holes above the entrance, close to the roof. Small drainage holes drilled through the floor will prevent flooding from rain that may otherwise occur, especially if the floor fits tightly against the sides.

Do paint or stain the house with color that will make it blend with its surroundings.

Do place birdhouses in locations that are suitable and safe from prowling cats. This means avoiding dense foliage and using either a post or tree trunk in the open as a support. Houses for chickadees, house wrens, woodpeckers, and swallows should be anywhere from 5 to 15 feet above the ground.

Don't make multiple dwellings (houses big enough for several families of birds) except for purple martins. Most birds that are attracted to houses like privacy for their families. For this reason too it is best not to set up many houses in a small area. Only in unusual situations should there be as many as five in an acre.

Don't allow a birdhouse to go to waste because it is dirty. After it has been used and the young have flown away, it must be cleaned before a new family will be attracted. The best time for this job is in the fall when old nests and debris should be removed. If you find there are lice in the house, the wood should be well scrubbed with soap and water.

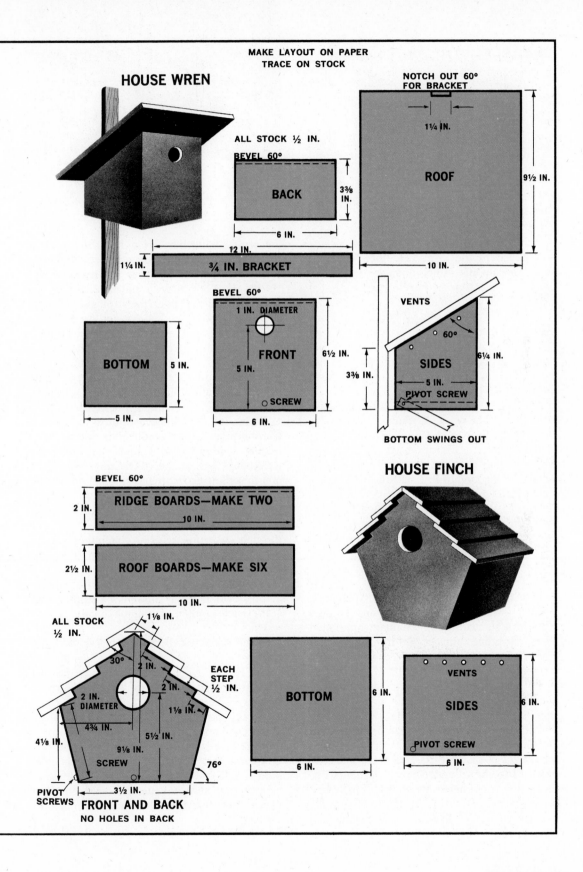

MAKE LAYOUT ON PAPER
TRACE ON STOCK

HOUSE WREN

NOTCH OUT 60°
FOR BRACKET

1¼ IN.

ROOF

9½ IN.

10 IN.

ALL STOCK ½ IN.

BEVEL 60°

BACK

3⅜ IN.

6 IN.

12 IN.

¾ IN. BRACKET

1¼ IN.

BOTTOM

5 IN.

5 IN.

BEVEL 60°

1 IN. DIAMETER

FRONT

5 IN.

6½ IN.

SCREW

6 IN.

VENTS

60°

SIDES

5 IN.

6¼ IN.

3⅜ IN.

PIVOT SCREW

BOTTOM SWINGS OUT

BEVEL 60°

RIDGE BOARDS—MAKE TWO

2 IN.

10 IN.

ROOF BOARDS—MAKE SIX

2½ IN.

10 IN.

HOUSE FINCH

ALL STOCK
½ IN.

1⅛ IN.

30°

2 IN.

2 IN.

EACH
STEP
½ IN.

2 IN.
DIAMETER

2 IN.

1⅛ IN.

4¾ IN.

1⅛ IN.

5½ IN.

4⅛ IN.

9⅛ IN.

SCREW

76°

PIVOT
SCREWS

3½ IN.

FRONT AND BACK
NO HOLES IN BACK

BOTTOM

6 IN.

6 IN.

VENTS

SIDES

6 IN.

PIVOT SCREW

6 IN.

BISMARCK, OTTO VON (1815–1898)

Otto Eduard Leopold von Bismarck-Schönhausen, the man responsible for the unification of Germany, was born on April 1, 1815, at Schönhausen, Prussia (now in East Germany). His father belonged to the Junkers, the old Prussian landowning class, and his mother came from a middle-class family.

As a schoolboy, Otto was a careless student, with a reputation for wild pranks. He later studied law at the universities of Göttingen and Berlin. After graduation in 1835, Bismarck worked in the Prussian civil service and served in the army. He then returned home to help his father manage the family estates. At this time he began to read a great deal and to study philosophy and religion.

In 1847 he married Johanna von Puttkamer, a member of an extremely devout religious sect. That same year, Bismarck became a member of the Prussian Diet (parliament), where he represented the conservative traditions of the Junkers.

The liberal ideas of the 1848 French Revolution set off a wave of change across Europe. Germany was still a collection of independent states. Liberals tried to turn the country into a constitutional monarchy headed by the king of Prussia. But the king rejected the constitution and the attempt failed.

In 1851 Bismarck was Prussia's delegate to the German Diet at Frankfurt. There he spoke for Prussia's interests against those of Austria—then the most powerful German state. In 1859 he became Prussian ambassador to Russia, and, 3 years later, to France.

In 1862 the new Prussian King, William I, clashed with parliament. When matters reached a standstill, King William appointed Bismarck prime minister and minister of foreign affairs. Now he had the power to put his foreign and domestic policies into effect.

To gain the tiny northern states of Schleswig and Holstein, which had large German populations but belonged to the Danish crown, Prussia and Austria fought Denmark in 1864. But in 1866, Bismarck turned Prussian military might against Austria to achieve sole control. In 1867 he set up the North German Confederation, dominated by Prussia, including all the states north of the Main River. He became chancellor and was soon nicknamed the Iron Chancellor, from his 1862 speech stating that "the great questions of the time are decided not by speeches and majority decisions . . . but by iron and blood."

He had made Prussia the strongest German state and now he looked further. In 1870 he created a situation in which France was forced to declare war. Within 3 months France had been defeated. The new German Empire was born, taking in all the German states except Austria. King William of Prussia became Kaiser (Emperor) William I of Germany.

To maintain a balance of power in Europe, Germany mediated conflicts between other nations. Alliances were made, and meetings were held (such as the 1878 Congress of Berlin) to settle European and colonial questions.

Within Germany, Bismarck played his political rivals off against each other. Though he never accepted liberal views, he put through sweeping reforms, including one of the world's first social security programs, in order to gain support from his opponents.

William II came to the throne in 1888. He had his own ideas on running the empire, and after much conflict, Bismarck finally had to resign.

When Bismarck died, on July 30, 1898, he had been retired from public life for 18 years. His will included instructions that his tombstone bear the words "A true German servant of Emperor William I." His legacy to the world was a united Germany and a web of alliances that involved every nation in Europe. Though an era of German and European history came to an end with his retirement, historians still enjoy guessing what would have happened in Europe if Bismarck had remained in power or if his successors had continued his policies.

BISON AND BUFFALO

Bison and buffalo are big, strong animals. They have horns on their heads. Each of their feet has two hooves. Bison and buffalo are members of the big group of animals called hoofed mammals. Cows and oxen are hoofed mammals, too. Cows, oxen, buffalo, and bison are all in the cattle family.

Like other cattle, bison and buffalo eat only plants. Those that live on plains eat mostly grass. Those that live in forests eat leaves.

Cows and oxen have been tamed for several thousand years. But only one kind of buffalo has ever been tamed. That is the Asian water buffalo. Bison have almost never been tamed and put to work for people.

▶BISON

Bison were the wild cattle that ran in huge herds across the plains of North America before the land was settled. A bison is a big, dark, shaggy animal. It has a thick mane of fleecy hair over its neck, shoulders, and front legs. It also has a topknot of hair, a beard, and short, curved horns. There is a hump of fat on its shoulders. Bison are nearly 1.8 meters (6 feet) tall at the shoulder.

As the West was settled, people hunted bison for hides and meat. The big herds were nearly wiped out. Then some people decided the animals must be saved. There are thousands of bison today. Most of them live in national parks and wildlife refuges.

You often hear people use the name "buffalo" for these animals. But "bison" is the correct name for them.

▶BUFFALO

Buffalo live in Asia and Africa. They look a lot like oxen except for their horns. For instance, two kinds—the Asian water buffalo and the African Cape buffalo—have big, sweeping horns. These horns are broad and flat at the base, where they grow out of the head.

The water buffalo is used in India and Southeast Asia to pull plows and do other heavy work. It likes to spend time in the water or to wallow in the mud, probably to keep flies away. These buffalo are also raised for milk, meat, and hides.

The Cape buffalo lives in Africa. Hunters

North American bison. Today herds live in national parks and wildlife refuges.

Tame water buffalo of India and Southeast Asia. It is very strong but can be handled even by children.

have called it the world's most dangerous hoofed animal. Two kinds of forest buffalo also live in Africa.

Pygmy buffalo live in the Philippines and certain islands of Southeast Asia. They are just under 1 meter high at the shoulder.

> Reviewed by ROBERT M. MCCLUNG
> Author, science books for children

See also HOOFED MAMMALS.

BLACKFOOT INDIANS. See INDIANS OF NORTH AMERICA.

BLACKS, HISTORY OF. See NEGRO HISTORY.

BLACK SEA. See OCEANS AND SEAS.

THE TIGER

Tiger! Tiger! burning bright
In the forests of the night,
What immortal hand or eye
Could frame thy fearful symmetry?

In what distant deeps or skies
Burnt the fire of thine eyes?
On what wings dare he aspire?
What the hand dare seize the fire?

And what shoulder, & what art,
Could twist the sinews of thy heart?
And when thy heart began to beat,
What dread hand? & what dread feet?

What the hammer? what the chain?
In what furnace was thy brain?
What the anvil? what dread grasp
Dare its deadly terrors clasp?

When the stars threw down their spears,
And water'd heaven with their tears,
Did he smile his work to see?
Did he who made the Lamb make thee?

Tiger! Tiger! burning bright
In the forests of the night,
What immortal hand or eye,
Dare frame thy fearful symmetry?

BLAKE, WILLIAM (1757—1827)

William Blake, the English poet and artist, was born on November 28, 1757, in London. His family were simple working people.

As a boy, Blake had little formal education. However, he read poetry and other literature, including the Bible, theology, mystical writing, and philosophy. In this way Blake formed his own mind and educated himself in a very personal and original way.

At 10, Blake spent what little money he had on inexpensive prints of paintings and drawings. He was able to go to a school for students who wished to learn to draw. At 12, he began writing poems. At about 15, he was apprenticed to an engraver, James Basire.

As Blake developed his skills at painting and drawing, the subjects and mood of his work became more and more unusual. Blake became a truly visionary artist and poet, a man who could bring alive, through words and pictures, the world of his own mind.

When he was a boy, Blake would speak casually of seeing angels among men at work in the hay fields. When his father heard him, he threatened to punish him for lying. Blake's father did not understand that the sights the boy saw, the creations of his own imagination, seemed as real to William as ordinary, everyday events seemed to other people.

In 1782, William Blake married Catherine Boucher. She had little education but proved wonderfully understanding and helped him throughout their long life together—a life often made hard by poverty. The Blakes had no children, which was a sorrow to both of them.

Blake trained his wife Catherine to assist him in the hand-coloring of the engravings he produced to illustrate his poems and books.

Blake was generally neglected in the literary world of his day. The full appreciation of his genius, the awareness that he was one of England's great artists and writers, came long after his death.

As a poet, Blake is best loved for the group of poems called *Songs of Innocence and Experience*. These works, published between 1789 and 1794, include his two most famous poems, "The Lamb" and "The Tiger."

Blake saw the world in all its dimensions. His comments on the ugliness, cruelty, and injustice of the world as he saw it play as much a part in his work as do his comments on the beauties and joys of life. Blake understood that both ugliness and beauty, joy and pain—all of these contrasting feelings and emotions—are always present in human life.

Blake's chief prose work is *The Marriage of Heaven and Hell* (1790–93), a satire on the pitfalls of religion and of religious thought. He also wrote many long, mystical poems, known as the *Prophetic Books*.

Blake's engravings enlarge and complete the meaning of his poems. Ideally, nothing that Blake wrote should be read without seeing his drawings. He also did engravings for the Biblical Book of Job and for works of other poets.

Blake once said: "I cannot think of death as more than going out of one room into another." In this belief, he died at the age of 70, on August 12, 1827. He was tired but he was tranquilly happy.

EDMUND FULLER
Kent School

BLEEDING. See FIRST AID.

BLIND, EDUCATION OF THE

One way to become acquainted with the problem of blindness is to put on a blindfold for a few minutes. Could you dial a telephone or eat a meal neatly? Could you find your way around the house or tell a penny from a dime? Without the use of sight, blind people must learn to use their other senses so skillfully that they can do all these things.

People who are blind cannot move about as quickly or as easily as they could if they could see, and sometimes they may have to seek help. But it is important to give them every chance to be as independent as they wish to be.

Sighted people can help the blind in many different ways. If you meet a blind person, give your name immediately. When your help is needed, offer your elbow and lead the blind person gently. Always pause at a step or a curb for a moment or two. If you are eating together, you can help by imagining the plate as a clock. To indicate the position of the food, you might say, "The meat is at six o'clock, the carrots at ten o'clock, and the potatoes at three o'clock."

Always be accurate when giving instructions to someone who is blind. The blind are dependent on the directions you give.

▶ BLINDNESS IN THE WORLD

There are many degrees of blindness. Some blind people have no sight at all and cannot even see light. Others have so little sight that they can tell only light from dark. Still others have a small amount of vision and can distinguish vague shapes.

In some countries only those who cannot see at all are considered blind. In other countries people who have a very limited degree of sight are also considered blind. Because there is no single definition of blindness, it is difficult to know exactly how many blind people there are throughout the world. Estimates reach into the tens of millions.

What we do know for certain is that the rate of blindness is highest in countries where medical care is poor and the diseases that cause blindness are not controlled. In many parts of the world, blindness occurs three to four times as often as it does in the United States and other countries where medical care is widely available.

▶ CAUSES OF BLINDNESS

Over two thirds of the people who are blind today might have had their sight saved if modern medicine and surgery had been available to them. Of all the blind people in the world, a small percentage were born blind. Blindness at birth is called congenital blindness. The causes of it are not all known. Blindness that occurs after birth is caused mainly by diseases of the eyes. Diabetes, while it is not a disease of the eyes, is an important cause of blindness. People with diabetes may develop disease of the retina of the eye. Accidents and explosions are two other causes of blindness.

In countries where good medical care results in longer lives, people often develop eye conditions in old age. Over half the blind people in the United States are over 65. Two eye conditions of old age are **cataracts** and **glaucoma**. A cataract is a clouding of the lens of the eye. The lens is a transparent part of the eye through which light rays pass. When the lens becomes cloudy, only strong light rays pass through it and there is a loss of vision. Cataracts can be removed by surgery.

Glaucoma is characterized by a hardening of the eyeball and great pressure inside the eye. Today there are medicines to control glaucoma if it is discovered in time. Sometimes surgery is necessary.

In nations with poor living conditions and little medical care, **trachoma**, **smallpox**, and **river blindness** are the three main causes of blindness. Malnutrition (vitamin A deficiency) is a leading cause of blindness among infants in developing countries.

Trachoma is the single greatest cause of loss of sight. It is said to have affected one sixth of the world's population. It is a contagious disease of the eyes that affects the inner lining of the eyelids. Blood vessels also grow over the cornea, a part of the outside coating of the eyeball.

At one time there were many cases of trachoma in the southern part of the United States. But antibiotics now control the disease in this area. It is still common in some parts of Africa and Asia.

Smallpox sores were once responsible for

Left: Blind pupil in regular classroom solves math problem, using braille and abacus.
Right: Physical education teacher directs blind pupil and sighted classmates in hula-hoop exercise.

millions of cases of blindness in India. But great strides have been made in controlling this disease. Onchocerciasis, or river blindness, is found mainly in Africa. It is caused by a wormlike parasite that is passed to people through the bite of a fly. Research to control the disease is under way.

▶ EDUCATION OF THE BLIND

The first school for the blind was started in France in 1784 by Valentin Haüy. Later several other schools were founded in Europe. Three schools for the blind in the United States were founded about 1832. Since then classes for blind children have been a part of the American school system.

One child out of every thousand in the United States has a sight loss serious enough to need help from a special teacher. Almost 30,000 children are legally blind—that is, they see no more than the large top letter on the standard eye chart used for testing vision. Of these, 75 percent attend community schools. The rest go to boarding schools for the blind.

Before blind children go to school, it is important for them to play and to attend nursery school and kindergarten with sighted children. Parents, brothers, and sisters are required to spend more time with the blind child. Blind children learn about the world around them by reaching out and touching things with their hands.

In school blind children receive an education equal to that received by sighted children. They follow the same course of studies. But some changes in materials must be made to make the course fit their special needs.

Maps and diagrams are outlined with raised lines. Dials and watches have raised dots placed on their faces so they can be read with the fingertips. Rulers also have raised dots to indicate the measurements. Blind pupils learn to listen closely, to type lessons for classes, and to develop skills in mental arithmetic. They learn to use a special alphabet called braille. Textbooks are prepared in braille, recorded on records and tapes, or read to the students. The children are taught enough handwriting to sign their names and write short notes.

▶ BRAILLE AND "TALKING BOOKS"

The braille alphabet was developed by Louis Braille (1809–52). He was a blind student in Haüy's school who later became a teacher. The letters of the braille alphabet are based on a system of six raised dots that the blind can read with their fingertips.

Braille codes have also been developed for music and mathematics.

Braille is produced by punching dots into heavy paper with a pencil-like stylus. Since the dots are pushed down into the heavy paper, the paper must be turned over to be read. One dot is A; another added below it forms B. To save space, combinations of dots may mean common words or parts of words, such as "for" or "-tion." The first 10 letters of the alphabet also stand for the numbers 1 through 10. Using a braille writer, it is possible to write as many as six dots at once by pressing six keys.

▶ WHAT IS A TALKING BOOK?

The world of books is open to the blind today through books prepared in braille and through long-playing recordings of books, called talking books. The largest producer of braille textbooks is the American Printing House for the Blind in Louisville, Kentucky.

The Library of Congress of the United States, Division for the Blind and Physically Handicapped, in Washington, D.C., has hundreds of thousands of braille volumes and talking books. Hundreds of new library titles are recorded and brailled each year. Throughout the country there are libraries that act as distributing centers for these books and records. They are mailed postage-free.

▶ DOG-GUIDES AND THE USE OF THE CANE

Being able to travel safely and independently is one of the major goals of the blind. At one time blind persons had to depend only on human guides. Large numbers of the blind still do. But when dog-guides were introduced into the United States, many blind persons were able to have new independence.

The first training school for dog-guides, established in 1929, is now known as the Seeing Eye, Inc., and is located in Morristown, New Jersey. There are several other training schools throughout the United States today.

To obtain a dog-guide, the blind person applies to one of these centers. All dog-guides have been specially trained. Most are German shepherds. For a month the dog and its new owner are trained to work together as a team.

Dog-guides learn to obey every command, and blind people learn how to care properly for their dogs. The two will spend all of their time together. Dog-guides are usually permitted to accompany the blind everywhere —in college classrooms, on trains, and in hotels and restaurants.

The blind person grasps a long handle rising from a harness on the dog's back as the two move through the crowded streets. Together they can travel even more swiftly than the average person. The dog does not actually lead but obeys commands to go left, right, and forward. Blind people must always remember where they are or know how many blocks they must walk in a certain direction, because a dog cannot read addresses and street signs or tell the color of the traffic lights. The command to cross a street comes from the blind person. The blind are trained to listen for signals or cues, such as the click of the traffic light as it changes and the sounds of the movement of traffic.

The dog is responsible for guiding the blind person safely. Dog-guides keep the blind from bumping into people or other obstacles. They circle around low-hanging awnings and tree branches and stop to indicate that they have come to a curb. Dog-guides are even trained to disobey a command to go forward if there is any danger in the path, such as construction work or a hole in the sidewalk. The dog stops and then guides the blind person around it. It is well to remember that when dogs are guiding, they are working and should never be treated as pets.

Not every blind person is able to work with a dog-guide. Only those who are in good physical condition can take part in the training program and keep up with the dog's fast pace. It is estimated that less than 5 percent of the blind can use a dog-guide. For this reason the correct use of the cane is taught more and more.

There are approximately 5,000 war veterans in the United States who became blind as a result of their wartime service. The method of using a cane that is taught to the blind today was developed by instructors working with blinded veterans at the end of World War II.

Before that time there was no special teaching in the use of the cane. Blind persons simply carried a white or white-tipped cane, of any length or weight, diagonally across the body. These canes identified blind persons. They also served as bumpers to keep blind persons from walking into obstacles.

The new use of the cane is based on a definite technique taught by carefully trained instructors. To learn to use the cane properly, the blind study an hour a day for two or three months. A lightweight cane, often made of aluminum is used. The length is important, since blind people reach out with their canes as they walk. Each cane must be fitted to the individual.

The cane is held in front of the body. As the blind person takes a step with the right foot, the tip of the cane is placed on the sidewalk in the spot where the left foot will touch down at the next step. Walking in this way, the blind person can make sure with each step that the next step will be a safe one.

▶ **EMPLOYMENT OF BLIND ADULTS**

Every blind person who can work should be given the necessary training and the opportunity to work. This is one of today's goals for the blind. In the United States there are programs under which the blind can receive advice about jobs, training for a job, and help in finding one.

It is estimated that over 7,000 different occupations are followed by the visually handicapped. Each year over 3,500 blind people find employment in some phase of business, industry, agriculture, and the professions. The blind are also employed in special workshops where they make articles such as brooms and mops. Some do craft work in their own homes. In the United States there are special training programs to teach vocations to the blind. These include music, piano tuning, and the operating of newsstands.

Sometimes the tools of work must be adapted to assist the blind in their jobs. There is a special switchboard for blind telephone operators. For cooks there are also special cooking thermometers and measuring devices with braille dots.

▶ **RECREATION**

In the use of leisure time blind persons are much like others. They follow their individual tastes and enjoy reading and listening to recordings; playing checkers, chess, and card games with brailled cards; clay modeling; weaving; knitting; and sewing. They can dance, bowl, golf, wrestle, hike, swim, and take part in many other physical activities and sports.

▶ **AID TO THE BLIND**

In the United States people who have up to one tenth of normal vision are considered blind. They are qualified to receive financial help. This help is provided by the federal government under the Social Security Act. The individual states are in charge of handling these benefits.

The national agencies active in the field of blindness include the American Foundation for the Blind and the National Society for Prevention of Blindness.

Many countries are working on ways to help the blind and to prevent blindness. Two organizations, the American Foundation for Overseas Blind and the Royal Commonwealth Society for the Blind, offer help to many nations with such programs. United Nations agencies concerned with blindness include the United Nations Education, Scientific and Cultural Organization (UNESCO) and the World Health Organization (WHO), and the United Nations Children's Fund (UNICEF).

EVERETT E. WILCOX
California School for the Blind
Reviewed by SUSAN SPUNGIN
American Foundation for the Blind

See also KELLER, HELEN.

BLOOD

Long before the beginning of recorded history, people realized that blood meant the difference between life and death. When cave dwellers speared an animal and blood gushed from the wound, the beast soon fell dead. A person who lost a lot of blood also died. It is no wonder that blood was often regarded as the mysterious secret of life. People came to believe that good or evil spirits were present in blood itself.

Today blood is no longer a mystery, but as everyone knows, it is vital to certain forms of animal life. For all such animals, blood is the stream of life.

BLOOD'S MAJOR TASKS

The human body contains a vast network of blood vessels. They are the arteries, veins, and capillaries. These vessels, extending throughout the body, carry the stream of blood. The average adult has about 5 liters (just over 5 quarts) in continuous circulation. A child has less. The blood serves the body's needs in the following ways:

The body is made of living cells that need food to grow and to reproduce themselves. Blood supplies food to the cells.

Cells "burn" food, thus producing energy for the body. To burn food, the cells need oxygen from the air. The blood carries oxygen to the cells.

Wastes, such as the gas carbon dioxide, are given off by the burning process. The blood carries these wastes away from the cells.

Cells live surrounded by a watery material called tissue fluid. Blood provides this fluid.

Every part of the body needs water to function. The blood brings water to all parts of the body.

When the body exercises heavily, a great deal of heat is given off by the muscles. Blood distributes heat evenly through the body. Blood also carries excess heat to the skin, where this heat is given off.

Some parts of the body make chemicals needed by cells and body organs. Blood distributes these chemicals.

The body produces cells and chemicals that fight harmful bacteria and viruses. Blood carries these "fighters" to the parts of the body that need them.

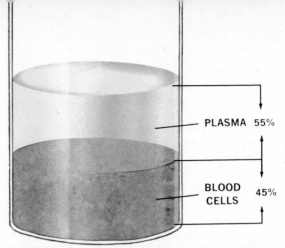

The clear liquid, plasma, makes up about half the blood.

For all these—and other—reasons, blood is called the stream of life.

WHAT IS BLOOD MADE OF?

When you cut yourself, some very small blood vessels—capillaries—break, and a little blood escapes. Soon the blood clots. It forms a thick jelly that plugs the cut. From such experiences we all learn that blood is red, thicker than water, sticky, and salty in taste. Blood contains platelets (one kind of blood cell) and chemicals that make it clot.

If a drop of blood is examined under a microscope, many round cells can be seen. These are the red cells. Seen singly, they appear faint pink or yellow rather than red. Only the thickness of many cells bunched together makes blood look red.

Red cells are only one kind of solid matter that is found in blood. Some of the solids are dissolved in the watery part. Other solids are in suspension. That is, they are distributed through the blood like grains of sand in a glass of water that has been stirred. In laboratories blood can be separated into two major parts: a jellylike mass of cells and a thin, straw-colored liquid.

Blood Plasma

The liquid part of the blood is called plasma. It is thin and clear because it is 90 percent water, but many chemicals are dissolved in it. These chemicals include forms of calcium (which builds bones) and potassium (which is needed by the heart and muscles). Plasma contains a salt, which accounts for the salty taste of blood. Plasma also carries sugar and tiny drops of fat—fuels for the body's cells.

Most of the solids dissolved in plasma are

molecules of the type known as proteins. Proteins perform some of the most important jobs in the human body. Certain ones play a vital part in building and repairing cells. Proteins called antibodies help fight certain disease-causing invaders of the body. Among the proteins are also certain hormones—chemicals that control the work of different parts of the body.

Solids in the Blood

While circulating throughout the body, the blood plasma also carries solids that are not dissolved. The most important of such solids are the corpuscles ("little bodies")—usually called blood cells. Mature blood corpuscles do not grow or reproduce themselves. Unlike most of the body's cells, blood corpuscles do not join together to form tissue. They float singly, in suspension. The blood corpuscles can be separated from plasma. When this is done, the corpuscles form a jellylike mass.

There are three kinds of solid bodies in the blood: red cells, white cells, and platelets. (The drawing shows what the different bodies look like.) Each kind performs one major task. The red cells carry oxygen throughout the body. The white cells attack infection-causing bacteria. And the platelets help to clot the blood.

Blood contains three types of cells: red cells, platelets, and white cells.

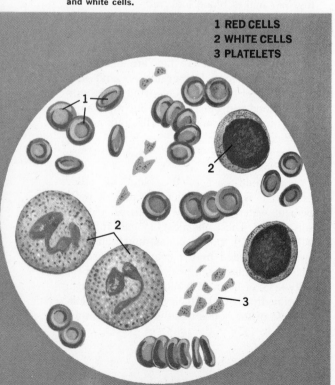

1 RED CELLS
2 WHITE CELLS
3 PLATELETS

Red Blood Cells. Most of the solids in the blood are red cells. Billions and billions of them circulate in the bloodstream. About 1,400 of them placed side by side would stretch one centimeter (about 3,500 to an inch). As they flow through the capillaries, red cells move in single file in these narrow blood vessels.

The red cells contain a protein called hemoglobin. Hemoglobin is a pigment (coloring matter) containing iron. In combination with oxygen, hemoglobin gives blood its red color. More important, hemoglobin also has the ability to combine loosely with oxygen.

This loose combining explains how red cells deliver oxygen to the body cells. Oxygen is part of the air breathed into the lungs. The hemoglobin picks up oxygen as blood passes through the lungs. Then, as the blood flows through capillaries among the body cells, the oxygen escapes through the thin capillary walls.

When the oxygen is released, hemoglobin takes up carbon dioxide from the body cells. This gas is waste formed when cells burn food. Loaded with carbon dioxide, the blood returns to the heart, which pumps it to the lungs. Here an exchange takes place. Carbon dioxide is dropped (to be breathed out) and fresh oxygen is picked up. Then the red cells continue on their way, carrying oxygen to cells throughout the body.

A red cell lives for about 120 days. By then it is worn out and can no longer do its work properly. Passing through the liver, it is caught and destroyed. While most of the red cell is destroyed, the iron from the hemoglobin is stored in the liver. The iron is later used in making new red cells.

New red cells are made in the red marrow of the bones. Bones have a spongy tissue inside the solid outer part. Red marrow fills the spaces in some of the spongy bone parts. New red cells are produced at about the same rate at which the worn-out old ones are destroyed.

White Blood Cells. White blood cells are colorless. They can be seen only when blood examined under a microscope has been treated with a special dye. Unlike the other blood cells, white cells have a nucleus. This is the inner core that enables the body's other cells to divide in two and reproduce themselves. But white cells do not reproduce themselves in the blood-

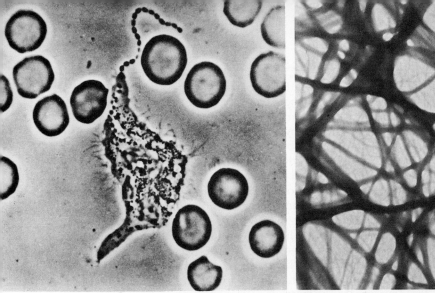

Left, living human blood cell ingesting a chain of streptococci, a type of bacteria. Right, microphotograph of blood clot showing network of fibrin in which cells become entangled.

stream. Most of them are formed in the red marrow and in the lymph glands.

Most white cells are phagocytes ("eating cells"). They can move about, even slipping through the walls of capillaries. They are also able to engulf and destroy (by "eating") invading organisms. So they make up one of the body's main defenses against infection.

If infectious bacteria enter the body— through a cut, for example—the white cells rush to the spot where the bacteria are. Great numbers of them gather around the bacteria. If they can engulf the bacteria fast enough, the infection is stopped. The dead tissue, bacteria, and dead and living white cells that collect at the point of infection all make up the matter known as pus.

Normally red cells outnumber white cells by several hundred to one. The number of white cells may increase slightly in response to physical exertion. But in a healthy person the white cells remain fairly constant. Some white cells are killed in the steady battle with harmful bacteria. Others get into the body's digestive and waste-disposal system and are lost to the body. But replacements for lost and destroyed white cells are produced in the bone marrow and in structures called lymph glands.

When harmful organisms infect the body, the total number of white cells may double or triple. One of the ways a doctor can tell whether someone is suffering from some unknown infection is to count the white cells in a tiny sample of blood.

Platelets. These are the third kind of solid in the blood. Their name describes their shape —little plates. These small, colorless bodies are fewer in number than the red cells, but more numerous than the white cells. Platelets are fragments of cells that are produced in the red bone marrow.

The platelets are needed for clotting—the process by which the blood turns into a sticky jelly and stops flowing. Blood clots most easily when exposed to air, rough surfaces, or nonliving matter, such as a bandage.

There are many steps involved in the clotting process. It begins when the platelets come in contact with the rough edges of a cut or other break in the skin. The platelets then release a chemical. This chemical starts a chain of reactions. As a result of these reactions, another chemical called fibrin is formed. Fibrin is a threadlike material. It forms a lacy mesh of fine threads. Blood cells and platelets are trapped in the mesh, like fish in a net. More cells pile up behind and a clot forms. The clot acts like a plug to stop the flow of blood.

▶ **BLOOD TYPES**

All human blood is made up of basically the same plasma, cells, and dissolved chemicals. But individuals differ in some of the arrangements and proportions of the chemicals in their cells and plasma.

Karl Landsteiner (1868–1943), an Austrian doctor, found in 1901 that the blood of every human being could be classed under one of four main groups, or types. The groups are called A, B, O, and AB. They are based on the presence or absence of certain protein molecules in the blood.

When blood from two different groups is mixed, the blood sometimes forms clumps. This results from a reaction between the protein molecules in the red cells of one group and the plasma of the other. Such chemical reactions make it dangerous for a person to receive a transfusion of whole blood from someone whose blood group is unknown. But if the cells are removed from blood, then the remaining plasma can be given to anyone, no matter what the person's blood group.

In the years since Landsteiner's discovery, scientists have found that the four major groups of blood can be classed chemically into various subgroups.

The presence or absence of certain other protein molecules separates all human blood into two other broad groups—Rh positive and Rh negative. The protein itself is called the Rh factor, after the rhesus monkey, in which the protein was first found.

Couples about to marry are tested for the Rh factor. This is done because of a possible danger that is faced by the baby of an Rh-negative woman and an Rh-positive man. If the baby is Rh-positive, the mother's Rh-negative blood produces substances that destroy many of the baby's blood cells. At one time doctors had to remove and replace all of such a baby's blood at birth to save its life. Today they have a way of learning whether the developing baby is Rh-positive. If it is, the baby is given a life-saving transfusion of concentrated Rh-negative red cells before it is born.

Blood can be exchanged among any human beings whose groups and subgroups have been matched. But certain large populations may have more of one particular group than another. Anthropologists who study human physical development use blood groups as one means of showing relationships among individuals and population groups. It is even possible to type a sample of blood taken from ancient bones or mummies. This helps anthropologists learn more about our ancestors.

Although human blood has many different groups and subgroups, it is basically all the same. Each species of animal, in fact, has its own blood. This blood can be exchanged only among animals of the same species. All cats, for example, have the same kind of blood, just as all dogs have the same kind of blood.

The study of blood types often helps scientists study relationships among animals. For example, most mammals live on the land. But a few, such as dolphins, live in the sea. Studies of the blood of dolphins and whales indicate that their ancestors once lived on land. It is not known how these distant ancestors adjusted totally to life in the sea—to become the only seagoing mammals completely divorced from the land.

EVOLUTION OF ANIMALS WITH BLOOD

Not all animals have blood. Many bloodless animals live in the water. Most of these creatures are one-celled. They get their food and oxygen directly from the water and give up their wastes to the water. The exchange takes place through the thin membrane (skin) that surrounds the one-celled animal.

All animal life began as bloodless forms in the ocean. Many millions of years ago all simple animals lived much as today's one-

Chart shows which types of blood will clump when mixed.

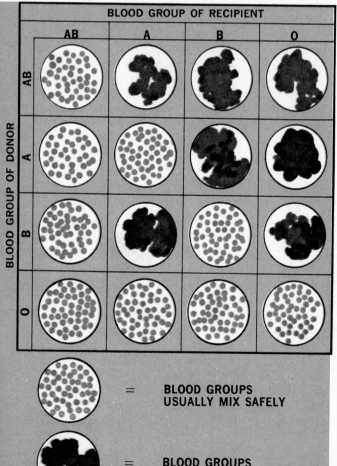

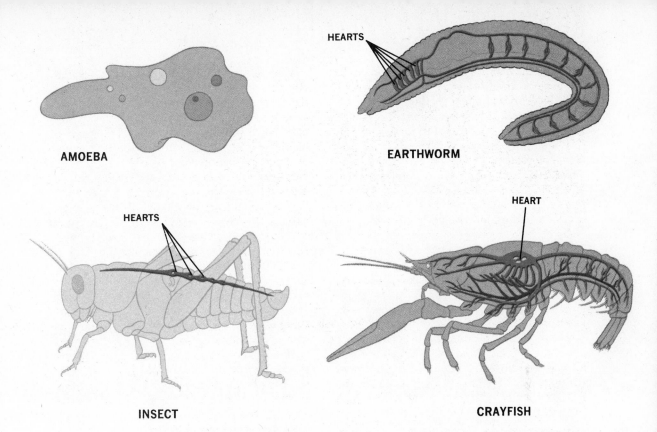

AMOEBA

EARTHWORM

HEARTS

HEART

HEARTS

INSECT

CRAYFISH

Amoeba has no blood system. Most other invertebrate animals have a heart-and-blood system.

celled animals still do. The ocean surrounding them did the major jobs that blood does.

During a long period of time, some ocean creatures developed with a central tube inside their bodies. Seawater went from the tube to all parts of the body. As more complicated animals developed, a system of tubes also developed. The liquid flowing through this system became more like plasma. And as blood cells developed, it became blood. All animals evolved from simple forms of ocean life. And blood plasma has a chemical makeup that is very much like the makeup of seawater. The big difference is in the far smaller amount of salt (sodium chloride) that the plasma contains.

Warm-Blooded and Cold-Blooded

Warm-blooded animals keep about the same body temperature, partly because the nervous system regulates it and partly because their blood contains hemoglobin in its red cells. The hemoglobin delivers enough oxygen to support the high rate of food burning that goes on in the cells of warm-blooded animals.

The body temperature of cold-blooded animals, such as fishes, goes up and down with the outside temperature. Their red cells are larger. But there are fewer red cells, and they contain less hemoglobin. Part of the cell is taken up by a nucleus, which a mammal's red blood cells do not have. This means that each cell carries less oxygen. Cold-blooded animals do not get enough oxygen in their blood to burn food quickly in the cold of winter. As the temperature outside falls, their body temperature lowers, and all their body processes slow down. Many cold-blooded animals hibernate or become inactive during the winter.

Birds are a different case. They are warm-blooded and their red cells ordinarily carry enough oxygen to keep their very active fuel-burning process going. But in winter the problem of finding food puts an extra strain on their bodies. This is one of the conditions that cause many species of birds to migrate to warmer climates during cold weather.

SARAH R. RIEDMAN
Author, *Your Blood and You*
Reviewed by THOMAS R. FORBES
Yale University School of Medicine

See also BODY, HUMAN; CELL.

BLOOD TRANSFUSION. See TRANSFUSION, BLOOD.

Above: A marina where every kind of small craft can be docked and serviced. Below: Summer on the water is fun in a speedy runabout.

BOATS AND BOATING

Boating is a fast-growing sport. Every year more young skippers pilot their craft on fresh-water lakes and rivers and on the bays and inlets at the ocean's edge. To keep pace with the rapid growth of boating, hundreds of marinas have been built to provide shoreside berths for small craft. *Marina* is a Spanish word meaning "seacoast," and is used in English to describe a modern boat basin with piers and slips for docking boats, launches, and yachts. In a marina large and small boats are repaired, serviced, and stored. Shore electricity, telephones, fresh water, ice, and fuel are available at dockside, and the pleasure-boat owner may shop for supplies and food and drink all within walking distance of his boat.

A visit to a marina is like a trip to a million-dollar boat show. Here every type of craft may be seen, from small rowboats and sailing dinghies to two-masted schooners, from outboard runabouts to big cabin cruisers with berths for six people or more.

The 14- to 18-foot runabouts are the most popular small powerboats. They are wonderful for fishing or for just having fun on the water. The larger ones, fitted with powerful outboard engines, are used for towing water-skiers.

Before the beginning boatman learns to run one of these craft or even goes for a ride in a dinghy or other small rowboat, he should know the basic rules of safety for himself, as well as for his boat.

▶ SAFETY RULES FOR YOUNG SAILORS

(1) Learn to swim. If you cannot swim, wear a life jacket.

(2) Do not go out in a boat alone. Young children should always be accompanied by an adult.

(3) Do not go out in bad weather, or when a storm is forecast, or in a fog. Beginning boaters should stay close to shore.

(4) Never overload your boat.

(5) Sit quietly when boating. Do not scuffle or try to practice boxing while aboard a boat. Do not change seats when the water is rough or when the boat is in deep water.

(6) Do not try to swim ashore from an overturned boat even though you are a good swimmer. Hold on to the boat and wait for help.

(7) Wear sneakers or rubber-soled shoes to avoid slipping, and wear a hat to protect yourself from the sun.

(8) Before diving off a boat into strange water, test for depth, rocks, and weeds. Swim in a safe place.

▶ RULES OF THE ROAD

It is important to know the rules of any sport, but in boating not to know the rules can mean disaster. The important rules concern whistle signals, the lights for different kinds of boats, and rights of way.

Signal Talk

One blast of the whistle means "I am going right (starboard)." Two blasts mean "I am going left (port)."

Motorboats are forbidden to use a cross signal—that is, to answer one whistle with two blasts or two blasts with one. The reason for answering with the same signal is that this indicates that you understand the other boat's signal. Whistle or horn signals are not exchanged between sailboats.

Four or more blasts make up the danger signal. If you disagree with a signal, blow the

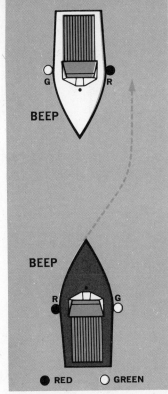
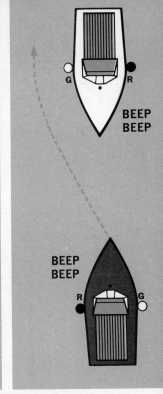

When boats approach head on, one blast of the whistle means "going right" (starboard). It is answered by one blast from the approaching boat. Two blasts mean "going left" (port), and are answered by two blasts.

danger signal, stop your boat, and do not proceed until the proper whistles have been given, answered, and understood.

Lights Required After Sunset

Class A boats (under 16 feet) and Class 1 boats (16 to 26 feet) carry a combination red and green light forward, the red showing to port, or left, and the green to starboard, or right. Each color should be visible from dead ahead and show for 10 points around the horizon on each side for a distance of 1 mile. (On a compass card 32 points represent a complete circle.) A 32-point white light at the stern should show all around the horizon and be visible for 2 miles.

Class 2 boats (26 to 40 feet) and Class 3 boats (40 to 65 feet) all have separate red and green side lights, which are screened so as not to shine across the bow. These boats require a white 20-point light showing at the bow, as well as a white 32-point stern light, which is placed higher than the bow light.

All classes carry a white lantern or small light to flash when they are in danger of colliding with another boat.

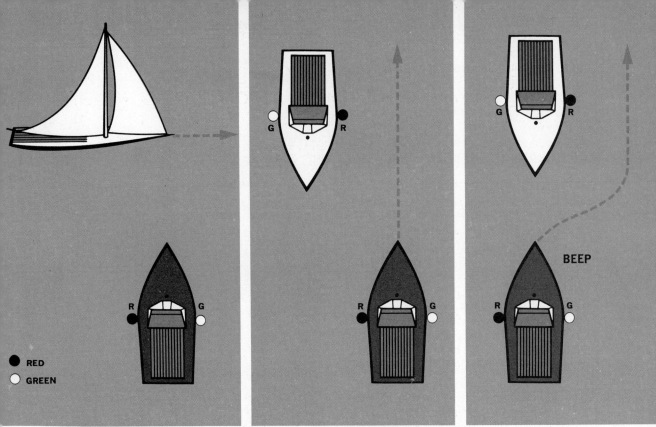

Left: Sailboats always have the right of way over powerboats. Center: Red to red (port to port) means safe to go ahead. Right: When you see both red and green lights, blow one blast and pass red to red (port to port).

Right of Way

If ever in doubt about which way to turn, remember that the first rule of the seaway is "Keep to the right." For instance, when two boats are about to meet head on, each skipper should give one blast on the whistle and swing his bow to starboard (right), and the boats will pass port side to port side (left side to left side.) This and other passing situations are shown in the illustration on page 263.

Sailboats always have the right of way over powerboats.

In any dangerous situation, even though you have the right of way, you should turn or back away to avoid collision. For further piloting rules there are many free pamphlets available from the United States Coast Guard Marine Inspection Office in Washington, D.C., or from your district Coast Guard commander or local unit of the United States Power Squadrons. In Canada boating information is available from the Canadian Department of Transport, Hunter Building, Ottawa, Ontario.

Safety also requires that a pleasure boat have emergency equipment. The gear should include a fire extinguisher, a small, well-stocked first-aid kit, life jackets, and buoy-

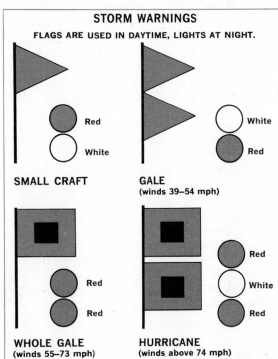

STORM WARNINGS
FLAGS ARE USED IN DAYTIME, LIGHTS AT NIGHT.

Red
White

White
Red

SMALL CRAFT

GALE
(winds 39–54 mph)

Red
Red

Red
White
Red

WHOLE GALE
(winds 55–73 mph)

HURRICANE
(winds above 74 mph)

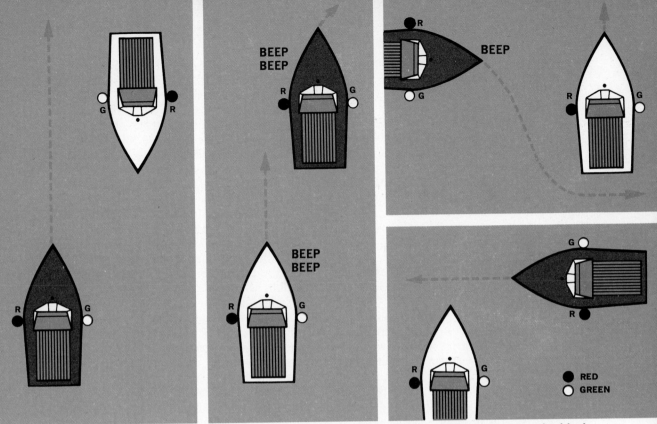

Left: Green to green means safe to proceed. Center: Boat astern asks to pass. Lead boat answers and moves to starboard. Upper right: Red to starboard gives other boat right of way; signal and go astern. Lower right: Green off your port bow gives you right of way.

ant cushions. A compass, too, is important for a small boat that navigates offshore.

▶ THE MANY ACTIVITIES OF BOATING

You can swim from almost any boat. The boat should be moored to a pier or lying at anchor, and the motor must be stopped before anyone goes in swimming. The boat should have a boarding ladder placed at one side so that the swimmers can climb back into the boat. Someone should remain aboard the boat, ready to throw a life preserver if a swimmer needs help. Children under 10 years of age should wear life vests and never swim in water over 5 feet deep.

Skin diving, like swimming, can be done from almost any kind of boat. However, water skiing requires the use of a fast powerboat because a water skier is a heavy weight and has to be pulled through the water rapidly.

Fishing is the most popular pastime for boatmen. To many people the boat is just a means of getting to the spot where the fish are. Most fishing from runabouts and other small boats is done with light poles and lines, and small reels. The boat can be stopped and the bait cast to the spot where the fish are thought to be, or the bait can be pulled along behind the boat as it moves through the fishing grounds. This last method is called trolling.

For fishing offshore, big boats with heavy fishing tackle are needed. A flying-bridge cruiser is used for going after marlin, sailfish, and even sharks. When one of these big game fish is hooked, the skipper must be able to twist and turn the boat quickly to keep the fishing line tight and to prevent it from getting under the boat. It may take the fisherman, strapped into a special "fighting" chair in the cockpit, several hours to bring a big sailfish into the boat.

Camping is a recreation that almost every boat owner may enjoy. Even a canoe or a small runabout can carry a tent, sleeping bags, a portable stove, a little ice chest, and a supply of food. Mosquito nets might be included, as insects are often a problem near the water, especially at night. On larger boats where everyone sleeps on board, screens may be used to keep out insects.

▶ POWERBOAT RACING

Some racing requires special boats and motors. Most races are run with hydroplanes on an oval course. Hydroplanes are light, flat-bottomed boats powered by either inboard or outboard motors. There are classes for each boat size and type of motor according to piston displacement.

The largest competition boats are the 25- to 40-foot hydroplanes with powerful engines that enable the boats to reach speeds of 200 miles an hour on a straight run. These boats compete in contests like the famous Gold Cup race, which is held at various cities in the United States. Another prize for which these boats contend is the British International (Harmsworth) Trophy. This cup was held for many years by American boats, and races were held at Detroit. In 1960 the course was moved to Pincton, Ontario. "Miss Supertest III," a great Canadian hydroplane, was the only boat to win in both countries.

Another famous boat was Donald Campbell's "Bluebird." For many years it held the world jet speedboat record of over 260 miles an hour. Its record was broken in 1967, when Lee Taylor drove a jet-powered hydroplane over 285 miles an hour.

The marathon is a long-distance event often raced on a river. Lately powerboats such as runabouts and cruisers have been raced over the open ocean. These races provide a rugged test of the boats, their equipment, and their drivers. One of the most famous races is the 163-mile Miami–Nassau race (Miami, Florida, to Nassau in the Bahamas). Others are the Hennessy Grand Prix, held around Long Island, New York, and the 170-mile race along the southern coast of England from the Isle of Wight to Torquay.

In 1921 Gar Wood raced 1,257 miles from Miami to New York in 47 hours and 15 minutes. After 41 years Wood's marathon record was finally broken in 1962 by Sam Griffith, who made the grueling journey in 38 hours and 28 minutes.

The newcomer to boating has many ways to find fun afloat before he starts racing. The waterfront has attractions for even the smallest sailor—he can use a boat for exploring, for nature studies, and for photography. And, as Kenneth Grahame wrote in *The Wind in the Willows,* "There is nothing—absolutely nothing—half so much worth doing as simply messing about in boats. . . . In or out of 'em, it doesn't matter."

TOM BOTTOMLEY
Executive Editor
Motor Boating and Sailing Books

See also DIVING; FISHING; ROWING; SAILING; SKIN DIVING; SWIMMING; WATER-SKIING.

BOBSLEDDING

How does it feel to shoot down the side of a mountain and around sharp curves at speeds of more than a mile a minute? You would know if you rode a bobsled down the ice-packed trough on Mount Van Hoevenberg, near Lake Placid, New York. It is one of the world's fastest bobruns.

A bobsled can carry two or four people. The four-man sled used in championship races is about 12 feet long. The weight of the sled and crew together cannot be more than 1,389 pounds (630 kilograms). A two-man racing sled is about 8½ feet long. The sled and crew together cannot weigh more than 827 pounds (375 kgs.).

The bobsled is a plank of steel or other metal alloy mounted on two sets of runners. The driver steers the front runners by means of either a wheel or ropes. He handles the sled as carefully as he would a racing car. The back runners do not turn.

The man on the back of the sled is the brakeman. The other two men on a four-man sled sit between the driver and the brakeman. In the early days of bobsledding, these riders used to bob back and forth together at times in order to make the sled go as fast as possible. That is why the sleds are called bobsleds.

The metal or plastic covering over the steering gear is called the cowling. It protects both the driver and the steering mechanism.

From a standstill, bobsleds can reach speeds as high as 90 miles an hour during a 1-mile run.

It also cuts down wind resistance, to make faster speeds possible. The cowling is usually painted with the colors and emblem of the club or country that enters the bobsled in a race. Push handles on each side of the bobsled help the crew to get the sled off to a fast start.

Modern bobsledders incorporate some of the most advanced engineering techniques into their sleds. Many of the best bobsleds have their runners mounted in rubber. They act like the shock absorbers on a car, taking up much of the shock at high speeds. Some bobsled racers make sleds for their own use, building special features into the sled in the hope that it will go faster. Each bobsled owner takes as much pride in his machine as an auto racer does in his car.

▶ HOW THE SPORT OF BOBSLEDDING GREW

People long ago discovered that it was easy to travel and carry loads over snow and ice on sleds. Early sleds were probably made of flat boards or animal skins stretched over frames. Then came sleds with narrow wooden runners on the bottom. These were faster and easier to control. Indians of North America used a kind of light, flat-bottomed sled that curved up in front. It was from Algonkin words that we got the name "toboggan" for this kind of sled.

During the 1880's some sportsmen in the Swiss Alps discovered the thrill of coasting down the mountains on toboggans. They then tried mounting the toboggans on runners. This made them go faster. In fact, they went so fast that they would run off course out of control. This caused many bad accidents. Then some members of the Toboggan Club at St. Moritz, a famous winter resort in Switzerland, found that by making their sleds much heavier they could control them better. So was born the bobsleigh, or bobsled, as it is called today. A bobrun was built at St. Moritz, and the first race was held there in 1898.

A better bobrun was later built at St. Moritz as the sleds became faster and faster. Many other bobruns have since been built in Europe, especially in the Alps. The first national championship races were held in Austria in 1908, and bobsledding became a world event in the first winter Olympic Games, held in France in 1924.

▶ NORTH AMERICA'S FAMOUS BOBRUN AT LAKE PLACID

The Van Hoevenberg bobrun was the first built in North America. It was finished a year before the 1932 winter Olympic Games, which were held at Lake Placid. The builder was Stanislaus Zentzytski of Germany, one of the world's greatest bobrun designers.

Van Hoevenberg is 5,013 feet long and has 16 curves. Between curves are narrow strips called straightaways. The straightaways are 5 feet wide, and the walls on either side are 3 feet high. These sidewalls are made of planks with a thin coating of ice. This type of sidewall does away with the time-consuming job of building sidewalls of large ice blocks.

The curves are from 10 to 22 feet high. Each curve is made of solid rock covered with a mixture of ice and snow. After this is frozen, it is sprayed with water until blue ice forms. When the run is in use it is sprayed each day with 20,000 gallons of water, which is pumped through 8,000 feet of pipe. Ice blocks are now used on the Shady, Zig-Zag, and finish curves.

The bottom of the run is usually covered with a thin frosting of snow. This gives the runners a better grip on the ice.

Shady is the largest curve at Van Hoevenberg, and one of the most famous in the world. Although Shady is the largest curve, Zig-Zag is the trickiest. The reason for this is that Zig-Zag is two curves, one right after the other and in opposite directions. You must have perfect timing in Zig; if you don't, you will have trouble going into or out of Zag. After you get through Zig-Zag, you feel safe because there is only one more small curve before you come to the long, sweeping finish curve.

▶ RACING AGAINST THE CLOCK

There is room for only one sled at a time on a bobrun. So a bobsled race is a race against time. The time of each sled is clocked with the aid of electric eyes.

The riders push their sled off from a point 50 feet from the electric eye, and leap aboard after the sled has passed the starting line. As the sled crosses the starting line electric eyes cause a clock in the timing booth at the finish line to start running. Other electric eyes along the run mark the time that the sled reaches intermediate points. At the end of the run still another pair of electric eyes stops the clock in the timing booth. Each run is timed to $\frac{1}{100}$ of a second.

Championship races are run in four heats (unless weather makes it necessary to stop after two heats). Each sled makes four runs. The sled with the shortest total time for four heats is the winner. The fastest times on the Mount Van Hoevenberg mile run are under 1 minute and 10 seconds for a single heat. However, on some parts of the course racing sleds reach speeds of 90 to 95 miles per hour.

From telephone booths along the run, information is relayed over a public-address system to the spectators at the race. "Approaching Shady," a man in one booth will say, "riding high—they're through!" In case of an accident the call "81!" goes out. An emergency crew is ready to rush to the scene. The call "82" brings an ambulance.

Bobsled racing is governed by the International Bobsleigh and Tobogganing Federation. A jury of three men has charge of the run and the sleds when races are held. If anything should happen to the run during the event, the jury would decide what to do.

World championship races are held at the same time as other winter Olympic events and yearly between Olympic Games. In the North American championships, usually held each year, four-man and two-man crews compete for the Lowell Thomas international trophies. The winner of the annual national Amateur Athletic Union four-man race receives the Billy Fiske Memorial Trophy. Billy Fiske was only 17 years old when he was driver for the winning American crew in the 1928 Olympics. He died in World War II of wounds he received while flying with the Royal Air Force in England. The A.A.U. two-man trophy is named for Harold "Bubs" Monahan, a bobsledder who served with the Royal Canadian Air Force in World War II and was later lost on a mission with the United States Army Air Corps over Italy.

▶ BOBSLEDDING FOR FUN

You don't have to be a racer to enjoy the sport of bobsledding. In winter the bobrun at Lake Placid is open for public pleasure riding. As a paying passenger, you can ride between an experienced driver and a brakeman. The Van Hoevenberg run, which is in the heart of the Adirondack Mountains, is owned and operated by the New York State Conservation Department.

Anyone who wishes to learn to drive a bobsled may do so if he can first pass a physical examination. He is taught by an expert Conservation Department driver. When he is ready for his test he must drive first from the ½-mile and then from the mile starting points. After he has done this in a satisfactory manner, he can be granted a license.

STANLEY BENHAM
Former World Bobsled Champion

BODY, HUMAN

In some ways the human body is like a machine. A machine, such as an automobile engine, needs energy to do its work. The engine burns fuel, usually gasoline. The fuel combines with oxygen from the air. Energy is released. The body's fuel is food. The food is combined with oxygen that is breathed in. Energy is released.

There are many other likenesses between machines and the human body. But it is the differences that make us better than machines. Because the body can change food into living material, it can grow. Machines can't do that. Cameras can "see" and computers can "learn" in a way. But machines cannot feel, see, think, and learn as humans do. The body can repair worn-out parts, and even produce new humans. The human body has a very special thing about it—it is alive.

▶ LIVING CELLS

All living things are made of cells. Your body is made up of billions of cells. This tells you something about the size of cells. Most of them are too small to be seen without a microscope. But they are alive.

Most cells have three main parts. The outside is like a thin skin. It is called the **cell membrane**. Inside it is a soft jelly, the **cytoplasm**. Within the cytoplasm lies the **nucleus**. The nucleus controls the making of new cells. It reproduces by dividing into two parts. Each part then becomes the nucleus of a new cell, complete with membrane and cytoplasm. You can grow because your body cells form new cells in this way.

The blood brings digested food to the cells. Within a cell the cytoplasm uses some of the food to get the energy the cell needs. It may also use part of the food for making new cell materials. In some kinds of cells food is stored for later use.

Six steps in cell division. 1: Cell nucleus about to divide. 2 and 3: Division begins. 4 and 5: Nucleus divided; cell membrane dividing. 6: Two complete cells. For more details, see the article CELL.

CELL DIVISION

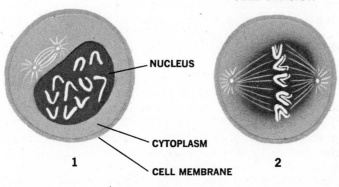

NUCLEUS

CYTOPLASM

CELL MEMBRANE

1

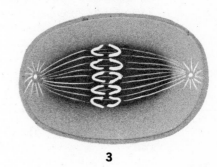

2

3

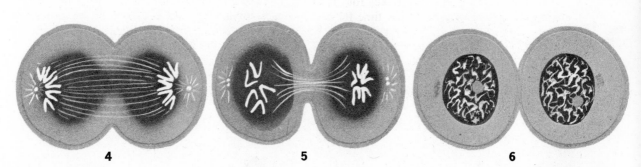

4

5

6

OUTER LAYER OF SKIN
(EPIDERMIS)

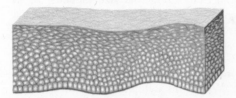

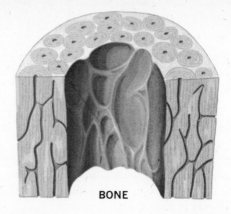

BONE

FOUR KINDS OF TISSUE

MUSCLE

NERVE

Tissue is made of many cells of one kind, all joined together. There are many different kinds of tissue in the body. Above: Four kinds of tissue. Drawings show how cells are joined into small pieces of epidermis, bone, muscle, and nerve. Muscle cells form fibers; nerve cells form bundles of nerves. Below: Major organs of the body.

SOME MAJOR ORGANS

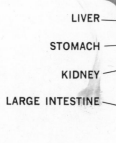

BRAIN

LUNG

HEART

SPLEEN

PANCREAS

SMALL INTESTINE

BLADDER

LIVER

STOMACH

KIDNEY

LARGE INTESTINE

The cell membrane acts as a wrapper and a sieve. It is like a sieve that lets some materials pass through while holding back others. Food and oxygen carried to the cell must pass through the cell membrane. Wastes given off by the cell when it has burned the food and oxygen pass out through this sieve back into the blood, which carries them away.

The human body has many kinds of cells. Each has a special form that makes it fit for the special job it has to do.

Cells of one kind are usually joined together to make **tissue**. (Blood cells are an exception. They are not joined, but travel alone.) A tissue is a fabric of the same kind of cells. For example, muscles are tissue made of muscle cells; nerves are tissue made of nerve cells.

Different kinds of tissue are combined in the body's **organs**. An organ is a body part that does one or more special jobs for the rest of the body; the heart, lungs, stomach, brain, and skin are all organs. The skin is the largest organ of the body, and it does many jobs. It seals fluids inside the body; it keeps air, water, and dirt outside. By giving off heat it helps to regulate the body's temperature. It contains nerves that report on the world, giving you information, pleasure, and warning.

Organs that work together make a **system**. For example, the heart, blood, and blood vessels make up the **circulatory** system. The nose, throat, windpipe, and lungs make up the **respiratory** (breathing) system. The systems are like the members of a team. Together they make it possible for the body to work, play, learn, grow, and carry out other functions.

▶ THE BODY PLAN

Your back is very different from your front. But your two sides are almost exactly alike. Each has an eye, ear, arm, leg, lung. A body plan with two similar sides is called **two-sided symmetry**. Most of the animals you know —grasshoppers, lobsters, cats, dogs, monkeys, and elephants—are built this way. Some animals are not. The starfish, for example, is built on a radial plan, which means that its body parts radiate from a central point.

The kind of skeleton that an animal has is included in the body plan. The lobster and the grasshopper wear their skeletons on the outside of their bodies. Instead of having bones inside, they have a hard shell outside. You,

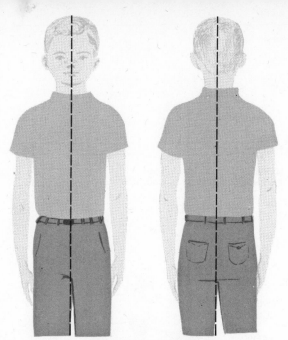

TWO-SIDED SYMMETRY

Higher animals, including man, have a two-sided body plan (*top*). One side is a mirror image of the other. The starfish (*bottom*) and certain other animals have a radial body, spreading out from a central point.

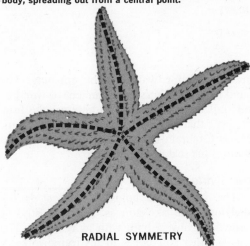

RADIAL SYMMETRY

the cat, dog, monkey, and elephant have an inside skeleton made of bones.

The cat, dog, and elephant have a body plan that permits them to walk easily only on all fours. Man and monkey have a body plan that lets them walk easily on two feet. However, the monkey more often walks on all fours. His toes are designed for clinging to branches. His forepaw is useful but is much like his hindpaw.

Man has certain features all to himself. Only man has developed a chin. He alone stands erect. His strong legs are as long as his trunk and head together. His feet and toes

SKIN

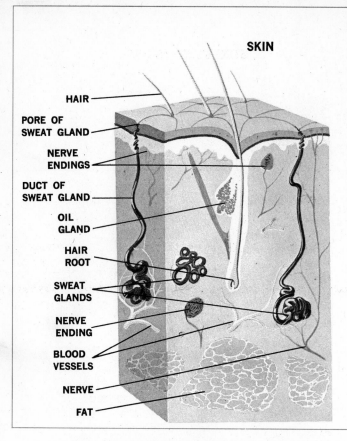

HAIR

PORE OF
SWEAT GLAND

NERVE
ENDINGS

DUCT OF
SWEAT GLAND

OIL
GLAND

HAIR
ROOT

SWEAT
GLANDS

NERVE
ENDING

BLOOD
VESSELS

NERVE

FAT

NAIL

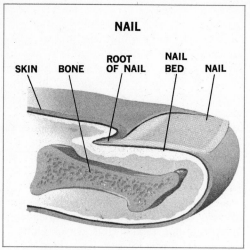

SKIN   BONE   ROOT
OF NAIL   NAIL
BED   NAIL

Left: Cross section of skin, greatly enlarged. Hair grows from roots in the skin and is made up of dead cells. Hairs of the head, brows, and lashes help protect the brain and eyes. Nails, like hair, are made up of dead cells. (That is why you can cut them without pain.) The nail bed (*above*) and the root of the nail are composed of live cells, and the nail itself grows from these areas.

are shaped for walking, not grasping. His hand has grown into an instrument of wonderful skill because the thumb apposes the four fingers; that is, it can push against them. Man's forebrain is also large; this part of the brain is the seat of intelligence.

▶ THE LIVING SKELETON

The frame that holds man erect is his **skeleton**. The skeleton is made mostly of bones. A baby is born with as many as 270 small, rather soft bones in his framework. A fully grown person usually has 206. The rest of the bones have fused (grown together).

Bones fit together at **joints** and are held fast by tough cords or straps, called **ligaments**. Some joints can be moved freely; others cannot be moved at all. When you run, you move your legs at the hip and knee joints. When you throw a ball, you move your arm at the shoulder and elbow joints. You can move your spine, too, though not as freely. However, in the base of the spine the bones are fused, forming one bony plate that fits into another. Neither moves. The joints in your skull are solid, too, except for those in the jaw.

The skeleton does two main jobs. It supports the body—without a skeleton you would be like a jellyfish. And it protects delicate organs. The hard, bony cap of the skull protects the brain. The rib cage protects the heart and lungs. The spinal cord—the body's trunk line of nerve cables—is shielded inside the hollow spinal column, or backbone. (The backbone is made up of a string of small bones. They give support, yet let you bend.)

The joints permit movement, and there are several kinds of them. Two main kinds are the ball-and-socket joint and the hinge. Arm and shoulder are attached with a ball-and-socket joint; it is the kind of joint that permits the greatest possible movement—you can swing your arm in a full circle. The knee is a hinge joint, which bends in only one direction.

Bone is living tissue, and it grows when a person is young. For example, the thighbone of a grown person is several times as long as that of a newborn baby. Bones grow in length and thickness as calcium and other minerals are added to them. Also, because bone is living tissue, it must be fed. If you look at a soupbone in a butcher's shop, you will

BONES AND JOINTS

1 BALL-AND-SOCKET JOINT (HIP)

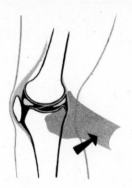

2 HINGE JOINT (KNEE)

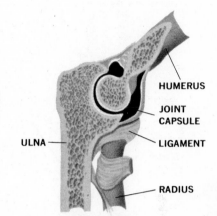

HUMERUS
JOINT CAPSULE
ULNA
LIGAMENT
RADIUS

3 ELBOW JOINT (CUT THROUGH)

HUMAN SKELETON

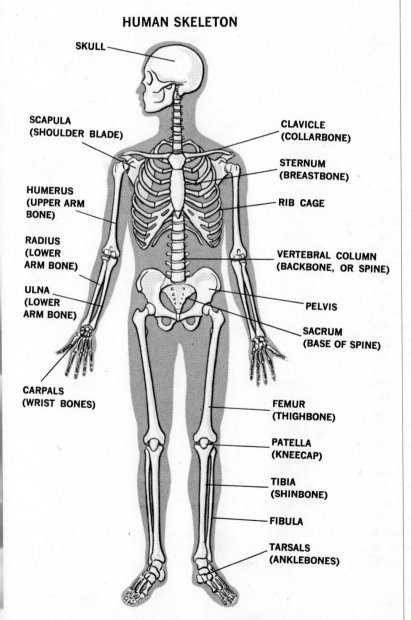

SKULL

SCAPULA (SHOULDER BLADE)

CLAVICLE (COLLARBONE)

STERNUM (BREASTBONE)

HUMERUS (UPPER ARM BONE)

RIB CAGE

RADIUS (LOWER ARM BONE)

VERTEBRAL COLUMN (BACKBONE, OR SPINE)

ULNA (LOWER ARM BONE)

PELVIS

SACRUM (BASE OF SPINE)

CARPALS (WRIST BONES)

FEMUR (THIGHBONE)

PATELLA (KNEECAP)

TIBIA (SHINBONE)

FIBULA

TARSALS (ANKLEBONES)

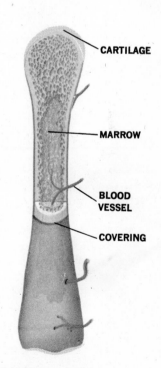

CARTILAGE

MARROW

BLOOD VESSEL

COVERING

4 BONE (CUT THROUGH)

SOME LARGE MUSCLES

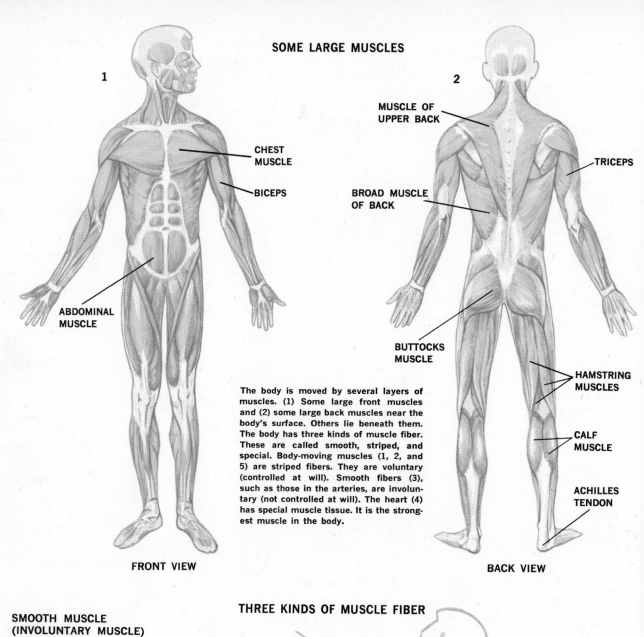

1

CHEST
MUSCLE

BICEPS

ABDOMINAL
MUSCLE

FRONT VIEW

2

MUSCLE OF
UPPER BACK

TRICEPS

BROAD MUSCLE
OF BACK

BUTTOCKS
MUSCLE

HAMSTRING
MUSCLES

CALF
MUSCLE

ACHILLES
TENDON

BACK VIEW

The body is moved by several layers of muscles. (1) Some large front muscles and (2) some large back muscles near the body's surface. Others lie beneath them. The body has three kinds of muscle fiber. These are called smooth, striped, and special. Body-moving muscles (1, 2, and 5) are striped fibers. They are voluntary (controlled at will). Smooth fibers (3), such as those in the arteries, are involuntary (not controlled at will). The heart (4) has special muscle tissue. It is the strongest muscle in the body.

THREE KINDS OF MUSCLE FIBER

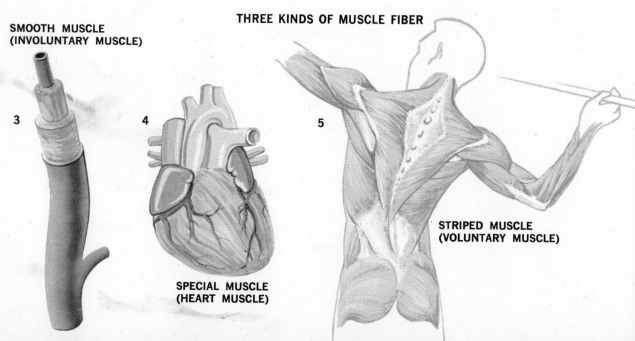

SMOOTH MUSCLE
(INVOLUNTARY MUSCLE)

3

4

5

SPECIAL MUSCLE
(HEART MUSCLE)

STRIPED MUSCLE
(VOLUNTARY MUSCLE)

see that much of the outside of the bone is covered with a thin, tough skin. The skin is pink because it holds many tiny blood vessels that carry food to the bone cells.

Look at the part of the bone that has been cut through. You will see that the bone is not solid. Because it is spongy in the middle, a bone is lighter in weight than it would be if solid, but it is still very strong. The holes in the spongy bone are filled with marrow. Some marrow is yellow; it is a storehouse for fat. Some marrow is red; it is a busy factory that makes red blood cells, as well as some of the white blood cells.

▶ BODY MOVERS

Bones are the framework of the body, but they cannot move by themselves. **Muscles** are the body's movers. For every bone that can move, there are muscles to move it. Muscles are firmly anchored to the bones by hard, ropelike tendons. A muscle moves a bone by pulling it. A muscle pulls because it has the ability to contract—to make itself shorter and fatter. When it contracts, it pulls.

Muscles pull, but they cannot push. So they must work in pairs. If you bend your arm, one set of muscles contracts and pulls the forearm up. To straighten the arm, you relax the first set of muscles. A second set pulls the opposite way, straightening the arm.

The body's largest muscles are in the back, arms, legs, abdomen, and chest. Usually you can see the outside layers of muscles at work under the skin.

The muscles described so far are all under the control of the will. They work because you decide to walk, pick up a ball, or take off your sweater. The body also has another muscle system that works without conscious orders from you. These muscles are found in many parts of the body. They do jobs like controlling the pupil of the eye and pumping blood through the circulatory system.

To do work, muscles must burn fuel. The fuel for humans is the food they eat.

Muscles work in pairs, by pulling. (1) How arm bends. Biceps muscle contracts. This pulls one of forearm bones toward shoulder on "hinge" of elbow. (2) Triceps straightens arm by pulling other forearm bone opposite way. Drawing also gives an idea of how triceps pulls to lock forearm in place. Next three drawings show three of the ways muscles are attached for pulling. (3) Broad, fan-shaped muscle pulls from a wide area. (4) Diagonal fibers pull slantwise on two long tendons. (5) In simplest form of all, parallel muscle fibers exert direct pull on tendons.

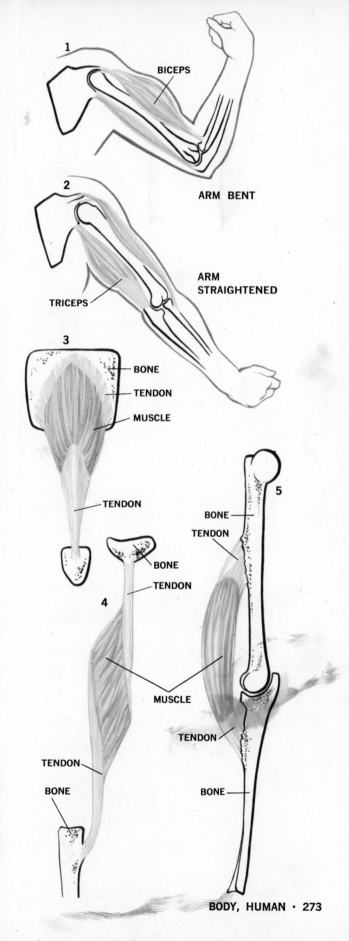

1 BICEPS
ARM BENT

2 TRICEPS
ARM STRAIGHTENED

3 BONE
TENDON
MUSCLE
TENDON

4 BONE
TENDON
MUSCLE
TENDON
BONE

5 BONE
TENDON
MUSCLE
TENDON
BONE

THE DIGESTIVE SYSTEM

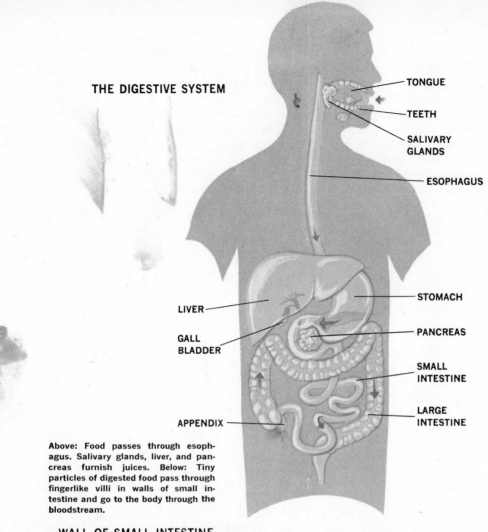

TONGUE

TEETH

SALIVARY GLANDS

ESOPHAGUS

LIVER

GALL BLADDER

STOMACH

PANCREAS

SMALL INTESTINE

LARGE INTESTINE

APPENDIX

Above: Food passes through esophagus. Salivary glands, liver, and pancreas furnish juices. **Below:** Tiny particles of digested food pass through fingerlike villi in walls of small intestine and go to the body through the bloodstream.

WALL OF SMALL INTESTINE

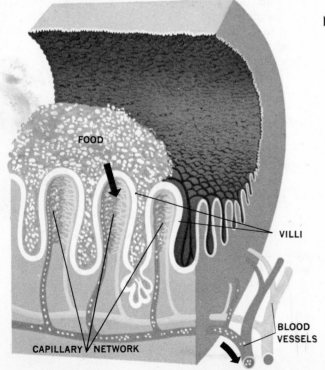

FOOD

VILLI

BLOOD VESSELS

CAPILLARY NETWORK

▶ IS THE FOOD READY?

When you're hungry and you smell dinner, your mouth waters. This is the first step in changing the food you eat into the kind of food that cells can use. This change is called **digestion**, and it begins in the mouth.

Suppose someone is making a meal of a meat sandwich, a glass of milk, and an apple. The front teeth cut and tear the sandwich. The molars grind it. Saliva, the juice in the mouth, gets everything moist. Saliva also contains a type of chemical called an enzyme. It starts breaking down the starch of the bread into sugar. (That is why bread tastes sweet if chewed long enough.)

The moist ball of food is carried to the back of the mouth by the tongue. Muscles force the food into the **esophagus**, a narrow tube behind the windpipe. Other muscles force the food down the esophagus. They do their work so well that the food would travel along even if the person were standing on his head.

Next the food enters the pouchlike stomach, where muscles push the food about. Acid and enzymes are made in the stomach. They curdle the milk, and start the digestion of the proteins in the milk and meat. All told, the stomach works on food for about 1 to 4 hours. By the time the stomach finishes its work, the food is almost liquid.

From the stomach the food is pushed into the **small intestine**. The small intestine is so called because it is only about an inch in diameter. Otherwise it is not small; it is so long that it fits in the body only because it is folded back and forth.

In the small intestine food is mixed with juices from the liver and the pancreas. The liver makes bile, which splits fats into tiny drops. The pancreas puts out three enzymes that are the most active ones in the digestive system. The small intestine also has juices of its own. And the last part of it holds millions of bacteria that help with digestion.

The digested food is semi-liquid. It is also chemically different from food. Starch has been broken down into simple sugars, proteins split into amino acids, and fats changed to fatty acids and glycerol. These digested materials can pass through cell membranes. Undigested foods cannot do that.

Food for the cells passes through the walls of the small intestine into the blood. What is left moves on into the large intestine. It is solid waste, which passes out of the body.

On the Way to the Cells

The small intestine does the main job of digestion. And it is from the small intestine that food starts its journey to the cells. Food for the cells leaves the small intestine this way: The inside of the small intestine is lined with microscopic threadlike projections. These are called **villi**. Every square inch of intestinal wall has hundreds of them. Tiny particles of digested food pass through the outer covering of the villi to very thin blood vessels called capillaries. There is a very thin network of capillaries inside each of the villi.

Food particles go from the villi into the blood. Some are ready to be used at once. Others are first carried to the liver. The liver, like a big chemical factory, causes changes in many of these particles. For example, it changes sugar into a substance called **glycogen** and stores the glycogen. When the body cells need more sugar, the liver changes the glycogen back into sugar.

The liver is a soft reddish-brown organ that may weigh up to 3 pounds or more. It lies in the upper part of the abdomen. Besides making bile, the liver makes substances needed in blood clotting and in overcoming many diseases. The liver protects the body from harmful substances formed during the process of digestion. It can even overcome certain types of poisonous drugs that may enter the body. The liver also helps to regulate the amount of blood in circulation. These are only a few of the many important jobs done by the liver.

▶ THE CIRCULATORY SYSTEM

The heart, blood, and blood vessels together make up the **circulatory system**. The heart pumps the blood through the miles of big and little blood vessels in the body. The blood makes deliveries, picks up wastes, and plays a big part in the body's defense system.

About half of the blood is a light yellow, clear liquid called **plasma**. It flows through the blood vessels carrying many dissolved materials and solid blood cells.

Most of these blood cells are **red blood cells**. They carry oxygen from the lungs to the cells of the body. There they pick up carbon dioxide, a waste gas, and carry it back to the lungs to be breathed out. **White blood cells** in the blood kill dangerous bacteria that may get into the body. **Platelets** are the third kind of solid material carried in the plasma. They start the blood clotting process when a blood vessel is torn or cut.

On its way to the body cells, blood travels in vessels called **arteries**. Returning from the cells, the blood flows through **veins**. The force needed to push the blood is supplied by a powerful muscular pump, the **heart**. It lies in the middle of the chest, between the lungs.

To hear the heart at work, roll a piece of paper into a long, thin tube. Place one end against a friend's chest and put your ear to the other end. You will hear a noise that sounds like lubb-dup, lubb-dup. The "lubb" is the sound of the heart muscle tightening.

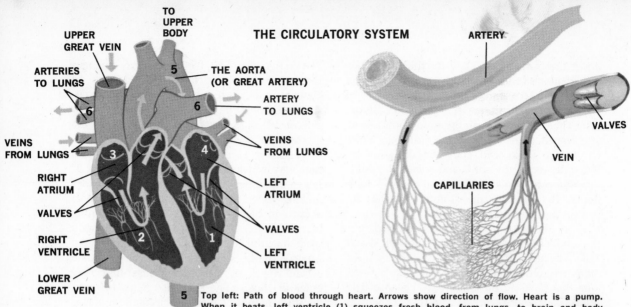

UPPER GREAT VEIN

TO UPPER BODY

ARTERIES TO LUNGS

5 THE AORTA (OR GREAT ARTERY)

6 6 ARTERY TO LUNGS

VEINS FROM LUNGS

VEINS FROM LUNGS

3 4

RIGHT ATRIUM

LEFT ATRIUM

VALVES

VALVES

RIGHT VENTRICLE

2 1

LEFT VENTRICLE

LOWER GREAT VEIN

5

TO LOWER BODY

ARTERY

VALVES

VEIN

CAPILLARIES

Top left: Path of blood through heart. Arrows show direction of flow. Heart is a pump. When it beats, left ventricle (1) squeezes fresh blood, from lungs, to brain and body through large artery, aorta (5). Right ventricle (2) sends blood from brain and body to lungs through lung artery (6). Between beats, right (3) and left (4) atria fill from veins. Valves keep blood from leaking backward. Right: Fresh blood (shown as orange) goes to cells through walls of capillaries. Blood from cells (shown as gray) goes back to heart. Below: Flow of arterial (orange) and venous (gray) blood through major vessels.

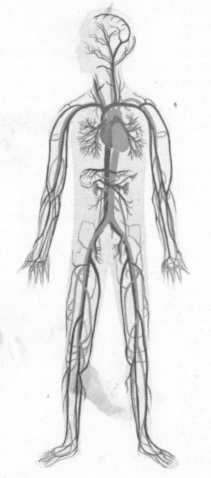

The "dup" is the sound of closing valves (the valves are flaps that close off the four hollow areas, or **chambers**, of the heart so that blood cannot flow backwards).

Blood from all over the body enters the **right atrium** through two great veins. It passes from this chamber into the **right ventricle**. The heart muscle tightens powerfully, forcing the blood out to the lungs. After picking up the oxygen from the breathed-in air, the blood flows to the **left atrium**. From there it passes down into the **left ventricle**. Then it is pumped into the aorta.

The **aorta** is the biggest artery in the body. It runs from the heart down the body, in front of the spine. Other big arteries branch from it, and still other arteries branch from them. Blood flows from the smallest arteries into tiny, thin-walled tubes, the **capillaries**. Oxygen and digested food materials can pass through the walls of these blood vessels. Thus the cells of the body get food and oxygen from the blood as it flows through the capillaries.

Some of the food is used for making and repairing cells, and some is stored. Most of the rest is burned for energy. This special kind of burning takes place at low heat and without flame. But as in all burning, oxygen is needed and wastes are formed. Waste gas from the cells passes through the walls of the capillaries into the blood. Waste-carrying blood moves on into tiny veins. The tiny veins lead into bigger veins. The bigger veins lead into still bigger ones, until the blood finally flows into a great vein that carries it back to the heart.

The heart pumps the body's 4 to 6 quarts of blood through more than 60,000 miles of blood vessels—most of them tiny. The round trip between the heart and some part of the body may take about a minute. During exercise the body needs more energy. The heart beats faster, pumping two or three times as much blood. Thus the body cells receive the extra food and oxygen they need.

▶ THE BREATH OF LIFE

The oxygen that the blood carries is part of the air we breathe. Air is usually taken in through the nose and is warmed and cleaned on its way to the throat. However, at times when the body needs extra oxygen, air can also be taken in big gulps through the mouth. From the throat air goes through the **voice box**, into the **windpipe**, and then to the lungs. The nose, throat, voice box, windpipe, and lungs make up the **respiratory system**.

The voice box is formed from plates and other pieces of stiff gristle. The windpipe is made largely of rings of gristle and is about 5 inches long. It lies between the esophagus and the front of the chest. The windpipe branches to form two tubes. Each tube, called a **bronchus**, leads to a lung. The bronchus branches into smaller and smaller **bronchial tubes**. Each of the tiniest bronchial tubes opens into a grapelike cluster of thin-walled **air sacs**. The air sacs are covered with networks of capillaries.

Waste-carrying blood is pumped from the heart into the capillaries of the air sacs. Here a quick exchange takes place. The waste gas, carbon dioxide, passes through the thin capillary walls into the air sacs. Oxygen from the air sacs passes into the capillaries. There it is picked up by the red blood cells. Then the blood moves on to the left side of the heart.

The circulatory and respiratory systems work very closely together. If someone runs,

1. Air is breathed in. It moves through the nose, windpipe, and bronchial tubes into air sacs in the lungs. 2. Closer view of air sacs. 3. Cluster of air sacs, much enlarged. Red blood cells move along within the capillaries. They pick up oxygen from the air in the sacs. At the same time they give off waste carbon dioxide gas. The gases pass through the thin capillary walls. 4. As breath is drawn chest muscles widen rib cage. Diaphragm flattens at same time, deepening chest cavity. Breath is let out as muscles relax.

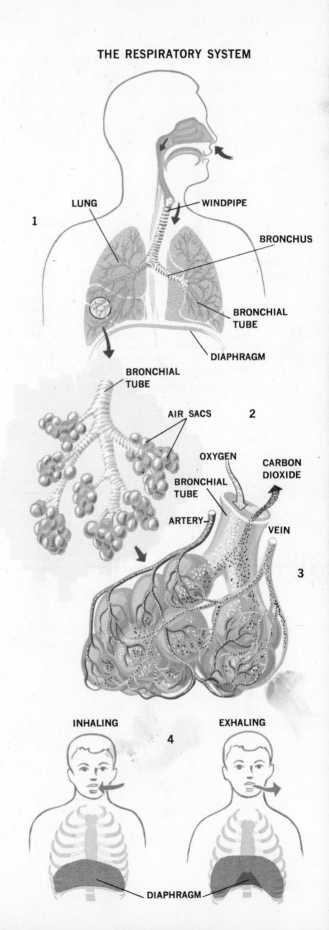

THE RESPIRATORY SYSTEM

1

LUNG

WINDPIPE

BRONCHUS

BRONCHIAL TUBE

DIAPHRAGM

BRONCHIAL TUBE

AIR SACS

2

OXYGEN

CARBON DIOXIDE

BRONCHIAL TUBE

ARTERY

VEIN

3

INHALING

4

EXHALING

DIAPHRAGM

URINARY SYSTEM

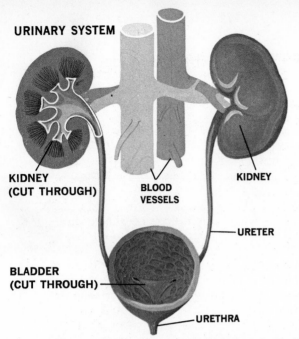

KIDNEY (CUT THROUGH)

BLOOD VESSELS

KIDNEY

URETER

BLADDER (CUT THROUGH)

URETHRA

Above: Kidneys and their tubes and the bladder. Inside of right kidney is shown. Below: How skin cools body. Body heat is carried near surface in enlarged blood vessels. Sweat evaporates, and cools the blood through the skin.

SKIN'S COOLING DEVICE

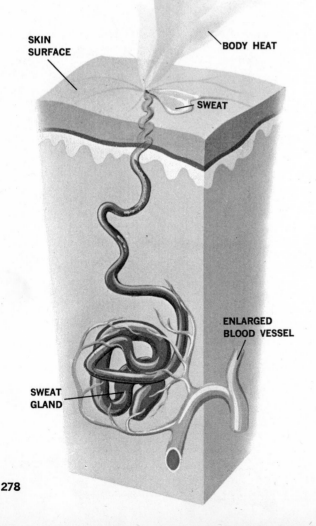

SKIN SURFACE

BODY HEAT

SWEAT

ENLARGED BLOOD VESSEL

SWEAT GLAND

he breathes faster and takes in bigger breaths than he does when resting. This means that more oxygen is reaching his lungs. At the same time his heart beats faster and harder. This means that blood is being pumped faster, is picking up more oxygen, and is delivering it to the rest of the body in faster trips.

Air is moved in and out of the lungs by the process called **breathing**. As in all body movements, muscles do the work that results in the air's rushing in and then being pushed out.

Breathing in takes place as muscles lift the front and sides of the ribs and the breastbone, making a bigger space in the chest. At the same time the **diaphragm**, a big muscle at the bottom of the chest, flattens out. This makes the space even bigger. Air rushes into the lungs. As a person breathes out, the chest space grows smaller and air is pushed out.

▶ WASTE-DISPOSAL SYSTEM

In a house windows are opened to let out stale air. Liquid wastes leave through the drain pipes. Solid wastes go out as garbage.

In the body, carbon dioxide is the stale air. It is thrown off by the lungs. Solid waste passes out through the large intestine. Much of this waste is what remains of the food after the body has removed what it needs.

Some of the liquid wastes of the body leave through the lungs. (Watch your breath on a cold day as the moisture in it condenses.) Some liquid waste evaporates from the skin as sweat. But most of the liquid waste is removed by the kidneys.

The kidneys, the bladder, and three tubes make up the **urinary system**. The **bladder** is a muscular storage tank for the urine. This is the liquid waste produced in the kidneys. A **kidney** is bean-shaped and dark red in color. It is about 4 inches long. Within the kidney there are hundreds of thousands of capillaries. Around each capillary there are kidney cells that act like living filters. As the blood flows through the capillaries the kidney cells remove certain substances from the blood.

Extra salts and minerals are among the substances removed. Wastes from worn-out cells are filtered out of the blood. One familiar substance that is filtered out makes up about 95 percent of the urine. It is water. By removing water, the kidneys help to keep the balance of water in the blood just right. With some illnesses, substances not normally in the urine are found there. A doctor often orders an analysis made of a patient's urine. The substances found (or not found) are clues to the patient's health.

▶ HEATING AND COOLING

A thermostat controls the temperature in a house by turning the furnace on and off. The human body has a "thermostat" too. It is in a part of the brain called the **hypothalamus**. The hypothalamus acts to keep the body at a temperature of about 98.6 degrees Fahrenheit.

Body heat is produced by the activity of the cells. Muscle cells are especially good heat producers. They get the energy they need by "burning" food. In this "burning" food is combined with oxygen from breathed-in air. As in burning lots of heat is produced, usually more than is needed to keep the body at normal temperature. There are several ways to get rid of the extra heat.

One of the ways that heat leaves the body is in exhaled air. Breathe onto your hand. Feel the warmth of the air. Solid and liquid wastes passing out of the body also remove some heat. But most of the heat is lost through the skin.

Millions of the smallest arteries, called **arterioles**, lie just beneath the skin. The blood in these arterioles has been warmed in passing through the heat-producing parts of the body. Some heat is lost from the arterioles to the skin, and from the skin to the surrounding air. If more heat must be lost, the hypothalamus orders the arterioles to widen. More heat escapes from the widened arterioles.

During exercise, or on hot days, a great deal of heat must be lost. A second system goes to work to cool the body. Sweat glands in the skin produce sweat—a salty liquid. It moves through narrow tubes to openings, or **pores**, in the skin surface. The sweat spreads over the warm skin. It evaporates, taking heat away from the skin.

In very cold weather, body heat may have to be saved. The arterioles narrow, so less heat escapes from the skin. The muscles may become more tense than usual. In tensing, they burn more fuel and produce more heat.

▶ CHEMICAL MESSENGERS

Sweat glands are just one of the many kinds of glands in the body. All **glands** are chemical factories. And they **secrete** (give off) substances that the body uses in some way.

Many kinds of glands have ducts (tubes) leading out of them. The pores in the skin are the ends of ducts that come from the sweat glands and the oil glands. A gland called the **pancreas** sends digestive juices to the small intestine through a duct.

Other glands do their work without ducts. Their secretions pass directly into the bloodstream. These are called **ductless glands**. The pancreas also functions as a ductless gland. It makes a second substance, called **insulin**, which passes directly into the bloodstream. Insulin enables the body to burn sugars.

The secretions of ductless glands are called **hormones**. The name comes from a Greek word meaning "to excite." Most hormones cause some organ or system of the body to be more active.

These ductless, hormone-producing glands make up the **endocrine system**. They are widely scattered over the body. All do the same kind of work—their hormones are chemical messengers that travel in the blood. The activity of the organs they excite keeps the body alive and in normal working condition.

The **thyroid** is an example of a gland that keeps the body working normally. It is a rather large gland in the neck. Its hormone stimulates the cells to produce more energy. Thyroid hormone controls the rate at which cells burn food and thus the rate at which they produce energy; it also affects growth and development of the mind.

A pair of glands lie above the kidneys. These are the **adrenals**. Each gland is in two parts. Each part does a different job, as if it were a separate gland. Whenever a person

Left: Adrenal glands are on top of kidneys. Right: Pancreas is beneath stomach.

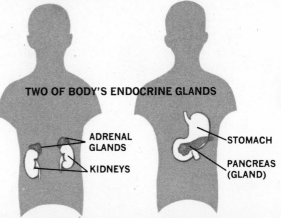

TWO OF BODY'S ENDOCRINE GLANDS

ADRENAL GLANDS

KIDNEYS

STOMACH

PANCREAS (GLAND)

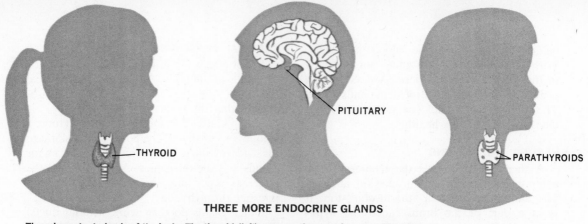

THREE MORE ENDOCRINE GLANDS

Three important glands of the body. The thyroid (*left*) governs the use of energy. The pituitary (*center*) controls growth and influences all other glands of the body. The parathyroids (*right*) are small glands (shown as dots on the thyroid) that control bone building.

is in danger, one part releases a hormone that prepares him for quick action. Suppose something happens that gives you a sudden fright. Your heart begins to pound. Your face turns pale, and the pupils of your eyes open wider. Your muscles tense. You feel "butterflies" in your stomach. Hormones cause these changes. Blood in large amounts is sent to the brain and muscles, where it may be needed. Digestion is shut down for the time being, so that parts of the body that need more blood can get it. The other part of the adrenals produces other hormones, too, whose work is necessary to life.

The **pituitary** is a pea-sized gland at the base of the brain. It is sometimes called the master gland because it makes hormones that control the other endocrine glands. For example, one of its hormones controls the action of the adrenal glands. Another makes the thyroid gland work faster. Still others control the growth of bones and help young people mature into adults. However, the pituitary itself takes orders from other parts of the body, particularly from the brain.

▶ **GUARDS ON THE ALERT**

Your **senses** are windows on the world about you. Through them you learn everything you know about that world. The information comes to you through your eyes, ears, nose, tongue, and skin—and in no other way. (Even a microscope or telescope is only an extension of the eyes.)

For a long time the human body was considered to have five senses: sight, hearing, smell, taste, and touch. But today scientists know that the body really has more senses.

Besides the senses that tell about the outside world, there are some that tell what is going on inside of you. For instance, you always know when you are hungry or thirsty. You know without looking whether you are lying down or sitting up. You know where your hand is and whether it is moving or still. You know whether an object that you lift is heavy or light. You know whether you are standing firmly or about to fall, spinning or bending over. Much of this information comes to you through muscle sense and the sense of balance.

However, no sense works alone. That is, we do not see with our eyes alone or hear only with our ears. The senses are reporters. They take in information and send it to the brain. Not until the message reaches the brain do we actually see, hear, taste, and so on.

When people think of the senses they usually think first of the sense of sight. The eyes report the size, shape, color, position, and movement of objects. The seeing process begins when light coming from an object reaches the eyes. The rays of light go through the lens to the **retina**, a sort of screen at the back of the eyeball. From there a message is sent to the brain—and the person sees.

Because the two eyes are a small distance apart, they report slightly different images. The two images merge, but the important result is that we see things in depth and can judge distances.

Having an ear on each side helps us to judge the direction from which a sound comes. We hear when something sends out the vibrations called **sound waves**. The sound waves enter the ear and hit the eardrum. A

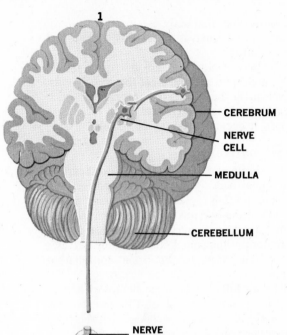

CEREBRUM

NERVE CELL

MEDULLA

CEREBELLUM

NERVE FIBER

NERVE SHEATH

CELL CASING

NERVE BUNDLE

SPINAL CORD

SPINAL NERVE

SYMPATHETIC CHAIN

VERTEBRA

vibration is set up that moves some small bones inside the head. The bones send a message along the hearing nerves to the brain.

Smelling and tasting work closely together, and much of what most people call tasting is really smelling.

Tastes are reported by the tongue. Look at your tongue in the mirror and you will see that it is covered with little bumps. Your taste buds are inside the bumps, and they do the reporting of taste sensations. All taste buds look alike, but there are four different kinds. Each kind reports on one of four different tastes—salt, sweet, bitter, and sour. All other "tastes" are really reported by the sense of smell.

Anything that has an odor is giving off tiny particles of gas, which mix with the air. By breathing you draw these particles into your nose, where the particles of gas are moistened. Nerve cells sense the wet particles and send a

The central nervous system, in diagram. Left: (1) Top half of brain. Brain cell at right edge of cerebrum is connected to cell reaching into spinal cord. The latter cell becomes part of a cable called a spinal nerve bundle (2). Cross section of spinal cord (3) shows how bundle forms part of cord; 3 also shows a chain of sympathetic nerves, part of the system controlling involuntary muscles and glands. Right: How nerve endings at body surface connect with central nervous system.

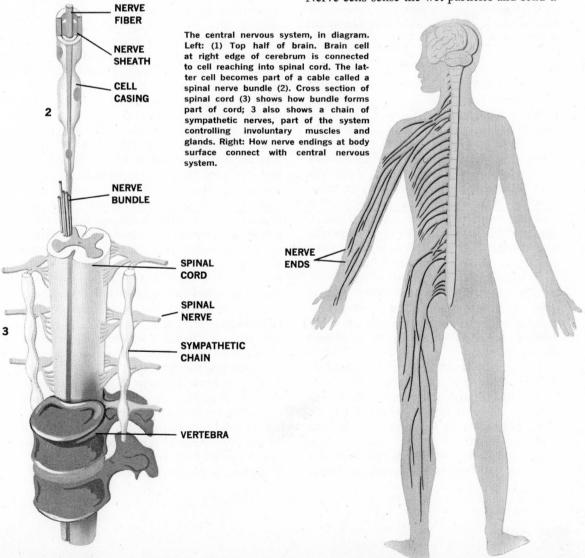

NERVE ENDS

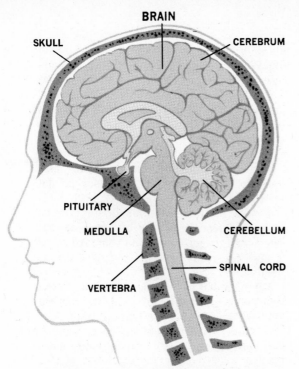

BRAIN

SKULL
CEREBRUM
PITUITARY
MEDULLA
CEREBELLUM
SPINAL CORD
VERTEBRA

Right half, or lobe, of brain inside skull. Largest part is cerebrum. It sits on top of medulla. Pituitary gland is below, cerebellum is at rear. White spaces are fluid-filled cushions.

message to the brain. Then you smell whatever the odor is.

When you are eating, the particles of gas rise through the back of your mouth to the nerve cells in your nose. That is how you know about "tastes" other than salt, sweet, bitter, or sour. And that is why, when you have a stuffed-up nose, food seems tasteless.

What used to be called the sense of touch is now known to be several senses. Through different kinds of nerve cells in the skin, the brain learns about pain, pressure, heat, cold, and touch. What is now called the sense of touch tells whether things are rough or smooth, hard or soft, sharp or rounded. When you feel your way through the dark, you are using your sense of touch. The same sense tells you about being stroked and about something that is pulling on the skin.

The nerve cells of the skin are scattered all over the body, but some parts of the body have especially large collections of them. The fingertips are such parts—you can get much more information by feeling with them than with your elbows.

Through nerve cells inside the body the brain learns of feelings like hunger and thirst.

It learns that the body is tired—or full of energy. Only when it learns this do you feel the sensation.

The senses alone do not tell us anything. They are reporters, and what they report must travel along the nerves to the brain before it means anything. When the brain receives a report, it decides what action to take, if any.

▶ BODY CONTROLS

The brain can get its signals, add them up, and signal back for action in a split second. Sensing, putting together, and responding are the job of the **nervous system**. In man and the higher animals the nervous system is made up of the brain, the spinal cord, and the nerves.

Different parts of the brain do different things.

The **medulla** lies between the lower part of the brain and the top of the spinal cord. Its nerve cells carry messages between the spinal cord and other parts of the brain. The medulla also controls an important set of nerves. These nerves are in charge of muscles and glands that must work day and night, no matter what you are doing. Even when you are sound asleep the medulla keeps your heart beating, your lungs taking in air, and your stomach digesting food.

The **cerebellum** controls body movement and balance. Many of the habits and skills you have learned are stored here. Once you have learned them, they become automatic. The cerebellum issues orders to the muscles that enable you to walk, ride a bicycle, play the piano, or pitch a baseball. Suppose you decide to take a bike ride. The **cerebrum**, the thinking part of your brain, makes this decision. It also decides where you will ride, what route you will take, and how fast you will pedal. It orders the muscles to work. After that, the cerebellum and other parts of the brain take over. These make muscles work smoothly and together. Because it controls learned body movements, the cerebellum frees the cerebrum for thinking.

The cerebrum is where thinking, learning, remembering, deciding, and being aware take place. The sensations of seeing, hearing, smelling, tasting, and touching are centered here. So are body feelings. The cerebrum enables you to enjoy things, speak intelligently, make up a poem, or design a rocket.

The cerebrum is grayish pink, soft, and full of folds. The folds give it a greater surface area than it would have if it were smooth. This is important because the surface is made of nerve cells, which do the brain's work.

No one understands how the brain does its work. However, scientists know that the messages that travel through the nervous system are a combination of chemical changes and weak electrical charges. Nerves are made up of nerve cells. A nerve cell consists of a central cell body with a number of threadlike parts reaching out from it. Messages are passed from cell to cell through these threads.

The billions of nerve cells in your body form a huge network that leads toward the spine. Along the way nerves from different parts of the body come together in thick bundles, rather like telephone wires in a cable. A thick cable of nerves runs up the hollow of your spine to the brain. One set of nerves in the cable carries messages from the senses to the brain. Another set carries messages from the brain to the muscles and glands. The brain functions something like a telephone switchboard, sorting out calls and making the right connections.

Suppose a small child runs into the street directly into the path of your bicycle. In a flash the eyes send a message to the brain. The memory centers are alerted. They warn of collision. The brain decides what the rest of the body must do. The adrenal glands are ordered into action, giving your muscles extra energy. Orders stream out to the muscles. You slam on your brakes and cut your wheel to one side. And you miss the child. The time that it took for all these messages to flash through your body is about as long as it takes to say "suddenly."

Even so, there are times of danger when that is not fast enough. Suppose you touch a hot stove. The message of pain passes through a small switchboard on the way to the brain. Your hand jerks away before the message reaches the brain. When the message arrives, the brain takes over to see if you have hurt yourself and to decide what must be done.

Scientists have not yet learned how the brain makes sense of all the messages that reach it. They know only that each kind of nerve cell reports to its own part of the brain. And they know that the brain is the most wonderful part of the human body.

Reviewed by THOMAS R. FORBES
Yale University School of Medicine

See also BLOOD; BODY CHEMISTRY; BRAIN; CELL; FEET AND HANDS.

BODY'S SENSES

Everything we know about the world comes to us through our senses. Senses tell us what is going on, warn of danger, and give pleasure. The human body has several kinds of senses. The best-known were first listed by Aristotle, a scientist of ancient Greece. They are sight, hearing, smell, taste, and touch. However, scientists now know that there are more than five senses. Also, the sense of touch has proved to be not just one sense but several senses, and so has the sense of taste.

There are **receptors** for every sensation. A receptor is an organ such as the eye or ear that has sensitive nerve endings. Each receptor takes in only one kind of information. That is why you cannot see with your ear or taste with your eye.

Messages or **impulses** from the receptors race through nerves at speeds of up to 325 feet per second, reaching the brain. Scientists do not know the exact nature of these impulses. However, they are able to detect chemical changes in a nerve as it carries an impulse. They can also measure small electrical currents in such a nerve.

Each kind of information reaches a particular part of the brain. Seeing, hearing, and so on really take place in the brain. In a way that scientists do not understand, the brain turns nerve impulses into sounds, tastes, and smells.

▶ THE LIVING CAMERA

If you have a camera, you know something about how the **eye** works. The eye is like a camera that constantly adjusts itself to take and develop an endless stream of pictures at a speed greater than you could imagine.

THE EYE

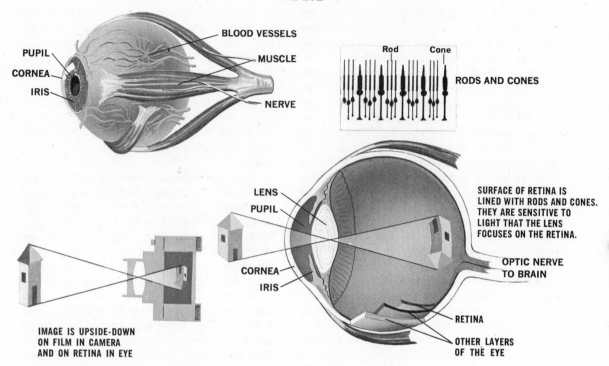

RODS AND CONES

SURFACE OF RETINA IS LINED WITH RODS AND CONES. THEY ARE SENSITIVE TO LIGHT THAT THE LENS FOCUSES ON THE RETINA.

OPTIC NERVE TO BRAIN

RETINA

OTHER LAYERS OF THE EYE

IMAGE IS UPSIDE-DOWN ON FILM IN CAMERA AND ON RETINA IN EYE

The eye works like a camera. Light enters a hole in the front of a camera and passes through a lens. The lens focuses the light on the film. In the same way, light enters a hole (pupil) in the front of the eye and passes through a lens. The lens focuses the image on the retina in the back of the eye. The retina is connected to nerves going to the brain.

A camera has a lens that gathers and focuses light to form images of objects; an adjustable opening to control the amount of light that will enter the camera; a dark chamber through which the light passes; and a film, like a screen, on which images are recorded by a chemical process.

The eye has somewhat similar parts. It has a lens, an adjustable opening called the **pupil**, a dark chamber, and a screen called the **retina**. Here is how the eye works.

Light coming from objects passes through the **cornea**, a clear protective shield. Then it goes through an opening, the pupil. In front of the pupil is the **iris**, which gives the eye its color. Muscles in the iris change the size of its central opening. In this way the iris controls the amount of light that gets through the pupil. The iris closes down in bright light and widens when the light is dim.

Behind the pupil is the **lens**. Muscles control the shape of the lens, thus focusing it to view objects at different distances.

The light rays then pass through the dark chamber to the screenlike retina at the back of the eyeball. The retina contains nerve cells. When light strikes them, they signal the brain through the optic (eye) nerve at the back of the retina. As the brain receives the message, you see.

The eye is remarkable for its ability to take countless pictures at various distances in rapid succession. But like a camera, it records its image upside down (see diagram above). However, the brain corrects this. Long before a person can remember, his brain has learned to turn the image right side up so that the person sees things as they are.

The retina has about 135,000,000 light-sensitive cells. They are of two distinct kinds —cones and rods. Cones react to color in bright light. They stop working in dim light. This is the reason we cannot see colors when the light is poor. Rods, the second kind of cell, are sensitive to dark and light—black and white—only. Rods work well in dim light. That is why we are able to see a little even at night.

However, rods and cones seem to function in the same way. Both have a special pigment (color) at their tips. When light strikes the tips, it bleaches them for a moment. That is, there is a change from color to lack of color. The sudden change releases a tiny charge of electrical energy. It excites an adjoining nerve cell, which passes on the charge to the next nerve cell, which also passes on the charge. In this way the message is sent to the brain. Meanwhile, the pigment at the tips of the rods or cones has renewed itself.

Because of the difference in what rods and cones report, some scientists think that sight may really be two senses, not one.

▶ INSIDE THE EAR

Sounds are caused by vibrations. You can hear because your ears detect these vibrations and report them to your brain.

You cannot see sounds, but sometimes you can feel them. Put your fingers to your throat as you talk and you will feel vibrations. These vibrations are set up in a part of the throat called the vocal cords. Strike a key on a piano, and touch its string. You can feel the vibrations. These vibrations set the surrounding air in motion. The air vibrates at the same rate as the vocal cords or the piano string.

The vibrations spread invisibly through the air in ever-widening circles. You can see circles like these by dropping a pebble into still water. The spreading lines of ripples are water waves. The vibrations that spread through the air are **sound waves**.

The part of the ear we can see is the outer ear. It acts as a cup that catches the sound waves. However, the job of hearing takes place deeper inside the ear.

Sound waves bounce off the outer ear into a canal. About an inch inside this canal, the sound waves meet a thin, tight sheet of tissue called the **eardrum**. The sound waves make the eardrum vibrate. The vibration is passed on to three tiny bones that fit together in a chain about a quarter of an inch long. The eardrum and these three little bones make up the middle ear.

The vibrations pass on into a snail-shaped part of the inner ear, the **cochlea** (Latin for "snail"). The cochlea is filled with a liquid that picks up the vibrations of the little bones. Thousands of cells in the cochlea, called **hair cells**, sense the vibrations. The hair cells set up nerve impulses. The impulses pass through nerves to the brain and we hear.

The ears bring you both warning and pleasure and also serve as organs for learning.

Ear has three sections. Sound waves pass through outer ear, cause eardrum and three tiny bones in middle ear to vibrate. Vibrations pass to cochlea in inner ear, where they cause nerve impulses that go to brain.

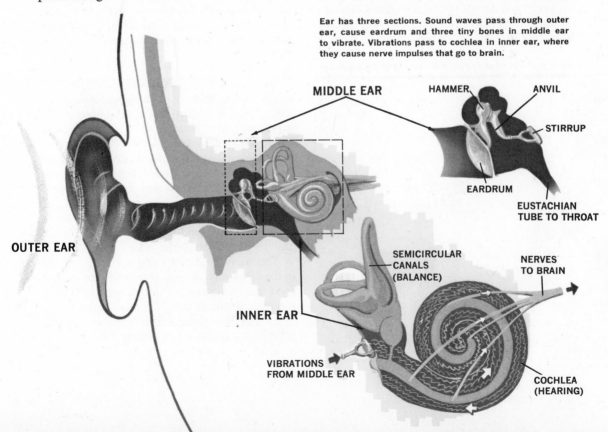

MIDDLE EAR

HAMMER

ANVIL

STIRRUP

EARDRUM

EUSTACHIAN TUBE TO THROAT

OUTER EAR

SEMICIRCULAR CANALS (BALANCE)

NERVES TO BRAIN

INNER EAR

VIBRATIONS FROM MIDDLE EAR

COCHLEA (HEARING)

▶TASTE AND SMELL

The senses of taste and smell are closely related and work together. What we call the flavor of food is experienced through our taste receptors and through our smell receptors. Very few foods act only on our taste receptors.

The Senses of Taste

Aristotle listed taste as one sense. Modern scientists count four senses of taste: sweet, salt, sour, and bitter.

With the help of a friend, you can easily explore the tasting abilities of the tongue. For the first part of the experiment you will need small quantities of sugar and water, salt and water, lemon juice and water, and coffee. You will also need four soda straws. Draw one of the liquids into a straw, ask your friend to put out his tongue, and release drops of the liquid on different parts of his tongue—the tip, sides, center, and back. Repeat with each of the other liquids. You will find that the tip reports chiefly on sweet and salt, the sides on salt and sour, the back on bitter. (The center does not report tastes at all.) By keeping track of your friend's reactions, you can make a taste map of the tongue.

Now take up a little dry sugar on the tip of your tongue and close your mouth. For a moment you do not taste the sugar. You taste it only when saliva, the liquid in the mouth, dissolves the sugar. When food is wet, a

With the help of a friend, you can easily map out the taste areas of the tongue, as shown here.

TASTE MAP OF THE TONGUE

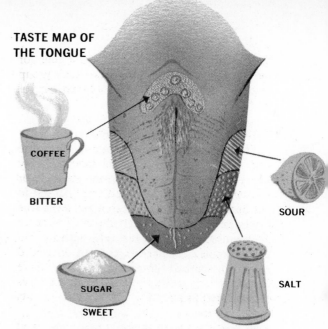

There are four kinds of taste buds in the tongue. Each kind reports on one taste: sweet, sour, salt, or bitter.

chemical reaction takes place with the taste receptors and a message is sent to the brain.

The taste receptors are usually called taste buds. They lie inside the little bumps on the tongue. All taste buds look alike, but each reports on only one kind of taste.

The tongue also has other kinds of receptors, which report on heat, cold, pain, and texture. But the tongue has no receptors that tell, for example, whether ice cream is vanilla, chocolate, or peppermint. This information comes to you through your nose.

Inside the Nose

The nose on your face is not the nose that smells odors. When you smell something, the sense of smell begins inside your nose where nerve cells line what is called the olfactory patch. These cells sense odors.

Anything that gives off an odor is giving off tiny particles of gas. The tiny particles of gas mix with the air. When you draw this air into your nose, the gas particles are moistened and a chemical reaction takes place with the nerve cells. The cells send a message to the brain, and then you smell the odor.

The many food tastes you know are sensed in the same way. As you chew and moisten the food, gas particles rise through the back of the mouth to the nerve cells that report odor.

Exactly how these nerve cells can tell one odor from another is not known. One theory is that the nose has different groups of cells for sensing different kinds of odors. Each group of cells would then report to its own part of the brain.

SENSING THROUGH YOUR SKIN

The skin contains several senses that were once all called the sense of touch. Today scientists divide these sensations into five or six separate senses. These different senses do not depend on anything so complicated as the eye or ear. Some are simply the ends of nerve fibers; others contain a few cells with a nerve fiber wrapped around them. These cells and fibers are scattered through the skin. Where especially large collections of them occur—as in the fingertips and the lips—the body is at its most sensitive.

One of the senses in the skin is still called the **sense of touch.** It tells you about texture. It tells you that things are hard or soft, sharp or smooth. At night when you feel your way in the dark, touch tells you that a chair or a door is just ahead. The same sense reports on stroking or pulling of the skin. However, many scientists think that tickling is reported not by touch but by a **sense of tickling.** And all agree that pressure (Is your belt too tight?) is reported through a **sense of pressure.**

Another kind of information that comes to you through your skin has to do with temperature. Some scientists say that there are two such senses—a **sense of heat** and a **sense of cold.** Others say it is only one sense—**sense of temperature.**

Another closely related sense is the **sense of pain.** Pain often results from touching something that is unpleasantly cold, hot, or sharp. It can also result from other injuries and from infections. Pain is an unpleasant but very useful sense. Without it we would often be unaware of the harm being done to our bodies and therefore would not take action to stop it. Like other messages of sudden warning, those of pain pass through reflex centers on their way to the brain. These centers react immediately, triggering a reflex action. If you accidentally touch something very hot, your hand jerks away in a reflex action. Then the brain takes over.

Although touch, temperature, and pain are closely related, each set of nerves reports only on its own sensations. For instance, the nerve fibers that report pain say nothing about the insect on your hand—unless it bites you.

DEEP BODY SENSES

You have some senses that report from inside the body. They tell of hunger, thirst, too much to eat or drink, being tired or rested, an aching stomach, the need to get rid of wastes, and other sensations within. These senses register information and work in much the same way that the senses of the skin do.

MUSCLE SENSE

Without looking, can you tell the position of your hands as you hold this book? Can you tell whether you are sitting down or standing up? If you turn a page, do you know how far your hand reaches from your body? Which fingers do you use to turn the page?

You know where all the parts of your body are and what they are doing, without looking. You can also tell which of two suitcases is heavier, whether a door is hard to open, and whether your bicycle tires need pumping.

You receive all this information through your muscle sense. Muscle sense is the oldest of the "new" senses. It was first identified by Sir Charles Bell, a British doctor, in 1826 and added to Aristotle's five senses.

Muscle sense is buried in your muscles, tendons, and joints. Here the ends of some nerves are coiled around muscle fibers. Messages from these nerve threads in the muscles become information about what the muscles are experiencing.

Muscle sense serves you in a number of ways. Without it you couldn't walk, run, throw a ball, swim, skate, or dance. In fact, you couldn't even remain standing up. Gravity would pull you to the earth unless your muscles reported this pull and the brain sent out orders to do something about it.

SENSE OF BALANCE

One other sense also helps to keep you upright. This is your sense of balance. Balance has to do with your position in relation to the center of the earth. Gravity pulls you toward the center and however you move, you move against this pull.

The human organ of balance is in the semicircular canals. The canals lie in the same skull bone that holds the inner ear and are connected with the cochlea. The semicircular canals are filled with liquid. When the body moves (the head goes along, of course), the liquid rushes past little hairs. These hairs set up nerve impulses. The impulses give the brain information about the body's movements up and down, from side to side, and forward and back.

If the brain learns that the body is about to fall, muscles are ordered to move to stop this. The sense of balance works closely with the muscle sense in keeping your body where you wish it to be. And both senses react to the pull of gravity.

Astronauts who experience weightlessness, or freedom from the earth's gravity, have a good many problems. Free of gravity, the sense of balance does not work and muscle sense does not give normal information.

▶ **RECENT STUDIES OF THE SENSES**

Since Aristotle first listed five human senses, scientific understanding of the senses has come a long way. We now know that the body has many senses but that we are still far from knowing precisely how many or what their limits are.

Also, no one fully understands how the senses work. An important discovery is that we do not see with the eyes alone or hear only with our ears. Our sense organs are only reporters. They respond to light, sound, touch, and so on by chemical changes. They also generate small currents of electricity. These electrical charges race through the nerves to the brain, each kind going only to one special area of the brain. There, and only there, do they become the sensations that we call sight, hearing, taste, smell, and hunger.

The interesting thing about these electrical charges is that they are all the same. Pattern, number, and rate vary, but all the messages are simply impulses (charges) of electricity. At the Rockefeller Institute of Medical Research, Dr. H. K. Hartline has made a tape recording of a person seeing. The recording sounds like someone rapidly tapping his fingers. But it is really a recording of electrical impulses traveling from the eye to the brain. Yet a tape recording of someone sniffing a rose or listening to music would sound the same. The important thing is the area of the brain that the impulses reach. When the impulses reach the "sweet taste" part of the brain, we become aware of a sweet taste in our mouths.

When the brain receives such a message, it checks the message out against past experience. That is, the brain holds a memory bank of experiences. It knows, for example, that apples are sweet or sour. If an apple tastes bitter, the brain becomes suspicious. Probably the apple is wormy and should not be eaten. Scientists think that every new sensation is checked with this memory bank of experiences in the brain.

Experiments with the Senses

Startling proof of the memory bank was provided by Dr. Wilder Penfield, world-famous Montreal brain surgeon. During brain operations he applied tiny charges of electricity to different parts of the patients' brains. (The patients were under the kind of anesthetic that kills pain but leaves a person fully conscious.) One patient reported seeing a baseball game. One heard a song. One heard children's voices "down along the river." Each patient was calling up a long forgotten sensation. He was experiencing it just as vividly as he had years before.

In spite of its memory bank the brain requires a steady series of new sensations. Evidence of this came from experiments at McGill University. Volunteers were cut off from almost all sensation. They were wrapped in soft cloths and placed motionless on beds. The beds were in dimly lighted, tiny, sound-proof rooms. No volunteer could bear to continue the experiment for more than 48 hours. Without a flow of sensations they began to have terrible hallucinations (visions).

Everything learned about the senses shows how they depend on the brain and how the brain depends on them. The brain gives meaning to the senses; the senses stimulate the brain and keep it working properly. Out of this relationship comes all we do, think, and know. For as Aristotle said, "The whole world comes to us through our senses."

SARAH R. RIEDMAN
Author, science books for children
Reviewed by THOMAS R. FORBES
Yale University School of Medicine

See also BRAIN; LENSES; SOUND AND ULTRASONICS.

BODY CHEMISTRY

The body is a complicated chemical machine. The cell is the engine that runs this machine. If we want to learn how the cell engine works, we must take it apart. We must find out what each part looks like and what job it does.

The body is made up of so many cells that it would be impossible to take each one apart to learn how it works. Fortunately, this is not necessary, because cells resemble one another in many ways. A liver cell, a kidney cell, and a brain cell have much in common even though they do very different jobs in the body. Much of what we learn about one kind of cell applies to others as well. Therefore, from now on we will talk about a typical cell. This is a cell that doesn't really exist but that has the properties of many different kinds of cells.

▶ WHAT CELLS ARE MADE OF

The cell is a collection of chemicals called compounds. At first glance these compounds don't seem very unusual. A typical cell is about 65 percent water, 15 percent fatlike material, 15 percent protein, ½ percent carbohydrate, and 4½ percent salt. You could make up a mixture like that for less than a penny's worth of chemicals, but of course you wouldn't have a living cell. These compounds must be arranged in a very special way to produce life.

The most ordinary compound in the cell, water, has several important functions. For one thing, water is a very good solvent, which means it will dissolve many different kinds of chemicals. This is very important because the cell engine runs on chemical reactions. And chemical reactions, in general, take place best when the chemicals are dissolved in some liquid.

Many salts are dissolved in the cell water. Of course, it wouldn't do for all the salts in the body to dissolve in water. If they did, our bones would dissolve and we would collapse like a wet rag. Our bones contain calcium salts, which do not dissolve very much in water.

These simple compounds, water and salts, are found everywhere—in the sea, in the ground, and so on—not just in living cells.

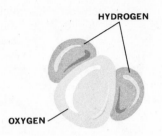

A molecule of water contains two atoms of hydrogen attached to an atom of oxygen. A typical cell is about 65 percent water.

Table salt is one of the simplest compounds known. It contains only two different kinds of atoms, sodium and chlorine. Water is simple, too. It contains two atoms of hydrogen attached to an atom of oxygen.

Not all the compounds in the body are this simple. Some of the most important molecules in the body contain thousands of atoms hooked together in a definite way. The compounds we are most interested in can be divided into four groups. These groups are called: the carbohydrates, the proteins, the lipids, and the nucleic acids.

A compound in a particular group is built on a definite plan. The carbohydrates have a plan, the proteins have another plan, and so on. A chemist can recognize this plan and can tell a carbohydrate from a protein as readily as you can tell an automobile from an airplane.

Within each group there are differences, too, just as there are differences between different makes of automobiles. You must learn a little about these different compounds before we can talk about how the cell works.

▶ CARBOHYDRATES

Carbohydrates are made up of carbon, hydrogen, and oxygen atoms. Lots of other compounds contain these same atoms. But carbohydrates can be recognized by the way the atoms are put together. **Sugars** are the simplest carbohydrates. When sugars were first discovered, scientists thought they were just carbon atoms combined with water. So they named the sugars carbo-hydrates, meaning carbon-water. Actually sugars are more complicated than this, and the carbohydrate group includes many compounds other than sugars.

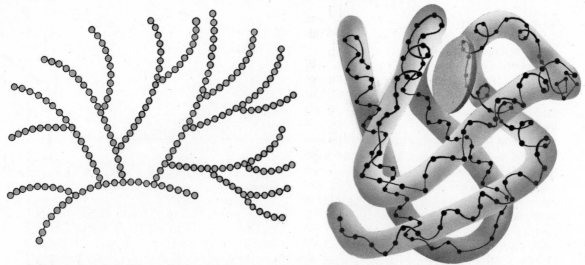

Left: Long, branched chains of glucose form glycogen. Right: Proteins are very important macromolecules. Amino acids (small dots) link together in complex chains and form huge protein molecules.

The word "sugar" makes everyone think of table sugar. But table sugar is actually a particular kind of sugar, which is called **sucrose**. There are many different kinds of sugar. The most important sugar in the body is **glucose**. Glucose is also called **dextrose**. It is one of the body's most important fuels. It is so important that the body stores up a good supply of it in a form called **glycogen**.

Glycogen is not a sugar itself, but is made up of sugar building blocks. Glycogen is produced when glucose molecules are hooked together into chains. The main glucose chain has many shorter chains that branch off it like the branches of a tree.

Starch is another important carbohydrate. Starch comes from plants, and starch molecules are very similar to glycogen. They are made up of glucose chains, too. Starch is the most important carbohydrate in the diet because it furnishes much of the glucose your body needs to function properly.

Compared to the sugars, starch and glycogen are huge molecules. Biochemists (scientists who study the chemistry of living organisms) have a special name for giant molecules like this. It is **macromolecules**. Macromolecules are so important that there cannot be any life without them.

▶ PROTEINS

Starch and glycogen are not the only macromolecules in the body. Proteins are macromolecules, too. Every cell of every living organism has protein in it. In fact, the word "protein" means "of the first importance" in Greek.

There are many different proteins in the body, and they have many jobs to do. Your skin and hair contain a tough structural protein called **keratin**. Keratin and other structural proteins hold the body together. They are like the frame of your house. Another group, the **functional proteins**, are actively working at all sorts of important jobs. **Hemoglobin**, a blood protein, carries oxygen from the lungs to the cells. A large group of proteins called **enzymes** helps the cell carry out hundreds of chemical reactions.

Proteins are made from simple building blocks, the **amino acids**. Like the sugars, amino acids contain carbon, hydrogen, and oxygen, but they also contain nitrogen. There is a common pattern of carbon, hydrogen, oxygen, and nitrogen atoms in the amino acids that sets them apart from other compounds. However, there are also different arrangements within this basic plan. And so there are many different amino acids. Twenty of them are of particular importance in the body.

The amino acids are hooked together in long chains. One or more of these chains makes up a protein. Sometimes the chains are stretched out like string. Many structural proteins, such as keratin, are like this. In other proteins the chains are coiled and folded into a ball-like structure. Hemoglobin and many other functional proteins have this globular form.

Protein chains are complicated, with 20 different kinds of building blocks. Most proteins contain all 20, but a few do not. Our bodies can produce 12 of the 20 amino acids needed to make cell proteins. The other 8 must come from proteins in our food. A prolonged diet deficient in any of these 8 **essential amino acids** causes serious disease.

The chains in even the simplest protein are more than 30 amino acids long. The chains of many proteins are several hundred units long. The order of amino acids in the chains and the way the chains fold up give the protein the special properties it needs to carry out its particular job in the body.

The sum total of all your body's proteins makes you what you are. They are responsible for both the similarities and the differences between you and your parents. You do not inherit your proteins directly from your parents. But you do inherit the information that tells your cells what kind of proteins to make. This hereditary information is carried by another important group of compounds, the nucleic acids.

▶ NUCLEIC ACIDS

Like proteins, nucleic acids contain carbon, hydrogen, oxygen, and nitrogen. But nucleic acids also contain phosphorus. And like proteins, nucleic acids are made up of long, chainlike molecules within the body's cells. The building blocks of nucleic acid chains are called **nucleotides**.

Nucleotides are divided into two groups, depending on the sugar they contain. One group has the sugar **ribose**; these nucleotides are called **ribonucleotides**. The other group contains the sugar **deoxyribose**; these nucleotides are called **deoxyribonucleotides**. Deoxyribose has one less oxygen atom than ribose.

Ribonucleotides join together and form one type of nucleic acid—**ribonucleic acid**. It is commonly known as **RNA**. The smallest RNA has about 75 nucleotides in a single chain. The largest RNA chains are thousands of nucleotides in length.

Deoxyribonucleotides join together to form the other type of nucleic acid—**deoxyribonu-**

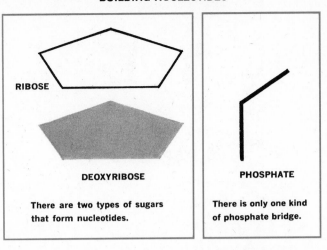

RIBOSE

DEOXYRIBOSE

There are two types of sugars that form nucleotides.

PHOSPHATE

There is only one kind of phosphate bridge.

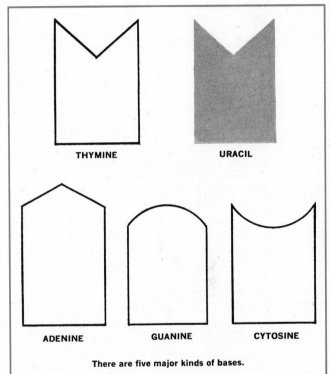

THYMINE

URACIL

ADENINE

GUANINE

CYTOSINE

There are five major kinds of bases.

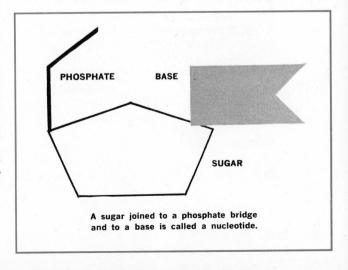

PHOSPHATE   BASE

SUGAR

A sugar joined to a phosphate bridge and to a base is called a nucleotide.

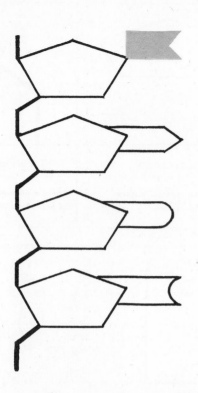

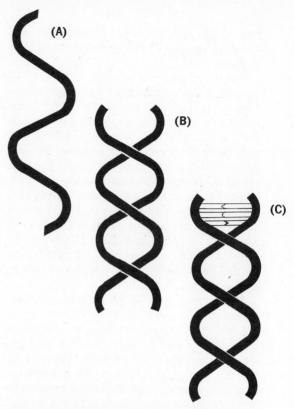

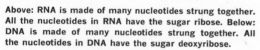

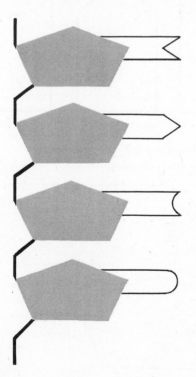

Above: RNA is made of many nucleotides strung together. All the nucleotides in RNA have the sugar ribose. Below: DNA is made of many nucleotides strung together. All the nucleotides in DNA have the sugar deoxyribose.

Above: (A) Nucleotides in DNA and RNA are arranged in a helix. (B) Nucleotides that make up DNA form two helices that wind around each other. (C) The helices are held together by bases that join in pairs. Two bases are always found together, one base on each helix. Below: Model of a DNA molecule.

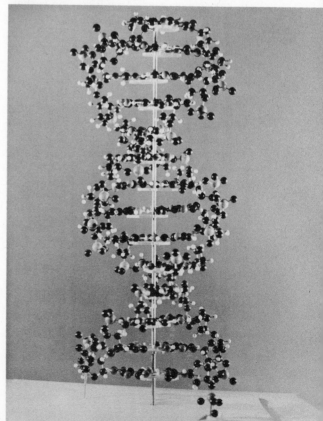

cleic acid, or **DNA**. DNA chains contain many thousands of nucleotides. Usually the DNA molecule has two nucleotide chains exactly the same length. The chains are wound around each other like two strands of rope and form a double helix.

DNA is found only within the nucleus of the cell. DNA carries all the body's hereditary information. All of us inherit DNA from our parents. When the two chains of the DNA helix split apart, each produces a new partner. The result is two DNA molecules exactly like the original one. As this process continues hereditary information is passed on from cell to cell.

Later in this article, you will learn more about the fascinating things nucleic acids do. But there is still one more group of compounds to talk about before we come to how the body machine works.

▶ LIPIDS

All the fatlike or "greasy" compounds in the body belong to the lipid group. The simplest lipids are the fatty acids. There are many different fatty acids in the body. They are building blocks for other lipids. For example, **fats** such as beef fat or lard and **oils** such as olive oil are made when three fatty acids become attached to a molecule of glycerol (glycerin). Fats are an important storehouse of energy in the body.

The **steroids** are also fairly simple lipids. Perhaps you have heard about the steroid **cholesterol**. It serves as the raw material for making many other important steroids such as the **sex hormones**. The body can't function normally without cholesterol. But when the amount gets too high, the cholesterol may deposit in the arteries and lead to the disease atherosclerosis (hardening of the arteries).

Not all lipids are simple. In fact, lipid macromolecules are perhaps the most complex (complicated) molecules in the body. They do not have just one building block, as in glycogen, or a few similar building blocks, as in proteins and nucleic acids. Rather, the **complex lipids** may contain many different kinds of building blocks. Fatty acids are almost always part of these lipids, but the lipids may also contain sugars, amino acids, phosphates, and some special compounds.

These complex lipids make up the various membranes of the cell. The membranes hold important parts of the cell machine together. The cell itself is encased in a lipid membrane —without this membrane there can't be a cell. The cell nucleus also has a lipid membrane. These membranes are so constructed that certain kinds of molecules can pass through them easily. For example, building blocks such as sugars must pass through the cell membrane in order for the cell machinery inside to use them. Waste products such as carbon dioxide must pass out of the cell.

There are other molecules that the cell must keep inside the membrane. The liver cell can't store glucose because glucose molecules pass through the cell membrane. But large glycogen molecules will not go through the cell membrane. So the liver can store glucose as glycogen. When glucose is needed, some glycogen is broken down into glucose.

As you can see, the cell is more than a complicated mixture of chemicals. And these chemicals are not just thrown together like nuts in a bag. They are carefully woven into the complicated chemical structures that make up the different parts of the cell machine.

Now that you know a little about the parts of the machine, we can go on to how they work at the chemical level. The cell machine runs on hundreds of chemical reactions. All these reactions, taken together, are called **metabolism**.

▶ ENZYMES

Many chemical reactions by themselves are quite slow. For example, if the gases hydrogen and oxygen are mixed, nothing happens. When a little finely ground platinum metal is added, the hydrogen and oxygen combine to form water. Sometimes they react so fast in the presence of platinum that the mixture explodes. When the reaction is finished, the metal can be recovered unchanged.

The platinum speeded up the reaction between hydrogen and oxygen without being permanently changed itself. Chemists call compounds that do this **catalysts**.

The body has hundreds of different catalysts. Almost every chemical reaction that occurs in the body has a special catalyst. These body catalysts are called **enzymes**. Enzymes, then, speed up the body's chemistry.

With all catalysts, including enzymes, a

little bit goes a long way. This is because they aren't changed by the reaction they catalyze. So a single molecule of catalyst can work over and over again. However, enzymes have special properties, which are different from those of other catalysts. First of all, enzymes are proteins. (Now you see one reason why proteins are so important.) Second, enzymes have **specificity**. This means that a particular enzyme catalyzes one particular reaction or, at most, one particular group of reactions. It will not work in any other reactions.

Specificity comes in when the enzyme and its **substrate** meet. The substrate is the substance on which the enzyme does its work. The substrate and the enzyme must fit together in the way that a lock and its key fit together. On the surface of the enzyme, the substrate is changed to some other compound. The new compound separates from the enzyme. And so the enzyme is again free to combine with another molecule of the substrate. This can happen again and again.

▶ ENZYME HELPERS

The protein molecules can't always act as catalysts by themselves. Sometimes they need help.

Very often an enzyme has two parts, a protein and a **coenzyme**. A coenzyme is a fairly complicated molecule, but much simpler than a protein. And it is the coenzyme that actually gets the job done. The protein part of the enzyme assures that the job is done on the right substrate.

The body can make coenzymes if it has the right building blocks. The building blocks must be furnished by the diet because the body can't make them. These building blocks are the **vitamins**. For example, vitamin B_2 (riboflavin) is changed into the coenzyme, flavin adenine dinucleotide, or simply FAD. Other vitamins are converted into other coenzymes. Now you can understand why vitamins are important in the diet.

▶ DIGESTION

Enzymes are made inside the cell. Most of them remain in the cell, where they catalyze the complicated cell reactions. A few of them, however, pass out of the cell to do their job. The digestive enzymes are **extracellular** (out-

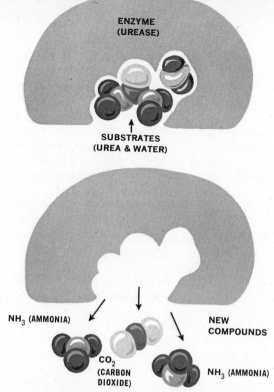

ENZYME (UREASE)

SUBSTRATES (UREA & WATER)

NH_3 (AMMONIA)

NEW COMPOUNDS

CO_2 (CARBON DIOXIDE)

NH_3 (AMMONIA)

Enzyme and substrates fit together like a lock and key. Chemical reaction alters the substrates while the enzyme remains unchanged. Products of reaction on substrates are separated from the enzyme. The enzyme is now free to act on other molecules of substrates.

side the cell) **enzymes**. Let's see how digestion works at the chemical level.

Suppose you have just had a ham sandwich. This sandwich contains protein and fat in the meat. It contains carbohydrate (starch) in the bread. An enzyme called **ptyalin** or **alpha-amylase** is present in your saliva. This enzyme begins to break down the starch chains. In the stomach the enzyme **pepsin** begins to work on the proteins, splitting the chains into shorter pieces. The finishing touches are carried out in the intestine. There still other enzymes finish the digesting. The protein chains are digested into amino acids. Starch is digested into glucose. Fats are converted to fatty acids and glycerol.

All of these are small molecules. They pass through the intestinal wall and are carried by the circulatory system to the various cells of the body. There they serve as fuel and building blocks for the cell engines. Without the digestive enzymes much of our food would remain as macromolecules. Since these are too big to pass through the intestinal wall, we would starve to death.

Unlike the digestive enzymes, most enzymes act inside the body's cells. There are enzymes that hook the glucose molecules together to form glycogen. There are enzymes that string the amino acids together again. The result is not proteins just like the ones in the meat but new proteins that are needed by the particular cell that is making them. Fatty acids and glycerol are combined again to make fat.

Now you can understand why proteins, carbohydrates, and fats are important in the diet. They are the raw materials. Digestion converts them to important building materials, such as sugars, amino acids, and fatty acids. As we shall see, they are also important fuels for the cell engines.

▶ MAKING PROTEINS

It is not too difficult to imagine how cells can make certain vital substances. Enzymes assist in much of the work. Enzymes in the cells can hook glucose units together to form glycogen. Enzymes in the cells can link fatty acids to glycerol to produce fat.

However, making a protein is much more complicated. (The process is called **protein biosynthesis**.) Even the simplest protein contains at least 30 amino acids in a chain. The more complicated proteins contain hundreds of amino acids. Furthermore, the amino acids must be arranged in just the right way if a protein is to carry out its particular job.

The problem of making proteins can best be understood through a comparison. Imagine you are told to make a string of beads representing a chain of amino acids. Each bead (amino acid) is numbered. You are told the string of beads must have a certain length and the numbers must run in a certain order. But you are not told what this length is or what the order of numbers is.

All the parts for solving the problem are set out (Fig. 1). The only information is given by the pattern. In the cell DNA is the pattern. This information is coded in units (nucleotides) of different shapes. There are six units, which means that the string of beads is to be six beads long.

Now the information of the DNA pattern must be decoded to find the order of the amino-acid beads in the chain. Of all the parts, only the shaded blocks (ribonucleotides) fit

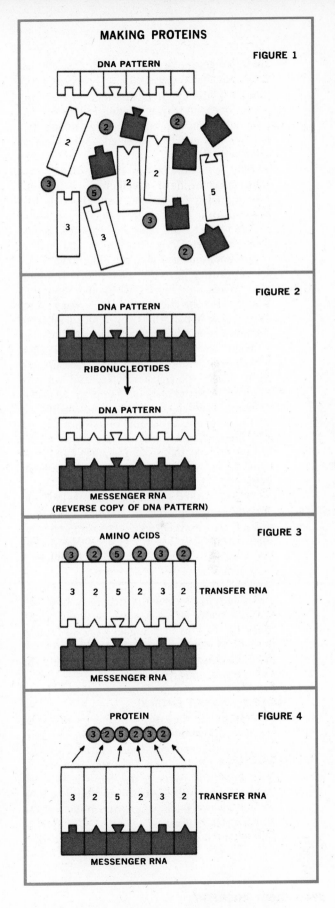

MAKING PROTEINS

FIGURE 1

DNA PATTERN

FIGURE 2

DNA PATTERN

RIBONUCLEOTIDES

DNA PATTERN

MESSENGER RNA
(REVERSE COPY OF DNA PATTERN)

FIGURE 3

AMINO ACIDS

TRANSFER RNA

MESSENGER RNA

FIGURE 4

PROTEIN

TRANSFER RNA

MESSENGER RNA

into the pattern. When the shaded blocks are joined together, the result is a copy of the pattern (Fig. 2). It is not the same as the pattern—everything is reversed. But it contains all the information that was in the pattern. In the cell this reversed copy is called **messenger RNA**.

This reversed copy is like a plaster cast taken of a head or a sculpture. When the proper material is poured into the cast, the original form can be reproduced.

The white blocks represent another kind of RNA, **transfer RNA**. The beads attached to them represent amino acids. There is a different transfer RNA for each different amino acid. When the transfer RNA and its amino acid fit into the messenger RNA copy (Fig. 3), the DNA pattern is reproduced and the order of amino acids is fixed (Fig. 4).

There are 20 kinds of amino acids. Then how does each kind of amino acid hook up with its own kind of transfer RNA and with no other? If a mistake should happen, the order of amino acids in the protein chain would be wrong. Suppose, for example, that a molecule of amino acid 2 becomes attached to a transfer RNA 3. As the protein chain is built, this amino acid will be fitted into a place where an amino acid 3 belongs.

Proteins called **activating enzymes** provide for the correct pairing of transfer RNA and amino acids. A specific activating enzyme links amino acid 2 with transfer RNA 2. Another enzyme does the same for the number 3 pair, and so on.

Arranging the amino acids in the correct order is only part of the problem, however. As you know, it takes work to make something. It requires mechanical work to build a house and electrical work to produce light. It takes chemical work to build proteins and the other compounds the body needs.

▶ **FROM FOOD TO ENERGY**

Work requires energy. The energy to do the body's work comes from the food we eat. Our food is mainly carbohydrate, fat, and protein. It took energy to make these food molecules. And energy is never really lost—it just appears in different forms. So we should be able to get energy back when our body breaks down these molecules.

Let's take a simple example and see how this energy cycle works. The sugar glucose contains 6 carbon atoms, 12 hydrogen atoms, and 6 oxygen atoms. Plants make glucose from carbon dioxide, water, and sunlight. The carbon dioxide provides the carbon atoms and some of the oxygen atoms. The water provides the hydrogen atoms and some of the oxygen atoms. The sunlight provides the energy that hooks these atoms together in a glucose molecule. (As it turns out, when the glucose molecule is finished, there is some oxygen left over. It becomes the oxygen in our air.)

We call this process **photosynthesis**. And we can summarize it as follows:

(plants)
carbon dioxide + water + energy → glucose + oxygen

If we reverse this process we should be able to produce energy:

(animals)
oxygen + glucose → energy + water + carbon dioxide

And that is exactly what people and animals do. Glucose is oxidized, or combined with oxygen, to give energy and waste products (water and carbon dioxide). This energy is used by the cells to make their macromolecules and to carry out their other work assignments, such as moving muscles.

This process of oxidation also occurs when we burn something. That's why a fire needs oxygen to burn. That's why you will often hear that the body "burns" its food to obtain energy. This "burning" is not exactly the same as a campfire, though. There are no tiny flames flickering inside the cell.

Furthermore, we build a fire to produce heat. We use this heat in many ways—to cook our food, to change water into steam that runs a steam engine, and so on. The body has no way to use heat to do work. It needs heat to keep the cells warm. But much of the heat produced by oxidation is a waste product because the body cannot use it directly.

If the body can't use heat to do work, how does it use its energy? The answer lies in a special molecule called **adenosine triphosphate** or **ATP**. ATP is a nucleotide. It is an RNA building block. But it is also able to trap the chemical energy released by oxidation and convert this energy into chemical work. ATP supplies the energy for building macromolecules. It also supplies the energy for muscle contraction, for nerve transmission, and so on.

THE ENERGY DYNAMO

Actually the cell is more like an electrical dynamo than a furnace. In a dynamo water flows over the turbine blades and turns the turbine. The turbine drives an electrical generator, which produces electricity. The electricity is used to produce light, run electric motors, and so on.

In the cell glucose is oxidized by a series of chemical reactions, which are like the turbine wheel. This chemical wheel turns another chemical wheel, which is like the electrical generator. This second wheel produces ATP, instead of electricity. The energy obtained from the ATP is used to do the cell's work.

So far we have talked only about the oxidation of glucose. But the other sugars are oxidized too. Except for the first few steps where preparation for oxidation occurs, all carbohydrates are oxidized by the same reactions. Fatty acids (from fats) and amino acids (from proteins) are oxidized inside the cell by the same energy dynamo.

Each different kind of food can furnish the cells with a definite amount of energy. Suppose you ate the same weight of each foodstuff in a meal. The fat would furnish one half the energy from that meal. The carbohydrate and protein would each furnish one fourth. In other words, fat can furnish about twice as much energy as the same amount of carbohydrate or protein.

As you remember, energy is never lost. What happens if you take in more potential energy in your food than your body can use up? The answer is simple. The body stores the extra food. The body can only store a certain amount of this food as carbohydrate and protein. The rest is stored as fat. It doesn't make any difference what this extra food is. Extra carbohydrate and protein can be converted to fat.

Clearly, if you eat more than your body needs, you will get fat. If you eat less than your body needs, it must draw upon its energy stores. The fat will be broken down to supply energy, and you will lose weight. When the carbohydrate and fat supplies are low, protein will be used to produce energy. If this breakdown of vital proteins continues for very long, a person will die.

CONTROLLING THE CELL ENGINE

When you run a race your muscles work hard. They need a big supply of fuel quickly. Your liver goes to work almost instantly changing glycogen, a carbohydrate that it normally stores, into glucose. The glucose enters the bloodstream, and in seconds it reaches the straining muscles. What controls this process? How does the liver know when to supply glucose for the muscles? Two systems control the work of the body tissues: the **nervous system**, and the **endocrine system**.

The nervous system provides a rapid response to an emergency situation. You know how fast you pull your hand away when you accidentally touch a hot stove. Your nervous system has told your muscles what to do.

The endocrine system acts less quickly, but for a longer time. The eight different glands that make up this system produce special chemicals called **hormones**. These are given off directly into the bloodstream, which carries them throughout the body. Each hormone acts on a particular organ to speed up or slow down its work. For example, the adrenal glands produce epinephrine (adrenaline). This hormone stimulates the liver to change glycogen into glucose. The hormones of the endocrine system act collectively to regulate the body's very complicated chemistry, producing a smoothly running machine.

SUMMARY

As you can see, the body is a complicated chemical machine. Simple chemicals are built into complicated macromolecules. Some macromolecules are woven into various structures that form the cell. Inside the cell hundreds of chemical reactions are going on and these reactions are catalyzed by other macromolecules, the enzymes. The chemical reactions provide the energy to make new cells and to carry out the functions of the body—moving muscles, thinking, and so on. Each cell is an independent unit, but it co-operates with other cells to make the body machine run smoothly and efficiently.

ROBERT WARNER CHAMBERS
New York University School of Medicine
See also BIOCHEMISTRY; CELL.

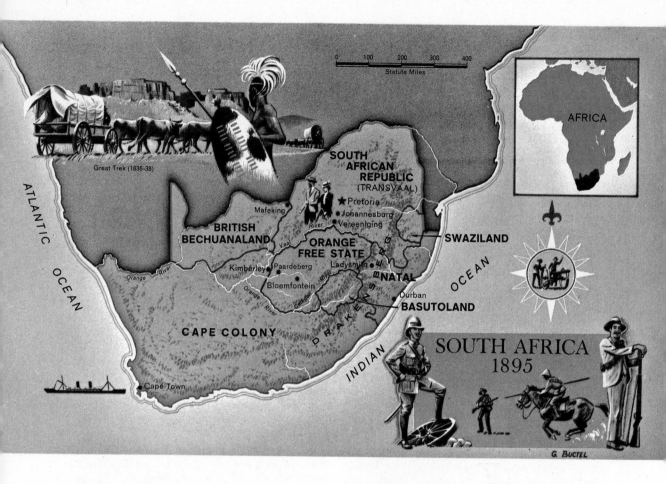

AFRICA

SOUTH AFRICA
1895

G. BUCTEL

BOER WAR

In 1899 Great Britain, a great power with a world-wide empire, found itself at war with two small states in South Africa.

The South African war had been brewing for many years. Originally South Africa had been settled by the Dutch, sometimes called Boers—the Dutch word for farmers. In 1814 the Dutch Cape Colony at the southern tip of Africa was officially ceded to Britain in return for a large payment of money. Large numbers of British immigrants soon arrived. The Dutch settlers grew dissatisfied with British rule. They objected when the British freed their slaves. Many moved north and founded two states of their own: the Orange Free State and the South African Republic (the Transvaal).

In 1886 gold was discovered in the Transvaal, and British gold seekers soon outnumbered the native Boers. The Boers feared

a British take-over, so they passed restrictive laws that prevented British settlers from voting.

The "outlanders," as the new British arrivals were called, protested against this treatment. They paid the greatest share of the taxes in the Transvaal, and yet they could not vote. Supported by the British Government, the "outlanders" plotted to overthrow the Boer Government. The plot convinced the Boers that they had to be on their guard. The two Boer republics formed a military alliance.

Trouble continued to build up. The British settlers demanded full political rights. The Boers remained firm in their refusal. Both sides began preparing for war. On October 9, 1899, President Paul Kruger of the Transvaal angrily ordered the British to withdraw all troops from the borders of Boer territory. An army of 35,000 Boer fighting men was mobilized.

The British Government refused to obey

the order, and on October 11 the war began. The Boers besieged Mafeking and Kimberley in the Cape Colony, and in Natal they surrounded Ladysmith. In the first few weeks, the British were badly beaten.

At the end of October, the British commander in chief, Sir Redvers Buller, began a counterattack. Unfortunately Buller was an old soldier with old-fashioned ideas. In fact, like General Buller, the whole British army was old-fashioned. Many of its officers were poorly trained, and British soldiers carried weapons that were out of date. The British were also hampered by the time and expense required to move troops and supplies the great distance from Britain to South Africa. In the so-called "Black Week" (December 10–15), the Boers defeated the British in three separate battles.

In Britain there was a feeling of despair. British public opinion was split. There were many pro-Boers who felt the war was unjust. Most people, however, supported the war. A major reason for this was that other European powers—especially Germany—were accusing England of bullying two small republics. The British resented this interference by other nations and rallied behind their government. The government was determined to win in South Africa. General Buller was replaced by Lord Frederick Sleigh Roberts, with Lord Horatio Herbert Kitchener as his chief of staff.

Roberts and Kitchener immediately began plans for a new offensive. On February 11, 1900, British troops marched north to help the besieged towns. In less than a month, the British recaptured Kimberley and Ladysmith and defeated a 4,000-man Boer army at Paardeberg.

By March the Boers were retreating. The British had reclaimed most of the Cape Colony and in May pushed forward into the Transvaal. On May 13 they rescued the besieged town of Mafeking. The following month Kitchener and Roberts entered Pretoria in triumph. By September President Kruger was in exile.

Roberts now considered the war to be over. He left for England in December, leaving Kitchener in command. But Kitchener soon found that the Boers had not given up. Instead they broke up into small groups called

SOME WORDS IN AFRIKAANS (a language spoken by the Boers)	
baas	master or boss
berg	mountain
biltong	dried meat
dorp	village or town
goeie-middag	good afternoon
goeie-môre	good morning
goeie-nag	good night
kêrel	young man
kraal	native village or cattle enclosure
laer	circle of covered wagons
Oom	sir (term of respect to older man)
spoor	trail or track of a wild animal
springbok	antelope (national animal of South Africa)
totsiens	good-bye or adieu
trek	long trip or journey
veld	field or meadow
wildebees	gnu (large antelope)

"commandos" and began 15 months of guerrilla warfare. For almost 2 years some 50,000 Boers held off a British army of almost 250,000 men.

To counter the Boer guerrilla tactics, Kitchener had to use harsh methods. British troops burned farms and carted off livestock and supplies to keep the Boers from using them. Refugees driven from their homes were then herded into concentration camps. There was much suffering in these camps. Poor sanitation caused disease, and 20,000 inmates died in a 14-month period.

Finally, worn out by almost 3 years of war, the Boers agreed to negotiate a peace settlement. In May, 1902, meetings were held at Vereeniging, and an agreement was signed on May 31. The Boers surrendered their arms and agreed to swear allegiance to the British crown. In return the British promised self-government, restored all possessions to their owners, and paid a sum of £3,000,000 to help rebuild the farms and buildings that had been destroyed.

The British granted the Boer states self-government under the British flag within a few years. This led to the creation of the Union of South Africa in 1910, which remained a part of the British Commonwealth until 1961, when it became an independent republic.

Reviewed by KENNETH S. COOPER
George Peabody College

See also SOUTH AFRICA.

BOHR, NIELS (1885–1962)

Early in the 1900's a young Danish physicist named Niels Bohr began to study the atom. His studies turned out to be both his life's work and extremely important. First he gave science a new view of the atom's structure. Some years later he helped to release the energy of the atom. Still later he worked to control that energy for peaceful uses.

Niels Bohr was born on October 7, 1885, in Copenhagen, Denmark. His father was a scientist and professor at the university there, and Niels was raised in a home where science was naturally of interest. In 1903 he entered the University of Copenhagen. His chief concern was physics, but he was also an outstanding soccer player. By 1907 Niels had won a gold medal from the Royal Danish Academy for his scientific work.

After receiving his doctor's degree in 1911, Bohr wanted to learn more about the atom. He decided to go to England and study with J. J. Thomson and Ernest Rutherford. Both these men were leaders in atomic physics. Bohr first studied under Thomson at Cambridge University; a year later he worked with Rutherford at the University of Manchester. In 1913 Bohr returned to the University of Copenhagen as a lecturer.

It was during this year that Bohr made his first great contribution to atomic physics. By that time many scientists had attempted to explain the atom. Rutherford, for example, had provided one theory. The great German physicist Max Planck had another.

Working from the ideas of Rutherford and of Planck, Bohr set forth a new theory of his own. It dealt with atomic structure and behavior. Bohr's theory became the basis of the branch of modern physics known as quantum mechanics. For his brilliant work Bohr received the Nobel prize for physics in 1922.

Meanwhile Bohr had married a Danish girl, started a family, and continued teaching at the University of Copenhagen. In 1920 he became director of the university's new Institute of Theoretical Physics. He made the institute into one of the world's major research centers. Scientists came from all over the world to study with Bohr. He was sometimes so busy with his work that he forgot about his meals. But he always managed to make time for his wife and five sons.

About 1930 the institute began important studies of the nucleus of the atom. In 1936 Bohr made another major advance in atomic physics: he gave the first correct description of a nuclear reaction. This work later helped the United States develop the atomic bomb.

Bohr arrived in the United States in 1939 to work at the Institute for Advanced Study in Princeton, New Jersey. Some of the world's leading scientists were there, including Albert Einstein. Bohr told them of the work going on in Europe in splitting uranium atoms. His reports spurred United States research in this field.

Bohr returned ·to Copenhagen a few months after World War II broke out. In 1940 the Germans conquered Denmark. Bohr refused to co-operate with them and closed his institute. In 1943, when he was threatened with arrest, Bohr fled. He went first to Sweden and then to the United States.

Bohr served as adviser at the first atomic bomb laboratory, near Los Alamos, New Mexico. He soon began to worry about the far-reaching effects of the new bomb. After the first atomic bomb test, in 1945, Bohr went to Washington to plead for immediate international control of atomic weapons.

When the war ended in 1945, Bohr returned to work at his institute in Copenhagen. In 1955 he became chairman of the newly founded Danish Atomic Energy Commission. Two years later Bohr received the first Atoms for Peace award—a fitting climax to his lifetime with the atom. Bohr died November 18, 1962.

JOHN S. BOWMAN
Author and Science Editor

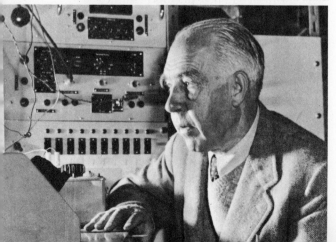

Niels Bohr helped form modern theory of atomic structure. He later served as adviser on the first atomic bomb.

BOILING POINT. See LIQUIDS.

BOLÍVAR, SIMÓN (1783–1830)

For nearly 300 years most of South America was under Spanish rule. Simón Bolívar vowed to free his native land, Venezuela, from Spain. When he died in 1830, he had freed not only Venezuela, but Ecuador, Bolivia, and Colombia as well.

Bolívar was born at Caracas, Venezuela, on July 24, 1783. His ancestors in Spain had belonged to the nobility, and young Bolívar was educated as an aristocrat. When he was 16, Bolívar was sent to Spain to continue his education. For the next seven years he studied and traveled in Europe. The example of the American and French revolutions stirred Bolívar deeply. He swore that he would not rest until he had broken the chains that bound his country to Spain.

In Venezuela a group of patriots, including Bolívar and Francisco Miranda, seized Caracas. On July 5, 1811, they declared Venezuela's independence. But the patriots were crushed by Spanish troops. Miranda died in prison and Bolívar fled from Venezuela.

Years of bloody fighting and heartbreaking defeat followed. Twice again Bolívar was forced to flee into exile. But his stern face and dark, piercing eyes showed a determination to win independence at all costs. In 1819 he boldly marched his patriot army over the snow-covered Andes mountains. It was winter, and in that terrible march many men and all the horses perished. But Bolívar surprised the Spanish Army and defeated it completely at Boyacá, in Colombia. The victory brought independence to Colombia. Two years later, Bolívar liberated Venezuela. And the following year, Ecuador was freed.

Venezuela, Colombia, and Ecuador were united into the republic of Gran Colombia, with Bolívar as its president.

Meanwhile, General José de San Martín, the liberator of Argentina, with Bernardo O'Higgins of Chile, had proclaimed the independence of Peru. Bolívar met with San Martín at Guayaquíl. San Martín generously gave Bolívar command of his army to complete the liberation of Peru. The next year Upper Peru was renamed Bolivia in honor of its liberator.

Bolívar soon had all the powers of a dictator, though his ideals were freedom and jus-

Simón Bolívar, South American patriot.

tice. He encouraged the creation of constitutional government and urged that more schools and universities be built. There were slaves in South America. Bolívar had freed his, and he insisted that other slave owners do the same.

Bolívar's dream had been to see all the liberated countries united. However, each country wanted its independence. New revolutions broke out and Gran Colombia fell apart. Bolívar's enemies accused him of being a tyrant, and an attempt was made to kill him.

In 1830, weary and ill after years of war and revolution, Bolívar resigned as president of Colombia. On December 17, 1830, he died at the age of 47.

Bolívar's dream of a united South America was a failure. He died a disappointed man, with few friends and many enemies. But to the people of South America he is still *El Libertador*—the liberator.

Reviewed by ERNESTO SÁBATO
Author, *The Graves and the Heroes*

BOLIVIA

Bolivia lies in the heart of South America. Dominated by the great snowcapped peaks of the Andes mountains, it is one of the highest countries in the world. In fact, it is sometimes called the Tibet of South America. The city of La Paz, one of the country's two capitals, is about 3,600 meters (12,000 feet) above sea level.

▶ THE PEOPLE

Most of Bolivia's 5,600,000 people live in the cold, snowcapped Andes in the western part of the country. Only about one quarter of the Bolivians make their home in the east, where the land slopes away into tangled tropical jungles and hot, dry plains.

Bolivia is the most Indian of the South American nations. More than one half of the population are Quechua and Aymará Indians. A quarter of the population are mestizos, people of mixed Spanish and Indian descent. Only a tiny fraction of the Bolivian people call themselves whites. These are mostly descendants of Spanish settlers.

Way of Life

More than 1,000 years ago a great Indian civilization grew up on the banks of Lake Titicaca in what is now Bolivia. The leaders of this civilization spoke Aymará, the language still spoken by Bolivia's Aymará Indians. Today the Aymará live mainly in the mountain area around Lake Titicaca. They work as farmers, shepherds, and miners.

Bolivia's other important Indian group, the Quechua, are descended from the Inca invaders who came to Bolivia in the 13th century A.D. The Quechua live mostly in the highlands and the deep valleys of the eastern Andes. Like the Aymará, the Quechua have their own language.

The life of the Bolivian Indian is generally harsh and monotonous. Families live in one-room houses of stone or baked mud brick called adobe. Windows are, at best, slits in the walls. The family shares its cramped quarters with its fowl.

Most Indians are farmers. Since 1952 the government has made many of them owners of their land. But the Bolivian Indians still have problems. If they are fortunate, they may have oxen to draw the wooden plows that they guide in the furrows, or rows. After the seed is sown, children often follow behind to cover the furrows with earth.

Children also tend the herds of llamas and alpacas. These long-necked animals are related to the camel and are found only in the Andes. The Indians use them as pack animals and for their meat and fur, and they burn the dung of these animals to heat their homes.

The foods the Indians eat most often are potatoes, corn, and beans. A basic food is called *chuño*. It looks like popcorn, but it is really a potato that has been left outdoors for several days to freeze and thaw. Then it is trampled to squeeze out the water, and frozen again. It can be stored for many months in this condition.

The life of the Indians who work in Bo-

FACTS AND FIGURES

REPUBLIC OF BOLIVIA is the official name of the country. Bolivia was named for Simón Bolívar, the liberator of South America.

CAPITAL: Sucre (legal capital), La Paz (actual capital).

LOCATION: West central South America. **Latitude**—9° 35′ S to 23° S. **Longitude**—57° 30′ W to 69° 34′ W.

PHYSICAL FEATURES: Area—1,098,581 km² (424,163 sq mi). **Highest point**—Mt. Ancohuma in the Andes, 6,550 m (21,490 ft) above sea level. **Lowest point**—El Beni, about 360 m (1,200 ft) above sea level. **Chief rivers**—Guaporé, Mamoré, Beni, Madre de Dios, Pilcomayo, Desaguadero.

POPULATION: 5,800,000 (estimate).

LANGUAGE: Spanish, Quechua, Aymará.

RELIGION: Roman Catholic.

GOVERNMENT: Republic. **Head of government**—president. **International co-operation**—United Nations; Organization of American States (OAS); Latin American Free Trade Association (LAFTA).

NATIONAL ANTHEM: *Bolivianos el hado propicio coronó nuestros votos y anhelos* ("Bolivians, propitious fate has crowned our oaths and hopes").

ECONOMY: Agricultural products—potatoes, barley, quinoa, broad beans, wheat, alfalfa, coca, corn, vegetables, oats, fruit, coffee, cacao, tobacco. **Industries and products**—textiles, food products, beverages. **Chief minerals**—tin, lead, petroleum, zinc, silver, copper, antimony, gold, asbestos. **Chief exports**—tin, wolfram, lead, copper, zinc, antimony, silver, gold. **Chief imports**—sugar, rice, flour, cooking oil, iron and steel products, mining machinery, automobiles and trucks, drugs, paper and paper products. **Monetary unit**—Bolivian peso.

livia's mines is a little better than that of the farmers. Miners live in houses built by the mining companies. They can also shop in special stores that sell low-priced goods. But the miners' work is very dangerous, especially in the tin mines that are at altitudes of 3,600 to 5,500 meters (12,000 to 18,000 feet). They are given a daily ration of coca, which is very important to them. Chewing the leaves of this tea-like plant relieves hunger. In 1952 the mines were nationalized, as the first step toward economic and social reforms for the miners.

Feasts and Fairs. The gayest days in the life of Bolivians are holidays and fairs. They delight in the Alacitas Fair, which is held in La Paz each January. The fair is held in honor of the Aymará god of abundance, Ekeko. Ekeko is a cheerful fellow. He looks a little bit like Santa Claus without a beard. Ekeko carries miniatures of all the things people may want or need: tiny sacks of rice and sugar, a miniature sheep or cow, a house, an automobile, a suit of clothes. According to legend, if a person buys one of Ekeko's miniatures, he will get its life-sized equivalent during the coming year.

Spanish missionaries long ago converted the Indians to Catholicism. But many ancient Indian festivals are still mixed with Christian rituals. For example, at carnival time in Oruro dancers perform the Diablada, or Devil Dance. The dance is dedicated to the Virgin of the Mines. The dance is the miners' way of asking the Virgin's protection against the devil, whom they fear meeting deep in the dark mines.

Religion. The majority of Bolivians are Roman Catholic. Catholicism is recognized as the state religion, but members of all religious groups may worship freely.

Language. Spanish is the official language of Bolivia, and most educated people in Bolivia speak it. Bolivia's Indians are taught Spanish in school. At home they may speak the language of their group, be it Aymará or Quechua.

Education. All children between the ages of 6 and 14 are supposed to go to school. But many Bolivian boys and girls are so busy helping their families that it is not always possible for them to attend school. There may not even be a school nearby. Many Indian

children drop their studies after a year or two. Only a handful continue as far as the university. The Bolivian Government now is working to reduce the huge number of people who are unable to read and write.

In Bolivia's cities many more children are able to attend school. Some schools are modern, especially the private and parochial schools. Boys and girls usually go to separate schools. In addition, there are universities in leading Bolivian cities such as Oruro, Potosí, Cochabamba, and La Paz. San Francisco Xavier University at Sucre was founded in 1624 and is one of the oldest universities in the Western Hemisphere.

▶**THE LAND**

Bolivia has three major land regions. They are the Andes, the Altiplano, and the lowlands.

The Andes are widest in Bolivia, stretching as much as 640 kilometers (400 miles) across at their widest point. The Bolivian Andes are divided into two main ranges, or cordilleras. The Cordillera Occidental, or Western Range, forms Bolivia's border with Chile. It is the barrier that cuts Bolivia off from the Pacific Ocean. Bolivia's highest mountain, Anco-

Balsas, small boats made of reeds, on Lake Titicaca.

A busy and colorful outdoor market in La Paz.

huma, rises in the Cordillera Oriental, or Eastern Range. Deep valleys called *yungas* have been cut by rushing rivers in the slopes of the Eastern Range. The mild climate of these deep valleys makes them good farming areas.

The Altiplano is the high, bleak, cold, and almost treeless plateau between the mountain ranges. Its average elevation is almost 3 kilometers (over 2 miles) above sea level. Three out of four Bolivians live in this region, many in La Paz and smaller towns.

The lowlands of Bolivia are entirely different from the highland zone, and much larger. The climate throughout this region is hotter. The northern lowlands are heavily forested. Close to the border of Brazil the jungle grows dense and the rivers are a home for giant crocodiles. The southern lowlands are drier than those in the north. Instead of jungles there are great plains where wild cattle roam. Near the Argentine border there are important oil reserves owned by the Bolivian Government.

Lakes and Rivers. Lake Titicaca, at the northern edge of the Altiplano, is the highest navigated body of water in the world. It lies 3,812 meters (12,507 feet) above sea level, on the border with Peru. Small native boats called *balsas* are used for fishing in the lake. Lake Titicaca drains into Lake Poopó, farther south. There is no drainage from Lake Poopó.

The water evaporates, leaving the lake very salty. Great salt flats dot the lonesome landscape south of the lake.

The Beni River and its tributaries drain the northern *yungas*. They flow north to join the Madeira River in Brazil and finally the great Amazon River. The southern *yungas* are drained by the Pilcomayo River and its tributaries. They are part of a river system that flows southeast to join the Paraguay River and the Río de la Plata in Argentina.

Climate. Because of Bolivia's altitude, there are great differences in temperature between day and night. The average annual temperature at La Paz, on the Altiplano, is only 8°C (47°F). At Trinidad, a city in the lowlands of eastern Bolivia, the average temperature is around 21°C (70°F). In Bolivia there is little difference in temperature between summer and winter. Wet and dry seasons are more important. The dry season lasts from May to November. Between December and February there are heavy rains on the Altiplano and drenching tropical storms in the lowlands.

Natural Resources. Bolivia has been described as "a beggar on a throne of gold." The country's mountainous terrain and its turbulent history have kept Bolivia from making full use of its great natural resources.

The little wealth Bolivia has enjoyed has come from the mines on or near the Altiplano. The Cerro Rico ("rich hill") of Potosí is a mountain that is almost a solid mass of tin, silver, tungsten, and other ores. Zinc, antimony, gold, iron, bismuth, sulfur, and asbestos are also mined in Bolivia. And at Corocoro there is one of the world's rare surface deposits of natural copper. Another increasingly important Bolivian resource is oil, which is found mainly in southern Bolivia.

Timber is one of Bolivia's most valuable and least-exploited resources. Timber covers nearly 40 percent of the land. The most valuable trees—mahogany, jacaranda, rosewood, balsa, and cedar—grow on the eastern slopes of the Cordillera Real.

▶ THE ECONOMY

Agriculture. The leading Bolivian occupation is agriculture. About one half of Bolivia's farms are on the Altiplano. But the crops have been poor because of the high altitude, the lack of rain, and the primitive methods of cultivation. However, potatoes, barley, a grain called quinoa, broad beans, wheat, and alfalfa are grown. Coca, coffee, cacao, and bananas are grown in the *yungas*. From the fertile valleys around Cochabamba, Tarija, and Sucre come corn, wheat, barley, vegetables, alfalfa, and oats. Only a very small portion of the lowlands east of Santa Cruz de la Sierra are under cultivation. Rice, sugar, cotton, corn, yucca, oil plants, and fruit are grown there. Cattle and hogs are raised in the lowlands.

Industry. Large-scale industries, except for mining, are as yet unknown in Bolivia. The chief source of Bolivia's industrial wealth comes now, as it has for centuries, from mining. Tin is mined in larger amounts than any other mineral, and Bolivia has long been one of the leading exporters of tin in the world. Petroleum and petroleum products are of growing importance to the economy.

Transportation and Communication. Bolivia's future as a united and strong country depends to a large degree on its success in improving its transportation network. At present Bolivia must import a great deal of food and lumber because these products cannot be transported cheaply from the lowlands to the cities of the Altiplano. The hardwood trees of the northern forests die of old age while Bolivia imports lumber because there is no road from the forests. Airplanes sometimes fly beef from the city of Trinidad to La Paz —the only way to get the meat to market.

Most of the communications system in Bolivia is privately owned. There is telephone service in the major cities, but more than half the total number of phones are in the city of

La Paz has the highest elevation of any large city in the world.

La Paz. There are many radio stations and a government-operated television network.

CITIES

Sucre, where the Supreme Court sits, is the legal capital. But La Paz is Bolivia's largest city and its center of government, commerce, and culture. The fastest-growing city in the country is Santa Cruz. Cochabamba, the center of the aviation industry, is honored for its women, for they fought for independence. Potosí, one of the great colonial cities, is still an important mining center.

HISTORY AND GOVERNMENT

The magnificent carved stone Gate of the Sun, ruined temples, and a few ancient roads are all that remains of Tiahuanaco, a great Indian civilization that once flourished on the banks of Lake Titicaca. From about A.D. 600 to 900 the Indians of this region reigned supreme. Then mysteriously their civilization vanished. By the year 1300 the powerful Incas of Peru ruled the region. The Inca Empire in turn was destroyed by the Spanish.

Bolivia was a Spanish colony for about 300 years. In 1545 the mineral-rich mountain at Potosí was discovered, and the Spaniards began to exploit its wealth for themselves. Indians were forced to work in the mines and were treated cruelly. The harshness of Spanish rule led to rebellions against Spain early in the 19th century.

In 1809 Bolivia's small white population, inspired by Simón Bolívar's heroic liberation of the northern part of the continent, led a revolt against Spain. But it was not until 1824 that Antonio José de Sucre (1795–1830), one of Bolívar's lieutenants, completely broke Spanish power in this region. The new nation declared its independence on August 6, 1825. It was named Bolívar in honor of the Liberator. Later the spelling was changed to its present form.

Bolivia's first president was General Sucre. He was followed in office by General Andrés Santa Cruz, who tried but failed to bring about a permanent union between Peru and Bolivia. The next half century of Bolivian history is scarred by a succession of military dictatorships.

The most terrible of these dictators was Mariano Melgarejo, who came to power in 1864. He was illiterate, cruel, dishonest, and tyrannical. During the years of his rule Melgarejo sold and leased national territory to neighboring countries. In later years, wars cost Bolivia much of her original territory.

The first 50 years of the 20th century in Bolivia were marked by some advances in industry and transportation. But since the Bolivian economy depended so much on the world demand for tin, events far from Bolivia shaped the course of Bolivian life. During the depression of the 1930's, when the tin demand was slight, Bolivians suffered. World War II brought a rise in the price of tin and some improvement in the Bolivian economy. But at the end of the war tin prices dropped, and Bolivia was once again in crisis.

A revolution in 1952 brought the National Revolutionary Movement to power and caused a deep change in the social and economic life of the country. Victor Paz Estenssoro, the leader, served as president from 1952 to 1956 and from 1960 to 1964, when he was overthrown. He nationalized the mines, the oil industry, and part of the railroad system. A program of land reform under which Indians were given land was begun. Indians were also given the right to vote, the lowlands were opened for colonization, and new miners' laws were passed. In 1966 René Barrientos Ortuño was chosen president in a popular election. But his expanded reform program was cut short by his death in a helicopter accident in 1969.

Under its constitution, Bolivia is a republic headed by a president who is elected by popular vote for a 4-year term. The legislature, called the Congress, is composed of two houses—the Senate, whose members are elected for 6-year terms, and the Chamber of Deputies, elected for 4-year terms.

During the instability that followed Barrientos' death in 1969, Congress was dissolved and the military took control. During the 1970's there were student protests and labor strikes. A return to civilian rule was scheduled for 1978. Elections were held, but the military again assumed control.

J. DAVID BOWEN
Author, *Hello South America*
Reviewed by MARINA NÚÑEZ DEL PRADO
Bolivian Ministry of Education

See also ANDES; BOLÍVAR, SIMÓN.

BOMBAY

Bombay, city of story and legend, is the capital of the state of Maharashtra as well as the major port and industrial center of the west coast of India. The main part of the city is built on Bombay Island, which is about 18 kilometers (11 miles) long and 5 kilometers (3 miles) wide.

At the southwestern end of Bombay Island, the coast is indented. It forms a shallow body of water known as Back Bay, which opens into the Arabian Sea. To the west of the bay is a high ridge known as Malabar Hill. The homes of the well-to-do are to be found on the ridge and along the slopes. The Hanging Gardens and Kamala Nehru Park with its giant Mother Hubbard shoe are also in the Malabar Hill area. The summit of the hill offers a superb view of the city. At night thousands of lights form a sparkling outline of Marine Drive, which runs along the northeastern edge of Back Bay. This brilliant view is named the Queen's Necklace.

Marine Drive is perhaps the most spectacular seaside road in Asia. This six-lane divided highway has rows of modern apartments on one side. On its other side are lovely palms and a wide promenade facing the bay. In the warmer part of the year the people of Bombay come to Marine Drive and walk along it in the cool of the evening.

The port of Bombay is on the eastern edge of the island. Its shore is lined with docks, piers, and warehouses. One of the world's finest natural deepwater harbors, the port covers an area of about 180 square kilometers (70 square miles). Most of India's petroleum and imported goods enter through this port. Cotton yarn, oilseeds, and manganese ore are exported.

At the entrance to the harbor is the Gateway of India, the most familiar landmark of the city. It is a huge and magnificent stone arch, which was built in 1911 in honor of King George V and Queen Mary of England.

Western architecture and wide avenues contribute to Bombay's cosmopolitan atmosphere.

Crowded street in the market district of Bombay.

Gateway of India, a famous large stone arch, stands at the entrance to Bombay Harbor on the Arabian Sea.

The major commercial center is west of the waterfront, in a part of the city known as The Fort. Most of the older and larger buildings in this area are of Gothic and other European architecture. Nearby is the famed Victoria Railway Station, which is the railway terminus of Bombay.

Among the special attractions of Bombay are the Prince of Wales Museum, the Jehangir Art Gallery, and the famous Bombay University, with over 50,000 students. Other places of interest include Brabourne Stadium, the Mahalakshmi racetrack, golf courses, and a well-stocked zoo.

About 6,000,000 people live in Bombay, which is considered India's most cosmopolitan city. The vast majority are Hindus, but the population includes Muslims, Christians, Jains, Zoroastrians, Jews, and Sikhs. The two major languages spoken are Marathi and Gujarati, although more than 50 different languages are in use.

From a small fishing village called Mumbai, Bombay grew into one of the world's great seaports.

DAVID FIRMAN
Towson State University
Reviewed by THE CONSULATE GENERAL OF INDIA

BONDS. See STOCKS AND BONDS.

BOOK AWARDS FOR CHILDREN'S LITERATURE

The following are the major awards for excellence in the writing and illustrating of children's books.

Book of the Year for Children Medal. Given annually since 1947 by the Canadian Association of Children's Librarians for outstanding books in English and French by Canadians.

1947 *Starbuck Valley Winter,* Roderick Haig-Brown.
1948 *Kristli's Trees,* Mabel Dunham.
1950 *Franklin of the Arctic,* Richard S. Lambert.
1952 *The Sun Horse,* Catherine Anthony Clark.
1954 *Mgr. de Laval,* Emile Gervais, S.J.
1956 *Train for Tiger Lily,* Louise Riley.
1957 *Glooskap's Country,* Cyrus Macmillan.
1958 *Lost in the Barrens,* Farley Mowat.
       Le chevalier du roi, Béatrice Clément.
1959 *The Dangerous Cove,* John F. Hayes.
       Un drôle de petit cheval, Hélène Flamme.
1960 *The Golden Phoenix,* Marius Barbeau and Michael Hornyansky.
       L'été enchanté, Paule Daveluy.
1961 *The St. Lawrence,* William Toye.
       Plantes vagabondes, Marcelle Gauvreau.
1962 *Les îles du Roi Maha Maha II,* Claude Aubry.
1963 *The Incredible Journey,* Sheila Burnford.
       Drôle d'automne, Paule Daveluy.
1964 *The Whale People,* Roderick Haig-Brown.
       Féerie, Cécile Chabot.
1965 *Tales of Nanabozho,* Dorothy M. Reid.
1966 *Tikta'liktak,* James A. Houston.
       Le chêne des tempêtes, Andrée Maillet.
1967 *Raven's Cry,* Christie Harris.
1968 *The White Archer,* James Houston.
       Légendes Indiennes du Canada, Claude Mélançon.
1969 *And Tomorrow the Stars: The Story of John Cabot,* Kay Hill.
1971 *Cartier Discovers the St. Lawrence,* William Toye.
1972 *Mary of Mile 18,* Ann Blades.
1973 *The Marrow of the World,* Ruth Nichols.
       Le petit sapin qui a poussé sur une étoile, Simone Bussières.
1974 *The Miraculous Hind,* Elizabeth Cleaver.
1975 *Alligator Pie,* Dennis Lee.
1976 *Jacob Two-Two Meets the Hooded Fang,* Mordecai Richler.
1977 *Mouse Woman and the Vanished Princesses,* Christie Harris.
1978 *Garbage Delight,* Dennis Lee.
       Loon's Necklace, Elizabeth Cleaver.
       (No award 1949, 1951, 1953, 1955, 1970)

Caldecott Medal. Given annually since 1938 by the American Library Association to the artist of the most distinguished American picture book.

1938 Dorothy P. Lathrop, *Animals of the Bible* (Bible selections by Helen Dean Fish).
1939 Thomas Handforth, *Mei Li.*
1940 Ingri and Edgar P. d'Aulaire, *Abraham Lincoln.*
1941 Robert Lawson, *They Were Strong and Good.*
1942 Robert McCloskey, *Make Way for Ducklings.*
1943 Virginia Lee Burton, *The Little House.*
1944 Louis Slobodkin, *Many Moons* (James Thurber).
1945 Elizabeth Orton Jones, *Prayer for a Child* (Rachel Field).
1946 Maud and Miska Petersham, *The Rooster Crows.*
1947 Leonard Weisgard, *The Little Island* (Golden MacDonald).
1948 Roger Duvoisin, *White Snow, Bright Snow* (Alvin Tresselt).
1949 Berta and Elmer Hader, *The Big Snow.*
1950 Leo Politi, *Song of the Swallows.*
1951 Katherine Milhous, *The Egg Tree.*
1952 Nicolas Mordvinoff, *Finders Keepers* (Will Lipkind).
1953 Lynd Ward, *The Biggest Bear.*
1954 Ludwig Bemelmans, *Madeline's Rescue.*
1955 Marcia Brown, *Cinderella* (Charles Perrault).
1956 Feodor Rojankovsky, *Frog Went A-Courtin'* (John Langstaff).
1957 Marc Simont, *A Tree Is Nice* (Janice May Udry).
1958 Robert McCloskey, *Time of Wonder.*
1959 Barbara Cooney, *Chanticleer and the Fox.*
1960 Marie Hall Ets, *Nine Days to Christmas* (Ets and Aurora Labastida).
1961 Nicolas Sidjakov, *Baboushka and the Three Kings* (Ruth Robbins).
1962 Marcia Brown, *Once a Mouse.*

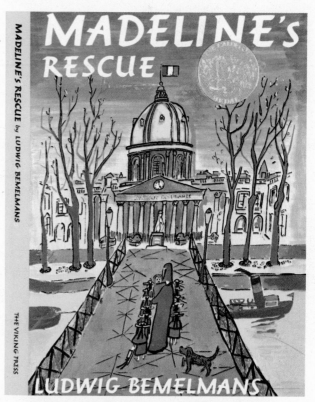

1963	Ezra Jack Keats, *The Snowy Day.*

1963 Ezra Jack Keats, *The Snowy Day.*
1964 Maurice Sendak, *Where the Wild Things Are.*
1965 Beni Montresor, *May I Bring a Friend?* (Beatrice Schenk de Regniers).
1966 Nonny Hogrogian, *Always Room for One More* (Sorche Nic Leodhas).
1967 Evaline Ness, *Sam, Bangs & Moonshine.*
1968 Ed Emberley, *Drummer Hoff.*
1969 Uri Shulevitz, *The Fool of the World and the Flying Ship* (Arthur Ransome).
1970 William Steig, *Sylvester and the Magic Pebble.*
1971 Gail E. Haley, *A Story, A Story.*
1972 Nonny Hogrogian, *One Fine Day.*
1973 Blair Lent, *The Funny Little Woman.*
1974 Margo and Harve Zemach, *Duffy and the Devil.*
1975 Gerald McDermott, *Arrow to the Sun.*
1976 Leo and Diane Dillon, *Why Mosquitos Buzz in People's Ears: A West African Tale.*
1977 Leo and Diane Dillon, *Ashanti to Zulu: African Traditions.*
1978 Peter Spier, *Noah's Ark.*

Carnegie Medal. Given annually since 1937 by the Library Association of England to the most outstanding children's book by a British author published in England.

1937 *Pigeon Post,* Arthur Ransome.
1938 *The Family from One End Street,* Eve Garnett.
1939 *The Circus Is Coming,* Noel Streatfeild.
1940 *The Radium Woman,* Eleanor Doorly.
1941 *Visitors from London,* Kitty Barne.
1942 *We Couldn't Leave Dinah,* Mary Treadgold.
1943 *The Little Grey Men,* D. J. Watkins-Pitchford.
1945 *The Wind on the Moon,* Eric Linklater.
1947 *The Little White Horse,* Elizabeth Goudge.
1948 *Collected Stories for Children,* Walter de la Mare.
1949 *Sea Change,* Richard Armstrong.
1950 *The Story of Your Home,* Agnes Allen.
1951 *The Lark on the Wing,* Elfrida Vipont.
1952 *The Wool-Pack,* Cynthia Harnett.
1953 *The Borrowers,* Mary Norton.
1954 *A Valley Grows Up,* Edward Osmond.
1955 *Knight Crusader,* Ronald Welch.
1956 *The Little Bookroom,* Eleanor Farjeon.
1957 *The Last Battle,* Clive Staples Lewis.
1958 *A Grass Rope,* William Mayne.
1959 *Tom's Midnight Garden,* Philippa Pearce.
1960 *The Lantern Bearers,* Rosemary Sutcliff.
1961 *The Making of Man,* Ian W. Cornwall.
1962 *A Stranger at Green Knowe,* Lucy M. Boston.
1963 *The Twelve and the Genii,* Pauline Clarke.
1964 *Time of Trial,* Hester Burton.
1965 *Nordy Bank,* Sheena Porter.
1966 *The Grange at High Force,* Philip Turner.
1968 *The Owl Service,* Alan Garner.
1969 *The Moon in the Cloud,* Rosemary Harris.
1970 *Flambards in Summer,* K. M. Peyton.
1971 *The God Beneath the Sea,* Leon Garfield and Edward Blishen.
1972 *Josh,* Ivan Southall.
1973 *Watership Down,* Richard Adams.
1974 *The Ghost of Thomas Kempe,* Penelope Lively.

1975 *The Stronghold,* Mollie Hunter.
1976 *The Machine Gunners,* Robert Westall.
1977 *Thunder and Lightnings,* Jan Mark. (No award 1944, 1946, 1967)

Hans Christian Andersen Medal. Given biennially since 1956 by the International Board on Books for Young People to an author of a book of fiction or for the author's complete work.

1956 Eleanor Farjeon, *The Little Bookroom.*
1958 Astrid Lindgren, *Rasmus and the Vagabond.*
1960 Erich Kästner, *When I Was a Boy* and his complete work.
1962 Meindert DeJong, complete work.
1964 René Guillot, complete work.
1966 Tove Jansson, complete work. Alois Carigiet (Illustrator's medal).
1968 James Krüss, complete work. José María Sánchez-Silva, complete work. Jiri Trnka (Illustrator's medal).
1970 Gianni Rodari, complete work. Maurice Sendak (Illustrator's medal).
1972 Scott O'Dell, complete work. Ib Spang Olsen (Illustrator's medal).
1974 Maria Gripe, complete work. Farshid Mesghali (Illustrator's medal).
1976 Cecil Bødker, complete work. Tatjana Mawrina (Illustrator's medal).
1978 Paula Fox, complete work. Svend Otto (Illustrator's medal).

John Newbery Medal. Given annually since 1922 by the American Library Association to the author of the most distinguished book for children. Author must be a citizen or permanent resident of the United States.

1922 Hendrik van Loon, *The Story of Mankind.*
1923 Hugh Lofting, *The Voyages of Doctor Dolittle.*
1924 Charles Boardman Hawes, *The Dark Frigate.*
1925 Charles J. Finger, *Tales from Silver Lands.*
1926 Arthur Bowie Chrisman, *Shen of the Sea.*
1927 Will James, *Smoky, the Cowhorse.*
1928 Dhan Gopal Mukerji, *Gay-Neck.*
1929 Eric P. Kelly, *Trumpeter of Krakow.*
1930 Rachel Field, *Hitty, Her First Hundred Years.*
1931 Elizabeth Coatsworth, *The Cat Who Went to Heaven.*
1932 Laura Adams Armer, *Waterless Mountain.*
1933 Elizabeth Foreman Lewis, *Young Fu of the Upper Yangtze.*
1934 Cornelia Meigs, *Invincible Louisa.*
1935 Monica Shannon, *Dobry.*
1936 Carol Ryrie Brink, *Caddie Woodlawn.*
1937 Ruth Sawyer, *Roller Skates.*
1938 Kate Seredy, *The White Stag.*
1939 Elizabeth Enright, *Thimble Summer.*
1940 James H. Daugherty, *Daniel Boone.*
1941 Armstrong Sperry, *Call It Courage.*
1942 Walter D. Edmonds, *The Matchlock Gun.*
1943 Elizabeth Janet Gray, *Adam of the Road.*
1944 Esther Forbes, *Johnny Tremain.*
1945 Robert Lawson, *Rabbit Hill.*
1946 Lois Lenski, *Strawberry Girl.*

Brian Wildsmith's

1947   Carolyn Sherwin Bailey, *Miss Hickory*.
1948   William Pène du Bois, *The Twenty-One Balloons*.
1949   Marguerite Henry, *King of the Wind*.
1950   Marguerite de Angeli, *The Door in the Wall*.
1951   Elizabeth Yates, *Amos Fortune, Free Man*.
1952   Eleanor Estes, *Ginger Pye*.
1953   Ann Nolan Clark, *Secret of the Andes*.
1954   Joseph Krumgold, *. . . and now Miguel*.
1955   Meindert DeJong, *The Wheel on the School*.
1956   Jean L. Latham, *"Carry On, Mr. Bowditch."*
1957   Virginia Sorensen, *Miracles on Maple Hill*.
1958   Harold Keith, *Rifles for Watie*.
1959   Elizabeth G. Speare, *The Witch of Blackbird Pond*.
1960   Joseph Krumgold, *Onion John*.
1961   Scott O'Dell, *Island of the Blue Dolphins*.
1962   Elizabeth G. Speare, *The Bronze Bow*.
1963   Madeleine L'Engle, *A Wrinkle in Time*.
1964   Emily Neville, *It's Like This, Cat*.
1965   Maia Wojciechowska, *Shadow of a Bull*.
1966   Elizabeth Borten de Treviño, *I, Juan de Pareja*.
1967   Irene Hunt, *Up a Road Slowly*.
1968   E. L. Konigsburg, *From the Mixed-Up Files of Mrs. Basil E. Frankweiler*.
1969   Lloyd Alexander, *The High King*.
1970   William Armstrong, *Sounder*.
1971   Betsy Byars, *The Summer of the Swans*.
1972   Robert C. O'Brien, *Mrs. Frisby and the Rats of NIMH*.
1973   Jean C. George, *Julie of the Wolves*.
1974   Paula Fox, *The Slave Dancer*.
1975   Virginia Hamilton, *M. C. Higgins the Great*.
1976   Susan Cooper, *The Grey King*.
1977   Mildred D. Taylor, *Roll of Thunder, Hear My Cry*.
1978   Katherine Paterson, *Bridge to Terabitha*.

Kate Greenaway Medal. Given annually since 1957 by the Library Association of England for the most distinguished work in the illustration of children's books published in Great Britain.

1957   Edward Ardizzone, *Tim All Alone*.
1958   Violet H. Drummond, *Mrs. Easter and the Storks*.

1959   No award.
1960   William Stobbs, *Kashtanka* (Anton Chekhov); *A Bundle of Ballads* (Ruth Manning-Sanders).
1961   Gerald Rose, *Old Winkle and the Seagulls* (with Elizabeth Rose).
1962   Anthony Maitland, *Mrs. Cockle's Cat* (Philippa Pearce).
1963   Brian Wildsmith, *Brian Wildsmith's ABC*.
1964   John Burningham, *Borka*.
1965   C. Walter Hodges, *Shakespeare's Theatre*.
1966   Victor C. Ambrus, *The Three Poor Tailors; The Royal Air Force*.
1967   Raymond Briggs, *The Mother Goose Treasury*.
1968   Charles Keeping, *Charley, Charlotte and the Golden Canary*.
1969   Pauline Baynes, *A Dictionary of Chivalry* (Grant Uden).
1970   Helen Oxenbury, *Quangle-Wangle's Hat* (Edward Lear); *Dragon of an Ordinary Family* (Margaret Mahy).
1971   John Burningham, *Mr. Gumpy's Outing*.
1972   Jan Pienkowski, *The Kingdom Under the Sea*.
1973   Krystyna Turska, *The Woodcutter's Duck*.
1974   Raymond Briggs, *Father Christmas*.
1975   Pat Hutchins, *The Wind Blew*.
1976   Victor C. Ambrus, *Horses in Battle; Mishka*.
1977   Gail E. Haley, *The Post Office Cat*.

Laura Ingalls Wilder Medal. First awarded in 1954 by the American Library Association. Since 1960, given every 5 years to an author or illustrator whose books, published in the U.S., have made a substantial and lasting contribution to literature for children.

1954   Laura Ingalls Wilder.
1960   Clara Ingram Judson.
1965   Ruth Sawyer.
1970   E. B. White.
1975   Beverly Cleary.

National Book Award. Given annually since 1969 for a children's book by a U.S. citizen, published in the U.S. (Award recognizes children's books as part of the national literature.)

1969   Meindert DeJong, *Journey from Peppermint Street*.
1970   I. B. Singer, *A Day of Pleasure: Stories of a Boy Growing Up in Warsaw*.
1971   Lloyd Alexander, *The Marvelous Misadventures of Sebastian*.
1972   Donald Barthelme, *The Slightly Irregular Fire Engine or The Hithering Thithering Djinn*.
1973   Ursula Le Guin, *The Farthest Shore*.
1974   Eleanor Cameron, *The Court of the Stone Children*.
1975   Virginia Hamilton, *M. C. Higgins the Great*.
1976   Walter D. Edmonds, *Bert Breen's Barn*.
1977   Katherine Paterson, *The Master Puppeteer*.
1978   Judith and Herbert Kohl, *The View from the Oak: The Private World of Other Creatures*.

BOOKKEEPING AND ACCOUNTING

No business could operate very long without knowing how much it was earning and how much it was spending. Bookkeeping and accounting are the methods business firms use to keep track of their earnings and expenses.

People have counted and kept records throughout history. In the ancient world, trade between merchants made necessary the creation of some kind of business records. Ancient clay tablets show that a system of positive and negative entries was used, in which the gain or loss of any business transaction was added to or subtracted from the total worth of the business.

▶ ORIGINS OF BOOKKEEPING

The modern system of bookkeeping originated in medieval Italy. Records were kept according to the modern system in the city of Genoa in 1340. Some historians believe that the origins of the system can be traced as far back as the 13th century. Genoa, Lombardy, and Tuscany were all thriving business centers in Italy, and any one of them could have been the birthplace of modern bookkeeping. Gradually merchants in other countries learned of the new bookkeeping system, and it spread throughout Europe.

▶ DEVELOPMENT OF ACCOUNTING

As the methods of the new bookkeeping system were developed some people became specialists in this kind of record keeping. They were known as accountants. With the increase of business activity, some accountants began to offer their services to any individuals or organizations that needed accounting work done. This was the origin of public accounting. Public accounting developed mainly in the British Isles, which were a leading center of trade. As early as 1720 an English public accountant was called in by Parliament to investigate a financial scandal.

During the 19th century, corporations became the most important form of business organization. A corporation has many owners. These are the stockholders, people who have bought shares, or stock, in the business in return for a share of the corporation's profits. The stockholders depended on published financial reports to learn how well their corporations were doing and whether the executives they hired to manage them were doing their jobs properly. During this period the basic principles of modern accounting were worked out to ensure that the stockholders got thorough and accurate reports.

In 1868 an English law was passed requiring all railroads to have audits made regularly and to submit them to the stockholders of the railroads. An **audit** is an examination of a business' financial record and a report on the findings. Public accountants were usually called on to prepare these audits.

Stockholders soon realized that if the reports were to have any value, there had to be a set of common principles for gathering and reporting the information. Without a standard method of reporting financial information, a misleading idea about the condition of a business could be given by reporting some facts and ignoring others.

Many unqualified people claimed to be accountants and attempted to do auditing work. Just as standard accounting methods were needed, properly qualified accountants were also found to be necessary.

▶ WHAT IS BOOKKEEPING?

Bookkeeping is a formal, organized system of recording financial transactions. It is done according to standardized rules. These rules make it easier to detect errors in the bookkeeping. The bookkeeper's record shows how much was spent in a certain transaction and how much was gained or lost in the transaction. The information is arranged so that it may be easily analyzed, that is, examined to determine the financial condition of the business or person involved.

Electronic bookkeeping machine stores information on magnetic tape or cards, solves accounting problems, and automatically prints results on forms.

A bookkeeper makes separate entries of all day-to-day transactions in a **journal**, or he may enter the data on an IBM or other punched card. These entries are totaled from time to time and entered, or posted, in a more permanent record called a **ledger**.

Our present system of bookkeeping makes it possible to present a great deal of information in relatively little space. This is an important advantage. A few pages of data can give a picture of the financial activity of even a large corporation such as General Motors for an entire year.

Two types of financial statements are used to report this information: the statement of financial position and the income statement.

The statement of financial position, often called the **balance sheet**, is a summary that shows the over-all condition of a business at a given point in time. It shows the assets of the business at that moment and specifies their value. Examples of assets are land, buildings, and equipment owned by a company. Money in the company's bank account is also an asset. So are services that have been paid for in advance.

The statement also shows **liabilities**, which are debts to persons or businesses. Examples of liabilities are wages owed to employees, money owed to a bank, unpaid bills for supplies, and stocks that have been sold to get money to run the business. The **equity**, or **capital**, is equal to the assets minus the liabilities.

The **income statement**, sometimes called the **profit and loss statement** or **operating statement**, shows the income and expenses of a business over a definite period of time, usually 1 year. From this statement the managers of the business can learn whether the company showed a profit or a loss for the period covered by the report. Information for the statement of financial position and the income statement is assembled from the records kept by the bookkeepers.

In order to keep track of a company's assets and liabilities, the bookkeeper groups them into **accounts**. There is an account for each of the different types of assets that the company has. For example, the money that a company owns is recorded in the "cash" account. The "accounts receivable" account is the record of the money owed to the com-

pany. The money paid for office equipment is recorded in a "Furniture, Fixtures, and Equipment" account. This account is a record of the value of the office equipment owned by the company.

Other accounts are records of the company's liabilities. For example, the "accounts payable" account is the record of money owed by the company for things such as purchases of goods and supplies.

In addition to the accounts that record the company's assets and liabilities, there is an "equity," or "capital," account. This account records how much of the company is owned by the owners or stockholders.

The system used in keeping the financial records of a business is the **double-entry** system, a method first developed by merchants of northern Italy during the 13th and 14th centuries. Behind this system is the basic idea that every business transaction affects the company's financial position in at least two ways. In the double-entry system every aspect of a transaction is recorded.

A bookkeeper records these transactions in terms of debits and credits. Every time a business transaction is made certain accounts are debited and others are credited. Increases in the liability or capital or decreases in the assets are credited. Decreases in the liability or capital or increases in the assets are debited. Any entry made under the heading of credits must be balanced by an entry under the heading of debits. The following are examples of this system:

(1) Suppose business A decides to pay off a loan of $1,000 made to it by business B. Payment of the loan decreases the liability account, so business A's bookkeeper will debit the liability account $1,000. Business A's "cash" account, an asset account, has also been affected by the transaction. It has been decreased by $1,000, so in order to record the transaction fully, the bookkeeper must also credit the "cash" account $1,000.

(2) Suppose a piece of land is sold for $2,000. The buyer pays $500 immediately and will pay the other $1,500 later. The bookkeeper credits the "land" account for $2,000. He debits the "cash" account for $500 and the "accounts receivable" account for $1,500.

The use of the double-entry system main-

JOSEPH H. SMITH

BALANCE SHEET, DECEMBER 31, 1968

ASSETS

Current Assets:

Cash		$ 7,400
Accounts Receivable		800
Sundry Materials and Supplies		1,200
Interest Receivable		100
Total Current Assets		$ 9,500

Other Assets:

Note Receivable, due Dec. 31, 1970		2,000

Fixed Assets:

Equipment	$ 4,000	
Store Building	10,000	
Land	1,000	
		15,000
Total Assets		$ 26,500

LIABILITIES AND CAPITAL

Current Liabilities:

Notes Payable		$ 2,000
Accounts Payable		1,000
Mortgage Interest Payable		100
Total Current Liabilities		$ 3,100

Long-Term Liabilities:

Mortgage Payable on Real Estate		4,000
Total Liabilities		$ 7,100

Capital—Joseph H. Smith:

		19,400
Total Liabilities and Capital		$ 26,500

tains an up-to-date record of the assets, liabilities, and owner's equity of a business. At any time an examination of the books will show just what the financial situation of a business is. An accountant periodically checks the books to see that the debit and credit entries are equal to one another. If they are not equal, it shows that an error has been made. This is called **balancing the books**. This is usually done before a statement of financial position is drawn up.

A bookkeeper often works under the direction of an accountant who has been trained in a university. While the bookkeeper's duties are mainly to keep a record of his company's business transactions, the accountant's work has a broader scope.

▶THE ACCOUNTANT AND HIS WORK

The accountant supplies the eyes and ears for business management. In order to know whether the company is making or losing money, management relies on the accountant's ability to supervise the recording of important financial information and to analyze this information.

The three main fields of accounting are public accounting, industrial accounting, and governmental accounting. Each of these fields has special characteristics.

A **public accountant** offers his services to the public rather than to one organization. His work often involves giving advice to businesses about investments or taxes; he may also help individuals in preparing their income tax returns. Most public accountants try to become C.P.A.'s (Certified Public Accountants) by fulfilling certain requirements of education and experience and passing a written examination. They do this because a C.P.A. certificate is the mark of expert competence in the accounting field. A C.P.A. certificate is required in order to certify financial statements.

The **industrial accountant** is employed by one business firm. He keeps the records and makes the reports on which the managers of a business rely in planning the operations of the business. The accounting department is, in effect, the nerve center of a company. A gain or loss in business is almost immediately revealed in the figures of the accounting department's records.

Government accountants hold important positions at all levels of federal, state, and local government. Their duties are often similar to those of public and industrial accountants.

In modern business, accounting has such a variety of duties to perform that there are accountants who specialize in certain types of jobs. **Tax accountants** keep tax records and prepare reports that must be sent to government tax agencies. They also advise management about the taxes that the company may have to pay as a result of a business transaction. Many individuals hire tax accountants to prepare their income-tax returns.

Cost accountants deal with the costs involved in all the operations of a business. These may be the cost of a product, a service, a manufacturing process, or the operating expenses of a business. The information provided by the cost accountant helps management to budget the company's money and to plan its future operations.

Much financial information can be assembled in a short time by using electronic data-processing equipment. Some accountants specialize in preparing information for recording by such equipment. As electronic equipment becomes more widely used in business, the jobs of these accountants will increase in importance.

Today a college degree in accounting has become essential for a successful accounting career. The possible rewards make it worthwhile to get the education. The accountant's familiarity with nearly all the basic operations of a business gives him a good opportunity for promotion to the management of a company. Many business executives began their careers as accountants.

EUGENE L. SWEARINGEN
President, University of Tulsa
Tulsa, Oklahoma

BOOK REPORTS AND REVIEWS

The book report or book review is one of the most frequent school assignments, from the early elementary grades through high school and college. The book reviews that appear in newspapers and other publications are very useful and are always eagerly read by people interested in books.

Book reports and book reviews have different purposes. The book report presents information, or facts, about a book. The book review goes further and reveals the way a reviewer feels about a book: he likes it, he disagrees with it, he recommends it—in other words, he judges it.

▶ BOOK REPORTS AS RECORDS

The simplest kind of book report is a record that on a given date a certain book by a certain author was read. Sometimes a pupil is given a card form on which to record the reading he does. Such a card may look something like the one at the top of the following page.

A reading record of this kind becomes more useful the longer it is kept. Both the reader

READING RECORD

Name of Pupil _____   Teacher _____

Author   Title   Date Read

_____   _____   _____

_____   _____   _____

_____   _____   _____

and his teacher can see at a glance whether the books recorded are all from one series or about one favorite subject—or whether they show a range of interests.

Some states give good-reader citations to boys and girls whose reading is extensive and varied. For instance, pupils may receive a certificate of membership in a state readers club for reading and reporting on a total of 10 books a year, divided into fiction and non-fiction such as biography, travel, and history. School librarians or teachers sponsor the club, assign and handle the reports, and determine eligibility for certificates. The report form used by one such librarian and filled out by a fifth-grade girl is shown at right.

When the reader completes his 10 books for the year, he is awarded a certificate with a red seal for his first year of membership in the club. Second-year members receive blue seals; third-year members have gold seals.

▶ **ORAL BOOK REPORTS**

One of the most important purposes of book reports is to encourage reading. Some students are inspired to read more when they hear books reviewed or reported on in class. Yet there are probably not so many effective oral book reports as there would be if high standards and efficient use of time could be combined.

Deciding what is most interesting to report, setting class standards for a report, and agreeing upon time limits for each individual report will make for more efficient use of time. Each pupil needs to make his own careful plans and practice what he is going to say, checking the time precisely. For this purpose an automatic timer of the kind used in the kitchen or for

monitoring telephone calls—or even a good alarm clock—will give the reviewer an exact idea of how much or how little he can say in his allotted 3 to 5 minutes.

Many different kinds of effective oral book-report plans have been tried in schools—some for group reports and some for solo work. Here are six different ideas for oral reports to arouse class curiosity and increase good reading.

(1) The book chat is a favorite among many classes. On a specified day boys and girls come to school prepared to take part in

Author	Pupil
Taber, Gladys	Jerre Stallcup
Title	**Teacher**
The First Book of Cats	Miss Garrish
Publisher	**Grade**
New York, Franklin Watts, Inc.	Fifth Grade
Date	**Type**
1950	Nonfiction

This book tells about different kinds of cats. My favorite kind is the Siamese. They were first raised in temples and palaces in Siam, so they're royal cats. A Siamese cat has more charm and intelligence than any other cat. Some people think they can really talk because they have several different sounds and will answer every remark made to them. Siamese kittens are white when they are born. They aren't plump, roly kittens, but are wiry and thin and extremely lively. Their bright sapphire eyes stay open more than those of a round little Persian kitten. Their faces are like pansies. Their look of vivid intelligence makes them adored by all who know them.

a small conversational group. Each person gives his own answer to a question like "What good book have you read lately?" The class sets standards for a good book chat: It gives one or two interesting parts of the book in detail—something really exciting or funny or sad; it gives some idea of what the main characters are like; it does not "tell the story"; it reveals what the reader thinks about the book; it is just long enough—3 to 5 minutes. When book-chat time comes, members of each group sit together and talk in turn about their books. Each group has a recorder to write down the time each speaker begins and ends his chat. At the end of the period, each person records his opinion of the most interesting book he has heard about. Since all the groups have their chats at the same time, the total time devoted to this project is about 20 minutes. The teacher spends a little time in each group and receives individual plans, reports, and reactions from all groups. Sometimes the whole class may later hear about the books most strongly recommended from the chat groups. This may be done by a panel made up of one person from each group. A tape recording of such a panel is good for later listening.

(2) When several boys and girls have read the same book, they can present a scene from the book in dramatic form. They must plan together, selecting the scene that best represents the book, then taking parts, learning or reading dialogue, and having a narrator give the necessary setting for the scene. The dramatization may be simple—a radio scene with sound effects but no scenery or costumes. Sometimes a group pantomimes its scene while one member reads the author's words. Puppets may be used in the dramatization. For an audience of another class or of parents, the students may agree to dress as the characters they represent.

(3) Describing the hero or heroine of a book of fiction or biography is interesting to classmates who might wish to read the book. The reviewer retells one situation that shows the character faced with an important decision. Here the goal is to whet the curiosity of the hearers, to make them read the book in order to find out what happens to the character.

(4) Reading aloud a favorite passage is sometimes a good way to attract others to read the book. Selecting a curiosity-arousing passage is important, as is good, carefully practiced oral reading.

(5) Planning a book report for a class of younger boys and girls is an activity that calls for simplifying language and choosing the really important ideas of the book to be presented.

(6) After a class has been working to increase their vocabularies, an oral book report stressing new and interesting words may be tried. Ten new words found in the book, each used in a sentence that shows its meaning and at the same time gives an idea of the book, will make a different kind of oral book report.

▶ EYE APPEAL

Interest in reading can be increased by "visuals" prepared by students. One caution to be observed is this: Avoid taking a great deal of time away from reading to devote to painting or pasting or constructing. Here are some ways to add eye appeal to the book report:

(1) Make a poster using the author's name, the book title, and a picture that suggests the story's action. Boys and girls may use many different media for posters—from crayons to cut paper.

(2) Design a book jacket with an original ad printed for the inside cover. A collection of these book jackets makes an interesting exhibit for Book Week or National Library Week.

(3) Construct a miniature stage setting or diorama. Start with a shoebox with one long side cut out and add scenery made of various materials and props and furniture either made of cardboard or borrowed from a dollhouse. Small dolls or pipe-cleaner figures can be dressed to represent story characters. This kind of project requires very careful reading of the book.

(4) Illustrate a book's historical background with a "time line." Colorful pictures showing events that occurred at dates important to the story will help the class to understand the times as well as the action. For *Johnny Tremain,* for instance, a time line showing the Boston Tea Party, the battle of Bunker Hill, and Paul Revere's ride might be helpful.

(5) For a travel book a number of postcards, pictures from travel folders, and photographs and slides of places described will make the book more real and interesting to members of the class.

(6) The reader may produce two or three original illustrations for the book. Once more it is important to read the author's descriptions carefully to be sure that the illustrations fit the scene or the characters.

(7) Sometimes a movie or television show can be suggested by mounting a series of pictures on a long strip of wrapping paper attached to rollers and pulled through a frame. This kind of project requires the teamwork of several boys and girls for dialogue and sound effects.

(8) A parade of storybook characters calls attention to favorite books for some occasion such as Book Week. Costuming may be simple —a hat, an apron, or shoes to suggest the character. Or the pupils may enjoy dressing from head to toe in the style of their selected characters.

WRITTEN BOOK REVIEWS

The book review in a magazine or newspaper is more than an announcement that an author has written a book. A good review is also a guide to the quality of the book. Often the reviewer, whose name is signed, is an expert on the subject that the new book discusses. But even when it is not signed, the book review does more than give facts—it conveys opinion as to the interest, the accuracy, and the scope of the book.

Thousands of book reviews printed annually in magazines and leading newspapers are briefly condensed in the *Book Review Digest*. There are also many reading lists and catalogs of recommended books for young people, compiled by specialists in juvenile literature. These lists and catalogs can be found in most school and public libraries. It is interesting to note that the reviews of the same book sometimes show opposite opinions.

Remember that the publisher's short description, often on the book jacket, is not a review. It is a blurb, a form of advertising. It does present some of the information a reader needs, but it never gives an unfavorable opinion. To help him to decide whether a particular book will be worth reading, the would-be reader should turn to a review in a magazine or book list he trusts.

Student book reviews are written for a much smaller audience than those of mass-circulation magazines. Sometimes only the teacher reads the review. But some classes make a collection of their own reviews of books they wish to recommend to next year's class. Here is a review prepared as part of a card file for this purpose:

Title	SC
Ghosts, Ghosts, Ghosts	(Story Collection)
Author	F
Fenner, Phyllis Reid	

Goblins, ghosts, and spirits take part in this story. They haunt houses, villages, and such. These stories, although scary, can be very funny too. They are all very good too.

Laurie Jones

The basic parts of a written book review are the same as those of a book report: the author, the title, the publisher, and information about the kind of book it is. In addition the reviewer gives his own opinion—in its simplest form a statement of why he likes or dislikes the book.

Many different kinds of short compositions can be used as book reports and are more interesting than a mere retelling of the story. Here are some suggestions:

(1) The pupil quotes from the book a sentence or two that describes a feeling he has had. Then he describes his own experience that produced the feeling.

(2) An exciting moment in the book may be described by the reader using the personal angle. Such a paper may begin, "I was there when Montezuma surrendered to Cortes." The rest of the page would contain a description of events from the pupil's point of view.

(3) In another personal kind of book report, the student deals with a dilemma, a hard but necessary choice to be made by one of the characters in a book. By describing the dilemma and explaining how he would act in a similar situation, the reader can write an interesting book theme.

(4) An imaginary letter can be written from one book character to another. Tom Sawyer might write a letter to a friend about the time he had to whitewash the fence.

(5) Real letters can be written, too. Living authors sometimes receive letters from children who have enjoyed their books. The town librarian might be sent a letter about a new book that is recommended for purchase.

VALUES OF BOOK REPORTS AND REVIEWS

Even though it may seem to be a great deal of work at the time, the experience of preparing and presenting a book review or book report—either oral or written—can be full of value. It gives the reviewer the chance to use a book subject for practice in writing or speaking—two important ways to express his ideas. The experience of reading or listening to a book report or review can suggest other books to be sampled. And the habit of reading and reacting to reading will help the student to have more things to talk about, to be a more interesting person, to give and receive more joy in living.

MARGARET WASSON
Director of Instruction
Highland Independent School District
Dallas, Texas

BOOKS

Early people wrote on rocks, tree trunks, and sand. But to make their knowledge available to others, they had to write on some-

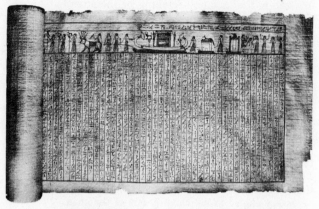

The *Milbank Papyrus*, a scroll, made in Egypt nearly 2,000 years ago, is now at the Oriental Institute, University of Chicago.

(1) The scroll, the oldest form of book. (2) The codex, a book of bound pages. (3) The accordion-folded book.

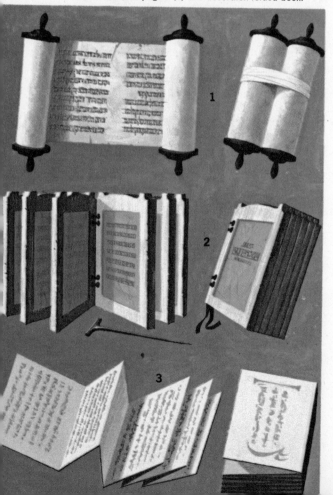

thing that could be passed from one reader to another. The people of ancient Mesopotamia wrote on tablets of wet clay. When the tablets were dried in the sun or baked in a hot oven, they became very hard. The hard tablets could then be passed around for many years.

But as people began to write more and more, the clay tablets became less suitable, for they were too heavy and bulky to be easily carried. What was needed was something light enough to be portable and yet contain many thousands of words. At the same time it had to be easy to read and had to last a long time. People needed books.

About 3500 B.C. the Egyptians developed the papyrus roll. Papyrus is a tall, grassy plant that grows along the shores of the Nile River. Our word "paper" comes from "papyrus," and the two products resemble each other. Strips of the plant were laid out lengthwise, side by side. Another row of strips was placed crosswise on top, and the two rows were glued together, soaked in water, and dried in the sun, forming cream-colored sheets of varying sizes. Then the sheets were glued end to end to make a strip 5 meters (15 feet) long, sometimes longer. Pens made of reed, a plant that resembles very thin bamboo, were used to write the text onto the side with the lengthwise strips. The book was then illustrated and rolled into a scroll.

By around 1300 B.C. the Chinese had books. Some were written on palm leaves. In others the pages were wood or bamboo strips fastened together with cord and folded accordion fashion. By the 2nd century the Chinese had invented paper. At first they used it to make scrolls, but by the 5th century they were using it for accordion-folded books similar to the older bamboo and wood books. Celebrated painters, using brushes and ink, wrote and illustrated the books, for the Chinese regarded calligraphy (elegant writing) as one of the fine arts.

In Greece the Egyptian papyrus scroll was adopted. The Greek scroll was approximately 25 centimeters (10 inches) wide and up to 11 meters (35 feet) long. Text was printed in columns separated by wide margins. Ancient writers mention illustrated scrolls, but none have been found from this pre-Christian era. For this reason we do not know the type of illustrations that were used.

THE BEGINNINGS OF MODERN BOOKS

The English and Romans wrote on wooden boards. In England boards of beechwood were used. The Anglo-Saxon word for beech tree is *boc,* and this is where our English word "book" comes from. The Romans learned how to join several boards together. They punched holes in each board and passed rings through the holes. *Codex,* meaning "tree trunk" in Latin, was the name given to the Roman books. Today "codex" is the word still technically used to mean books that are made of pages rather than rolled into scrolls.

Text was inscribed onto Roman pages in an unusual way. The boards were covered with several coats of gesso, a liquid mixture of chalk and glue. When the gesso had dried to a hard finish, a thin coat of black wax was applied. With a stylus, a pointed instrument, the writer scratched the lettering through the wax. The text was therefore white on black. The codex was used mainly as a notebook. For permanent records the Romans used the Greek-style papyrus scroll.

Pages and Binding Replace the Scroll

In the 1st century A.D. someone in Rome fastened flat sheets of papyrus between two boards, and the book as we know it was born. Roman lawyers liked this type of book because the ease of handling permitted several texts to be compared at once. The early Christians were interested in comparing various translations of a text, and they soon adopted the codex. By the 4th century the scroll had been replaced.

Skins Replace Papyrus

Writing on animal skins had been practiced in the ancient world. Some of the Dead Sea Scrolls, religious texts found in Palestine, were written on leather. In the 2nd century B.C. parchment and vellum came into practical use. Parchment is skin from sheep and goats; vellum is calfskin. The skins were washed, covered with lime to loosen the hairs, stretched, scraped, dusted with chalk, and scrubbed with pumice, a kind of stone, to make them smooth.

Although skins had been used almost everywhere, it was not until the codex came into general use that parchment and vellum were used more than papyrus. Skin was expensive, and preparation was a difficult job, but it was

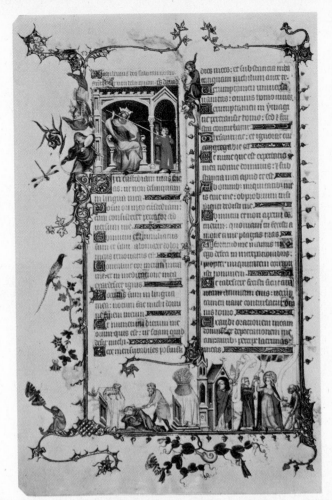

A page from the *Belleville Breviary* (1343), an illuminated manuscript in the National Library of France.

more practical than papyrus in the making of paged books. Its main advantage was the fact that it could be used on both sides. Artwork in books had always been important, but only watercolor and ink could be used on papyrus. Parchment and vellum could be painted with gouache, a thick paint made with gum, which lasts longer than watercolor or ink.

BOOKS IN CHRISTIAN EUROPE

In the 6th century in Italy, Cassiodorus, court secretary to Theodoric the Great, king of the Ostrogoths, created scriptoria (writing rooms) in which monks could copy and design manuscripts. In the same century Saint Benedict had the members of his Monte Cassino monastery copy manuscripts as part of their regular duties. Each monk copied from a book in front of him. This was the root of medieval scholarship.

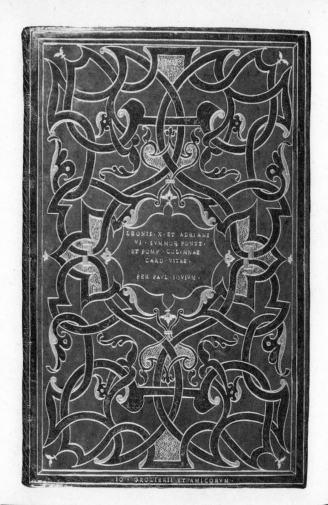

The practice of making manuscripts spread to monasteries throughout Europe. Until the 13th century nearly every book made on the continent was created by monks.

How Medieval Books Were Made

Books made by monks during the Middle Ages (the name given to the period roughly between the 5th and 15th centuries) were usually written on parchment or vellum. Four sheets of skin were put together and folded in half. This made a section of eight leaves—16 pages. The writer, called a scribe, worked on one page at a time. Either the scribe or a specialist added headings in fancy red, yellow, or blue lettering and elaborate initials for the first letters of sentences. After the accuracy of the text had been checked, the sections were sent to the binder.

Each section was sewn through the fold. Then the binder placed the sections between two wooden covers and drew the ends of the sewing cords through holes in the covers. One large piece of leather, or a sheet made from small pieces sewn together, was glued to the wooden covers so that it covered the sewn

Left, a typical Grolier binding, named for the book collector Jean Grolier de Servières (1479–1565). Below, the Gutenberg Bible, probably the first book printed by a press with movable type (1456?).

ends of the sections while it joined the two covers. Sometimes the leather was decorated with designs burned in with a hot iron. Gold, silver, jewels, and carved ivory were used to decorate important books. Books printed before 1501 are called **incunabula**, from the Latin word meaning "cradle," because this period represented the infancy of bookmaking.

Books for Knowledge and Books for Beauty

Throughout history the making of fine books has been an art requiring much skill and imagination. Many of the medieval pages made by the monks were richly decorated and are truly works of great artists.

At the start of the 13th century universities were being formed in Europe. Monasteries continued producing books, but the need for educational books was increasing rapidly. Universities hired scribes called stationers to make and keep books for use by students and teachers, who would rent their textbooks. As paper replaced parchment the cost became less, and more books were produced. Stationers began to sell their books rather than rent them.

Book manufacture became very profitable, and the publishing industry was founded. Skillfully decorated books were still being created in the monasteries. Wealthy patrons hired the finest artists of the day to illustrate their books because the hasty work of the publishers' copyists led to a lower level of beauty in books. To produce books cheaply, the manufacturers had to produce them fast. The idea that books were works of art seemed to be dead.

▶THE PRINTING PRESS

In 1456, around the start of the Renaissance, Johann Gutenberg (1400?–68) produced in Germany what is probably the earliest known book printed with movable type. It was a Bible, and Gutenberg's printing press opened the way to mass production of books and to the return of beauty in books. The most popular printing type at first looked like handwritten script. Later, new, elegant, and easy-to-read styles were created. The invention of movable type and the printing press revolutionized not only the book but the entire world. For with many books available, more and more people could learn to read.

Woodcut illustrations were practical in early printed books. This page is from a German book of 1494, the *Narrenschiff,* which in English means "Ship of Fools."

Illustrations

Medieval scribes could change colors by wiping their pens. But printed books needed a separate printing for each color. For this reason printers soon stopped trying to imitate old, colorful manuscripts. Black-and-white illustrations were most often used, although some illustrations were still colored by hand.

Woodcutting was the most suitable system of printing pictures. The drawing was carved into a block of wood, and the block was locked in the press with the text. Text and illustration could then be printed together.

The city of Florence, Italy, was a publishing center where printers achieved a harmony of illustration, type style, and size of margins. Florentine books were especially pleasing because designers stopped imitating the appearance of the ancient manuscripts and developed type styles and illustrations suited to the printing press. In Venice pocket editions were invented. In 1501 Aldus Manutius (1450–1515) began the publication of a series of small books of the Greek classics.

Layout

When books were made by hand, even rich people could afford only a few volumes, and they knew each by sight. But as libraries grew, title pages were needed. Other information, such as the name of the author, printer, bookseller, illustrator, and so on, had to be given in printed books, too. By 1550 a form of book layout had developed that, with only slight changes, is still in use today. The first page is the half title, giving a short or condensed title. Then comes the title page, which gives the whole title, the author, publisher, and date and city of publication. On the reverse side (verso) of the title page may be copyright information and the name of the printer if it differs from the publisher. Then, in order, come a page for dedication, the table of contents, illustration list, preface or introduction, text divided into chapters, notes (if they were not located at the foot of each page within the text), appendix, bibliography giving the books used for reference, and an index.

Type

Typography developed three distinct styles: black letter (or gothic), roman, and italic. Black letter resembles manuscript writing and was popular in England and Germany for a while. The Germans still use it occasionally today, but after the 17th century the English dropped it except for Bibles. Roman grew to be the most popular. It is the style in which this article is printed, *while these words are in italics.*

Binding

Until this century binding was often arranged for by the purchaser, but at the end of the 15th century a few books appeared with their bindings stamped with the printer's name. However, in most cases binding styles were designed or commissioned by collectors, and the styles bear their names. In the 16th century Thomas Mahieu and Jean Grolier de Servières (1479–1565) of France were among the most noted collectors of fine books.

The hand binding of books has changed little during the past 500 years. Each folded printed section is sewn down the fold. The sections are then sewn to tapes, which are fastened to stiff boards. Finally the cloth or leather is glued on. The cover fabric can be decorated with plain lines pressed in with a fillet (a metal wheel) and with gold or colored trimming stamped on with brass stamps.

Sometimes one or two edges of a book are coated with gold or silver, or dyed a color to match the binding. This is still done by hand by the binder. During the 17th century the Englishman Samuel Mearne produced a trick edge for his books. Tightly closed, the book appeared to have an ordinary gilded edge. But when the pages were slightly fanned, a landscape, portrait, or decorative design became visible.

▶ CHANGES IN RECENT CENTURIES

For centuries books were made much as they were in the days of Gutenberg and other pioneers of printing. Gradually, printing became faster and easier, and less work was done by hand. Today phototypesetting and offset methods are often used to print books. These processes rely on photographic film rather than metal type. Bookbinding is usually done by machine, and the wooden boards have been replaced by cardboard. Many books are issued in softbound editions, with covers of heavy, stiff paper. But in layout and general appearance, books have not changed greatly.

The 19th century brought few changes. A great amount of engraving was used, and since it is difficult to print large engravings, books became smaller. New type faces and ornaments were designed.

Cost-cutting methods of mass production reduced the artistic quality of 19th-century books. But in England the artist William Morris (1834–1896) joined with the best typographers and binders he could find and founded the Kelmscott Press. Wishing to recreate the beauty of medieval books, they published books using the best materials available. Many people feel that their books had an old-fashioned look, but their efforts inspired many others and opened the way for a new trend in book design.

RICHARD W. IRELAND
Maryland Institute College of Art

See also GRAPHIC ARTS.

BOOK DESIGN

Book design is a term for the selection and arrangement of all the materials that make up a book. "Design" is what we mean by the size, shape, color, weight—the appearance of any object. Why should a book need to be well designed? The answer is that any book, whether expertly planned or just thrown together, has its own design; but if it is well designed, it is more useful.

The designer of books is somewhat like an architect. An architect plans the size and shape and interior arrangement of a building to suit its intended use. A home must be comfortable, an office convenient, a factory efficient. He also tries to make the building good looking inside and outside, and strong and durable. And the structure must be built within a planned budget.

The book designer works toward similar goals. Each different kind of book (encyclopedia, textbook, novel, children's story, biography, poetry collection) gives him special problems that he must study and solve. His purpose is to make the novel pleasant to read and appropriate looking in relation to its contents. The textbook should present facts and ideas in a clear and orderly way. The encyclopedia must be a convenient source of information that is easily located and logically arranged.

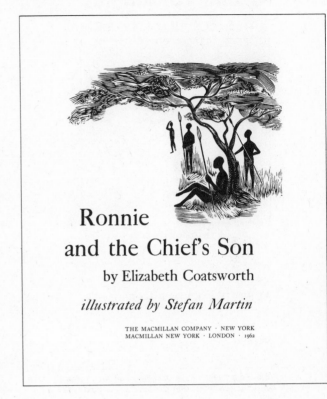

Ronnie
and the Chief's Son

by Elizabeth Coatsworth

illustrated by Stefan Martin

THE MACMILLAN COMPANY · NEW YORK
MACMILLAN NEW YORK · LONDON · 1962

Today well-designed books are available to more people than ever before. In this children's book, designed by David Paul and Ursula Suess, the picture on the title page (*right*) is from a double-page illustration (*below*).

They were of all colors, and the shapes of their horns were never alike, though all were enormous. Some rose up into the air, curved like lyres. Some spread sideways into a scimitar sweep like the horns of wild buffalo, and some grew forward in upturned spikes.

Gunnar's Daughter

BY SIGRID UNDSET

TRANSLATED FROM THE NORWEGIAN BY
ARTHUR G. CHATER

1936
ALFRED A. KNOPF *NEW YORK*

Title page from a book designed and illustrated by W. A. Dwiggins, an influential 20th-century typographer.

▶ WHAT DOES A BOOK DESIGNER DO?

The chief duty of the book designer is to aid the reader to understand the author's ideas. The designer studies the text to learn what the author is saying and how he is trying to communicate with the reader. He estimates the length of the text and considers what size, shape, thickness, and weight will be appropriate and convenient for the book. Except in the design of expensive limited editions, economy and efficient use of machinery for printing and binding must also be taken into account.

The book designer is sometimes called a typographer, meaning a specialist in the choice and arrangement of type matter. He has made a study of the many styles of type, called typefaces, each of which has slight but important differences. To use these typefaces to best advantage, he should know their origins and history. In designing each book, he selects the typeface and type size he considers most appropriate. He makes layouts (as the architect makes drawings for blueprints) to indicate every detail of how the book shall be made. The size of the type is very important in making a book easy to read. Equally important is the length of the line of type, the space between the words, the space between the lines, and the margins around the outside of the type. Too much or too little margin space will tire the reader's eyes, but just the right amount of white space in each place will make reading easier. The easier the reading the more clearly the reader understands what the author has to say. Typographers sometimes refer to the white space on a printed page as "air," so we can say that each book design must provide just the right amount of "air conditioning."

▶ MODERN BOOK DESIGN

The roots of modern book design were planted in England toward the end of the 19th century. There a rebirth of interest in fine printing was taking place. Some of the great printer-designers of the time were William Morris (Kelmscott Press), St. John Hornby (Ashendene Press), and Emery Walker, who with T. J. Cobden-Sanderson produced the masterpieces of the Doves Press.

These men and their work aroused great interest in fine craftsmanship and the appreciation of beautiful books in the United States. As a result, some American printers, publishers, and illustrators undertook the production of better-planned and better-looking books than the United States had so far produced. A movement developed that is sometimes referred to as the American revival of printing. Among the memorable names of the movement is that of Theodore L. De Vinne (1828–1914) of New York, who was notable for the fine quality of his printing rather than the design of his books. There was D. B. Updike (1860–1941), who became America's greatest scholar-printer to date. He designed and printed the books that have given his Merrymount Press in Boston an important place in American printing because of both their typographic design and their influence on others. Updike wrote the classic history of printing types in Western Europe, Great Britain, and the Americas. Both Updike and, later, Bruce Rogers worked for the Riverside Press

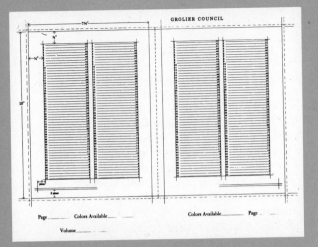

Every book presents special problems to the book designer. Consider, for example, this encyclopedia. First the size of the book, the style of type, and the general format (overall appearance) of the set is decided by the designer. Then pages are assigned to each article. Only after the text is written and the illustrations obtained can the designer and his staff of artists plan the appearance of the pages.

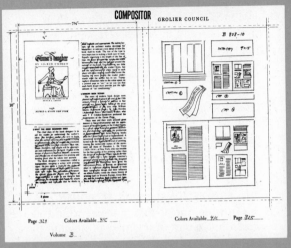

The article is laid out on a board marked with the column widths and margin spaces of the book page. All illustrations and text must be fitted within these lines.

Text is printed in widths of one book column on long sheets called galleys.

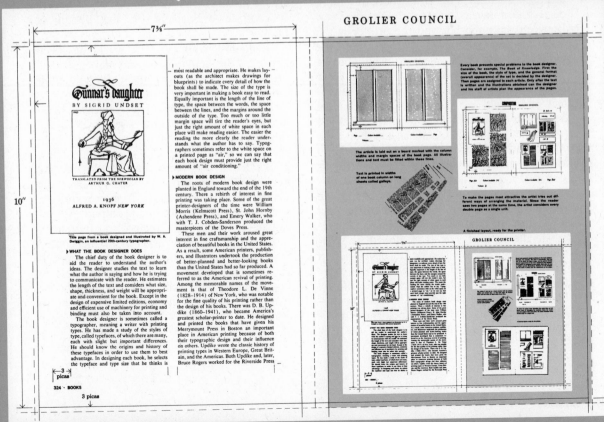

To make the pages most attractive the artist tries out different ways of arranging the material. Since the reader sees two pages at the same time, the artist considers every double page as a single unit.

A finished layout, ready for the printer.

of the Boston publishing house Houghton Mifflin and Company. This publisher played an important part in the revival of printing.

Another outstanding figure in American graphic arts during the first third of the 20th century was Frederic W. Goudy (1865–1947). Goudy was less a printer than a designer of printing types. He designed more than 100 different typefaces for various type foundries and for special uses. Some of his best are called Goudy Old Style, Goudy Modern, Goudy Text, Hadriano, and Deepdene. Goudy's importance was not only in type design; he became a symbol of careful work. His attention to detail influenced many American printers toward higher standards of craftsmanship.

▶ THE PROFESSIONAL BOOK DESIGNER

Growing out of this movement and at the same time a part of it, a new profession developed—that of the book designer separate from the printer. It developed as a result of a new awareness of design as a skill different from printing. This separate profession has developed because of the increasing complexities of 20th-century printing and publishing. The publisher of books is most concerned with authors, editorial matters, and sales. The printer has had to concentrate more and more on technical developments and on manpower. Between the publisher and the printer is the book designer. He must be aware of both the publisher's and the printer's problems, but he is not exclusively concerned with either. Here again we see the similarity between the architect and book designer. The architect must be aware of the builder's problems, but his profession is not the same as the builder's.

The father of book design as a profession separate from printing was Bruce Rogers (1870–1957). Trained as a commercial artist, Rogers had great skill in the use of type. He studied the great printing masters of the past with such understanding that he could re-create the style of Tory (developed in 16th-century France), of Baskerville (developed in 18th-century England), or of almost any other type appropriate to the subject matter of any book. His creative power kept him from copying former masters; he absorbed their traditions and reformed the spirit of the past for modern readers.

Among Rogers' outstanding books were the Bible, the *Odyssey,* a new edition of the writings of James Boswell, books by Joseph Conrad, and a complete set of Shakespeare.

Bruce Rogers and W. A. Dwiggins (1880–1956) were two distinguished American designers of books who worked professionally for various publishers and printers and were not exclusively attached to any one company.

Dwiggins concerned himself less with the past than did Rogers. He had a lively sense of humor and experimented a great deal. Dwiggins' fresh, modern design—like all good book design—accepted the discipline of type and gave full importance to the ideas of the author and the needs of the reader. His best work included editions of Balzac and Rabelais, Robert Louis Stevenson, H. L. Mencken, and Thomas Mann. Dwiggins also wrote books and articles on advertising design, postage stamp and money design, and related subjects.

▶ BOOK DESIGN TODAY

The great variety in appearance of books today is largely due to the fact that there are different kinds of book designers with many different ideas. Some are still printers as well as designers. Others are principally advertising artists who design books only occasionally. By far the largest group consists of those who concentrate exclusively on the design of books.

Book design all over the world has been aided by the activities of national and local organizations. These organizations hold exhibitions, discussions, and trips to inspect new technical developments. The American Institute of Graphic Arts holds a series of annual exhibitions. In one of these the institute chooses and displays 50 outstanding new books from the standpoint of design and quality. The exhibition is sent all over the United States and to many foreign countries. In this way other nations can compare American book design with their own. In return, other nations send exhibitions to the United States. By making these constant comparisons, book designers everywhere are able to improve their own skills and to design books that will be more attractive and useful to readers.

M. B. GLICK
Graphic arts consultant

BOOKBINDING

In the days when books were copied out laboriously by hand, they were rare and prized possessions. The covers were often decorated with gold and jewels, and the few people who could afford books cared as much about the handsome bindings as the contents.

These decorative covers hid a painstaking binding process. The first step was to tie the pages together with cords. Our word "bookbinding" is derived from this process. The cords were then drawn through holes in a wooden case. A leather covering was glued onto the case and trimmed and decorated with skill and patience.

Some books today are still bound in leather by hand, but in order to turn out large quantities of books at a price the ordinary reader can afford, bookbinding has developed into a highly mechanized industry.

Let us follow a book through the binding process. The pages of a book come off the press on large sheets of paper. From 4 to 64 pages may be printed on each side of the sheets, but the usual number is 16 or 32. The pages do not follow each other in order. Instead, they are arranged so that they will fall into the proper order when the sheet is folded. This arrangement is called an **imposition**.

The flat sheets are fed into the folding machine. This machine has a menacing appearance, with a large knife that looks ready to slice the paper in half. Actually the knife is so dull that it will not cut the paper. Instead, when it falls, it creases the paper in the middle and pushes it down between two rollers that squeeze it flat. Inside the machine a series of hidden knives and rollers repeat the process until the sheet is folded into pages.

Each folded section is called a **signature,** and a book is usually made up of groups of 16- or 32-page signatures. Putting the signatures together in the proper numerical order to make a complete book is called **gathering.** The signatures are sometimes gathered by hand and sometimes by machine.

The book then goes to a sewing machine, where its back (or spine) is sewn together. There are three methods of sewing a book.

Books with only one signature are often **saddle sewn**—that is, they are opened out on a peaked frame called a saddle and stitched through the center from back to front. Open a saddle-sewn book to its center pages and you can see the line of stitching. Saddle sewing is not very strong because no reinforcing glue is used on the spine and the pages easily work loose from the single line of stitching. These books open flat.

Smyth sewing is commonly used for larger books. A series of signatures, perhaps in groups of 32 pages, are first individually saddle sewn. Then they are placed next to each other, and several needles working together sew across the back of the book, attaching the first signature to the second and so on. A Smyth-sewn book will open flat like a saddle-sewn book, but a Smyth-sewn book is stronger because it has a strip of cloth glued across the backs of the signatures.

Side sewing gives the strongest binding. The book is left closed, and a line of stitching is run along the back fold from top to bottom. The stitching cannot be seen and will not pull loose. Most textbooks are side sewn.

After sewing comes the important step of **smashing.** No matter which method is used, the sewing makes the signatures bulge slightly along the rear edge. If this were not corrected, the finished book would be unsightly and hard to handle. In smashing, the books are squeezed in a powerful compressor. A fraction of a second is long enough to flatten them out.

Smashing is usually followed by **gluing off.** A mechanical roller and brush force glue between the rear edges of the signatures for a short distance—usually about $\frac{3}{16}$ inch. By gluing the signatures together in this manner, the strength of the book is increased.

Some books, such as paperbacks, have no sewing at all. In this method, which is called **perfect binding,** the folded rear edge of each signature is trimmed off and the pages are glued directly to the cover. As used in paperbacks and other books that are not designed to be kept permanently, perfect binding is not very durable. However, telephone directories and large mail-order catalogs, which must be able to stand heavy use, are also perfect bound.

Pamphlets and magazines are usually fastened with wire staples.

If the book has been sewn, it goes to another knife machine called a **trimmer,** which

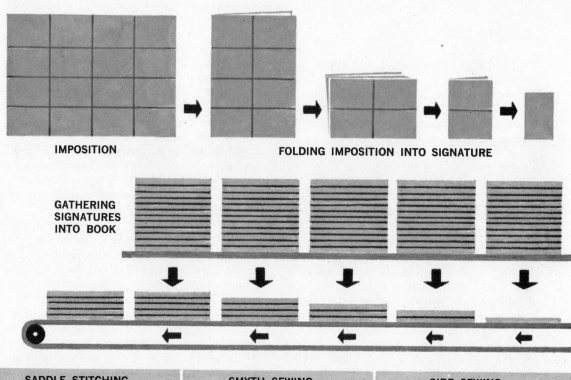

IMPOSITION

FOLDING IMPOSITION INTO SIGNATURE

GATHERING SIGNATURES INTO BOOK

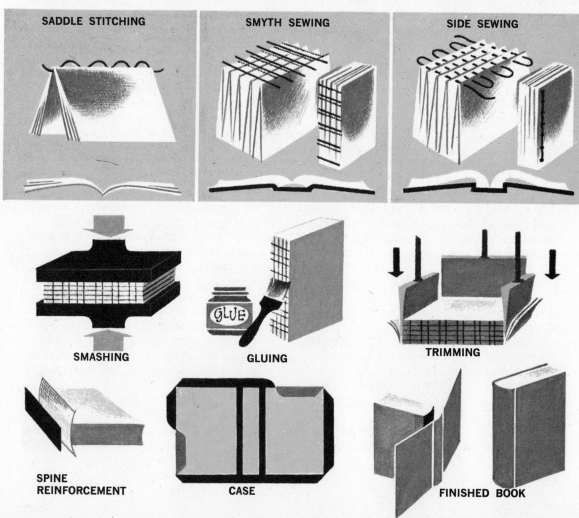

SADDLE STITCHING

SMYTH SEWING

SIDE SEWING

SMASHING

GLUING

TRIMMING

SPINE REINFORCEMENT

CASE

FINISHED BOOK

trims all the edges so that they are even, and all pages are cut.

Books are constantly being opened and shut, left open, and moved from place to place. A book must have a flexible spine to withstand this hard treatment. To make sure that the spine is flexible, the book is put through a process called **rounding and backing.** Rollers push the outside signatures forward to form a hollow while a heavy bar crushes and slightly flattens the backs of all the signatures.

A lining machine further strengthens the spine by adding layers of glue and a material similar to cheesecloth, called **crash.** A strip of strong brown paper called kraft paper is sometimes added for extra durability.

Covers for most books are made of starch-impregnated cloth. Since this type of cloth becomes dirty easily, textbooks and other reference works are often covered with plastic-impregnated cloth that can withstand wear and tear and can be sponged clean when it is soiled. Strong paper is often used, too. Some covers are simple, with only the author's name, the title, and the publisher's name stamped on them. Others have more elaborate designs and even colored illustrations to make the book more attractive.

How can hardbound books be kept from coming apart?

Often the backs of books crack, and the pages fall out. This happens because the threads that hold the pages together have snapped under the strain of opening and shutting the book. Books can be made to last much longer by the following simple steps: Open the cover of the book, and run your hand along the place inside where the cover joins the pages (front and back). Then leaf through the book, smoothing down the pages. This loosens the threads, and they will give as the pages are turned.

Two pieces of heavy cardboardlike material called **binder's board** act as backing to stiffen the cover. To hold the book together, workers in the bindery glue the first and last pages (called **end sheets**) to the cover. For extra strength more strips of crash cloth are glued along the hinges (the places where the cover meets the pages).

After their covers have been attached, books are ready for the next stage on their way to the reader: the publisher's warehouse, where orders for books are filled.

MARGARET SAUL
Education Research Director, R. R. Bowker Co.

See also BOOKS: FROM AUTHOR TO LIBRARY; PRINTING; PUBLISHING.

BOOKS: FROM AUTHOR TO LIBRARY

In each of the books you read, there are really two stories. There is the one told by the type and pictures, and there is the story behind the story—that of the book itself. The new book that appears one day on the library shelf already has quite a life story. It has been months and sometimes years in the making.

Fifty or more people may have a part in this story, but it usually begins with just one, the author. The author is the person who has the idea for the book. More important, the author is the person who puts the idea into words and sentences, paragraphs and pages. This is fun, but it is not easy. And it takes a lot of time.

It took Jeanne Bendick 6 weeks to finish her manuscript for *The First Book of Time.* Not all of this time was spent in writing. First came the research. She knew before beginning that she wanted to write a book about what time means.

Soon after she began her research, Mrs. Bendick found this quote: "What is time? If nobody asks me, I know, but if I try to explain it, plainly I know not." Saint Augustine said this hundreds of years ago, but it is still the way most people feel about time. Mrs. Bendick made a note of this quote so she could use it in her book. It would, she thought, help to point up why time is such an interesting subject to think about. She needed more than one quote, however. She needed all kinds of facts and interesting information about such things as clocks, calendars, tides, and light-years. Most of this research she could do in books. But experiments were also part of her research, since she wanted to be able to explain how to build simple clocks.

Jeanne Bendick at work on *The First Book of Time.*

Mrs. Bendick was writing a factual book, but authors writing fiction often do research as well, to add color and reality to their descriptions. To do their research, authors must on occasion travel to special libraries, museums, or historical places.

After weeks or possibly months of research, the author collects and sorts his pages and pages of notes. Often, like Mrs. Bendick, the writer makes a rough outline of the whole book.

Then comes the time to sit down at the typewriter and begin to write. Sometimes the words come easily, sometimes they come slowly, sometimes they don't come at all. Often a part that sounds fine one day seems confusing or uneven the next day. It must be rewritten. Sentences, paragraphs, and whole sections may be rewritten several times before they are just as the author wants them. When Mrs. Bendick finds something hard to explain, she might read that part to her children or their friends to be sure that it is clear. Slowly, chapter by chapter, the book grows, until one day the writing, the reading, and the rewriting is completed, and the manuscript is finished. With a sigh of relief the author slips the manuscript into an envelope and sends it by registered mail to her editor at the publishing house.

▶THE EDITOR

Jeanne Bendick has done many books. She knew before she began writing *The First Book of Time* that her editor was interested in publishing it. Editors are pleased to have books by their established authors, but they are always on the lookout for good manuscripts by new authors. Each year 500 or more manuscripts are submitted to a publishing house. One of the jobs of editors and their staffs is to read and consider these. What a thrill it is to find a good one that everybody agrees should be published!

The editor read Mrs. Bendick's finished manuscript several times. As she did so she thought about how the story was told. Were the facts organized in a clear and interesting way? The second time she went through the manuscript, the editor stopped at a few spots that seemed confusing or difficult. In the margin she penciled questions or suggestions. Later Mrs. Bendick came in and talked with the editor about these suggestions. Then, tucking the manuscript under her arm, she headed for home. Mrs. Bendick needed the manuscript for two reasons. One, she had to make a few changes. Two, she had to plan the illustrations. For, unlike most authors, Jeanne Bendick is also an illustrator of books.

▶THE ILLUSTRATOR

At home Mrs. Bendick put away her typewriter and pulled out her pens and brushes. Before she began the actual drawings for the book, she had to plan carefully what she wanted to show and where. To do this, she made a **dummy book,** exactly the size and length her book was to be. After figuring the number of lines of type that would be on each page, she sketched in her ideas for the drawings. The dummy went back to the editor with the revised manuscript. Here and there the editor suggested possible changes.

Each of the illustrations was to be in two colors, black and either blue or gold. The sketches in the dummy were in color, but the final drawings were done all in black. Furthermore, each drawing was done in two pieces, called **separations.** To do this, Mrs. Bendick first drew everything that would be printed in black on one piece of paper. Then over this she placed another piece of paper. By working on a piece of frosted glass over a bright light, she could see the black drawing through the second sheet. Very carefully she painted in the spots that were going to print in blue. But she painted these spots in black ink, not blue. Once the light was turned off, this second drawing looked like pieces of a jigsaw puzzle.

Every drawing that is going to be printed in more than one color must be separated. For most children's books the artist does it. If the artist does not do it, the printer must do the separating with photography. He photographs the colored drawing several times, each time using a filter that allows the camera to record just one of the colors. This is done because the colors are printed one at a time. Before the drawings are finally finished, the type has been set, and the lines for each page can be carefully pasted on the drawing that will print in black.

▶ THE DESIGNER, THE COPY EDITOR, AND THE PRODUCTION MANAGER

Mrs. Bendick prefers to be the one to paste the type with her drawings. But in many cases it is the designer or even the printer who does this. The designer is the person in the publishing house who is responsible for planning just how a book will look. He decides what size and shape the book will be. He decides such things as how many lines there will be on a page, how wide the margins will be, and where the page numbers will go. He also picks the typeface a book is to have. Type comes in many different styles, called faces, and it is important to pick one that fits the subject of the book and also the kinds of readers who will be using it. The designer works closely with both the editor and the illustrator, for it is important that the book look just right.

The designer must also draw up plans for the front matter. These are the pages that come in the front of the book, before the story begins. There may be many pages in the front matter, but the first important one is the title page, the book's formal introduction. Here are the full title, plus the name of the author and the artist, the publisher, and the city of publication. The year of publication is on the next page, called the copyright page. This page carries a short statement saying that no one may copy anything out of the book for publication without permission. Next comes the page listing the table of contents.

After Mrs. Bendick returned her revised manuscript, the editor looked at it once more.

Then the manuscript was ready for copy editing. Some editors do their own copy editing; others pass it on to a copy editor. Copy editors make certain that the manuscript's punctuation and spelling are correct and consistent. They also read carefully to see if the author and editor have overlooked any mistakes in fact. Frequently authors and editors are so deeply involved in a manuscript that some details escape their attention. Copy editing is another step toward exactness in style and content.

Copy edited and approved by the editor, Mrs. Bendick's manuscript went to the designer. The designer carefully drew up his plans and marked the manuscript to show the printer what he wanted done.

Next the manuscript went to the production manager. Most publishing houses do not print and bind their own books. Instead they hire other specialized companies to do this. It is the production manager who makes all these arrangements and sees that everything runs smoothly. From this point on, the manuscript begins to change shape in a most dramatic way. On the next two pages you will see how *The First Book of Time* looked as it turned from a manuscript into a printed book. It took about 2½ months for these changes.

▶ NEWS OF THE BOOK

Publicity, promotion, and advertising are the three means a publishing house has to let people know about new books. Once *The First Book of Time* was bound, there were several thousand copies of it neatly stacked in a warehouse, waiting to be purchased and read. Before this could happen people had to hear about the book, and stores and libraries had to order it.

Even before the book was printed, the publicity and promotion manager began to send news of it to book reviewers and book sellers. He prepared a special place for it in the children's book catalog, which the publishing house sends out twice a year. He also made plans to have the book exhibited along with other new books at special conventions and in traveling exhibits.

Later, copies of the book were sent to book reviewers who might perhaps mention it in a newspaper or magazine article or on radio or television. Organizations that make booklists

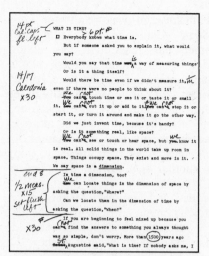

On the page of notes above is the quotation from Saint Augustine. In the margins of the manuscript are the editor's notes and the designer's instructions to the printer.

Here is Mrs. Bendick's plan for two pages. She has sketched her ideas for the drawings that should go on these pages. From one set of galleys she cut the text that belongs here and pasted it in place.

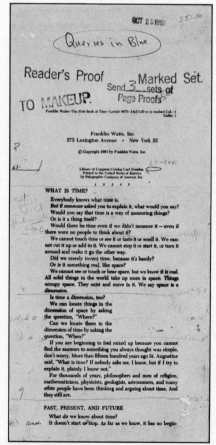

Once the type is set, it is printed on long sheets of paper. These are called galley proofs, and only a few sets are printed. These go to the editor and the author for any small last-minute changes or corrections.

Below is the final two-part drawing for the same pages. In the top drawing is everything that will print in black. In the bottom one is everything that will print in blue. The two parts are called separations.

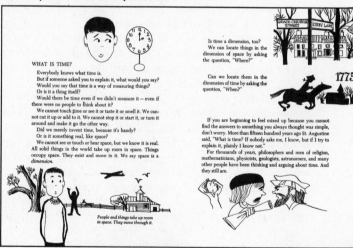

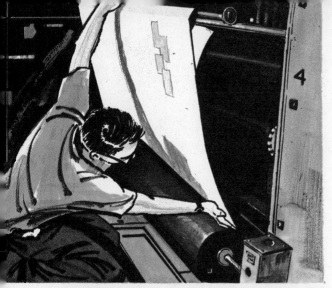

To print this book by offset lithography, the drawings and type are reproduced on large metal plates. There is one plate for each color. Here a printer fastens a plate onto the printing press.

Next the sections are sewn together. This book is sewn along the side with what is called sidestitching. At the back is the cover, ready to be glued on. It is made of cloth glued over boards made of fibers.

The press can print 2,700 sheets every hour. Part of a sheet is shown above. The pages on it are arranged in a special pattern, so that a binding machine can fold the large sheets into three sections. Each section has 24 pages.

The cover is now glued on. With this step the finished book is ready to make a journey to bookstores, libraries, and homes, where it will meet its readers.

The book reaches one of its destinations—the children's room of a public library.

also received copies. Advertisements for the new book were prepared.

For the catalog, the ads, and also the book jacket, special "copy" about the book was written. Writing such copy takes a special skill. The copy writer must choose his words and put them together in such an intriguing way that people will not only read all the copy but also the book.

Most books are published either in spring or fall. Mrs. Bendick's book was published in the spring. Several months before it was finished, the salesmen of the publishing house gathered at the publisher's offices in New York to hear about the coming books. At this meeting the editor introduced each of the new books, telling what it was going to be about and showing some of the drawings for it. These are an important few minutes in the life of a book.

From this sales conference until the next one in early summer, the salesmen traveled around the country calling on bookstores, wholesalers, and sometimes libraries. Some libraries buy books directly from the publishing houses. Many others buy them through a wholesaler who handles the books of many different publishing houses.

Orders for *The First Book of Time* had come in even before it was finished. As soon

as the warehouse had copies of the book, they filled these orders so that they might reach their destination close to the publication date. The publication date is the book's official birthday, and it usually comes several weeks after the book is bound.

Perhaps one carton of new books went to a school library, where the librarian pulled out a copy of *The First Book of Time* and put it on the worktable. Here it was checked off the list, given a book pocket, a card, and a Dewey decimal number that makes it easy to find on the library shelf. Before too long it was making its debut in a "New Books" display.

▶A THIRD STORY

Along with the story in the book and the story about the book, there is perhaps a third story. That is the story the book's card would tell if it could talk. Who are the people who borrowed this book? Did they all read it? Did they like it? Perhaps they didn't. Perhaps it was one of their special favorites. Hopefully this third story—of the completed book's life—is a long one. If a great many readers get something from the book, then all the time, thought, and care that go into its making are more than worthwhile.

JOANNA FOSTER
Author, *Pages, Pictures, and Print*

BOONE, DANIEL (1734–1820)

Daniel Boone has become a legend as America's greatest pioneer. He was a dead shot with a rifle and a skillful hunter who could glide through the forests as swiftly and silently as an Indian. Some men said Boone could even think like an Indian.

Boone was born on November 2, 1734, at Oley, a frontier settlement in Pennsylvania. Indians roamed the nearby woods. Daniel knew that if he were caught by Indians on the warpath against intruders on their land, he would either be tomahawked or taken prisoner. So the woods became Daniel's school. He never learned how to spell correctly. But he did learn how to walk through the forest without making a sound and how to tell if a noise was a deer—or an Indian. At the age of 12, Daniel owned his first rifle, and he was soon hunting game for the dinner table.

When Daniel was 16, the Boones decided that Pennsylvania was becoming too crowded. They set out by wagon and in 1751 settled in North Carolina. The French and Indian War broke out in 1754, and a year later Daniel joined General Edward Braddock's expedition against the French. The British soldiers, unused to Indian fighting, were ambushed and slaughtered. Boone and a hunter named John Finley escaped into the woods. Finley told Daniel about a land west of the Appalachian Mountains that the Indians called Kentucky. It was a land shrouded in mystery—only a few hunters and trappers had ever been there. The forests were thick with turkey, deer, and bear, and buffalo thundered across the prairies. Finley's stories inspired Daniel to go to Kentucky.

But first Daniel returned home and married 17-year-old Rebecca Bryan, whose family lived near the Boones. For the next 10 years they rarely lived in one place for long. Daniel was often away on hunts. He would return with deerskins and beaver pelts, which he sold to provide for his growing family.

One winter day John Finley arrived at the Boone's cabin still talking about Kentucky. In 1769 Boone, Finley, and five other men set out across the mountains. For 2 years Boone hunted and trapped and explored Kentucky. When he returned home, he gathered several families to establish a settlement there. On the way they were attacked by Indians. Daniel's son James and several others were killed, and the settlers turned back. However, Boone was determined to settle Kentucky. He cleared the Wilderness Road into the territory and built a fort, Boonesborough. Then he returned and led another group across the mountains. Boone's wife and daughter were among the first women settlers in Kentucky.

Once, while Boone was away from Boonesborough, he was captured by the Shawnees. Their chief, Blackfish, was proud at having caught the famous Boone, and he adopted him as his son. For several months Boone lived with the Indians. One day he overheard them planning a raid on Boonesborough. He escaped and reached Boonesborough just in time to warn the settlers.

In later years the land that Boone had explored was taken from him because he had no legal title to it. About 1799 Boone turned westward again and moved to Missouri. There he lived peacefully for the rest of his life. He died on September 26, 1820, at the age of 86.

Reviewed by DANIEL ROSELLE
State University College (Fredonia, New York)

BORNEO

Borneo is a giant among the islands of the world. Only Greenland and New Guinea are larger. Borneo is big enough to hold all of the states of Texas, New Hampshire, and Vermont. The island has an area of about 743,000 square kilometers (287,000 square miles).

Borneo straddles the equator at the western end of the Pacific Ocean. Its neighbors to the northeast are the Philippine Islands. To the west, across the South China Sea, are Vietnam and the narrow finger of the Malay Peninsula. To the south and southwest are the large Indonesian islands of Java and Sumatra. To the east are Celebes; the fabled spice islands, the Moluccas; and New Guinea.

Politically Borneo is made up of the territories of three countries. Sabah (formerly North Borneo) and Sarawak are states of Malaysia. Brunei is a tiny sultanate (ruled by a sultan). The third political unit of Borneo is known as Kalimantan and is part of Indonesia.

▶ **THE LAND**

Most of this huge island is mountainous. Many areas are 1,800 to 2,400 meters (6,000 to 8,000 feet) above sea level. Mount Kinabalu, Borneo's highest peak, towers to 4,100 meters (13,455 feet). The island's interior is a complex mass of mountain ranges. Travel is difficult, and large areas are still unmapped and unexplored.

Vast areas of swamp and tidal flats greet travelers when they approach the coast of Borneo. There are no good deepwater harbors, and all the chief ports are located upstream. Captains of ships coming to these ports must carefully seek out deepwater channels through the shallow river mouths, or their ships will run aground in mud.

Climate

Borneo's location on the equator is an important clue to its climate. Its equatorial location means that Borneo is warm all year round. Except in the cooler highlands, the temperature seldom falls below 21°C (70°F). But like most tropical lands, Borneo rarely has a temperature above 36°C (96°F).

Borneo has two seasons—a wet and a less wet season. The wet season, when the heaviest rains fall, lasts from November to May. During the remainder of the year, rainfall is not quite so heavy. Rainfall varies from place to place, depending chiefly on elevation and exposure to rain-bearing winds. Most places receive 2,500 to 5,000 millimeters (100 to 200 inches) of rain a year.

Plants and Animals

Much of the island is covered with a dense tropical forest. Along some coastal areas are tangled mangrove swamps. Sago and coconut palms grow in other sections. Valuable teak and other tropical hardwood trees grow in the forests of the interior. But because cutting and moving the logs out of the rugged mountains is difficult and costly, the lumbering industry is small and undeveloped.

Vegetables are sold in open-air markets in Borneo.

Borneo is famous for the variety of its wild animals. One is a giant ape whose name, orangutan, comes from a Malay word that means "jungle man." Borneo is also the only home of the proboscis monkey, a large, long-nosed monkey that lives in the coastal swamps. Many other species of monkeys live in the dense forests of Borneo, as do the gibbons, smallest of the apes.

Other animals of Borneo include the Asiatic two-horned rhinoceros, the elephant, the wild ox, the leopard, and the tiny honey bear. Crocodiles lurk in the rivers and coastal swamps; and there are many different kinds of snakes, including the huge python and the deadly king cobra. The magnificent peacock and more than 600 other kinds of birds add their brilliant colors to Borneo's forests.

▶ THE PEOPLE

More than 6,000,000 people live in Borneo. But there is plenty of room for everyone. This makes Borneo unique among the densely populated lands of Asia. Banjermasin, with over 280,000 people, is the largest city.

Two kinds of people are native to Borneo—Malays and Dayak. The Malays live near the coastal regions. Here they have come in contact with Europeans and with Asian people who have migrated to Borneo from China, Indonesia, India, and Malaya. The Malays of Borneo have been greatly influenced by these people and have adopted many of their customs. Many Malays are able to speak Chinese and English as well as Malay.

Their chief occupations are fishing and working in rice fields. Some have become shopkeepers, and others work on rubber plantations, in petroleum fields, and for the government.

Most of Borneo's schools are in the coastal regions. The only university on the island is at Banjermasin, in Kalimantan. Pupils attend schools where they are taught in one of the island's three major languages—Malay, Chinese, or English. In the remote parts of the island, children receive their lessons by means of radio broadcasts.

Some children wear their native loincloths or half-sarongs to school, but most boys and girls now wear more citified clothes. The boys wear khaki shorts and shirts, and the girls wear high-necked, Chinese-style sarongs.

BORNEO

The Dayak are very different from the Malays. They are primitive people who live in the interior of Borneo. They belong to many different tribal groups and speak many different languages. Unlike the Malays, the Dayak have little contact with the outside world and follow the old ways of their tribes.

As many as 50 families live together in one long house that may be 275 meters (300 yards) in length. The house is usually located on a riverbank. It is raised about 4.5 meters (15 feet) off the ground by hardwood stilts. The house is easy to defend and high enough so that an enemy cannot jab a spear through its bamboo floor. Each family has its own room. A porch runs the entire length of the long house. Here the members of the tribe gather to talk.

Dayak men use blowguns and poison darts to hunt for birds and wild animals. Dayak women spend their days tending rice, yams, and sugarcane, planted in tiny forest clearings near the long house. The cleared land can be cultivated only for 3 or 4 years. Tropical rains wash away important minerals. When crops begin to do poorly, the Dayak slash and burn the trees in another part of the forest and make another clearing.

The Dayak are highly superstitious and practice various forms of spirit worship. Until

Water buffalo are used as a means of transportation.

Mats of pandanus fiber have a ready market in cities.

Goods and sometimes children are transported in baskets on the island of Borneo.

Modern apartments in Kota Kinabalu, northern Borneo.

recently some were headhunters. Today the government has strict laws against headhunting, and this practice is a thing of the past.

▶ HISTORY AND GOVERNMENT

More than 2,000 years ago, traders from India visited the coast of southern Borneo. In the 12th and 13th centuries came the Chinese, who settled on the west coast. Arab missionaries came shortly before 1600 and brought the Muslim faith to Borneo. Europeans began coming to Borneo in the 17th century. Borneo was then ruled by several different sultans. Dutch, Portuguese, and Spanish traders persuaded the sultans to give up parts of their territories. The Dutch were the most successful, and by 1800 they controlled three fourths of the island. The British gained control of the northwestern quarter of Borneo.

Japanese troops captured and occupied most of the coastal areas of Borneo during World War II. After the war Sarawak and North Borneo (now Sabah) became protectorates of Britain. Dutch Borneo (now Kalimantan), which had been a colony of the Netherlands, became part of the Republic of Indonesia in 1949. The Sultanate of Brunei is an independent state, but it has a special relationship with Britain, which is responsible for its foreign affairs. In 1963 Sabah and Sarawak joined Singapore and the Federation of Malaya to form Malaysia. Singapore seceded from Malaysia in 1965 and is now an independent country.

PHILLIP BACON
Teachers College, Columbia University

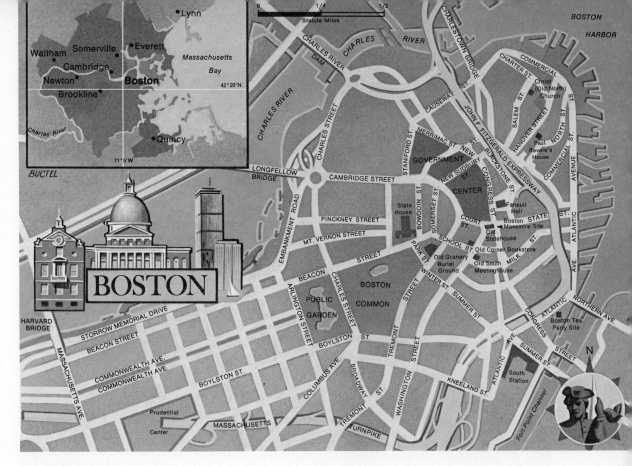

BOSTON

Wandering through the streets of downtown Boston, one can understand why this city—the capital of Massachusetts—has been nicknamed the Cradle of Liberty. Along a marked path called the Freedom Trail, visitors come upon landmarks of the Revolutionary War and the early history of the United States. Members of the Massachusetts Bay Colony founded Boston in 1630 on a peninsula where the Charles River flows into a sheltered bay of the Atlantic Ocean. They had crossed that ocean from England in search of religious freedom. Today Boston is the home of more than 625,000 people and the center of a metropolitan area of more than 3,000,000.

The wealth of historic places in Boston sparks a visitor's imagination. It was at the Old South Meetinghouse that the Boston Tea Party of 1773 was planned. The Boston Massacre (1770) took place opposite the Old Statehouse. A visit to Faneuil Hall brings to mind the fiery speeches of colonists who wanted their independence. Looking up at the tower of Christ (Old North) Church, one almost expects to see the lantern signal that started Paul Revere on his famous ride. Paul Revere's grave is in the Old Granary Burial Ground, along with those of Samuel Adams, John Hancock, and other patriots. Nearby is Boston Common. Benjamin Franklin used this park as a pasture for his cow.

During the 19th century Boston was a leader in religion, literature, and social reform. Christian Science was established at the Mother Church in Boston, and King's Chapel was the birthplace of American Unitarianism. William Lloyd Garrison made his first antislavery speech in 1829 at the Park Street Church. And the Old Corner Bookstore was the meeting place for Henry Wadsworth Longfellow, Ralph Waldo Emerson, and other writers.

Today a modern City Hall looks out on a city that is a busy seaport as well as a center of industry, commerce, and finance. Boston's major industries include publishing, food processing, and the manufacture of electronics equipment, leather goods, textiles, and machinery.

At the same time, Boston maintains its position of leadership in education and culture.

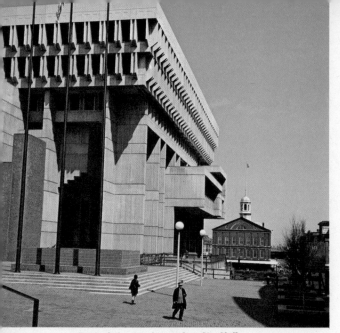
Boston's impressive modern City Hall.

Students still attend the famous Boston Public Latin School, which five signers of the Declaration of Independence attended. It was founded in 1635 and is one of the oldest free public schools in the United States. Harvard University, in nearby Cambridge, was founded in 1636. Other institutions of higher education in the Boston area are the Massachusetts Institute of Technology, Tufts University, Boston University, Boston College, Brandeis University, Wellesley College, and Simmons College.

Boston provides many opportunities for enjoyment of museum and library collections, music, and the theater. Plays that are bound for Broadway in New York City often try out in Boston. The Boston Symphony Orchestra is world-famous. The spring season brings concerts by the Boston "Pops" Orchestra. Sports are not neglected. The city has professional teams in baseball, hockey, and basketball. To many New Englanders, Boston still seems to deserve another of its old nicknames —the Hub of the Universe.

Reviewed by RICHARD O. RIESS
Salem State College

See also MASSACHUSETTS.

BOSTON MASSACRE. See REVOLUTIONARY WAR.
BOSTON TEA PARTY. See REVOLUTIONARY WAR.
BOTANICAL GARDENS. See ZOOS AND BOTANICAL GARDENS.

BOTANY

Have you ever wondered what's inside a flower? Or what the veins in a leaf are for? Or why a plant will not grow without water? If you have, you have asked the same sorts of questions as those asked by a botanist. A botanist is a scientist whose field is botany— the study of plants.

Plants form the basis of all life on earth. Only plants can capture the energy of the sun and use it—in a process called photosynthesis —to make food. Animals cannot do this and so must depend on plants for food. No animal life could exist on earth without plants.

This essential world of plants is a large and varied one. There are over 300,000 different kinds of plants. They range in size from tiny diatoms, rarely over 0.5 millimeter ($\frac{1}{50}$ inch) long, to the giant redwoods, the largest living things on earth. Some plants, such as carrots, are rooted in soil. Others—orchids, for example—grow in air. Some plants reproduce from seeds, others from underground stems, and others in still different ways.

The subject matter of botany includes every aspect of plant life. A botanist may study the plant itself—its structure and the function of its various parts. Other botanists may be interested in the development of plants on earth—when they first appeared and how they changed over long periods of time.

Some botanists study the plant in relation to its environment—the living and nonliving things that surround it. They may, for example, try to determine how soil and water affect the growth and reproduction of plants.

A botanist may specialize in one area of botany, but whatever his or her specialty, the work can benefit people. Thus, botanists may discover plants that yield important new medicines or improve crops by developing new and better varieties of plants.

See also ALGAE; BACTERIA; CACTUS; FERNS, MOSSES, AND LICHENS; FLOWERS AND SEEDS; FOSSILS; FUNGI; GENETICS; GRASSES; KINGDOMS OF LIVING THINGS; LEAVES; LIFE; PHOTOSYNTHESIS; PLANT DEFENSES; PLANT ENEMIES; PLANT PESTS; PLANTS; PLANTS, FOOD; PLANTS, MEDICINAL; PLANTS, ODD AND INTERESTING; PLANTS, POISONOUS; REPRODUCTION; TREES; TREES (Tree Rings); WEEDS.

BOTSWANA

BOTSWANA

Botswana was formerly the British protectorate of Bechuanaland. On September 30, 1966, it was granted independence and became the Republic of Botswana.

▶ PEOPLE

There are about 630,000 people in Botswana. A great majority are Botswanas (or Bechuanas), a Negroid people belonging to the Bantu group. Some 30,000 Bushmen inhabit the Kalahari Desert. About 20 percent of the adult male Botswanas work in the mines of South Africa, Zambia, and Rhodesia.

About 50 percent of the school-age children attend primary school. Enrollment in secondary schools increases each year as the school system expands. Botswana has two vocational schools and a teacher training college. A university in Roma, Lesotho, is shared by Botswana, Swaziland, and Lesotho.

Most Botswana families raise cattle. The government controls the raising of cattle in order to prevent the outbreak of sleeping sickness, caused by the tsetse fly. The Botswana farmers grow kaffir corn, maize, and sorghum. Where irrigation is possible, some wheat and citrus fruits are also grown. Gold, asbestos, and manganese are mined.

▶ THE LAND

Botswana has an area of 231,804 square miles—slightly larger than France. Most of Botswana is a vast plateau with an average elevation of about 3,300 feet. A large valley running from north to south cuts through the center. The elevation increases toward the southeast and reaches about 5,000 feet in the hills bordering the Transvaal province of South Africa. In the northwest corner the Okavango River overflows and creates a number of huge swamps. In the far north are the grasslands of the Zambezi basin. Southern Botswana is part of the Kalahari.

Botswana receives an average of 18 inches of rain a year, mostly from October to April. The land varies from arid to semidesert, except for the Okavango Swamps, where the tsetse fly and mosquito are health problems.

A railroad connecting Botswana's neighbors South Africa and Rhodesia runs along Botswana's eastern border.

Cities and Towns

The new capital of Botswana is Gaborone, in the southeast. The most important towns are Lobatse and Francistown. They are both located in the east, along the railroad. There is a gold mine near Francistown.

▶ HISTORY AND GOVERNMENT

Very little is known of the region before the 19th century, when Robert Moffat of the London Missionary Society first set up a mission. During the next 50 years, tribal warfare and raids by the Boers from South Africa disturbed the peace of the area.

In 1885 the chiefs of Bechuanaland requested British protection against the Boers. The whole territory was then proclaimed a British protectorate. During World War I and World War II the people of Bechuanaland demonstrated their loyalty to the British by actively participating in the wars.

In 1964 the British Government accepted Bechuanaland's proposals for independence as a basis for revision of Bechuanaland's constitution. In September, 1966, the protectorate became the sovereign state of Botswana and a member of the Commonwealth.

The head of state in Botswana is the president. He is assisted by a cabinet. The legislative body is the National Assembly, which acts after consultation with a council of chiefs. Botswana is the 119th member of the United Nations.

HUGH BROOKS
St. John's University (New York)

BOTTICELLI, SANDRO (1444?–1510)

The poetic paintings of the Renaissance master known as Botticelli often describe the beginnings of things. With grace and delicacy Botticelli depicted not just love but the birth of the love goddess, not simply faith but the birth of Christ, not only the beauty of nature but the blooming of spring. He turned for subject matter to history and religion, to poetry and legend.

Botticelli's life is somewhat like a legend. Little about it can be proved since much of what we know has come down through the ages by word of mouth. He was born in Florence and died there when he was about 65. His real name was Alessandro Filipepi, but he took the name Botticelli from his older brother, whose nickname was *Botticello,* meaning "little barrel." By 1460 he was probably studying with the well-known artist Fra Lippo Lippi. By the time he was 25, Botticelli had already become teacher to Lippi's son and was considered one of the best painters in Florence.

Among his many admirers was Pope Sixtus IV. In 1481 the Pope invited Botticelli to Rome to help decorate the Sistine Chapel, which had recently been completed. Botticelli's contributions to the chapel include wall paintings illustrating the life of Moses.

The Medici family, rulers of Florence, were the greatest supporters of artists and scholars in the world at the time. Botticelli received support and encouragement from them and may even have lived in the Medici palace. The scholars who surrounded the Medicis were studying the ancient Greek philosopher Plato. They were trying to unite the ideas of Christianity with Plato's. Botticelli's work shows that he was interested in the scholars' studies. The spiritual quality of his religious paintings can also be seen in his portrayals of the gods and heroes of ancient Greece.

In his later years Botticelli was influenced by the fanatic monk Savonarola, who preached against the vanity and extravagance of the Florentines. Botticelli became very religious, painted only religious subjects, and may even have destroyed some of his nonreligious pictures.

Botticelli's paintings are famous for their dancing lines, flowing forms, and delicate details, admirably represented in the painting *Primavera.* His golden-haired Venus, goddess of love, has the faraway look in her eyes of one lost in daydreams, which appears so often in Botticelli's work.

Primavera ("Spring") by Sandro Botticelli, painted around 1478. This famous picture, on a huge, rectangular wooden panel, hangs in the Uffizi Gallery, Florence.

BOTTLES AND BOTTLING

Bottles are made in an endless variety of forms—tall, squat, round, and slender. They range in size from tiny perfume bottles that hold a fraction of an ounce to large industrial bottles that hold many gallons. There are useful bottles and decorative bottles.

Ancient man's first containers for liquids were crude sacks made of animal skins. Next came bottles of pottery, stone, and metal. Glass bottles came into use very slowly over a span of many hundreds of years.

The Egyptians had known how to make glass since before 3000 B.C. Around 1500 B.C. they began to make bottles of glass. They formed molten glass around a core of sand or clay. When the object had been fashioned and decorated, the core was scraped out. Making bottles this way was difficult and expensive. Glass bottles were a luxury item for 1,500 years, until the Romans developed cheaper and quicker methods of production. Skilled Roman workmen blew the glass into bubble shapes with blowpipes. A speedier method was to blow the bottle inside a mold, which produced bottles of uniform size and shape.

After the fall of the Roman Empire in the 5th century A.D., glass bottles again became a scarce and sought-after luxury for people in Europe, to be displayed like a prized painting.

Particularly prized were the beautifully decorated colored glass bottles produced by Venetian glass blowers around the 15th century. These bottles were sold at exorbitant prices throughout Europe. The Venetian glassmakers were kept under strict guard in order that others might not learn the secrets of Venetian glassmaking. In spite of this, the Venetians

Why do bottles have different shapes?

Individual bottles have different shapes for different reasons. Some bottles are shaped in odd ways for advertising purposes. The manufacturer wants people to remember his bottle and be able to pick it out among all the others in the store. Other bottles are designed from a practical standpoint. They may have very broad bases to keep from being toppled over and long narrow necks to make for easy pouring. Many bottles are also so beautifully designed that they may be used solely as ornaments.

were unable to preserve their trade secrets. European rulers succeeded in luring Venetian glassmen to settle in their countries and teach their skills to native glass blowers.

Ordinary bottles were green. This was caused by traces of impurities, such as iron oxide, in the minerals from which the glass was made. Bottle-green glass remained the least expensive and therefore the most common type of glass for centuries. The green color ranged from dark olive-amber to aquamarine, depending on the impurities present. The dark color of the glass was actually an advantage, for it protected wine and other liquids from the action of light.

Even though clear glass can be made inexpensively today, many bottles are still purposely made dark to protect their contents from the action of light.

Some of our most familiar glass containers date from the 19th century. The first baby bottle was patented in 1841; John L. Mason put his famous Mason jar on the market in 1858; and Dr. Hervey D. Thatcher perfected the milk bottle in the mid-1880's.

▶ BOTTLE MANUFACTURING

Although bottles became more of an everyday item in the 18th century, they were still made by hand by the same methods the Romans used nearly 2,000 years before. Even with the help of molds, the most an experienced glass blower and his crew of assistants could turn out was about 20 dozen bottles a day.

Glass manufacturers experimented with various types of mechanical equipment. In 1865 the pressing and blowing machine was invented. In this machine a plunger forces the molten glass against a mold. Then compressed air blows the glass into its final shape. At first the blowing had to be done by human lung power. Later, mechanical air compressors took over the job of blowing.

The pressing and blowing machine is good only for making wide-mouthed containers. This is because the neck must be wide enough for the plunger to fit into. By varying the size of the mold and plunger, the machine can turn out products ranging from sturdy canning jars to tiny medicine vials.

The first fully successful automatic blowing machine was the Owens Bottle Machine, invented in 1903 by Michael J. Owens of Toledo, Ohio. The machine sucks the exact amount of molten glass needed for each bottle into the molds, where puffs of air enlarge, elongate, and partially shape the glass into bottle form. Another set of molds completes the bottle.

The Owens machine was the first step toward real progress in the manufacture of glass containers since the invention of the blowpipe. Once it had proved successful, many factories adopted similar "iron glass blowers," and today blowing machines make a tremendous variety of products including jelly glasses, fruit jars, and soft-drink bottles.

Plastic bottles and cardboard containers have replaced glass bottles for many uses because they are not breakable and can be easily disposed of.

▶ BOTTLING

After bottles have been made, they must be filled and prepared for shipment to stores. This task, called bottling, involves a number of steps. These are washing, filling, capping, labeling, and packing. Today almost all the work is done by machines. Conveyor belts move the bottles from one machine to another in an orderly parade, like soldiers marching on a drill field.

The bottles must first be cleaned so that the liquid poured into them will stay pure. This is especially important with returnable glass containers that are used over and over again. Some soft-drink, milk, and beer bottles are re-used as many as 30 times before they are broken or lost. Before being washed, returned bottles are examined, and any that are chipped or cracked are discarded.

There are two main types of bottle-washing machines. The **hydro washer** cleans bottles by spraying them inside and out with hot water and cleaning solutions. In **soaker washers** bottles are submerged in tanks of cleaning solution, scrubbed with automatic brushes, and rinsed. The hot water and chemicals used for cleaning kill all germs and leave the bottles sterile.

After being washed, the bottles move along a conveyor belt to the filling machine. They travel around the circular machine, each stopping below a filling nozzle. Small lifting plat-

Conveyors carry bottles to be filled and capped by machine.

forms raise the bottles and press them tightly against the nozzles. The soft drink, milk, or other beverage pours in. Then the bottles are lowered and moved on to the capping machine.

Before William Painter invented the ordinary soft-drink bottle cap in 1891, sealing a bottle was a difficult job. There were more than a thousand different kinds of bottle stoppers: springs, levers, and wires to keep the bottle sealed. Painter's invention, simple and inexpensive to make, replaced most of these gadgets. His design of a round, crimped piece of metal with a cork disc inside has remained basically unchanged to this day. The crown cork, as Painter called it, does two important jobs. It seals the bottle tightly and keeps the pouring mouth from getting dirty. Nowadays bottle caps are often lined with soft, flexible plastic instead of cork.

The capping machine presses a cap onto the mouth of each bottle, sealing the cork snugly. Then the machine squeezes the sides of the cap together. This presses the metal skirt around the bottle's locking ring, the groove around the top of the neck. Not all bottles are capped this way. Some have screw caps. Some have cardboard discs or corks inserted in the neck.

New bottles or old ones that have been washed need to have labels glued onto them. This job is done by a labeling machine that has sets of automatic "fingers." The fingers pick up a label, put glue on it, and press it onto the correct place on the bottle.

After being washed, filled, capped, and labeled, bottles are ready to be packed for shipment to stores. Packing is done by machines that drop the bottles into cases or cartons, seal the boxes, and send them on their way to the shipping platforms.

ANNE HUETHER
Curator of Education
The Corning Museum of Glass

See also FOOD PRESERVATION AND PROCESSING; GLASS.

BOW AND ARROW. See ARCHERY.

Antonio, became a Mexican citizen, and married the richest girl in town, the daughter of the Texas vice-governor. In a short time, through clever land dealings, Bowie owned almost 400,00 hectares (1,000,000 acres). Once he led a search for the fabled San Saba mines, said to contain Spanish gold. On the way Bowie and 10 men had to fight off an attack by more than 160 Indians. No one knows whether Bowie ever found the San Saba treasure. To this day people are still looking for the lost mine.

About 1832 Bowie joined other Americans in Texas to fight for independence from Mexico. His courage and ability soon made him a colonel in the Texas army. In 1836 the Mexican general Santa Anna with an army of several thousand besieged the Alamo in San Antonio. There were fewer than 200 Texans to defend the mission-fortress. Although sick with pneumonia, Bowie killed several Mexicans before he was fatally wounded. He died on March 6, 1836. All the other defenders of the Alamo lost their lives as well.

Bowie's favorite weapon was a hunting knife with a long blade slightly curved at the end. The blade and handle were so well balanced that the knife could be thrown with great accuracy. Whether or not Bowie actually invented the knife, it was named after him because he used it with such skill.

Reviewed by DANIEL ROSELLE
State University College (Fredonia, New York)

BOWIE, JAMES (1799?–1836)

James Bowie was a famous American adventurer and a leader in the Texas revolt against Mexico. He was born about 1799 (some historians say 1796) in Burke County, Georgia, but grew up in the backwoods of Louisiana, where his parents moved when he was a baby.

All sorts of stories have been told about young Bowie. It was said that he roped and rode alligators and speared wild cattle. There are tales of fights in which Bowie killed men with thrusts of his long knife, and of the $65,000 Bowie made slave trading with the pirate Jean Laffite. How much truth there is in these stories it is impossible to say.

In 1828 Bowie traveled to Texas, which then belonged to Mexico. He settled in San

What is the origin of the bowie knife?

Tradition tells us the bowie knife was invented because frontier hero James Bowie lost his grip and cut his hand on a butcher knife while fighting Indians. Bowie decided the old-style knife needed a metal guard, or crosspiece, between the blade and the handle, to keep the hand from slipping to the blade. About 1825 a blacksmith named James Black is said to have added the extra piece (the "bolster") and sharpened the blade to razor keenness. Another legend credits John Sowell of Gonzales, Texas, with making the first bowie knife.

Frontiersmen nicknamed the knife the Arkansas Toothpick. They used it to defend their lives from enemies and to kill animals in close fighting. They skinned buffaloes with it and used it to cut up the meat for food. It was an all-purpose tool. About 100 years later commandos were using a similar knife in World War II.

BOWLING

The game of bowling has been played for more than 7,000 years. Objects similar to our modern tenpins were discovered in the grave of an Egyptian whose burial has been placed at 5200 B.C.

Just how the sport came to be called bowling is not known. The word "bowl" may have come from the Saxon *bolla* and the Danish *bolle,* meaning "bubble," and through usage, "round."

In its earliest form bowling was a crude recreation and was played with primitive equipment in any space that provided suitable conditions.

Today we have automatic pinsetters and smooth, well-balanced balls and pins. We bowl in air-conditioned centers amid attractive surroundings. Bowling is very popular with children and women, as well as with men. In the United States, where there are over 26,000,000 bowlers, it ranks as the number one participant sport.

▶ **EQUIPMENT FOR THE GAME**

The basic idea of bowling is to roll a ball down a wooden lane and knock down the 10 pins set in a triangle. The American Bowling Congress sets the following standards for the equipment used in bowling tenpins.

The length of a bowling lane is 60 feet from the foul line to the head pin. The width of a lane is 42 inches, and the normal approach is 15 feet from the rear edge to the foul line. Tenpins are 15 inches in height and must weigh not less than 2 pounds 14 ounces. The distance between pins set for play is 12 inches from center to center. A bowling ball cannot weigh more than 16 pounds or less than 9. Its circumference must be 27 inches.

The correct attire for bowling is important. Since the sport involves activity of the entire

A three-finger ball is recommended for beginners. Grip is very important. If span is too wide, it strains the hand and reduces ball control. If too narrow, it cramps the hand and tires it, causing loss of control. The best grip test is to try the ball for a couple of frames to be certain it feels comfortable.

TOO WIDE   TOO NARROW   JUST RIGHT

BOWLING ALLEY

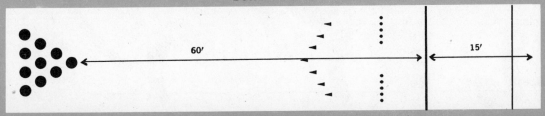

60'   15'

FOUR-STEP APPROACH

(A) Stance—shoulders square to the pins. Hold ball just above waistline. (B) First step—take small step forward with right foot. Push ball forward in smooth motion. (C) Second step—this is slightly longer than the first step. The ball should be swinging back past right leg. (D) Third step—this is a full step. The ball is at the height of its backswing. (E) Fourth step—this step, on the left foot, brings you to the foul line in a graceful glide. Get the ball well out over the foul line. Then release the ball—don't throw it. (F) Follow-through is necessary for good bowling form.

body, your clothes can affect your scoring. Clothing should allow freedom of movement of arms, shoulders, and legs.

Special bowling shoes should be worn on the lanes. One of these shoes has a leather sole and one a rubber sole. The leather sole allows you to make the necessary slide on the last step of your approach. The rubber sole is used as a brake to control the slide. The shoes can be rented for a nominal fee or purchased at a local bowling center. The use of a bowling ball is included in the price of the game.

▶ USE A BALL THAT FITS

A three-finger ball, preferred by most bowlers, is especially recommended for beginners. Bowling balls come in weights of 9 to 16 pounds. Use a ball weight with the "right feel." Never bowl a ball that is too heavy, for it will tend to make you drop your shoulder and thus put you off balance before you release the ball. Start with a lightweight ball and gradually work up to the heavier weights.

For ball grip, study the diagram.

▶ THE FOUR-STEP APPROACH

The most popular style of bowling is called the four-step approach. Although five-step and three-step approaches are used, the

(1) The most natural and safest delivery is the straight ball. Thumb is on top and fingers underneath. (2) The hook ball is delivered with a twist to the left by the wrist. Thumb comes out of the ball first and fingers apply spin with a sharp lift of the ball. (3) The curve is thrown like a hook with less twist.

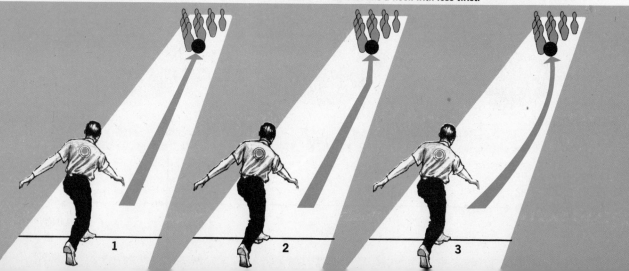

1   2   3

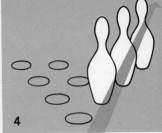

1 and 2 — SPARES COVERED BY THE STRIKE BALL

3 and 4 — CONVERTING RIGHT-HAND SPARES

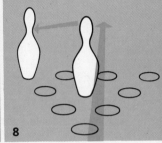

5 and 6 — CONVERTING LEFT-HAND SPARES

7 and 8 — CONVERTING SPLITS

four-step has proved to be the best for 90 per-cent of the bowlers.

Champions agree that every bowler eventu-ally develops his or her own style, but for beginners the illustrated way to learn the four-step delivery is strongly recommended.

To determine where you should begin your approach, go to the foul line and place your left foot so that the toes are from 2 to 6 inches on the near side of the line. Then turn around, take one long step, one full step, one half step, and one small step. Again turn around and face the pins. This position indicates approxi-mately where you should start your four-step delivery. If you are left-handed, start with your right foot on the near side of the line.

▶ **TIMING**

To excel in bowling, as in other sports, you must develop good timing. For example, in baseball a batter will hit the ball far only if his bat connects with the pitched ball at exactly the right moment. If his timing is off, he will miss the ball or merely pop it to the infield.

In bowling, timing is equally important. It consists of the ability to co-ordinate the for-ward motion of your body with the pendulum swing of your arm. Develop your timing and your bowling scores should improve.

To understand better the value of timing, study some fast-action-sequence photographs of champion bowlers. Be sure to note the smooth, rhythmic flow of their delivery as ball and body work together.

▶ **GOING AFTER SPARES**

In each turn you are allowed to roll your ball at the pins twice if necessary. If you knock down all the pins on your first try, it is scored as a strike. If you knock down all 10 pins with two balls, it is scored as a spare. Spares are important in bowling, both to be-ginners and to expert bowlers. They can make the difference between a 190 and a 90 bowling average.

Spares fall into four categories: right-side spares; left-side spares; spares that can be converted with your strike ball; and splits, the most difficult spares. Study the illustrations that show how to convert spares—that is, to knock down all pins that remain standing after your first bowl. In spare situations where your strike-ball delivery is required, you should take the position you normally apply to your first ball. Splits are very difficult, but with the proper determination and concentration, and confidence in your bowling style, you will find yourself converting more spares than you are missing.

▶ **HOW TO SCORE**

A game consists of 10 frames. Each bowler rolls two balls per frame unless he strikes, which makes a second ball unnecessary. The symbols used for scoring are X, strike; /, spare; —, possible spare not converted; O, split that is difficult to convert; and Ø, split that has been converted.

For a strike a player receives 10 pins plus a pinfall on the next two balls. A spare entitles a player to 10 plus a pinfall on the next ball. Now let's score a game you might bowl.

In the first frame you spare.

1	2	3	4	5	6	7	8	9	10
/									

In the second frame you roll your first ball into the pocket for a strike. This gives you 20 in the first (a spare in the first plus a pinfall on the next ball).

1	2	3	4	5	6	7	8	9	10
/	X								
20									

In the third frame you split, but you bring one in with your second ball for a pinfall of 9. Score in the second is 39 (10 from a strike in the second plus a pinfall of the next two balls, added to the score in the first frame). Add your 9 for a third-frame total of 48.

1	2	3	4	5	6	7	8	9	10
/	X	o							
20	39	48							

In the fourth frame you strike.

1	2	3	4	5	6	7	8	9	10
/	X	o	X						
20	39	48							

In the fifth frame you strike (no score is recorded; a pinfall of one more ball is due you).

1	2	3	4	5	6	7	8	9	10
/	X	o	X	X					
20	39	48							

In the sixth frame you bring in 8 on your first ball, then convert for your spare. The score, which is 48 from the third, plus 10 for a strike in the fourth, plus 10 for a strike in the fifth, plus 8 for a pinfall of the first ball in the sixth, totals 76 in the fourth. Score in the fifth frame, which is 10, plus a pinfall from two balls in the sixth, which was 10, makes the total score 76 plus 20, which is 96.

1	2	3	4	5	6	7	8	9	10
/	X	o	X	X	/				
20	39	48	76	96					

In the seventh frame you bring in 8 on your first ball, then miss two standing pins on your second ball. Score 96, plus 10, plus 8 pins on first ball, gives 114 in the sixth, plus 8, gives 122 in the seventh frame.

1	2	3	4	5	6	7	8	9	10
/	X	o	X	X	/	–			
20	39	48	76	96	114	122			

In the eighth frame you spare.

1	2	3	4	5	6	7	8	9	10
/	X	o	X	X	/	–	/		
20	39	48	76	96	114	122			

In the ninth frame you bring in 7 on your first ball, then convert. Score 122, plus 10, plus 7, is 139 in the eighth.

1	2	3	4	5	6	7	8	9	10
/	X	o	X	X	/	–	/	/	
20	39	48	76	96	114	122	139		

In the tenth frame you strike for 10 pins for your spare and a total of 159 in the ninth. Striking in the tenth frame allows you two more balls, of which you make good use and spare. Your total for the game is now 179 (159 from the ninth, plus 10 for your strike, plus 10 for your extra 2 balls).

1	2	3	4	5	6	7	8	9	10
/	X	o	X	X	/	–	/	/	X /
20	39	48	76	96	114	122	139	159	179

▶ **BOWLING ORGANIZATIONS**

The American Bowling Congress (ABC) of Milwaukee, Wisconsin, is the official organization for adult male bowlers. Standards laid down by the ABC govern all sanctioned bowling in North America. The Woman's International Bowling Congress (Columbus, Ohio) is the counterpart of the ABC for the adult women bowlers. The American Junior Bowling Congress (Chicago, Illinois) is under the guidance of the ABC. It regulates bantam and teen-age bowling in the United States. All three organizations give special awards.

▶ **OTHER BOWLING GAMES**

Germans of the Middle Ages played a game in which balls were rolled to knock over wooden clubs, or *kegels*. The players were called *keglers*. From Germany this game spread to other parts of Europe. Varying numbers of pins were used, but the most common game in Germany and Holland was (as it is today) ninepins. The pins were set up to form a diamond.

Early Dutch settlers in New York played ninepins. This is the game that made the sound of thunder Rip Van Winkle heard in the famous story by Washington Irving. By about 1840 ninepin bowling had become such a popular gambling game that some states banned it. In order to get around the laws against ninepins, a tenth pin was added.

Tenpins is the standard bowling game in the United States. It is good recreation for young people and adults alike.

Fivepins is a favorite form of bowling in Canada. The pins, 12⅜ inches tall, are arranged in a V. Balls are 5 inches in diameter and weigh 3½ pounds. A bowler rolls three balls in each of the 10 frames.

Another bowling game, popular in New England and eastern Canada, is candlepins. It is played with long, tapering pins.

Skittles is a game sometimes confused with bowling. It is like ninepins, but played on a smaller scale and with disks instead of balls. The disks are tossed or slid toward the pins.

▶ DUCKPINS

Duckpins is a variation of bowling in which smaller pins and smaller balls are used. It is popular in the eastern part of the United States.

The game is played on a regulation bowling alley, but the ball used in duckpins is no more than 5 inches in diameter and weighs 3 pounds 12 ounces. It is completely smooth, without grooves for the player's fingers. The 10 bottle-shaped pins are 9¹³⁄₃₂ inches high. Some duckpins have a band of rubber around the middle, but the game using all-wooden pins is considered the real test of skill.

Each player bowls three balls in a frame, rather than two. Even though there are three chances to score in each frame, the total score is usually lower than that in regular bowling because the ball is so much smaller and lighter.

In duckpins you hold the ball comfortably and firmly, but not very tightly. You must be able to let it go easily. The ball is rolled straight off the tips of the fingers, without any twisting motion. After the ball has been bowled, the back of your hand should be turned down.

▶ BOWLS, OR LAWN BOWLING

The game called bowls is the most popular form of bowling in Britain, Australia, New Zealand, and some other Commonwealth lands. In the United States and Canada, where it is also widely played, it is called lawn bowling, or bowling on the green, to avoid confusion with the tenpin game.

Bowls is usually played on a smooth, level grass court. The object is to roll balls, which are themselves called bowls, as close as possible to the jack, a white ball 2½ inches in diameter. Bowls are made of a composition material or lignum vitae and weigh not more than 3½ pounds each. They are about 5 inches in diameter. One side of a bowl bulges less than the other, giving it what is called bias. This causes the bowl to lean to one side and curve as it loses rolling speed. A player can roll his bowl so that it will approach the jack in a curve from either side.

In singles or doubles games each player uses four bowls; in triples, three bowls. When full teams of four play, each person rolls two bowls. To start, the first player rolls the jack from a rubber mat at one end of the rink, a division of the green on which the game is played, at least 75 feet toward the other end. In team play two opposing players, called the leads, roll their bowls alternately. Then two other opposing players bowl. Last to bowl are the skips (captains) of the teams, who have been directing the play of their teammates. If a bowl touches the jack, it is marked with chalk to show that it is still alive, even if it goes into the ditch at the end of the rink. Any other bowl going into the ditch is out of play.

When all players have bowled, an end (inning) is over. The team that then has a bowl closest to the jack scores a point for every bowl that it has closer to the jack than the nearest of the opponents' bowls. (Each set of bowls has a special marking so they can be identified.) The players then bowl toward the opposite end of the rink, the side that scored last bowling first. A game consists of 21 points in singles, or in team play a number of ends (usually 21) agreed on at the start.

Similar games were played with balls of stone in very early times. One called "bowles" was popular in England in the 13th century or earlier. The bowls used were generally of wood, and by the 1500's they were made with bias. From England the game spread to Scotland and to the British colonies.

Bowls was played in Jamestown as early as 1611. It was also enjoyed by early New Yorkers in a small area at the lower end of Manhattan that is still called Bowling Green. Lawn bowling has grown in popularity in the United States in the present century. The American Lawn Bowling Association was formed in 1938.

LOU VRANA
Brunswick Corporation

BOXER REBELLION

In 1900 a group of Chinese staged a violent uprising against foreigners and Chinese Christians. These men were members of a patriotic organization that called itself the Righteous Harmony Fists. Newspapermen shortened the name to "Boxers" and called their uprising the "Boxer Rebellion."

Trouble began in 1895, when Japan quickly defeated China in the Sino-Japanese War. As a result, China had to give up its domination of its neighbor Korea. China was also forced to give Japan the large island of Formosa, the Pescadores Islands, and the Liaotung Peninsula in Manchuria—although European powers forced Japan to return this last territory.

The humiliation of defeat at the hands of Japan was bad enough. But in addition China had to suffer new inroads by the European powers. England, France, Russia, and Germany had been extending their power in China for some time. After the Sino-Japanese War, they became greedier than ever. Seeking to control vast portions of China's mines, railways, and trade, the European nations staked out economic claims in 13 of the 18 Chinese provinces and in the three provinces of Manchuria. Foreigners now traded and traveled freely, exempt from Chinese laws. Missionaries went throughout the land, winning people away from their ancient faiths. To many Chinese it seemed that their whole nation would be lost if they did not find a way of limiting the influence of foreigners.

In these circumstances it was easy to blame foreigners for many of China's major problems—food shortages, floods, dry spells. When the cry went up to "kill the foreign devils," the fanatical Boxers were ready to do it.

The Boxers were convinced by their leaders that they could not be harmed. They wore special sashes, carried special paper charms, repeated special prayers, and performed ritual exercises. They were sure these would protect them from the bullets of the "foreign devils." In demonstrations Boxer leaders stood up before a hail of bullets to prove no hurt could come to them. They did not tell their followers that the bullets were blanks.

In the early months of 1900 the Boxers gradually worked themselves up into a frenzy. The Chinese Government chose not to suppress their activity—partly because Boxers had worked their way into many government offices. The old empress dowager particularly approved of the Boxers. She had always resented the attempts of foreigners to control her country and limit her own power.

Finally, in June, 1900, the Boxers' reckless campaign of burning, killing, and looting reached its high point. Scores of missionaries and thousands of Chinese Christians were killed, mainly in North China. In Peking the Boxers laid siege to the walled legation section, where the representatives of foreign governments lived.

▶ DIPLOMATS FIGHT BACK

Up to this time the diplomats and their families did not believe that the Boxers would dare to attack them. But once the attack came, they fought back bravely. Joined by missionaries from the area and some Chinese Christians under their care, they set up barricades and gathered a supply of weapons, mainly hunting rifles and shotguns. They stored their food in a central place and rationed it out daily. Water supplies were closely guarded. Once the fighting began there would be little chance of getting water through the barricades.

For 55 days a force of about 500 men from an American missionary group and guards from the British, Russian, American, French, Japanese, and German legations held off a mob of at least 20,000 Chinese Boxers. During the siege over 200 of the defenders were killed or wounded.

On August 14, 1900, relief came. Troops from several nations fought their way into Peking and rescued the diplomats, missionaries, and their families.

A year later the Chinese Government agreed to pay a total of $330,000,000 to settle all claims. The government also promised that no more harm would come to foreigners. By 1925 the United States and the other nations that had suffered losses in the rebellion agreed that at least part of the money due them would be used for educational and cultural purposes.

Reviewed by HYMAN KUBLIN
Brooklyn College

BOXING

Boxing is a contest in which two opponents wearing padded gloves attempt to strike one another and keep from being struck. Each boxer tries to score more points than his opponent by the intelligent use of skills in which he has been trained. In amateur boxing, especially, skill is more important than strength.

Boxers wear gloves made of soft leather padded with heavy sponge rubber. Gloves weigh from 6 ounces (for professional title bouts) to thickly padded 16-ounce gloves. A boxer's hands are wrapped in soft cotton or linen for protection from the impact of his own blows. Amateur boxers wear headgear to protect their heads and ears from injuries. All boxers use a rubber mouthpiece that helps prevent injuries to the lips and teeth.

The space in which a boxing match takes place is called a ring. It is generally 16 to 20 feet square, closed in by lengths of muslin-wrapped rope. The ropes are 2, 3, and 4 feet above the floor of a platform on which the ring is mounted. A canvas floor covering is laid over padding 2 inches thick. The cornerposts and turnbuckles that hold the ropes are also heavily padded.

The length of a round in college and most other amateur boxing is 2 minutes or less. In professional and some international amateur contests, 3-minute rounds are used. There is a 1-minute rest period between rounds, during which the fighters go to their corners of the ring opposite one another and are tended by their seconds. Most amateur matches are scheduled for three rounds, while professional championship bouts go as many as 15 rounds. A timekeeper marks the beginning and end of each round by sounding a bell, gong, or buzzer.

The referee is a very important third man in the ring during a bout. He sees that the rules are obeyed and separates the boxers if they clinch one another. Blows below the beltline, on the kidneys, or on the back of the neck (rabbit punches) are fouls. So too are pushing or butting, or hitting an opponent when he is down (on the floor, getting up, or outside, between, or hanging helpless over the ropes)

If a fighter is knocked down, his opponent must go to a neutral corner—a corner of the

ring not occupied by either fighter between rounds. The fighter who is down must get back on his feet within the ring before the referee counts to 10 at 1-second intervals. If he does not do this, his opponent is declared the winner by a knockout (KO). However, if the round ends before the count reaches 10, the man who is down is said to be "saved by the bell" and may fight in the next round.

The referee is expected to stop a fight any time he feels that either boxer is too badly hurt to continue. The opponent is then declared the winner by a technical knockout (TKO). A physician must be on hand to help the referee determine whether or not an injured fighter should be allowed to continue.

If there is no knockout, usually two judges, who sit outside the ring, and the referee decide the bout's winner on a basis of rounds won or points. They note how effectively each man strikes his opponent and how well he conducts himself in the ring. They also allow for knockdowns and for fouls and such minor faults as hitting in a clinch. The decision may be based on the number of rounds won or on total points. In case of a tie, a bout is declared a draw.

▶ BOXING AS AMATEUR AND PROFESSIONAL SPORT

As in any physical contact sport, there are bound to be injuries in boxing. In 1938 the Society of State Directors of Physical and Health Education found the basis on which interschool boxing was being promoted in some communities to be "potentially dangerous to the welfare of boys participating." Therefore, the directors adopted an official policy disapproving of boxing as an interscholastic sport.

Supporters of amateur boxing claim that when it is conducted under proper rules and supervision, it is a safe competitive sport. They point out that it is a contest in which each man must pit his own ability, stamina, and resourcefulness against these same qualities in his opponent.

Many colleges and youth and athletic clubs provide instruction in basic boxing skills. They stress sound body condition, proper training, knowledge of the rules, and principles of fair play. They match only opponents of nearly equal size and experience.

BOXING WEIGHT LIMITS

	International		AAU and College	Professional
Flyweight	51	kg.	112 lb.	112 lb.
Bantamweight	54	kg.	119 lb.	118 lb.
Featherweight	57	kg.	125 lb.	126 lb.
Lightweight	60	kg.	132 lb.	135 lb.
Light welterweight	63½	kg.	139 lb.	No class
Welterweight	67	kg.	147 lb.	147 lb.
Light middleweight	71	kg.	156 lb.	150 lb.
Middleweight	75	kg.	165 lb.	160 lb.
Light heavyweight	81	kg.	178 lb.	175 lb.
Heavyweight	No Limit		No limit	No limit

International (Olympic) weight is given in kilograms and is about equal to AAU and professional weights given in pounds.

Olympic and other amateur boxing competition around the world is governed by the International Amateur Boxing Federation. In the United States, the Amateur Athletic Union and National Collegiate Athletic Association are the chief governing bodies. The Golden Gloves Association conducts amateur tournaments throughout the country, and the winners compete in national championships.

Professional boxers are those who fight for cash prizes. Their activity is regulated in the United States by the World Boxing Association (WBA) and various state and local boxing commissions. Since professional boxers do not wear head protectors in bouts, some of them have been badly hurt or disfigured. A series of fatal fights during the early 1960's led to widespread feeling that boxing should be banned as a sport.

▶ BOXING PAST AND RECENT

The people of Sumer in ancient Mesopotamia made many carvings in stone. Archeologists have found one of these that shows two boxers in combat. Greek and Roman athletes fought with their hands wrapped in a kind of leather covering called a cestus. To this the ancient gladiators attached murderous metal studs or spikes. A Roman boxer was called a *pugil,* from which we get "pugilism," another name for boxing.

Little is known about fistfighting from the end of the Roman Empire until the 17th century. Then Englishmen gave the name boxing to a contest in which men boxed, or beat, one another with their bare fists. In 1719 James Figg became the first British champion. Figg established a boxing school for young men in London, and interest in the sport spread quickly. Men often fought for prizes, hence the term "prizefighting." Jack Broughton, a champion from 1743 to 1750, drew up the first London Prize Ring Rules.

Boxers of the bareknuckle era stood toe to toe and wrestled, shoved, or struck each other until one man was knocked down. That marked the end of a round. After a brief rest the fight began again. When one man could no longer fight, his opponent was the victor. Many bouts lasted 50 rounds or more.

If a boxer's second, or assistant, in his corner decided to give up the match for his boxer, he could inform the referee by throwing a towel into the ring. From this practice comes the saying that a person who gives up some effort is "throwing in the towel."

In 1865 the Marquis of Queensbury drew up rules that are the basis for those in use today. The rules provided for 3-minute rounds with a 1-minute rest period between rounds. They required fighters to wear "fair-sized" boxing gloves, banned wrestling holds, and set the 10-second count for a knockout.

Bareknuckle prizefighting did not disappear at once. However, with the adoption of the Queensbury rules and the use of padded gloves, boxing gradually became acceptable in the United States, where prizefighting had been against the law.

The greatest interest in modern professional boxing lies in the world heavyweight title. American fighters have held this title most of the time since Paddy Ryan took it from the British champion Joe Goss in 1880. John L. Sullivan, who defeated Ryan in 1882, was the last of the popular bareknuckle champions. In 1892 he was knocked out by James J. "Gentleman Jim" Corbett in the first heavyweight title fight with gloves under the Queensbury rules. From Corbett the title passed to Bob Fitzsimmons of England (1897), James J. Jeffries (1899), Marvin Hart (1905), Canadian-born Tommy Burns (1906), Jack Johnson, the first Negro champion (1908), and Jess Willard (1915). All were Americans unless otherwise indicated.

William Harrison "Jack" Dempsey launched the golden age of boxing by knocking out Willard in 1919. His bouts began to draw huge crowds. James J. "Gene" Tunney won the title from Dempsey by a decision in 1926 before 120,000 onlookers. The next year a crowd paid a record $2,658,660 to see a return match. Dempsey knocked Tunney down in the seventh round; but because Dempsey did not go at once to a neutral corner as he should have, the referee did not start the count for several seconds. Tunney got to his feet at the famous "long count" of 9 and went on to win by a decision.

Tunney retired in 1928. After that the championship was claimed in turn by Max Schmeling of Germany (1930), Jack Sharkey (1932), Primo Carnera of Italy (1933), Max Baer (1934), and James J. Braddock (1935).

Joe Louis knocked out Braddock in 1937. Louis went on to a brilliant career with knockout after knockout. He retired undefeated in 1949 but lost when he tried to return to the ring in 1950. The next champions were Ezzard Charles (1949), Jersey Joe Walcott (1951), and Rocky Marciano (1952), who retired undefeated in 1956.

Floyd Patterson became champion in 1956 and lost to Ingemar Johansson in 1959. Patterson then knocked out Johansson in 1960 to become the first modern champion to regain the heavyweight title. In 1962 Patterson was defeated by Sonny Liston, who lost the title in 1964 to Cassius Clay (Muhammad Ali).

In 1967, following his refusal to enter the armed forces, Ali was stripped of the title. Elimination bouts were held to find a successor. Jimmy Ellis, World Boxing Association titlist, met Joe Frazier, recognized by some as champion, in 1970. Frazier won in the fifth round. In 1971, after Ali was allowed to box again, Frazier and Ali met, with Frazier winning a unanimous decision. In 1973 George Foreman scored a technical knockout over Frazier and took the title.

Among noted world champions in other classes have been light heavyweight Archie Moore (1952–61); middleweight Sugar Ray Robinson, who was also welterweight champion (1946–51) and who won, lost, or gave up and regained the middleweight crown five times (1951–59); lightweight Joe Brown (1956–62); and featherweight Sandy Saddler (1948–49; 1950–57).

ROCKY MARCIANO
Former World Heavyweight Boxing Champion
Reviewed by NAT S. FLEISCHER
The Ring Magazine

BOYLE, ROBERT (1627–1691)

Robert Boyle was a self-taught amateur who became one of the world's great scientists. During the 1600's he carried out experiments that helped found modern chemistry and modern physics.

Boyle was born on January 25, 1627, at Lismore Castle in the province of Munster, Ireland. He belonged to a large and well-known family. His father was an Englishman who had been made Earl of Cork. Robert was the 7th son and 14th child in a family of 15 children.

An unusually bright and studious child, Robert studied Latin and French at an early age. At 8 he went to Eton, the famous boys' school. When he was 11 he set out to travel in Europe with a tutor. He spent most of the next 6 years in Geneva, Switzerland. It was during this time that Boyle developed an interest in science · and began to study the works of Galileo.

When his father died, Robert Boyle inherited a rich estate in England. In 1644 he settled there. He was now in a position to do anything he wanted. Having what he called "an unsatisfied appetite for knowledge," he decided to explore the unknowns of science. Since there were no textbooks and few teachers, Boyle had to proceed on his own. He moved into his new home and set up a laboratory. It was the first of several he was to have. He worked on his own, paid for his projects, and hired assistants when he needed help. (One assistant was Robert Hooke, who became an important scientist himself.)

For more than 40 years Boyle investigated questions in biology, chemistry, and physics. He studied how animals breathe and how blood circulates. He showed how matter burns, boils, and freezes. His investigations ranged from the barometer and crystals to light and sound. The results of these experiments are no longer very important. What matters is that Boyle was among the first to use careful scientific methods.

Boyle's work with the air pump is probably best known. The pump was a new device that could both compress air and produce near vacuums. With it Boyle could control the quantity of air in a closed container. His experiments demonstrated the role of air in burning, breathing, and sound. During these experiments Boyle discovered what happens when pressure on a given quantity of air is increased: The volume of air becomes smaller. This finding became the basis of what is now known as Boyle's law: If the temperature and quantity of a gas remain constant, the volume varies inversely with the pressure.

At this time other men were becoming active in scientific research. As early as 1645 Boyle had begun to meet with some of these men in London. Out of these meetings grew the Royal Society, still one of the world's leading organizations for the encouragement of science.

Boyle was a deeply religious man. He learned Greek and Hebrew so that he could read the Bible in the original. He wrote books on religious matters. He spent great sums of money to have the Bible translated into foreign languages and he also supported missionary work in both New England and India.

Though always a very active man, Boyle tended to be sickly. He had weak eyes and was troubled by a bad memory. But his interest in science was such that he worked steadily almost until he died, on December 30, 1691.

JOHN S. BOWMAN
Author and Science Editor

Robert Boyle was one of the first men to use scientific methods. He discovered an important law of gases.

BOYS' CLUBS

Among the many organizations serving young people, few offer a greater number and variety of activities than the Boys' Clubs in the United States and Canada.

Each club has a very complete sports program. Most clubs have fully equipped gymnasiums, and many have full-size swimming pools. Almost every club has a wood shop and a library. The clubs are open each day after school, every night, and all day on Saturdays. Each is supervised by full-time professional youth workers.

Arts and crafts, music, painting, radio and television repair, printing, science, astronomy, automobile mechanics, and even cooking—all are taught at Boys' Clubs. Talented members have many opportunities to improve themselves. Hundreds of scholarships are awarded to them each year.

Those who show talent in music or art may obtain scholarships through the Steven David Epstein Memorial Foundation. A member once had his paintings exhibited at New York City's famous Grand Central Art Galleries. Another member made his debut at Carnegie Hall as a violinist and received fine compliments from the music critics.

During the summer months many clubs operate major camp programs. Others have day or overnight camping facilities.

The Boys' Clubs are privately operated. Their support comes mainly from voluntary contributions.

▶ ANY BOY CAN JOIN

Membership in a Boys' Club is open to all boys 7 through 17 years of age, regardless of race or religion. All a boy needs to do to join a club is to apply at the one nearest his home. He receives a membership card that entitles him to all privileges of the club, provided he observes the club rules. Each club charges small annual dues.

You will recognize a Boys' Club by its keystone emblem. Members proudly wear their keystone insignia. In Canada it is a keystone with a red maple leaf. This worldwide Boys' Club emblem was inspired by the statement attributed to Disraeli, "A boy is the keystone in the arch of a nation's destiny."

Boys' Club members repair toys to be distributed to needy children at Christmastime.

Many famous men have grown up as members of Boys' Clubs. Among them have been Joe Di Maggio, Brooks Robinson, and other baseball players; football stars Albie Booth and Sid Luckman; composers Irving Berlin and George Gershwin; actors Eli Wallach and Ben Gazzara; and comedians Eddie Cantor, George Burns, Danny Thomas, and Joe E. Brown.

Millions of former Boys' Club members are now doctors, lawyers, clergymen, teachers, skilled craftsmen, government officials, and businessmen. These community leaders from all walks of life prove that Boys' Clubs have been successful in working toward their goal of "building better citizens."

▶ THE BOYS' CLUBS OF AMERICA

There are over 900 Boys' Clubs in more than 640 cities throughout the United States. These clubs serve almost 1,000,000 boys.

The first Boys' Club was founded in Hartford, Connecticut, in 1860. The Boys' Clubs of America was founded as a national organization in 1906. In 1956 it received a charter from the Congress of the United States.

Herbert Hoover, a former president of the United States, served as chairman of the board of the Boys' Clubs of America for 28 years. He once said, "After the home, the church, and the school, Boys' Clubs are the greatest character building institutions in our country today."

The national office of the Boys' Clubs of America is in New York City. There are 10 regional offices throughout the country.

E. J. STAPLETON
Boys' Clubs of America

BOY SCOUTS

Not long ago a 12-year-old Boy Scout was leaving a tidal pool when he saw two small children bobbing helplessly in the water. The Scout rescued the children from the pool, laid them on the beach, and began mouth-to-mouth resuscitation. One child began to breathe, but the other did not. The Scout instructed people on the beach to continue working on the second child while he called for an ambulance. Both children lived, thanks to the Scout's actions.

This is but one of hundreds of real cases in which Boy Scouts have saved lives as a result of their Scout training. They knew what to do in emergencies. They lived up to their Scout motto, "Be prepared."

Boys get much from Scouting besides training for emergencies. They find fun and fellowship with other boys and the men who lead them. They find adventure in hiking, camping, boating, and the other outdoor sports. They gain useful knowledge and skills, and have many chances to take part in the life of their community and nation.

The Beginnings of Scouting

The man who started Scouting was born in England in 1857. His name was Robert Baden-Powell. He was one of the 10 children of an Oxford University professor. As a boy, he loved outdoor life, especially camping. His hobby was sketching.

At 19 Baden-Powell joined the Army and became an officer. His duties took him to the frontiers of India and South Africa. There he spent much of his time training his men for military scouting. They learned to operate on their own in small groups and to remember and report what they saw. Baden-Powell made up many training games and contests, which he later described in a book called *Aids to Scouting*.

In 1899 and 1900, during the Boer War in South Africa, Baden-Powell led a garrison of 1,250 men that held Mafeking through a 217-day siege. When he returned to England he was a hero. He was surprised to find that some leaders of boys had started using his scouting games and contests. He was asked to work out a program of scouting more directly suited to the needs of boys. He began to think of scouting as a game. But he wanted it to be a game with a goal, so his program was built around the high ideals of the Scout Promise and Law.

In 1907 Baden-Powell held a camp on Brownsea Island in southern England, to test his ideas. He then wrote his handbook, *Scouting for Boys,* published in 1908. With only this handbook to guide them, troops of

Boy Scouts take part in an anti-litter drive.

Boy Scouts began to spring up at once throughout Britain and the British Empire and in many other countries.

Baden-Powell was made a knight in 1909. In the following year he retired from the Army as a lieutenant general to give all his time to Scouting. In 1922 he was made a baronet and in 1929 a baron. Lord Baden-Powell, the Chief Scout of the world, died in Kenya in 1941.

Shortly after the Boy Scout movement started in Britain, William D. Boyce, a United States publisher, became lost one day in a London fog. An English Scout helped him find the address he was looking for. This led Boyce to become interested in Scouting. Upon his return to the United States he got help from leading citizens, and on February 8, 1910, the Boy Scouts of America was organized. In 1916, Congress gave the organization a federal charter.

Among those who helped found the Boy Scouts of America was Daniel Carter Beard (1850–1941). "Uncle Dan" had formed an earlier outdoor organization for boys, the Sons of Daniel Boone, about 1905. He became the first National Scout Commissioner. James E. West (1876–1948) was the first Chief Scout Executive. When he retired in 1943, the Boy Scouts of America had about 1,600,000 members. Today it has nearly 3,500,000 members.

The first Scout troop in Canada was formed in 1908. Six years later the Canadian General Council of the Boy Scouts Association was formed by an act of Parliament. In 1961 this name was changed to Boy Scouts of Canada. By that time there were more than 300,000 Canadian Scouts and leaders.

World Scouting Today

There are about 13,500,000 Scouts and leaders in the world today. They are found in nearly all but the Communist countries. They have different uniforms, badges, and customs. But their aims and ideals are alike. The motto "Be prepared" is known in many languages. The headquarters of the Boy Scouts World Bureau is in Geneva, Switzerland.

World jamborees are held every four years. These are huge camps that bring together Scouts from many nations in friendship. The first world jamboree was held in England in 1920. Many countries also hold national jamborees. The Boy Scouts of America held its first jamboree in 1937. Canada held its first in 1949.

▶ THE BOY SCOUTS OF AMERICA

The National Council of the Boy Scouts of America is made up of persons who come from about 420 local councils across the country. This body meets each year. It makes the rules of Scouting. The president of the United States is the honorary president of the Boy Scouts of America.

The home office is at North Brunswick, New Jersey. A full-time staff, headed by the Chief Scout Executive, publishes handbooks and magazines for boys and leaders. It prepares films and other materials for training leaders. It controls the manufacture and sale of uniforms and equipment through stores. The staff also aids the local councils.

Each local council is made up of volunteers who offer to help Scouting in a city, county, or larger area. The council must have, among other things, a camp for its members. A small group of professional Scout leaders works full time on council tasks.

Scouting reaches boys through churches, schools, and other organizations. Each group that sponsors a troop or any other Scout unit offers a meeting place, good leaders, and other needed support. Today there is an active interest in Scouting in the inner cities. Many city youngsters join Scouting because of the outdoor activities it offers, such as camping and water safety programs.

The Boy Scouts of America provides a long-term program for a boy from the time he is 8 years old until his 21st birthday. At 8 he may become a Cub Scout, at 11 a Boy Scout, and at 14 an Explorer.

Cub Scouts—Boys 8 to 10

The Boy Scouts of America started Cub Scouting for younger boys in 1930. At that time the lowest age limit was 9.

The home is the center of activity for the Cub Scout. There a boy learns to do many things, with the encouragement of adults in the household. He starts out as a Bobcat. By completing 12 achievements, he can earn his Wolf badge. Then, for earning elective credits in a variety of activities, he

SCOUT INSIGNIA AND BADGES

SALUTE

CUB SCOUT

SIGN

HANDCLASP

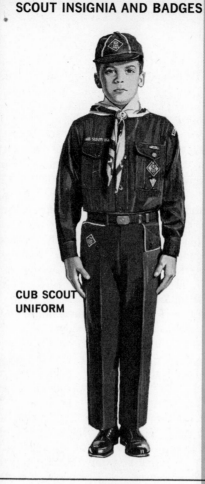

CUB SCOUT UNIFORM

CUB SCOUT BADGES

- BOBCAT
- WOLF
- BEAR
- WEBELOS
- ARROW OF LIGHT
- ARROWPOINTS

SALUTE

BOY SCOUT

SIGN

HANDCLASP

BOY SCOUT UNIFORM

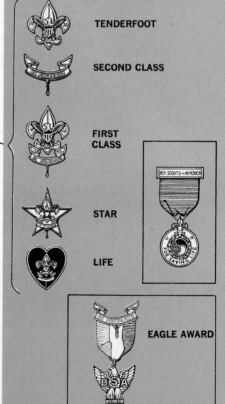

BOY SCOUT BADGES

- TENDERFOOT
- SECOND CLASS
- FIRST CLASS
- STAR
- LIFE
- EAGLE AWARD
- EAGLE PALM

Cubs at a Den meeting make the Cub sign.

Cubs compete in field-day events.
Scouts at a National Jamboree build a table.

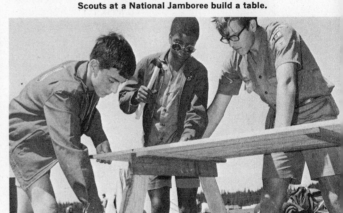

receives arrow points to wear under his badge. When he is 9 years old he begins to work for the Bear rank. At age 10 he may join a Webelos den and earn the Arrow of Light, the highest award in Cub Scouting. Webelos Scouts can also earn activity badges for learning special skills. "Webelos" stands for "We'll Be Loyal Scouts."

A Cub belongs to a neighborhood group of boys called a den. The den meets each week at the home of one of the boys, under the guidance of its Den Leader, who is helped by a Scout called the Den Chief.

Once a month the several dens that make up a Cub pack meet together. Their leader is the Cubmaster. Often the pack meetings take the form of group outings.

The Cub uniform is dark blue with yellow trim. A yellow and blue neckerchief is worn by all Cubs.

Cub Motto: "Do your best."

Cub Promise: "I, [name], promise to do my best to do my duty to God and my country, to help other people, and to obey the law of the pack."

Law of the Pack: "The Cub Scout follows Akela. The Cub Scout helps the pack go. The pack helps the Cub Scout grow. The Cub Scout gives good will." ("Akela" means "good leader.")

Boy Scouts—Boys 11 and Older

A boy may become a Boy Scout as soon as he is 11 years old. By understanding the Scout Oath and Law and by passing a few simple tests, he may join and be called a Scout. Skill awards and merit badges lead him on to Second Class and then on to First Class. Scouts may earn merit badges in any of over 100 different fields. Certain merit badges help him meet the requirements for Star (9 merit badges), Life (15 merit badges), and Eagle (24 badges). Eagle is the highest award in Scouting.

A small group of Scouts forms a patrol. Several patrols make up a troop. The troop usually meets once a week with its adult leader, the Scoutmaster.

Hiking and camping are part of the adventure that Scouts enjoy. They learn how to take care of themselves in the open and how to help others in case of accidents. They also learn to be useful citizens.

The Scout uniform is khaki. Neckerchief colors and designs are chosen locally.

Scout Oath: "On my honor I will do my best to do my duty to God and my country and to obey the Scout Law; to help other people at all times; to keep myself physically strong, mentally awake, and morally straight."

Scout Motto: "Be prepared."

Scout Slogan: "Do a good turn daily."

SCOUT LAW

A Scout is Trustworthy.
A Scout is Loyal.
A Scout is Helpful.
A Scout is Friendly.
A Scout is Courteous.
A Scout is Kind.
A Scout is Obedient.
A Scout is Cheerful.
A Scout is Thrifty.
A Scout is Brave.
A Scout is Clean.
A Scout is Reverent.

Exploring—for Young Adults

Exploring is a division of the Boy Scouts of America that meets the needs of young men and women from high school age to 21. Members—and they need not be Scouts—may join a general- or major-interest Explorer Post or Sea Explorer Ship. Exploring offers a choice of activities and a chance for adventure, vocational experience, education, and recreation. Explorers plan their own programs with the help of an adult Advisor or Skipper. Young women became full members in 1971.

Over a third of all posts are organized around a career interest such as law enforcement, medicine, banking, space exploration, computer programming, and other occupations. Explorers have many interesting national events, among which are the Explorer Olympics, the National Safe Driving Road Rally, Exploration Awards, and the National Explorer President's Congress.

Scouting for the Handicapped

Today more than 60,000 physically or mentally disabled Scouts are active in various programs throughout the United States. Anyone who has been certified as disabled by a proper medical authority may enroll in Scouting and remain in its program beyond the regulation age limits. This provision allows all members to advance in Scouting as far as they wish.

▶ SCOUTING IN COMMONWEALTH COUNTRIES

Scouting in the member countries of the Commonwealth of Nations has gone through a period of transition. Many changes have taken place. These changes have been directed toward a boy-centered movement rather than a program-centered movement. Each country has its own national organization and is represented at the World Scout Conference.

The Boy Scouts of Canada are governed by a national council, which has its headquarters, or secretariat, in Ottawa, the capital. French-speaking Scouts belong to *L'Association des Scouts du Canada*. This association is affiliated with the Boy Scouts of Canada through the office of the Chief Scout, who is traditionally the governor-general. The French Association and the Boy Scouts have an exchange of members of their national councils. Councils are at the provincial, regional, and district levels.

The Scout promise is: "I promise to do my best, to love and serve God, my Queen, my country and my fellow men, and to live by the Scout Law."

The Canadian Scout law differs from the American one that appears on this page. The Canadian Law is: "A Scout is helpful and trustworthy, kind and cheerful, considerate and clean, wise in the use of his resources."

The Scout motto is "Be Prepared," and the Scout slogan, "Do a Good Turn Daily."

The Boy Scouts of Canada has five age groupings: Beavers, Wolf Cubs, Boy Scouts, Venturers, and Rovers. The former Tenderfoot, Second Class, and First Class grades have been replaced by grades known as Pioneers, Voyageurs, and Pathfinder Scouts.

Reviewed by BOY SCOUTS OF AMERICA
BOY SCOUTS OF CANADA

BRAHE, TYCHO (1546–1601)

Tycho Brahe, the great Danish astronomer, was born into an aristocratic family on December 14, 1546. Early in life Tycho decided to become an astronomer. His family disapproved strongly because in those days this was not considered a suitable profession for an aristocrat.

Tycho's early years were spent in the village of Knudstrup, which then belonged to Denmark but is now part of Sweden. In 1559 he entered the University of Copenhagen. While he was there an eclipse took place, as predicted by astronomers. There is a story that this so impressed him that he decided to become an astronomer. At any rate, he did begin to study astronomy and mathematics.

Three years later his family sent him to study law in Leipzig, Germany. Tycho continued to study astronomy in secret. He bought a fist-size globe of the heavens, carried it around with him, and in a month's time had learned all the constellations.

Tycho was not only stubborn but also hot-tempered and arrogant, and he made a number of enemies during his life. In his student years he fought a duel with another young nobleman, who cut off part of his nose. Tycho replaced it with one of gold and silver.

When Tycho returned to Denmark, he set up quarters in an uncle's castle and began his study of the heavens. He used only his eyes, for the telescope had not yet been invented. There, in 1572, he became the first Western astronomer to sight a supernova—an old star that suddenly becomes brilliant because it has exploded. The star was in the constellation of Cassiopeia.

In 1573 Tycho published his observations of the star. That year he also married a peasant girl. Neither of these acts won the approval of his family.

His growing fame as an astronomer drew the attention of King Frederick II of Denmark. To make sure Tycho stayed in Denmark, the King built him an observatory, called Uraniborg, and paid him a salary. Here for 21 years Tycho taught, wrote, studied the heavens, and made astronomical instruments. Night after night he studied the sky, recording the stars and the movements of the planets.

During these years Tycho made many ene-

Old engraving shows Tycho in his observatory at Uraniborg. There was no telescope, since it had not yet been invented.

mies. One result was that when Frederick II died, the new king took away Tycho's observatory and stopped his salary.

Tycho left Denmark. He spent 2 years at universities in Germany. Then, in 1599, the Holy Roman Emperor, Rudolph II, invited Tycho to Prague. There he installed all his instruments from Uraniborg in a castle. In 1600 he hired as his assistant a young German astronomer, Johannes Kepler, who later became famous himself. A year later, on October 24, 1601, Tycho died.

Tycho's great work was completed by Kepler. This was the publication of the Rudolphine tables. The tables summed up Tycho's observations of the positions of the fixed stars and of the motions of the sun, moon, and planets. Working without a telescope and with only the simplest of instruments, Tycho had recorded the positions of 777 fixed stars.

Tycho himself believed that the earth was the center of the universe. The sun, he thought, revolved around the earth, and the other planets around the sun. Yet his careful observations laid the groundwork for men like Kepler, who revealed the true nature of the solar system.

JOHN S. BOWMAN
Author and Science Editor

BRAHMS, JOHANNES (1833–1897)

Johannes Brahms, the son of a poor musician, was born on May 7, 1833, in Hamburg, Germany. With his sister and younger brother, he grew up in the slums of the city. His mother, a major influence in his life, encouraged him in his studies.

At a very early age Brahms showed that he had unusual musical ability. When he was 13, he began to help his family by playing the piano in taverns and restaurants of the city. Two years later, already well known for his skill at the keyboard, he gave a public recital. By the time he was 16, Brahms decided that his chief interest was composing music rather than performing it.

When he was 20, Brahms met Joseph Joachim, the great violinist, and they became lifelong friends. Through Joachim, Brahms met Robert and Clara Schumann, who immediately recognized his talent as a composer.

In 1853 Schumann wrote a famous magazine article entitled "New Paths" in which he hailed Brahms as the coming genius of German music. Aside from being a great composer, Schumann had great influence as a music critic, and his praise of Brahms helped the young composer become better known.

Brahms's native city failed to appreciate his talents, so he went to Vienna in September, 1862, to try his success. Except for conducting engagements, Brahms lived in Vienna for the rest of his life.

The Viennese quickly accepted him for his musical ability, and he soon won an appointment as a choral conductor. After his mother died in 1865, Brahms composed the *German Requiem,* which brought him widespread recognition as a composer. From 1872 to 1875 Brahms was musical director of the famed Viennese Society of the Friends of Music. Brahms, a shy and modest man, lived a simple life in a two-room apartment, content with the companionship of musical friends.

In the later part of his life, Brahms's fame as a composer spread throughout Europe. In 1876 his first symphony, which he had started to work on 22 years before, was finally performed. Three years later Brahms introduced his violin concerto, a tribute to his friend Joachim, who gave the first public performance of the work. The great second piano concerto was finished in 1881, and in 1885 Brahms completed the fourth and last of his symphonies.

For the last 12 years of his life Brahms concentrated on chamber music, compositions for the piano, and songs. His daily life fell into the comfortable routine of the confirmed bachelor. All of Vienna knew and loved him, and his favorite restaurant, The Red Hedgehog, became a center of musical society. The concerto for violin and cello of 1887 was his last orchestral work. Two years later his native city, Hamburg, finally gave Brahms full recognition, and at the age of 56 he received the Honorary Freedom of the City.

In 1894 Brahms was offered the post he had wanted all his life, conductor of the Hamburg Philharmonic Orchestra. But Brahms felt he was too old for the position and declined the offer. He took satisfaction, however, in the many festivals dedicated to his music. When his final illness began in 1896, Brahms faced it calmly, feeling that his life's work had been completed with success. He died on April 3, 1897.

Reviewed by KARL GEIRINGER
Author, *Johannes Brahms*

Johannes Brahms in his home in Vienna.

BRAIN

The brain is the master organ for control and communication within the body. And it is the master organ for communication between the body and its surroundings. It is an important part of the nervous system and is found in all but the most primitive animals.

In a way the brain is unlike any other organ of the body. The brain alone receives, handles, and sends out information.

Flowing into every brain is a never-ending stream of signals carrying sensory (from the senses) information about the world outside the body and about the inside of the body. The brain turns this into another stream of signals, which are commands. This new information is then sent to the muscles and glands by nerves that connect the brain to the rest of the body.

The total complex pattern of activity in muscles and glands of an animal is what we call its **behavior**. Therefore, the brain is responsible for behavior. The different types of behavior that we see in various animals are partly the result of differences in brain structure and organization.

One-celled organisms, such as the amoeba, do not have a nervous system or a brain. (However, they can and do react to stimuli such as light, heat, and food.) Simple, many-celled animals, like sea anemones, have a primitive nervous system. But they have no real brain. That is, they have nerves that connect various parts of the body, but they lack the central grouping of cells that forms a brain.

Larger and more complicated animals have a greater need for an organ to control the activities of the body. In general, therefore, more highly developed animals have more highly developed brains.

No two animals ever have exactly identical brains. But related species may have brains that are much alike. Though there are countless species of insects, their brains share many common features. All fish have similar brains. And because fish, amphibians, reptiles, birds, and humans are distantly related, their brains are basically organized in much the same way.

▶ **THE BASIC FEATURES OF A BRAIN**

In spite of their great differences, all brains have some features in common.

(1) All brains are composed of nerve cells, or **neurons**.

(2) All brains have at least three major sections: a **sensory section**, which supplies the information on which the brain acts; an **integrating** (putting together) **section**, where the incoming information is processed; and a

These animals have simple nervous systems that receive information, put it together, and react to it. But they lack the complex nerve cluster, or brain, that vertebrates have.

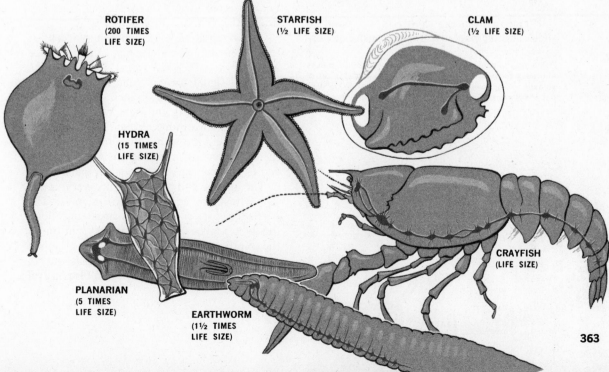

ROTIFER
(200 TIMES
LIFE SIZE)

STARFISH
(½ LIFE SIZE)

CLAM
(½ LIFE SIZE)

HYDRA
(15 TIMES
LIFE SIZE)

CRAYFISH
(LIFE SIZE)

PLANARIAN
(5 TIMES
LIFE SIZE)

EARTHWORM
(1½ TIMES
LIFE SIZE)

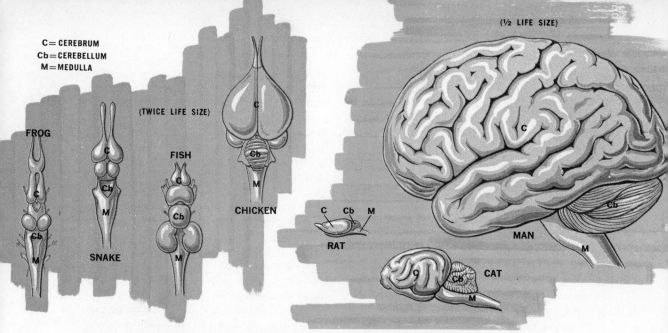

C = CEREBRUM
Cb = CEREBELLUM
M = MEDULLA

(½ LIFE SIZE)

(TWICE LIFE SIZE)

FROG

SNAKE

FISH

CHICKEN

RAT

CAT

MAN

In general, the cerebrum, or forebrain, increases in size as it goes up the evolutionary scale, through fish, frog, snake, bird. The cat's cerebrum is bigger than the rat's and more wrinkled. This means that more nerve cells are crowded together at the surface. The human brain is the most complex.

motor apparatus, which generates the final output signals to muscles and glands.

The overall function of the brain, which we see as behavior, is determined by two things: the precise way in which these three divisions are connected and the presence (or absence) of other special brain centers.

To understand the operation of the brain as a whole, you must first know something about the nerve cells themselves and how they are combined into systems.

The Neuron

Primitive brains, such as those found in snails and their relatives, may consist of only

Delicate, threadlike dendrites pick up incoming pulses and pass them to the cell body. When a particular set of signals arrives, cell becomes active and pulses are sent out along axon.

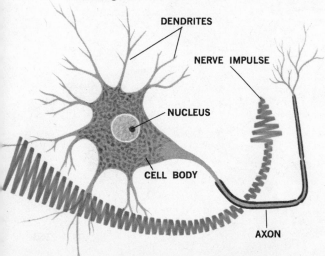

DENDRITES

NERVE IMPULSE

NUCLEUS

CELL BODY

AXON

a few thousand nerve cells (neurons). In man the number of neurons is probably around 10,000,000,000 (billion).

Although usually too small to be seen without a microscope, each neuron is itself a tiny communication system. A typical neuron consists of a central portion, or **cell body**, within which is the nucleus. Coming out of the cell body may be numerous delicate, threadlike parts. Certain of these are called **dendrites**. They conduct signals arriving from other neurons toward the cell body. If a particular set of signals arrives along the dendrites, the cell becomes active.

The remarkable fact about nerve cells is that when they become active, they produce a tiny, brief, electrical signal. This pulselike electrical signal travels along a main branch leaving the cell; this branch is called the **axon**. On reaching the next cell, the signal does one of two things. Either it causes other cells to relay the signal onward (by causing them to generate their own pulses) or it causes the neurons to stop firing pulses.

The axons and dendrites act very much like wires that carry electrical signals. The particular pattern of pulses streaming along the axon makes up the "message" sent on by the cell. Each cell may fire hundreds of pulses each second, because each one lasts only a small fraction of a second. The pulses travel at great speeds along the axon (up to several hundred feet a second). The fastest nerves in a human will conduct impulses at a speed of several hundred miles an hour. This means that a message can go from the brain to the toe in much less than a second.

A neuron may send different messages by changing the number or pattern of its pulses, but the individual pulses themselves are always identical.

The axon, which carries the pulses from one cell to the next, is the connecting link between cells. These axons may be very short if they connect cells lying near each other. But they can also be quite long. For example, a single sensory axon going from the toe of the elephant to his spinal cord may be several yards long.

Sensory Systems

Sensory systems are those parts of the nervous system that supply the brain with information about the world outside the body. In humans they include such special senses as sight, smell, and hearing. The first link in this chain is usually a specialized nerve cell, or **receptor**, which is sensitive to certain kinds of stimuli. Receptors in the retina of the eye are extremely sensitive to light. Various receptors in the skin may be sensitive to touch or pressure; others may be sensitive to heat or pain. The receptors send signals to the central nervous system about particular kinds of events. Our brains interpret these signals as heat, pain, or other stimuli.

In addition, there are receptors that report on the state of the body to the brain. There are receptors that signal body temperature, position of the arms and legs, blood pressure, and many other kinds of information. A person is not aware of all these signals. But they are always arriving at the brain, night and day. As a result, the brain is able to regulate what goes on within the body.

Each sensory system has its own set of receptors and axon pathways within the brain. Each system is always actively sending information to the brain. For example, from the cells of the retina of the human eye alone, about 1,000,000 axons lead to the brain. These are necessary for sending visual information to the brain. Many of them are always at work, even in the dark. (After all, there must be some signal that the brain can interpret to mean "dark.") These axons are grouped along special pathways in the brain concerned with the processing of visual information. Actually, much information processing is done by the cells in the retina itself. So "busy" is the retina that, for its size, it uses up more energy than any other part of the body.

Integrating Centers

The brain must keep bringing about behavior that is suited to the situation. So there are brain centers into which a large part of the sensory information is fed. These centers decide which sensory signals are the most important. They relate what one sense reports to information from other senses.

When you ride a bicycle, for example, you do not rely on what sight alone tells you. The actions that your body takes depend on sight, sounds, sense of balance, and many other things. All this information must be integrated (put together). Only then are the final commands sent by your brain to your muscles.

The integrating centers are organized differently in various animals. But their general function is present in every brain.

Motor Centers

Within every brain there is a section called the motor apparatus. This is the set of nerve cells that acts directly on muscles and glands, putting them to work. These cells carry the brain's commands to the rest of the body.

Some of these command signals are followed quickly, taking only a fraction of a second to be completed. The fastest muscles, such as the wing muscles of insects, take less than $\frac{1}{1000}$ of a second to contract. The record for slowness probably belongs to some of the muscles in the sea anemone; these may take 5 or 6 minutes to contract after they have been excited by their nerves. The fastest human system is the one that controls eye movements.

There is also a great range in the strength that different muscles can produce. These differences in strength are brought about by slight changes in the command signal from the brain. As a result, we can use our hands for such different tasks as picking up a ripe tomato or hanging from a bar.

DIFFERENCES BETWEEN BRAINS

Although all brains share certain features, they also differ in a number of important ways.

First of all, some brains contain a great many more nerve cells than others. Also, the more highly developed brains have many more connections between cells. In simple nervous systems a given neuron may directly receive signals from only a few other cells. In man some cells are believed to receive signals directly from thousands of other cells.

Brain size is an important difference. So is the size of individual neurons. The entire brain of some insects is so small that it could fit inside a single large neuron, such as the giant neurons found in the sea slug. (These are about $\frac{1}{25}$ of an inch in diameter.) One of the largest brains belongs to the elephant, and it weighs more than 10 pounds.

The thickness of axons also differs greatly. This is important. The larger the diameter of the axon is, the faster impulses can be sent along it. Therefore, thicker axons mean that different parts of the brain can communicate faster with one another.

Temperature is another factor. The warmer the body is, the faster most nerve activity is. This gives the warm-blooded animal an advantage over his colder and more sluggish competitors.

Some animals have brains with sensory systems not possessed by others. The rattlesnake, for example, has highly specialized and sensitive receptors in his face for detecting warm objects. With these receptors, he can detect warm-blooded prey, such as mice, many feet away. Relying on these receptors, he can hunt in total darkness.

Bats have specially adapted vocal organs for producing very high-pitched sounds—far too high for our own ears to hear. The bat, however, can detect the echo of its own voice bouncing off distant objects. That is why a bat can fly in the dark without bumping into things and why a bat can pick out tiny insects as prey. This bat system is very much like radar and is of great interest to scientists.

THE HUMAN BRAIN

The human brain is the most complex and highly developed of all brains. It commands the body's hundreds of different muscles, so

---

Does a larger brain mean greater intelligence?

Not necessarily. For instance, man is the most intelligent member of the animal kingdom. Yet his brain is smaller and weighs less than those of some animals. Man's brain weighs about 3 pounds, while an elephant's weighs about 10 pounds. The clue to intelligence is in the cortex, the surface covering of the brain. Intelligence seems to be related to the amount of folding in the cortex.

---

that we can run, talk, and hold things. The brain also commands the thousands of glands that produce vital substances. For example, sweat, tears, and saliva are all under the brain's control.

The brain is located in the head, protected by the skull. It weighs a little more than 3 pounds in an adult. Like most parts of the body, it consists mainly of water. To the touch, a brain feels very much like a balloon filled with water. Because the brain is delicate in structure, it must have extra protection from bumps and injury. This protection is provided by tough membranes that surround it and by a special fluid that supports it and buoys it up in the skull.

Divisions of the Brain

The largest part of the brain is the **cerebrum**. It has a peculiar surface: twisted, wrinkled, and knotted. This surface is the **cerebral cortex**. Its pink color is due to the presence of very tiny blood vessels. The foldings of the surface are called **convolutions**. They serve to increase the surface area of the cortex. Thus they increase the total number of cells in the cortex. This is important because, in a way, intelligence is related to the total number of nerve cells in the cortex.

The cerebrum, also called the **forebrain**, consists of two hemispheres. At the base of the hemispheres, and surrounded by them, is a region of the brain called the **diencephalon**, or "between-brain." It connects with the **midbrain**. Overlying the midbrain is the large **cerebellum** (which means "little brain"). The midbrain continues back into the **medulla** and finally into the **spinal cord**. Strictly speaking, the spinal cord is not considered to be part of the brain.

These various parts of the central nervous

system are connected by long bundles of axons. These relay messages back and forth to the collections of nerve cells that are grouped together. Because of their color, these groupings are called **gray matter**. (The bundles of axons, because of their color, are called **white matter**.)

Local Brain Functions

The **spinal cord** is the great link connecting the brain with much of the body. From receptor neurons throughout the body, messages travel up the cord to the brain, carrying information about touch, pain, temperature, and body position. Alongside these **sensory pathways** are the **motor pathways**, coming down from the brain. These relay messages from the cortex, midbrain, and cerebellum, which command activity in muscles and glands.

Higher up, in the **medulla**, are vital centers that automatically control the rate and depth of breathing, heart rate, and blood pressure. Without these centers, life would cease.

In the **midbrain** are important centers for the major sensory systems and important motor centers. (In lower animals, such as fish, amphibia, and reptiles, the cerebrum is not well developed. The midbrain is the most highly developed part of the brain.) In addition, there are recently discovered centers here that act in the control of sleeping, waking, and attention.

The deepest part of the **diencephalon** is the **hypothalamus**. It is involved in such matters as hunger, thirst, regulation of body temperature, and, to an extent, emotional behavior. Hanging down from the hypothalamus is the **pituitary gland**. It acts much like a master control organ for many of the other important glands of the body.

Higher up in the diencephalon is the **thalamus**. It is an important relay center for sensory signals on their way to the cortex and to centers where different sensory signals come together.

From these centers in the thalamus, sensory signals are relayed to the **cerebral cortex**. Many parts of the cortex seem to be concerned with only a single sense. At the back of each hemisphere are areas concerned with vision. At the side of each hemisphere are areas concerned with hearing and touch. Just ahead of these are the main motor centers, which may be concerned with voluntary control of muscles and movement.

Left: A section of the brain, showing some of its inner parts. Right: Position of the brain within the head. The delicate tissue of the brain is protected from injury by the hard bony skull that surrounds it and by the shock-absorbing fluid. The spinal cord is also protected by fluid and by the bones of the spine.

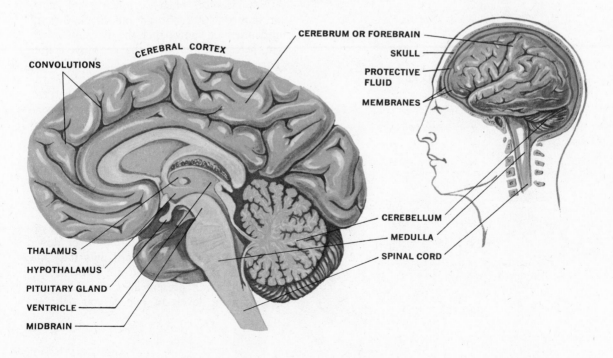

CEREBRAL CORTEX

CONVOLUTIONS

CEREBRUM OR FOREBRAIN

SKULL

PROTECTIVE FLUID

MEMBRANES

CEREBELLUM

MEDULLA

SPINAL CORD

THALAMUS

HYPOTHALAMUS

PITUITARY GLAND

VENTRICLE

MIDBRAIN

Strangely enough, all these centers in the cortex are chiefly concerned with sensation and movement on the opposite side of the body. That is, a touch on the left arm is relayed to the right cortex; movements of the right hand involve the left cortex.

Why, if you tap one spot on a relaxed knee, does the leg jerk? This is one of the body's reflexes. Signals go from knee to lower spinal cord and down to thigh muscles in a fraction of the time they take to reach the brain. Such a reflex lets the body protect itself quickly. The brain acts later on the information.

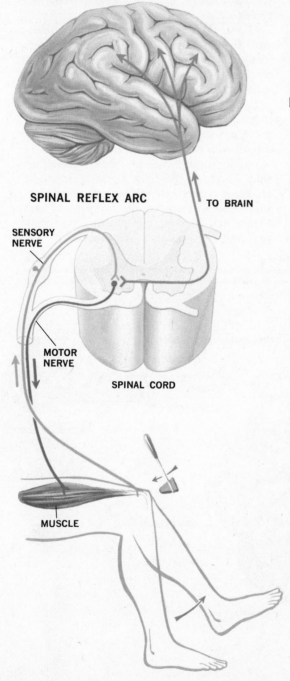

SPINAL REFLEX ARC

TO BRAIN

SENSORY NERVE

MOTOR NERVE

SPINAL CORD

MUSCLE

In humans certain parts of the cortex are necessary for speech, writing, memory, learning, and various kinds of emotional behavior. But the functions of these centers are poorly understood.

It is not yet possible to say which part of the brain "thinks," "sees," "learns," or "wants." We can only say that these activities require many different parts of the brain working together. But at every level of the brain, from the spinal cord to the cortex, there are sensory, motor, and integrating centers. Each has a particular kind of activity. These centers are fairly simple in the spinal cord and unbelievably complicated at the cortex. But scientists are a long way from completely understanding even the spinal cord.

▶ **COMPLEX BEHAVIOR**

All brains have sensory and motor functions. These are fairly well understood by scientists. However, all brains have other functions that are very complicated and poorly understood.

The Reflex

Most animals, for example, have automatic responses to certain types of stimuli, called **reflex responses**. These are patterns of activity that are produced whenever certain stimuli appear. And they are largely beyond control of the animal.

For instance, when we touch a hot stove, we immediately withdraw our hand. Careful measurement shows that the movement begins before we are aware that the stove is hot. This is because there are **reflex centers** in the spinal cord. They receive sensory warning signals before the signals have reached the conscious parts of our brain. The reflex centers in the cord immediately send signals to the nearby motor centers in the cord. These cause withdrawal of the hand.

The entire mechanism is present in the cord. And it is brought into action whenever a painful event occurs. This obviously helps to protect the body. Precious time would otherwise be lost by the signals' having to travel farther up in the brain and back down again. The reflex in the cord cuts the time to a tenth of what it would otherwise be.

The reflex is present in many functions and at many levels of our nervous system.

There is also a great amount of activity that is under conscious, or voluntary, control.

Instinctive Behavior

Many nervous systems produce very complex patterns of behavior that have not been learned by the animal. This is called instinctive behavior. Many insects and birds, for example, build complicated nests, although they have never seen another animal do so. This must mean that the directions are stored somewhere in the brain at birth. At the right time the proper pattern of activity is "triggered" somewhere in the brain. It may take a long time to build the nest, but each animal of the species will complete the task. (And once they have started, it is hard to stop them.) Instinctive patterns of behavior are very much like phonograph records; once they start, they play through to the end, always the same.

In some animals scientists have discovered which parts of the brain control instinctive behavior. They have learned what stimuli are necessary to start the process. But otherwise very little is known.

Less well-developed brains rely very heavily on reflexes and instinctive behavior. But as the nervous system becomes more advanced the brain is able to become somewhat more independent of the stimuli reaching it. This means also that the animal becomes more independent of its environment.

▶ LEARNING AND MEMORY

Brains can learn different kinds of tasks. Better developed brains can learn more complicated tasks. In the simplest brains learning is very crude. Humans show the greatest learning abilities. Among all animals, only humans can learn verbal (speaking, writing) behavior.

Memory

How and where does the brain store the information that we call memory? That is an easy question to ask, but very difficult to answer. In the human brain, areas of the cortex appear to be involved. When these areas are excited by a weak electrical current, the person "relives" past experiences. Apparently these electrical stimuli force the brain to reproduce experiences that are stored within it

from the past. It is also known that injury to certain areas will result in loss of memory.

But this does not mean that these are the places in the brain where the information is stored. Nor does it tell us anything about the way information is stored. Some scientists think that memory storage is chemical in nature. That is, they think that individual nerve cells have chemically coded information within them. Other scientists believe that memory is a result of some permanent change in the structure of the nerve—in the dendrites, for example.

▶ CONSCIOUSNESS

In humans we have a whole set of functions like consciousness, emotion, verbal expression, and thinking. These functions are the object of much study, and a great deal is known about them. But they are far too complicated to be understood in terms of the activities of nerve cells.

▶ RESEARCH ON BRAINS

Today scientists in many countries are studying the brain of man and other animals. In recent years electronic equipment has been developed that lets scientists observe the tiny electrical signals produced by nerve cells. These signals provide much important information about the operation of the brain. Other instruments permit experimenters to use tiny amounts of electricity to stimulate or prevent activity in certain parts of the brain. These methods have been used to trace pathways through the brain, to discover the connections between cells, and to see how signals are sent from one center to another. These experiments also tell us what functions are served by different areas of the brain.

Nevertheless, we have only begun to uncover the basic processes going on within the brain. As more and more of our questions about the brain are answered the number of unanswered questions becomes larger. The brain is the most complicated of all organs. And it will continue to be a challenge to scientists as long as man wonders about the workings of the living body.

GEORGE P. MOORE
Brain Research Institute, U.C.L.A.

See also BODY, HUMAN (Body's Senses).

BRAKES. See HYDRAULIC MACHINERY; RAILROADS.

BRANCUSI, CONSTANTIN (1876–1957)

The sculptor Constantin Brancusi was born in Rumania in the village of Pestisani Gorj. His parents were peasants and were so poor that after his father died, Brancusi left home at the age of 11 to support himself.

When he was older he worked for a furniture maker in order to pay his way at a school of arts and crafts. At 22 Brancusi won a scholarship to the Academy of Fine Arts in Bucharest, the Rumanian capital. In 1904 he enrolled in the Ecole des Beaux-Arts in Paris. To reach Paris, Brancusi had made the long journey across Europe on foot, earning money along the way as a stonemason and builder's laborer.

By the 1920's many far-sighted people recognized the importance of his work, but Brancusi's style marked such a break with the past that most people did not understand it. When one of his most famous sculptures, *Bird in Space,* was sent to the United States for an exhibition, the customs officials looked at its streamlined, polished shape and said that it was not art. To defend his work Brancusi sued the United States Customs Service. In 1928 the court decided in Brancusi's favor.

Brancusi led a solitary life of great simplicity. He carved the simple wooden furniture and stone tables that furnished his studio and even made his own tools. For 40 years he lived in Paris in the same studio, rarely leaving it, surrounded by his sculpture.

Brancusi prepared himself for his work by hours of contemplation. In his sculpture details are ignored and shapes are pared down to their simplest forms. Trying to express the essential spirit of his subject, he concentrated on only a few themes. He worked in stone, metal, and wood. In wood he used rough, forceful strokes, but most of his stone and metal sculptures are highly polished.

When he died at the age of 81, Brancusi left his studio and all the sculpture in it to the city of Paris.

BRANDEIS, LOUIS DEMBITZ (1856–1941)

Louis Dembitz Brandeis lived three decisive lives. He was a great American judge, a social philosopher, and a great Jewish leader.

Brandeis was born in Louisville, Kentucky, on November 13, 1856. His parents had fled from German political oppression. Brandeis was a brilliant student of the law, winning highest honors at Harvard. He became a successful lawyer and in 1916 was named to the Supreme Court by President Woodrow Wilson. Immediately a struggle began to prevent Brandeis' confirmation by the Senate.

Brandeis had unorthodox views. He believed that the law must be fashioned not only by previous legal decisions, but by a changing society. He was a persistent enemy of "bigness." He felt that the overwhelming power of giant economic structures crushed the initiative and the opportunity of the little man. These views terrified the conservatives. They fought Brandeis' confirmation for what they called his "lack of judicial temperament."

Ultimately Brandeis' appointment was approved and he sat on the Supreme Court for 22 years, joining Justice Oliver Wendell Holmes in dissenting opinions that became historic. The two strong-willed men persevered; in time their views became the court's prevailing philosophy, and the whole structure of American society was transformed. President Franklin D. Roosevelt, deeply influenced by Brandeis, often referred to him as Isaiah and as the father of the New Deal.

Brandeis also played a decisive role in Jewish life as a leader in the Zionist movement. He had a very large influence on President Wilson at the Paris peace conference of 1919. He was partly responsible for the declarations that pledged Britain and the United States to the support of a Jewish homeland in Palestine. In 1939 Brandeis retired from the Supreme Court. He died 2 years later, on October 5, 1941.

Brandeis was considered the greatest American Jew of his generation. It was inevitable, when a university was founded by the American Jewish community, that it should be named for him as a tribute to his influence.

ABRAM L. SACHAR
President, Brandeis University

BRANT, JOSEPH (1742–1807)

Joseph Brant was a Mohawk Indian and a war chief of the Six Nations. His Indian name was Thayendanegea. A brave warrior and a wise chief, Brant was also an educated man who translated the Anglican prayer book and part of the Bible into the Mohawk language.

In 1742 the Brant family left their Mohawk Valley home in New York and went to the Ohio Valley. Joseph Brant was born and grew up in what is now the state of Ohio.

When he was 12, Joseph met Sir William Johnson, the British superintendent of Indian affairs. Johnson took the young boy into his home, treating him almost as a son. At 13 Joseph was fighting on the side of the British during the French and Indian War. Later he was sent to school in Connecticut.

When the Revolutionary War began, Brant and most of the Iroquois Indians of the Six Nations remained loyal to Great Britain. Brant received the rank of captain in the British Army. After the war ended, Brant led his Mohawk tribe into Canada, seeking a new home for his people. The British Government granted him a large tract of land in what is now Ontario. There Brant settled most of his tribe and built Ontario's first Protestant chapel, which is still used today.

Brant made two trips to England. His tall, strong figure and handsome face attracted great attention, and the artist George Romney painted his portrait. Brant was presented to King George III. As a king of the Mohawks, Brant refused to bow to another king, but he graciously kissed Queen Charlotte's hand.

In 1792 Brant was invited to visit George Washington. The next year he attended a great conference of Indian tribes. Brant urged the Indians to live in peace with the settlers. But many of the tribes deserted him and continued to war against the settlers.

Brant died on November 24, 1807, in Hamilton, Ontario, Canada. A replica of his home can be seen there today. The city of Brantford, Ontario, which was named in his honor, has a Brant museum.

JOHN S. MOIR
University of Toronto

BRAQUE, GEORGES (1882–1963)

During World War I a French soldier named Georges Braque was blinded from a serious wound. Blindness is tragic for anyone, but for an artist it is a tragedy that can affect the whole world. Before long, however, his sight was restored.

Braque's interest in art began when he was a child in Argenteuil, France. His father was an interior decorator and an amateur painter. The young boy watched and copied his father, and art became the center of his life.

The Braque family moved to the city of Le Havre in 1890, and Georges continued to draw and paint and study. Ten years later he went to Paris, where a great revolution in art was taking place. In a few years he exhibited with a group called *les fauves,* which means the wild ones.

In 1907 Braque met the great young painter Pablo Picasso. They became close friends and for years worked together, experimenting with modern techniques. They helped develop **cubism**, a kind of painting that shows many sides of an object at once, and the **collage**, a work of art that is made by assembling scraps of different materials.

After the war Braque continued to work with cubism, simplifying it as the years passed. However, he did not limit his energies to painting, and his stage scenery, book illustrations, and sculpture are widely admired. His later work is as fresh and vigorous as his earliest paintings. He died on August 31, 1963.

BRASS. See BRONZE AND BRASS.

BRASS INSTRUMENTS. See WIND INSTRUMENTS.

Still Life: The Table (1928) by Braque. National Gallery of Art, Washington, D.C., The Chester Dale Collection.

BRAZIL

Long ago sailors told tales of a mythical island in the Atlantic Ocean. There the ground was shaded by dense forests of a wood called *bresilium,* or "brazilwood." This wood was highly prized as a dye for the bright red cloth worn by the kings and nobles of Europe. Sailors hunted in vain for the island for hundreds of years. Then in 1500 a Portuguese navigator strayed off his course for India and accidently ended the search.

The navigator, Pedro Alvares Cabral, landed on the shores of a vast, tropical land which he claimed for the King of Portugal. The land was named for the dyewood, pau-brasil, found there. Now known as the Federative Republic of Brazil, the country is one of the world's giant nations. Brazil has an area of 8,511,965 square kilometers (3,286,478 square miles). Its 21 states, four territories, and the federal district of Brasília cover an area nearly as large as that of all the other South American nations put together. Only four countries—the Soviet Union, China, Canada, and the United States—are larger than Brazil.

Brazil lies mainly in the tropics. It ex-tends from north of the equator to south of the tropic of Capricorn. Most Brazilians, however, live near or along the Atlantic coast, which stretches for a distance of about 7,400 kilometers (4,600 miles). This is partly because the climate along the coast is suit-able for settlement. In addition, the Great Escarpment, a mountain wall that runs paral-lel to the coast, has made travel to inland Brazil difficult.

Brazil is unique in one way among all the independent republics in the New World. It alone won its independence without having to fight a war, and for 67 years it was a progres-sive monarchy. Then in 1891 it became, like the United States, a federal republic.

In the 18th and 19th centuries, Brazil, like the United States, had its "gold rush" and pioneers. It also became a "melting pot," where people of every race and of different nationalities made their home.

▶ THE PEOPLE

The population of Brazil is approximately 107,000,000. Brazil has about half of the total population of South America. About

Brazilians relax on Copacabana Beach in Rio de Janeiro.

BRAZIL

three quarters of the people live on the eastern edge of the country—between the Amazon River and the border of Uruguay.

More than half the Brazilians—about 61 out of every 100—are of European ancestry; and the majority of these are of Portuguese descent. Since the middle of the 20th century Europeans of many other nationalities have also settled in Brazil. European Brazilians live for the most part in the eastern, southeastern, and southern regions of the country.

Sugarcane was Brazil's most important crop during the early days. Portuguese plantation owners at first used Indians to work in the fields, but found that they resisted settling down and were not skillful farmers. In 1538 the colonists began to bring in large numbers of Negro slaves to work on the sugar plantations. Many Negroes came from a part of Africa where farming and metalworking were highly developed. As a result, the Brazilian Negroes, first as slaves and later as freedmen,

Carnival, celebrated before Lent, is a 3-day festival enjoyed by rich and poor, young and old.

made many important contributions to the growth of the country. Today about 11 out of every 100 Brazilians are Negro; 26 out of every 100 are of mixed Negro and European ancestry.

Fewer than two out of every 100 Brazilians are descended from the country's first settlers—the Indians. Most of the pure-blood Indians now live in the Brazilian and Guiana highlands. Brazilians of mixed white and Indian ancestry are found mainly in the interior of the country.

The remainder of Brazil's population includes various other racial mixtures. A number of Lebanese, Syrians, and Japanese also make their home in Brazil.

Many different ways of life are found in Brazil. But Brazilians respect tradition, and they have many customs and ideals in common. They speak the same language; nearly all worship according to the same faith; they are educated in the same way.

Language

"*Buenos días*" is the way to say "hello" in every South American country except Brazil. In Brazil they say *"Bom día,"* which is Portuguese for "good morning." Brazil is the only Portuguese-speaking nation in the Western Hemisphere. But because there are so many Brazilians, Portuguese has become a major world language. Brazilian Portuguese is much like the language spoken in Portugal except that it is spoken with a different accent. A visitor from Portugal would also have to learn new words that have been added to the language by Brazilian Negroes and Indians.

Most educated Brazilians also speak Spanish, and many are fluent in English and French. Descendants of European settlers often speak their native language at home. German and Italian are spoken by several million in the southern states. Magazines and newspapers are published in many different languages.

Education

Brazilian law requires all children to attend elementary school for at least 3 years. Well-to-do elementary school students can be recognized easily by their uniforms: boys wear khaki shirts and shorts; girls wear navy-blue skirts and white blouses. They study Brazilian history, arithmetic, science, social studies, and Portuguese. English is taught as a second language in the higher grades; so is French.

Secondary school consists of 4 years of junior high school, called *ginásio,* and 3 years of senior high school, called *colégio.* Most secondary schools are privately run, and only well-to-do Brazilians can afford to send their children to them.

Advanced education is available at technical schools, state colleges, and at national and Catholic universities. Specialized institutes for graduate study in the fields of diplomacy, civil service, government, and medicine located in Rio de Janeiro attract students from all over South America.

Although Brazil has many fine schools and

colleges, there are not nearly enough for all of its fast-growing and widely scattered population. At present a large percentage of the population can neither read nor write. The government is trying to reduce the number of illiterates through a program of school building and teacher training. Adult education courses are being given in some of the larger cities. And there are even mobile schools that carry teachers, books, and school supplies to remote villages by truck. But lack of schools is, and probably will continue to be, one of Brazil's major problems.

Religion

About 90 percent of all Brazilians are Roman Catholics. This gives Brazil the distinction of having the largest Catholic population of any nation in the world. Freedom of worship is guaranteed by the constitution. Many Protestants, as well as smaller numbers of Buddhists and Jews, make their home in Brazil. Furthermore, an unusual mixture of African cults and Catholicism is practiced by many Brazilian Negroes in the big cities and the Northeast.

The family is the center of everyday life in Brazil. Most couples marry when they are quite young, often when they are still in their teens. Children are welcomed and loved; little boys are sometimes even a bit spoiled. But the household revolves around the father, who is treated with great respect and politeness by his wife and children.

Social life in Brazil is often built around family holidays. The birthdays, christenings, and weddings of the immediate family and vast numbers of aunts, uncles, and cousins are occasions for celebrations and parties.

All Brazilians share in the many Catholic holidays, such as saints' days, when festivals, pageants, and dances are held. The most famous of these holidays is Carnival—the 3-day festival before the beginning of Lent. Carnival is celebrated in all Brazilian towns and cities. The most famous is the one that is held in Rio de Janeiro; the most typical, in Recife. Schools and businesses close, and the whole city is given over to parades, street dances, and masked balls. Strolling musicians play the *samba, marchina,* and *frevo;* confetti and streamers fill the air. *Cariocas,* as the people of Rio are called, and tourists join in

this huge city-wide celebration during which no one sleeps and nearly everyone dances. Even as Lent begins, everyone in Rio, from the wealthiest apartment dweller to the poorest person in the *favelas,* or "slums," starts to plan his costume for the great event of the next year.

Sports

Nearly all Brazilians are enthusiastic sportsmen and good athletes. Boating, sailing, and

Youngsters play soccer, Brazil's most popular national sport, on a beach in Rio.

swimming are popular activities. Baseball is a popular spectator sport, but nothing excites a Brazilian so much as a good *futebol* ("soccer") match. *Futebol* is the national sport, and every school and town has its own team. Professional soccer players are national heroes in Brazil just as baseball players are in the United States. No one is surprised to see a soccer fan weep if his team loses or celebrate if it wins.

What Brazilians Eat

Cafézinhos—tiny cups of sweet, steaming-hot coffee—are as important a part of daily life in Brazil as *futebol*. Brazilians stop several times a day to sip their *cafézinho* in outdoor restaurants, at home, and even in factories and offices, where trays of the small cups are brought to workers for a *cafézinho* break.

The national dish of Brazil is called *feijoada* and contains black beans, pork sausage, spices, and manioc powder. Manioc is made from mandioca, the root of the non-poisonous cassava, a tropical plant that is native to Brazil. No one would enjoy eating the root raw, but Indians long ago discovered that when cooked and dried it could be used in many ways. Brazilians sprinkle it on soups, meat, stews, and use it as flour in bread and puddings. It is exported as tapioca.

Every region of Brazil has its own special foods. *Charque* (dried and salted beef) is made in southern Brazil. In the Northeast and along the Amazon River, fish dishes are popular. The gauchos (cowboys) of the southern grasslands eat a kind of barbecued beef and drink *maté,* a kind of tea, instead of coffee. Everywhere in Brazil oranges, pineapples, peaches, bananas, and other varieties of tropical fruits are inexpensive and far more popular than vegetables.

The Arts in Brazil

The Portuguese colonists brought a love of music and art from their mother country that has become a vital part of Brazilian life. As the colony grew into a nation, many Brazilians won fame in the arts.

One of the first well-known Brazilian artists was the 18th-century sculptor, Antônio Francisco Lisboa, who was known as Alei-

---

SOME BRAZILIANS PROMINENT IN THE ARTS

ART

Aleijadinho (Antônio Francisco Lisboa); **Cavalcanti,** Emiliano di; **Costa,** Lúcio; **Niemeyer,** Oscar; **Portinari,** Cândido.

MUSIC

Fernández, Oscar Lorenzo; **Gomes,** Antônio Carlos; **Guarnieri,** Camargo; **Novaes,** Guiomar; **Villa-Lobos,** Heitor.

LITERATURE

Alves, Antônio de Castro; **Amado,** Gilberto; **Amado,** Jorge; **Andrade,** Mário de; **Bandeira,** Manuel; **Costa,** Cláudio Manuel da; **Cunha,** Euclides da; **Freyre,** Gilberto; **Goncalves Dias,** Antônio; **Guimarães,** Rosa; **Lima,** Jorge de; **Lins do Rêgo,** José; **Machado de Assís,** Joaquim Maria; **Monteiro Lobata,** José Bento; **Meireles,** Cecilia; **Veríssimo,** Erico.

jadinho—the "Little Cripple." Aleijadinho was a leper. When he could no longer use his hands, he had his tools strapped to his wrists so that he could go on sculpting. His most famous works are the statues of the 12 prophets on the steps of a church in Congonhas, a small town in Minas Gerais.

Brazilian painters have only begun to win world-wide fame in this century. Among the best known are Emiliano di Cavalcanti, Lasar Segall, and Cândido Portinari, whose murals can be seen not only in Brazil but also at the Library of Congress in Washington, D.C., and at United Nations headquarters in New York City.

In the field of architecture too, Brazilians have won international fame. The dramatic new capital city of Brasília is the work of Brazil's leading designers—the city planner Lúcio Costa, the architect Oscar Niemeyer, and the landscape architect Roberto Burle Marx.

Brazilian dances and music, such as the samba, baião, and bossa nova, are known all over the world. But only two Brazilian composers have won international fame. One is António Carlos Gomes, a 19th-century composer whose opera about a proud Indian is called Il Guarany. Another well-known Brazilian, Heitor Villa-Lobos, composed more than 2,000 works based on the folk music of the Brazilian Negroes and pioneers.

Only a few Brazilian writers are known outside their own country. One of them, Joaquim Maria Machado de Assís, is considered one of the greatest South American writers. His portrayals of life in Rio de Janeiro during the early 19th century are found in Epitaph for a Small Winner, Dom Casmurro, and Quincas Borba. Euclides da Cunha is another of Brazil's better-known writers. His most famous book, Rebellion in the Backlands, is an essay on man and the land in the Northeast, and the third part tells of a military adventure there. Distinguished Brazilian writers of the 20th century include the poets Carlos Drummond de Andrade, Manuel Bandeira, Augusto Frederico Schmidt, and Guimarães Rosa; and the novelists Graciliano Ramos, Erico Veríssimo, Rachel de Queiroz, and Jorge Amado. The sociologist-historian Gilberto Freyre is well known in the United States. His classic works are The Masters and the Slaves and The Mansions and the Shanties.

▶ THE LAND

Brazil, like all large countries, has many different kinds of landscape. An easy way to view this variety is by dividing the country into uplands and lowlands. The two main areas of uplands—the Brazilian Highlands and the Guiana Highlands—cover more than one half of Brazil. The three major lowland

São Paulo and Santos, long separated by high mountain walls, are now connected by a highway.

areas are the Amazon Basin; a small area in southern Brazil drained by the Río de la Plata system; and a small area of the upper Paraguay river system in the southwest.

Brazilians usually divide their large and varied country into five regions that have a geographic unity and share a common history, economy, and way of life. These regions are the Northeast, the Central East, the South, the Central West, and the Amazon Basin. Each region contains several states.

The Northeast

In the region known as the Northeast are the states of Maranhão, Piauí, Ceará, Rio Grande do Norte, Paráiba, Pernambuco, Alagoas, Sergipe, and Bahia.

Here on the hot, rainy coastal plain Portuguese planters of colonial times grew wealthy raising cane sugar on their *fazendas* ("plantations"). The *fazenda* was home to the planter, his family, and the crews of Indian and Negro slaves who worked the fields. The port cities of Salvador (formerly Bahia), Brazil's first capital, and Recife flourished. The sons of wealthy planters became the leaders of the colony. Their descendants are still among the leaders of the nation today.

The coastal plain soon became crowded, and settlers pushed inland to the *sertão,* or "backland." The *sertão* is a forbidding region of extremes in climate. It has either too much or too little rain, and in some years the drought is so severe that people must move away or die of hunger and thirst. In rainy years cotton can be grown and the land is green with fodder for cattle.

The cowboys on the ranches of the *sertão* must wear leather clothing to protect themselves from the thorny plants that are typical of the region. Many unusual plants grow in the caatinga, a tropical thorn forest of the Northeast. One, the carnauba palm, stays green even during severe droughts because its leaves are coated with a thin film of wax. This wax is used in the manufacture of lipstick, self-polishing floor waxes, and phonograph records.

Other valuable products of the Northeast include sugar, cotton, tobacco, and rice. In addition, all of Brazil's crude oil (though insufficient for the country's needs) comes from the state of Bahia.

The Central East

The Central East region is made up of Rio de Janeiro, Espírito Santo, Minas Gerais, and São Paulo. A combination of good climate, rich soils, and abundant natural resources has made these states, with the exception of Espírito Santo, the richest and most important in Brazil.

Thousands of settlers were attracted to this region after the discovery of gold in Minas Gerais ("General Mines") in 1698. During the next 100 years almost half the gold mined in the world came from Brazil. Today gold is mined only in small quantities. There are, however, tremendous iron reserves at Itabira as well as a wealth of industrial diamonds, aquamarines, beryls, topazes, and tourmalines elsewhere in the region.

One important result of Brazil's gold rush was that the Northeast lost in importance and the Central East gained its position as the heart of the nation. In 1763 the capital was moved from Bahia to Rio de Janeiro on the central coast. Rio, which had been a sleepy village before the discovery of gold, became the chief port for the shipment of the precious metal abroad. Other businesses grew too, and soon it was the commercial center of the country. Today Rio is considered one of the world's most beautiful cities. Its fine harbor, steep mountains, and magnificent modern apartment houses strung along the beaches and wide, tree-lined avenues have made Rio one of the most visited and photographed cities in South America.

The most important city of the Central East is São Paulo. Founded more than 400 years ago, it was a frontier town until the 19th century, when *terra roxa,* the purplish-red soil of the region, was found perfect for growing coffee trees. Thousands of European immigrants swelled the population of São Paulo, and the number of coffee plantations in the region mushroomed. São Paulo and its port city, Santos, became rich as centers of the coffee industry.

Today São Paulo is the chief industrial city of Latin America. It is the nation's textile center, producing more than half of Brazil's cotton cloth. Other factories in and near the city produce chemicals, electrical goods, automobiles, appliances, and processed foods. The people of this bustling, modern city, the

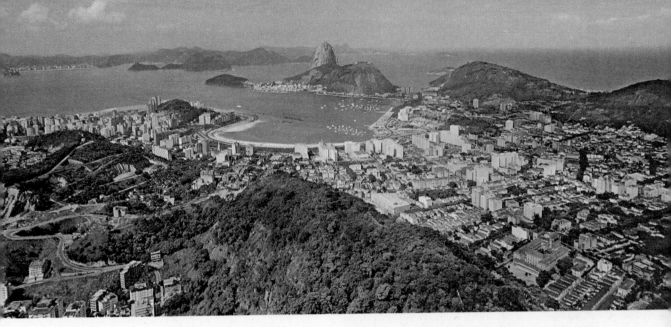

Paulistas, are proud to be known as the Yankees of South America; they are also proud of their city's growing importance in the world.

For hundreds of miles around São Paulo the countryside is dotted with huge coffee plantations. The headquarters of these vast *fazendas* are often small towns with movie houses, health centers, churches, and clubs. The people of the *fazenda* are busiest at coffee harvest time when everyone, including the children, goes out to pick the ripe coffee berries from the trees and prepare them for shipment to São Paulo and Santos. You will find an article on Rio de Janeiro in Volume R and one on São Paulo in Volume S.

Santos lies southeast of São Paulo. Building a highway and a railroad to link the two cities was a major feat of engineering because of the great difference in elevation. An electric-cable railroad and a highway carved into the Great Escarpment now connect the *fazendas* of the plateau with the port. In Santos the air is perfumed with coffee, and nearly everyone makes a living in an activity related to coffee production. Coffee tasting, coffee packing, coffee shipping, and many other types of work are related to Brazil's most important export.

The South

The three southern states are Santa Catarina, Paraná, and Rio Grande do Sul. A pleasant, temperate climate and fertile land

Mountains, sea, the modern city, and the jungle beyond it, all meet in a unique way at Rio's Guanabara Bay. Below, the Central Plaza in São Paulo, Brazil's industrial city.

The Congress and Senate Chamber in Brasília—the new capital city of Brazil.

attracted large numbers of European settlers to this region in the 19th and 20th centuries. The narrow coastal plain and rolling grasslands of the interior are today the most European parts of Brazil. Some southern towns such as Blumenau and Joinvile look like transplanted German villages; other cities are mostly Italian or, in Paraná, Polish.

The immigrants brought many of their European skills to the new land. The Italians have made grapes and wines important products of the region. Germans have built breweries and cultivated large farms in the area.

The leading cities of the South are Pôrto Alegre, the capital of Rio Grande do Sul, famous for its beautiful women and long, colorful sunsets, and Curitiba, the capital of Paraná. Pôrto Alegre ("Happy Port") is a modern city whose leading products are leather, textiles, beer, and wine. Curitiba is becoming a rival of São Paulo as a center of coffee growing.

In parts of the South, rolling grasslands like the Pampas of Argentina are used to raise Brazil's largest herds of sheep and high-grade beef cattle. Rio Grande do Sul is the center of the beef industry, and wheat and soybeans are leading products.

Brazil's only source of coal is in the state of Santa Catarina. Low-grade coal mined here is used in the manufacture of steel at Volta Redonda in the Central East. Araucaria pine, which is found in Santa Catarina and Paraná, is the chief source of income for those states. Cotton, sugar, rice, beans, onions, potatoes, and tobacco are raised throughout the South.

The Central West

Brazil's frontier states are Goiás and Mato Grosso ("Great Forest") on the western plateau. This vast, thinly populated region was first settled by men hunting for gold and diamonds. Only in recent years have travelers been able to go into this region unarmed.

Many people have tried to settle in this region. But huge distances and poor communications have discouraged settlers. In the southern part of the region there are coffee plantations, but most of the land is used for ranching. Cattle roam the large, unfenced ranches and provide the chief source of income for Brazil's westerners.

The government believes that this vast region may become the heart of the nation. This explains the location of the new capital, Brasília, in Goiás. For hundreds of years Brazilians had spoken of moving their capital to the center of their nation, but it was not until Juscelino Kubitschek de Oliveira became president that the dream turned into a reality. In 1956 the Brazilian Congress decided to build a new capital city. On April 21, 1960, Brasília officially became the capital of Brazil in place of Rio. All Brazilians hope that with the movement of the capital their last frontier has been permanently opened for settlement.

The Amazon Basin

The territories of Rio Branco, Amapá, Rondônia, and the states of Amazonas, Acre, and Pará lie in the huge basin formed by the Amazon and its tributaries.

So much rain falls in the Amazon Basin that Brazilians divide the seasons into the "time of the big rains" and the "time of the little rains." The rains and high humidity feed the trees of the world's largest tropical rain forest, which sometimes grow as high as 160 feet. The selva, or rain forest, is home to many unusual forms of wildlife, including rare butterflies, giant spiders, huge beetles, boa constrictors, a rat that grows up to 4 feet long, and a kind of jaguar called an *onça*. More than 1,000 different species of fish live in the river. One of these is the pirarucu, a giant codfish that often grows to 1.5 meters (5 feet) in length. Another is the piranha, a small flesh-eating fish.

Many of Brazil's Indians still make their home in remote parts of the tropical rain forest. The Indians of Brazil have always lived in scattered groups and have never developed a great civilization like that of the Aztecs or Incas.

Most of the settlers in the Amazon Basin are of mixed Portuguese and Indian descent. They live in family groups or in small clusters of houses built on the river banks. In the places where the rains are heaviest, the houses are raised off the ground on stilts.

Because the tropical rains have washed away minerals that make the soil good for agriculture, settlers usually cannot farm one place for more than 3 years. The people of the upper Amazon Basin get much of their food through hunting and gathering. They hunt tapirs, peccary, monkeys, and parrots for meat. The river provides turtles and many kinds of edible fish.

The Amazon people gather the products of the forest and river such as latex, palm and brazil nuts, cayman (a type of alligator) skins, and medicinal plants that provide many different kinds of drugs, including cocaine, cumarin, curare, and strychnine. When the people have enough goods to sell, they travel

Houses along the Amazon are on stilts because of floods.

on the river by canoe, boat, or steamer to the nearest trading post. Here they exchange their goods for manufactured products such as knives, needles, and pots.

There are only a few large cities on the Amazon. One of them, Belém, is an important port at the mouth of the river. Another is Manaus, on the central Amazon, which was very important during the 19th century when the Amazonian forest was the leading source of natural rubber. The opera house and mosaic sidewalks of Manaus are reminders of the city's great days before Brazil lost its rubber

In Salvador (Bahia), the past and present, the African and Portuguese, meet and mingle.

Pots are sold along the old streets of Belém, capital of Pará (*left*). At right, coffee beans from Pará are spread out to dry in the sun. Brazilians have become world experts in the coffee-growing industry.

monopoly and Malaya began rubber cultivation.

Some of the resources of the Amazon Basin are believed to be great, but none of them, except rubber, has ever been developed. The timber of the great forests may someday form the basis of a lumber industry. The drugs that can be made from the medicinal plants of the forests may also become important. Manganese is now mined in Amapá, but oil exploration has not yet become successful.

▶ INDUSTRIES AND PRODUCTS

Throughout its history, Brazil's economy has depended mainly on one product at a time. In the late 16th and 17th centuries sugar was king. Just when the soil on the sugar plantations was losing fertility, large gold veins were discovered in Minas Gerais, and throughout the 18th century, Brazil was in the grips of "gold fever." As the riches from gold lessened, Brazil turned to agriculture, which still provides the basis of the economy. Only manganese and iron are mined in large quantities.

Agriculture and Stock Raising

A little less than half of the Brazilian people work in agriculture. Brazil is now a major cattle-raising nation. Other livestock, including hogs and horses, are raised extensively. The importance of farming is shown by Brazil's main exports. Coffee, cacao (the source of cocoa and chocolate), and sugar head the list. At least a third of the world's coffee comes from Brazil. In spite of Brazil's rich agriculture, a number of foods, including wheat and flour, must be imported.

Cotton, tobacco, bananas, and citrus fruits are also produced for export. Cotton is widely grown in the northeastern and central states and supplies Brazil's largest manufacturing industry—textiles. Tobacco is sold in large quantities, especially to the nations of northern Europe. Brazil is the second largest grower of oranges in the world, after the United States. Beans, rice, and manioc are widely grown for local use. Jute, used for making cord and rope, was introduced by Japanese immigrants.

Industry

Brazil has greatly increased its industrial capacity in recent years. The government has invited many foreign companies to build factories in Brazil. About 18 percent of the labor force is engaged in industry.

Food processing and textiles are the industrial giants. The main centers of industry are

São Paulo and Rio de Janeiro, but other cities are growing rapidly. Volta Redonda, for example, was once a village but today has one of the largest steel works in South America. Another fast-expanding industry is the manufacture of automobiles.

The most serious obstacle facing industry is the lack of mineral fuels. There is little coal, and petroleum is even more scarce. The building of hydroelectric plants on Brazil's rivers will help provide electricity. Brazil is also turning to nuclear power as a source of energy.

Trade

Brazil sells its farm products on the world market to pay for imports of fuels and lubricants, machinery, vehicles, chemicals, wheat, and metals and metal products. Imports come mainly from the United States, West Germany, Venezuela, and Argentina. The chief exports are coffee, iron ore, cotton, sugar, and pinewood. Many exports go to the United States, West Germany, and Argentina.

Transportation and Communications

Transportation and communications in Brazil need to be made better because the country is very large; settlements, towns, and cities are far from each other, and mountains, jungle, and deserts often separate them. The Great Escarpment has made the construction of roads and rails slow. Most highways and railroads are found on the eastern fringe of the country, where most of the people live. But air travel helps to link all parts of Brazil and is expanding rapidly. Brazil's domestic air network has become one of the world's greatest. There are many excellent harbors, which are important for world trade.

All major cities are linked by telephone and telegraph. Brazil has many hundreds of radio stations. In 1950 it became the first country in Latin America to have a television station.

▶ GOVERNMENT

Brazil is a republic composed of 21 states, four territories, and the federal district of Brasília. The head of the government is the president. He is elected for a 5-year term. The national congress is made up of two houses: the federal Senate and the Chamber of Deputies. Three senators are elected from each state for 8-year terms. The number of deputies a state or territory elects depends upon the size and population of the state or territory. Deputies serve 2-year terms.

▶ HISTORY

In 1500 a Portuguese explorer, Pedro Alvares Cabral, claimed Brazil for Portugal. Portugal had been given the right to colonize this part of the New World by the Treaty of Tordesillas in 1494. By this treaty Spain and Portugal, the leading seafaring nations of the day, divided the Western Hemisphere neatly between themselves.

For about 30 years after Cabral's voyage to the New World, the Portuguese paid little attention to their new colony, and only a few trading posts grew up along the coast. Portugal's main interest still lay in trade with the Orient. However, Portugal's attitude changed after 1530 for two reasons: a new source of wealth was needed, and other European powers were threatening to take Brazil.

The Portuguese king started the settlement of Brazil by giving favored nobles grants that stretched far inland from the coast. The early settlers had difficulties with hostile Indians. The settlers also had to face a new and strange tropical environment and unfamiliar soil conditions. The large landowners soon discovered that if they were to run successful settlements they needed better farm laborers than the Indians. Negro slaves were brought to Brazil in large numbers from Africa. Before long the sugar plantations of the Northeast were flourishing.

Meanwhile, in the Central East and the South, a new kind of person appeared. He was a mestizo, of mixed Portuguese and Indian ancestry. Bands of these hardy peoples, called *bandeirantes*, roamed the interior in search of gold and men to sell as slaves to the plantation owners of the north. The *bandeirantes* found both gold and slaves—and in doing so helped to explore and settle large regions in the present states of Minas Gerais, Mato Grosso, and Goiás.

By the beginning of the 19th century, Brazil's gold mines had been nearly exhausted, but a large part of the country was permanently settled. Farming was the major occupation. The descendants of the Portuguese settlers now thought of themselves as Brazilians rather than subjects of the King of Portugal.

Just as the first Brazilian movements for independence were developing, the French emperor Napoleon invaded Portugal. In 1808 the Portuguese royal family and more than 1,000 members of the court fled to Brazil. For the next 14 years Rio de Janeiro was the capital of the Portuguese empire. At last, in 1821, the King returned to his native land and left his son, Dom Pedro, to rule Brazil. The next year Dom Pedro, following the advice of José Bonifácio de Andrada, his minister of the interior, declared Brazil independent of Portugal. Peaceful change became the pattern of Brazil's political life.

Independence

Brazil remained an empire from 1822 until 1889. Dom Pedro was emperor for 9 years and then turned over his throne to his 5-year-old son, Dom Pedro II, who became emperor in 1840 at the age of 14. Dom Pedro II ruled Brazil for 49 years, during which the nation became larger and richer. Wars with Argentina (1851–52) and with Paraguay (1865–70) were finally settled peacefully. Railroads were built. Rubber from the Amazon jungle doubled foreign trade during Dom Pedro's reign. Six hundred thousand immigrants swelled Brazil's population between 1874 and 1889.

This peaceful growth ended in 1888, the year the Emperor's daughter Isabella abolished slavery. Many of the large landowners and slaveholders called for an overthrow of the government. But some wanted a republican form of government. The Army itself, exceptionally republican in spirit, favored the change, and in 1889 the old Emperor peacefully left Brazil for the good of the new republic. Ruy Barbosa, leader of the anti-slavery movement, prepared the first constitution of republican Brazil in 1891.

The Republic

During the early years of the republic, when the Army ruled Brazil, there was civil war and the risk of chaos. But by 1891 Brazil had a new constitution, and order had been restored to the country. Brazil became increasingly important in world politics, and in 1917 entered World War I on the Allies' side.

The years 1919 to 1939—between the two world wars—were troubled ones for Brazil. The overproduction of coffee and the fall of world coffee prices during the Depression brought new difficulties to the country. In 1930 the president was overthrown, and Getúlio Vargas became dictator of what he called a "disciplined democracy." Under Vargas' rule living conditions were improved and trade grew. During World War II, Brazil was a firm ally of the United States and sent a force of 25,000 men to fight in Italy.

The Second Republic

The Army forced Vargas to resign in 1945. Eurico Dutra was elected as his successor; but in 1950 Vargas ran for office and was elected. At the culmination of a very serious political crisis, in which he was close to being ousted again, Vargas took his own life. As a result of the next election, Juscelino Kubitschek de Oliveira became president.

Kubitschek told the Brazilians that they would "enjoy in 5 years the progress of 50 years," and worked hard to live up to his promise. The government helped to develop hydroelectric plants and some industries. Brasília, the beautiful new capital, was built. But rising costs and a fall in world coffee prices brought new problems to Brazil.

In 1960 Jânio Quadros was elected president, but his attempts to improve conditions were blocked. Quadros resigned within a year, and his vice-president, João Goulart, took his place. In 1964 discontent with Goulart's leftist policies caused serious problems throughout the country. The result was a revolution that brought the military to power. Since then Brazil's presidents have been members of the armed forces. They are selected by an electoral college made up of Congress and delegates from each state legislature.

In the past decade Brazil has made great economic progress. Investment of foreign capital has spurred production and brought increased employment. As the gap between rich and poor narrows, Brazil promises to become the "land of the future."

PETER O. WACKER
Louisiana State University (New Orleans)
Reviewed by ERICO VERÍSSIMO
Author, *Crossroads*

BRAZING. See SOLDERING AND BRAZING.

BREAD AND BAKING

Bread in some form is eaten practically everywhere in the world. It has been called the staff of life. Bread is so important that the word has taken on symbolical meanings. To break bread is a sign of friendship, and "More bread!" has been the slogan of many revolutions.

Before man had grain, he lived on fish, meat, wild berries, and nuts. Archeologists believe that man may have existed for 400,000 years before he knew how to plant grain. When he learned how to turn the grain into bread, he moved one step closer to civilization.

The first tools for making bread—stone mortars (hollow bowls) and pestles (pounders)—date from about 10,000 B.C. After the grain had been crushed, it was mixed with water and patted into slabs. These slabs of coarse grain were baked in hot ashes or on stones heated by the sun. Later, people discovered how to grind the grain by placing it on a flat or slightly hollowed stone and rubbing another stone back and forth across the grain. The next step forward was to bake the bread in ovens instead of in hot ashes.

Archeologists have found a sample of early bread that had been preserved in the ruins of Thebes. The bread was nothing more than a pressed cake of barley flour with the husks still in it. Man had not yet discovered leavening, and the bread was flat, like some religious breads of today—the matzoth eaten by Jews at Passover and the wafers used in Communion.

Leavening is the action of yeast in moist, warm dough. Yeast is made up of tiny one-celled organisms that feed on sugars and starches. The yeast cells convert the starch of the dough into sugar, which they then digest. As they do this they give off carbon dioxide as a waste product. This gas is trapped by gluten, a rubbery substance in the dough. Gluten is formed when water is mixed with flour that contains two protein materials called gliadin and glutenin. The gas blows the gluten into bigger and bigger bubbles, and makes the fermenting dough rise.

Wild yeast spores are almost always present in the air and will land naturally on the dough. The first people to discover the value of yeast were the Egyptians. They tried baking fermented dough and were pleased with the lighter, tastier bread. However, bread that rises with the aid of wild yeast may turn out quite differently each time. This is because

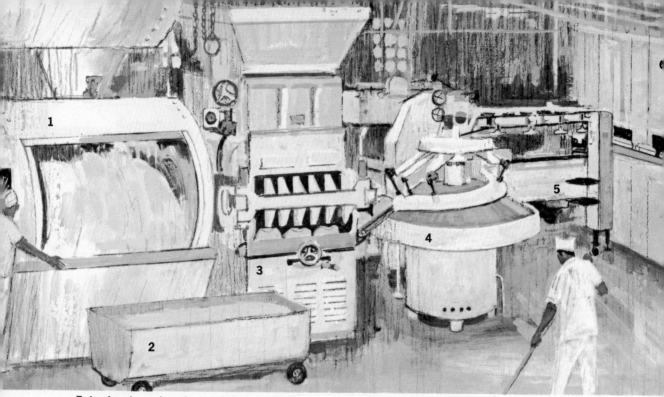

Today bread can be mixed, baked, and wrapped in a completely automatic process. Dough is turned out by the revolving paddles of the mixing machine (1). After fermenting in a trough (2), the dough is transferred to the divider (3), which divides the mass of dough into loaf-sized pieces. The rounder (4) forms the dough into balls. From the rounder the dough passes to a proof box (not shown), where it rises. Conveyor belts carry the

different kinds of yeast may fall on it.

The Egyptians discovered a way to control the kind of yeast in their bread. Each time they baked, they set aside some of the leavened dough to mix with the next batch. In this way they could be sure of using the same kind of yeast. Each batch of bread would then have the same taste and texture. The sour dough carried by prospectors in the California and Klondike gold rushes was used for the same purpose.

The Egyptians tried other experiments with their bread. They put in sesame or lotus seeds and added milk, wine, or oil to vary the flavor. Around 1000 B.C. Phoenician traders carried the art of making leavened bread to the Greeks, who became the master bakers of antiquity. The Greeks had over 70 different recipes for bread.

The Romans turned baking into a large-scale industry and passed many laws governing the quality of the bread. The bakers belonged to a society called the College of Pistors, which had the right to a seat in the senate. They were so proud of the superior taste of their bread that each baker marked his loaves

with his name, just as bakeries put their brand name on the wrappers today.

The Roman expression "bread and circuses"—bread for nourishment, circuses for amusement—shows how important bread was in Roman life. However, the poor people had to be content with coarse, dark bread. Fine, white bread was only for the wealthy.

Although the art of baking had been spread throughout Europe by Rome's conquering armies, the practice of making white bread was abandoned after the fall of the Roman Empire. As Europe revived during the Middle Ages white bread again took its place as the bread of the rich and privileged, but dark, often sour, rye bread was the mainstay of most of the people.

Wheat was sent to the cities, where the growing demand for bread led to the development of bakeries and eventually bakers' guilds. The guilds trained apprentices, controlled prices, and supervised the quality of the bread. Not all bread was sold in shops. Some was sold on the streets by venders who rang bells and chanted songs about the good taste of their wares.

dough from machine to machine. In the molding machine (5), rollers flatten the dough into pancake shape, then form it into loaves. The loaves rise once more in a final proof box (6), then move into a traveling oven (7). When the bread comes out of the oven about ½ hour later, it is fully baked. The loaves are sliced by the steel blades of a slicing machine (8), then wrapped automatically (9).

The Industrial Revolution brought many changes in baking. Large bread factories gradually took the place of little neighborhood shops. As the standard of living rose and wheat became more abundant, people demanded more refined bread. They considered that the whiter the bread, the better the quality. This was not actually true, because as bakers sifted out the impurities they were also removing some of the vitamins and minerals. However, since 1940 the flour has been enriched by adding the vitamins and minerals lost during the sifting.

▶ BREAD MANUFACTURING

In the automatic bakeries of today, bread can be handled without being touched by human hands. Instead of the flour being carried in in bags, a whole carload of loose flour is blown into the bakery storage tanks by a machine similar to a giant vacuum cleaner. Tank carloads of melted shortening are also pumped into the bakery. By pressing a button the baker can open the tanks, and the exact amount of shortening and flour needed falls into the mixers.

Sponge Method. Most of the bread manufactured in the United States is mixed by the sponge method. The sponge, the base for the dough, is a combination of flour, yeast, and water.

The sponge goes through a carefully timed fermenting process in a special room and is then returned to the mixer. More flour and enriching ingredients—butter, sugar, eggs, milk—are added to the sponge, and the sticky combination is kneaded until it is elastic. Then a series of machines shape it into loaves or rolls.

A slowly moving conveyor belt carries the dough from machine to machine. This permits the dough to "rest" between steps. If bread dough is worked too much, it becomes tough.

Straight-Dough Method. In the straight-dough method all the ingredients are mixed at once, and the dough ferments a shorter period of time. There is more yeast and fewer enriching ingredients because the yeast would eat them up. Since all the wheat ferments, the bread has a hard crust and a heartier, stronger taste.

Although straight dough makes good bread, it is harder to move it through modern machinery. Usually only the smaller bakeries use this method for handmade bread, but good rye or pumpernickel must be made with straight dough.

Another way to give bread flavor is to save a piece of dough from each day's baking to start off the next day's batch. This is common practice in bakeries mixing French bread, rye bread, and handmade bread of all kinds. The ancient Egyptian method of adding leavening has not been improved on yet.

Continuous-Mix Method. Some of the newest bakeries use a continuous system of mixing bread that eliminates many steps and many workers. In this system a liquid ferment or brew is made containing all the ingredients that go into the bread and part of the flour. This brew is fermented in tanks and then pumped into a continuous-mix machine, which looks something like a kitchen meat grinder but is very much bigger. Here it is mixed with the rest of the flour into dough.

The continuous-mix machine makes about 6,000 pounds of bread an hour and automatically puts the right amount of dough in each pan. Bread made in this way has a very smooth, even grain and is very soft. Bakers sometimes add softeners and salt to dough to prevent the bread from getting moldy or hard while it is waiting in the shop to be bought.

Proofing and Baking

After the dough has been mixed and shaped by one of these three methods, it rests in a proof box, where it rises. A proof box is kept at about 100 degrees Fahrenheit and with a humidity high enough to keep the bread from drying out and forming a crust. From the proof box the bread goes into a very hot oven (over 400 degrees), where it keeps rising until the yeast is killed by the heat and stops making gas. As the sugar on the dough surface caramelizes, the bread starts to turn brown. If steam is let into the oven, the bread comes out shiny.

Traveling ovens keep the bread moving even while it is being baked. The traveling oven is built like a long steel tunnel, lined with heating units. The bread bakes as it moves slowly through the oven on a wire-mesh conveyor belt. When the loaves reach the end of the oven, they tumble off the belt and fall onto another conveyor. The loaves have time to cool as they ride along on their way to the slicing and wrapping machines.

Other Bakery Products

The Roman honey bread and the later medieval sweet cakes were the forerunners of the iced layer cakes and spongecakes of today. Pies or tarts were made by medieval cooks, but most of the pies they brought to their masters' tables were meat pies. Gradually pastry cooks began to turn sweet desserts into elaborate creations. In the 19th century the Viennese and French made such artistic and tasty desserts that people traveled to Vienna and Paris to try their pastries.

Most commercially baked desserts are produced by local companies that specialize in putting out cakes, pies, and other sweet concoctions. However, some large bread factories make cakes, pies, and doughnuts as well as bread.

Surprisingly enough, these big companies make many of their baked goods by adding water to a mix, just as housewives do. Instead of buying a box of cake mix, the baker buys it in huge sacks by the freight carload. Using prepared mixes means both the housewife and the commercial baker can be certain of how their baked goods will taste and can save time in their preparation.

Frozen baked products and brown-and-serve rolls are usually put out by specialty companies. They are shipped throughout the country and give the housewife a wider choice than she found 10 years ago on her grocery shelf. Now she can serve fresh cakes and crisp rolls without spending hours making them. Twelve minutes in a hot oven, and the rolls are baked for dinner. Thirty minutes on a kitchen counter, and a chocolate cake is defrosted.

Many types of cakes, such as poundcake, fruitcake, and Boston brown bread, are packed in cans. Canned bread was developed to meet a very practical problem. The Army had to find a way to keep bread in combat rations from going stale.

Canned bread is made by baking the dough right in the can rather than in baking pans. The lid is loosely clinched onto the can to permit steam and leavening gas to escape during baking—otherwise the can would explode. As soon as the can leaves the oven, a machine seals it hermetically (airtight). This keeps out bacteria and molds that cause decay. The can is then rapidly cooled to protect the flavor and color of the bread inside it.

▶ COOKIES, CRACKERS, BISCUITS, AND PRETZELS

Cookies, crackers, biscuits, and pretzels certainly do not look or taste alike, but they actually are alike in many ways. They are all small and crisp, and keep well. They are even made on the same kinds of machines and packaged in the same way. Special baking plants turn out all four with only slight changes in equipment and recipes.

They are made with the same ingredients—flour, leavening, shortening, sweetening, and liquid. Usually the leavening in these products is baking powder instead of yeast. In the oven the baking powder creates carbon dioxide gas, which makes the baked goods light without making them rise too high.

During the Middle Ages French travelers, soldiers, and sailors carried a strange, hard bread. The bread had been cooked twice to keep it from spoiling. No one needs to cook bread twice today, but we do eat hard biscuits. The name "biscuits" comes from the early French word for twice cooked. Another form of hard bread, hardtack, was the traditional fare for British sailors.

Crackers appeared in the United States about the time of the Civil War. Soon every grocery store had a cracker barrel filled with square soda crackers or round butter crackers. Grocery stores were the center of social life in small towns during the 1800's and early 1900's. The people who gathered there to exchange news and opinions were called cracker-barrel philosophers.

Part of the fun in eating cookies is their shape. Hearty oatmeal cookies are cut into their big, round shapes by knives on a cutting machine. The designs on some cookies are stamped as the sheet of dough is pressed over the rollers of another cutting machine. Novelty cookies, such as four-leaf clovers or hearts, are often made by forcing the dough through nozzles shaped like the design of the cookie. A wire under the nozzle snips off the cookies, and they drop onto the belt that carries them into the oven. There are even machines to sprinkle sugar, salt, or other toppings on the cookies or crackers.

You may have noticed the tiny rectangular punctures in soda crackers. A special roller made these holes to let some of the steam out while the rest of the steam bubbled up in the dough. Those little holes help make the crackers crunchy.

Pretzels have a long history. They date back to the early Christians in the Roman Empire and were used at that time solely for religious purposes. Fat, milk, and eggs were forbidden during the Lenten season, and people ate dry pretzels instead of bread. They were especially popular on Ash Wednesday. It was only in modern times that they became snacks to nibble on.

In northern Europe and the Scandinavian countries the pretzel has become the sign of the baker, and a large golden pretzel is usually seen hanging outside each bakery.

The original pretzel was a large twist with a soft inside and a crusty outside. By baking out almost all of the moisture, manufacturers produce the crisp, hard pretzel we eat today. Made from very stiff dough, the pretzels are actually salty baked biscuits. They are twisted or shaped into sticks.

Packaging

Packaging is one of the most important steps, for these products must be well wrapped to stay fresh. Crackers particularly must be thoroughly cooled and dried before they are packed. As they leave the ovens they are stacked on edge in rows. Some crackers are double wrapped in lined boxes with wax paper and outer wrapping of transparent film. Biscuits and cookies are sealed with the same care to protect the package from air and moisture. Months on the shelf will not harm their flavor.

It is interesting that while bread is wrapped to keep the moisture in, cookies, crackers, and biscuits are wrapped to keep the moisture out so that they will come to you as crisp as when they left the oven.

Reviewed by RICHARD PRINCE
President, Gottfried Baking Co.

See also FLOUR AND FLOUR MILLING; FOOD AROUND THE WORLD; GRAIN AND GRAIN PRODUCTS; WHEAT.

BREATHING. See BODY, HUMAN.
BREWING. See BEER AND BREWING.

BRICKS AND MASONRY

Bricks are a common, cheap, and very useful building material made of baked clay. Bricks are one of man's oldest permanent building materials.

Bricks are durable, easy to build into walls, and cost little to make. Ordinary brick can stand the direct flames of a fire with little damage, and firebrick (a special brick used for lining furnaces) can stand temperatures as high as 4000 degrees Fahrenheit. The clay in brick is highly resistant to acids, so that brick walls can withstand the smoky, corrosive air of cities better than some kinds of stone and painted metal.

With a simple wooden mold, workers in Togo, Africa, make bricks by hand. The finished bricks are spread out in the sun to dry.

Bricks have been made in many sizes and shapes since they were first used over 5,000 years ago. At the present time the standard brick in the United States is a rectangular block measuring about 2¼ by 3¾ by 8 inches. Most bricks shrink a little during baking, so that few are exactly this size.

Bricks range in color from nearly white, through tan, red, and red-brown, to dark purple and blue. The color is determined by the amount of iron and other impurities in the clay and by the method of baking, or firing, the brick. Usually the higher the baking temperature used, the darker the brick will be. Bricks may also be glazed in various colors, like pottery.

The strength of brick also varies a great deal. Brick has high compressive strength; that is, it can withstand forces that press in on it. But brick does not have tensile strength —it cannot withstand forces that tend to pull it apart. The average brick can take a load of about 5,000 pounds a square inch before it is crushed. Several types of brick can stand a load as high as 10,000 pounds a square inch.

▶ FROM CLAY TO BRICK

All bricks are made from clay. Clay is a common mineral substance composed of very small rock particles. Some types of clay are formed by the disintegration of rocks by weathering. Other types of clay were formed during the Ice Age by the action of glaciers grinding boulders to fine powder. Clay is found over most of the earth's surface, often in lake beds and riverbeds. It is frequently mixed with other substances, such as sand and silt. Clay becomes slippery and plastic (easily molded) when it is wet. When it is dry, it becomes hard and stony.

When clay is heated to a high temperature (about 850 degrees), it changes chemically so that it no longer becomes plastic when it is wet. This means that bricks of baked clay will not soften and lose their shape when they become wet, and a wall made of these bricks will not collapse into a sticky heap during a heavy rain. Bricks are baked, or burned, at 1600 to 2200 degrees. At about 1000 degrees the brick turns red; its color becomes darker as the temperature increases.

Until the 19th century bricks were made by hand. In one common method clay was dug up from the ground and exposed to the air from fall to spring. After the clay was thoroughly dried, the brickmaker spread a small quantity of it on the ground, added a little water, and mixed it into a paste. He pressed the mixture into wooden forms, or molds, which gave the bricks the correct size and shape. Then he removed the sides of the mold and laid the moist brick on the ground to be dried and hardened by the sun. In Biblical times chopped straw was usually mixed with the clay to help hold it together.

Since rain might slow up the process or even ruin the soft clay, brickmakers realized that they had to find a better process of drying. As early as 2500 B.C. the technique of baking the brick in ovens, or kilns, was being used in Mesopotamia and India. (Sun-dried bricks, or adobe, are still used in regions where it seldom rains.)

Over the centuries a number of different types of kilns were invented. Most bricks today are made in continuous kilns. Continuous kilns are designed so that they can turn out bricks 24 hours a day if necessary. In older types of kilns only one batch of brick could be made at one time. The tunnel kiln, a heated tunnel through which the bricks are pulled slowly on little railroad cars, is a leading type of continuous kiln.

Basically the manufacture of bricks has changed little since ancient times, except that machines now perform most of the tasks that were once done laboriously by hand. The clay is now dug by power shovels. After drying, it is ground in power-driven mills and screened to get particles of uniform size.

In the **stiff-mud** process the clay is mixed with water into a stiff paste, then forced out under pressure through shaped nozzles, like a giant square-cornered strip of toothpaste. The strip is automatically cut into pieces of the proper size by knives or wires. The soft brick is then dried in heated tunnels and finally carried in small railroad cars to the kilns for firing.

The **soft-mud** process is older than the stiff-mud process. As the name tells us, the clay-and-water mixture is quite soft. The soft paste is shaped in individual molds either by machine or by hand. The soft-mud process is slower than the stiff-mud process, and it is little used today.

In the **dry** process the ground-up clay is barely moistened with water—just enough to make it hold together. Powerful hydraulic presses squeeze the clay into brick shape. Brick made by this method is just as durable as brick made by the stiff-mud process, and the time of manufacture is shortened because the bricks do not have to be dried before they are fired.

▶ **MASONRY**

Masonry is the name for walls, pillars, arches, and other structures made by laying bricks, stone blocks, and other stonelike materials, such as concrete blocks, in a cementing material.

Long ago, primitive man discovered that he could pile naturally occurring stones together to make a rough wall. Later, men hit upon the idea of trimming the stones so that they would fit together better. This made a firmer and more solid wall. At about the same time, people in regions where stone was scarce discovered how to turn clay into artificial stones—bricks. Bricks were easy to build with because they were the same size and shape, and did not need trimming to fit together. And, being small, they were easy to handle. The final step in the evolution of masonry was taken when builders learned that they could use various materials to cement bricks or stone blocks together. In this way they could build rigid walls and more complicated structures, such as arches and vaults.

Brick Masonry

To make a rigid wall of brick, individual bricks are laid together in horizontal layers, or **courses**. The bricks are bound together by a cementing material, or **mortar**.

The mason spreads a layer of mortar with a wide, flat trowel. He then sets the bricks on the mortar, pressing them down lightly. If a brick is out of line, he taps it gently into place with the handle of his trowel. Mortar is also placed between each brick in a course. When the first course is laid, the mason spreads mortar on top of it and lays the second course on this mortar. He repeats this process until the wall is built.

It is important that each course should be level and that the wall should be straight. An uneven wall is not only unsightly but it is

Pressing a brick into place, a bricklayer uses his trowel to scrape off excess mortar.

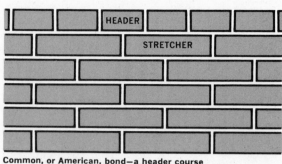

Common, or American, bond—a header course is placed at every sixth stretcher course.

English bond—a course of stretchers and a course of headers alternate up the wall.

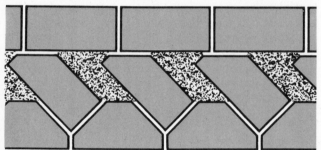

Diagonal raking bond—(seen from the top) for building a thick hollow wall. The shaded area is mortar and brick chips.

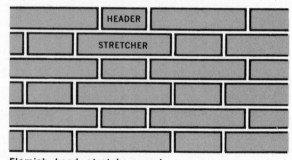

Flemish bond—stretchers and headers alternating in each course.

weak. As he works the mason uses a spirit level to make sure that the bricks are set level in the mortar. He uses a plumb line (a string with a weight at one end) as a vertical guideline. A string stretched tightly from one end of the wall to the other helps the mason line up the bricks horizontally.

The thin horizontal and vertical layers of mortar between the bricks are called the **joints**. The early masons learned that they could build a stronger wall by overlapping the bricks so that the vertical joints of one course stood at the centers of the bricks below. These are called **staggered joints**. The different arrangements in which the bricks are laid are called **bonds**. Bricks laid with the ends toward the face of the wall are called **headers**. Bricks laid with the lengths parallel to the face of the wall are called **stretchers**. (See illustrations above.)

Because of the force of wind, bearing walls (walls that support a building) made of brick are not suitable for high buildings. Wind pushing against such large walls would tumble them down unless the walls were extremely thick. The highest building in the world with brick bearing walls is the 16-story Monadnock Building in Chicago, completed in 1891. Its walls are 72 inches thick at the base. Constructing such thick walls is expensive and time consuming. This is one of the reasons that builders began to use steel or reinforced concrete for the frames of later skyscrapers.

Today brick is used as a basic structural material only in small buildings. Modern builders use it mainly as a facing, or veneer, over the wooden frames of houses and the concrete or steel frames of large buildings. So many buildings of every type are constructed, however, that the manufacture of brick is still a major industry.

Stone Masonry

Stones vary widely in size, shape, and composition. Most stone used in buildings is cut from quarries and dressed, or trimmed, to an exact rectangular shape. However, natural stones occurring on the surface of the ground or in stream beds are also used. These may be rough chunks of rock or rounded boulders worn smooth by glaciers, streams, or ocean waves.

A person who works with stone is called a stonemason. The stonemason's work is more difficult and exacting than the bricklayer's. The stones have rough, jagged edges. To get a smooth surface, the stonemason trims off the projections. This is called dressing the stone and requires experience and skill.

Setting the stones in place in the walls is an art in itself. Since building stones are usually cut in large sizes (to save labor in trimming), they are very heavy. For example, a granite block 6 feet long by 3 feet wide by 1 foot thick weighs about 3,060 pounds—more than a ton and a half.

Obviously, such stones are too heavy to lay by hand. They must be lifted by powerful derricks and guided into place by the stone setter as they are gently lowered. If the stone is out of line, it cannot simply be tapped into line like a brick. It must be lifted up and lowered into place again.

Stone, like brick, was once a major structural material. It was used where great strength and weight were required, as in dams, bridges, fortresses, foundations, and important build-ings. Today steel and concrete have taken the place of stone as a basic construction material. However, stone is still important as sheathing (outside covering) for buildings, as flooring where there is heavy traffic, and for many decorative uses.

▶ HISTORY OF MASONRY

The history of masonry goes back as far as that of civilization. Bricks were apparently first used around 3500 B.C. by the people who lived in the flat, low-lying plain between the Tigris and Euphrates rivers in what is now Iraq. Wood and stone fit for building were scarce in that region, but there was plenty of clay, which the people made into sun-dried, unbaked bricks shaped like loaves of bread. They used these oddly shaped bricks to build their great cities.

The next great civilization to use brick was that of Egypt, where brick making began about 3100 B.C. Although the Egyptians had vast supplies of fine building stone, it took so much labor to quarry the stone, cut it to size, and transport it to the building sites that stone was used only for temples, palaces, and monuments. Ordinary buildings were made of sun-baked brick.

From Egypt and the Near East brick making spread over the Mediterranean world. The Romans became the master brickmakers of antiquity. Roman bricks were relatively thin and broad, and they were made in a variety of different shapes: rectangular, square, triangular, and semicircular.

One of the worst problems faced by builders in the ancient world was the lack of a strong mortar to bind their bricks and stones together. The earliest Egyptian brick buildings, for example, were held together by nothing more substantial than a paste of mud. Later the Egyptians developed a slightly stronger mortar of clay and sand. The Babylonians used asphalt or lime mixed with clay and ashes. Yet in spite of their poor mortar ancient builders constructed some remarkable brick temples and palaces, with walls 10 to 20 feet thick. The builders depended mainly on the weight of the walls to hold the bricks in place.

Masonry construction was revolutionized by the Roman discovery of concrete in the 2nd century B.C. With this strong cementing

A mud-brick wall in the ruins of Nebuchadnezzar's palace in Iraq. The figure of the horse was formed by using molded bricks.

A 12th-century castle at Carcassonne, France. The walls and towers, still strong and solid, show the durability of stone masonry.

material builders no longer needed to make their walls enormously thick to keep them from toppling over. In fact, the Romans' concrete was so strong that they were able to use it for the heart of their masonry construction. Most important Roman buildings were made of concrete with a thin decorative facing of brick or stone.

Perhaps the most famous examples of ancient stone masonry are the pyramids of Egypt, some of which are more than 4,500 years old. Some of the blocks of stone in the pyramids weigh over 1,000 tons each.

Other ancient civilizations besides the Egyptians developed great skill in handling very large blocks of stone. The Myceneans, who lived in central Greece between 2100 and 1300 B.C., built fortifications and tombs of rough stone blocks that weighed several tons apiece. Later Greeks could not believe that ordinary men were capable of handling such huge stones; so they decided these walls had been built by one-eyed giants called Cyclopes. This type of masonry is still called cyclopean masonry.

The Greeks became the master stone workers of the ancient world. They were especially skilled at designing and trimming stone blocks. Their columns were cleverly built up of short sections pinned together by metal rods. The Greek masons fitted the sections so exactly that they needed no mortar. Another favorite device of the Greeks was the use of hidden metal clamps to hold stones together.

The Gothic cathedrals of the late Middle Ages are the most intricate structures in pure stone ever attempted. The skill of the men who built these cathedrals has never again been equalled.

CARL W. CONDIT
Co-editor, *Technology and Culture*

See also ARCHITECTURE; BUILDING CONSTRUCTION; CEMENT AND CONCRETE; STONE.

BRIDGES

Man has been using bridges since very early in history. At first these were natural bridges, such as a tree that had fallen across a stream or a rock formation stretching across a gorge. Then men learned to make their own bridges with logs, stones, and vines. Eventually primitive man learned how to make in a crude form every type of bridge that we know today.

The earliest bridges of which there are any records were beam bridges—the simplest type to construct. More complicated structures, such as suspension and cantilever bridges, were built in India around 3000 B.C. The arch bridge was the last type to be developed, because of the difficulty of construction.

The first great bridge-builders of the Western world were the Romans, who excelled in all kinds of building. The Romans had developed a good cement mortar that enabled them to erect very remarkable and durable structures. For one thing, they could build larger arches than earlier builders had been able to do. Arches were a good way to support a bridge, because with arches a builder could span long distances with a minimum of materials. Most of the great Roman bridges were supported on arches. Around the city of Rome alone, six bridges built by the ancient Romans are still standing. The oldest of these bridges was built in 179 B.C.; the most recent dates from A.D. 307. Many other Roman structures still exist in countries that were once part of the Roman Empire.

After the collapse of the Roman Empire, there were no officials to keep bridges in repair or to build new ones. The bridges gradually fell into ruin. Rivers and gorges that once were easily crossed on bridges became hazardous obstacles for travelers. Communications were disrupted and sometimes were cut off altogether. At the end of the 12th century, a religious order was founded in Europe that became known as the Brothers of the Bridge (Frères Pontifes in France, Fratres Pontifices in Italy). Besides building bridges, the monks kept them in repair and established shelters on the riverbanks where travelers could rest. One of the famous bridges constructed by the brotherhood was the bridge over the Rhône River in Avignon, France. So solidly was it built that some parts of the bridge are still standing after 7 centuries.

In England also the clergy led the way in bridge-building. The construction of London Bridge, one of the most famous structures in history, was directed by the clergyman Peter Colechurch. The bridge was begun in 1176 and completed in 1209. Until the 18th century

The Pont du Gard, which is still standing, was built by the Romans about the year A.D. 150 as part of an aqueduct to bring water to the city of Nimes, France.

Most of the world's great cities grew up on rivers. Above are some of the bridges that carry the traffic of Paris across the Seine River.

it was the only bridge across the Thames in London. Not only was it used for crossing the river; it became one of the centers of London life. People lived on the bridge, fought duels there, and even had their heads displayed there if they were executed.

Although there had been small wooden bridges on the Thames, London Bridge was the first to be built entirely of masonry. The citizens of London gave money to help pay for the work. After the bridge was finished, houses were built on it, and in time it became lined with buildings. The houses were rented out to help pay for maintaining the bridge.

The houses on the bridge were several stories high. Some had basements that were dug out of the huge masonry piers. When the people who lived in the houses wanted water for household chores, they let down buckets attached to ropes and drew up water from the Thames. Occasionally they had to use their ropes to rescue sailors whose boats crashed into the bridge. Such accidents happened quite often, especially at night, because the arches of the bridge had narrow openings.

Maintenance of the bridge was a continual

problem. Some scholars think the song "London Bridge Is Falling Down" originally referred to the bridge's constant need for repairs. The old bridge continued in use, however, until the 1830's, when it was replaced by a new London Bridge.

But with the passing of time, this bridge, too, had to be replaced. The foundations were causing problems, and the bridge had become too narrow for modern traffic. A new London Bridge spanning the Thames was begun in 1968 and completed in 1973. Some of the stone from the previous bridge was shipped to Lake Havasu City, Arizona, where it was used in a small reproduction of London Bridge across an arm of the Colorado River.

London Bridge was not the only bridge of the Middle Ages on which people lived. The Ponte Vecchio in Florence, built in 1345, still is lined with houses along each parapet, with an arcade over the top of the roadway. Most of these houses are now used for shops. The famous Rialto Bridge over the Grand Canal of Venice, erected in 1591, is built in the same way. It is a single-arch bridge with a span of 89 feet.

▶ TYPES OF BRIDGES

Throughout centuries of bridge-building, man has developed a variety of bridge types for different needs or conditions. These types may be classed in two broad groups—fixed bridges and movable bridges.

Fixed Bridges

Fixed bridges are anchored in one spot and cannot be moved. They are made of supports called **piers** that hold up the roadbed of the bridge and **foundations** that support the piers. The distance between the piers, or supports, is called the **span**. The simplest types of fixed bridges are the simple-beam bridge, the arch bridge, and the suspension bridge.

The Simple-Beam Bridge. The roadbed on a simple-beam bridge is supported by beams that rest on the piers. A fallen tree lying across a stream forms a kind of simple-beam bridge. Since the beam bridge is easy to build, it was formerly the most-used type of bridge where the loads on the bridge were light. Heavier loads called for more complicated structures.

The Truss Bridge. Adding a framework of beams called a truss to the simple-beam bridge creates a truss bridge. The truss framework adds stability and strength to the basic structure and helps transmit the load from the roadbed to the piers. A series of trusses, each supported by a set of piers, is called a simple-truss bridge. A continuous-truss bridge has one long truss that extends the entire length of the bridge.

Arch Bridges. Bridge-builders as early as Roman times found that the arch was useful because it allowed them to span greater distances than they could with beams. The arch was also an efficient way to distribute the load to the piers. Arch bridges are of two basic types. The **deck-arch** bridge has the roadway supported on top of the arch; the **through-arch** bridge has the roadway suspended from the inside of the arch. Most arch bridges are of the deck type.

The arch bridges of the Chinese are outstanding for the beauty of their design. The Chinese are thought to have learned the use of the arch from the people of the Near East with whom they began to trade in the 1st century A.D. The great 13th-century traveler Marco Polo expressed admiration for the Chinese bridges he saw. An arch bridge that he ob-

SIMPLE-BEAM BRIDGE

THROUGH-ARCH BRIDGE

DECK-ARCH BRIDGE

CANTILEVER BRIDGE

TRUSS BRIDGE

SUSPENSION BRIDGE

The Golden Gate Bridge, spanning the entrance to San Francisco Bay in California, is one of the world's best-known suspension bridges.

served ouside Peking was wide enough for 10 horsemen to ride abreast on it.

The first metal arch bridge (of cast iron) was built in England in 1775. However, until late in the 19th century most arch bridges continued to be made of stone. An arch bridge of steel was not built until 1867, when Captain James B. Eads spanned the Mississippi River at St. Louis with a steel deck-arch bridge.

Suspension Bridges. The suspension bridge has support towers holding long steel cables that are anchored at each end of the bridge. Vertical steel cables attached to the main cables hold up the bridge roadway.

The suspension bridge existed in a primitive form in ancient times. It was usually made of vines that supported a walkway or roadway. Another crude type of suspension bridge is the hammock type, which consists of two pairs of cables (usually of vine or rope) all woven into a web. Bridges of this type are still in use in parts of Asia, Africa, and South America.

The modern suspension bridge, supported by steel wire cables, was introduced when John A. Roebling designed the Brooklyn Bridge in New York City. In 1869, as construction was begun, Roebling died in an accident. His son, Washington A. Roebling, completed the work in 1883. The bridge has a span of 486 meters (1,594½ feet).

Because the suspension bridge is less heavy than other kinds of bridges, it can be built to span greater distances. Some of the longest and best-known bridges in the world are suspension structures.

Measurements given for suspension bridges are usually of the central span, between the two main support towers. The Golden Gate Bridge in San Francisco, California, with a central span of 1,280 meters (4,200 feet), once held the record for the world's longest single span. But now there are two newer bridges with longer central spans. One is the Verrazano-Narrows Bridge, with a span of 1,298 meters (4,260 feet), crossing New York Bay from Brooklyn to Staten Island. The other is the Humber Bridge over the Humber River in eastern England. Its span of 1,410 meters (4,626 feet) is the longest in the world. In total length, Michigan's Mackinac Bridge is the longest. Including the two side spans, it is 2,256 meters (7,400 feet) long. In Asia, the Kanmon Bridge linking the Japanese islands of Honshu and Kyushu is the longest suspension bridge, with a central span of 712 meters (2,336 feet).

For a long time the chief problem in building a suspension bridge was keeping it stable. If the bridge was not rigid enough, it would sway in the wind or under a heavy load. If it swayed too much, the bridge could pull loose from its moorings or break apart. Such a catastrophe actually occurred with the Tacoma Narrows Bridge over Puget Sound in 1940, only 4 months after it was completed. Long before this, however, Roebling had shown that with the proper design the suspension bridge could be as safe as any other kind of bridge. Before Roebling proved this, the most popular type of bridge had been the more rigid cantilever type.

Cantilever Bridges. The cantilever bridge basically consists of beams or trusses extending toward one another from piers and connected by a short, suspended span. Because they are rigid, cantilevers have been extensively used as railroad bridges.

A Bridge That Goes Underwater. An unusual bridge is the 17.6-mile Chesapeake Bay Bridge-Tunnel, completed in 1964. It crosses the mouth of Chesapeake Bay, linking Norfolk, Virginia, with Virginia's eastern shore. It has 12.2 miles of trestle and two bridge spans over ship lanes. The roadway dips under the water in two tunnels, each over a mile long. Four man-made islands provide access to the tunnels. The bridge was designed in this way so as to leave clear channels for warships from nearby naval bases in Virginia.

Movable Bridges

Bridges are often needed across bodies of water where ships sail. Sometimes it is not possible or convenient to build a bridge high enough for ships to pass under it. If this is the case, the bridge must be built so that it can be moved out of the way or raised so that the ships can pass under it. There are four main types of such movable bridges—floating bridges, swing spans, drawbridges, and lifts, or vertical drawbridges.

Floating Bridges. Since they are easy to assemble and move, floating bridges have been widely used by armies ever since the time of the ancient Greeks. The Greeks and Romans supported their floating bridges on boats that were anchored in a row across the river.

Modern floating bridges are supported on hollow floats of steel, rubber, or concrete

This truss bridge carries a railroad across the Corinth ship canal in Greece. The trussing is below the roadway.

Above, stone arches support the 600-year-old Ponte Vecchio across the Arno River in Florence, Italy. Below, the steel through-arch Sydney Harbour Bridge spans the harbor entrance in Sydney, Australia.

The Tower Bridge in London, England, is a double-leaf bascule bridge. The center spans tilt up to allow ships to pass.

called pontoons. Floating bridges may be permanently anchored in one spot or they may be built in sections for easy removal to another location.

During World War II the British engineer Donald Bailey designed a bridge made of prefabricated sections for rapid assembly and removal. The **Bailey bridge** was adapted for use as a floating bridge by the military. It has since been used for emergency rescue work after natural disasters, such as floods that have washed away regular bridges.

Swinging Bridges. The **swing-span bridge** rotates on a pivot on a pier, swinging aside to allow ships to pass. A swing span usually turns on one pivot on a pier in the middle. There are, however, swing-span bridges with two rotating spans.

Drawbridges. Instead of swinging aside, a drawbridge opens in the middle and swings up into the air to allow ships to sail through. The bridge has counterweights called bascules at either end. For this reason it is sometimes called a **bascule bridge**. If only one span of a bascule bridge opens, it is called a single-

leaf bascule; if two spans open, it is called a double-leaf bascule. Because of their counterweights, bascule bridges are relatively easy to operate and are among the most common types of movable bridges.

The lift, or vertical drawbridge, is raised straight up into the air to allow ships to pass under it. The lifting devices usually are counterweights contained in towers at each end of the span. When the weights are lowered, the span is lifted into the air.

Transporter Bridges. A transporter bridge consists of a high, fixed span stretching between towers and a movable platform or cars suspended from the span. Passengers and vehicles are transported from one side to the other on the moving platform or cars. Transporter bridges are most useful where traffic is rather light, since passengers have to wait until the moving cars pick them up and carry them across.

▶ **PROBLEMS OF BRIDGE DESIGN**

One of the chief problems facing a bridge designer is the kind of material he should use to support the load that the bridge will have to bear. A bridge not only has to support a load of people and vehicles but it also has to support its own weight. The longer the bridge is, the more material will be used in building it, and the heavier it will be. Thus a long bridge will have to be constructed of especially strong material. Light, strong metals and alloys have allowed modern builders to erect bridges with longer spans between the supports. Even these

---

Why were some of the early bridges in America covered?

Covered bridges once dotted the American countryside from the Atlantic coast to the Ohio River. The bridges looked like square tunnels with peaked roofs. Some people claim that the bridges were covered so that horses would not be frightened by the water underneath. Others say that they were built as a shelter for travelers in bad weather. Actually the coverings were designed to protect the wooden framework and flooring of the bridges and keep them from rotting. Some of these covered bridges are still standing—after more than 100 years. Many bridges have been destroyed to make room for modern highways. To protect the bridges that are left, the National Society for the Preservation of Covered Bridges has been established. The society publishes information on covered bridges and works to save them from being torn down. The states also try to protect the bridges by making them historical landmarks.

long, sweeping spans must be firmly supported at some points, however.

No matter how strong a bridge is designed to be, it is no better than its foundations. Poor foundations will cause a bridge to collapse. The piers must be capable of supporting the load of the bridge and traffic, and also of resisting the forces of wind and water. The foundations of the piers must be solidly based on rock or on ground that is as firm as possible. Many bridge foundations have to be sunk into the bottom of a river or bay, where there are layers of mud, sand, silt, and rocks. To support the foundation, the builder has to drive long timbers called piles through these upper layers of loose material to the solid bedrock underneath. This is done usually by a powerful hammering machine called a **pile driver**. Sometimes a steel pipe instead of a solid beam is driven down to the bedrock. The water is pumped out of the pipe, and it is filled with concrete for extra strength.

Another method is to dig away the loose mud and silt and build concrete pillars or walls on the bedrock. For this underwater construction, large watertight compartments called **caissons** are sunk to the bottom. The water is pumped out of them and air is pumped in. Then workmen can enter the caisson, excavate the loose soil, and build the foundation pillars on the bedrock.

Materials

When man first began to build bridges, he had to use whatever materials were available for the construction. He supported his suspension bridges with vines at first. Ropes took the place of vines as civilization progressed. If greater strength was needed to support heavier loads, more strands were added to the ropes. But there was a limit to how thick the ropes could be made before they became too cumbersome to use. Metal link chains were then used because they were stronger than ropes and they were not so thick. Eventually cables composed of woven strands of iron or steel wire were developed. Roebling's main accomplishment with the Brooklyn Bridge was in showing how steel wire cable could be used to hold up a suspension bridge.

For the main structure of a bridge, wood was one of the earliest materials. But wood is worn away by weather and friction, and it is

The Aerial Lift Bridge in Duluth, Minnesota. The bridge has been raised to let ships pass underneath.

not strong enough to be used in bridges that have extremely heavy loads to support. Covered bridges were developed to protect the wooden structure from the weather. These bridges can still be seen in some areas of North America, particularly in eastern Canada and in New England.

Stone is more durable than wood but it also has a disadvantage—it will break easily if very much tension or bending force is applied to it. Concrete is as durable as stone and it can be given greater resistance to bending (tensile strength) by being reinforced with steel rods. Concrete has another advantage from the bridge designer's point of view. It is easy to pour into almost any shape. For these reasons concrete has become one of the most useful materials for bridge construction.

Possibly the greatest advance in bridge-building materials came with the invention of a cheap way to make steel. This metal and the alloys formed from it offer the builder a relatively light and very strong material. When properly protected against rust, steel is also very durable.

Bridges of the future will probably make more and more use of such light materials as aluminum, magnesium, and plastics. Welding instead of riveting the separate parts together and advances in prestressed concrete design promise to give even cleaner and simpler lines to new bridges.

GEORGE N. BEAUMARIAGE, JR.
Research Director, Engineering Division
Sacramento State Teachers College

See also TRANSPORTATION.

BRITISH COLUMBIA

British Columbia, the most westerly province in Canada, faces the Pacific Ocean. The coast is indented with hundreds of narrow inlets. Some of them extend inland as far as 100 kilometers, or 60 miles. Vancouver Island and the Queen Charlotte Islands, which are part of British Columbia, lie between the coast and the open sea. The Inside Passage, a natural waterway that extends from Washington to Alaska, separates the islands from the mainland.

▶ THE LAND

British Columbia is the most mountainous province in Canada. Row after row of jagged peaks must be crossed to travel from one side of the province to the other. In the northeast corner of the province are the forested, rolling plains of the Peace River district. Many rivers have cut narrow passes through the Rocky Mountains. Such passes as Crowsnest, Kicking Horse, Yellowhead, and Pine are used now as road and railway routes across the Rockies.

FACTS AND FIGURES

LOCATION AND SIZE: Western Canada. **Latitude—** 49° N to 60° N. **Longitude—**114° W to 139° W. **Area—** 948,600 km²; 366,255 sq mi. **Rank among provinces—** 3rd.

JOINED CONFEDERATION: July 20, 1871, as 6th province.

POPULATION: 2,457,000 (estimate). **Rank among provinces—**3rd.

CAPITAL: Victoria, pop. (metropolitan area) 208,000 (estimate).

LARGEST CITY: Vancouver, pop. (metropolitan area) 1,137,000 (estimate).

PHYSICAL FEATURES: Rivers—Peace, Liard, Fraser, and Columbia. **Lakes—**Atlin, Babine, Kootenay, and Okanagan. **Highest mountain—**Fairweather, 4,663 m; 15,300 ft.

INDUSTRIES AND PRODUCTS: Lumbering and the manufacture of forest products; mining; farming and the processing of food products; commercial fishing.

GOVERNMENT: Self-governing province. **Titular head of government—**lieutenant governor, appointed by Governor-General of Canada in Council. **Actual head of government—**premier, elected by people of province. **Provincial representation in federal parliament—**6 appointed senators; 23 elected members of House of Commons. **Voting age for provincial elections—**19.

PROVINCIAL MOTTO: *Splendor sine occasu* (Splendor without end).

PROVINCIAL FLOWER: Dogwood.

The Coast Mountains form the western rim of British Columbia's mainland. These forest-covered mountains rise steeply from the shores of the coastal inlets and the Inside Passage.

In central British Columbia there is an area of rolling plateaus and valleys from 600 to 900 meters, or 2,000 to 3,000 feet, high. This is the Interior Plateau. The towering mountains that encircle the plateau make it appear as a huge, oval basin, if it is seen from the air.

Climate

British Columbia has a great variety of climates. In winter the climate along the coast is the mildest in Canada. Air masses moving eastward across the Pacific Ocean bring mild winters, cool summers, and much rainfall to the coastal area. The average annual rainfall on western Vancouver Island is more than 2,540 millimeters, or 100 inches, the heaviest in North America.

Summers are hotter and winters are colder in the interior of the province. There is much less rainfall than there is on the coast.

Natural Resources

Forests. The mild, wet coastal climate helps the growth of British Columbia's most abundant natural resource—the great forests of coniferous trees. These forests cover the eastern lowlands of Vancouver Island and the Queen Charlotte Islands, and the lower slopes of the Coast Mountains. The most valuable tree is the gigantic Douglas fir, which may reach a height of 60 m, or 200 ft. Western hemlock, Sitka spruce, and western cedar also are commercially important.

Waterpower. Swift, snow-fed rivers and many lakes provide an abundance of waterpower. The largest hydroelectric projects are near Kitimat and Vancouver, along the Columbia River and its tributaries, and on the Peace River.

▶ THE PEOPLE

The population of British Columbia is small for so vast an area. Many parts of the province are without people because the land is too

Vancouver, the largest city in British Columbia, is Canada's major Pacific port.

rugged and steep for settlement. Seventy-five percent of the people live in or near the cities in the southwest and on Vancouver Island. The remainder live in towns or small cities in the southern valleys or along roads or rail lines crossing the Interior Plateau and the northern plains. Only 5 percent of the provincial population lives on farms.

The city people work in sawmills, in wood and metalworking factories, and in industries connected with the ports. The agricultural lands of the Fraser River valley are used mainly for dairy farming. Most of the 300,000 residents of Vancouver Island live in or near Victoria or in Nanaimo and Port Alberni. Others live in small coastal villages and work at farming, fishing, and forestry. About 100,000 people live in the fertile Okanagan Valley in the interior. Fruitgrowing is their chief occupation. In the southeast mining district, in or close to the cities of Trail and Kimberley, live another 100,000 people. In the Interior Plateau the population is strung out in small settlements near the few railroads and highways. These people are engaged in beef-cattle ranching and forestry. The population in the Peace River district has been increasing steadily since the discovery of petroleum and natural gas in the 1950's. But grain farming and cattle raising are still the major occupations in this area. In the remote north-

ern part of the province there are fewer than 5,000 people living in an area of 135,000 square miles.

British Columbia is well named because most of the early settlers were of British origin. This is true of 60 percent of the present-day British Columbians. But many other Western Europeans have moved to the province since the end of World War II.

In the 1880's Chinese laborers were brought to British Columbia to help build the western section of the Canadian Pacific Railway. Afterward many of them settled in Vancouver and began forming the largest Chinese community in Canada. Later other immigrants came to Vancouver to work in the manufacturing industries that were being developed. By 1901 half the people were living in or near Vancouver. This is still true, although the population of the province has increased by almost 2,000,000 persons.

People Noted in British Columbia's History

Sir James Douglas (1803–77) is sometimes called the "Father of British Columbia." Born in British Guiana (now Guyana), he was involved with the Hudson's Bay fur-trading company for over 35 years and was instrumental in establishing Victoria as an important trading center. He was governor of Vancouver Island (1851–63) and also of the mainland

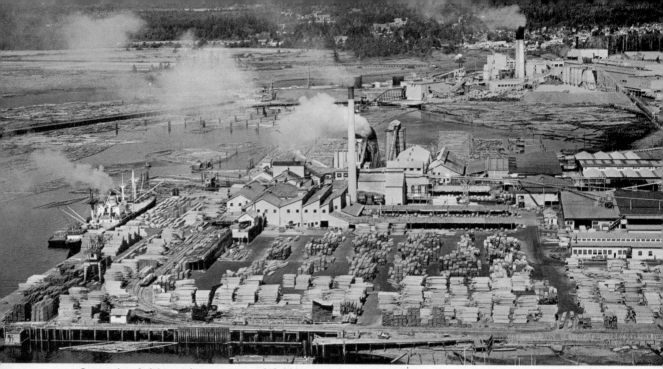

Oceangoing freighter takes on cargo of freshly-sawed lumber at Port Alberni sawmill, Vancouver Island.

Many yacht basins are found in the inlets and fiords along the coastline of British Columbia.

colony of British Columbia (1858–66). He worked to keep British Columbia and the other British Pacific colonies from becoming part of the United States.

Simon Fraser (1776–1862) explored much of the territory of British Columbia for the North West Company and established several fur-trading forts, including Fort George and Fort Fraser. In 1808, in an extremely perilous journey, he traveled the length of the river that now bears his name. He retired in 1820 and died a poor and lonely man.

Amor De Cosmos (1825–97) was born William Alexander Smith in Windsor, Nova Scotia. His name, meaning "lover of the universe," was acquired during the California gold rush of 1853. He joined the gold rush in British Columbia in 1858, and in that year founded *The Colonist,* one of the oldest newspapers in western Canada. He was premier of British Columbia from 1872 to 1874.

Emily Carr (1871–1945) was a noted painter and writer. Born in Victoria, she was known as Canada's leading woman painter, and took as her subjects the west coast Indians and the forests of British Columbia. Her paintings are on display in Vancouver. Her prose pieces are collected in *The Book of Small* (1942), *The Heart of a Peacock* (1953), and *Pause* (1953).

Mary Ellen Spear Smith (1861–1933), born in England, was one of British Columbia's most noted social reformers. Politically active from 1918 to 1928, she was instrumental in the fight for woman suffrage and reforms for women and children. The first woman to sit in British Columbia's legislature, she was also the first woman to hold cabinet rank (as a minister without portfolio), in 1928.

Malcolm Lowry (1909–57), a noted English novelist, spent 15 years in Canada in a squatter's cabin at Dollarton, east of Vancouver. Drawing on his experiences there, he wrote his most famous novel, *Under the Volcano* (1947).

Ethel Davis Bryant Wilson (1890–   ) is known for her novels of life in British Columbia. Born in Port Elizabeth, South Africa, she came to Vancouver in 1910. Her novels, noted for their wit and sympathetic character portrayals, include *Swamp Angel* (1934) and *Love and Salt Water* (1956).

Peter Vasilievich Verigin (1858–1924) was a Russian-born leader of the Doukhobors, a Russian religious sect that settled in Saskatchewan and British Columbia after 1909. The Doukhobor communities were thriving collective societies under Verigin's leadership for more than 10 years. Verigin was killed by an explosion, probably set by followers who became disenchanted with his increasingly dictatorial leadership.

William Bruce Hutchison (1901–   ), one of Canada's leading journalists, was born in Prescott, Ontario, and grew up in Victoria. A reporter since 1925, he was editor of the Victoria *Times* from 1950 to 1963, when he became editorial director of the Vancouver *Sun*. He has also written several books about Canada, including *The Fraser* (1950).

H. R. MacMillan (1885–1976) was a forester in British Columbia prior to 1915, when he toured the world finding markets for British Columbia's forest products. He later formed lumber companies, which by the 1960's were the largest in Canada, sending lumber products all over the world.

A biography of fur trader and explorer Sir Alexander Mackenzie, who helped open British Columbia to settlement, appears in Volume M. A biography of George Vancouver, who explored and mapped the northwest coast of North America and gave his name to Vancouver Island and the city of Vancouver, appears in Volume V.

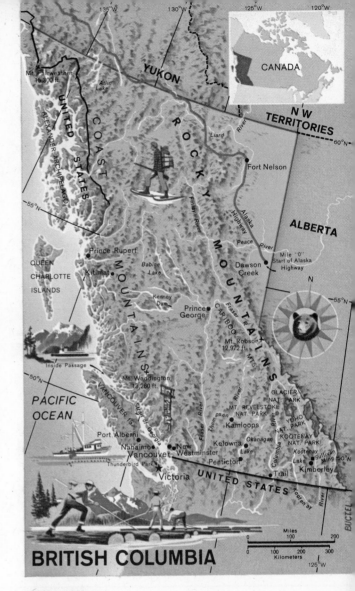

BRITISH COLUMBIA

▶ EDUCATION

Education is free and compulsory for all children between the ages of 6 and 15. Most of the schools have a 12-year system made up of elementary schools and junior and senior high schools. Numerous community colleges have been established to provide vocational courses or the first two years of university education. The British Columbia Institute of Technology offers post-secondary career programs only.

By the early 1970's, more than 22,000 students were attending the University of British Columbia, at Vancouver. The University of Victoria, in the capital city, had an enrollment of about 6,000 students. Simon Fraser University, in Burnaby, had an enrollment of 5,000 students.

Parliament Buildings, Victoria. Flower-filled baskets decorate many street lamps in this lovely capital city.

Towering totem pole dominates Prospect Point in Vancouver's huge Stanley Park. Park contains zoo, aquarium, and theater.

Mount Maxwell Provincial Park in the Gulf Islands of the Inside Passage.

Libraries. Public libraries are maintained in all the larger cities, and mobile libraries serve distant communities. The library of the University of British Columbia in Vancouver, and the provincial archives in Victoria are noted for their collections of historical material on British Columbia.

▶ **PLACES OF INTEREST**

The International Festival of the Arts, held annually in Vancouver, includes concert, symphony orchestra, and dramatic presentations.

Maritime Museum, in Vancouver, has displays emphasizing the importance of the ocean in British Columbia's past and in its present economy. Near this museum is housed the RCMP *St. Roch,* the first ship to navigate the Northwest Passage in the Canadian Arctic from west to east. New additions to the complex of museum buildings include a city archives and museum and a planetarium.

Provincial Museum of Natural History and Anthropology, in Victoria, contains fine collections of Indian relics and exhibitions on British Columbia's early days. Adjoining the museum is Thunderbird Park, which has a large collection of Indian totem poles.

British Columbia also has some of Canada's most magnificent scenery and extensive recreational areas. There are four national parks, located in the eastern mountains, as well as two national parks marking historic sites.

Glacier National Park is located in the Selkirk Mountains of southeastern British Columbia. The Rogers Pass section of the Trans-Canada Highway crosses through this park, which is known for heavy snowfall and many avalanches.

Kootenay National Park, more than 540 square miles of forest preserve, was developed in the Canadian Rockies at the source of the Kootenay River. Big game, deep canyons, and waterfalls are among its major attractions.

Mount Revelstoke National Park is a winter sports center in the western Selkirk Mountains. Its ski slopes are a tourist attraction.

Yoho National Park was established in 1886 on the west side of the Continental Divide. It is the site of Takakkaw Falls, with a drop of 1,200 feet. This park also has many lakes and a natural stone bridge, as well as the Yoho and Kicking Horse valleys. The park adjoins Banff National Park in Alberta and is crossed by the Trans-Canada Highway.

Pacific Rim National Park was established in 1971 on the central west coast of Vancouver Island. It includes the longest continuous stretch of sand beach in British Columbia.

Fort Langley National Historic Park is the site of the first government of British Columbia. The fort was built as a trading post in 1827 and has been restored as a museum.

Fort Rodd Hill National Historic Park, near Esquimalt, is a 19th-century stone and concrete fortification.

There are also more than 200 provincial parks in British Columbia, with a total area of nearly 10,000 square miles. Vancouver Island has many of these parks. The largest provincial park is Tweedsmuir, in the Coast Mountains. It extends from the Bella Coola River to the Nechako River, and is left mainly as a wilderness park.

▶ **INDUSTRIES AND PRODUCTS**

Forestry and the manufacture of wood products are the leading industries in British Columbia. The mining, agricultural, and fishing industries are next in importance.

Forestry. Sixty percent of Canada's lumber products come from British Columbia's forests. More than 60,000 people are employed either directly or indirectly in the forest industries. Many of the pulp and paper mills are located around Georgia Strait, but the newest mills are located in the interior, which now produces almost 40 percent of provincial lumber.

Mining. The gold rush of 1858 up the Fraser River and later into the Cariboo country brought the first large wave of settlers into the province. Gold no longer adds much to the income of the province. The most valuable minerals are copper, zinc, lead, asbestos, molybdenum, silver, and tungsten. Most of Canada's lead and about 50 percent of its zinc are produced at the Sullivan mine near Kimberley. The biggest smelter in the Commonwealth is at Trail on the Columbia River. Copper is shipped to Japan from several mines in southwestern British Columbia.

Agriculture. Most good farmland is found in four main areas: the lower Fraser River valley, the Okanagan valley, the central Interior Plateau, and the Peace River district. The lower Fraser River valley is the center of the provincial dairy farming. Truck farms in that area produce vegetables, fruits, and

A salmon catch. Most of Canada's Pàcific salmon comes from the waters of British Columbia.

poultry for the nearby cities. Specialty crops of flowers and flower bulbs are raised on Vancouver Island and are exported to eastern Canada. The irrigated Okanagan valley is a major apple-growing area in Canada. It also produces peaches, cherries, pears, plums, and the only apricots in the nation. Beef cattle are raised on ranches in the Interior Plateau. The Peace River district produces many grain crops, including some of the world's finest wheat and legume seed crops.

Fishing. Almost all the Pacific salmon—Canada's most valuable fish—comes from the river mouths and coastal inlets of British Columbia. The large salmon canneries are near Vancouver. Prince Rupert is an important port for the halibut-fishing fleets.

▶ **CITIES**

The number of people in British Columbia passed the 2,000,000 mark between the census years 1966 and 1971. This was part of a long-term growth in population. Most recently, population increases have occurred in the cities, particularly in the southwestern part of the province.

Victoria is the capital of British Columbia. It grew from a Hudson's Bay Company trading post built in 1843. It is a quiet city of fine homes and beautiful flower gardens. Many of the residents do government work, but there are also sawmills and small manufacturing plants. The metropolitan area has a population of more than 200,000.

Vancouver is one of Canada's largest cities and its major Pacific port. Over 1,000,000 people live in the metropolitan area of Vancouver, which was named for the British explorer and mapmaker George Vancouver. The city, with its magnificent harbor, has most of British Columbia's industry, finance, transportation, and trade. It is also the center of education and cultural activities, and the headquarters for most businesses. The various municipalities that make up the Vancouver metropolitan area hold half of the population of British Columbia. Sawmilling, fish and food processing, petroleum refining, shipbuilding, and a variety of metal-using businesses are among Vancouver's chief industries. The city's Chinatown is the second largest on the Pacific coast. An article on Vancouver is in Volume V.

New Westminster, on the north bank of the Fraser River near its mouth, was founded in 1859. It was the capital of British Columbia until 1868. The city has a good freshwater port, several large sawmills, and is a commercial center for the residents of the lower Fraser River valley. It has a population of more than 40,000.

Nanaimo, on Vancouver Island, was an important coal-mining town in the last half of the 19th century. It was once known as the Newcastle of the Pacific. Its major industries today are sawmills and a working pulp mill. It is the main wholesale and distribution center for central Vancouver Island. Nanaimo has a population of about 15,000.

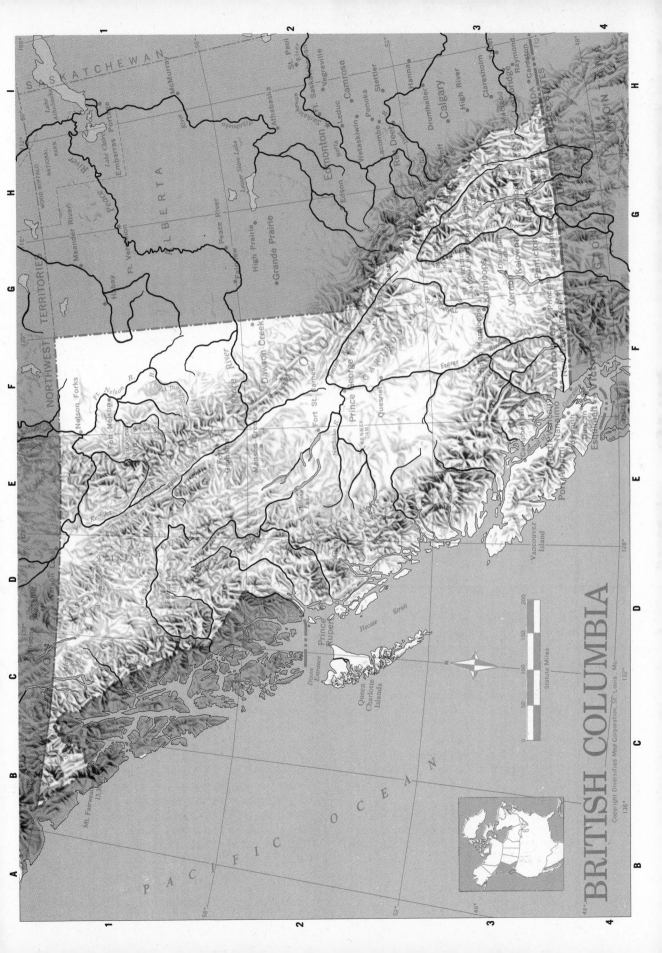

BRITISH COLUMBIA

Copyright Diversified Map Corporation, St. Louis, Mo.

Statute Miles

0   50   100   150   200

Emerald Lake in Yoho National Park. The park is especially popular with mountain climbers.

Prince George, with a population of about 30,000, is a commercial and transportation center for central British Columbia. It has more sawmills and pulp and paper mills than any other city in the interior of the province. Simon Fraser established a fur-trading post at Fort George in 1807, near the city's present site at the confluence of the Fraser and Nechako rivers.

Prince Rupert was laid out as a planned city in 1909 to be the northern terminal of the railway. It has salmon canneries and halibut-freezing plants. Nearby is a pulp and cellulose mill.

Trail is located on the Columbia River near the Washington border. It has important smelters, refineries, and fertilizer plants. Lead, zinc, silver, and mineral by-products are produced.

Kimberley is the site of the Sullivan mine, one of the largest lead-zinc mines in the world. The city is located on the St. Mary River in southeast British Columbia.

Kamloops is a major transportation and wholesale city for the province's ranching industry.

▶ TRANSPORTATION AND COMMUNICATION

Transportation in British Columbia has always been a problem because of the moun-tains, the scattered population, and the high costs of construction. The historic Cariboo Road into British Columbia's gold country, built in the 1860's, had to be cut through many miles of the Fraser canyon's rock wall. But by the time the Trans-Canada Highway was completed in 1962, there were paved roads through most of the settled regions. The Alaska Highway starts at Dawson Creek, the end of the railway in the Peace River district, and extends more than 600 miles through northern British Columbia before entering Yukon Territory.

The Canadian Pacific and the Canadian National transcontinental railroads connect British Columbia with the rest of Canada and are vital to the province's economy. Vancouver is the western terminal for both these railways. The provincially owned Pacific Great Eastern railway crosses the province from Vancouver to the Peace River and carries many of the resources of the interior.

Passenger boats and cargo vessels stop at the coastal ports between Vancouver and Prince Rupert. Ferries make regular runs between Victoria, Nanaimo, Vancouver, and ports in Washington state. Many ships sail from Seattle, Washington, and Vancouver through the Inside Passage to Skagway, Alaska—a voyage of about 950 miles.

Airplanes are used extensively, as they are throughout all of Canada. There are commercial airports in the major cities.

More than 30 radio stations and 9 major television stations serve British Columbia. *The Colonist,* one of the first newspapers in British Columbia, began publication in Victoria in 1858 and remains today one of the province's major newspapers. Other major newspapers include the *Times* of Victoria; the *Province* and the *Sun,* both of Vancouver; and the *Columbian* of New Westminster.

▶ GOVERNMENT

British Columbia is a self-governing province with a legislative assembly of 55 members. A lieutenant governor, appointed by the Governor-General of Canada in Council is titular head of the province. The actual head of government is the premier of the province, who is elected by the people. British Columbia has 6 appointed senators in the Canadian Parliament, and 23 elected members of the

House of Commons. The voting age for provincial elections is 19.

▶ HISTORY

In 1774 the Spanish voyager Juan Pérez became the first European known to have reached the coast of British Columbia. Pérez claimed the land for Spain. Four years later Captain James Cook arrived and claimed the land for Britain. For many years Spain and Britain contested the territory, but during these years both countries carried on a lively fur trade with the Indians.

In 1792 Captain George Vancouver explored Puget Sound and surveyed the coastal inlets. A year later Alexander Mackenzie, a trader with the North West Company, completed the first overland journey from eastern Canada to the Pacific coast. Finally Spain was forced to give up her claim and to recognize Britain's right to the territory.

In 1808 Simon Fraser explored the river that now bears his name. By 1811 David Thompson had explored the southeast interior and the Kootenay and Columbia rivers. During these years the only European settlers were fur traders. Trading posts were established along the Columbia River and in the north. In 1843 Victoria on Vancouver Island became the center of the coastal fur trade. Settlers arrived and farming began.

In 1858 the discovery of gold in the Fraser River brought prospectors from eastern Canada and the United States. By 1861 the gold rush to the Cariboo Mountains was in full swing. Ranching and farming began in the interior plateaus and river valleys, and sawmills began harvesting the coastal forests.

Vancouver Island and the mainland settlements were separate crown colonies until 1866, when they were united by the British Government into the single crown colony of British Columbia.

In 1871 British Columbia became Canada's sixth province. In 1885 the Canadian Pacific Railway was completed, and the next year the first transcontinental train arrived at Port Moody. The water around Port Moody was too shallow for an ocean port, so the rail terminal was moved to the little sawmilling town of Granville. Later, Granville was renamed Vancouver.

During the 1890's another mining boom brought settlers to the southeast Kootenay country. Commercial fishing began off the river mouths, and lumber from the tall forests was exported east of the Rockies to build the towns in the prairie provinces. Early in the 20th century, farming began in the irrigated Okanagan valley, and dairy farming expanded across the lower Fraser River valley.

Over the years British Columbia has become ever more closely linked with the economic expansion of all Canada. And the province's wealth of resources is only now coming into full development.

J. LEWIS ROBINSON
University of British Columbia

IMPORTANT DATES

1774	Juan Pérez, Spanish voyager, reached the coast of British Columbia.
1778	Captain James Cook claimed the coastal area for Great Britain.
1792	George Vancouver began explorations along the Pacific coast.
1793	Alexander Mackenzie reached the Pacific coast.
1795	Spain renounced claims to the area.
1805–1808	Simon Fraser explored area of British Columbia; followed Fraser River to the sea.
1843	Fort Victoria established at present site of capital city.
1846	Oregon Treaty set boundary between British Columbia and the United States.
1849	Vancouver Island established as British Crown Colony.
1858	Colony of British Columbia established on the mainland during gold rush to Fraser River.
1866	British Columbia and Vancouver Island united.
1868	Victoria became provincial capital.
1871	British Columbia joined Canadian Confederation as the 6th province.
1885	Canadian Pacific Railroad completed to west coast of Canada.
1903	Alaska boundary dispute arbitrated.
1914	First grain elevator was built in Vancouver harbor.
1915	Railway completed across southern British Columbia.
1942	Alaska Highway linked Dawson Creek with Yukon Territories and Alaska.
1957	Natural-gas pipeline completed between Peace River District and Vancouver.
1962	Trans-Canada Highway completed; Rogers Pass section opened.
1965	Columbia River power project, joint venture between the United States and Canada, begun.
1969	Electric power from the Peace River Dam was transmitted to Vancouver and points between for the first time.

BRITISH COMMONWEALTH. See COMMONWEALTH OF NATIONS.

BRITISH GUIANA. See GUYANA.

BRITISH HONDURAS. See BELIZE.

BRITISH ISLES. See UNITED KINGDOM.

BROADCASTING. See RADIO (Radio Programs); TELEVISION (Television Programs).

BRONTË SISTERS

The three Brontë sisters—Charlotte (1816–55), Emily (1818–48), and Anne (1820–49)—and their brother Branwell (1817–48) lived with their father, the Reverend Patrick Brontë, and a maiden aunt who kept house for them. Their mother had died when Anne was a year old. The parsonage, their home, stood high above the village of Haworth on the moors of Yorkshire, England. There were no other children for the Brontës to play with. They walked on the moors, read books and newspapers, and wrote stories about imaginary places called Angria, Gondal, and Gaaldine. The stories, which they wrote even after they grew up, were more real to them than their own lives.

When Charlotte was 30 years old she decided to publish some poems that she, Emily, and Anne had written. To hide their true identities, she used the names Currer, Ellis, and Acton Bell. The poems did not sell.

Meanwhile the three sisters had been working on novels. Anne's and Emily's novels were accepted for publication, but Charlotte's novel *The Professor* was rejected everywhere. Finally one publisher expressed interest in any future writing, so Charlotte finished *Jane Eyre,* a second novel she was working on, and sent it off. It was published in 1847 and was an immediate success. Emily's *Wuthering Heights* and Anne's *Agnes Grey* appeared later the same year.

Fame made little difference in the lives of the Brontë sisters, since their identities were still unknown to the public. In fact, their father did not know of their success until much later, and Branwell never knew. Branwell, a failure at painting and writing, took to drink and opium and died September 24, 1848.

Emily caught cold at his funeral and became very ill. She refused all care and 3 months later died. Then Anne died after another 5 months.

Charlotte lived on for 6 more years, but life seemed empty to her without her sisters and brother. Her father kept to himself, and the new friends she made through her novels never became close friends. She had let her real name be known after a rumor had spread that Currer, Ellis, and Acton Bell were the same person, but she was too shy to enter into society. She published two more novels, traveled to London, met literary celebrities such as Thackeray and Mrs. Gaskell, and finally married her father's curate. Less than a year later she fell ill and died.

BRONZE AND BRASS

Sometime between 3500 and 3000 B.C. men discovered that mixing copper and tin would yield a new metallic substance, harder and tougher than either copper or tin. This new substance was bronze, and its discovery was an important event in human history. Bronze was man's first truly strong and durable material for making tools and weapons.

Before the discovery of bronze, most tools and weapons were made of stone, wood, or bone. Stone could be given a sharp edge, but it was hard to shape. Stone was also likely to break if a sharp blow was struck. Bone and wood, being softer than stone, were easier to shape. But they also wore out more quickly.

Another disadvantage was that stone, wood, and bone—particularly stone—could be made into only a few shapes without the risk of breaking when they were used.

Copper, which was discovered around 5000 B.C., made better tools and weapons than stone, wood, or bone. It could be cast or hammered into many different shapes. When a copper knife broke, it did not have to be thrown away. It could be melted down and used to make a new knife. However, copper was soft and bent easily, and it grew brittle with use.

Bronze was different. Bronze could be cast into complicated shapes more easily than copper. It would hold a sharp edge much longer. It did not bend in use or grow brittle quickly, as copper did. Durable bronze hoes and spades helped farmers to cultivate their fields better and thus raise more food. Bronze sickles made the work of harvesting easier. Bronze saws and chisels made it possible for carpenters to cut and trim wood accurately.

Machine trims rough edges off 350-foot coils of brass strip. Each coil weighs 6½ tons.

Many of our familiar hand tools date from the **Bronze Age.**

Bronze brought other changes, too. Armies equipped with bronze swords and battle-axes and protected by bronze armor easily crushed their more primitive neighbors. From these conquests the first empires were formed.

Archeologists believe that bronze originated somewhere in the mountainous regions of southwestern Asia. Both native copper nuggets and tin ore were found there, often in the beds of mountain streams together with gold. Scholars think that tin was probably discovered shortly before bronze. It is believed that tin was first produced accidentally when some early gold hunter tried to melt the gold out of a load of stream-bed gravel containing tin ore. However, the soft, pliable, white metal was apparently not used by itself, since no tin objects from that time have been found.

Metallurgy in those times was a mysterious art with overtones of sorcery. Primitive metalworkers experimented freely with new combinations of metals and ores, just as a sorcerer might try new ingredients in his "magical" potions. Copper was already being alloyed with lead and antimony to make it easier to cast. Eventually someone tried adding tin, and bronze was the result.

The knowledge of how to make bronze spread gradually from the Near East to other parts of the ancient world. Eventually people from China to the British Isles were using bronze.

The period in history when bronze was the most important material for tools and weapons is called the Bronze Age. The Bronze Age lasted until about 1000 B.C., when iron became plentiful and cheap enough for everyday use and took the place of bronze.

Although the Bronze Age ended nearly 3,000 years ago, bronze has remained an important material down to the present time.

▶ **BRONZE MAKING TODAY**

Bronze is made by mixing molten copper with molten tin. The most commonly used bronzes contain up to 10 percent tin. Adding more tin makes the bronze too hard for working by ordinary methods. However, bells and cymbals are made of bronze containing 20 to 25 percent tin, because this very hard bronze produces a clear, ringing tone when struck.

Traces of other elements are often added to the basic copper-tin mixture to obtain bronzes with special qualities. Phosphorus, for instance, yields a hard, springy bronze that has high resistance to fatigue and corrosion. (Fatigue means that the metal becomes brittle under stresses such as repeated bending or twisting.) Phosphor bronzes are used for products in which these qualities are important, such as bearings, shafts, and diaphragms. Silicon bronze is used for piston rings, metal screens, and propeller shafts for ships because of its corrosion resistance. Aluminum bronze is also used for engine parts and fittings for ocean-going ships.

Bronze may range in color from reddish brown to silvery white, depending on its composition. However, the most usual color is golden brown. Bronze is a favorite material for statues and other works of art.

Although "bronze" really means an alloy

whose chief ingredients are copper and tin, the name is also used now for some copper alloys that do not contain any tin at all. Aluminum bronze, for example, actually contains no tin. These tinless bronzes do have some of the characteristics of true bronze, especially its typical golden-brown color. Tinless bronze is often used in architectural trim for buildings, as in lobbies and store fronts.

▶ BRASS

Brass, an alloy of copper and zinc, was developed much later than bronze. It appears to have been first used by the peoples of the Middle East around 700 B.C.

Much of our present knowledge of brass comes from the alchemists of the Middle Ages. Their attempts to turn common metals into gold (or at least gold-colored alloys) yielded much information about mixtures of copper, zinc, tin, and lead.

During the 18th and 19th centuries, hundreds of different copper alloys were developed. Most of them were brasses. Today brass is the most widely used copper alloy.

Brass is made like bronze except that zinc is used instead of tin. The two metals cannot be melted together because copper melts at a much higher temperature than zinc. Otherwise the zinc would boil away by the time the copper melted.

Usually solid ingots of zinc are added to the molten copper. The two metals may also be melted separately and then mixed.

The resulting alloy ranges in color from deep red through gold to creamy white. The zinc content ranges from 5 to 42 percent. The more zinc, the harder the brass is. Small quantities of other elements—lead, tin, silicon, manganese, or iron—may be added to produce special qualities.

Brasses are divided into two main types, based on the amount of zinc they contain. Brasses with up to 37 percent zinc are called alpha brasses, and those with more than 37 percent are called beta brasses. Alpha and beta brasses have different crystal structures and therefore different properties.

Alpha brasses are malleable, or easily worked. They are especially suited for cold-working (forming or rolling the metal without softening it by heating). Beta brasses are very soft and malleable when hot, but at normal temperatures they are hard and not easily worked.

Low-zinc, or alpha, brasses are used for such products as water pipes, costume jewelry, women's compacts and lipstick cases, and artillery shells. High-zinc brasses are used for musical instruments, lamps, doorknobs, locks, and hinges.

A small amount of lead makes brass more easily machinable (easier to cut and drill with machine tools). The lead spreads through the alloy in microscopic particles. When the metal is machined, the lead particles cause it to peel off in small chips rather than in long, curling spirals that would clog and dull the tools. Leaded brass is used in parts that must be accurately shaped, such as watch and clock parts, gears, plumbing materials, and engraving plates for fancy printing work.

▶ METHODS OF WORKING

In addition to casting and machining, there are several ways of shaping brass and bronze that also alter the properties of these alloys. **Forging,** for instance, increases the strength of the metal. In forging, the hot metal is pressed with great force between a set of dies. A die is a type of mold that shapes objects by squeezing them. Dies are used to shape relatively soft materials like hot metals or plastics.

In **cold-rolling,** the unheated metal is passed back and forth between two heavy rollers, growing longer, wider, and thinner each time. The rolling hardens the metal, but it also creates stresses that make it brittle. **Annealing** (heating the metal and slowly cooling it) relieves the stresses and softens the metal. The cold-working process can then be repeated without danger of cracking or breaking the metal.

Seamless tubing and pipe are made by extrusion. The heat-softened alloy is squeezed out of a circular die with a plug in its center. As the metal is forced through the die and around the plug it takes the shape of a hollow tube. While still soft, it is then drawn, or stretched, down to the desired size. The drawing makes the tube or pipe longer and thinner.

ROBERT C. CARMODY
Copper and Brass Research Association

See also ALLOYS; COPPER; DIES AND MOLDS; METALS AND METALLURGY; TOOLS.

BROWN, GEORGE (1818–1880)

George Brown was a tall, red-haired, hard-driving journalist and the owner of Canada's most powerful newspaper of his day, the Toronto *Globe*. He was a leader of the Liberal Party and one of the Fathers of Canadian Confederation.

Brown was born in Scotland on November 29, 1818, and came to the United States when he was 18. In 1843 the Browns moved to Toronto in Upper Canada. There in 1844 Brown founded the *Globe*. The *Globe* supported the Liberals, or Reformers, in their struggle for responsible government—the right of Canadians to rule their own affairs within the British Empire. After responsible government was won in 1848, Brown decided to enter politics. In 1851 he was elected to Parliament.

Canada was then a union of two provinces—Upper Canada and Lower Canada. Since both sections had an equal number of representatives in Parliament, either side could block the other. And during the early 1850's there were bitter sectional quarrels in Canada. Brown felt that the country was being controlled by Lower Canadian votes. Yet Upper Canada had the larger population.

He demanded representation by population to give Upper Canada the greater number of seats in Parliament. He also urged Canada to acquire and settle the vast northwest wilderness. Brown won increasing support in Upper Canada and rebuilt a Liberal Party nicknamed the Clear Grits. In 1858 he became premier, but his government only lasted 2 days. During the next few years no government lasted long. And by 1864 neither Liberals nor Conservatives could govern.

Then Brown boldly approached his chief foes, Conservative John A. MacDonald and George Cartier, a leader of Lower Canada. Brown offered to work with them to solve Canada's problems. This great step eventually led to a federal union, or confederation, of all the British provinces in North America and the vast northwest territory. Brown played a major part at the Charlottetown and Quebec conferences, which were held to settle the design of the new union. Brown left the government before confederation came into effect in 1867. But he remained a power on the *Globe* and in the Liberal Party, and he was named a senator in 1873.

Brown died in Toronto on May 9, 1880.

J. M. S. CARELESS
The University of Toronto

BROWN, JOHN (1800–1859)

John Brown was a strange, violent man who tried to fight a one-man war against slavery. He considered himself an instrument in the hands of God and believed that only through force and bloodshed would the slaves be freed.

John Brown was born in Torrington, Connecticut, on May 9, 1800, but grew up in Ohio. To support his 20 children, Brown moved from place to place, working as a farmer, leather tanner, sheep raiser, and surveyor. Brown's father had taught him to hate slavery, and over the years his feelings against it grew stronger. In Pennsylvania his barn was a station in the Underground Railroad—an escape route for slaves fleeing to the North.

In 1855 Brown moved to Kansas, which was then being settled by both slaveholders and anti-slavery men. So much violence broke out between them that the territory was called "bleeding Kansas." Brown's strong anti-slavery feelings led him to take part in the violence. On the night of May 24, 1856, Brown and a group of men, including four of his sons, attacked and killed five helpless pro-slavery settlers. From then on the name of Brown caused terror in Kansas. In the fighting that followed, one of his sons was killed. Others were to die the same way—fighting at their father's side.

About this time Brown conceived a plan for a revolt of the slaves. On October 16, 1859, Brown and 21 men began the revolt with an attack on the United States arsenal at Harpers Ferry, Virginia (now West Virginia). A company of United States Marines, led by Colonel Robert E. Lee, was sent to capture Brown's band. After desperate fighting in which 10 of his men, including 2 sons, were killed, Brown was captured. When he was brought to trial for murder and treason, even Brown's enemies were impressed with his dignity. He declared that his only wish had been to free the slaves. Many people were convinced that he was insane. Nevertheless, Brown was convicted, and on December 2, 1859, he was hanged. But the controversy over Brown did not stop with his death. Some people said he was a murderer. Others said he was a martyr. Not many years later, during the Civil War, Union soldiers sang,

> John Brown's body lies a-mouldering
> in the grave,
> His soul goes marching on.

BROWNING, ELIZABETH BARRETT (1806–1861) AND ROBERT (1812–1889)

Two of England's finest poets, Robert Browning and his wife, Elizabeth Barrett Browning, are remembered as much for their love as for their poetry. Elizabeth was born on March 6, 1806, in Durham, England. She was the first of 12 children and her father's favorite. He encouraged her to read, took pride in the rhymed verses she composed when still a child, and let her be tutored in Greek and Latin along with her brother Edward. When at 13 she composed a long epic poem, *The Battle of Marathon,* he had it printed.

Elizabeth was impetuous, and one day, eager to go out riding, she tried to saddle her pony by herself. The pony stumbled, and the saddle fell on top of Elizabeth, injuring her spine. That injury and an infected lung made her a semi-invalid. From then on she spent most of her time indoors reading and writing poetry.

Robert Browning was born 6 years after Elizabeth Barrett on May 7, 1812, in Camberwell, near London. Like Elizabeth's father, Robert's had a well-stocked library and encouraged his son to read. Like Elizabeth, Robert began writing verses at an early age. He studied art, music, languages, and literature and published his first poem, *Pauline,* in 1833.

As poetry by both Elizabeth Barrett and Robert Browning began to appear in print, they grew acquainted with each other's work. Then in 1845 Browning found himself mentioned in one of Miss Barrett's poems. He wrote to her, told her how much he admired her poetry, and said he had long wished to meet her. He had, in fact, been as far as her door, but had been told she was not well enough to receive him. They began corresponding, and on May 20, 1845, Browning called on Miss Barrett in the house on London's Wimpole Street where the Barretts were living. He visited her frequently afterwards, his visits carefully hidden from Mr. Barrett, who had selfishly forbidden his children to marry.

Although Elizabeth loved her father, her love for Robert Browning was stronger. On September 12, 1846, the two were secretly married. A week later they left for Italy. Mr. Barrett never forgave his daughter and returned her letters unopened.

The Brownings were extremely happy, and Mrs. Browning's health improved greatly. They both worked on their poetry, although they never discussed or showed their poems to each other until they were finished. They traveled a good deal, yet always returned to Casa Guidi, their home in Florence. It was there that their only child, Robert Wiedemann Barrett Browning, called Penini or Pen, was born on March 9, 1849.

Shortly after the Brownings' third wedding anniversary, Mrs. Browning slid something into her husband's pocket while he stood looking out a window. It was the manuscript of sonnets she had written before they were married. Browning felt they should belong to the whole world and urged his wife to publish them. To hide the identities of the lovers, he suggested she call them *Sonnets from the Portuguese.* No one would know that he sometimes called her his "little Portuguese" after the heroine of her poem "Catarina to Camoens." The sonnets are Mrs. Browning's best-known work.

For 16 years Elizabeth Barrett and Robert Browning knew a life together of such happiness that it has become legendary. Then on

June 30, 1861, Mrs. Browning died at Casa Guidi. A month later Browning left for England with his son, but his heart lay buried with his wife. He could not bring himself to return to Italy until 1878, but from then on he spent most of his time there. He died on December 12, 1889, in the palace his son and daughter-in-law had bought in Venice. His body was taken to England and buried in the Poets' Corner of Westminster Abbey.

Reviewed by REGINALD L. COOK
Middlebury College

This is one of Elizabeth Barrett Browning's *Sonnets from the Portuguese:*

How do I love thee? Let me count the ways.
I love thee to the depth and breadth and height
My soul can reach, when feeling out of sight
For the ends of Being and ideal Grace.
I love thee to the level of every day's
Most quiet need, by sun and candle-light.
I love thee freely, as men strive for Right;
I love thee purely, as they turn from Praise.
I love thee with the passion put to use
In my old griefs, and with my childhood's faith.
I love thee with a love I seemed to lose
With my lost saints—I love thee with the breath,
Smiles, tears, of all my life!—and, if God choose,
I shall but love thee better after death.

Robert Browning's *Pied Piper of Hamelin* is based on an old legend. The following passage tells how the rats followed the piper out of the town of Hamelin.

Into the street the Piper stept,
Smiling first a little smile,
As if he knew what magic slept
In his quiet pipe the while;
Then, like a musical adept,
To blow the pipe his lips he wrinkled,
And green and blue his sharp eyes twinkled
Like a candle-flame where salt is sprinkled;
And ere three shrill notes the pipe uttered,
You heard as if an army muttered;
And the muttering grew to a grumbling;
And the grumbling grew to a mighty rumbling;
And out of the house the rats came tumbling.
Great rats, small rats, lean rats, brawny rats,
Brown rats, black rats, gray rats, tawny rats,
Grave old plodders, gay young friskers,
Fathers, mothers, uncles, cousins,
Cocking tails and pricking whiskers,
Families by tens and dozens,
Brothers, sisters, husbands, wives—
Followed the Piper for their lives.
From street to street he piped advancing,
And step by step they followed dancing,
Until they came to the river Weser
Wherein all plunged and perished
Save one, who, stout as Julius Caesar,

Swam across and lived to carry
(As he the manuscript he cherished)
To Rat-land home his commentary,
Which was, "At the first shrill notes of the pipe,
I heard a sound as of scraping tripe,
And putting apples, wondrous ripe,
Into a cider press's gripe;
And a moving away of pickle-tub boards,
And a drawing the corks of train-oil flasks,
And a breaking the hoops of butter casks;
And it seemed as if a voice
(Sweeter far than by harp or by psaltery
Is breathed) called out, Oh, rats! rejoice!
The world is grown to one vast drysaltery!
To munch on, crunch on, take your nuncheon,
Breakfast, supper, dinner, luncheon!

And just as a bulky sugar puncheon,
All ready staved, like a great sun shone
Glorious scarce an inch before me,
Just as methought it said, come, bore me!
—I found the Weser rolling o'er me."

You should have heard the Hamelin people
Ringing the bells till they rocked the steeple.
"Go," cried the Mayor, "and get long poles!
Poke out the nests and block up the holes!
Consult with carpenters and builders,
And leave in our town not even a trace
Of the rats!"—when suddenly up the face
Of the Piper perked in the market-place,
With a, "First, if you please, my thousand
    guilders!"

BRUCE, ROBERT (1274–1329)

Robert Bruce was one of Scotland's great heroes in the struggle for unity and independence from England. Bruce was born on July 11, 1274, probably in the Scottish county of Ayrshire. He lived at the court of Edward I (1239–1307) of England, and had little interest in Scotland's struggle for freedom—even though he had a claim to the Scottish throne.

During Edward's reign, control of Scotland was in the hands of feuding chieftains. One of these, John Comyn, was an old rival of the Bruce family. In 1306 Bruce secretly agreed to meet with the Scottish nobles. In an argument at the meeting in the church at Dumfries, Bruce murdered Comyn, and was later crowned King Robert I at Scone. He vowed to lead Scotland to freedom.

At first the Scots suffered grave defeats. Many of Bruce's supporters were captured and killed by the English. Bruce himself was forced into hiding.

The disheartened leader took refuge on an island off Ireland. One day, according to legend, he watched a spider spin a web. Many times the spider began its labor and many times the web broke. As Robert watched the spider start the web again, his hope was restored. He knew that he, like the spider, would have to be patient and steadfast to finish his task.

Soon the tide of battle changed. In 1314 England suffered a crushing defeat at Bannockburn. A treaty signed in 1328 established the sovereignty of Robert I and granted greater freedom to Scotland.

King Robert died a year later. The affairs of his country had kept him from leading a crusade to the Holy Land. Before his death he had asked his friend, Sir James Douglas, to take his heart to Jerusalem, but Douglas did not live to accomplish the mission. King Robert's body was buried at Dumfermline, his heart at Melrose Abbey.

BRUEGHEL, PIETER (1525?–1569)

Very little is known about the life of Pieter Brueghel (or Bruegel) the Elder, one of the great masters of Flemish painting. Although the exact date of his birth is uncertain, it is known that he was born in a small village in what is now Belgium. He spent most of his life in Antwerp, where he was a member of the guild of master painters. In 1563 he married the daughter of a well-known painter and with her made his home in Brussels until his death in 1569.

Brueghel had already gained some note as a landscape painter when he suddenly became interested in painting the human figure. In

The Wedding Dance (1566) by Pieter Brueghel the Elder. Oil on wood panel, 47″ by 62″; Detroit Institute of Arts. The arrangement of the figures reflects the rhythm of the dance.

many of his paintings crowds of people cover the canvas, creating a pattern of brightly colored figures. He painted farmers at work in the fields and village folk at feasts and festivals. His religious paintings too are peopled with peasants. He used the everyday life of the Flemish peasants to illustrate stories from the Bible and to portray the sins and follies of mankind,

Brueghel's sons, Pieter and Jan, and his grandsons, Jan and Ambrose, carried on the great tradition of Flemish painting.

BRYAN, WILLIAM JENNINGS (1860–1925)

William Jennings Bryan ran three times for the presidency of the United States, and three times he was defeated. Yet for nearly 20 years he remained a leader of the Democratic Party. His speeches were so eloquent that he was called "the silver-tongued orator."

Bryan was born in Salem, Illinois, on March 19, 1860. In 1887 he moved to Nebraska, where he became interested in politics. In 1890 he was elected to the House of Representatives.

During the last quarter of the 19th century, political controversy over the question of silver money swept the United States. Silver-mine owners and farmers wanted the government to issue silver as well as gold money. The farmers, hard pressed by low prices, felt that free (unlimited) silver coinage would increase the amount of money in circulation and raise the prices for their crops. Businessmen, however, wanted money backed by a gold standard. Bryan became the leader of the Free Silver Democrats. At the Democratic convention of 1896 the party was badly divided on the gold and silver question. When the 36-year-old Bryan spoke, he roused the quarreling delegates to applause with these words from his famous Cross of Gold speech:

We will answer their demand for a gold standard by saying to them . . . you shall not crucify mankind upon a cross of gold.

Bryan's speech won him the Democratic presidential nomination, and he began a strenuous campaign to win the election. Traveling through 29 states, he made hundreds of speeches to farmers and workers who came from miles away to hear him speak. The farmers felt that Bryan understood their problems better than anybody else. But in spite of their support, Bryan lost the election to Republican William McKinley.

In 1900 Bryan was again the Democratic candidate—and again he lost to McKinley. In 1908 he ran against William Howard Taft and was defeated for a third time. Yet Bryan still had great political influence, and he used it to help Woodrow Wilson win the presidential nomination in 1912. When Wilson became president, he appointed Bryan secretary of state. Bryan worked out a plan that he hoped would prevent war by arbitrating international disputes. But his efforts failed to prevent the outbreak of World War I in 1914. A year later Bryan resigned because of a disagreement with President Wilson. He feared that Wilson's foreign policy would force the United States into the war.

In 1925 Bryan became involved in the famous Scopes "monkey" trial in Dayton, Tennessee. Bryan was a deeply religious man. He opposed Darwin's theory of the evolution of man, which he felt denied the teachings of the Bible about man's creation. John Scopes, a high school biology teacher, was brought to trial for teaching Darwin's theory in violation of the Tennessee law. Bryan went to Dayton to help in the case against Scopes. Though Bryan won the case, many people laughed at his old-fashioned ideas. Five days after the trial, on July 6, 1925, worn out by his labors, Bryan died.

BRYANT, WILLIAM CULLEN (1794–1878)

William Cullen Bryant, American poet and editor, was born November 3, 1794, in Cummington, Massachusetts. His father was a physician who played the violin and wrote verse. It was he who had Cullen's poem "The Embargo" published when Cullen was 13, and he who gave "Thanatopsis," written when Cullen was 17, to the *North American Review*.

Cullen attended school in Cummington and was tutored in Latin by his uncle, Reverend Thomas Snell, and in Greek by Reverend Moses Hallock. He entered Williams College as a sophomore in 1810. He planned to go to Yale the next year, but lack of funds forced him to give up college. In 1811 he was apprenticed to a lawyer. He passed his bar exams before he was 20 and began practicing in 1815. After moving to Great Barrington in 1816, he became very successful. He married Frances Fairchild in 1821.

He continued to write poetry and literary criticism. He was invited in 1821 by the Phi Beta Kappa Society of Harvard College to compose a poem for commencement. This led to publication of a collection of his poems. He contributed regularly to the *United States Literary Gazette* in 1824, and in 1825 accepted a position in New York City as co-editor of the *New York Review and Athenaeum Magazine*. A little over a year later he stepped in as sub-editor of the New York *Evening Post* when the editor was injured. In 1829 he became editor.

In 1832 a visit to his brothers in Illinois inspired "The Prairies." In 1834 he went with his wife and two daughters to Europe. There Bryant became a friend of the poet Henry W. Longfellow. In the spring of 1836 he was called home suddenly to take personal charge of the *Post*.

His editorials in the *Post* set a high standard for journalistic writing. He campaigned for a public park in New York City (land for Central Park was set aside in 1853, and later, in 1884, Bryant Park was named after him). During the Civil War he took a strong stand against slavery. Following his wife's death in July, 1865, he worked on a popular translation of the *Iliad* and the *Odyssey,* published in 1870 and 1872. He died June 12, 1878, from injuries received in a fall.

JAMES BUCHANAN (1791–1868)

15TH PRESIDENT OF THE UNITED STATES

BUCHANAN, JAMES. James Buchanan, the 15th president of the United States, served his country as a congressman, senator, ambassador, and secretary of state. But many people remember mainly two things about him: that he was the only president who never married; and that the Civil War followed his administration.

▶ EARLY LIFE

Buchanan was born on April 23, 1791, in a log cabin near the frontier settlement of Cove Gap, Pennsylvania. His father, a Scotch-Irish immigrant, had come to America in 1783. When James was 6, the family moved to Mercersburg, Pennsylvania, where his father opened a general store. James's mother had little schooling, but she loved to read, and she inspired her son with a love of learning.

James was able to go to school in Mercersburg. When he was not studying, he helped his father in the store. James's father was fond of his son, but he made him work hard and pay close attention to business. Mr. Buchanan taught James that he must be ready to care for his nine younger brothers and sisters if their parents should die. In later years, after his father died, James Buchanan became responsible for the care of his mother and four of his brothers and sisters.

James learned to be very careful about money. It was a habit that never left him. Once, when he was president, he discovered that he had been charged too little for a White House grocery order. He insisted on paying the difference, saying that he wanted to pay exactly what he owed—neither too little nor too much. The amount he owed was 3 cents.

When James was 16 his father sent him to Dickinson College in Carlisle, Pennsylvania. Young Buchanan was a serious student, but he also wanted to have a good time. He began to drink and smoke with some of the other students. Even though his marks were excellent, he was expelled for bad conduct at the end of his first term. James pleaded to be taken back and promised to turn over a new leaf. He was allowed to return, and went on to graduate with honors.

Buchanan then went to Lancaster, Pennsylvania, to study law. Hard work and intelligence made him a very good lawyer. Before long he was earning over $11,000 a year, a huge sum in those days.

In 1814 Buchanan became a candidate for the Pennsylvania legislature. But the War of

Buchanan's birthplace as it now stands at Mercersburg Academy, Pennsylvania.

Ann Coleman (1796?–1819).

1812 was raging, and the British had just burned Washington. Buchanan felt that the United States should not have gone to war against Great Britain. However, he knew it was his duty to serve his country, and he joined a volunteer cavalry company.

Buchanan returned in time for the election and won his seat in the legislature. He served a second term and then returned to Lancaster to continue his law practice.

▶A TRAGIC LOVE STORY

As his practice grew, Buchanan became an important figure in town. He was invited to parties at some of the best homes in Lancaster. At one party he met and fell in love with beautiful Ann Coleman. In 1819 Ann and James were engaged to be married, but their happiness was destined to end quickly.

During the fall of 1819 Buchanan often had to be out of town on business. While he was away rumors spread that he wanted to marry Ann only for her money. There was gossip about another woman. All of this was untrue, but Ann was heartbroken. Because of a misunderstanding, she broke her engagement to James.

A short time later Ann died. Buchanan was so grief-stricken that he vowed he would never marry. Years later, after his death, a package of Ann's letters, yellow with age, was found among his papers. They were burned, according to his last wishes, without being opened.

▶HE RETURNS TO POLITICS

Buchanan turned to politics to forget his sorrow. The Federalist Party was looking for a candidate for Congress. Buchanan agreed to run, and in 1820 he was elected to the House of Representatives, where he served for 10 years. During his years in Congress, Buchanan changed his political party. He joined the Jacksonian Democrats (named for Andrew Jackson), and became a leader of the Jacksonians in Pennsylvania.

In 1831 President Jackson asked Buchanan to become minister to Russia. Buchanan went to Russia the following year. While there he negotiated the first trade agreement between Russia and the United States.

On his return to the United States, Buchanan was elected to the Senate. He served until 1845, and became chairman of the important committee on foreign affairs.

Buchanan applied all his training as a lawyer to his work in the Senate. The Constitution, he said, was the basis of all political power. But the Constitution also strictly limited the powers of the federal government. Buchanan believed that a constitutional republic could adjust serious differences between its people only by compromise and legal procedure.

▶SECRETARY OF STATE

By 1844 Buchanan had become an important political figure. Though he hoped for the presidential nomination, he gave his support to James K. Polk, who won the nomination and the election. President Polk appointed Buchanan secretary of state.

During Polk's term as president, war broke out between the United States and Mexico. Buchanan, as secretary of state, helped to arrange the treaty of peace in 1848. By this Treaty of Guadalupe Hidalgo the United States purchased from Mexico the region

Photograph of President Buchanan, taken about 1859.

President Pierce made Buchanan minister to Great Britain in 1853. Shortly thereafter Pierce instructed the American ministers in Europe to draw up proposals to "detach" Cuba from Spain. This led to the Ostend Manifesto, named after the Belgian city where the ministers met. The Manifesto defined a plan to purchase Cuba. But it also included a proposal many people condemned: that the United States would be justified in seizing Cuba if Spain refused to sell the island. Buchanan's political opponents severely denounced the Ostend Manifesto, and nothing ever came of the plan. Buchanan wrote of it: "Never did I obey any instructions so reluctantly."

While Buchanan was in England, Congress passed the Kansas-Nebraska Act, permitting slavery in regions of the Northwest from which the Missouri Compromise of 1820 had formerly excluded it. This new law marked the beginning of the Republican Party, which vowed to prevent any further expansion of slavery, and it split the Democratic Party into northern and southern groups. As Buchanan had been in England during the Congressional fight over the Kansas-Nebraska bill, he remained friendly with both sections of his party. When the Democrats met in 1856 to pick a new candidate for president, they needed someone who would be accepted by both the North and the South. Buchanan proved to be the man. This time he won the nomination and the election.

▶ PRESIDENT BUCHANAN

On March 4, 1857, Buchanan was inaugurated as president. Since Buchanan had no wife, his 27-year-old orphan niece, Harriet Lane, acted as his hostess. She was very popular, and Buchanan's administration was a great social success. White House guests included the first Japanese representatives to the United States and the Prince of Wales (who later became King Edward VII of England). The Prince arrived with such a large party that the President had to give up his own bed and sleep on a couch.

The Dred Scott Decision

But the political situation was getting worse. Two days after Buchanan's inauguration, the Supreme Court gave its historic

extending west from Texas to the Pacific Ocean.

Another problem concerned the vast Oregon territory, which both Great Britain and the United States claimed. The dispute became so bad that war threatened. But Buchanan arranged a compromise, and the Oregon Treaty of 1846 settled the Northwestern boundary between Canada and the United States.

When Polk left office, Buchanan also retired. For 4 years he lived the life of a country gentleman. He bought the famous mansion, Wheatland, near Lancaster, Pennsylvania, partly to have a suitable place to entertain political guests, but mainly to care for a growing family. Although Buchanan remained a bachelor, he had over the years become a kind of foster father to a score of nephews and nieces, seven of them orphans. They often visited him at Wheatland, and two made their home with him there, cared for in his absence by his faithful housekeeper, Miss Hetty Parker.

But Buchanan could not stay out of politics for long. In 1852 he was again a candidate for the presidential nomination. He was beaten by a little-known candidate, Franklin Pierce.

President Buchanan received the first Japanese delegation to the United States in 1860.

decision in the case of the Negro Dred Scott. The court decided that Congress had no power to keep slavery out of federal territories.

Buchanan thought slavery was wrong, but unfortunately the Constitution recognized it. He hoped that the Dred Scott decision would quiet the country. However, people in the North refused to accept the Supreme Court's decision. Thus the North and the South became more divided than ever.

South Carolina Secedes from the Union

The crisis came in December, 1860. Abraham Lincoln had just been elected president, but he did not take office until March, 1861. Until that time Buchanan was still president.

When the news of Lincoln's victory reached the South, the state of South Carolina seceded from the Union, declaring that it was no longer a part of the United States. By February, 1861, six more southern states had broken away from the Union. The split in the nation that Buchanan feared had taken place.

In this crisis Buchanan wanted to keep the remaining eight slave states loyal to the Union. To achieve this, he said he would do nothing to provoke a war but he would try to protect federal property and enforce the laws in the South. He asked Congress to call a Constitutional Convention and to vote him the men and money needed to enforce the laws. But Congress rejected all these requests.

▶ THE COMING OF WAR

On March 5, 1861, Buchanan left Washington and returned to Wheatland. He was happy to leave the presidency and hopeful that the president who followed him could maintain peace and restore the Union. But 5 weeks after Lincoln's inauguration, the South fired on Fort Sumter and the Civil War began.

Buchanan spent his last years writing a book about his term as president. He died at Wheatland on June 1, 1868.

Could Buchanan have prevented the Civil War? Historians do not agree. Some say that a stronger president, one with more imagination, could have prevented the war. Others argue that the Civil War was inevitable: it would have happened no matter who was president, and if Buchanan had used force against the southern states, the war would only have started earlier.

Buchanan tried to solve the problems of the United States by acting within its laws. He failed. Whether any man could have succeeded will never be known.

Reviewed by PHILIP S. KLEIN
Author, *President James Buchanan*

See also DRED SCOTT DECISION; KANSAS-NEBRASKA ACT; MISSOURI COMPROMISE.

BUCK, PEARL (1892–1973)

Pearl Sydenstricker Buck, American author, was born on June 26, 1892, in Hillsboro, West Virginia. Her parents, Presbyterian missionaries in China, were home on leave. They returned to China 5 months later.

China was Pearl Buck's home for 42 years. She learned to speak Chinese before she learned English. Her closest friends were Chinese. All her schooling was in China until she attended Randolph-Macon College and, later, Cornell University.

Her marriage to Dr. John Buck, an agricultural missionary, took her to a small town in northern China. She described the region in her best-known novel, *The Good Earth* (1931). After 5 years she moved to Nanking and taught English literature to university students. When revolutionary soldiers invaded Nanking in March, 1927, she was rescued by an American gunboat and went to Japan. The next winter she returned to China, but by 1934 the situation was so dangerous for foreigners that she knew she must leave. She decided to make her home in Pennsylvania. She was divorced from Dr. Buck in 1935 and married Richard J. Walsh.

Mrs. Buck received many honors for her writing. *The Good Earth* won her the Pulitzer prize and the Howells medal of the American Academy of Arts and Letters. In 1938 she became the first American woman to win the Nobel prize for literature. Among her many good works she founded Welcome House in 1949. It is a home for American children of Asian ancestry who are waiting to be adopted.

▶ THE BIG WAVE

Pearl Buck wrote *The Big Wave* (1948) after living in Japan. It tells what happened to Jiya when a big wave rose out of the sea and destroyed all the homes and families in his Japanese fishing village. The part about the wave is given below.

At two o'clock the sky began to grow black. The air was as hot as though a forest fire were burning, but there was no sign of such a fire. The glow of the volcano glared over the mountaintop, blood-red against the black. A deep-toned bell tolled over the hills.

"What is that bell?" Kino asked his father.

"I never heard it before."

"It rang twice before you were born," his father replied. "It is the bell in the temple inside the walls of Old Gentleman's castle. He is calling the people to come up out of the village and shelter within his walls."

"Will they come?" Kino asked.

"Not all of them," his father replied. "Parents will try to make their children go, but the children will not want to leave their parents. Mothers will not want to leave fathers, and the fathers will stay by their boats. But some will want to be sure of life."

The bell kept on ringing urgently, and soon out of the village a trickling stream of people, nearly all of them children, began to climb toward the knoll.

"I wish Jiya would come," Kino said. "Do you think he will see me if I stand on the edge of the terrace and wave my white girdle cloth?"

"Try it," his father said.

"Come with me," Kino begged.

So Kino and his father stood on the edge of the terrace and waved. Kino took off the strip of white cloth from about his waist that he wore instead of a belt, and he waved it, holding it in both hands, high above his head.

Far down the hill Jiya saw the two figures and the waving strip of white against the dark sky. He was crying as he climbed, and trying not to cry. He had not wanted to leave his father, but because he was the youngest one, his older brother and his father and mother had all told him that he must go up the mountain. "We must divide ourselves," Jiya's father said. "If the ocean yields to the fires you must live after us."

"I don't want to live alone," Jiya said.

"It is your duty to obey me, as a good Japanese son," his father told him.

Jiya had run out of the house, crying. Now when he saw Kino, he decided that he would go there instead of to the castle, and he began to hurry up the hill to the farm. Next to his own family he loved Kino's strong father and kind mother. He had no sister of his own and he thought Setsu was the prettiest girl he had ever seen.

Kino's father put out his hand to help Jiya up the stone wall and Kino was just about to shout out his welcome when suddenly a hurricane wind broke out of the ocean. Kino and Jiya clung together and wrapped their arms about the father's waist.

"Look—look—what is that?" Kino screamed. The purple rim of the ocean seemed to lift and rise against the clouds. A silver-green band of bright sky appeared like a low dawn above the sea.

"May the gods save us," Kino heard his father mutter. The castle bell began to toll again, deep and pleading. Ah, but would the people hear it in the roaring wind? Their houses had no windows toward the sea. Did they know what was about to happen?

Under the deep waters of the ocean, miles down under the cold, the earth had yielded at last to the fire. It groaned and split open and cold water fell into the middle of the boiling rocks. Steam burst out and lifted the ocean high into the sky in a big wave. It rushed toward the shore, green and solid, frothing into white at its edges. It rose, higher and higher, lifting up hands and claws.

"I must tell my father!" Jiya screamed.

But Kino's father held him fast with both arms. "It is too late," he said sternly.

And he would not let Jiya go.

In a few seconds, before their eyes the wave had grown and come nearer and nearer, higher and higher. The air was filled with its roar and shout. It rushed over the flat still waters of the ocean and before Jiya could scream again it reached the village and covered it fathoms deep in swirling wild water, green laced with fierce white foam. The wave ran up the mountainside, until the knoll where the castle stood was an island. All who were still climbing the path were swept away—black, tossing scraps in the wicked waters. The wave ran up the mountain until Kino and Jiya saw the wavelets curl at the terrace walls upon which they stood. Then with a great sucking sigh, the wave swept back again, ebbing into the ocean, dragging everything with it, trees and stones and houses. They stood, the man and the two boys, utterly silent, clinging together, facing the wave as it went away. It swept back over the village and returned slowly again to the ocean, subsiding, sinking into a great stillness.

Upon the beach where the village stood not a house remained, no wreckage of wood or fallen stone wall, no little street of shops, no docks, not a single boat. The beach was as clean of houses as if no human beings had ever lived there. All that had been was now no more.

Jiya gave a wild cry and Kino felt him slip to the ground. He was unconscious. What he had seen was too much for him. What he knew, he could not bear. His family and his home were gone.

BUDDHA AND BUDDHISM

More than 2,500 years ago, a man in India made a discovery. He discovered the cause of unhappiness and its cure. The man was named Siddhartha Gautama, but he is much better known as the **Buddha**, which means "the wise one" or "the enlightened one." The Buddha's teachings are the basis for one of the world's great religions, Buddhism.

▶ HOW SIDDHARTHA BECAME "THE WISE ONE"

Siddhartha Gautama was born about 563 B.C. His father ruled a small state in northern India near the Himalayas. Strangely enough, the man who discovered the cause of unhappiness knew little about it when he was young. His father tried to protect him from all knowledge of sickness, pain, suffering, and death. Siddhartha spent his early years within palaces and gardens where all was beautiful and pleasant. When he left the palace grounds, his father sent servants to clear the road of any painful sights. As a result, Siddhartha knew nothing about unhappiness.

In spite of all his father did, Siddhartha did eventually learn of unhappiness. Once as he was riding in his chariot he came upon a frail old man. Then he saw another man suffering from a dread disease. Later he met some men carrying the body of one who had died. When Siddhartha asked about those who suffered from old age, disease, and death, he was told: "This happens to all men." For the first time Siddhartha understood that unhappiness was a part of life.

Siddhartha thought about what he had learned. He realized that he could no longer live cut off from the sight of all suffering, as he had in the past. Now that he had begun to learn about life, he could never be content until he understood the whole truth. One night Siddhartha left his father and his wife and child and gave up his great personal fortune. He thought that wealth and comfort would only interfere with his search for understanding.

At first Siddhartha tried to learn wisdom from some holy men, but after 6 years he knew that this was not the way. He then decided to look for the truth within himself. He seated himself beneath a tree (which Buddhists now call the Bo Tree) and vowed that he would not leave until he understood the whole meaning of life. He sat there for 49 days, and then the truth came to him. Siddhartha, the seeker for wisdom, had become the Buddha—the wise one.

The Buddha spent the next 45 years teaching men what he had learned under the Bo Tree. He died about 483 B.C., when he was 80. Shortly before his death he reminded his followers that they should not grieve because "everything must die."

▶ WHAT THE WISE ONE TAUGHT

The Buddha wrote no books. He taught his followers, and they taught their followers, who in turn did the same. For hundreds of years the Buddha's teachings were passed on by word of mouth. When men did finally try to write down the teachings in books, they no longer agreed about them. Some had learned one thing; some had learned another. For this reason there is no single collection of writings that serves as a Buddhist bible.

However, most Buddhists do agree about certain teachings. They agree that the Buddha taught that pain, suffering, and unhappiness must be expected as a natural part of life. They tell of a woman who came to the Buddha hoping that he could bring her dead son back to life, for she had heard that he had remarkable powers. The Buddha told her to borrow a cup of mustard seed from a family that had not known of death. The woman went from door to door, but, of course, she could find no such family. She then understood what the Buddha was trying to teach her. No one could escape death and unhappiness. We must expect it and accept it. Men expect only happiness and they are disappointed when they do not receive it. To avoid disappointment, the Buddha taught that one should expect nothing.

If one knows the cause of unhappiness, the Buddha said, one also knows its cure. One can escape unhappiness by getting rid of all selfish desires. How can this be done? By thinking as much of others as we do of ourselves. The man who understands the whole truth and accepts it will understand that he should never steal or cheat or grow angry. He will

The famous gold statue of the Buddha in Bangkok, Thailand.

not stir up trouble by repeating hurtful things. The man who understands what the Buddha taught will "bear the burdens of those who are tired and weary," and he will "harm no living thing."

Once a man completely overcomes all selfishness, he will know a kind of freedom from care that the Buddhists call **nirvana**. The word "nirvana" means "the going out of fire," especially the fire of anger, greed, and desire. It is evidently hard to describe nirvana to those who do not know it. It is like trying to explain how salt tastes to someone who has never tasted it.

▶ DIFFERENT KINDS OF BUDDHISM

A hundred years after the Buddha's death, men already had different ideas about what he had taught. Each man believed what he had learned from his own teacher, and he taught this to his own students.

One group insisted that they remain true to the **Theravada**, which means "the way of the elders." The Buddha had taught, they said, that each man must find his own way to nirvana. No one can help him, not even the gods and spirits. The Buddha did all that one person can do for others; he showed them what they must do for themselves.

Buddhist nuns—their heads shaved—receive a spoonful of rice (*left*) in return for their prayers. The Japanese monk (*right*) sits in silent contemplation.

Another group said that the Theravada was only a part of the Buddha's teachings. He taught these "lesser ideas" first, but to those able to understand them he gave a greater teaching called the **Mahayana**, which means "the greater vehicle." Mahayana Buddhists refer to Theravada teachings as the **Hinayana**, "the little vehicle."

Mahayana Buddhists also teach that men should follow the Buddha's example of doing good to others. But they believe that the Buddha did more than provide an example. Mahayana Buddhists believe that the Buddha is a god who aids and protects those who pray to him and call upon him. They also believe that men can call upon a number of good spirits, called **Bodhisattvas**, who devote themselves to helping suffering mankind.

From these two divisions of Buddhism have come a number of others. It is said that there are more than 60 different Buddhist groups in Japan today. The differences among the various kinds of Buddhism are great. There are Buddhists, such as those of Tibet, who combine belief in the Buddha with a belief in a large number of spirits and demons. They believe that these spirits and demons can be controlled by magic. Other groups, such as Zen Buddhists of Japan, say very little about gods and spirits. Zen Buddhists, in fact, say

that it is impossible to explain Buddhist teachings in words at all. Either you understand what enlightenment is, or you do not. If you do not, there is nothing that can be said to make it clear to you.

Since Buddhism includes such a variety of branches, it has been described as a group of religions and of ways of thinking rather than a single religion.

▶BUDDHIST MONKS

During the Buddha's lifetime some of his followers gave up all they had and shared their master's way of life. They spent their time learning the teacher's words and trying to do as he did. We call these men **monks** and the houses they live in **monasteries**.

Some men still choose to live as Buddhist monks. A Buddhist monk owns nothing except his yellow or orange robe, his bowl, his razor, and a few other personal items. Many monks depend entirely upon gifts of food for their living. They spend their time learning and reciting the Buddha's teachings. Monks also teach others, both by their words and by the example of their lives. Some monks care for the sick, for the Buddha once said, "He who would care for me should care for the sick."

Some monks spend their entire lives in the

monasteries. Others may live as monks for a short time. This has been true in Burma, where many boys have spent a few weeks or months living as monks.

▶ BUDDHISM IN THE WORLD TODAY

It is impossible to say how many Buddhists there are in the world today. All that can be said for sure is that Buddhism is one of the world's major religions. A Buddhist is simply a person who believes that there is truth in some form of Buddhism.

Almost all Buddhists live in Asia, but only a small number live in India, where Buddhism began. Most Buddhists are found in Sri Lanka, Burma, Thailand, Cambodia, Tibet, China, and Japan. There are only a few people practicing Buddhism as a religion in Europe and America. But many Europeans and Americans have read and studied Buddhist teaching.

The Buddhists of the country of Sri Lanka follow the Theravada—the way of the elders. They take pride in the fact that Buddhism has been in their country for a long time. Buddhist missionaries went to Sri Lanka 2,200 years ago, bringing with them a cutting from Buddha's sacred Bo Tree. Sri Lankan Buddhists say that the cutting grew into a tree that still stands.

In Tibet the everyday life of the people revolves around a form of Buddhism known as Lamaism. The lamas, or monks, were once very powerful. The highest monk of one order, the Dalai Lama, was both the spiritual and political head of Tibet for several centuries. Although he was forced to leave Tibet for political reasons, the present Dalai Lama is still a spiritual leader.

Travelers carried Mahayana Buddhism to China before A.D. 100, where it became one of the three main religions. The Chinese adopted Buddhist teachings without giving up their old Confucianist beliefs. Some persons might consider themselves both Buddhists and Confucianists. This is why it is so hard to decide how many Buddhists there are.

In about A.D. 372 Buddhist monks carried their teachings to Korea, China's eastern neighbor. About 200 years later Buddhists from both Korea and China carried Buddhist books and images to the island kingdom of Japan. Today Buddhism is one of Japan's two major religions.

KENNETH S. COOPER
George Peabody College

BUDGETS, FAMILY

Most families have far more money than they realize. The ones who get the most from their money seem to have learned how to manage the money they have very well.

A plan for spending the money is called a budget. You, as a member of a family, share in the money spent for food, shelter, clothing, medical care, education, and recreation in your family. It is well to know how much thought and planning often has to be done to provide for the family's basic needs and the individual wants of each member.

Each family must decide for itself exactly how much planning it wants to do. However, there are useful steps that any family can follow for this purpose.

Step 1. Decide whether to divide the budget into periods of 1 week, 2 weeks, or 1 month. Most people find that the time between paydays is the best budgeting period.

WEEKLY BUDGET	
Fixed Expenses	Cost
Rent and Mortgage	
Insurance	
Transportation	
Taxes and Savings	
Time payments	
Living Expenses	
Food	
Clothing	
Utilities	
Recreation	
Contributions	
Medical	
Automobile	
Others	
Total	

Step 2. List all fixed expenses. Include every bill for which the exact amount is known in advance, such as payments for rent, mortgage, insurance, the car, and any other installment purchases.

Step 3. List all regular living expenses for which the amounts vary. Estimate how much each costs during a pay period. Accurate estimates will require time and experience since the amount spent on living expenses depends on such things as the care shown by the shopper and the time of year. For example, food costs can be kept down by the woman who shops and cooks wisely; more water is used in summer, and more fuel and electricity in winter. The cost of clothing and its care can be spread out over the whole year instead of spending large amounts in the fall and spring. The homemaker who knows what to look for in selecting clothing, who has a wardrobe plan that will prevent unwise purchases, and who can sew, will need less money than another person.

Step 4. List any expected major expenses too large to be paid in a single pay period. Decide how much should be set aside each payday to meet such expenses when they occur. Taxes can usually be estimated in advance, and enough money saved to pay them. Home appliances and furnishings can be bought with savings.

Step 5. Total all expenses. Compare this total with the family's income for the budgeting period. If the expenses are too high, look for ways to cut them. If there is money left, some of it should be set aside regularly in an emergency fund and some in a savings or investment program.

Step 6. Use a budget book or make a chart. Write down the family's plans for using its money. In the following weeks and months, compare this budget with what is actually spent and make any necessary changes.

Even a good budget will not help the family control its spending unless all family members co-operate. Young people who get experience in good money management as they grow up will have little difficulty in working out a family budget of their own.

KATHERINE R. CONAFAY
Author, *Family Budgets*

See also INSTALLMENT BUYING.

BUENOS AIRES

Buenos Aires is Argentina's largest city, its capital, and its gateway to the world. It is situated on the Río de la Plata (the River Plate), about 275 kilometers (170 miles) from the sea. Buenos Aires is one of the largest ports in the Americas. Greater Buenos Aires has about 9,000,000 people—over one third of Argentina's total population. The city itself has about 3,000,000 people. Most of the country's roads, railroads, manufacturing plants, ocean shipping, and commerce are centered in Buenos Aires.

The name of the city was given to it by the early Spanish explorers. Buenos Aires means "good airs." A first settlement in 1536 failed because of Indian attacks. A permanent settlement was finally achieved in 1580.

Buenos Aires was a modest city until the end of the 19th century. In time thousands of immigrants—Italians, Germans, Swedes, and people of other nationalities—made it the wonder city it is today. Buenos Aires is set

on a flat plain like a huge, sprawling giant. Its highways and streets stretch out in all directions as far as the eye can see. Seen from above at night, with its countless lights stabbing at the darkness, the city looks like a vast field of glittering diamonds.

On a sunny day the center of the city bustles with sound and movement. Automobile horns honk sharply, and river freighters whistle mournfully. Cheerful, busy people go about their errands, talking in Spanish

Buenos Aires is the bustling capital and commercial center of Argentina. Shoppers (*below left*) throng the city streets. Avenida 9 de Julio (*below right*) is one of the widest streets in the world. Above is the Palace of the National Congress.

and as many other languages as are likely to be heard in New York. There is also the dull rumble of the subway trains from deep beneath the sidewalk.

Buenos Aires is a great port whose ships go all over the world. Cement docks line the Río de la Plata. Warehouses, meat-packing plants, grain elevators, and the smokestacks of oceangoing ships loom against the sunny sky. Long freight trains pull into busy yards. Some of these trains have come hundreds of kilometers across the pampas, or plains, with wool to be shipped to distant countries. Most imports also come through the city.

Buenos Aires is a city of sunny plazas and wide boulevards. It is a city of pleasant living. People stroll to the many sidewalk cafés, sit at outdoor tables, and sip black coffee. Many of the streets and avenues are bordered with flowers.

Buenos Aires is the home of the tango. It is a city of music, of drama, of fine libraries and modern schools. World-famous opera stars come to the luxurious Teatro Colón to perform. Open-air performances of ballet are given at the Palermo Gardens. And here a symphony orchestra plays for crowds of appreciative listeners.

It is a city that loves to watch and play sports—golf, tennis, swimming, rowing, polo, and above all soccer, car racing, and horse racing. Champion sports figures become national heroes. One of the largest stadiums in the world, said to have a capacity of about 100,000 people, is in Buenos Aires.

These are some of the sights and sounds of the largest city in the Southern Hemisphere. This is Buenos Aires.

Reviewed by ERNESTO SÁBATO
Author, *Heroes and Graves*

BUFFALO. See BISON AND BUFFALO.

BUFFALO BILL (1846–1917)

Buffalo Bill was the last of the famous American frontier scouts. He was a dead shot with a rifle and an expert guide, hunter, and Indian fighter.

Buffalo Bill, whose real name was William Frederick Cody, was born in Scott County, Iowa, on February 26, 1846. At the age of 14 he was carrying mail for the Pony Express across country where Indians and bandits were a constant danger. During the Civil War, Cody was a Union Army scout. Later he hunted buffalo to supply meat for workmen building a railroad across Kansas. It is said that Cody killed 69 buffalo in one day, and over 4,000 in 17 months. He became known everywhere as Buffalo Bill. When war with the Sioux and Cheyenne Indians broke out in 1875, Cody again became a scout for the cavalry. He is said to have fought a hand-to-hand duel with Yellow Hand, the son of a Cheyenne chief, and killed him.

In 1883 Cody produced the first of his famous Wild West shows. The show included a huge cast of cowboys, Indians, and sharpshooters, with herds of buffalo, elk, ponies, steers, and wild horses. Historic events such as Custer's Last Stand were re-enacted. Sitting Bull, the Sioux chief whose braves had helped defeat General Custer's soldiers, was one of the attractions. Annie Oakley, the most famous woman rifle and pistol shot, was another. Thousands of people in the United States, Canada, and Europe saw the show before Cody gave it up in 1913.

Cody died on January 10, 1917. His grave and the Cody Memorial Museum are on top of Lookout Mountain in Colorado. There is also a Buffalo Bill museum in Cody, Wyoming. Scenes from the old Wild West shows are re-created there every summer.

FIVE POPULAR BUGLE CALLS

ASSEMBLY

CALL TO QUARTERS

ATTENTION

BOY SCOUT CALL

TAPS

BUGLE

The bugle is a brass wind instrument that looks very much like a trumpet. Unlike the trumpet, however, the bugle has no valves or keys. It consists of a cylindrical tube with a bell-shaped opening at one end and a cup-shaped mouthpiece at the other. Since it has no valves or keys, the notes available on a bugle are limited to the natural, or so-called "open tones," of the scale. Only five different notes are required to play the various bugle calls. The sound is produced by the pressure of the player's breath and the tension on the mouthpiece of his lips, which act as reeds. Bugles have a treble, or high, range in pitch and are usually tuned to the key of B flat.

The word "bugle" comes from the Latin word *buculus,* meaning "young bull." In early times when people wanted to signal one another, they blew through the tip of a hollow animal horn. The horn of a young bull was most frequently used for this purpose.

The bugle of today is a descendant of the ancient battle horns used by men thousands of years ago. One such instrument is mentioned in the Bible. The Hebrew shofar—a ram's horn—was used by Joshua at the battle of Jericho, and Gideon used hundreds of shofars to terrify the Midanites.

Around the middle of the 18th century, the bugle became the chief signal instrument of military regiments in Europe. Bugle calls of that time resembled those of today. Although it is now less important in military life than it used to be, the bugle has retained strong military associations.

Bugle calls are familiar melodies that announce certain duties in military camp life. Reveille, a quick, lively tune, means "time to get up." Taps, a slow, sad melody, means "go to sleep" and is commonly played at military funerals. The armed forces of most countries have their own bugle calls.

The Boy Scouts use the bugle at camp to announce such activities as swimming, meals, and raising or lowering the United States flag. Each troop has its own bugler. An especially good Scout bugler can win a merit badge for his talent.

BUILDING CONSTRUCTION

There are many different kinds of buildings, ranging in size from tool sheds to immense skyscrapers and factories. They are built in a number of ways, out of a great variety of materials. But in spite of these differences all buildings can be classified into a few types, according to their function, their structure, and their materials.

The **function** of a building means the purpose for which it is constructed. Some of the main functions of buildings are to shelter people from the weather, to provide them with living and working space, to store goods, and to house machinery. Special purposes are served by buildings like churches, schools, and museums. The size and structure of a building depend on the building's function. A one-family house is quite different from a high school where 1,500 children study.

The term **structure** means the parts that support the building and the way they are arranged and fastened together. The structure of a building must be planned so that the building will be able to support itself and whatever it contains, such as people, furniture, or heavy machinery.

There are a variety of structural forms that can be used in constructing a building. After a builder decides on the structural form he wants, he then determines the materials he will use in the actual construction.

▶ THE MATERIALS OF BUILDING

The materials are the basic elements of any building. Building materials may be classified into three groups, according to the purposes they are used for. Structural materials are those that hold the building up, keep it rigid, form its outer covering of walls and roof, and divide its interior into rooms. In the second group are materials for the equipment inside the building, such as the plumbing, heating, and lighting systems. Finally, there are materials that are used to protect or decorate the structural materials.

The basic structural materials are wood, clay, stone, steel, and concrete. Wood is the oldest of the structural materials. It has been used since prehistoric times. Wood can be shaped with simple tools, and it can be easily fastened with nails, screws, or adhesives.

Wood has three important characteristics that make it useful as a building material. It resists being broken by bending or being pulled apart; brick and stone do not have this quality. Wood can withstand a heavy load pressing directly down on it. And it has elasticity, which means that it can regain its shape after being bent, stretched, or twisted. However, wood is not as durable as other building materials. Unless it is protected by paint or chemicals, it can be warped and split by weather, eaten by insects, or rotted by fungi.

Clay is used in the form of bricks and tile. To make a rigid wall of bricks, the individual bricks are laid in rows, or courses, and held together by a cementing material called mortar. A wall made of bricks or stones held together by mortar is called masonry. A brick-and-mortar wall can bear heavy loads that press directly down on it. However, it cannot withstand forces that tend to cause bending, such as high winds, unless it is built extra thick. The great advantage of brick construction is its low cost. Clay is cheap and plentiful, and bricks are small enough to be laid easily by hand.

Stone is strong and durable. In many respects it is an ideal building material. However, it is difficult to handle. For use in a large building, stones must be cut from the solid rock in a quarry. Then they must be shaped into blocks, trimmed to the correct size, and smoothed so that they fit closely together. All this labor makes stone very expensive. Stone blocks of the size used in buildings are so heavy that they cannot be laid by hand. Instead, they must be lifted into position by cranes. Because it is expensive and difficult to work with, stone is used today mainly as a thin outside covering for large buildings and for the decorative walls and floors of entrance lobbies.

Steel and concrete are the most widely used structural materials today. Steel is truly an all-round material. Steel is nearly as durable as stone (although it must be painted to protect it from rust). It has some of wood's elastic quality. And it can be formed into almost any imaginable shape. In modern construction steel is used for the supporting framework of large buildings.

Concrete, a mixture of cement, sand, and

gravel, is actually an ancient material that has found new uses. Concrete was invented by the Romans shortly before the beginning of the Christian Era. After the fall of the Roman Empire, concrete was not used again until the early 19th century.

Concrete sets, or hardens, into a dense, stonelike substance. Unlike stone, however, it does not have to be cut and shaped into individual blocks that are then fitted together to make a wall. Instead, it can be poured into wooden forms to make solid, one-piece structures of almost any shape.

By itself concrete, like stone and brick, has only compressive strength. That is, it can support great loads pressing down directly on it. But it cannot withstand forces that cause it to bend. For example, a flat roof of plain concrete would soon crack under its own weight. This is because the weight of the roof would act so as to push it down in the center, while the edges of the roof were held up by the walls. One way of solving this problem is to support the concrete roof with pillars. A better way is to reinforce the concrete with steel rods. Concrete reinforced in this way takes on steel's ability to withstand bending and stretching forces.

Every part of a building—vertical columns, walls, horizontal beams, and floors—can be made of reinforced concrete. And because the concrete can be poured into forms, it can be used to make many useful structural shapes, such as one-piece domes, that would be impossible to build with other materials.

Many other kinds of materials besides the basic structural materials are needed for a building. There is window glass, to admit light and provide a view. There is insulation, to keep the building warm in winter and cool in summer. A big office or apartment building contains vast and complicated heating, air conditioning, plumbing, electrical, and lighting systems. These use up great quantities of metals and alloys, plastics, adhesives, wood, and fibers. Partitions between rooms account for a small mountain of plaster. There are also protective and decorative coatings, such as paint for walls and tar to keep roofs from leaking. By the end of World War II the nonstructural materials used in a building added up to more than half the total cost of the building itself.

▶THE WORK OF CONSTRUCTION

The construction of a large office or apartment building is a long process. It requires many different talents and skills. Before construction can begin, architects and engineers must design the structure and all the things within it that are fixed parts of the building, such as heating and electrical systems. The first step is to learn how the building is to be used (as a hotel, factory, apartment house, or movie theater, for example) and how much money the owner is prepared to spend. These factors influence the type of construction and materials that will be used.

Next, the experts must study the site, or location, of the building. They must find out the nature of the soil, to learn whether it will support the weight of the building or whether special foundation work will have to be done. They must also learn the relation of the building to its surroundings, the area it will cover, and the maximum height that local regulations allow. Only then can the engineers and architects begin to draw their plans.

For a large building the architect prepares several hundred drawings, or plans, that show the building in various ways. Some are drawn as though we were looking down on a particular floor from above. These show the location of corridors, rooms, doors, windows, elevators, and stairways. Some show the outside appearance of the building. Another kind of plan is drawn as though the building has been sliced through from top to bottom. Still another kind of plan shows special features of a building, such as window frames, stair rails, elevators, and lighting fixtures.

Several kinds of engineers take part in designing a building. The structural engineer calculates the size, shape, and location of the foundations and structural parts of the building. His drawings show the columns, beams, and other parts of the supporting structure. They also show how the parts of the frame are connected. The mechanical engineer designs the heating, plumbing, and air conditioning systems, and all the wiring for the electrical equipment. There are so many jobs for engineers to do in designing a building that more of the cost of a building arises from engineering than from architectural work.

When the plans of a building are com-

A blasting mat of steel rope (*above*) keeps rocks from flying about when excavations are dynamited.

Right: An excavation is ready for the foundations to be laid.

High above the city streets, steelworkers guide a girder into place, then bolt and rivet it securely.

1 EXCAVATING FOR FOUNDATION

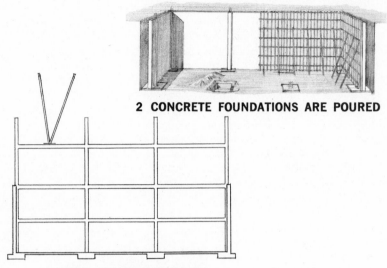

2 CONCRETE FOUNDATIONS ARE POURED

3 STEEL FRAMING GOES UP

4 FIREPROOFING AND CONCRETE FLOOR SLABS FOLLOW CLOSE BEHIND STEEL

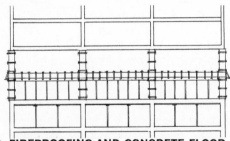

5 PREFABRICATED SECTIONS OF SIDING AND GLASS ARE ADDED

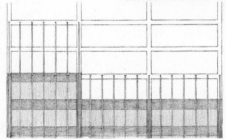

KEY TO SYSTEMS:

ELECTRIC WIRING (BLACK)——

HEATING (BLACK) ———

SUPPLY → →

RETURN ← ←

PLUMBING (RED) ———

ELEVATORS (RED) ------

6 HEATING, PLUMBING, ELECTRIC, AND ELEVATOR SYSTEMS ARE INSTALLED

Above: Steel girders and other materials are stacked ready for use in building a skyscraper. Below: Workers guide precast concrete wall panels into place on New York's Pan Am Building.

BUILDING CONSTRUCTION · 433

pleted, the contractor can begin his job. The contractor is the man who carries out the actual work of construction. The first step is to excavate for foundations and basements. If the soil of the building site is soft, an underpinning must be constructed to keep the foundation from sinking. There are two ways of doing this. The older and simpler way is to drive wood poles or steel pillars, called piles, down through the soil to the underlying rock. Then the concrete foundation is poured on top of the piles. A newer, stronger technique is to dig a narrow well down to bedrock at the location of each column. The wells are filled with concrete. These concrete pillars are called caissons.

With the foundation laid, the erection of the building frame begins. In steel-framed buildings cranes lift the columns, girders, and beams into place. They are riveted, welded, or bolted together story by story, to form a rigid, cagelike structure. If the frame is concrete, steel reinforcing bars are fixed in wooden forms and concrete is poured around the bars. When the concrete has hardened, the forms are stripped away, leaving the concrete frame.

As soon as the frame is completed, the floors and roof are constructed. In some buildings the floors are constructed as the framework for each story is completed. In large buildings the floors and roof are usually made of reinforced concrete. A temporary wooden floor supports the concrete until it hardens. When the floors have hardened, the outside walls are put up. In framed buildings the outside walls do not have to carry any of the building's weight. They simply act as a skin or curtain to enclose the building. For this reason they are called curtain walls. In many modern buildings the curtain walls are largely of glass.

Now begins the long process of installing interior partitions, heating and air conditioning equipment, water pipes, elevators, lighting fixtures, and wiring. Interior walls must be plastered. The ceilings may be covered with soundproofing material. Then painters and decorators go to work. When they have finished, the building is ready to be moved into. In office buildings tenants often move in as each floor is finished, while work is still being done on the floors above or below.

There are, of course, many differences between the construction of a large business or apartment building and a private home. A private home is small enough so that it does not need to be supported on piles or caissons. Its frame can be made of wood instead of steel. Most of the construction work can be done without heavy machinery.

Not all modern small buildings have frame structures. If the building is to be fairly low, for example, a one- or two-story garage or store, the builder may use bearing walls. A bearing wall supports the loads of the roof and floors, as well as its own weight. Bearing walls are usually made of brick or stone masonry, cinder block, or poured concrete. Windows and doors must be small and few in number, to avoid weakening the wall. Bearing walls are not practical for tall buildings because they must be built very thick to keep from toppling over.

▶ FROM BRUSH HUTS TO SKYSCRAPERS

Building began as soon as human beings emerged from caves. The most primitive form of building was the piling up of pieces of turf on logs to form a roof over a shallow hole in the ground. Later, huts were made of woven branches plastered with mud or clay. This is called the **wattle-and-daub** method.

Primitive man eventually began to learn the fundamentals of frame construction. He probably began by driving branches into the ground in a circle, bending them together at the top, and covering them with bark, grass, or animal skins. Some of the Indian tribes of the northeastern woodlands were still building their lodges this way when the first Europeans reached America.

Later, Neolithic man invented a true system of framing. This consisted of three parallel rows of posts, along which beams were laid. The beams along the high center row formed the ridgeline of the roof. From the ridge logs called rafters sloped down to the outer, lower rows. Woven twigs or grass formed the roof, and bark was used for the side walls—if any were erected. This frame was the ancestor of the wood framing that is still used in the construction of houses. Other kinds of primitive structures are tents, domed huts made of reeds and grass, and the igloo of the Eskimos.

Buildings of brick were constructed in small villages around the eastern end of the Mediterranean Sea as early as 6500 B.C. Stone buildings were created by the Egyptians about 3000 B.C. Egypt has large quantities of building stone, especially limestone and granite. Egyptian builders learned how to cut the stone and lay it in columns and walls. The stones were held in place by their weight alone. The pyramids and a number of temples still standing are examples of Egyptian stonework.

Stone was scarce in the region of ancient Mesopotamia, so that Babylonian and Sumerian builders had to use clay, which they formed into bricks. The first bricks were simply dried in the sun. Later it was discovered that baking them in kilns made them harder, stronger, and more durable.

Methods of building in stone and brick were perfected by the Greeks and Romans. The Greeks created many beautiful architectural designs, although they had little interest in developing new structural methods.

The Romans were the great builders of the classical world. They borrowed many of their ideas from other peoples, but they used them in original ways to construct new kinds of buildings. It was the Romans who perfected the arch, vault, and dome. It was also the Romans who invented concrete. (The secret of Roman cement and concrete was lost during the Middle Ages and was not rediscovered until the 19th century.)

In the Middle Ages fortified castles, palaces, churches, and other important buildings were generally constructed of stone; for ordinary houses builders used whatever was locally available. Thus stone and adobe were common materials in regions around the Mediterranean Sea, brick and stone in western Europe, and wood in northern Europe. The picturesque half-timbered houses of medieval Europe were actually a way of saving on expensive wood. Heavy timbers were used for the framing. But instead of covering the frame with boards or shingles, medieval builders filled up the spaces between the timbers with bricks or rough chunks of stone. The surface was then plastered over to make it look smooth. In cheaper houses wattle-and-daub was used to fill the space between the timbers. Farmhouses were usually covered with thatch (reeds or straw tied in bundles and arranged to overlap like shingles). In order to reduce the danger of fire, town and city houses had roofs of slate or tile.

Fine craftsmanship was used in building the great cathedrals and palaces of the Middle Ages. Rich people also had well-built houses, but the common people lived in crudely built huts.

Construction was done almost entirely by hand. There were no machines for cutting or shaping wood or stone. Machinery was used only for hoisting heavy loads of stone onto large buildings. These crudely built cranes and derricks were usually cranked by hand, although animal power was sometimes used to raise the load. Bricks and mortar were carried up rickety ladders to the workmen on the scaffolds in hods. (A hod is something like a small trough with one end open. It is mounted on the end of a long pole and carried over the shoulder. Hods are still used on small construction jobs.)

There was little change in construction methods as Europe emerged from the Middle Ages, except that ordinary houses were better built. The old handicraft techniques continued to be used. To lessen the danger of fire, town authorities began to require that town houses be built of brick or stone instead of wood.

The great revolution in building construction began at the end of the 18th century, when the Industrial Revolution brought about changes in the whole process of building. The development of large-scale manufacturing brought a need for new kinds of buildings. These buildings had to be fire-resistant, they had to be quickly and economically put up, and they had to be strong enough to bear heavy machinery.

The development of the iron and steel industry provided builders with large quantities of new materials that met these needs. At first production was limited, and prices for iron and steel were high. As a result, they were used mainly in buildings like factories, where great strength and fire resistance were needed. As better production methods were developed the prices fell, and iron and steel became common building materials.

The first type of iron used in building factories was cast iron. Cast iron was used

At a housing project, carpenters erect wooden frames.

Fireproof asbestos shingles are tacked on the walls.

Below, left: A carpenter works on the framework of the roof while a plumber (*below, right*) installs water pipes.

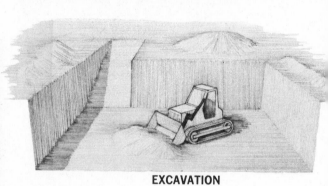

EXCAVATION

The last job on the roof—putting on the shingles.

WALLS AND ROOF ARE FRAMED

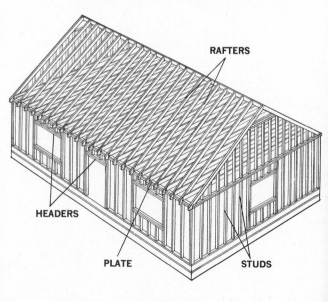

RAFTERS

HEADERS

PLATE

STUDS

Left: A bricklayer uses a level and trowel in straightening the wall he is building. Right: Around the new house a bulldozer operator shapes and smooths the yard.

STEPS IN BUILDING A PRIVATE HOUSE

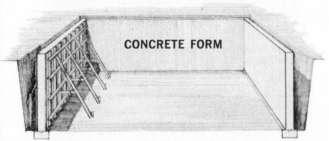

CONCRETE FORM

CONCRETE FOUNDATION IS POURED

SUBFLOOR — JOISTS — SILL — BEAM — FOUNDATION — COLUMN — CONCRETE FLOOR SLAB — FOOTING

FIRST FLOOR FRAMING

HEATING, PLUMBING, AND ELECTRICAL SYSTEMS

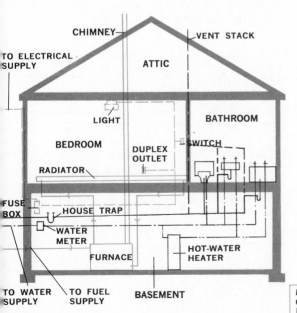

CHIMNEY — VENT STACK
TO ELECTRICAL SUPPLY
ATTIC
LIGHT
BATHROOM
BEDROOM
SWITCH
DUPLEX OUTLET
RADIATOR
FUSE BOX
HOUSE TRAP
WATER METER
FURNACE
HOT-WATER HEATER
BASEMENT
TO WATER SUPPLY
TO FUEL SUPPLY

ROOF AND WALLS ARE COMPLETED

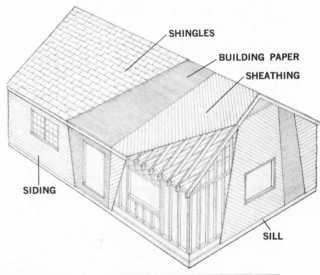

SHINGLES
BUILDING PAPER
SHEATHING
SIDING
SILL

KEY TO SYSTEMS:
COLD WATER — · —
HOT WATER — · · — · · —
WASTE ———
PLUMBING SYSTEMS — · — TOILETS
AIR-CONDITIONING SYSTEM — —
ELECTRIC WIRING — — — — —
HEATING

437

for vertical columns because of its high compressive strength. However, it could not be used for long floor beams because it breaks under a heavy bending load.

Around 1840 wrought iron became available to builders in large quantities. Wrought iron is a form of iron that contains very little carbon. It can stand much heavier bending loads than cast iron. However, wrought iron was not the final answer to builders' problems. It does not have great compressive strength, so that an upright column of wrought iron tends to buckle under a heavy load. Often builders used cast iron for upright columns and wrought iron for horizontal beams.

Steel gave builders an all-round material that could take both compressive and bending loads. During the first half of the 19th century steel could be made only in small batches, a few pounds at a time. It was too scarce and expensive to be used in buildings. But the invention of the Bessemer process in 1856, and the open-hearth process soon afterward, made steel available at low cost. By the end of the 19th century steel was the chief structural material—as it is today.

The use of iron was important in another way too. It helped to turn building from a tradition-bound craft to an exact science. Over the centuries men had learned from experience how wood, brick, and stone behaved in buildings. Iron was something new and strange for builders. No one could predict how this new material would act. At first a number of bridges and buildings collapsed because builders did not know how to use iron correctly. For the sake of safety it was necessary for scientists and engineers to spend years studying the properties of iron. Builders began to rely on scientific method rather than on the old, traditional craftsman's lore. The engineer took over as designer of the structure of buildings, while the architect now dealt mainly with the appearance of the building.

Some of the old handicraft techniques are still used on small construction jobs. But for most large structures, construction is a highly mechanized process.

Iron, steel, and reinforced concrete made it possible for builders to create framing systems of slender columns and beams, stretching across wide areas. With this type of frame they could construct many-storied buildings. Fireproofing and windbracing made steel frames even stronger. The elevator was one of the inventions that made tall buildings practical. Few people would have been willing to walk up 20 flights of stairs every day! The first skyscraper, made possible by these inventions, was built in Chicago in 1885.

Another advance in building technology was the development of prestressed concrete shortly after World War I. Prestressing is a method of compressing a concrete beam or slab before it is put into place in a building. This technique makes the concrete stronger and more durable.

In the 20th century so many structural and mechanical inventions have been made that the design of buildings is more than ever the work of engineers. Architects have also contributed to modern building by designing a variety of beautiful structures that take advantage of the new construction methods and materials.

CARL W. CONDIT
Co-editor, *Technology and Culture*

See also ARCHITECTURE; BRICKS AND MASONRY; CEMENT AND CONCRETE; IRON AND STEEL; STONE.

BULGARIA

BULGARIA

Bulgaria, once a great European power, is now a small nation on the Balkan Peninsula in southeast Europe. For almost 500 years the Turkish Empire controlled and occupied the Balkan Peninsula. In 1878 Bulgaria was liberated by Russia, and most of the Turks were driven from the land.

▶ PEOPLE

Approximately 9,000,000 people live in Bulgaria. About 90 percent are Bulgarians. The Bulgarians inherited their name and some of their vigorous spirit from the Bulgars, people related to the Huns. The Bulgars moved westward from Central Asia. During the 7th century they conquered the Slavs who lived in what is now Bulgaria. They adopted the Slavic language and absorbed many Slavic customs. Today Bulgaria is mainly a Slavic land. Turks make up most of the remaining 10 percent of the population. They are descended from the Turks who settled in Bulgaria when Bulgaria was a Turkish province. There are also other minority groups, such as the Gypsies and Armenians, but they are small in number.

Before the Communists took over, Bulgaria was mainly agricultural. Most peasants owned small strips of land. Although most of the Bulgarians are still peasants, village life has changed greatly since the Communists took control of Bulgaria in 1944. The land is now owned by the state and by collective farms. Peasants receive wages or share in the farm income. But they lack the freedom of a landowner, and their income is low.

Many young people have given up farming for jobs in mines, industry, and the government. Hundreds of others have been forced to leave the villages and to move to the rapidly growing cities. Even the villages are beginning to look like towns. This has greatly changed the rural atmosphere and way of life. Elaborate wedding ceremonies, colorful national costumes, folk dances such as the *horo,* and religious observances are among the traditional customs that still survive.

FACTS AND FIGURES

PEOPLE'S REPUBLIC OF BULGARIA is the official name of the country.

CAPITAL: Sofia.

LOCATION AND SIZE: Southeastern Europe. **Latitude**—41° 14′ N to 44° 13′ N. **Longitude**—22° 22′ E to 28° 37′ E. **Area**—110,912 km² (42,823 sq mi).

PHYSICAL FEATURES: Highest point—Musala Peak, 2,925 m (9,596 ft). **Lowest point**—sea level. **Chief rivers**—Danube, Maritsa, Iskar. **Chief mountain peaks**—Musala, Vikhren.

POPULATION: 9,000,000 (estimate).

LANGUAGE: Bulgarian.

RELIGION: Bulgarian Eastern Orthodox.

GOVERNMENT: People's republic. **Head of state**—chairman of the State Council. **Head of government**—chairman of the Council of Ministers. **Inter-** **national co-operation**—United Nations, Warsaw Pact, Council for Mutual Economic Assistance (COMECON).

NATIONAL ANTHEM: *Bulgario meela, zemya na geroi* ("Dear Bulgaria, land of heroes").

ECONOMY: Agricultural products—wheat, corn, oats, barley, potatoes, sugar beets, grapes, tomatoes, sunflower seeds, tobacco, fruits, roses, cotton. **Industries and products**—food processing, textiles (cotton, wool, and silk), iron and steel, light engineering, chemicals, cement, building and transportation equipment. **Chief minerals**—lignite, coal, iron ore, lead, zinc, copper, crude petroleum. **Chief exports**—tobacco, fruits and vegetables, rose oil, eggs, nonferrous ores and metals, machinery and equipment, electric motors, chemical products (calcined and caustic soda). **Chief imports**—heavy machinery and equipment, vehicles, ferrous metals, coke, petroleum products, chemical products (aniline dyes and fertilizers), rubber, cellulose, cotton and wool. **Monetary unit**—lev.

Language

Most people speak Bulgarian. This is one of the Slavic languages, similar to the languages in neighboring Yugoslavia and in Russia. Different dialects are spoken in many parts of Bulgaria, but Bulgarians from all regions have no difficulty understanding each other.

Bulgarian was the first Slavic language to use the Cyrillic alphabet. This alphabet is derived from the Greek and Hebrew alphabets. It was devised in the 9th century A.D. by two monks, Cyril and Methodius, so they could translate religious works for the Slavs. The alphabet is now used in the Soviet Union and parts of Yugoslavia.

Children enjoying a ride in a horse-drawn cart. In the background is an 11th-century church.

Religion

The Communists discourage religious practices, but most Bulgarians still belong to the Bulgarian Church. This is a branch of the Eastern Orthodox Church but is completely independent. The head of the Bulgarian Church is called the Patriarch. Most of the Turks in Bulgaria, and also some Bulgarians, are Muslims. Bulgarian-speaking Muslims are called Pomaks. There are also small communities of Jews, Roman Catholics, and Protestants. Religious groups are not permitted to maintain separate school systems, and the government must approve the appointment of clergymen.

Education

Great progress has been made in education since Bulgaria's freedom from Turkish domination. In 1878 only 3 percent of the people over school age could read and write. Before World War II the number jumped to 75 percent. Today complete literacy is claimed. Schooling is compulsory for all children between the ages of 7 and 15. Communist doctrine is taught in every grade. Students must also spend one third of their school time working in factories or on farms.

Nearly every village has a public library. The University of Sofia was founded in 1888, and many other cities now have schools of higher education. Technical education is stressed, and many Bulgarian students attend technical schools in the Soviet Union. Bulgaria's medieval paintings at Rila, Tǔrnovo, and Boyana are famous throughout the Western world. Before World War II Bulgaria was also well known for its writers, but today's writers are allowed to write only what the government wants its people and the rest of the world to read.

▶ LAND AND CLIMATE

The Balkan Mountains run east and west and split Bulgaria in two. They act as a divide between the two main climatic regions. North of the mountains the Danube Plateau slopes gradually to the Danube River, which separates Bulgaria from Rumania. The climate of the Danube Plateau is continental, with hot summers and cold winters. The fertile Maritsa River Valley lies between the Balkan Mountains and the rugged Rhodope Mountains on

Old and new buildings are found in Bulgaria. Above is a new circus building. Below is part of the Rila Monastery, a national sanctuary. Rounded arches are decorated in fresco—painting done on wet plaster.

the southern boundary between Bulgaria and Greece. The valley is protected by the Balkan Mountains from the cold winds of the Russian plains. The Maritsa Valley is influenced by the Mediterranean climate, with mild but rainy winters and dry, hot summers.

The Danube Plateau, especially the Dobruja region, is an important agricultural area, where wheat, corn, sunflowers, and sugar beets are grown. The Maritsa Valley, suitable for Mediterranean crops, raises tobacco, rice, cotton, poppy seed, mulberry trees, and silkworms.

The famous Valley of Roses in Middle Bulgaria is the center of Bulgaria's rose-growing industry. It produces attar of roses, an ingredient used in making perfumes. Bulgaria has nearly a world monopoly in the production of this attar.

Natural Resources

One third of Bulgaria is covered with valuable forests. About 75 percent of the forests in the mountains are broadleaf; the rest are coniferous. Beech forests and evergreen scrub plants are found along the Maritsa

Valley and the Turkish border. Bears, wolves, foxes, squirrels, elk, and wildcats roam in the mountain forests.

Bulgaria has a variety of mineral resources. Low-grade coal, low-content iron ore, lead, zinc, and copper are among the principal raw materials. Gold, chrome, manganese, uranium, and pyrites are also mined. Some petroleum was discovered recently but plays a minor role.

▶ **INDUSTRIES AND PRODUCTS**

About 50 percent of the working population is engaged in agriculture, and about 40 percent of the land is usable for farming. The rest of the land is too dry, too marshy, or too mountainous. Irrigation, drainage, and land improvement programs have been started in

Handmade bricks are set out to dry in the sun.

an effort to increase the fertility of farmland. The government now stresses the growth of industrial crops such as tobacco and sugar beets instead of cereal grains. But wheat and corn still occupy over 70 percent of the farmland. Grapes, fruits, and vegetables are also grown, mainly for export. But for many reasons agriculture, especially livestock raising, is faring poorly. One reason is the concentration on heavy industry at the expense of agriculture.

There was little heavy industry in Bulgaria before 1947. Then the Communist government nationalized existing industries. The government drew up plans for building heavy industry, regardless of costs and the lack of adequate raw materials in Bulgaria. Now there are steel and engineering plants, and 20 percent of all Bulgarian workers are employed in manufacturing. But food processing still remains the largest industry.

Bulgaria now produces many types of lighter machine tools and electrical equipment, small ships, railroad cars, building materials, and a variety of processed food products, as well as its traditional textile and leather goods. Coal and iron-ore production have been greatly increased, but much of the needed coke, iron ore, and steel must be imported. Attention has also been given to methods of increasing electricity production. Rivers like the Struma, Mesta, Vŭcha, and Arda may one day provide valuable hydroelectric power for Bulgaria's industries. Little regard is paid to the needs of the domestic consumer. Living standards are low, and even food shortages are not unusual.

Transportation and Communication

Government-owned railroads are the chief means of transportation. Most of the routes connect the capital, Sofia, with other parts of the country. While the number of railroads, paved roads, and modern bridges is steadily increasing, travel in Bulgaria is still difficult.

Traffic on the Danube, Bulgaria's only navigable river, is increasing. The main Danube ports are Ruse, Vidin, Lom, and Svishtov. The Bulgarians also have ports on the Black Sea at Varna and Burgas.

The Bulgarian Government owns and operates the telephone, telegraph, postal, radio,

A scene in Sophia, the capital. The new square has wide, tree-lined streets. Buildings include a department store, Communist Party headquarters, and a hotel.

and television facilities. Publishing is also owned and controlled by the government. The leading newspaper is the *Rabotnichesko Delo,* the official newspaper of the Communist Party.

▶ **GOVERNMENT**

According to the Bulgarian Constitution, the supreme organ of state power is the National Assembly, whose members are elected for terms of 5 years. The National Assembly, however, meets only a few times a year. Real legislative power is exercised by the State Council, which is elected by the Assembly. The chairman of the State Council serves as head of state. Executive authority rests with the Council of Ministers, or Cabinet, whose chairman is the head of government. Citizens are eligible to vote at 18.

The leading force in the country is the Bul-garian Communist Party, headed by a first secretary. The top positions in all governing bodies are held by Communist Party members. All candidates for elected office must be approved by the party.

▶ **HISTORY**

The history of the Bulgarian state in the Balkans began in the 7th century A.D. The Bulgars were tribes who came from Central Asia. They conquered the part of the Balkan Peninsula inhabited by Slavs from the Byzantine Empire. In 679 the Bulgars founded the First Bulgarian Kingdom, which lasted until 1018. Although they ruled the country, they adopted the language and most of the customs of the conquered Slavs.

Medieval Bulgaria was one of the great military and cultural powers. It fought many wars against the Byzantine Empire and against other neighbors and invaders. Boris I accepted Christianity (865), established the independent Bulgarian Church (870), and introduced the Cyrillic alphabet. His son, Czar Simeon I (893–927), one of Bulgaria's greatest rulers, conquered many new territories. At the end of his rule Bulgaria stretched from the Black Sea on the east to the Adriatic on the west; and from present-day Croatia, in Yugoslavia, to Salonika, on the Aegean Sea. Under his rule Bulgaria flourished as a center of Slavic culture and learning.

Bulgaria declined in importance after Simeon's death. In 1018 Basil II (1415–62), the Byzantine emperor who later took the title *Bulgaroctonos,* or "Bulgar killer," conquered the country and ended the First Bulgarian Empire. Bulgaria became part of the Byzantine Empire and remained so until 1186.

In 1186 John Asen I (?–1196) and his brother, Peter (?–1197), attacked Byzantium and regained Bulgaria's independence. Their descendant Czar John Asen II (reigned 1218–41) established the Second Bulgarian Empire, which included most of the Balkan Peninsula. Art, commerce, and literature flourished during the Second Bulgarian Empire, and many new churches and monasteries were founded. But the second empire began to fall apart. In 1396, along with the rest of the Balkan states, Bulgaria was conquered by the Turks.

The Turks ruled Bulgaria for nearly 500 years. Constantinople, the capital of Turkey, was so close to Bulgaria that the Turks were able to control Bulgaria longer than any other nation that they had conquered. The Muslim minority and the style of many Bulgarian buildings reflect these years of Turkish rule.

The Bulgarians almost lost their national identity when the Turks gave the Greek Patriarchate the right to represent all Christian subjects. Bulgarian books were replaced by Greek, and few could remember the past history of their people. But a Bulgarian national revival started in the 18th century and was followed by cultural and religious freedom.

Russia helped Bulgaria to win political independence from the Turks in the Russo-Turkish War of 1877–78. Russia re-established the medieval frontiers of the country, but the Western European powers feared possible Russian expansion. Therefore, only the northern part of Bulgaria was made independent. In 1885 the southern part of the country, called Eastern Rumelia, broke away from Turkey and was reunited with Bulgaria. Prince Ferdinand of Saxe-Coburg-Gotha (1861–1948) was chosen as the new ruler.

In 1908 Ferdinand took the medieval title of Czar and decided to claim the rest of the areas of medieval Bulgaria, especially Macedonia. A Balkan alliance between Bulgaria, Serbia, Montenegro, and Greece was formed. This alliance fought against the Turks in the First Balkan War of 1912. Victorious over the Turks, the Balkan allies quarreled among themselves in the Second Balkan War of 1913. Bulgaria lost this war.

In World War I, Bulgaria was again on the losing side, this time with Germany and Austria-Hungary. It lost more territory. Ferdinand was forced to abdicate, and the throne was inherited by his son Boris III (1894–1943). Heavy reparations and a flood of refugees from Macedonia caused economic and political instability. Secret organizations sprang up. The military and then the king took over the country, and arrests and murders were frequent. Bulgaria was a German satellite during World War II, but Boris managed to keep the army out of the war and helped save Bulgarian Jews from extermination.

Boris died mysteriously in 1943. In September, 1944, a government friendly to the West took over. But the Soviet Union unexpectedly declared war on Bulgaria and occupied the country. A government friendly to the Soviet Union was set up. Many of the leaders of the nation were either imprisoned or put to death. Then Georgi Dimitrov (1892–1949), a Communist leader from the Soviet Union, had the head of the opposition party, Nikola Petkov (1891–1947), executed. Dimitrov turned the country into a Soviet-type people's republic. The young Czar Simeon II (1937–   ) was exiled. Since then Bulgaria has generally followed the Soviet Union in its political, economic, and social policies. In recent years Bulgaria has signed trade agreements with several Western nations. During the 1970's, agricultural and industrial production have expanded, and tourism has developed.

GEORGE W. HOFFMAN
University of Texas at Austin

BULLDOZERS AND OTHER CONSTRUCTION EQUIPMENT

At the construction site of any new building, bridge, or road, the roar of powerful machinery is heard. Snorting bulldozers are pushing over trees or shoving large piles of earth from place to place. Power shovels thrust their huge digging buckets into the ground, scooping up half a ton of earth and rock in one stroke. Dump trucks grind their way up and down muddy slopes as they carry away the dirt excavated by the shovels. Clanking pile drivers hammer away at pilings (heavy steel pipes or huge logs that are driven deep into the ground for foundations). Tractors and cranes haul and lift the steel, stone, or concrete needed to erect the structure.

Construction work would be much more difficult than it is already without these machines and many others as well. Making an excavation, laying a foundation, and erecting a structure mean heavy labor.

For thousands of years the burden of such work was mostly on human shoulders. The ancient Egyptians, for instance, cut, transported, and laid over 2,000,000 stone blocks to build the Great Pyramid of Cheops. Most of the work was done by human muscle power. It took 100,000 men about 20 years to complete the task.

The Egyptians and other ancient peoples did have animals to help with the heavy hauling. Men learned long ago that animals could be trained to carry loads and perform other tasks. Horses, donkeys, mules, oxen, camels, and elephants were used to carry burdens, pull wagons, and turn wheels for grinding grain or pumping water. But animals could not be used for many tasks. Men still had to wield picks and shovels to dig out earth and put it into carts, and they had to lift beams, stones, bricks, and mortar into place to erect buildings or bridges.

Machines eventually were devised for some heavy lifting jobs. By the time of the Roman Empire, cranes and derricks were being used. But even these machines were often operated by human power. Old drawings show men as well as animals turning large treadwheels or cranking windlasses to provide the power for the cranes.

Not until early in the 19th century was a

A bulldozer smooths a path for a new mountain highway.

device invented to ease the backbreaking work of excavation. The invention was a scraper with steel blades, mounted on wheels and drawn by a team of horses. Such scrapers were used to dig the Erie Canal between Albany and Buffalo, New York, from 1817 to 1825. The canal was 362 miles long, 40 feet wide at the top, 28 feet wide at the bottom, and 4 feet deep. Without the scrapers thousands of workers would have had to dig nearly 260,000,000 cubic feet of earth and rock a shovelful at a time.

A labor-saving machine such as the scraper was still not very efficient. It could work only as fast as horses or mules could move it, and getting the horses to pull was work, too. The great change in construction came only when engines were developed to power the machinery.

The first application of power to the heavy work of construction came in 1838, when William S. Otis of Philadelphia patented an earth digger that was powered by a steam engine—the first steam shovel.

The steam engine helped make construction faster and less difficult. Steam shovels could excavate with great speed, and small stationary steam engines called donkey engines gave ample power for lifting or dragging heavy loads. But steam was not the final answer.

At left, a loader digs away at a huge pile of wood chips in a lumber yard. The chips will be made into fiberboard. At right, a sheepsfoot roller packs down the earth for a highway.

Steam engines were heavy and clumsy, and trained engineers were needed to run them. These problems were solved with the development of the internal-combustion gasoline engine. It was much lighter and more compact than the steam engine, and almost anyone could learn to operate it.

An even more dependable source of power was the diesel engine, invented near the end of the 19th century by the German engineer Rudolf Diesel. The efficient diesel engine, which burns a cheaper grade of fuel than the gasoline engine, soon proved itself to be a good source of power for heavy-duty machinery. Diesel engines now provide power for machines that handle every kind of construction job.

▶ EARTH-MOVING MACHINES

One of the most useful machines for the early stages of construction work is the **crawler tractor**. It is a vehicle mounted on endless metal belts called treads. These treads enable the tractor to go through sand or mud, over rough terrain, and up steep slopes. The tractor ranges in size from 5 to 20 tons. It can be used to pull or push other equipment or, through its power takeoff, as a source of power for other machinery. Crawler tractors are often called caterpillar tractors. However, this name is the registered trademark of the Caterpillar Tractor Company and should not be used for other makes.

A **bulldozer** is a movable steel scraping blade mounted on a tractor. Some bulldozers are fitted with a heavy beam that can be used to uproot trees and push heavy objects. The bulldozer is used mostly for clearing and smoothing rough ground. It pushes trees over, shoves large rocks aside, scrapes down hillsides, and pushes earth to fill in low spots in the terrain.

If the surface of the ground is not too rough, **scrapers** can be used to level the ground instead of bulldozers. Scrapers are mounted on rubber-tired wheels and are drawn by a tractor. They have blades for scraping the earth and a bin in which the earth is carried for dumping and spreading elsewhere.

On long, flat stretches of ground, digging machines called **belt loaders** can quickly dig away large amounts of earth. These machines are equipped with a conveyor belt onto which the earth is thrown. The belt carries the earth away from the digger and dumps it into trucks. A belt loader can dig a continuous strip of ground up to 24 inches deep and more than 1 foot wide.

The machines we have just described are used mainly for scraping and moving earth when only shallow digging is required. For deeper excavations, such as for the foundations of large buildings, heavier equipment is used. The **dragline excavator** has a long steel arm, or boom, extending from the front of an operator's cab. The swiveling cab is mounted

 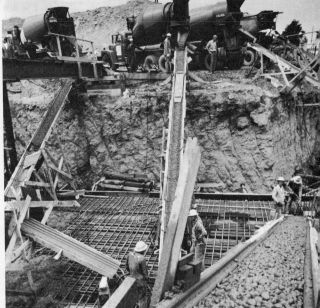

At left, three loaded earth scrapers haul dirt down a steep road. Each is powered by two diesels. At right, concrete mixer trucks pour the foundations for the Seattle World's Fair.

on a chassis carried by either crawler treads or rubber tires. Powered by a diesel engine, the cab can turn in a complete circle, and the boom can be raised and lowered. Cables attached to the boom operate the digging bucket. The bucket may be either a simple scoop bucket or a clamshell bucket, which has jaws that open and close.

Where there is not much room for digging, the **power shovel** works better than the dragline excavator. The power shovel, like the dragline excavator, has a boom, but instead of cables it has a short arm extending from the boom. On the end of the short arm is the digging bucket. The arm can travel back and forth while the boom moves up and down. This arrangement allows the operator to get the digging bucket into spaces where dragline excavators could not easily work.

If there is not enough room for the large excavators to operate, smaller equipment such as the **tractor shovel** is used. This is a tractor fitted with a shovel on the end of movable steel arms. It operates in much the same way as a power shovel, but it needs far less space in which to work.

The work of scrapers and excavators is often hindered by stumps, roots, or rocky earth. These obstacles are pushed out of the ground by tractor-drawn **rooters**, which resemble giant plows.

Sometimes during digging, solid rock is encountered and must be blasted out with explosives. The first task is to make holes in the rock in which to place the explosives. Until late in the 19th century, the holes were made with a hand drill and sledge hammer. Drills powered by steam or compressed air were invented in the 1880's. The standard drill today is the **pneumatic rock drill**, which is powered by compressed air. The air compressor is run by either a diesel engine or electricity.

In most places the earth and rock that have been dug up cannot be allowed to pile up in unsightly heaps around the construction site. They must be moved away. A vehicle often used for this job is the **dump truck**. The truck has up to 10 wheels with oversize tires, which enables it to climb steep grades and go through loose earth and mud. The load of earth is dumped out by tilting the truck's body. The trucks may be designed to dump from either the side or the rear. Larger amounts of earth and rock can be transported by semitrailer wagons, which are usually drawn by tractors.

Digging and scraping the earth is only part of the job of preparing the construction site. Other jobs that may need to be done, depending on the type of structure being built, are rolling and ditch digging.

Rollers are used to compact, or pack down, the surface of the ground. The sheepsfoot roller has a large steel drum studded with projections that look somewhat like the hooves of sheep. The drum can be filled with sand or water to increase the weight of the roller. The pneumatic-tire roller has a row of rubber tires to pack down the earth. A tank mounted over the tires may be filled for extra weight. Both of these rollers are drawn by tractors. In the early 19th century, rollers were drawn by horses. During the 1860's a steam roller powered by its own engine was developed in France and England. The steam roller is believed to have been first used in the United States in 1869. Steam rollers today are powered by gasoline or diesel engines.

At almost any construction site, ditches are needed for such things as drainage or laying down power lines. Two kinds of ditch-digging machines are used for this digging. The **ladder ditcher** is a tractor fitted with a boom that has a rotating chain of scoop-like buckets. The buckets move down the boom, scoop up earth, and carry it back to the top. As they turn over to start their descent again the buckets spill the earth onto a conveyor belt, which carries it off to the side. The **wheel ditcher** works in a similar way, but its digging buckets are mounted around the edge of a large wheel. As the machine moves slowly ahead the wheel revolves and the buckets scoop up the earth.

After the work of excavation has been completed, the next phase of construction is laying the foundations. If the ground is too soft to support the weight of a building or bridge, long, heavy steel pipes called piles must be driven deep into the earth to provide a stable base. Sometimes logs are used for temporary piles. Before a machine was invented to do the job, workmen had to pull a heavy weight off the ground by rope and pulley and let it crash onto the pile to drive it in. This was slow, tedious labor. Each time the weight fell, it had to be raised again by the workmen. In the 1880's a steam-powered **pile driver** was developed. Today pile drivers run on steam, compressed air, or electricity.

▶ ROAD-BUILDING EQUIPMENT

Specialized machines have been devised for particular construction jobs. Road builders, for instance, have a variety of machines to help them at each stage of their work. They use **power sweepers** to clear away dust and loose material from the surface of a road

before paving it. These sweepers, which are equipped with stiff revolving brushes, are larger versions of the curb sweepers used to clean city streets.

Paving a road involves a procession of machines, one following the other and each doing its special job. Most concrete road surfacing today is done with **concrete pavers**, which mix and pour the concrete as they move along the road. The paver has two drums. In one drum the mixing of the concrete is started. When the mixing is about half finished, the concrete is poured into the other drum, where it continues to mix until it is ready to be poured. In the meantime a new batch of concrete has started mixing in the first drum. This method saves time because the ingredients for new batches can continually be added without having to stop the machine.

Close behind the concrete paver comes a **spreader** to distribute the concrete evenly over the road surface. A **finishing machine** follows the spreader and smooths down the concrete. The final smoothing is done with a **longitudinal float**, a long trowel-like tool, which can be operated either by power or by hand.

▶ EQUIPMENT FOR BUILDING CONSTRUCTION

Special machinery is also used in building construction. **Cranes** and **hoisting engines** lift materials to the upper floors of the building. **Riveting machines** and **welding torches** are used by workmen to assemble the steel superstructure.

Truck mixers bring concrete to building sites in crowded cities, mixing the concrete as they drive from the storage plant to the building. The concrete is poured into a container called a hopper and hoisted to the upper floors, where small tractors with dump buckets shuttle the concrete to wherever it is needed.

There is a great variety of construction machines. We have mentioned only a few of the more important ones. Newer and more ingenious machines are being worked on continually in an effort to save labor, time, and money in construction.

WALTER F. BUEHR
Author, *First Book of Machines*
Reviewed by E. P. KRAG
Caterpillar Tractor Company

See also BUILDING CONSTRUCTION.

BULLFIGHTING

Bullfighting has often been called Spain's favorite sport. But to call it this is wrong for two reasons: first, soccer (called *fútbol* in Spain) is the most popular sport; and second, bullfighting cannot really be called a sport. It should be called, more properly, a spectacle, an exhibition, or a performance, like a ballet. However, this ballet is like dancing on a tightrope, because if the bullfighter makes a mistake, he will quite likely be injured or killed.

A bullfight is not really a contest between a man and a bull. Actually it is a contest between a man and himself. The audience goes to the ring to see a man conquer his own fear of the horns and take as many chances with the bull as possible. It is very much like the audience that goes to see acrobats do tricks on the flying trapeze at the circus. The crowd does not want to see the men miss the bar and fall; what it wants is the thrill of seeing the performers almost miss and then save themselves by their skill. It is the same in the bullring. The men who most gracefully execute the most daring maneuvers become the stars.

Bullfighting is one of the few ways a poor boy can become rich and famous in Spain and Latin America—and many *matadores* have become millionaires. But for every successful *matador* there are hundreds who have fallen by the wayside and are forgotten. Many do not have the necessary grace and skill. Some are crippled by the bulls, and some are killed.

▶ HOW DID BULLFIGHTING BEGIN?

Bullfighting has existed in one form or another for more than 2,000 years. The ancient Cretans used to perform what they called bull dancing. Both men and women would leap over the bulls' horns in graceful, reckless exhibitions.

One of the reasons that Spain has been the leading place for bullfighting is that the fighting bull first lived there. Bullfighting cannot be done with ordinary animals. It requires the special *toro de lidia,* or *toro bravo,* which is as different from a domestic bull as a cobra is from a gopher snake, or a wolf is from a dog. For centuries herds of these fierce bulls roamed wild over Spain; the Romans imported them for their savage battles against men and other animals in the Colosseum. The bulls usually won, even when pitted against lions and tigers. The Arabs in Spain helped make bullfighting popular around the early 12th century. In those days the spectacle consisted of a skillful horseman killing a wild bull with a lance while guiding his horse so as to avoid injury both to his mount and to himself. It is said that the famous cavalier El Cid was the first Spaniard to take part in organized bullfighting in an arena.

Bullfighting quickly became very popular, and for centuries rich Moors and Christians, nobles, and even kings practiced it. No feast day was complete without a *corrida de toros*.

The common people used to help the nobles fight the bulls, but they did so on foot. They used capes to distract the bull and keep it from charging at their bodies. Little by little this part of the act became the more exciting to watch, and the ritual developed as we know it today.

▶ THE ARENA AND THE TOREROS

The first thing a person sees when he goes to the *plaza de toros,* or arena, is the gaily dressed and excited crowd. When the band strikes up, generally late in the afternoon around four or five, the *toreros* stride into the arena, and parade around it while the *aficionados,* or fans, cheer.

All people who fight bulls are called *toreros.* The *matadores* are the stars of the show, and there are usually three in an afternoon's program. Each one has two *picadores* and three *banderilleros* to help him. It is old-fashioned and incorrect to refer to bullfighters as *toreadores.* (The "toreador" of Bizet's opera *Carmen* is actually a *matador.*)

A successful *matador* may make as much as $35,000 for one afternoon's work, while his helpers make only several hundred dollars. This is because the *matador* takes nearly all the risks.

The *matadores* are dressed in beautiful costumes of gold or silver spangles on different-colored silk. The *banderilleros* are not allowed to wear gold costumes. A good costume, or "suit of lights," is very costly, and every *matador* has several of them.

THE CONTEST

The men stride across the sand of the arena, and then the ring is cleared and the bull charges in. The bull has not been trained or tortured or starved; yet, because of its centuries of breeding, it knows it is supposed to fight. A *banderillero* will run out and swirl his cape a few times in front of the animal to demonstrate to his *matador* how this particular animal charges, since each bull has a different style of fighting.

Now the *matador* goes out. Where the *banderillero* was awkward and stayed safely several feet away from the bull's horns, the *matador,* being the star, must stand very close to the animal. He swings the cape gracefully and lets the horns slice by his legs just a few inches away. On each pass that the *matador* performs well, the crowd yells and cheers. If the *matador* bends over awkwardly and steps back out of the path of the bull as the *banderillero* did, the crowd boos loudly. The audience would like to see the bullfighters behave exactly opposite from the way they would behave if they had to stand in front of half a ton of bull with only a cape for protection. The bull goes at the cloth not because it is red, but because the *matador* knows just how to shake the cape to attract the animal and make it go at the lure instead of his body. The cape is yellow on one side and red on the other, but because bulls are color blind it makes no difference which side the matador presents to the animal.

It is often said that cows are more dangerous than bulls because bulls shut their eyes when they charge. This is not true, as is shown by almost any photo of a charging bull; both cows and bulls keep their eyes open.

After the *matador* does several passes, called *verónicas,* a trumpet blows and the *picadores* enter on horseback. They prick the bull with their lances in order to weaken his neck muscles. They do this so that at the end the *matador* will be able to reach over the horns and place the sword blade where it should go—between the bull's shoulder blades. The horses have been safely padded since 1930, so the performance is no longer as cruel as it was.

Next, each of the three *banderilleros* places two *banderillas* ("barbed sticks") in the animal's shoulders. These further weaken the bull's neck muscles.

Finally the *matador* goes out with the sword and a little cape called the *muleta*. This is the most dangerous time of the fight, in spite of the fact that the bull is tired. There have been about 125 great *matadores* since 1700, and 42 of them have been killed, generally during this part of the bullfight. This is because the little cape is so small, the bull has learned so much during the course of the fight, and the man must make his most dangerous passes at this time.

THE KILL

Killing the bull, called "the moment of truth," is the most dangerous maneuver of all. The man must run at the bull at the same time that the bull runs at him, and plunge the sword between the shoulder blades. When this is done correctly, the bull will drop over dead almost instantly.

If the *matador* has done his job well, the crowd applauds, and he is awarded the ear of the bull as a trophy. If he has done a superior job, he is given both ears and the tail. The meat of the bulls is sometimes given to the poor, but usually the animals are butchered in back of the arena and sold for steaks.

Joselito and Manolete, two of the greatest bullfighters of the 20th century, were killed by bulls. Joselito died when he was only 25; Manolete at the age of 30. Many other *matadores,* like the great Antonio Ordóñez and El Cordobés of Spain, have been severely injured in the bull ring. The ambition of most bullfighters, who usually come from poor families, is to make enough money to buy a bull ranch and retire at about the age of 30.

The best fights in Spain are held in Madrid, Seville, Valencia, and Málaga during the spring and summer. In Latin America the best fights can be seen in Mexico City or Lima, Peru. In Portugal the only ring of importance is in Lisbon.

The Portuguese also enjoy a form of bullfighting with no killing. It is a test of horsemanship in which the horse is unarmed and the bull's horns are padded or the points dulled.

BARNABY CONRAD
Author, *La Fiesta Brava, The Death of Manolete*

Paseo, or entrance parade, into the bullring in Madrid. Each *matador* heads his *cuadrilla*, or assistants—three *banderilleros* and two *picadores*.

Pedro Martinez does a *pase cambiado por alto*—two rapid passes, the second going over the bull's horns.

A classic *verónica* by Antonio Ordonez. The bull charges hard, passing before the *matador* as the cape is swung in front of its nose.

BUNCHE, RALPH (1904–1971)

In 1945 delegates from 50 nations of the world met at San Francisco, California. The conference was dedicated to world peace, and from it the United Nations was born. One of the United States delegates was Ralph Bunche, a former college professor and an expert on colonial affairs.

Bunche was born in Detroit, Michigan, on August 7, 1904. His parents died when he was 13, and young Ralph and his sister went to live with their grandmother in Los Angeles, California. Although his grandmother encouraged him to get as much education as possible, Ralph had to work after school, and he soon became self-supporting.

Because he was a good athlete and an excellent student, Ralph won a scholarship to the University of California. There it continued to be necessary for him to take odd jobs to pay for his books, meals, and carfare. Nevertheless, he received high grades and made the varsity basketball team. He won three prized golden basketballs for his performance on winning teams.

After graduating from college with highest honors in 1927, he won a second scholarship, to Harvard University. He received his M.A. (master of arts) degree from Harvard in 1928 and then taught at Howard University

Dr. Ralph Bunche at a press conference in the Congo.

in Washington, D.C. Soon after, he married Ruth Harris, who had been one of his students. They had three children—Joan, Jane, and Ralph, Jr. Jane died in 1966.

In 1931 Bunche was awarded a fellowship that allowed him to go to Africa, where he studied the governments of colonies and mandates. On this work he wrote his thesis for the Ph.D. degree, which he received at Harvard. He returned to teaching at Howard and during 1938–40 he worked with the Swedish sociologist Gunnar Myrdal on a survey of blacks in America. The result was an important book called *An American Dilemma* (1944). During World War II he worked with the United States Government as a specialist on Africa.

He joined the State Department and was a member of the United States delegation at the Dumbarton Oaks Conference in 1944. At the San Francisco conference in 1945, Bunche helped prepare the parts of the United Nations Charter that dealt with colonies. In 1946 his services were requested by the United Nations, where he accepted a permanent post. Not long after, trouble arose in the Middle East, and in 1948 war broke out between Israel and its Arab neighbors. Count Folke Bernadotte of Sweden was appointed to act as mediator to try to end the dispute. When Count Bernadotte was assassinated, Ralph Bunche, his deputy, was assigned to continue his efforts to stop the fighting.

At first neither the Arabs nor the Israelis would even talk to each other. Finally, after months of negotiations, the Arabs and Israelis agreed to sign an armistice.

In 1950, for this great contribution to peace, Ralph Bunche received one of the world's highest awards—the Nobel peace prize. In 1955 he was appointed an undersecretary of the United Nations, and in 1957 he became what is now called Undersecretary-General for Special Political Affairs. In the 1960's his efforts were directed toward achieving peace in the Congo (now the Republic of Zaïre) and in Cyprus. Bunche died on December 9, 1971.

Reviewed by MARGUERITE CARTWRIGHT
Hunter College, City University of New York

BUNKER HILL, BATTLE OF. See REVOLUTIONARY WAR.

BUOYANCY. See FLOATING.

BURBANK, LUTHER (1849–1926)

Luther Burbank once remarked: "I shall be contented if because of me there shall be better fruits and fairer flowers." In 50 years of work he more than achieved his goal. He developed 618 new varieties of plants.

Burbank was born on a farm near Lancaster, Massachusetts, on March 7, 1849. His father had married three times, and Luther was the 13th of 15 children. In his early years Luther attended a one-room school taught by a half sister. At 15 he entered Lancaster Academy, where he received some instruction in science. But Luther's interest in plants really grew from his life on the farm and his own reading in the Lancaster public library.

It was in this library that Burbank—at the age of 19—discovered the writings of Charles Darwin. He later recalled this as the turning point of his life. From Darwin, Burbank learned how man could develop better varieties of plants. The secret was to select seeds from those plants with the most desirable traits and to breed for those traits.

A few years later Burbank was able to put Darwin's principle of selection into practice. Using money he had inherited from his father, Burbank purchased 17 acres of land near Lunenburg, Massachusetts. There he set about developing his first "new creation," as he was to call every new plant. His aim: a larger and firmer potato. Burbank planted potato seeds and selected the best potatoes from the resulting crop. These were replanted, and from them came a crop of larger and firmer potatoes. The variety he developed in this way is still known as the Burbank potato.

Meanwhile, three of his older brothers had settled in California, and in 1875 Burbank decided to join them. He sold his farm and moved to Santa Rosa. There he set up a small nursery garden where he grew and sold plants to support his research. What Burbank had done with the potato, he now began to do with many plants. He gathered numerous varieties, selecting those with what he considered favorable qualities. He also developed plants by crossbreeding varieties. For example, Burbank's famous Shasta daisy combines the best traits of three other daisies.

A good deal of land was required for such work. Burbank bought more acres and estab-

Burbank with the spineless cactus he developed as a cattle feed for dry regions. He was 74 when photo was taken.

lished what became a world-famous experimental farm. The yearly catalog, *New Creations,* that he issued from 1893 to 1901 describes his experiments and indicates the quantity of his work. Although he used scientific principles and methods, Burbank's main interest was in practical results.

He noted, for instance, that plums had large pits and little flesh. So he set out to develop a fleshier plum. From a large number of plums, he selected the one with the thinnest pit. He planted this and then grafted the young seedling onto a mature plum tree. (Grafting speeded up the bearing of fruit, which could then be replanted.) Eventually Burbank was able to produce a plum with such a thin pit that it is called the "stoneless" plum.

Many visitors came to marvel at Burbank's farm. He himself especially enjoyed the young people who came, for though he was twice married he had no children.

Burbank worked tirelessly until he died on April 11, 1926. His work lives on wherever his plants are grown. In California alone, Burbank varieties form the basis of a major industry.

JOHN S. BOWMAN
Author and Science Editor

BURMA

The golden shrine of the Shwe Dagon Pagoda rises high above the roofs of Burma's capital city, Rangoon. The pagoda shines so brightly in the sun that the poet Rudyard Kipling called it "a golden mystery, a beautiful winking wonder." Shwe Dagon is only one of many pagodas that tell of the Burmese devotion to Buddhism. They have won Burma the nickname Land of the Pagodas.

▶ THE PEOPLE

The more than 31,000,000 people of Burma come from many different ethnic groups. The major ethnic group is the Burmans, who came from Tibet nearly 2,000 years ago. Later the Shan-Thai, who also settled in Laos and Thailand, migrated to Burma. They live in the eastern part of Burma. Other important ethnic groups include the Karens, who live in the southern and eastern part of the country; the Kachins, who live in the north; and the Chins, who live in the northwest. Altogether, the non-Burman people make up about one quarter of the population.

During the British occupation of Burma, which lasted for more than a hundred years, many Indians arrived in the country. There are today large numbers of Indians, Pakistanis, and Chinese in Burma. Most live in the cities, where they work as skilled craftsmen and shopkeepers. They have traditionally been dominant in trade and industry.

More than 120 native languages and dialects are spoken by the people of Burma. Burmese, the nation's official language, is used in the public schools. Three fourths of the non-Burmese understand Burmese. The well-to-do and better educated people also speak English.

The Buddhist religion, like the Burmese language, helps to unite the people of Burma. About 90 percent of the population are Buddhists, and their religion plays an important part in everyday life.

Almost every village has a Buddhist monastery, called a *pongyi-kyaung*. The *pongyi-kyaung* serves as a religious center, a school, a rest home for travelers, and sometimes as a hospital for the village. The monk in charge of the monastery is called a *pongyi*. He is the teacher and spiritual leader of the village.

Before Burma became an independent country in 1948, most children in villages received elementary education in the monastery schools. It is still the custom for Burmese Buddhist boys over 7 to live for a time in the monastery as novices. Some boys stay a year, others for as little as 2 weeks. Because so many Burmese learn to read and write from the monks, Burma has one of the highest literacy rates in all Asia.

Today many more public elementary schools are being built in the larger villages

---

FACTS AND FIGURES

SOCIALIST REPUBLIC OF THE UNION OF BURMA is the official name of the country.

CAPITAL: Rangoon.

LOCATION AND SIZE: Southeast Asia. **Latitude**—28° 29′ N to 9° 58′ N. **Longitude**—101° 10′ E to 92° 11′ E. **Area**—678,033 km² (261,789 sq mi).

PHYSICAL FEATURES: Highest point—Hkakabo Razi, 5,881 m (19,296 ft). **Lowest point**—sea level. **Chief rivers**—Irrawaddy, Chindwin, Sittang, Salween. **Chief mountain peaks**—Hkakabo Razi, Saramati, Mt. Victoria, Sirohifara Peak, Nattaung.

POPULATION: 31,300,000 (estimate).

LANGUAGE: Burmese, English, various dialects.

RELIGION: Buddhism; also Islam, Hinduism, Christian minorities.

GOVERNMENT: Socialist republic. **Head of state**—president. **Head of government**—prime minister. **International co-operation**—United Nations, Colombo Plan.

NATIONAL ANTHEM: *Kaba Makye* ("Our Free Homeland").

ECONOMY: Agricultural products—rice, sugarcane, groundnuts, pulses, sesame, tobacco, cotton, jute. **Industries and Products**—wood and rice processing, fishing, textiles, handicrafts. **Chief minerals**—petroleum, lead, zinc, manganese, copper, tungsten, tin, gold, silver, gems (rubies, sapphires, jade). **Chief exports**—rice, teak, cotton, rubber, petroleum products, minerals. **Chief imports**—machinery, transport equipment, various manufactured goods, textiles, iron and steel, pharmaceutical products, peanut oil, paper. **Monetary unit**—kyat.

and cities. But there is still a serious shortage of public schools and teachers. There are colleges in a number of cities and universities in Rangoon and Mandalay.

Way of Life

Most of the country people live in villages of a few score or more houses. The houses are often built close together along narrow, unpaved streets, or in groups of five or six along a river or on the coast. The typical Burmese country home is built on a framework of bamboo poles and has a steep, thatched roof made of straw and reeds. Many of the houses are built on stilts and have a long porch running the length of the house. The porch is used both as a living and a dining room.

The Burmese eat their meals at low tables, seated on floor mats. Rice, their chief food, is eaten at each meal. It is considered polite for a person to take rice from a common bowl, press it into a small ball, and then push it into his mouth with his thumb. Sometimes fish, poultry, or meat is served as well as fresh fruits such as bananas, mangoes, and papayas. The Burmese like their food to be moderately spiced with curry and pepper.

Many Burmese men and women wear a long saronglike skirt, which is called a *longyi*. A short, single-breasted jacket is also worn. The difference between the outfits worn by the men and women is that the men tie a brightly colored, thin, silk strip, called a *gaungbaung*, around their heads. Women go bareheaded with their long, shiny black hair tied in a knot on top of their heads. Boys and girls usually wear dark *longyis* and short, white jackets. But some boys are used to wearing European-style, dark shorts instead of the traditional *longyis*. Nearly everyone wears sandals or goes barefoot.

Holidays and Sports. Burmese children like to swim and paddle boats. They play hide-and-seek, fly kites, and play with balloons, balls, and toy musical instruments. The Burmese love holidays and sometimes celebrate for several days. If a holiday falls on Friday, they celebrate on Friday, Saturday, and Sunday. Young and old feast, sing, dance, tell tales, play games, and laugh together. Important national holidays are Peasants' Day (January 1), Independence Day (January 4), and Union Day (February 12).

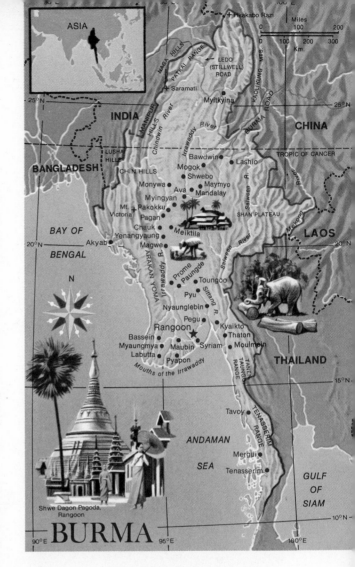

Shwe Dagon Pagoda, Rangoon

BURMA

The two most important religious holidays are the Burmese New Year, or Water Festival (Thingyan), in April, and the Festival of Lights (Thadingyut), in October. It is the custom during the Water Festival to sprinkle water on images of the Buddha and on one another as a sign of blessing. This custom often becomes the excuse for a water fight. For the 4 days of the festival, young people douse all vehicles and passersby within sight. Even the adults join in the fun.

The Festival of Lights marks the end of the Buddhist Lent. It celebrates Buddha's return to earth from the home of the gods. The people on earth were so happy to have him back again that they decorated the whole city with lights for 3 days to welcome him. To this day the people light their homes and shops to celebrate the event.

Water buffalo and sometimes modern tractors are used to plow paddy fields before transplanting rice. Grown in water, rice is Burma's leading crop and major export. It is also the chief food of the Burmese people, who eat it at every meal.

▶THE LAND

Burma is located in Southeast Asia. It shares borders with Thailand and Laos on the east; China on the north and northeast; and with India and Bangladesh on the northwest. Burma is hemmed in and almost cut off from its neighbors by hills and mountain ranges several miles high. But Burma's long coastline of 1,500 miles provides many outlets to the Bay of Bengal and the Andaman Sea (part of the Indian Ocean).

The country's largest river, the 1,300-mile-long Irrawaddy (Elephant) River, begins where the borders of Burma, China, and India meet. The Irrawaddy starts with the melting waters from the snowfields and glaciers on the mountain slopes, and flows to the Bay of Bengal. The Burmese say that the Irrawaddy has its head in nature's refrigerator and its mouth in one of the earth's ovens—a steaming hot mangrove jungle near the equator. The Salween River, one of the longest in Southeast Asia, begins in Tibet and flows south through eastern Burma to the Andaman Sea. The Sittang River drains the eastern part of central Burma. The Irrawaddy drains the western part.

Most of the Burmese people live on the delta and lower floodplain of the Irrawaddy and Sittang rivers. In this region as many as 500 people live on each square mile of land.

Climate. Burma has three seasons. The almost rainless cool season lasts from the end of October until February. This is the season for harvesting, weddings, travel, and celebrations.

The rainless hot season lasts from March to the end of May. Hot, drying winds evaporate the moisture from the earth and from living things. Marshes and lakes shrink and some disappear. Shallow rivers dry up. Even the largest rivers become shallow in many places and snarl river traffic. At this season the air is hot and dusty, and fires often burn out of control. Trees shed their leaves. Wells, cisterns, and reservoirs often get very low or dry up entirely.

The rainy season begins in June and lasts until October. It starts with thunderstorms over the land near the coast. Inches of rain are dumped on the land each week, moistening the dry, rock-hard earth so that it can be plowed.

But rainfall is very unevenly distributed over Burma. Where the winds blow in from the ocean and are forced to rise over high mountains, the air is cooled and heavy precipitation takes place. Inland from the Bay of Bengal, over 200 inches of rain fall annually. At Rangoon, on the Irrawaddy delta, nearly 99 inches of rain fall each year. But in the northern part of the Central Basin, far from the coast on the dry side of the Arakan Yoma mountains, as little as 24 to 35 inches of rain fall.

Natural Resources

Burma's two greatest natural resources are water and soil. The rains provide water for home use, crops, and for animals and plants. The rivers provide water for transportation, irrigation, homes, and industry. During the rainy and flood seasons, rivers also deposit sediment on their floodplains and deltas. Most of the farms and crops are located on the rich soils deposited by the rivers.

The forests, which cover over half of Burma, are another valuable resource. Tropical forests are found at elevations of less than 3,000 feet, where there are more than 80 inches of rain. The monsoon forests that lose

The Shwe Dagon Pagoda, sacred Buddhist shrine, sits atop a 168-ft. mound and rises to a height of 368 ft. in Rangoon, the capital city of Burma.

The Engineering College of the University of Rangoon.

Tin is mined along the Tenasserim coast. Rubies, jade, sapphires, and other gemstones have been mined for centuries at Mogok, just north of Mandalay.

▶ INDUSTRIES AND PRODUCTS

Burma is an agricultural country. About 70 percent of the people make their living as farmers. A small percentage are craftsmen, factory workers, or merchants.

Agriculture. Most of Burma's farms are on the Irrawaddy and Sittang river deltas and in the drier parts of central Burma. Rice is the principal crop in the wet region, where it is grown underwater in paddy fields. The chief crops of the dry region are grain sorghums, and oil seeds, such as sesame, peanuts, and soybeans. Cotton, beans, and pigeon peas are also grown.

Industry. Mining, lumbering, and handicrafts are the leading Burmese industries. A search for additional supplies of petroleum offshore has begun. Other minerals such as lead, tin, silver, gold, zinc, and copper are mined in different parts of the country. Many precious and semiprecious gems are mined in Burma, including the finest "Chinese" jade. The lumber industry is based on Burma's valuable teak forests. Beautiful lacquer ware, silk cloth, gold and silver

their leaves during the dry season generally grow where the rainfall is less. Teak trees cover about one quarter of the forested area. Other valuable commercial trees are also to be found here.

Petroleum is the most valuable mineral resource. The crude oil comes from the oil field at Yenangyaung, in central Burma. Silver, together with some lead and zinc, is mined at the Bawdwin mines, near Lashio, one of the largest silver deposits in the world.

Elephants are trained to work in the lumber industry in Burma, where there are many valuable teak forests.

jewelry, and carved ivory are produced by skilled Burmese craftsmen.

Exports. Rice and teak are two of Burma's most valuable exports. Burma earns most of its income from its rice exports. It is also the world's leading supplier of teak, a wood used in making furniture and in shipbuilding. Other important exports include rubber, cotton, and petroleum products.

Transportation and Communication. Most of the commerce within Burma and between Burma and other countries moves by boat. Rangoon handles nearly all of the import traffic and most of the exports. Bassein, Burma's fourth largest city, is an important rice port. Other ports and cities, like Moulmein, Tavoy, and Mergui, are shipping points for silver, lead, zinc, tin, and tungsten.

Burma has a system of navigable rivers and canals, including an all-season route from north Burma to Rangoon over the Irrawady and its tributaries and canals. Thousands of boats bring rice to Rangoon and other cities on this river highway during the harvest and threshing season, from December to February.

Minerals are also carried to the ports by boats and by pipelines and railroads. Pipelines have been built to carry the crude petroleum from the northern part of central Burma, where the oil fields are located, to the refineries in Rangoon, and in Syriam, on the opposite bank of the Rangoon River.

Burma's railroad network is concentrated mainly in the central part of the country. Burma is without a modern highway system and only about one fourth of the roads are all-weather roads. Most land travelers walk, ride a mule, or ride in a cart pulled by mules or water buffalo.

Burma has several international airfields and many other landing areas. Most air traffic within the country is on the government-owned Union of Burma Airways.

Burma's postal, telegraph, radio, and telephone systems are state-owned. A number of daily newspapers are published, and there are several book and magazine publishers in Rangoon and Mandalay.

▶ HISTORY AND GOVERNMENT

Burma's early history is a long record of wars and struggles. The capital of the country was first at Pagan and later at Pegu and Ava. These ancient capitals are now famous archeological sites and tourist attractions.

Many European traders came to Burma during the 17th century. First came the Portuguese and then the Dutch and the English. Burma at this time was an independent kingdom. During a series of wars in the 19th century, the British captured Burma and made it a part of the British Indian Empire. At the end of the 19th century, Burma was made a province of British India.

The country was ruled by the British until 1948. During the years of British rule, many of Burma's natural resources were developed by British and foreign investors. New wealth from sugarcane and cotton cultivation came to the country, and oil fields and railroads were built. In 1937 Burma was given dominion status within the British Empire.

The Burma Road was built in 1938 to make it easier to transport war materials into China for the war against Japan. In 1941, shortly after World War II began, the Japanese invaded Burma. Burma remained under Japanese occupation until 1945. It gained its independence in 1948.

During its early years of independence, Burma was a parliamentary democracy, but the nation's political life was disorderly and confused. Economic problems, Communist guerrilla activity, and opposition to the national government by various minority peoples added to Burma's difficulties. For the first 10 years, U Nu served as prime minister of the country. In 1958 General U Ne Win, commander in chief of the armed forces, came to power. In 1960 U Nu was elected to office again. He served until 1962, when he was deposed by General U Ne Win, who again took control of the government.

Burma today is governed under a constitution adopted in 1974. There is only one legal political party—the Burmese Socialist Program Party. The government is headed by the State Council, whose chairman is president of Burma. The chairman of the Council of Ministers serves as prime minister. Members of the People's Assembly, the Burmese legislature, are elected for terms of 4 years.

THOMAS F. BARTON
University of Indiana

BURNS. See FIRST AID.

BURNS, ROBERT (1759–1796)

Robert Burns, Scotland's greatest poet, becomes the world's favorite each New Year's Eve with the traditional singing of his "Auld Lang Syne." It is fitting tribute to a poet who loved good company, good song, and simple pleasures.

Robert was born January 25, 1759, in Ayrshire, Scotland. His father was a poverty-stricken farmer, but a man of great character who valued education and strict morality. Although Robert's help was needed on the farm, his father encouraged him to read and gave him as much schooling as he could.

Robert read everything from collections of songs to Shakespeare and Milton. He carried small volumes in his pocket and studied them while he was in the fields or at the table. He began writing his own verses and collected them in a scrapbook.

When his father died in 1784, Robert and his brother Gilbert tried to make a success of farming, but failed. Robert fell in love with Jean Armour, the daughter of a builder, but her father refused to have him as a son-in-law. Robert then planned to seek his fortune in Jamaica. Before he left, he published, in August, 1786, *Poems, Chiefly in the Scottish Dialect*. The poems were so successful that he was urged to try his luck in Edinburgh instead. He became a great favorite of high society there, and in April, 1787, he published a second edition of his poems. He also began collecting, adapting, and composing the lyrics of old folk songs for a publication called *The Scots Musical Museum*. For this and for George Thomson's *Select Collection of Original Scottish Airs,* published in 1793, he composed over 300 lyrics.

Robert began a new life of farming at Ellisland, near Dumfries, in 1788 and finally married Jean Armour. Once more unsuccessful at farming, he obtained an appointment as an excise officer and moved to Dumfries in 1791. His sympathy for the French Revolution and his rebellion against the Calvinist Church, put into songs and witticisms, lost him friends among the gentry. Ill health added to his misfortunes, and when he died on July 21, 1796, he was a bitter, broken man.

Two of Robert Burns's poems follow. The first is in the Scottish dialect.

A RED, RED ROSE

O, my luve is like a red, red rose,
That's newly sprung in June
O, my luve is like the melodie,
That's sweetly played in tune.

As fair art thou, my bonie lass,
So deep in luve am I,
And I will luve thee still, my dear,
Till a' the seas gang dry.

Till a' the seas gang dry, my dear,
And the rocks melt wi' the sun!
And I will luve thee still, my dear,
While the sands o' life shall run.

And fare thee weel, my only luve,
And fare thee weel a while!
And I will come again, my luve,
Tho' it were ten thousand mile!

SWEET AFTON

Flow gently, sweet Afton, among thy green braes!
Flow gently, I'll sing thee a song in thy praise!
My Mary's asleep by thy murmuring stream—
Flow gently, sweet Afton, disturb not her dream!

Thou stock-dove whose echo resounds through the glen,
Ye wild whistling blackbirds in yon thorny den,
Thou green-crested lapwing, thy screaming forbear—
I charge you disturb not my slumbering fair!

How lofty, sweet Afton, thy neighboring hills,
Far marked with the courses of clear, winding rills!
There daily I wander, as noon rises high,
My flocks and my Mary's sweet cot in my eye.

How pleasant thy banks and green valleys below,
Where wild in the woodlands the primroses blow!
There oft, as mild Evening weeps over the lea,
The sweet-scented birk shades my Mary and me.

Thy crystal stream, Afton, how lovely it glides,
And winds by the cot where my Mary resides!
How wanton thy waters her snowy feet lave,
As, gathering sweet flowerets, she stems thy clear wave!

Flow gently, sweet Afton, among thy green braes!
Flow gently, sweet river, the theme of my lays!
My Mary's asleep by thy murmuring stream—
Flow gently, sweet Afton, disturb not her dream!

BURR, AARON (1756–1836)

Aaron Burr was a brilliant lawyer, a hero of the Revolutionary War, and a vice-president of the United States. He was also one of the greatest failures in American history. His career was marred by poor judgment, uncontrolled ambition, and wasted opportunities. Most Americans remember Burr only as the man who killed Alexander Hamilton in a duel.

Burr was born in Newark, New Jersey, on February 6, 1756. His father was president of Princeton University in the days when it was called the College of New Jersey.

Burr was ready to enter college when he was 11 years old. But he had to wait until he was 13 before Princeton would admit him. He was graduated with honors when he was 16. Later, he studied law. Burr was a handsome young man with dark, flashing eyes. He had a ready smile and made friends easily.

▶ REVOLUTIONARY SOLDIER

At the outbreak of the Revolution, the 19-year-old Burr joined the Continental Army. He served as an officer in the ill-fated American march on Quebec in 1775. When General Richard Montgomery led an attack on the Quebec fortress, Aaron Burr was at his side. The Americans were defeated, and Montgomery was killed. Burr was the last man to leave the battlefield. He tried, unsuccessfully, to carry the body of his fallen commander through the knee-deep snow under a hail of British bullets.

Later, Burr served as a staff officer with George Washington. Once, by disobeying orders, he saved an entire army brigade from capture by the British. But poor health cut short his military career, and Burr resigned from the army in 1779.

▶ MARRIAGE AND A LAW CAREER

In 1782 Burr married Mrs. Theodosia Prevost, the widow of a British officer. She was 10 years older than Burr. They had one child, a girl, named Theodosia after her mother. Burr carefully educated his daughter since he believed girls should be as well educated as boys. His wife adored him, and he in turn was a model husband and father. Although Burr's ambitions made him ruthless in public affairs, he was a man with a warm heart who loved and helped young people throughout his long life. Burr's wife lived only 12 years after their marriage, but she was a steadying influence on her husband, whom Washington once called impetuous and reckless.

For 20 years Burr was a leading figure in the legal, social, and political life of New York. He served in the United States Senate and in the New York State Assembly. In his early years in New York, Burr had become

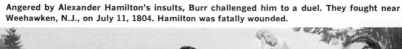

Angered by Alexander Hamilton's insults, Burr challenged him to a duel. They fought near Weehawken, N.J., on July 11, 1804. Hamilton was fatally wounded.

friendly with another prominent young lawyer, Alexander Hamilton. But political rivalry soon turned the two men into bitter enemies.

VICE-PRESIDENT AND TRAGEDY

In the presidential election of 1800, Burr and Thomas Jefferson both received the same number of votes. So the election was decided by the House of Representatives. After 36 ballots Jefferson was elected president, and Burr became vice-president.

Hamilton had led the fight to block Burr's election. He called Burr a cold-blooded conspirator and compared him to Julius Caesar. Later, Hamilton also played a leading role in Burr's defeat for the governorship of New York. The hatred between the two men smoldered. Finally it burst into the open when Hamilton bitterly attacked Burr's career and his character in the New York newspapers. Burr demanded an apology, but Hamilton refused. Then Burr demanded satisfaction on the dueling field. On July 11, 1804, Burr and Hamilton faced each other on the heights above Weehawken, New Jersey. At a signal both men fired, and Hamilton fell to the ground. Burr made an impulsive gesture toward the fallen man but was pulled back and hustled away by the man who acted as his second.

Hamilton died the next day in New York, and Burr fled the city to avoid an angry mob of Hamilton followers. After the hue and cry died down, Burr returned to his duties as vice-president.

AMBITION IN THE WEST

After leaving the vice-presidency in 1805, Burr found private life dull. He could not live again in New York because of the duel. When war threatened to break out with Spain over Florida, Burr began to plan an expedition against Spain's Mexican possessions. In 1805 and 1806 he traveled down through the Ohio and Mississippi river region. He exchanged views with leaders like Andrew Jackson and General James Wilkinson, governor of the Louisiana Territory.

What Burr's real intentions were are cloaked in mystery. Some people said that he planned to set up his own empire in the Southwest, with himself as emperor. Burr did propose that Americans seize and colonize the Spanish lands west of the Mississippi River. And he returned to the East to try to raise money for his scheme. He even turned to the British for financial help.

Meanwhile, General Wilkinson, who was secretly in the pay of the Spaniards, was afraid that his own traitorous conduct would be exposed. In 1807 he denounced Burr to Jefferson. The President, largely on Wilkinson's charges, ordered Burr's arrest for treason.

Burr was tried at Richmond, Virginia, with Chief Justice John Marshall of the Supreme Court as judge. He was accused of trying to separate the western states from the Union. But Marshall ruled that there was no clear proof of treason, and Burr was freed. However, his reputation was now tarnished beyond repair.

EXILE AND FINAL YEARS

Burr spent 4 years wandering across Europe. He finally returned to the United States in 1812. In New York his old friends welcomed him, and Burr soon built up a new law practice. Burr had hoped to devote his declining years to his daughter, Theodosia, and his grandson, "Gamp." But the 11-year-old boy died after a short illness. In that same year Theodosia was lost at sea. The death of his grandson and daughter were tragedies that haunted Burr for the rest of his life.

Burr spent the last 24 years of his life practicing law in New York City. Always gay and witty, he rarely betrayed his true feelings. When General Sam Houston defeated a Mexican army in 1836, Burr, remembering his own dreams of Mexican conquest, remarked: "I was only 30 years too soon."

Burr died in obscurity on Staten Island, New York, on September 14, 1836. He was buried at Princeton, New Jersey, near his father.

Perhaps Thomas Jefferson best summed up the fatal flaw in Burr's character when he wrote: "No man's history proves better the value of honesty. With that, what might he not have been?"

Reviewed by RICHARD B. MORRIS
Columbia University

See also HAMILTON, ALEXANDER.

BURUNDI

Burundi is a small, crowded country whose people live in farm villages clustered in the central highlands of equatorial Africa. For about 75 years Burundi was part of the colonial empires of Germany and Belgium. In 1962 it became an independent nation.

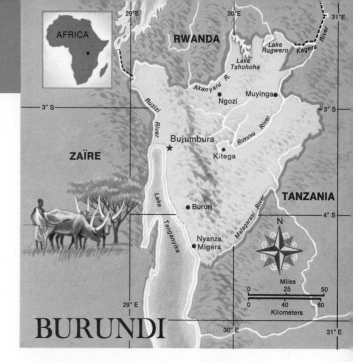

BURUNDI

▶ THE PEOPLE

The people of Burundi are known as the Barundi. They belong to three major ethnic groups—the Hutu (or Bahutu), the Tutsi (also known as Batutsi or Watusi), and the Twa (or Batwa).

Most of Burundi's people are Hutu. The Hutu live mainly by farming. Tutsi, who make up about 15 percent of the population, are cattle raisers. Most of the Tutsi are extremely tall. In the past they were the warriors who controlled and defended the land, dominating their Hutu neighbors. The Twa are Pygmies who live by hunting and fishing. They were the earliest inhabitants of the region. Today they make up a small part of the population.

Over three quarters of the people of Burundi are Christians, mostly Roman Catholics. Some of the Barundi are Muslims. The rest of the people practice tribal religions.

Some children do not attend school because of a shortage of neighborhood schools or because they are needed at home. Even very young children herd cattle, sheep, and goats in the mountain pastures. But the educational system is expanding. There is a university in Bujumbura, the capital city.

While many people wear Western dress in the city of Bujumbura, the rest of the Barundi wear cloth garments that hang loosely from their shoulders like togas. Tutsi men usually wear full-length white cotton robes, but the Tutsi are abandoning the traditional ways. Tennis shoes, berets, bicycles, and radios have become very popular.

Families live in mud-brick houses that look like beehives. Each house has a high, cone-shaped roof of split bamboo. Often the houses are grouped into villages, and around the villages are the fields in which the food crops are grown.

The most important foods are bananas, coffee, sweet potatoes, manioc, beans, peas, maize (corn), and sorghum.

The Barundi farmers grow the food they eat and a little coffee, sugar, and tea to sell. There are so many cattle, sheep, and goats that there are two animals for every three people living in Burundi. The cattle are valued not only for their milk and hides but as signs of importance and wealth.

▶ THE LAND

Burundi lies in the mountains that form one side of the great Rift Valley in the heart of

FACTS AND FIGURES

REPUBLIC OF BURUNDI is the official name of the country.

CAPITAL: Bujumbura.

LOCATION: East central Africa. **Latitude**—2° 19′ S to 4° 27′ S. **Longitude**—28° 51′ E to 30° 54′ E.

AREA: 27,834 km² (10,747 sq mi).

POPULATION: 3,900,000 (estimate).

LANGUAGE: French, Kirundi.

NATIONAL ANTHEM: *Hymne National du Burundi* ("National Hymn of Burundi").

GOVERNMENT: Republic (under military rule since 1976). **Head of state**—president. **International co-operation**—United Nations, Organization of African Unity (OAU).

ECONOMY: Agricultural products—coffee, bananas, sweet potatoes, manioc, maize (corn), beans, peas, sorghum, sugar, tea. **Industries and products**—milk, hides, fish, nickel. **Chief exports**—coffee, sugar, tea. **Chief imports**—machinery, petroleum, manufactured goods. **Monetary unit**—Burundi franc.

Africa. Long, narrow Lake Tanganyika borders the country on the southwest.

Most of Burundi is between 1,500 and 2,400 meters (5,000 and 8,000 feet) above sea level. Although the country is near the equator, the high altitude makes the climate quite pleasant. Temperatures average 10 to 27°C (50 to 80°F) all year long. Only in the lowlands near Lake Tanganyika is the weather warmer. Rainfall in the mountains is heavy, about 1,000 to 1,500 millimeters (40 to 60 inches) a year. Burundi's rainy season comes between September and May. During many months of the dry season there is no rain at all.

There is much air travel in Burundi because there are no railroads and few passable roads. Most villages are linked merely by footpaths. Bujumbura, the only large town, is a port on Lake Tanganyika from which boats go to meet the Tanzania and Congo railroads. Burundi's few Europeans and Asians have their homes and businesses there.

▶ **HISTORY AND GOVERNMENT**

Burundi was one of the last parts of Africa to become a European colony. In the 19th century Germany annexed Burundi and made it part of the German East Africa colony (together with Ruanda and Tanganyika). After Germany's defeat in World War I the League of Nations placed Burundi and Ruanda under Belgian rule. Belgium called the region Ruanda-Urundi and ruled it under a League of Nations mandate. After World War II, Ruanda-Urundi became a United Nations trust territory and Belgium continued to govern it until the Barundi asked for their independence. The United Nations wanted Ruanda-Urundi to become a single nation because the people in the two areas are much alike. But in 1962 Ruanda-Urundi became two independent nations—Burundi and Rwanda. Independence Day, July 1, is now a national holiday in both countries.

Burundi was a constitutional monarchy until 1966, when Prime Minister Michel Micombero, a former army officer, overthrew the *mwami* (king), Ntare V. Micombero declared Burundi a republic with himself as president. The constitution and legislature were suspended. A new constitution, adopted in 1974, confirmed Micombero as sole leader of the country. In 1976, Micombero was deposed by an army coup. Jean-Baptiste Bagaza was appointed president by the Supreme Military Council, a group of army officers.

ANN E. LARIMORE
Rutgers, The State University
New Jersey

See also RWANDA.

Farmers in Burundi cultivate terraced hillsides.

Crops are sold at local markets.

BUSES AND BUS TRAVEL

Every day buses carry millions of people to work from their homes in the cities or the suburbs and back again in the evening. Thousands of other passengers take long bus trips for business or pleasure. And millions of children rely on the bus to get them to school.

Yet the bus is relatively new as a means of travel. Motor buses came into use only when automobile travel began to gain popularity, about 60 years ago. But the bus does have ancestors that are much older.

In colonial days stagecoaches traveled over muddy, rutted roads between Boston, New York, and Philadelphia. Six or eight passengers were crowded inside the coach, and several more sat on top with the driver and the baggage. Horses were changed at posthouses at the end of each part, or stage, of the journey. That is why the coaches were called stagecoaches. The trip from Boston to New York took anywhere from 2 days to 1 week, depending on the weather and the condition of the roads. From New York to Philadelphia was a journey of 1½ days.

A form of the stagecoach was used for public transportation in the growing cities. The first such vehicle was operated in New York City in 1829. Known as the Accommodation, this vehicle was a horse-drawn wagon with benches for 12 passengers, a roof, and windows. The idea was such a success that similar conveyances, called omnibuses, began to be used in Philadelphia, Boston, and Baltimore as well as in New York. *Omnibus* is a Latin word meaning "for all," and the omnibus served everyone who had the fare. These omnibuses were eventually replaced by horse-drawn streetcars that ran on rails laid in the street.

During the 19th century, steam engines and electric motors began to replace horses as the power for vehicles. For long-distance travel people used steamships and trains instead of coaches. In the cities horsecars were eventually replaced by trolley cars. These cars were driven by electric power that was supplied by an overhead wire or a sunken third rail beneath the surface of the street. Trolley cars were also used for short trips between cities and towns.

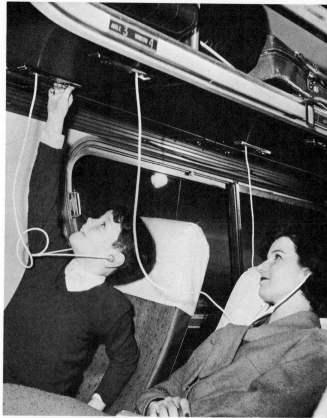

On modern luxury buses, individual radio receivers allow each passenger to listen to his own program.

But trolley cars could go only where there were tracks for them. The automobile could go wherever there was a road, and it became the favorite type of transportation.

Some people began to use their automobiles to carry passengers for a fare. They called attention to their services by painting signs saying "5¢" on their cars. These vehicles were called jitneys, from the slang term for a nickel, which was the fare. Jitneys competed with regular motor bus lines, which were in service in big cities as early as 1905.

The early buses were built by truck manufacturers and were designed to haul heavy loads rather than to provide for passengers' comfort. The heavy-duty truck springs gave a bumpy ride, and dust came in through cracks in the floorboards. There was no heating system to keep passengers warm in winter.

The first bus that was designed specifically for passengers' comfort appeared in 1920. Unlike the truck-type buses it was to replace, it was built close to the ground. This design gave a smoother ride with less swaying, and it lessened the danger of tipping over. It was also easier for passengers to board. During the next 40 years buses were constantly improved to make the ride more comfortable for passengers.

The long-distance bus that travels today's highways is comfortable and convenient. Under the floor there is a huge baggage compartment into which the driver or baggage man stows the heavy luggage instead of piling it on racks over the seats. There is heating and air conditioning for winter and summer use. The passengers sit in upholstered chairs that can be tilted back for resting or sleeping.

Each seat has its own reading light, so that a passenger can read while the person alongside who may want to sleep is left in darkness. The large windows are tinted to keep out the sun's glare without cutting off the view.

Most of the long-distance buses now have washrooms with hot and cold running water. Some deluxe buses have hostesses who serve orange juice, coffee, sandwiches, and cake. The engine is in the rear so that the noise and heat do not bother the passengers. To make the ride smoother, the modern bus is cushioned on cylinders of compressed air instead of being mounted on springs.

What is it like to travel on a long-distance bus? You and your baggage arrive at the bus terminal by car, taxi, or local bus. You buy your ticket from a clerk. If you want, he will arrange stopovers and will plan your route so that you can travel through the most scenic parts of the country.

At departure time the heavy baggage is stowed away, and on some buses the driver or hostess shows you to your reserved seat. The bus pulls out of the terminal and soon is rolling smoothly along the highway. At mealtimes the bus stops at a restaurant or cafeteria that has arrangements for serving the many bus passengers. On deluxe buses the hostess serves snacks between meals just as on an ocean liner or airplane. On very long trips passengers can stop overnight to rest at a motel.

Today large companies operate long-distance bus lines all over the United States. Their routes extend from Maine to California and from Canada to Mexico, as well as in Hawaii and Alaska. Their large bus terminals resemble railroad stations, with checkrooms, restaurants, barbershops, and newsstands.

Bus travel has also developed greatly in Europe, Africa, and South America since World War II.

Buses play an important part in local transportation. In most cities buses have almost entirely replaced trolley cars for short trips within the city or to neighboring cities and towns. The modern city bus is much like the long-distance bus, but it does not have the comfort features of the long-distance bus because its passengers are aboard only for a short time. The seats are not adjustable, and they are set close together in order to accommodate more passengers. There is no baggage compartment. City buses pick up and discharge their passengers at the curb at regular stops. Passengers pay their fare as they board the bus, instead of buying tickets at a bus terminal.

The school bus has changed the life of schoolchildren in the country. Once there were thousands of small one-room schools with one teacher for all the classes. This was because every child who lived on a farm had to be near enough to a school to be able to walk to it. These one-room schoolhouses have now been replaced by large central schools that serve a wide territory.

School buses pick up children each day at their homes, take them to the school, and bring them back home when school is over. School buses are usually painted bright yellow or orange so that they can be seen easily. As a further safety measure, most states forbid automobile drivers to pass a school bus that has stopped to pick up or let off children.

A new feature of bus travel is the chartered tour. A group of people can hire a bus and driver to take them wherever they want to go. They can make long stopovers and side trips, and take their time seeing scenery and historic sites. In America and Europe some bus lines specialize in running guided tours. The bus company makes all the arrangements for meals and hotel rooms. Hostesses care for the passengers' needs.

WALTER F. BUEHR
Reviewed by F. G. KECK
Eastern Greyhound Lines

See also AUTOMOBILES; TRANSPORTATION.

BUTTER

Years ago when a farmer made butter he first left the cream to cool and ripen in an earthenware crock in the springhouse. After several days he poured the slightly sour, or ripe, cream into a bell-shaped wooden churn. He whipped the cream with a long plunger until the butterfat separated from the rest of the cream into lumps about the size of peas. After draining off the leftover liquid, or buttermilk, he washed and kneaded the butter until it was smooth. Then the butter was packed in wooden tubs and taken to town. The buttermilk was usually fed to the live-stock.

Making butter was a long and tiring job, and there was not a large market for it. Butter was too expensive for many people. It did not keep well. Also, butter never tasted quite the same twice, since the farmer never knew how much butterfat was in the cream. Some butter turned out too rich, and some not rich enough. Butter had to be made by guesswork.

In 1890 an American scientist, Stephen M. Babcock (1843–1931), invented a way to test for the amount of butterfat in milk and cream. He treated a sample with acid and then spun it mechanically in a long-necked bottle. The fat rose to the top of the bottle and filled the neck. By looking at a measuring scale on the bottle's neck, the tester knew how much fat was in the milk. The Babcock test and the development of a mechanical cream separator (1878) made butter production an easier and more efficient operation.

Although some farms still do their own churning, most butter sold in the markets today is made in creameries that buy milk and cream from many farmers. After the cream is unloaded, it is weighed, tested, graded, and pasteurized. Most butter is made from sweet cream. Sometimes a starter—lactic-acid-pro-ducing bacteria mixed with other organisms that create good flavor—is added to the cream. The starter causes the cream to ripen. When churned, the butter develops a desir-able flavor and aroma. Some coloring is usually added, too.

The old-fashioned churn has been replaced by a revolving drum that shakes the cream back and forth until it is a grainy mass. Even though butter is now made mechanically,

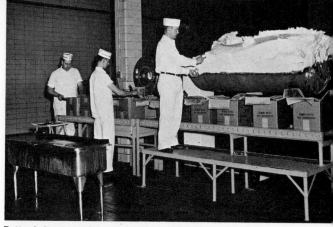

Butter is inspected for quality before packaging.

great care must still be taken to make sure that it has the right consistency and taste. Cooling the cream is one of the most important steps in making butter. Churning temperature depends on many factors, such as the time of year, the fat content of the cream, and the breed of cow from which the milk came.

The buttermaker has to be careful not to fill the churn too full, or the cream will have no room to swish around. If the churn is run too fast, the cream will spin around the walls and not thicken. If it is run too slowly, the cream settles on the bottom.

Creams vary. Creams from Jersey and Guernsey cows churn more quickly, because they have a high fat content and big fat par-ticles. The fats in milk given by cows that have eaten summer grass are softer than those in milk given by cows fed on dry winter rations.

Churning takes about an hour. The butter-milk is then rinsed off by spraying the butter-fat with water. The churn is filled with water and rotated for a few seconds to wash the butter. Salt is sometimes added. The butter is then kneaded mechanically until it has the right texture and the proper amount of mois-ture. The butter is then smooth and firm and ready for packaging.

Butter is usually packed in bulk containers weighing about 60 pounds and shipped to central markets. There it is repackaged into smaller pound or quarter-pound boxes or bars. The boxes are sold or held in storage until the butter is needed. Some large cream-eries often sell butter under their own brand names and do their own packaging and shipping.

Reviewed by JULIA PALMER
National Dairy Council

See also DAIRYING AND DAIRY PRODUCTS.

Butterfly at rest, left, has fully erect wings. Resting moth, above, folds back wings.

BUTTERFLIES AND MOTHS

Anyone who touches the wings of a butterfly or a moth finds that something like dust comes off on his fingers. The dust is actually made up of tiny scales. The scales grow in rows and give the wings their patterns of colors. The scales also account for the scientific name for butterflies and moths. Together they are called Lepidoptera, which means "scaly winged."

There are about 112,000 different kinds of moths and butterflies in the world, and they live almost everywhere. In the United States and Canada there are probably about 700 kinds of butterflies and 7,000 to 9,000 kinds of moths.

As microscope shows, a butterfly's wing has rows of scales that give it color and pattern.

How Can You Tell a Butterfly from a Moth?

Many butterflies and moths look very much alike. Yet it is possible to tell them apart. In general, butterflies are brighter in color than moths, although a few moths are as bright and beautiful as any butterfly. Butterflies are active during the day. Most moths are active only at night and are attracted by lights.

Butterflies and moths differ in other ways, too. Moths have thicker, more hairy bodies. Both have two pairs of wings. But a resting moth usually folds its front wings back upon its hind ones. A butterfly at rest leaves its wings full and erect. A butterfly, like a moth, has two antennae (feelers) on its head. A butterfly's antennae have slightly enlarged tips. A moth's antennae do not; in some moths the antennae have featherlike plumes, but the tips are never enlarged.

▶ LIFE CYCLE

Butterflies and moths are among the insects that pass through four stages in their life cycles.

The first stage is the egg. Adult females lay eggs on the kind of plant their young will later need as food.

The eggs hatch into wormlike creatures known as **larvae**. The common name for the larvae of butterflies and moths is caterpillar. Caterpillars are busy and hungry. They may

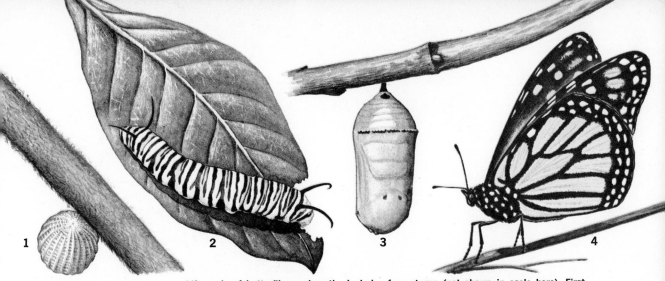

Life cycle of butterflies and moths includes four stages (not shown in scale here). First comes the egg (1), which hatches into a larva (2), familiar as a caterpillar. Larva then becomes pupa (3), a resting stage that lasts until body develops and adult emerges (4). Butterfly shown is a monarch. Third pair of legs is too small to show on thorax.

eat once or twice their own weight in leaves each day. After several days of such feeding, they outgrow their own skins. Then they molt, splitting the skin and crawling out of it. Caterpillars may shed their skins four or five times in this second stage of the life cycle.

In the third stage the caterpillar goes into a resting state and is called a **pupa**. Different caterpillars pupate in different ways. For example, many moth caterpillars burrow into the ground; others hide behind loose bark or in hollow logs. Some caterpillars rest in cocoons, which they make by spinning thread from their mouths. (Natural silk is made from the threads in the cocoon of the silkworm moth.) The pupa does nothing except rest. This stage may last 2 weeks; it may last a whole winter. During this period the caterpillar changes into a full-grown butterfly or moth.

In its new and adult form, it emerges wet and shaky from the cocoon. As blood flows into the veins of the wings the adult flutters and dries them. In a few hours, when the wings are strong and dry, the butterfly or moth flies off to live out its fourth, or adult, stage.

▶ WHERE THE COLORS COME FROM

The colors that mark an adult may be of several types. Some scales hold pigment, or colored matter; it accounts for the blacks, browns, reds, oranges, yellows, and whites. Other scales catch the sunlight and separate it into different colors. This second effect may be caused by a thin, oily film on the scales or by a scale's fine lines or ridges. (The green of many caterpillars is caused by their diet of plants.)

▶ THE SENSES

Both moths and butterflies have keen senses of sight, smell, and taste. A few moths are able to hear, too. The organs of taste in most butterflies and moths are in the mouth. Most organs of smell are on the antennae. However, the mourning cloak, the red admiral, and some other butterflies smell things through "noses" on their feet.

Sight

The eyes of butterflies are very sensitive to colors. Butterflies are especially attracted to red flowers. Moths, most active at night, are attracted to light-colored flowers. Most night-blooming flowers are white.

Scents and Smell

Many butterflies or moths have odors, or scents, which they use for two purposes. One kind of scent is used to attract the opposite sex; the other is used to drive away enemies.

The scents of male butterflies come from scales in pockets on their hind wings. During courtship a male monarch butterfly may scatter these scent scales over the female. The scents of many male butterflies resemble those of flowers or spices and are often pleasing to humans.

Female butterflies produce their scents in

Skipper butterfly has uncoiled its long, hollow "tongue" to suck in the sweet nectar from a zinnia.

special glands in their bodies. Most of these female odors are disagreeable to the human nose.

Taste

The taste organs of a butterfly are far more sensitive to sweet things than our tongues are. Their chief food, flower nectar, is a sugar solution, and they are easily able to find it. When a butterfly finds nectar in a flower, it uncoils its long, hollow "tongue" and sucks in the liquid.

Not all butterflies live on nectar. Some are attracted to rotting fruits. A few prefer the flesh of dead animals.

▶ MIGRATING BUTTERFLIES AND MOTHS

People have known for hundreds of years that birds travel over special routes during certain seasons. Such travel is called migration. Recently it has been learned that many butterflies, and some moths, also migrate. For example, the painted-lady butterfly travels from Mexico to California each spring. The same kind of butterfly flies across the Mediterranean Sea in spring, from North Africa to Europe. In butterfly migration thousands, even millions, of insects travel together.

The Monarch Butterfly

The best-known of the migrating butterflies is the monarch that winters along the Gulf of Mexico and other southern areas. In spring the young female lays her eggs on the milkweed plants that have begun to grow. The caterpillars that hatch from the eggs feed on the milkweed leaves. When the adult butterflies develop, they fly some distance north. There they mate and lay eggs on the milkweed that has just begun to grow with the advance of spring. Thus, within a few months' time, several generations of monarch butterflies travel farther and farther north in search of milkweed. By late summer, descendants of the original monarchs reach Canada.

With the cooler weather of autumn, surviving monarchs fly back south in great swarms. There are reports of monarchs spread out in a swarm 20 miles wide. Year after year such masses of butterflies follow the same routes. Every night they settle on trees and bushes. Trees where they roost are often known as butterfly trees.

▶ ENEMIES AND DEFENSES

Butterflies and moths have many enemies. There are tiny wasps that lay their eggs inside the much larger eggs of the butterfly. The wasp larvae then feed on the butterfly eggs. Caterpillars also have their enemies. They are eaten by birds and bats. They are invaded by tiny flies and wasps that live inside the caterpillars. Farmers and gardeners also kill the ever-hungry caterpillars.

From all the eggs that hatch, only two caterpillars out of every hundred live to become butterflies. If this were not so, caterpillars would be much more serious pests than they are. Caterpillars eat the leaves and fruit of growing plants and bore into the trunks and roots. The larvae of the clothes moth chew holes in wool and silk and also eat fur.

A few kinds of butterflies and moths have developed defenses against their natural enemies. Some are nearly invisible because they look like twigs or dead leaves. Some caterpillars have stinging hairs or poison spines that drive off enemies; others release bad odors. The monarch butterfly seems to taste bad to birds, and so the birds leave the handsome orange and black creature alone.

Ross E. Hutchins
Author, *Insects*

See also INSECTS; METAMORPHOSIS.

Adult life of butterfly begins when it emerges from pupal case, as shown in these photos of monarch butterfly. Legs break out, grab case, and pull rest of body free.

Within about 2 minutes, butterfly is free and hangs on empty pupal case. Newly emerged butterfly, still crumpled and wet, has small, fleshy wings and a flat abdomen.

As butterfly hangs there, its abdomen pulsates vigorously. This causes body fluids to circulate. After 10 or 20 minutes, wings will have expanded to full size.

Even after wings are fully expanded, adult butterfly remains clinging to pupal case for several hours, depending on weather, before it tries its first flight.

BUTTERFLIES OF THE WORLD

AGRIAS
SARDANAPALUS

EUROPEAN
SWALLOWTAIL
(PAPILIO
MACHAON)

BLUE MOUNTAIN
BUTTERFLY
(PAPILIO ULYSSES)

CHRISTMAS
BUTTERFLY
(PAPILIO
DEMODOCUS)

ORCHARD
SWALLOWTAIL
(PAPILIO AEGEUS)

ANCYLURIS
FORMOSISSIMA

SILVERSTRIPE
(PANDORIANA
PANDORA)

PEACOCK
(NYMPHALIS IO)

PAPILIO
SEMPERI

APOLLO
(PARNASSIUS
APOLLO)

MESENE
PHARAEUS

TAILED
BIRDWING
(PAPILIO
PARADISEA)

472

MORPHO
CYPRIS

BRIMSTONE
(GONEPTERYX
RHAMNI)

BUTTERFLIES OF THE UNITED STATES

QUESTION MARK
ANGLEWING
(POLYGONIA
INTERROGATIONIS)

MORNING CLOAK
(NYMPHALIS
ANTIOPA)

WOOD NYMPH
(MINOIS ALOPE)

PAINTED LADY
(VANESSA CARDUI)

MONARCH
(DANAUS
PLEXIPPUS)

DOG FACE
(COLIAS
CESONIA)

GREAT PURPLE
HAIRSTREAK
(ALTIDES HALESUS)

LEONARDUS SKIPPER
(HESPERIA LEONARDUS)

GIANT SWALLOWTAIL
(PAPILIO CRESPHONTES)

WHITE ADMIRAL
(LIMENITIS
ARTHEMIS)

VARIEGATED FRITILLARY
(EUPTOIETA CLAUDIA)

CABBAGE

CABBAGE LARVA
(PIERIS RAPAE)

BLACK SWALLOWTAIL
(PAPILIO POLYXENES
ASTERIUS)

ZEBRA SWALLOWTAIL
(PAPILIO MARCELLUS)

MOTHS OF THE WORLD

PSEUDOSPHEX
ICHNEUMONEUS

HORNET CLEARWING
(MELITTIA BOBBYLIFORMIS)

POLKA DOT MOTH
(SYNTOMEIDA EPILAIS)

URANIA MOTH
(URANIA FULGENS)

DUOMITIUS
LEUCONOTUS

GIANT HERCULES
(COSCINOSCERA
HERCULES)

TUSSOCK
(PORTHESIA SIMILIS)

COPIOPTERYX
DERCETO

EMPEROR MOTH
(SATURNIA PAVONIA)

AFRICAN PEACH MOTH
(EGYBOLIS VAILLANTINA)

CHINESE SILKWORM
MOTH AND LARVA
(BOMBYX MORI)

MOTHS OF THE UNITED STATES

STRIPED MORNING SPHINX
(DEILEPHILA LINEATA)

POLYPHEMUS
(ANTHERAEA
POLYPHEMUS)

LUNA
(ACTIAS
LUNA)

IMPERIAL
(EACLES
IMPERIALIS)

GYPSY MOTH
(PORTHETRIA
DISPAR)

HAWK MOTH
(SMERINTHUS
GEMINATUS)

IO
(AUTOMERIS IO)

CLOTHES MOTH
AND LARVA
(TINEOLA
BISSELLIELLA)

GLOVER'S SILKWORM
(SAMIA GLOVERI)

ARMY WORM MOTH
AND LARVA
(CIRPHIS UNIPUNCTA)

AMERICAN TIGER
MOTH AND LARVA
(ISIA ISABELLA)

FOREST TENT—
CATERPILLAR AND MOTH
(MALACOSOMA DISSTRIA)

CECROPIA MOTH AND LARVA
(HYALOPHORA CECROPIA)

475

BUTTERFLY COLLECTING

On a summer day, how many kinds of butterflies can you find within a mile of your house? The number may be higher than you think. There are more than 11,000 kinds of butterflies and moths in North America alone.

The best way to study butterflies and to learn to name some of the thousands of kinds is to start a butterfly collection.

Most collectors catch their specimens in a light net. Then they prepare the butterflies for mounting. Once the insects are mounted with their wings outspread, they can be identified and studied.

▶ COLLECTING YOUR SPECIMENS

A still, sunny day in summer or fall is the best kind of day for butterfly collecting. If you train yourself to look for butterflies, you will

---

EQUIPMENT

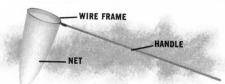

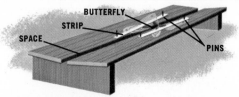

THE NET. To make your own net, use a light material like nylon net or Dacron, so that the net can sweep easily through the air. The bottom of the net should be rounded to allow enough room for the butterfly without damaging it. Once you have caught a butterfly in the net, loop the net over the ring from which it is hung. The net must be deep enough to permit this—at least twice as deep as the distance across the wire ring.

The length of the net handle is a matter of choice, but since you are going to catch insects that fly, it is best to have a fairly long handle—about 2 or 3 feet.

SPREADING BOARD. To make a spreading board, use two flat pieces of soft wood. You must be able to stick pins in the wood. The two pieces of wood are placed so that they lie alongside one another with a narrow space between them. The insect's body will lie in this space, under which another strip of very soft wood or cork is attached and into which the pin is placed. The pieces of wood are mounted on wooden blocks. Each piece of wood must slope gently downward from its outside edge to the center space, so the wooden blocks should be sawed to form a slightly V-shaped cradle.

KILLING JAR OR BOTTLE. Use a ½- or 1-pint jar with a wide mouth and a tightly fitting cover. Butterflies' wings are covered with scales that come off like dust when they are touched, so don't crowd the specimens together.

TWEEZERS. Use tweezers whenever you want to move or handle the butterflies. If you move the butterflies with your fingers, their scales may be removed.

RELAXING JAR. To make a relaxing jar or box, use a pint or quart wide-mouthed jar or a covered tin cookie box. In the bottom of the jar or box place a layer of wet sand 1½ inches deep. Put a wire rack on top of the sand so that the specimen does not rest on the wet surface.

PAINTBRUSH. It is important to have a clean specimen, as well as an undamaged one. A few moth flakes put in a box on the rack will prevent mold. A fine camel's-hair brush can be used to brush loose scales or particles of dirt from your specimens.

ENVELOPES. Use triangular envelopes made from small sheets of paper for storing and carrying the butterflies after they are removed from the killing jar. It is best to mount specimens at once, but when this is not possible, the envelopes are good storage places. **LABELS.** Labels are made from stiff white paper or white cards. Use India ink and a fine pen for labeling.

INSECT PINS. Ordinary pins are too short and thick to use in mounting butterflies. Special pins, called entomological or insect pins, must be used. The pins are rustproof and come in a number of sizes. For general use, sizes #2 and #3 are best. You will have to buy these from a supply house.

STORAGE BOXES. Line the bottom of a cigar box with a piece of corrugated cardboard cut to fit the space. On top of the first layer of cardboard paste a second piece of corrugated cardboard, making sure that the corrugations run at right angles to one another. This will be the surface into which you will pin your specimens with their labels. You can line the lid and sides of the box by pasting on them sheets of plain white paper cut to fit.

be surprised at the number of places in which they are to be found. But in the beginning look for them in fields in which wild flowers grow, and in flower gardens. Many butterflies take nectar from flowers.

The best time to catch a butterfly in your net is when the insect has come to rest. Don't let your shadow fall on the butterfly, or it may fly away. Bring your net down directly over the butterfly. You can scoop up some butterflies from the side; others may dart up and fly away if you do this. Once the butterfly is in the net, quickly flip the hoop to one side so that the rim falls across the lower part of the bag and keeps the butterfly inside.

▶ HOW TO USE THE KILLING BOTTLE

When a very active butterfly has been caught, it can be put into the killing bottle in several ways. One method is to get the butterfly at the top of the net and hold the net closed beneath it. Then open the net enough to get the mouth of the jar over the butterfly. It will usually fly into the jar. Or the fold of the net containing the butterfly can be put into the jar or bottle until the insect is stunned. Then it can be picked out of the net and put into the bottle. Another way is to get the butterfly into a fold in the net and stun it by pinching the thorax. The thorax is the middle region of the three divisions of the body of an insect. Once stunned, the butterfly is picked out of the net with the tweezers and put into the covered jar.

All killing bottles, no matter what kind of killing agent they contain, should be labeled "POISON." The beginner might use a few drops of lighter fluid on a piece of cotton or felt placed in the jar. On top of the cotton, place a round piece of cardboard or blotting paper. This will prevent the butterfly from resting directly on the cotton and possibly becoming damaged. Never leave bottles and jars uncovered any longer than is necessary to put insects in or take them out. The insides of the bottles should be kept clean and dry. A piece of cleansing tissue may be used to wipe them out.

The beginner must learn by experience the length of time the specimens should be left in the killing bottles. Some insects may require only a few minutes, while others may take longer. It is advisable to remove the insects within 1 or 2 hours at most.

▶ HOW TO PIN AND MOUNT

Butterflies should be mounted as soon as possible after they are collected. Those which have been stored in envelopes for any length of time will dry out and become brittle. In order not to break them you must first put them in the relaxing jar for at least 24 hours before they are mounted.

Pinning is a good way of keeping specimens. They continue to look natural and are easy to handle and study. Butterflies are pinned through the thorax between the bases of the front wings. The easiest way to pin an insect is to hold it with the tweezers and push the pin into the butterfly until its back is ½ inch from the top of the pin. Place the butterfly in the center space of the spreading board, and then spread or open its wings by pushing down on the wings with transparent paper until they lie flat against the board. To position the wings for mounting, put a thin pin behind the vein in the front part of the wing and slide the wing partway forward until the hind margins of the front wings form a straight line. Do not put the pin clear through the wing if you can help it, for you may tear it. When the wing is in the proper position, fasten it by placing paper strips over the wing and pinning the strips to the board. Do the same thing with the hind wing before you do the other front and hind wing. Once the wings are in position, the antennae may be held in place by crossed pins, or if the antennae are long enough, they may be held in place by the strips that hold the wings.

The time it takes for a spread butterfly to dry will depend upon its size, the temperature, and how humid or dry the weather may be. One way to tell if the specimen is ready to be taken off the spreading board is to touch the body gently with a needle. If the body is rigid and does not move, it is dry and can be removed from the board.

▶ STORING AND CARE

For each butterfly in your collection, print a small label. It should tell where you found the butterfly and the date you caught it, as well as the name of the butterfly. You may also add your name as collector. The label is placed on the pin below the insect.

Pinned and labeled, your butterflies are ready to be stored in a storage and display box. This box can be bought, but a beginning collector can make one from a cigar box. You may cover the bottom of the box with corrugated paper, as described. Or you may want to use cork, balsa wood, or any soft material into which you can stick a pin and have it stand upright.

The arrangement of the butterfly collection should be neat, and the specimens should be placed according to family and common names. The specimens should be in rows, with the labels placed low on the pins against the bottom of the box.

Many good collections have been ruined by beetles, ants, and other pests. They are always ready to attack and destroy mounted insects. A mothball on a pin or in a small cloth bag fastened in the corner of the box will keep pests away.

All butterfly specimens must be handled with care if they are to be kept intact. If a part of a specimen breaks off, it may be fastened back on with a little bit of glue.

Collecting is the first step in getting to know something about insects. The suggestions given here for collecting butterflies may be extended to many other insects, which can be collected and preserved in much the same way.

Reviewed by Ross E. Hutchins
Author, *Insects*

BUTTONS AND BUTTON COLLECTING

Buttons were probably first used to hold clothes together in the 13th century. At that time most people still fastened their clothes with clasps, but the nobility used beautiful buttons of silver and gold, hammered out by craftsmen.

Pictures can be made by covering drawings with buttons.

In the next few centuries an almost endless variety of materials and designs were used by buttonmakers. Louis XIV (1638–1715) had silver-covered bone buttons made for the soldiers serving him. Since Louis was called the Sun King, the silver was hammered into a picture of the King with sunlike rays coming from his head. The courtiers in the court of Louis XVI (1754–1793) had their own peculiar way of proving their elegance and wealth. They tried to outdo each other by seeing who could wear the most ridiculous buttons made of the most expensive materials.

Most buttonmakers, however, made graceful, delicate buttons. A popular button covering in the 1700's was made of metal threads wound into an intricate pattern. The buttonmaker needed all his skill and patience to weave the threads of different colors into tiny stars or triangles. Miniature scenes were painted on buttons of ivory or glass. Some buttons were covered with beads and pearls. Buttonmakers also cut designs in hard button bases and filled the cuts with silver.

The buttons that took almost the longest time and most painstaking care to make were surprisingly enough made of paper. The pieces of paper were cut with fine paring tools into the shapes of tiny houses, people, or various other forms. These were made into

 TOM SENT AND TO

SUE

scenes and fastened onto strong button bases. Trees in these scenes even had tiny paper leaves on their branches.

Buttons were made by hand in these elaborate styles until the 19th century. Manufacturers then began to use powered machines to turn out large quantities of buttons cheaply. Brass buttons became very popular because designs could be stamped on them quickly. Many of the brass buttons were made for work clothes and had railroad signs or colorful slogans on them. Children's buttons were often stamped with a tiny Jack Horner or some other nursery hero.

New materials changed button manufacturing, too. Hard-rubber buttons were tried in the 1840's, but they did not wear well. Celluloid, a synthetic compound that looks like ivory, was developed towards the end of the 19th century. Delicate buttons that seemed to be hand painted could be mass-produced in the new material.

Buttons today are made of plastics or natural materials such as wood, leather, metal, pearl, and shell. Shanks, which are the fastening loops on the backs of buttons, can be put on in minutes by machines. Other buttons have holes punched out so that they can be sewn on clothes. Automatic machines cut and shape most buttons, but some buttons are still finished by hand. There are as many different ways of making buttons as there are kinds of buttons. Buttonmaking still demands the imagination and skill of the craftsman.

Reviewed by THEODORE ABRAMS
Associated Button Company, Inc.

▶ **BUTTON COLLECTING**

Collecting pretty and unusual buttons is a popular hobby and an easy one to start. To have an interesting collection and not just a lot of buttons rattling around in an old shoe box, it is best to work according to some plan.

Many button collections start with one or two admired items out of the family spare-button box. At the button counter in a store you will find the newest button fashions. If you decide to collect old buttons, you can often find them at rummage sales and in secondhand stores. For the advanced collector there are dealers who buy and sell every kind of button. The dealers are often helpful in supplying missing items. The beginning collector should watch for button shows or exhibits. Attending a show is a fine way for you to become acquainted with adult collectors and perhaps get some new ideas for your collection.

How Buttons Are Grouped

The National Button Society of the United States has set up a system of classification that separates the various kinds of buttons into groups. There are four general divisions.

Division I—General. These are old buttons of various materials, shapes, patterns, and pictorial designs. The materials may be fabrics, metal, glass, enamel, pearls, shell, china, and so on. The designs may be of animals, plants, or pictorial subjects. The patterns include basket weave, fleur-de-lis, filigree, and paisley.

Division II—Uniform. These buttons are classified as United States, foreign, and livery. The United States buttons are divided into armed forces, police, railroad, and societies. Foreign buttons include armed forces, British court dress, and hunt club. Under livery are grouped heraldic (coats of arms, crests), achievements, monograms, and initials.

Division III—Modern. Buttons in this division fall into the same general categories as the general buttons. Collectors may limit themselves to one type—glass buttons, for example—or they may select assorted kinds.

Many collectors prefer to keep modern and antique buttons apart, taking World War I as the dividing time.

Division IV—Specialties. These are divided into bridle rosettes, cuff buttons, netsukes (carved buttons used on kimonos), obi domes, costume trimming, and studs.

Selecting and Sorting Buttons

Historical events, such as the French Revolution, have been the subject of button designs, and famous people like George and Martha Washington are pictured on buttons. So are characters from the Bible and mythology. Fairy-tale people like Hansel and Gretel and Little Red Riding Hood are pictured on buttons, and there are even colorful sets that illustrate Mother Goose nursery rhymes and include Humpty Dumpty and the Three Little Kittens.

Other attractive sets of buttons are shaped like flowers, fruits, vegetables, birds, animals, flags, food, and many other things. Collectors call them realistics or goofies. These designs of objects are true to form in every detail except size.

The important thing to see, when you group your buttons, is that no two are exactly alike. They can all be of the same color, shape, material, or subject, as long as no two match.

Uniform buttons are sorted and kept separately from other buttons. The foreign buttons are kept together, and when the collection is large, those of each country should be separated. This can only be done after the buttons are identified, so be sure to learn what each one is.

Buttons not belonging on uniforms are called dress or costume buttons, no matter what kind of clothes they belong on. Dress buttons have been made from hundreds of different materials in every possible size, shape, and color, and with hundreds of thousands of different designs. The variety is so great that even the largest collection is barely a sample.

You may want to collect buttons made of certain materials such as pewter, brass, enamel, bone, glass, wood, porcelain, silver, or gold. Or you may prefer to collect according to subjects, choosing perhaps fairy tales, animals, flags, ships, or your favorite sport. Perhaps covered buttons will interest you most, or you might want variety. Whatever you decide upon, you will certainly want to display your collection.

Displaying Your Collection

Buttons lying loose in a box or strung on cord are hard to see. They should be mounted if they are to be seen to the best advantage. A good way to mount them is on 9-by-12-inch cards. Posterboard is a good weight. Plain cardboard that is faced with colored paper is often used.

Buttons with holes may be sewn on or glued to the card. To make a button with a shank (the part of the button that juts out and by which it is attached) lie flat, punch a hole in the card for the shank. A 2-inch piece of pipe cleaner or wire run through the shank and clinched (the ends turned back) will hold the button firmly in place.

The pin-on buttons worn during political campaigns do not belong in collections of clothing buttons. Collecting pin-backs is an entirely different hobby.

The neater and more artistically your buttons are mounted, the more attractive they will be. Different ways suit different types of buttons, and it is always worthwhile to have variety.

Military and other uniform buttons are among the kinds that look best mounted in well-spaced rows. In contrast, tiny dress buttons look best when laid out in an elaborate design such as a snowflake or a fleur-de-lis.

The realistics or goofies are perfect for mounting on maps or scenes. Goofies are also excellent for making a button rebus, which is a printed story with buttons taking the place of some of the words. Here is an example: "Yesterday he read a book about coin collecting. It said that gold coins were dear." To make a rebus, mount a red button for the word "read," a coinlike one for "coin," and a goofy shaped like a deer for "dear."

Another popular style of mounting is to make buttons into mosaic pictures. The method is simple. For a mosaic bird, draw or paste the picture of a large bird on a card. Then cover the whole picture as much as possible with buttons. Ordinary plain buttons, and any number of the same kind, may be used.

The general collection should be mounted to bring out its variety. This can be done by having parts of the cards feature materials, other parts give attention to pattern, and another area show both. Well-chosen plain buttons are often ideal for exhibiting a material. This would be true in the case of mother-of-pearl, with its shimmering iridescence. Pictorial patterns are impressive when mounted by subject, as for instance an entire card of animals, one containing only flowers, or one that shows methods of transportation.

The National Button Society has a junior division for boys and girls ages 8 to 18. It publishes the *News-Sheet* and provides adult leadership. For information write to the Secretary, 7940 Montgomery Avenue, Elkins Park, Philadelphia 17, Pennsylvania.

JANE F. ADAMS
Editorial Consultant, *National Button Bulletin*

LILIAN SMITH ALBERT
Editor, *National Button Bulletin*

BYRD, RICHARD EVELYN (1888–1957)

Rear Admiral Richard E. Byrd was a daring aviator and America's greatest Antarctic explorer. He was the first man to fly over both the North and South Poles. His five expeditions to Antarctica helped to unlock the mysteries of that vast, frozen continent.

Byrd was born on October 25, 1888, in Winchester, Virginia. In 1912 he graduated from the United States Naval Academy. A leg injury forced him to retire from active sea duty in 1916, but he was soon back in the Navy as an aviator.

On May 9, 1926, Byrd and his copilot, Floyd Bennett, took off from Spitzbergen in the Arctic Ocean. They circled the North Pole and returned almost 16 hours later. For their achievement Byrd and Bennett each won the Congressional Medal of Honor. The following year, with a crew of three men, Byrd attempted a nonstop flight from New York to Paris, carrying the first transatlantic airmail. But bad weather forced him to crash land on the coast of France.

In 1928 Byrd led his first expedition to Antarctica. He established his base, Little America, on the Ross Ice Shelf near the Bay of Whales. The camp of more than a dozen huts was equipped with electricity and telephones. Airplanes were used to explore large areas of the continent. On November 28, 1929, Byrd and three crewmen took off from Little America. Their destination was the South Pole. From a height of about 10,000 feet, Byrd looked down at a vast expanse of snow and ice. He had conquered the South Pole by airplane.

Little America was to be Byrd's home on and off for over 25 years. During the second expedition, from 1933 to 1935, great emphasis was placed on scientific research. Science nearly cost Byrd his life. In order to make weather observations, he lived alone during the long polar night. His tiny cabin was built deep under the snow, over 100 miles from Little America. Fumes from a leaky stove almost poisoned him before he was rescued.

Byrd headed a third expedition from 1939 to 1941. In 1946 he led the largest Antarctic expedition in history—the United States Navy's Operation High Jump. Over 4,000 men and a large force of ships and planes continued the work of exploring and mapping the South Polar region.

Byrd's last journey, in 1955, was as head of the Navy's Operation Deepfreeze. He died in Boston, Massachusetts, on March 11, 1957.

Reviewed by LT. CMDR. D. M. COONEY
Office of Information, Department of the Navy

See also EXPLORATION AND DISCOVERY; POLAR REGIONS.

BYRON, GEORGE GORDON, LORD (1788–1824)

George Gordon Byron, English poet, was born in London on January 22, 1788, when his mother was on her way home to Scotland from France. His father died in France 3 years later. Born with a lame foot, Byron tried all his life to disguise it by acts of physical daring. When his great-uncle died in 1798, he became the sixth Baron Byron.

He received his schooling from tutors and in preparatory schools. In 1805 he entered Trinity College, Cambridge. He had a volume of his poems printed privately in 1806. A year later his first published work, *Hours of Idleness,* appeared. When it received an unfavorable review in the *Edinburgh Review,* he wrote a satire, *English Bards and Scotch Reviewers* (1809), in reply.

In the summer of 1809 he and a Cambridge friend, John Cam Hobhouse, set out to travel through Europe and the Middle East. Byron returned to England 2 years later. The first two cantos of *Childe Harold's Pilgrimage* are a poetic record of his first year's experiences. After the poem was published in 1812, Byron was received enthusiastically by London society. Tales based on his travels in Asia Minor increased his popularity, but scandalous love affairs damaged his reputation. He married Anne Isabella Milbanke in 1815. They were separated a year later, shortly after the birth of a daughter. Byron lost his place in society, and in April, 1816, he left England forever.

In Geneva he met the poet Shelley, finished the third canto of *Childe Harold,* wrote *The*

Prisoner of Chillon, and began the poetic drama *Manfred.* In October, 1816, he left with Hobhouse for Venice, Italy. The fourth canto of *Childe Harold* is about a visit to Rome in the spring of 1817. *Beppo,* published anonymously in February, 1818, is a satire on life in Venice. When Byron began his greatest work, *Don Juan,* in September, 1818, he planned it to be in the style of *Beppo.*

In 1819 he met Countess Teresa Guiccioli, whose devotion gave him a new steadiness. During their years together he completed *Don Juan* and wrote *The Vision of Judgment,* a number of poetic dramas, and minor poems.

In 1823 he was elected to a committee working for Greece's liberation from Turkey. He decided to go to Greece and was eager to lead an attack. Instead he died of fever in the Greek city of Missolonghi on April 19, 1824.

CHILDE HAROLD'S PILGRIMAGE
(excerpt from Canto III)

There was a sound of revelry by night,
And Belgium's capital had gathered then
Her Beauty and her Chivalry, and bright
The lamps shone o'er fair women and brave
   men;
A thousand hearts beat happily; and when
Music arose with its voluptuous swell,
Soft eyes looked love to eyes which spake again,
And all went merry as a marriage bell;
But hush! hark! a deep sound strikes like a
   rising knell!

Did ye not hear it?—No; 'twas but the wind,
Or the car rattling o'er the stony street;
On with the dance! let joy be unconfined;
No sleep till morn, when Youth and Pleasure
   meet
To chase the glowing Hours with flying feet—

But hark!—that heavy sound breaks in once
   more,
As if the clouds its echo would repeat;
And nearer, clearer, deadlier than before!
Arm! Arm! it is—it is—the cannon's opening
   roar!

Within a windowed niche of that high hall
Sat Brunswick's fated chieftain; he did hear
That sound the first amidst the festival,
And caught its tone with Death's prophetic ear;
And when they smiled because he deemed it near,
His heart more truly knew that peal too well
Which stretched his father on a bloody bier,
And roused the vengeance blood alone could
   quell;
He rushed into the field, and, foremost fighting,
   fell.

THE PRISONER OF CHILLON
(excerpt)

There are seven pillars of Gothic mold,
In Chillon's dungeons deep and old,
There are seven columns, massy and gray,
Dim with a dull imprisoned ray,
A sunbeam which hath lost its way,
And through the crevice and the cleft
Of the thick wall is fallen and left;
Creeping o'er the floor so damp,
Like a marsh's meteor lamp:
And in each pillar there is a ring,
And in each ring there is a chain;
That iron is a cankering thing,
For in these limbs its teeth remain,
With marks that will not wear away,
Till I have done with this new day,
Which now is painful to these eyes,
Which have not seen the sun so rise
For years—I cannot count them o'er,
I lost their long and heavy score,
When my last brother drooped and died,
And I lay living by his side.

They chained us each to a column stone,
And we were three—yet, each alone;
We could not move a single pace,
We could not see each other's face,
But with that pale and livid light
That made us strangers in our sight:
And thus together—yet apart,
Fettered in hand, but joined in heart,
'Twas still some solace, in the dearth
Of the pure elements of earth,
To hearken to each other's speech,
And each turn comforter to each
With some new hope, or legend old,
Or song heroically bold;
But even these at length grew cold.
Our voices took a dreary tone,
An echo of the dungeon stone,
  A grating sound, not full and free,
  As they of yore were wont to be:
  It might be fancy, but to me
They never sounded like our own.

BYZANTINE ART AND ARCHITECTURE

Byzantine art is the art of the Eastern Roman Empire. Constantine, the first Christian emperor of the Roman Empire, moved his capital from Rome to the old Greek city of Byzantium. He renamed the city Constantinople after himself. But the art of the Eastern Roman Empire that he founded is known as Byzantine.

Byzantine art extends from the founding of Constantinople in A.D. 330 until the Turks captured the city in 1453. However, long after the fall of Constantinople, artists in the Greek islands, in the Balkans, and in Russia continued to create works in the Byzantine style.

In the days of its glory, Constantinople was the most magnificent city in the world. Above the gates and towers of the city walls rose the golden domes of the churches and the tall, shining columns set up by the emperors. Some of the most famous statues of ancient Greece had been brought to the city. The huge palace of the emperor blazed with gold and silver, marble and mosaics. There the emperor, covered with jewels, was surrounded by priests in shining robes and by men-at-arms of every barbarian race.

The Byzantine Empire was a religious state. The emperor was not only the ruler of his people but God's representative on earth. The ceremonies of the church and of the court were meant to show the emperor's sacred character. His magnificent jewels, robes, and crown were intended to give him a majestic and saintly appearance.

The purpose of Byzantine art was to glorify the Christian religion and to express its mystery. All of Byzantine art is filled with a kind of spiritual symbolism—things on earth are meant to stand for the order of heaven. Another characteristic of the art of this rich empire is a love of splendor.

Byzantine art is a combination of Eastern and classical Western art. The Byzantine Empire inherited the ideas and forms of art of the classical world of Greece and Rome. However, part of the empire was in Asia and Africa. The shores of Asia could be seen from Constantinople. It was natural that the art of this empire should be greatly influenced by the art of the Near East.

The art of Greece and Rome was naturalistic—artists wanted to show the world about them as it actually looked. Their greatest interest was in the human body. To create an ideal beauty, they showed the body as it would look if it were perfect.

The art of the ancient Near East was more an art of decoration. Artists filled large, flat areas with patterns that were repeated again and again. Instead of copying nature, they made natural forms into flat patterns. They did not have the great interest in the human body that classical artists had, and they did not hesitate to change the shape of the body to fit into their designs. Another characteristic of Eastern art was a use of glowing color.

▶ THE LATE ANTIQUE PERIOD: THE BEGINNING OF THE BYZANTINE STYLE (330–527)

For the first 200 years of the Byzantine Empire, artists worked in the same style as the artists of ancient Greece and Rome. Because the art was still based on that of the old classical world, these years are called the Late Antique period. During these years the new Byzantine style gradually grew out of the decaying art of the classical world.

In this period the Roman Empire lost its lands to the barbarian invaders from the north. Much of the art of this time of violence and disorder shows a loss of skill and craftsmanship. Artists were no longer able to make the human body look like that of a living person. They could no longer achieve the realism or ideal beauty that Greek and Roman artists had. Instead, for representing heads and bodies, they used certain rules that made human figures look unreal—stiff and wooden. This unreality was made-to-order for expressing the spiritual ideals of Christianity.

▶ THE FIRST GOLDEN AGE (527–726)

The earliest true Byzantine style appeared in the First Golden Age. By the 6th century Byzantine artists had broken away from the classical styles. They had created a new style to show the supernatural nature of Christ and the sacredness and grandeur of the emperor.

Justinian

The most important ruler of the First Golden Age was the Emperor Justinian. He is remembered for his code of laws and his

Above: *Theodora and her Court,* a 6th-century mosaic in the church of San Vitale, Ravenna. Below: A mosaic of the Emperor Justinian in the same church.

great building projects in Constantinople and Italy. After recapturing much of Italy from the Goths, Justinian chose the city of Ravenna as the center of Byzantine rule in Italy.

There is a famous mosaic picture of the great emperor in the church of San Vitale at Ravenna. He is shown surrounded by his attendants. His stiff pose and rich robes make him a symbol of majesty. On the opposite wall is a picture of his wife, the Empress Theodora, with her ladies-in-waiting. At the end of the church, in the half dome behind the altar, Christ is shown among the angels. Christ, the All-Ruler, is surrounded by the members of his court in heaven just as Justinian and Theodora are surrounded by a court on earth.

These pictures are done in mosaic. A mosaic picture or design is made of thousands of small glass or marble cubes, called **tesserae,** set in cement. The walls and domes of the great churches of Ravenna and Constantinople were decorated with glass tesserae, brilliantly colored or covered with gold.

A picture made out of many pieces of glass cannot be as freely done or copy nature as exactly as a painting. In the pictures of Justinian and Theodora in San Vitale, the figures are stiff. The bodies are flat, and the magnificent robes do not seem to cover any solid shapes. The feet point downward on the flat ground, giving the illusion that the bodies are floating in air. However, the stiff poses of the rulers, and their long, flat shapes, are not simply the result of the use of mosaic. These are characteristics of the new Byzantine style. We can see by the heads that the artist could have been much more realistic if he had so wanted—the faces are almost like portraits in the old Roman tradition. However, Byzantine artists were not interested in realism, in showing solid forms in real space. Instead, they developed a formal style, a style in which the body is just another part of a flat design.

Built in the 6th century, Hagia Sophia (now a museum) was one of the world's great Christian churches.

Hagia Sophia, the Church of Holy Wisdom

The greatest building of the whole Byzantine world is the church of Hagia Sophia, in Constantinople. Hagia Sophia, known as the church of holy wisdom, was built on the site of an ancient temple to Pallas Athene, the Greek goddess of wisdom. It was dedicated to the Virgin Mary.

The church was designed by the architects Anthemius of Tralles and Isidorus of Miletus. Construction was begun in A.D. 532, and it is believed that the Emperor Justinian himself personally supervised the work. A legend tells that he followed the orders of an angel.

Hagia Sophia is so large that the human eye cannot take in the whole huge shape of the interior. If you stand inside the great church, you must look at it one part at a time. Your eyes are led from the pillars to the vaults, then to the smaller domes, finally to the central dome 180 feet above the floor. Probably this is just what the architects wanted. The eyes of the worshiper finally come to rest on the great mosaic figure of Christ in the dome, looking down as though from heaven itself. The feeling of endless space in Hagia Sophia makes it one of the most impressive buildings in the world. The many marble columns are enormous, but in the huge interior they seem small. At the same time the mounting of domes of increasing sizes up to the great central dome gives a feeling of order.

The splendor of Hagia Sophia also comes from color. The columns, brought from every corner of the empire, are of stone and marble of many different colors—blue, green, and blood-red. Even more brilliant in color is the mosaic decoration. The floor is covered with marble mosaic and the walls glitter with glass mosaics. The mosaics have designs of vines and pomegranates—the fruit of the

Icons—religious images—were popular among early Byzantine artists. This 6th-century icon shows Saint George killing the dragon.

pomegranate was a symbol of life after death —and imaginary beasts. Below the central dome are mosaic pictures of great, star-eyed angels. On the golden background of the vast, topmost dome is the figure of Christ as judge and ruler of all.

The Dome on Pendentives

Byzantine architects did not invent the plans or building methods that they used; they adapted them from the architecture of the Near East and Rome. However, the architects of Hagia Sophia did solve the problem of plac-

The wooden throne of Bishop Maximian at San Vitale, Ravenna, is ornamented with carved ivory panels.

ing a round dome on the square plan of the walls that support it. They did this by building up masonry from the corners of the walls in the shape of a triangle. This construction is called a pendentive. Pendentives not only support the dome but join the dome to the walls in one continuous sweep.

The pendentives of Hagia Sophia rest on four massive piers. The stone blocks of these piers are set in lead rather than in mortar. The dome is also made stronger by half domes that carry its outward-pushing weight to huge buttresses, or supports, on the outside. To make it lighter the dome was built out of a special kind of light brick.

Some scholars believe that Byzantine architects learned how to build domes from earlier Roman buildings. Others think that they learned from Near Eastern architecture. However, the meaning of the dome in religious architecture came from Persia. In the ancient Near East, men thought that heaven was like a cup placed upside down over the earth. In Persia from the 3rd to 7th centuries A.D., architects used the shape of the dome to suggest the architecture of heaven. Since Byzantine architects also used this idea, it seems likely that both the knowledge of how to build a dome and the meaning of this shape came to Byzantium from her eastern neighbors.

Ivory Carving: A Bishop's Throne

The Byzantine Church did not approve of sculpture in the round—sculpture that can be seen from all sides. The Church feared that it would recall the idols of the Greek and Roman religions. However, small carvings in relief (raised from a flat surface), especially in ivory, were allowed as church decoration. One of the most beautiful examples of ivory carving of the First Golden Age is the throne of the Bishop Maximian at Ravenna. He is the priest to the right of Justinian in the mosaic at San Vitale.

The wooden chair is covered with many ivory panels of different sizes. In the center of the long rectangular panel on the front of the throne is the monogram of Christ. On either side are carved peacocks, symbols of paradise or everlasting life, and grapevines, symbols of the wine of Communion. Byzantine designs of birds and animals placed among the curling branches of vines are like the complicated patterns in Oriental rugs. Byzantine artists probably adapted these designs from textiles or carvings made in the Near East.

Four ivory carvings on the front of the throne show Saint John the Baptist and the four Gospel writers. The thinness of the saints and their haggard appearance is typical of Byzantine art. In the early centuries of Christianity, many holy men fasted and tormented themselves. One famous hermit, Saint Simeon Stylites, even spent many years sitting on top of a column. The bodies of such holy men were very different from the healthy bodies of the Greek athletes. Extreme thinness came to be a sign of holiness, and this is one reason that the artist has carved such tall figures. By making the bodies of the saints very tall and fragile, they appear to be more spirit than flesh. The flat pattern of the saints' robes also makes their bodies look weightless, as if the cloth did not fall over any solid shapes.

The entire chair is carved with great precision and delicacy. The patterns of vines, birds, and beasts are wonderful examples of the Byzantine craftsman's creativeness in making a rich and exciting pattern.

▶ THE PERIOD OF ICONOCLASM (726–843)

In the 8th century the mosaics of the churches of Byzantium were covered with whitewash, and the sculpture was destroyed. This was done by the iconoclasts (image-breakers), who did not approve of representations of the saints or the Holy Family. They believed that many people really worshiped the picture or statue instead of the holy figure it represented. During the period when the iconoclasts were in power, no pictures of the Deity were allowed. The iconoclast movement not only interrupted the development of Byzantine art, but caused the destruction of nearly all the great treasures of the First Golden Age.

▶ THE SECOND GOLDEN AGE (843–1204)

When the iconoclasts lost power, a new golden age began. Constantinople was still a city of great treasures, shimmering with gold. It was the richest city in the world. The art of this period shows an Eastern fondness for things that are richly ornamented and perfectly made. Everything is on a smaller

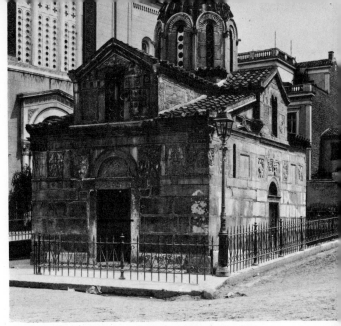

The Little Metropolitan was built in Athens in the 11th century. It is the world's smallest cathedral.

scale. Artists made small, beautiful things that are delicate rather than impressive. Compared with the grand monuments of the time of Justinian, the churches of this period are tiny. Religious art was made to appeal to the worshiper in much more human terms. Instead of the solemn grandeur that made Christ unapproachable, there was a new emphasis on his sufferings as a man.

Architecture

The churches of the Second Golden Age are like little jewel boxes in stone. They are most impressive from the outside, where the harmony and logic of the construction can be seen. The plan is square. Within the square is a cross with arms of equal length. A typical example is the Little Metropolitan in Athens. Three stories high, the church has a blocklike ground floor. The arms of the cross plan project into the second story. On the third level a small dome is placed over the center of the cross. Domes are also built between the arms of the cross plan on the second level, but these cannot be seen from the outside.

Another feature of the buildings of the Second Golden Age is the texture of the walls. In some places the surface is rough, in others smooth. This kind of surface causes an ever-changing activity of light and shade. The walls of the church at Athens are decorated with fragments of ancient Greek carving as well as reliefs of that time.

Saint Mark's. The famous church of Saint Mark's in Venice has nearly the same plan as the Little Metropolitan but is many times larger. Begun in 1063, it was probably copied from a church in Constantinople. The domes, like those in Hagia Sophia, have a ring of windows at their bases to let in light. The sunlight shining on the gold mosaics makes the domes look like golden shells hung in the air. The glow of gold mosaics and the sheen of colored marble make the visitor feel that he is really in a heaven brought to earth. On the outside the round domes are covered by domes of fantastic shape that make Saint Mark's look like an Eastern fairy palace. Marbles and mosaics of many different periods decorate the outside of the church.

The Mosaics at Daphni

The style of the mosaics of the Second Golden Age is like an echo of the great age of Greek art. In Greece, not far from Athens, is the church of Daphni. Inside the church are some of the finest mosaics in the whole history of Byzantine art.

In the dome there is a large picture of Christ. Only his head and shoulders are shown. His hand is raised in blessing, but his bearded face is solemn, even frightening. The large size of this picture, the beard, and the fearful solemnness of the face are like an ancient representation of the Greek god Zeus. The artist wanted to show Christ as the tremendous power that rules over the fate of man. It was natural that he should have turned to the noble beauty of Greek art for inspiration. He may even have been influenced by the bearded head of a statue of a Greek god.

On the pendentives are four scenes from the life of Christ. In the Crucifixion scene there are only three figures: Christ is on the cross, and Mary and Saint John are at the foot of the cross, one on each side. The figures are arranged in the shape of a triangle against the empty golden background. Each figure is separate and yet unified with the other figures.

Begun in the 11th century, Saint Mark's cathedral in Venice took centuries to build. The last details of this colorful church were added in the 1400's.

An 11th-century Italian cross
made of enamels and gold.

A 14th-century mosaic in a Constantinople church shows
the Holy Family paying taxes.

The balanced arrangement is like that used by Greek sculptors in placing their figures in the pediments of temples. Also, the position of Saint John—bending, with his weight on one leg—is a pose often used by Greek sculptors. The body of Christ is almost like that of a classic athlete. However, unlike Greek sculpture, the anatomy is not true to life. The Byzantine artist changed the body into a pattern of flat shapes. In doing this he tried to show Christ as perfect, unlike any ordinary human being.

The faces of Saint John and the Madonna have the flatness and heavy lines of the Byzantine style, but they express the calm of Greek statues. The emptiness of the background and the nobility of the figures show that this is an event that is not part of the everyday world. The artist has not tried to make a picture of the actual happening or to show what the real scene was actually like. Instead he has made a symbol of the Crucifixion.

Our Lady of Vladimir

Few examples of paintings on wooden panels have survived from the Second Golden Age. One of them is the famous Madonna of Vladimir, one of the first paintings to depict the Madonna and Child as mother and son, showing affection for each other. The picture reveals a new interest in human feeling. The softness of the features and the expression of

sadness in the eyes are like the technique and feeling of late Greek painting.

Our Lady of Vladimir was taken to Russia in the 11th or 12th century and became the model there for many later representations of the Madonna. This new, more human idea of divinity also influenced the religious painting of Italy in the 14th century.

Byzantine artists were not supposed to invent new compositions but to repeat as closely as possible the shapes of famous images. The Church wanted the representations of religious figures always to look the same. Artists followed rules written in manuals. In a beautiful ivory carving of the Madonna and Child, we can see that the artist has followed certain of these rules. The Madonna is carved in one of the standard poses—standing, she holds the Christ Child on her left arm. The carver has also used the Byzantine system of proportion for the body. The Madonna's body is extremely long and drawn out—9 or 10 times as long as the head. In ancient Greece artists usually made the bodies of athletes or gods seven times as long as the head.

The ivory carving has features that are typical of the Second Golden Age. The carved Madonna has the same sad, wistful look as the Madonna of Vladimir. Her oval head is delicate, with large, almond-shaped eyes and a tiny mouth. The strange, ghostly face under a heavy hood makes us feel that we are looking at a being from another world.

A delicately carved ivory panel of a Byzantine empress holding her scepter and orb.

A particularly beautiful feature of this ivory is the flattened pattern of the drapery arranged in a fanlike design.

The End of the Second Golden Age

The Second Golden Age came to an end with the capture of Constantinople by the Venetian crusaders in 1204. Like earlier crusades, it had been organized to fight the Turks in the Holy Land. Instead the crusaders attacked the most powerful city in the Christian world. When Constantinople fell into their hands, the invaders plundered the churches and palaces and burned the libraries. Many ancient works that had lasted from Greek and Roman times were lost in the flames. When the Venetians were finally driven out,

the last period of Byzantine civilization, the Third Golden Age, began.

▶ THE THIRD GOLDEN AGE (1261–1453)

The architecture typical of the Third Golden Age can be seen in many churches in the Balkans. These buildings differ from earlier churches like the Little Metropolitan because they give the impression of being tall, soaring buildings. Tiny domes are set on tall bases that sprout from the first story. The upward feeling is increased by the number of **pilasters** on the outside of the church. Pilasters are column-like strips built into the side of a wall. These churches do not look massive and solid like the churches of the Second Golden Age.

The Paintings of Kharieh Djami

In the paintings of this period, we seem to be looking at real dramatic happenings. The painters of the wall paintings of the church of Kharieh Djami in Constantinople were interested in storytelling. The figures in the Christian stories are placed in actual settings instead of on an empty golden background. Many of the old rules survive, but there is a new life and movement and a real beauty of color. Byzantine painters finally became interested in experimenting with realism, and in this respect they are the equals of their famous contemporaries in 14th-century Italy.

The End of Byzantium

Hagia Sophia was the spiritual center of the Byzantine Empire for 900 years. There the sacred emperors were crowned; there the priests celebrated the mass until that last dark night in Byzantine history, May 29, 1453. On that night the crowds prayed for the last time in the shadow of the great dome as the armies of the Turkish sultan attacked the city. Gathered inside the church, waiting for a miracle, they must have heard the crumbling of the city's walls. They must have heard the rattle of bridle chains in the streets, the clamor of the Turkish soldiers, the sound of axes hewing down the great doors as the sultan came to still forever the heart of the Byzantine world.

BENJAMIN ROWLAND, JR.
Harvard University

See also ARCHITECTURE; DECORATIVE ARTS; PAINTING; SCULPTURE.

BYZANTINE EMPIRE

A thousand years ago Constantinople was probably the largest and richest city on earth. It was the capital of the great Byzantine Empire. About a million people lived in Constantinople, and visitors marveled at its huge palaces, beautiful churches, and many shops. One visitor, writing for those who had never seen the city, said that if he described a hundredth part of its wealth, it would seem like a lie and no one would believe it.

In A.D. 330 Constantine, the Roman emperor, had moved the seat of government from Rome to the old Greek city of Byzantium. Constantine named his capital New Rome, but most people called it Constantinople (Constantine's city), or still used the old name, Byzantium.

After Constantine died, the emperors who succeeded him found it difficult to rule the vast Roman Empire. In 395 the empire was officially divided; the lands in the east were ruled from Constantinople and those in the west from Rome. In the 100 years that followed the division, Rome lost most of the lands of the Western Empire (Italy, Spain, France, Britain, northwest Africa). In the east, however, the emperors still ruled. This part of the Roman Empire, ruled by emperors living in Byzantium, is known as the Byzantine Empire. The rulers of the Byzantine Empire, however, still called themselves Romans, and for a time the Byzantine Empire was still called the Eastern Roman Empire. The language of the Eastern Empire was largely Greek, rather than Latin, the Roman language.

▶ DEFENDING THE EMPIRE

The Byzantine Empire lasted for hundreds of years. It had a long life, but not an easy one. Its neighbors tried for centuries to overrun it. The Persians threatened the empire at one time. They had scarcely been defeated in 628 before the Arabs began a conquest of the East. The Byzantines at different times had to stand off attacks by a number of peoples from Asia, such as the Avars, Bulgars, and Turks. Because of the invasions the size of the empire varied from time to time. Generally the Byzantine emperors ruled most of the Balkan Peninsula and Asia Minor.

▶ THE ARMY

The Byzantine Empire lasted as long as it did because of its military strength. The armies were usually well organized and equipped. They had medical and ambulance services, signalmen who flashed messages with mirrors, and even marching bands to keep up their spirits. The navy possessed a secret weapon, "Greek fire." This was an inflammable mixture that was thrown on enemy ships in hand grenades or sprayed, flaming, from tubes in the prows of Byzan-

The people of Constantinople wore the brightly colored and richly embroidered clothes of the Byzantine Empire. Even their chariots were decorated in a special Byzantine style.

tine ships. Greek fire was a fearful weapon in the days of wooden ships. It was no wonder that the Byzantines kept the directions for its manufacture a carefully guarded secret.

THE WONDERS OF THE CAPITAL CITY

The Byzantines encouraged foreign rulers and ambassadors to visit their capital. They went to great lengths to impress the visitors with the wealth and power of the emperors. When an ambassador was presented to the emperor, he was ushered into a large, richly decorated hall. Before the throne stood a gilded bronze tree. On its branches were little mechanical golden birds that whistled beautiful songs. On either side of the throne stood lifelike bronze lions that roared and beat their tails. As the awe-struck foreigner bowed to the floor the throne on which the emperor sat rose slowly toward the ceiling. Ambassadors who had never seen such marvelous devices were always impressed by the clever Byzantines. Foreign visitors also gazed in wonder at the gold- and marble-covered walls of the palaces and churches. In particular they noticed the great church of Hagia Sophia, which still stands today. Although Constantinople had many poor people, visitors gave them little attention. They were more impressed with the large number of rich people, who rode fine horses and wore silk garments.

THE TRADE OF THE EMPIRE

Most people within the empire worked on the land, but the wealth of the capital came largely from trade. The city stood at a crossroads. All ships carrying goods between the Mediterranean Sea and the Black Sea had to pass Constantinople. The main road from Europe to the Middle East also passed through the city. The emperors taxed all goods carried in or out of their crossroads capital.

Goods from far-off places filled the markets of Constantinople. There were furs from Russia, spices from Ceylon, rugs from Asia, leather from Morocco, and ivory from East Africa. Skilled craftsmen made the fine cloth, jewelry, and other rich goods sold in the shops. The emperors owned the only workshops permitted to make silk cloth. The shops were grouped together according to their business. The perfume shops were all located near the palace so that their wares would sweeten the air.

SCHOOLS AND BOOKS

Constantinople had schools as well as shops. Since Greek was the language of the Byzantines, they studied the writings of such ancient Greeks as Plato and Aristotle. Many ancient books would have been lost had they not been kept and studied in the Byzantine schools, for scarcely anyone could read Greek in the West at this time. Byzantine authors also wrote new books, especially histories.

THE BYZANTINE CHURCH

The Byzantine Empire was a Christian empire. Its missionaries spread Christianity among the Slavic peoples of eastern Europe, including the Russians. Byzantine Christians disagreed with those of the West about a number of matters. The pope at Rome condemned the Eastern emperor's great powers over the church. Eastern Christians, however, did not recognize the pope's authority. Disagreements between the Eastern and Western churches grew so great that they divided in 1054. Churches that grew from the church of the Byzantines are known as the Orthodox churches—for example, the Greek Orthodox Church and the Russian Orthodox Church.

THE END OF THE EMPIRE

The struggle to rule was often a bitter one. Sometimes an emperor's son inherited his father's place, but often the throne was seized by a strong man. Some men would stop at nothing to be emperor—not even murder.

These struggles weakened the empire. It was during a struggle for the throne that an army of Crusaders from the West captured Constantinople in 1204. The rule of the Westerners lasted only until 1261, but the Byzantine emperors never became powerful again. A Muslim people, the Turks, conquered the Byzantine lands piece by piece until only Constantinople remained, a capital without an empire. Finally, in 1453, a Turkish army using cannons took the city. The last piece of the old Roman Empire had finally fallen.

KENNETH S. COOPER
George Peabody College

B, second letter of the English alphabet   **B** 1
  See also Alphabet
Baa, Baa, Black Sheep, nursery rhyme   **N** 407
Baal (BAY-al), pagan god   **E** 176
Baal and the Dragon, apocryphal book of Bible   **B** 159
Baalbek (BA-al-beck), Lebanon
  Temple of Bacchus, picture   **L** 124

Baal Shem-Tov (BOL SHEM-tove) (Israel ben Eliezer) (1700?–1760), Jewish teacher and founder of Chasidism in Poland, b. Ukraine, Russia. He appealed to common people as well as scholars in his belief that God exists in all things and is approachable through joyous and sincere prayer rather than merely through intellect.

Baarle-Hertog (BAR-L'HER-tok), Belgium   **B** 129
Babcock, Alpheus, American piano builder   **P** 242

Babcock, Stephen Moulton (1843–1931), American agricultural chemist, b. Bridgewater, N.Y.: developed the Babcock test for determining amount of butterfat in milk (1890). He was professor of agricultural chemistry at University of Wisconsin (1887–1913), chief chemist (1887–1913) and assistant director (1901–13) of Wisconsin Agricultural Experiment Station.
  Babcock test   **B** 467;   **W** 199

Babcock test, determined amount of butterfat in milk   **B** 467
  Wisconsin dairy industry   **W** 199
Babe, blue ox of Paul Bunyan   **F** 312

Babel (BAY-bel), **Tower of,** in old Testament (Genesis 11, 1–9), a tower in the plain of Shinar, or Babylonia, in ancient Mesopotamia, built by descendants of Noah, who wished to build a tower reaching to heaven. This angered God, and He brought it to pass that the builders of the tower could no longer understand each other's speech. Unable to continue their work, they scattered over the earth in small groups, each speaking a tongue alien to its neighbor. According to Scripture, this is reason for diversity of races and languages.
  ziggurats of the Chaldeans   **A** 241

Babelthuap (BA-bel-tu-op), fertile, forested island in western Pacific, the principal island of the Palau group, in Caroline Islands. The chief export is bauxite.

Babenburg, House of, Austrian royal family   **A** 524
Baber, Mogul emperor of India   **I** 133
Babirusa (bab-i-RU-sa), wild pig   **P** 249
  hoofed mammals   **H** 209; picture   **H** 212
Babi Yar, poem by Yevtushenko   **U** 62
Baboons   **M** 420; pictures   **L** 224;   **M** 421
  social organization   **A** 280–81
Babur ("Tiger") see Baber, Mogul emperor of India
Baby   **B** 2–4;   **C** 231–34
  Eskimo, picture   **A** 304
  human reproduction   **R** 180
  in a hospital nursery, picture   **H** 249
  locomotion, picture   **A** 292
  origins of family life   **F** 37
  zoo babies   **Z** 375–76
Babylonia (bab-il-O-nia), ancient empire, now Iraq
  ancient civilizations   **A** 218–20
  ancient music of Sumerians and Babylonians   **A** 245
  art   **A** 236–37, 241–42; pictures   **A** 235
  building methods   **B** 435
  creation myths   **M** 557
  Jewish community of exile   **J** 104, 107
  mail service   **P** 406
  medical writings   **M** 203
  numeration system   **N** 394–96, 391
  science, advances in   **S** 60
  sculpture   **S** 93
  tunnels, earliest built   **T** 314

Baby's breath, decorative plant native to Europe and northern Asia, introduced into North America. Two to three ft. tall, it has numerous small white flowers. It is used by florists in trimming bouquets.

Baby teeth   **T** 47
Bacchus (BACC-us), Greek and Roman god   **G** 360;   **W** 188
Bacchus, Temple of, Baalbek, Lebanon, picture   **L** 124
Bach (BOCK), **Johann Sebastian,** German musician and composer   **B** 4–5;   **G** 182–83
  baroque period   **B** 66
  chorales   **H** 312
  choral music   **C** 278, 279
  electronic arrangements of his works   **E** 142h
  Mendelssohn revived music of   **M** 219
  organ music   **O** 209
Bach, Karl Philipp Emanuel, German composer   **C** 330;   **G** 183–84
Bachelor's degrees see Degrees, university and college
Bach Festival, Bethlehem, Pennsylvania   **M** 552
Bacillus (ba-CILL-us), a rod-shaped bacteria   **B** 10

Back, Sir George (1796–1878), English explorer, b. Stockport. He explored Spitsbergen seas with Sir John Franklin. While searching for Captain Ross in Arctic, he discovered Great Fish River. He wrote *Narrative of an Expedition in H.M.'s Ship Terror, in the Years 1836–7.*
  Northwest Passage   **N** 338

Backbone, or spine, of animals   **K** 251
  animals with and without backbones   **A** 264
  birds   **B** 201
  body's skeleton   **B** 270–71
  snakes have long backbones and short tails   **S** 204
Backer, Americus, London musical-instrument maker   **P** 242
Backgammon   **B** 5–6
Backhand, tennis stroke   **T** 91, 93
Backpack, space suit   **S** 340L–341; diagrams   **S** 388, 340L
Backpacker, camping   **C** 40, 41
Back saws, tools   **T** 212
Backstaffs, navigation instruments   **N** 65
Backstage, space behind the stage in a theater   **T** 156
Backstage crews, of plays   **T** 158
Back stitches, in sewing   **S** 129
Backstroke, in swimming   **S** 492; picture   **S** 490
Back to normalcy with Harding, campaign slogan   **H** 39
Backwoodsmen, frontier inhabitants   **W** 142–43
Bacon, Francis, English philosopher and essayist   **B** 7;   **E** 253–54, 292, 293
  contributions of his method to science   **S** 67–68
  heat theory   **H** 86d
  New Atlantis, The   **U** 256
  quotation from   **Q** 19
Bacon, Francis, Irish painter   **E** 242
Bacon, Nathaniel, English colonist in Virginia   **V** 359
  leader of Bacon's Rebellion   **B** 8–9

Bacon, Peggy (1895–   ), American artist and writer, b. Ridgefield, Conn. Known for her caricatures of American society, she wrote and illustrated books for children, such as the *Lion-Hearted Kitten and Other Stories* and *Mercy and the Mouse.* Her works are exhibited in permanent collections of Metropolitan Museum of Art and Whitney Museum of American Art.

Bacon, Roger, English scientist and author **B** 7; **E** 389
  writings on the science of optics **O** 166
Bacon's Rebellion, 1676 **B** 8–9; **V** 359
Bacteria **B** 9–13; **M** 208, 280–82
  aid digestion **B** 275
  antibiotics **A** 310
  bacteriostatic antiseptics **D** 222
  fermentation **F** 90
  food spoilage **F** 344, 352–54
  meteorite yields unknown bacteria **C** 421
  pasteurization of milk **D** 9
  place in the food chain **L** 242–43
  plant enemies **P** 287
  possible fourth kingdom of living things **K** 251
  soils, microorganisms in **S** 232
  vitamin K produced by **V** 371
  yogurt **D** 11
  See also Antiseptics; Disinfectants; Microbiology
Bacterial diseases **D** 187
  gonorrhea **D** 196
  Koch discovers microbes causing anthrax **K** 293
  lockjaw **D** 200–01
  pneumonia **D** 203–04
  streptococcal sore throats **D** 207–08
  tonsillitis **D** 210
  trench mouth **D** 210
  tuberculosis **D** 211–12
Bacterial viruses, or bacteriophages **V** 364

Bacteriological warfare (also called germ, or biological, warfare), warfare in which living organisms are used to transmit disease to enemy. Bacteria of such diseases as diphtheria, typhus, and smallpox are introduced into air or drinking water of enemy. Infected animals also can be used to transmit disease. Although techniques are available for such warfare, it has rarely been used.
  Soviet Union and U. S. resolution, 1971 **D** 185

Bacteriology, science that deals with bacteria
  Koch, Robert **K** 293
  medical laboratory tests **M** 201, 209
Bacteriophages (bac-TER-i-o-phages), or bacterial viruses **V** 364; picture **V** 361
Bactrian camels **C** 34; **H** 210; picture **H** 213
Baden-Powell (BADE-en PO-well), **Agnes,** English founder of Girl Guides **G** 213
Baden-Powell, Robert, English soldier, founder of scouting movement **B** 356–57
  Girl Guides **G** 213
Badgers **O** 242
Badger State, nickname for Wisconsin **W** 197
Badges, in heraldry **H** 118
Badges of honor see Medals
Badlands, area in Great Plains region, North America
  Alberta, Canada **A** 146a; picture **A** 146b
  Montana, in Makoshika State Park **M** 431, 439
  North Dakota **N** 325; picture **N** 333
  South Dakota **S** 315; picture **S** 314
Badlands National Monument, South Dakota **S** 322; picture **S** 314
Badminton **B** 13–15
Badr, battle of, 624 **M** 405

Baedeker (BAY-dek-er), **Karl** (1801–1859), German publisher of travelers' guidebooks, b. Essen. He started his book business in Coblenz (1827) and wrote guidebook about that city (1829). Later he moved to Leipzig and published a series of world-famous guidebooks in German, English, and French about European countries, the Orient, and parts of North America. The name "Baedeker" is identified with the most authentic travel information.

Baekeland (BAKE-land), **Leo Hendrik** (1863–1944), American chemist and inventor, b. Ghent, Belgium. He went to United States (1889) and became a citizen (1893). Baekeland invented an improved method of manufacturing photographic paper. He is noted especially for his discovery of synthetic resin Bakelite (announced 1909), a substitute for hard rubber and amber that has been important in development of plastics industry. **P** 324

Baer (BARE), **Karl Ernst von** (1792–1876), German biologist, b. Estonia. This pioneer in embryology (the study of animal development in its early stages before birth) was first to see the human egg. Von Baer's law states that each animal in its early development goes through stages similar to those gone through in its evolutionary history.

Baez (BA-ez), **Joan** (1941–), American folk singer, b. N.Y. She has performed on concert tours, at colleges, and on TV, singing and accompanying herself on the guitar. Her recordings include *Joan Baez* and *Joan Baez in Concert.* She has also taken part in a number of civil rights and anti-war demonstrations.

Baffin, William, English navigator
  Northwest Passage **N** 338

Baffin Bay, part of the North Atlantic Ocean between Greenland and the Canadian Northwest Territories. The bay is partially ice-free during summer months. The bay was discovered by the English explorer William Baffin during his search for a northwest passage (1616).

Baffin Island, Arctic Ocean **I** 427
  Arctic Archipelago in Canada's Northwest Territories **C** 51; **Y** 361
  Northwest Territories, Canada **Y** 361
Bagasse (ba-GASS), fibrous part of sugarcane **S** 454
  sweet grasses **G** 319
Bagatelle, musical form **M** 535
Bagaza, Jean-Baptiste, Burundi political leader **B** 464
Baggataway (bag-GAT-a-way), Canadian Indian game **C** 67
  lacrosse, a national sport of Canada **L** 20–21
Baghdad, capital of Iraq **I** 382
  Kadhimain, a suburb, picture **M** 302

Baghdad Pact, mutual defense pact signed by Turkey and Iraq and later joined by Iran, Pakistan, and the United Kingdom (1955). Also known as the Middle East Treaty Organization (METO), it was formed mainly for military purposes but works for economic development as well. When Iraq withdrew in 1959, headquarters was switched from Baghdad to Ankara and the name was changed to Central Treaty Organization (CENTO).

Bagpipe **F** 329; pictures **F** 330, **W** 182
Baguios (BOG-yos), hurricanes in Philippine Islands **H** 292

Baha'i (BA-ha-i) **Faith,** or the Faith of Baha'u'llah, was founded (1844) in Persia (now Iran) by Ali Mohammed of Shiraz, called the Báb ("the Gate"), who announced the coming of a new prophet. In 1863 Mirza Husayn Ali proclaimed himself the awaited Messiah. He took the name Baha'u'llah ("Splendor of God"), and it is on his teachings that the religion is based. World headquarters is in Haifa, Israel, and the Universal House of Justice is the international governing body. Members believe in one God, one evolving religion, one mankind, and strive to eliminate all forms of prejudice.
  later religions **R** 152

Bahamas (ba-HA-mas) **B** 16–17
Bahia, city in Brazil *see* Salvador, Brazil
Bahia Hona Bridge, Key West, Florida, picture **I** 424
Bahrain (bah-RAIN), emirate in Persian Gulf **B** 18–18a
  flag **F** 237
Bahutu *see* Hutu
Baida or **Beida**, Libya **L** 204
Baikal (by-KALL), **Lake**, Siberia, U.S.S.R. **L** 26
Bail, in law **C** 527

Bailey, Carolyn Sherwin (1875–1961), American author, b. Hoosick Falls, N.Y. She is known for children's books, such as *Children of the Handcrafts*, *Pioneer Art in America*, and *Miss Hickory*, which was awarded the Newbery medal (1947).

Bailey, of a castle **F** 375
Bailey, Donald, English bridge designer **B** 400

Bailey, Pearl (1918–), American entertainer, Negro, b. Newport News, Va. Known for her distinctive singing style, in which she half sings, half talks, and frequently ad-libs, she has appeared on Broadway (*St. Louis Woman*, *Hello, Dolly*), in movies (*Carmen Jones*, *That Certain Feeling*), in nightclubs, and on TV.

Bainbridge, William, American naval officer **N** 179

Baird, John Logie (1888–1946), Scottish inventor, b. Helensburgh. A pioneer in the development of television, he gave the first public demonstration of true television in London in 1926. He also pioneered in transatlantic and color television and invented the Noctovisor, a device for seeing in the dark.

Baird, Spencer Fullerton (1823–1887), American zoologist, b. Reading, Pa. As secretary of Smithsonian Institution, he greatly increased collections, improved cataloging methods, and founded the National Museum. As first head of U.S. Fish Commission, he founded Woods Hole Marine Biology Station and promoted use of hatcheries and laws against overfishing to protect fish resources. One of America's greatest naturalists, Baird wrote *Catalogue of North American Birds* and *Catalogue of North American Mammals*.

Bait, for fishing **F** 206
Bait casting, fishing **F** 206, 208–09
Baja (BA-ha) **California**, Mexico **M** 242
Bajans, or **Barbadians**, name for people of Barbados **B** 53
Baji, l'Masoudi al-, Tunisian writer **A** 76d
Baji, Muhammad al-, Tunisian writer **A** 76d
Baked Bean State, nickname for Massachusetts **M** 135
Bakelite (BAKE-el-ite), a plastic **P** 324
Baker, Dorsey S., American railroad builder **W** 27
Baker, Elwood T., American inventor of gin rummy **C** 115
Baker, George Pierce, American educator **D** 300

Baker, Josephine (1906–1975), American entertainer, Negro, b. St. Louis, Mo. She spent most of her adult life in Europe, where she developed an international reputation. During World War II, Josephine Baker served in the Air Auxiliary of the Free French Forces and was awarded the French Legion of Honor medal. She adopted 12 orphans of different races and nationalities, and she sponsored a children's village at Les Milandes in France.

Baker Island *see* Howland and Baker Islands
Bakewell, Robert, English agriculturalist **A** 100
Baking and bakery products **B** 385–89
  recipes for cookies and cupcakes **R** 116
  See also Flour and flour milling

Baking powder **B** 389

Baking soda, sodium bicarbonate ($NaHCO_3$). Baking soda is used in cooking to make baked goods rise, and it is often found as one of the ingredients in baking powder.

Bakke decision, a U.S. Supreme Court ruling on minority college admissions, *see* affirmative action.

Bakongo, African people **A** 260
Bakota, a people of Gabon **G** 2
Bakr, Ahmad Hassan al-, president of Iraq **I** 383
Baku, Union of Soviet Socialist Republics **E** 323; **U** 36
  Azerbaijan, capital **U** 45
Balaguer, Joaquin, Dominican Republic president **D** 283

Balakirev (ba-LA-kir-ef), **Mily Alekseevich** (1837–1910), Russian composer, b. Nizhni Novgorod (now Gorki). Balakirev was the leader of "The Mighty Five," a group of Russian composers, including Mussorgsky, Rimsky-Korsakov, Borodin, and Cui, who developed a distinctive Russian style of music. He was also director of the Imperial Capella in St. Petersburg (1883–94). He is best known for his orchestral works *Russia* and *Tamara* and for his arrangements of Russian folk songs. **U** 63

Balaklava (bal-ok-LA-va), **battle of**, Crimean War battle in which a British cavalry unit was nearly wiped out by Russians as the result of a misunderstood command. The disaster inspired Lord Tennyson's poem *The Charge of the Light Brigade*, which glorifies obedience of soldiers.

Balance, in design **D** 133
Balance, sense of **B** 287–88
  animals: locomotion **A** 291–93
Balance of nature **E** 272b, 272f; **L** 258–59
  cat family important in **C** 135
  communities of living things affect each other **K** 259
  dog family **D** 243
  food chain broken **L** 242
  insecticides **I** 258
Balance of payments, of trade **I** 329
Balance of power, among nations **I** 322
Balance scales, for weighing **W** 112
Balance sheet, in bookkeeping **B** 312, 313
Balance wheels, watches and clocks **W** 45
Balanchine (BAL-an-chene), **George**, Russian-born American choreographer **B** 28; **D** 26
Balante, African people **G** 406a
Balata (ba-LA-ta), a gum **R** 185
Balaton (BALL-a-ton), **Lake**, Hungary **H** 285; **L** 26
Balboa (bol-BO-a), Panama Canal Zone **P** 48
Balboa, Vasco Núñez de, Spanish explorer **B** 18b;
  E 382–83

Balchen (BOL-ken), **Bernt** (1899–1973), American aviator, b. Topdal, Norway. Balchen went to the United States (1926) and became a citizen (1931). As chief pilot of Byrd's Antarctic Expedition (1928–30), he piloted first flight over South Pole. Active in Norwegian underground during World War II, he entered U.S. Army Air Corps in 1941, rising to rank of colonel. Balchen wrote *The Next Fifty Years of Flight* and *Come North with Me*.

Balcones (bal-CO-nes) **Escarpment**, Texas **T** 124
Balcony, second floor of a theater **T** 156
Bald cypress, tree, picture **T** 276
  state tree of Louisiana **L** 348
  See also Cypress
Bald eagles **E** 2
  on front Great Seal of the United States **G** 330
  threatened species **B** 232; picture **B** 230

Balder, Norse god **N** 279
Baldness, loss of hair **H** 2–3
Baldwin, Abraham, American statesman **G** 145

Baldwin I (1058–1118), French crusader and king of Jerusalem. With his brother Godfrey of Bouillon, he was one of original leaders of First Crusade. He succeeded Godfrey as ruler of Jerusalem (1100). Jerusalem became the most important Latin state in the East.
   Crusades, history of **C** 539

Baldwin I (1171–1205?), French crusader and emperor of Constantinople. As Baldwin IX of Flanders, he joined Fourth Crusade and was elected first Latin emperor of Constantinople when the city was captured (1204). He was defeated at battle of Adrianople (1205).

Baldwin, James (1924–), American writer, b. New York, N.Y. A prominent leader and spokesman in the civil rights movement, Baldwin gives insight into what it means to be a Negro today. His novels include *Go Tell It on the Mountain* and *Another Country;* his books of essays include *Notes of a Native Son* and *The Fire Next Time;* and his plays include *Blues for Mr. Charlie,* first produced on Broadway in 1964.
   Negro in American literature **A** 213; **N** 102

Baldwin, Matthias William (1795–1866), American industrialist and philanthropist, b. Elizabethtown, N.J. Baldwin was the first U.S. manufacturer of bookbinders' tools and calico printers' rolls. He built "Old Ironsides," one of the first American locomotives; founded M. W. Baldwin Co. (now Baldwin Locomotive Works); established a school for Negro children; and helped found Franklin Institute.

Baldwin, Robert, Canadian statesman **O** 125
   Canada, history of **C** 73

Baldwin, Stanley, 1st Earl Baldwin of Bewdley (1867–1947), English statesman, b. Bewdley. Baldwin was elected Conservative member of Parliament (1908). As chancellor of the exchequer (1922–23), he negotiated settlement of Britain's war debt to United States. He served three terms as prime minister (1923–24, 1924–29, 1935–37) and also was lord president of the council (1931–35).

Balearic (bal-e-ARR-ic) **Islands,** east of Spain **I** 427; **S** 356; picture **I** 431
Baleen (ba-LEEN), or whalebone **W** 147, 152
Baleen whales, or mysticetes **W** 149
   special food adaptations of mammals **M** 66
   whaling **W** 152
Balers, farm machinery **F** 60; pictures **F** 61

Balewa (ba-lay-WA), **Alhaji Sir Abubakar Tafawa** (1912–1966), Nigerian political leader, b. Bauchi. He was elected to the House of Assembly of the Northern Region of Nigeria (1946) and served as representative of the Northern Provinces in the Legislative Council (1947–51). A founder (1951) of the Northern Peoples Congress (NPC) Party, he was elected to the federal House of Representatives. He held several ministerial posts (1952–57), becoming prime minister of the Federation of Nigeria (1957–63) and of the Federal Republic of Nigeria (1963–66). He was killed in a military coup in 1966.

Balfour, Arthur James, 1st Earl of Balfour and Viscount Traprain (1848–1930), English statesman, b. Whittinghame, East Lothian. Balfour served as Conservative member of Parliament (1886–1911) and head of his party for over 20 years (after 1891) and as prime minister

(1902–05). He retired (1911) but resumed office in coalition government of 1915 as first Lord of the Admiralty and later as foreign secretary (1916–19). He wrote Balfour Declaration, stating that British Government favored establishment of a Jewish state in Palestine (1917). He was also representative to the League of Nations (1920). Writings include *Foundations of Belief* and *Theism and Thought.*

Balfour Declaration, 1917 **J** 112
   support for Zionism **Z** 371
   Weizmann, Chaim **W** 118
Bali (BA-li), Indonesia **I** 219–20
   dancing an ancient art **D** 31–32
   funeral ceremony, cremation, picture **F** 495
   Hindu ceremony, picture **H** 131
Balkans **B** 19
   Albania **A** 145
   architecture, late Byzantine churches **B** 490
   Bulgaria **B** 439–44
   Rumania **R** 355–60
   World War I **W** 275
   World War II **W** 290
   Yugoslavia **Y** 354–59
Balkan Wars **B** 19, 444
Balkhash (bol-KASH), **Lake,** Kazakh Republic of U.S.S.R. **L** 26
Ball **B** 20–21
   antique baseball started museum **B** 80
   bowling ball **B** 345, 346
   dodge ball, game **G** 14
   golf **G** 254, 262
   official baseball **B** 70
   official basketball **B** 82
   softball **S** 229
   volleyball **V** 387
   See also names of individual ball games, as Baseball

Ball, George Wildman (1909–), U.S. lawyer and public official, b. Des Moines, Iowa. He began his career as a government lawyer (1933–35), practiced law in Chicago (1935–42), and was associate general counsel for the Lend-Lease Administration (1942–44). He directed the U.S. Strategic Bombing Survey in London (1944–45). Ball was under secretary of state for economic affairs, then under secretary of state (1961–66). He served as U.S. representative at the United Nations, 1968.

Ball, Lucille (1911–), American actress, b. Jamestown, N.Y. She appeared in numerous films during the 1930's and 1940's, but she is perhaps best-known as one of television's top comediennes. Her shows *I Love Lucy, The Lucy Show,* and *Here's Lucy* have been consistently top-rated. In 1967–68 she won an Emmy Award for *The Lucy Show.* She is president of Desilu Productions (1962–).

Balla (BA-la), **Giacomo,** Italian futurist painter **M** 391
   Dog on a Leash, painting **M** 390
Ballade (bal-LOD), a musical form **M** 535
Ballade, a poetic form **P** 353
Ballads (BAL-lads) **B** 22–23; **M** 535
   American folk ballads **F** 310–11
   folklore **F** 303
   folk music **F** 318
   narrative poems suitable for singing **P** 354
   sagas and Scandinavian literature **S** 51
   See also Folk music
Ballast, for railroad roadbeds **R** 77, 78

Ball bearing, circular part of a machine containing small steel balls that roll on a track. The ball bearing is fitted into moving parts of a machine for smooth running and less friction. It is used in bicycles, for example, to make wheels turn easily. This is also the name of the ball used in such a bearing.

Ball clay C 178
Ballet (BAL-lay) B 23–29
  Canada C 63
  dance music development D 36–37
  dance spectacles D 25–26
  festivals M 551
  Leningrad Ballet School, picture U 40
  Midsummer Night's Dream, A, picture D 25
  musical comedy, first use as part of plot M 543
  New York City Ballet's home, Lincoln Center L 298
  Petrouchka U 64
  Serenade, picture D 22
  Stravinsky's ballet music S 437
Ballets Russes de Monte Carlo B 28; M 406
Ballinger, Richard A., American politican T 8
Ballistic Missile Early Warning System (BMEWS) U 161
Ballistic missiles M 344
Ball lightning F 286
Balloonfish, picture F 183
Balloons and ballooning B 30–34
  aerodynamics of A 40
  aviation history A 567
  hydrogen used in H 305–06
  IGY use for weather studies I 317; picture I 316
  Missouri's role in ballooning history M 374–75
  mistaken for flying saucers F 285
  observatories send up telescopes O 13–14
  Piccard, Auguste P 244
  races, first international balloon M 374
  solar research with E 29
  Why do balloons float? F 251–52
Ballot (BAL-lot) E 114–15
  origin of the word B 21
Ball-point pens P 146–47
  ink I 255
Ballroom dancing, or social dancing D 26–28
Ball's Bluff, Virginia, site of Civil War battle C 322
Ball valves, diagram V 269
Balmaceda (bal-ma-SADE-a), **José Manuel,** president of
    Chile C 255
Balsa (BALL-sa), tree
  lightest wood in commercial use W 228
  wood used for airplane models A 104
Balsam fir, tree
  leaves, needlelike, pictures L 119
Balsas, fishing boats P 163; pictures A 252, B 304,
    L 30, 50
Balta (BOL-ta), **José,** president of Peru P 166
Baltic (BALL-tic) **languages**
  Union of Soviet Socialist Republics U 27
Baltic Sea O 45

Baltic States, countries of Lithuania, Estonia, and Latvia, situated on the Baltic Sea. Formerly part of the Russian Empire, they became independent in 1918, but were reannexed by the Soviet Union in 1940. They are now republics of the Soviet Union.
  constituent republics of the U.S.S.R. U 43–44
  World War II W 287–88

Baltimore, Lord see Calvert, George
Baltimore, Maryland B 35; M 120, 125
  Star-Spangled Banner Flag House F 248
Baltimore and Ohio Railroad R 89
  first electric locomotive L 331
  first in U.S. to provide public transportation T 264
  Maryland section M 121–22

Baltimore orioles, birds B 219–20; picture B 233
  Maryland, state bird of M 115
  nest, picture B 213
Balto-Slavic languages L 39; U 27
Baluba (ba-LU-ba), a people of Africa A 76
Balustrades
  escalators E 174–75
Balzac, Honoré de, French novelist B 36; F 441
  great European novelists N 348
  Rodin's *Monument to Balzac,* picture M 387
Bamako (BAM-ak-o), capital of Mali M 59
Bambara (bom-BAR-a), a people of central West Africa
  African sculpture A 70, 72, 76
  Mali M 58
Bamboo, giant grass G 318
  jungle growth J 154
Bamboo Curtain, imaginary barrier between Communist
    Asia and the West I 323
Banana B 36–38; F 484
  Costa Rican export, picture C 514
  Ecuador, world's largest producer E 56; picture
    L 59
  flower, picture F 276
  Guatemalan crop, picture G 394
  Honduras H 195, 197
  Puerto Rican crop, picture P 520
  Somali crop, picture S 254
Banaras, India G 25
Bancroft, George, American historian H 137
  historical writing in American literature A 202
Band, The, American rock music group R 262d

Banda (BON-da), **Hastings Kamuzu** (1906–), 1st president of Malawi, b. Kasungu District, Nyasaland. He was prime minister of Nyasaland (1963–64) and remained prime minister when Nyasaland became the Commonwealth nation of Malawi (1964). When Malawi became a republic (1966), Dr. Banda was elected its 1st president.
  Malawi, history of M 51

Bandages and bandaging
  tourniquets, splints, use of, pictures F 157, 162
Bandai-san, volcano, Japan V 382

Bandaranaike, (bon-da-ra-NY-kee), **Sirimavo Rawatte Dias** (1916–), Sri Lankan (Ceylonese) political leader, b. Balangoda. She was the first woman prime minister of a modern nation, serving Sri Lanka in this office 1959–65 and 1970–77. She succeeded her husband, **Solomon West Ridgeway Bandaranaike** (1899–1959; b. Colombo), who was assassinated. He founded the Sri Lanka Freedom Party and became prime minister in 1956.
  Sri Lanka, history of S 392d
  women, role of W 213

Banda (BON-da) **Sea,** part of the Pacific Ocean encircled by the Indonesian islands. The sea contains the Banda Islands, noted for spices since their discovery by the Portuguese in the 16th century.

Bandeira (bon-DAI-ra), **Manuel** (1886–1968), Brazilian writer, b. Pernambuco. Bandeira was director of Sociedade Brasileira de Música de Câmara. He won literary prize (1946) of Brazilian Institute of Education and Culture. His works include *Poesia e Prosa, Biografia de Gonçalves Dias,* and *Pasásgala,* his memoirs.

Banderillos (bon-dai-RI-lyos), in bullfighting B 449–51
Bandicoots, marsupials K 174
Bands and band music B 38–41
  circus music C 301

Bands and band music (continued)
drum **D** 333–36
how bands differ from orchestras **O** 182, 183
jazz bands **J** 59
military marches of Elgar **E** 176, 271
percussion instruments **P** 151–53
rock music **R** 262a–262b, 262d
The President's Own, U.S. Marine Corps Band
U 182
wind instruments **W** 182–83
See also Orchestra; Percussion Instruments; Wind Instruments
Band saws, tools **T** 218
Bandung, Indonesia, picture **I** 220

Bandung (bon-DOONG) **Conference,** meeting in Bandung, Indonesia (April, 1955), of 29 Asian and African nations to discuss common problems. The conference, the first of its kind ever held, symbolized the desire of Asian and African peoples for a voice in world affairs. The participants discussed economic and cultural co-operation, world peace, human rights, and colonialism.

Banff National Park, Alberta, Canada **B** 42–43
Valley of the Ten Peaks, picture **A** 146f
Banff School of Fine Arts **B** 43
Bangaway of Sirrah Crest, champion boxer dog **D** 261
Bangkok, capital of Thailand **T** 151; pictures **C** 308,
S 332; **T** 147, 148
Buddha's statue, picture **B** 423
permanent headquarters of SEATO **S** 335
Bangladesh (BANG-la-desh), formerly East Pakistan
B 44–44c; **P** 41
flag **F** 237
Bangor, Maine **M** 44
Bang's disease, of cattle **C** 149
Bangui, capital of Central African Empire **C** 173
Banjarmasin (bon-jer-MA-sin), Indonesia **B** 337; **I** 221
Banjo **F** 329; picture **F** 330
Banjul, formerly Bathurst, capital of Gambia **G** 9
Bankhead, William Brockman, American statesman **A** 125
Bank holidays, in Great Britain **H** 152
Banking Act, 1933 **B** 48
Bank notes, issuing of **B** 47
Bank of England **B** 47; **L** 335
nationalized in 1946 **U** 78
Bank of North America **B** 47
Bank of the United States **B** 47
Andrew Jackson opposes **J** 7
Tyler, John **T** 341
Banks, of the continental shelf **F** 218
Banks and banking **B** 44d–51
automation employed in **A** 531–32
depressions and recessions **D** 122
inflation and deflation, control of **I** 253
installment buying, rates on loans for **I** 289
interest **P** 149–50
international trade operates through **I** 329
Jackson's pet banks **J** 7
Roosevelt institutes deposit insurance **R** 321
Rothschild family **R** 337
See also Inflation and deflation; Money

Banks Islands, South Pacific volcanic island group. A part of the New Hebrides chain, they are administered jointly by Great Britain and France. The islands were discovered (1793) by English naval officer William Bligh.

Bannack, Montana **M** 442
Banneker, Benjamin, American mathematician **N** 93
Banners, flags **F** 225
heraldry **H** 115, 117

Bannister, Sir Roger Gilbert, English champion miler
B 51
Bannockburn, battle of, 1314 **S** 88
wins sovereignty for Robert Bruce **B** 414
Banquets
food in ancient times **F** 333

Banshee, or **banshie,** in Celtic folklore, supernatural being or spirit whose appearance or wailing foretells the death of some person. The word comes from the Gaelic *bean,* meaning "woman," and *sith,* meaning "fairy." The banshee is portrayed in Irish folklore as either a lovely weeping maiden or an ugly old hag.

Bantam chickens **P** 420
Bantamweight, in boxing **B** 352
Banting, Sir Frederick Grant, Canadian doctor and scientist **B** 52; **D** 217; picture **D** 216

Bantu, aboriginal inhabitants of central and southern Africa. Numerically and geographically they are the most important ethnolinguistic group in Africa. The various Bantu tribes share no particular racial or cultural characteristic other than language. The Bantu language family includes over 200 languages and dialects, among them Zulu and Swahili.
African literature in Bantu languages **A** 76b
Congo **C** 462
South West Africa **S** 336
Swazi tribe **S** 480b
Zaïre **Z** 366a

Bantustans, or homelands for Bantus of South Africa
S 268–69
Banyan trees **G** 203; picture **G** 202
aerial roots of trees **T** 279
Great Banyan Tree, in Calcutta **C** 11
Baobab trees, or **bottle trees** **P** 283
famous trees in the Sudan **S** 447
Bao Dai, emperor of South Vietnam **V** 334c, 335
Baptism **E** 41
Jesus Christ **J** 83
sacrament of Roman Catholic Church **R** 301
Baptist Church **P** 484
Baptistery of Florence Cathedral, Ghiberti's doors **I** 467;
R 163–64; picture **R** 165
Bar, or measure, in musical notation **M** 531

Barabbas (bar-AB-as), in New Testament (Matthew 27: 16–21), criminal released by Pontius Pilate upon the request of the people of Judea at the time that Jesus was condemned. Pilate, the Roman governor customarily permitted the people of Judea to choose one prisoner who should go free each year during Passover.

Barada River, Syria, picture **S** 505

Barak (ba-ROK) (from Hebrew, meaning "lightning"), in the Old Testament (Judges 4–5), the son of Abinoam of the tribe of Naphtali. Under the direction of Israelite judge Deborah he commanded a force of 10,000 men from Zebulun and Naphtali against Canaanite forces under Sisera at the Plain of Esdraelon. He conquered Sisera, relieving Israel of Canaanite oppression.

Baranof (ba-RA-nof), **Alexander,** first Russian governor of Alaska **A** 142, 143
Barataria (bar-a-TAR-ia) **Bay,** Louisiana **L** 23
Barb, a type of horse **H** 238
Barbados (bar-BAY-doze) **B** 53; **C** 116–19
flag **F** 241
Barbara Fritchie, poem by Whittier **M** 125

Barbarian tribes, in Europe during Middle Ages **M** 296
  art as a record **A** 438b, 438c, 438e
  Italian art of early Middle Ages **I** 458
  sculpture **S** 96

Barbarossa ("Redbeard"), name of two Barbary pirates. **Barbarossa I** (Horush, or Arouj) (1473?–1518) was head of a band of pirates who raided Spanish and North African coasts. After his death, his brother **Barbarossa II** (Khizr, or Khair ed-Din) (1466?–1546) became head of pirates and formed alliances with several Turkish sultans. He was appointed admiral of Turkish fleet (1533) and captured Tunis for Turkey (1534).

Barbarossa, Frederick *see* Frederick I, or Frederick Barbarossa
Barbary corsairs, pirates **P** 263
  early history of U.S. Marines **U** 177
Barbary States, North Africa
  piracy **P** 263
Barbecueing O 247
Barbed wire
  World War I **W** 274
Barbells, weights used for exercise **W** 107
Barbels, feelers of fish **F** 193
Barber, Samuel, American composer **O** 139
Barber of Seville, The, opera by Rossini **O** 140
Barberry, plant
  wheat rust, host of **F** 498
Barbers
  early doctors and surgeons **M** 205
Barbieri, Francisco Asenjo, Spanish composer **S** 373

Barbirolli (bar-bir-O-li) **Sir John** (1899–1970), English symphony and opera conductor, b. London. Barbirolli began his career as a cellist (1911). He formed Barbirolli Chamber Orchestra (1925) and was conductor of New York Philharmonic Orchestra (1936–42). Knighted in 1949, he was conductor in chief of the Hallé Orchestra, Manchester, and conductor emeritus of Houston Symphony.

Barbiturates (bar-BIT-u-rates), drugs **D** 326
  abuse of **D** 330
Barbizon School, of French painting **F** 426; **P** 29
  modern art **M** 387

Barbosa (ber-BORJ-a), **Ruy** (1849–1923), Brazilian statesman, jurist, and writer, b. São Salvador. An advocate of individual freedom, Barbosa was active in establishing Brazilian republic (1889). He was representative to The Hague Peace Conference (1907) and member of Permanent Court of International Justice (1921–23).
  Brazil, history of **B** 384

Barbuda, Caribbean island (Lesser Antilles group) **C** 118
Barca, Pedro Calderón de la *see* Calderón de la Barca, Pedro
Barcarolle, a musical form **M** 535
Barcelona (bar-cel-O-na), Spain **S** 355–56; pictures **S** 350, 354, 365

Bardeen, John (1908–   ), American physicist, b. Madison, Wis. He was the first person to receive two Nobel prizes in the same field. In 1948, Bardeen, W.H. Brattain, and W. Shockley invented the transistor. In 1956 they received the Nobel prize in physics for work on semiconductors, from which transistors are made. In 1972, Bardeen shared a second Nobel prize with Leon N. Cooper and John R. Schrieffer for work in superconductivity. Picture **E** 147

Bards, wandering poet-singers of British Isles and Gaul, chiefly during early Middle Ages. They composed and recited verses about heroic deeds and important people while accompanying themselves on the harp.
  Africa's bards or minstrels **A** 76a
  early Irish literature **I** 392

Barefoot skiing W 63

Barenboim, Daniel (1942–   ), Israeli pianist and conductor, b. Buenos Aires. He made his first public appearance in Buenos Aires at the age of 7. His family settled in Israel in 1952. Barenboim has played and conducted with the Israel Philharmonic Orchestra, the English Chamber Orchestra, and many other leading orchestras.

Barents (BAR-ents), **Willem,** Dutch navigator **E** 384
Barents Sea O 45–46
Bar examinations, for lawyers **L** 92
Bargain basements, in department stores **D** 119
Barges, boats
  dump scows for dredging **D** 309
Bar graphs G 309–11
Bariba, African people **B** 139
Barite, mineral **G** 138
  Arkansas, leading producer **A** 426
Baritone, male voice **C** 277
  voice training **V** 375
Barium (BARR-ium), element **E** 154, 159
  barium sulphate, use for X ray pictures **M** 208h
Bark, of trees **T** 280
  cork oak tree **C** 505
  defense against weather **P** 283
  wood and wood products **W** 225
Barkley, Alben W., American statesman **T** 301; **V** 331;
  picture **V** 330
Barley, grain **G** 284, 287
  Colombian farm, picture **C** 381
  grasses **G** 318
  seeds and ear, pictures **G** 283
Barlow, Joel, American poet and diplomat **A** 198
  quoted on patriotic songs **N** 15
Bar magnets
  demonstrating magnetic lines of force **E** 129–30, 132
Bar Mitzvah, ceremony in Judaism **J** 118, 119
Barnacles, a kind of crustacean **S** 171

Barnard, Christiaan Neethling (1922–   ), South African surgeon, b. Beaufort West, S.A. He performed the first successful human heart transplant at Cape Town in December, 1967. The patient lived 18 days. Dr. Barnard, who received a Ph.D. at the U. of Minnesota Medical School, had his most notable success with transplant patient Dr. Philip Blaiberg, who lived for 19 months with his new heart. Dr. Barnard is the creator of the Barnard valve, used in open-heart surgery.

Barnard, Henry, American educator **C** 475

Barnburners, progressive reform faction of New York State Democratic Party during 1840's. The nickname (from Dutch story of farmer who burned his barn to eliminate rats) was coined by opponents who felt the group's proposed plans would destroy institutions they were trying to save. Barnburners nominated Martin Van Buren for president (1848) and then united with Free Soil Party. Many joined Republican Party when it was formed (1854).
  Van Buren, Martin **V** 275

Barn dances *see* Square dances
Barnegat (BAR-ne-gat) **Lighthouse,** New Jersey, picture **N** 174

Barns, for farm animals
   stanchions versus loose housing **D** 7; picture **D** 6
Barn swallows, birds **B** 219; picture **B** 218

Barnum, Phineas Taylor (1810–91), American showman, b. Bethel, Conn. As a boy, he worked in his father's grocery store. An ardent abolitionist, he published a Danbury newspaper, the *Herald of Freedom.* In 1834 he entered show business. An imaginative promoter, he won fame by sponsoring such attractions as Tom Thumb and Jenny Lind. In 1881 he and John Bailey produced the famous circus now run by Ringling Bros.
   exhibited Jumbo, the elephant **E** 171
   was mayor of Bridgeport, Conn. **C** 477

Barographs, weather instruments **W** 83
Baroja (ba-RO-ha), **Pío,** Spanish writer **S** 371
Barometer (ba-ROM-et-er) **B** 54
   make a barometer **E** 366
   pressure observations of weather **W** 82–83
   Torricelli's barometer **E** 351
   use of vacuum principle **V** 263
Barons, members of the nobility, feudal lords
   England, power struggle with king **E** 217–19, 220
   Magna Carta and King John **M** 22
Baroque (ba-ROKE) **architecture** **B** 55–62
   architecture, history of **A** 383
   City Hall, Brussels, picture **B** 131
   Latin America **L** 64
   Russian architecture **U** 53
   Spain **S** 363
Baroque art **B** 55–62
   Bernini, Giovanni Lorenzo **B** 148
   decorative arts **D** 77
   French Academy combats **F** 437
   furniture design **F** 508
   Italian art and architecture **I** 472
   Latin America **L** 63
   painting **P** 23
   Rubens, Peter Paul **R** 348
   sculpture **S** 101
   Spanish art influenced by Caravaggio **S** 361–62
Baroque music **B** 62–66
   German composers **G** 182–83
   opera, development of the aria **O** 131–32
   sonata, before classical age **C** 331
   sonatas **M** 539
Baroque pearl **B** 55
Barracudas (barr-a-CU-das), fish **F** 188; picture **F** 183
   swimming speed **A** 290
Barranquilla (bar-ron-KI-ya), Colombia **C** 383
Barre (BAR), for ballet practice, picture **B** 24
Barre (BARRIE), Vermont **V** 318
Barred galaxies **U** 198
Barrel cacti **C** 4
Barrels, of guns **G** 425
Barrels, wooden **D** 89
Barren Grounds, Northwest Territories, Canada **Y** 363
   Barren Ground caribou **H** 219
   See also Tundra
Barrie, Sir James Matthew, Scottish writer **B** 67
   dressed his realism in fantasy and humor **D** 298
   children's literature **C** 241
   English literature, place in **E** 267–68
   Peter Pan, excerpt **P** 167–68
Barrientos Ortuño, René, president of Bolivia **B** 306
Barrier beaches
   Atlantic City, N.J. on Absecon Beach **N** 166
   New York's Fire Island **N** 215
Barrier reefs
   coral **C** 504
   Great Barrier Reef, Australia **A** 503

Barristers, lawyers **L** 93
   courts **C** 529
Barro Colorado, island, Panama Canal Zone **P** 44
Barrow, Alaska **A** 140

Barrow, Errol Walton (1920–), political leader, b. Barbados, West Indies. He was elected premier of Barbados in 1961. After the island achieved independence in 1966, he became prime minister and served until 1976.

Barry, Charles, English architect **E** 241

Barry, John (1745–1803), American naval officer, b. County Wexford, Ireland. Barry went to America (1760) and was one of first to be commissioned captain (1776) in Revolutionary War. As commander of the *Lexington,* he captured the *Edward,* first British ship taken by Americans. He was commissioned senior captain (1794), then the navy's highest rank, and supervised construction of frigate *United States,* which he later commanded.
   Revolutionary War, at sea **R** 205

Barry, Philip, American playwright **A** 216
Barrymore family, Ethel, Lionel, and John, American actors **B** 67–68
Bar soaps, manufacturing process **D** 148
BART, transportation system **S** 30
Barter, system of economics **T** 242
   use of money replaces barter **M** 409–10
   William Penn trades tools for land, picture **A** 191
Bartered Bride, The, opera by Bedřich Smetana **O** 140
Barter Theater, Abingdon, Virginia **V** 353

Barth, Karl (1886–1968), Swiss Protestant theologian, b. Basel, Switzerland. Professor of theology at the University of Basel, Barth stressed that man could not know God through the power of reason, but only through the Bible and through Christ.

Barthé (bar-TAY), **Richmond** (1901–), American sculptor, Negro, b. Bay St. Louis, Miss. Barthé executed a bust of Booker T. Washington for Hall of Fame and various coins for Republic of Haiti. His other works, which have been viewed in most major U.S. museums, include *African Boy Dancing* and *Negro Mother.*

Bartholdi (bart-ol-DI), **Frédéric Auguste,** French sculptor **L** 168
Bartholomew (bar-THOL-o-mew), **Saint,** one of the 12 Apostles **A** 333
Bartholomew Fair, England **F** 10; picture **F** 11

Bartlett, Captain Bob (Robert Abram Bartlett) (1875–1946), American Arctic explorer, b. Brigus, Newfoundland, Canada. Bartlett commanded *Roosevelt* on Arctic voyage (1905–09) and also made expeditions to Arctic, Ellesmere Land, Siberia, and Labrador (between 1917 and 1945). He wrote *Last Voyage of the Karluk* and *Sails over Ice.*

Bartlett, Josiah, American physician and Revolutionary War patriot **N** 161
Bartlett pear **P** 112
Bartók (BAR-toke), **Béla,** Hungarian composer **B** 68; **H** 283
   modern music **M** 401

Bartolommeo (bart-o-lo-MAY-o), **Fra** (Bartolommeo di Pagolo del Fattorini) (1475–1517), Italian painter, b. Savignano, Tuscany. He was also called Baccio della Porta. An important figure in Florentine school in High Renaissance, he excelled in painting drapery and in coloring. Most of his works are found today in Pitti Palace, Florence, including his masterpiece, *St. Mark*.

Bartram, John (1699–1777), American botanist, b. Chester County, Pa. Known as father of American botany, he founded country's first botanical garden near Philadelphia, Pa.

Baryshnikov, Mikhail Nikolayevich (1948–), Russian dancer, b. Riga, Latvia. He studied dance in Riga and in 1966 joined the famed Kirov Ballet of Leningrad. Although he received wide acclaim in the Soviet Union, he felt his artistic expression was limited. In 1974, while with the Bolshoi Ballet in Canada, he defected. He later joined the American Ballet Theatre.

Barzun, Jacques (1907–), American historian and educator, b. Paris, France. He came to United States (1919) and became citizen (1933). He is a member of Columbia University faculty (since 1927), and was dean of faculties and provost (1958–67). His works include *Teacher in America* and *The American University.*

Basal metabolism, the minimum amount of energy needed by an animal or plant to carry out basic processes such as breathing. It is measured in terms of the rate (basal metabolic rate) at which oxygen is taken in by the organism when at rest.

Basic English, system using 850 normal English words, designed by British scholar C. K. Ogden about 1925. It was devised for use in international communication and is used to teach English and to clarify and simplify writings in English.

Basilica (ba-SIL-ica) (from Greek word *basilikos*, meaning "royal"), a long rectangular building with interior colonnades and at least one apse (semicircular projection). Basilicas were originally Greek and Roman justice or assembly halls. Their architectural plan was widely used for churches.

Basil (BAZ-il) **the Great, Saint** (330?–379), doctor of the Christian Church, b. Caesarea, Cappadocia. He founded first monastery in Asia Minor at Pontus (about 360) and became known as the Patriarch of Eastern Monasticism. He was ordained a priest (about 365), and later became bishop of Caesarea (370). Basil tried to stamp out heresies within the Church, especially Arianism, which denied the divinity of Christ. His feast is celebrated on January 1 in the Eastern Church and January 2 in the Western.

Basov (ba-SOV), **Nikolai** (1922–) Soviet radiophysicist. He has been Deputy Science Director, Lebedev Physics Institute, since 1958. In 1964 he won the Nobel prize in physics for discovering how to produce high-intensity beams of radiation through use of masers and lasers.

Battle of Constantine, The, painting by Piero della Francesca, detail   **R** 167
Battles   **B** 100–02
National Battlefields, parks, and sites, lists   **N** 51
See also names of battles
Battleships *see* Warships
Battuta, or **Batuta, Ibn** *see* Ibn Battuta
Batutsi *see* Tutsi
Batwa *see* Twa, a people of Rwanda
Baucis *see* Philemon and Baucis
Baudelaire (bode-LAIRE), **Charles,** French poet   **F** 440
Baudot (bo-DO), **J. M. E.,** French inventor   **T** 53

Baudouin (BO-dwan) (1930–), king of the Belgians, b. Brussels. Baudouin became Prince Royal (1950) when his father, Leopold III, transferred royal constitutional powers to him because of postwar political unrest. He was crowned king when his father abdicated (1951).

Bauer, Georg *see* Agricola, Georgius
Bauhaus (BOU-house), former German art school
B 103–05;   **G** 171
architecture, history of   **A** 385
furniture design   **F** 510
industrial design   **I** 231
influence on decorative arts   **D** 78
Kandinsky, Wassily   **K** 166

Baum (BOHM), **L. Frank** (Lyman Frank Baum) (1856–1919), American journalist and author of children's stories, b. Chittenango, N.Y. He is best known for series of fantasies for children about the land of Oz, beginning with *The Wonderful Wizard of Oz.* That book and 13 other Oz stories that followed were an attempt to create a distinctly American fairyland. The first Oz book was made into a movie in 1939.

Bauxite (BOK-site), ore of aluminum   **A** 176; picture **R** 272
Arkansas first in U.S. production   **A** 424, 425, 426
bauxite-producing regions of North America   **N** 294
Guyana   **G** 428a
Jamaica   **J** 16
Bavaria (ba-VAIR-ia), Germany   **G** 158
costumes, traditional, picture   **C** 349
Thompson, Benjamin, service in government   **T** 166
Bavarian Alps, in Austria and Germany   **A** 174;   **G** 153
Bay, geographic term *see* by name, as Fundy, Bay of
Bayard, James Asheton, American statesman   **D** 99
Bayard, Thomas F., American statesman   **D** 99
Bay Area Rapid Transit System (BART), transportation system   **S** 30

Bayberry, shrub of eastern coastal North America. It has dark-green leaves about 3 inches long, small flowers, and round, waxy, grayish-white berries. Wax myrtles of southeastern and western coastal North America are similar, belonging to same genus (*Myrica*). The berries are used in making candles and soap.
candles, how to make   **C** 97, 399

Bayeux (ba-YER) **tapestry,** medieval embroidery   **E** 187
Bay leaves, spice   **S** 382; picture **S** 381

Baylor, Elgin (1936–), American basketball player, Negro, b. Washington, D.C. All-American player from Seattle University, he played for Los Angeles Lakers of the National Basketball Association. He was among the league's all-time leading scorers and was frequently named to the NBA All-Star team.

Bay lynxes, or bobcats   **C** 139

Bay of Pigs Invasion *see* Pigs, Bay of
Bayous (BY-os), marshy creeks
Louisiana's bayous   **L** 348; picture **L** 353
Bayou State, nickname for Louisiana   **L** 349

Bay Psalm (SALM) **Book** (correct title, *The Whole Book of Psalms Faithfully Translated into English Metre*), book of psalms adapted by several Puritan ministers in Massachusetts Bay Colony for use with familiar hymn tunes. It is famous as the first book in English printed in the New World (1640).   **H** 313

Bayreuth (by-ROIT), Germany, Federal Republic of
Festival of Wagner's operas   **M** 550;   **W** 2
Bay State, nickname for Massachusetts   **M** 135
Bazaars, pictures   **C** 8;   **I** 381
Bazán, Emilia Pardo *see* Pardo Bazán, Emilia
BB gun, or air rifle   **G** 424
BCG, vaccine against tuberculosis   **D** 212
B-complex vitamins   **V** 370c–370d
Beaches
Australia's Manly Beach, picture   **A** 496
Bahamas' Eleuthera Island, picture   **B** 16
barrier beaches of Louisiana   **L** 351
Brazil's Copacabana, picture   **B** 372
erosion   **E** 283
left by ice ages   **I** 17
New York City, picture   **U** 101
oil pollution, picture   **E** 272d
Tossa del Mar, Spain, picture   **S** 353
Beaconsfield, Earl of *see* Disraeli
Beads, jewelry
early glass articles   **G** 226
Indian beadwork   **I** 157–59
Beagle, dog, picture   **D** 254
Beagle, H.M.S., British ship   **D** 40
Darwin's voyage   **E** 344–45
Beaks, or bills, of birds   **B** 221
eagles   **E** 2
Beal, Frank Peer, American clergyman
inventor of paddle tennis   **P** 11
Bean, Alan L. American astronaut   **S** 345, 346
Beans   **V** 289
biological rhythms in life   **L** 248–49; picture **L** 247
classification   **T** 30
seed, structure of, picture   **F** 283
See also Soybeans
Bear cats, mammals related to mongooses   **G** 89, 91

Beard, Charles Austin (1874–1948), American historian, writer, and educator, b. near Knightstown, Ind. Beard was professor of politics, Columbia University (1915–17) and helped found New School for Social Research. Books written with his wife, **Mary Ritter Beard** (1876–1958), include *A Basic History of the United States* and *The Rise of American Civilization.*

Beard, Daniel Carter, a founder of Boy Scouts of America   **B** 357

Beardsley, Aubrey Vincent (1872–1898), English book illustrator, b. Brighton. Beardsley is known for his stylized, decorative line drawings in black and white. His works include illustrations for Ben Jonson's *Volpone,* Oscar Wilde's *Salomé,* and the English periodical *Yellow Book.*

Bear Festival, of the Ainu   **J** 42
Bear Flag Revolt, California   **T** 112
Bearings, machinery
made of diamonds   **D** 155
watches and clocks   **W** 48

Bearing walls, of buildings **B** 434
  bricks and masonry **B** 392–93
Bear Mountain Bridge, New York, picture
  N 215
Bear Run, Pennsylvania
  Falling Water, house, picture **A** 385
Bears B 106–08
  circus act, picture **C** 300
  dancing bear, picture **G** 433
  foot bones, diagram **F** 81
  partial hibernation of **H** 122
  polar bears, picture **P** 363
  tracks, picture **A** 271
  Yellowstone National Park **Y** 346
Bears and bulls, in stock exchanges **S** 432
Beast, bird, or fish, group game **I** 226
Beast epics F 4
Beasts of burden
  early means of transportation **T** 257
Beasts of prey
  cats **C** 134–41
Beat, in music **S** 262–63
  orchestra conducting **O** 188
Beater goes round, circle game **G** 14

Beatification (be-at-if-ic-A-tion), in Roman Catholic Church, papal act by which a virtuous or holy person is declared blessed after his death. Often this is the first step to canonization. To become beatified, a person must have led a life of heroic virtue and have performed at least two miracles.

Beatles, The, popular English rock group. John Lennon, Paul McCartney, Ringo Starr, and George Harrison began singing together in Liverpool, England (1962), and became known the world over for their originality and versatility as musicians and composers as well as for their singing. They made several movies including *A Hard Day's Night.* They received the Order of the British Empire in 1965. The Beatles officially broke up in 1971 to pursue their individual musical careers. Picture **R** 262b.
  rock music **R** 262c, 262d

Beaton, Cecil Walter Hardy (1904–   ), English photographer, writer, and designer, b. London. His work became known through magazines in England and America. He is noted especially for his photographs of beautiful women and is official photographer of British royal family (since 1939). He wrote *Air of Glory* and other books while working for the British Ministry of Information during World War II. His other books include *The Book of Beauty* and *Cecil Beaton's New York.*

Beatrice, Dante's ideal and inspiration **D** 38;
  I 476
Beats, sections of a city
  assignments of newspaper reporters **N** 201
  covered by patrolmen **P** 375

Beatty (BEAT-ty), **David,** 1st Earl Beatty of the North Sea and of Brooksby (1871–1936), British naval officer, b. Nantwich, Cheshire. Beatty commanded battle cruiser fleet, which led the attack against German fleet at battle of Jutland (1916) in World War I. He was commander in chief of British Grand Fleet (1917–18) and accepted surrender of German Navy (1918). He was admiral of the fleet (1919) and first sea lord (1919–27).

Beauchamp (bo-SHON), **Charles Pierre,** French ballet dancer and choreographer **B** 24, 29
  history of the dance **D** 25

Beaucourt (bo-COOR), **François Malepart de** (1740–1794), Canadian painter, b. Lapraisie, Quebec. The earliest known of native Canadian artists, he specialized in portraits and religious works. His best-known, *Portrait of a Negro Slave,* hangs in National Gallery, Ottawa.

Beaufort (BO-fort) **Sea,** part of the Arctic Ocean lying between Alaska and the Arctic Archipelago. It was partially explored (1915) by Vilhjalmur Stefansson (1879–1962) of Canada.

Beaufort wind scale W 84
Beauharnois (bo-HARN-wa), Quebec, Canada **C** 57
Beaujoyeulx (bo-jwa-YER), **Balthazar de,** Italian-born
  French choreographer **B** 24
Beaumarchais, Pierre, French writer **F** 439

Beaumont (BO-mont), **Francis** (1584–1616), English dramatist, b. Leicestershire. Although he wrote some plays on his own, his best-known works were collaborations with John Fletcher. Beaumont and Fletcher co-authored more than 50 plays, of which the best-known are *The Knight of the Burning Pestle, Philaster,* and *The Maid's Tragedy.*
  drama, history of **D** 296

Beaumont, William, American frontier surgeon **B** 109
  contribution to medicine **M** 207

Beauregard (BO-re-gard), **Pierre Gustave Toutant de** (1818–1893), American Confederate general, b. near New Orleans, La. Beauregard ordered firing on Fort Sumter, which began Civil War (1861). He led South to victory at Bull Run (1861), defended Charleston (1862–64), and together with General Bushrod Johnson surrendered to General Sherman (1865). His writings include *Principles and Maxims of the Art of War.*
  Civil War, history of **C** 318, 322

Beauty culture B 110–11
  See also Cosmetics; Perfumes
Beaver, Indians of North America **I** 164

Beaverbrook, Lord (William Maxwell Aitken, 1st baron of Beaverbrook) (1879–1964), English newspaper publisher and politician, b. Maple, Ontario, Canada. He made his fortune in cement industry and moved to England to enter politics. A Conservative member of Parliament (1910–16), he was raised to peerage (1917). He held various government positions during both world wars and was publisher of three of London's leading newspapers: *Daily Express, Evening Standard,* and *Pall Mall Gazette.* He was known for his strongly conservative views. His works include *Canada in Flanders* and *Men and Power.* **N** 138c

Beaver Island, in Lake Michigan **M** 268
Beavers B 112–14
  aplodontia, or mountain beaver **R** 277; picture
    R 278
  fur **F** 517
  hats **F** 511
  homes of **M** 67
  Indian hunting beaver, picture **C** 68
  tracks, picture **A** 272
Beaver Scouts B 360
Beaver State, nickname for Oregon **O** 193
Bebop, early name for modern jazz **J** 60
Becharof Lake, Alaska **A** 133
Becharre (bish-AR-re), Lebanon, picture **L** 123
Bechet (besh-AY), **Sidney,** jazz musician **J** 58
Bechuanaland see Botswana

Beck, Sir Adam (1857–1925), Canadian financier, b. Baden, Ont. He served as mayor of London, Ont. (1902–04); Conservative member of the Ontario Legislative Assembly (1902–19, 1923–25); and as a provincial cabinet minister without portfolio (1905–14, 1923–25). He led a commission investigating development and distribution of power from Niagara Falls (1903), and introduced the bill creating the Hydro-Electric Power Commission (1906), of which he was chairman until his death.

Becket, Saint Thomas à, English churchman **B** 115
  kings versus clergy in English history **E** 219

Beckett, Samuel (1906–), Irish writer, b. Dublin. He settled permanently in France in 1937 and has written in French since 1945. He has translated several of his own works into English. His best-known play is *Waiting for Godot.* In 1969 he received the Nobel prize.

Beckmann (BECK-monn), **Max** (1884–1950), German expressionist painter, b. Leipzig. His pictures, many taken from incidents during World War I, portray brutality of human nature. His works include *Christ in Limbo* and triptychs *The Actors, Blindman's Buff,* and *Departure.*
  Departure, painting **G** 168

Becknell, William, American pioneer, father of Santa Fe
  trail **O** 257

Beckwourth, James Pierson (1798–1867), American fur trapper, b. Virginia. He accompanied fur-trading expeditions to West. Influential among Crow Indians, he joined expeditions to Missouri, Colorado, and California and fought in Cheyenne War (1864).

Bécquer (BAKER), **Gustavo Adolfo,** Spanish poet **S** 370

Becquerel (BECK-rel), **Antoine Henri** (1852–1908), French physicist, b. Paris. Known for his discovery (1896) of radioactivity, he shared Nobel prize in physics (1903) with Pierre and Marie Curie for work on radioactivity. His physicist father, **Alexandre Edmond** (1820–1891), is known for work on light and its chemical effects. His grandfather **Antoine César** (1788–1878), also a physicist, is considered one of the founders of electrochemistry.

Bedbugs, insects **H** 262; picture **H** 263
Bede, the Venerable, English historian-monk **E** 246–47
  children's books **C** 236
  Christianity, history of **C** 284

Bedford, Gunning, Jr. (1747–1812), American statesman and lawyer, b. Philadelphia, Pa. Prominent in Delaware politics, he served as delegate to the Continental Congress (1785–86) and the Annapolis Convention (1786). At the Constitutional Convention (1787) he strongly supported states' rights and equality in voting.

Bed in Summer, poem by Robert Louis Stevenson **S** 424
Bedivere, knight of King Arthur's court **A** 442

Bedlam, hospital of Saint Mary of Bethlehem in London (name became slurred in popular usage: "Bethlem" and then "Bedlam"). It was built as a monastery (1247) and was later used as a lunatic asylum. Hence the term also refers to a madhouse or any place of noise and confusion.

Bedloe's Island (now Liberty Island), Upper New York
  Bay **L** 168
Bedouins (BED-du-ins), nomadic Arabic tribes **D** 128;
  picture **J** 138

Egypt **E** 90c
Saudi Arabia **S** 45
Syria **S** 506
Beds
  canopy bed, picture **C** 389
  Chinese, picture **D** 73

Beebe (BEE-be), **William** (Charles William Beebe) (1877–1962), American naturalist, explorer, and author, b. Brooklyn, N.Y. He was director of New York Zoological Society Department of Tropical Research (1900–52) and curator of birds at New York Zoological Park (Bronx Zoo). He led many wildlife expeditions to South America and elsewhere. With O. Barton, he was first to explore ocean region of perpetual darkness in record dive (3,028 ft.) with his bathysphere, reported in his book *Half Mile Down.* Other notable books of his are *Jungle Peace* and *The Bird.*
  Beebe and the bathysphere **O** 44; **U** 16

Beech, tree
  uses of the wood and its grain, picture **W** 223

Beecham, Sir Thomas (1879–1961), English symphony and opera conductor and impresario, b. St. Helens, Lancashire. He used his personal fortune to back several orchestras and opera companies, including Covent Garden Opera Company, London Philharmonic Orchestra, and Royal Philharmonic Orchestra. He introduced many operas to English audiences and toured extensively. Beecham was knighted (1915). He wrote his autobiography, *A Mingled Chime.*

Beecher, Henry Ward, American clergyman **B** 115
  "Beecher's Bibles" shipped to Kansas **C** 320

Beecher, Lyman (1775–1863), Presbyterian clergyman; b. New Haven, Conn. He served as pastor of churches in East Hampton, N.Y., Litchfield, Conn., and Boston, and was first president (1832–50) of Lane Theological Seminary in Cincinnati, Ohio. A controversial figure, Beecher won fame for his revivalist preaching, but his views were attacked by more conservative clergymen. He was the father of Henry Ward Beecher and Harriet Beecher Stowe.

Beechey, Frederick William (1796–1856), English explorer. He commanded ship *Blossom* on Arctic expedition (1825–29). He wrote an account of earlier Arctic expedition (1818) on which he accompanied Sir John Franklin.
  Northwest Passage **N** 338

Beef, meat of cattle **M** 192; cuts of, picture **M** 193
  baby beef **C** 148
  cow beef **C** 148–49; **D** 4
  what you eat depends on where you live **F** 332
Beef cattle C 147–49
Beefeaters see Yeomen of the Guard
Beehive State, nickname for Utah **U** 241, 254
Beekeeping H 202

Beelzebub (be-EL-ze-bub) (from Hebrew *Baal-zebub,* meaning "Lord of Flies"), Philistine god worshiped at Ekron. Considered a false god by Jews in Old Testament (II Kings 1: 3,6), he is mentioned in New Testament (Matthew, Mark, and Luke) as prince of devils. He appears in Milton's *Paradise Lost* as a fallen angel ranking second only to Satan.

Beer, Jakob Liebmann see Meyerbeer, Giacomo
Beer and brewing B 116–17
  malt extract from barley **G** 286
Beerbohm (BEER-bome), **Sir Max,** English writer **E** 268

Bees **B** 117–24
  adaptations to other organisims **L** 220–21
  biological rhythms **L** 248
  clock-compass **H** 193
  homing, meaning of **H** 185
  honey **H** 200–02
  How do honeybees make honey? **H** 200
  strength of **I** 273
  See also Honey
Beeswax **W** 70
  candles made of **C** 97, 399
  storing of honey **H** 202
Beethoven (BATE-ho-ven), **Ludwig van**, German com-
      poser **B** 124–25
  chamber music **C** 186
  choral music **C** 278
  classical age, compositions of **C** 330, 332, 333
  Fidelio, his only opera **O** 134, 144
  German music **G** 185
  symphonies **M** 541
Beetles, insects, pictures **I** 272, 281
  boll weevil **C** 523
  carpet beetles **H** 262
  freshwater creatures, pictures **L** 257
  ground beetle, picture **I** 262
  leg, diagram **I** 273
  luminescent tracks, picture **B** 197
  plant enemies and pests **P** 284–85, 288–89
  strength of **I** 273–74
  used as biological control for weeds **W** 106
Beets **V** 289; picture **P** 306
  sugar beets **S** 456–57
Beet sugar **S** 456
B.E.F. see British Expeditionary Force
Befana (bay-FA-na), **La**, Italian Santa Claus **C** 292

Begbie, Sir Matthew Baillie (1819–1894), British colonial
judge, b. Edinburgh, Scotland. He was appointed a judge
in colony of British Columbia (1858), where he was
instrumental in maintaining law and order during gold
rush. He was chief justice of mainland of British
Columbia (1869) and of whole province (1870–94).

Beggar's Opera, by John Gay **E** 257; **H** 280; **O** 132

Begin (BAY-ghin), **Menahem** (1913–   ), Israeli prime minister, b. Brest-Litovsk, Russian Poland (now Brest,
U.S.S.R.). Begin grew up in Poland and led a Zionist
youth group in the 1930's. After World War II he led forces
fighting for an independent Jewish state in the Middle
East. He became a member of parliament after Israel was
established and in 1977 was elected prime minister. In
1978 he shared the Nobel peace prize for his efforts toward peace between Israel and Egypt.

Begonia (be-GO-nia), plant **H** 269
  festival in Belgium, picture **B** 128
  tuberous begonia centerpiece, picture **J** 51
Béhanzin (bay-HON-zin), king of Dahomey **B** 140
Behavior
  brain function **B** 363, 369
  impulses to take drugs **N** 13–14
  learning **L** 98–106
  sociology, study of **S** 226–27
Behaviorism, psychology **P** 496–97

Behring (BEAR-ing), **Emil von** (1854–1917), German bac-
teriologist, b. Hansdorf. Known for his work on diphtheria
and tetanus, he discovered that blood serum of an
animal infected with one of these diseases, when
injected into a healthy animal, provided immunity
against that disease. He was first to apply word

"antitoxin" to these substances and was awarded first
Nobel prize in medicine and physiology (1901). **D** 215

Behring, Vitus see Bering, Vitus

Behrman (BEAR-man), **S. N.** (Samuel Nathaniel Behrman) (1893–1973), American playwright known for his
comedies, b. Worcester, Mass. His works include *The
Second Man, No Time for Comedy, and Fanny* (with
Joshua Logan). He also wrote motion picture scenarios.

Beida, Libya **L** 204
Beiderbecke, Leon ("Bix"), American jazz musician **J** 59
Beijerinck (BAY-jer-ink), **M. W.**, Dutch scientist **V** 362
Beirut (bay-ROOT), capital of Lebanon **L** 122; picture
    L 123
Bel see Baal, pagan god

Belafonte (bel-af-ON-te), **Harry** (Harold George Belafonte,
Jr.) (1927–   ), American folk singer and actor, Negro, b.
New York, N.Y. He popularized calypso music. He
appeared on Broadway in *Three for Tonight* and on the
screen in *Carmen Jones, Island in the Sun*, and *The Angel
Levine*. He has also made many concert, nightclub, and
TV appearances. His best-selling records include
"Matilda," "Scarlet Ribbons," and "Try to Remember."
He has been active in civil rights work. Picture **N** 102.

Belasco, David (1854–1931), American theatrical producer and playwright, b. San Francisco, Calif. He was
stage manager of various New York theaters before he
opened first of his own theaters (1902). His success is attributed to careful attention to stage detail, and he was
first to conceal footlights from the audience. He was author and collaborator of many plays, including *The Return
of Peter Grimm* and *The Girl of the Golden West*. **D** 299

Belaúnde (bay-la-ON-day) **Terry, Fernando**, president of
      Peru **P** 166
Belém (bel-EM), Brazil **B** 381; pictures **A** 179; **B** 382

Belep Islands, coral group in southwestern Pacific. A
dependency of New Caledonia, the islands are administered by France.

Belfast, capital of Northern Ireland **U** 73
Belgian Congo **B** 131
  See also Zaïre
Belgian horse, picture **H** 240
Belgium **B** 126–31
  flag **F** 239
  Flemish and Dutch art **D** 349–62
  Industrial Revolution **I** 241
  invasion by Hitler, 1940 **W** 288–89
  invasion in World War I **W** 271–72
  national anthem **N** 21
  Zaïre **Z** 366d
Belgrade, capital of Yugoslavia **Y** 357
Belize, British dependency, Central America
      B 132–33
Belize City, former capital of Belize **B** 132
Bell, Alexander Graham, Scottish-born American inventor
      and scientist **B** 134–35
  airplane research **A** 572
  Alexander Graham Bell Museum, Nova Scotia **N** 344d
  Bell Homestead, place of interest in Ontario **O** 125
  deaf, education of the **D** 52
  dictation machine **O** 57
  telephone **C** 438–39; **T** 56
Bell, Charles, Scottish-born British physician **B** 287
Bell, Chichester, American inventor **P** 197
Bell, Currer, Ellis, and **Acton** see Brontë family

Bell, James Madison (1826–1902), American poet, Negro, b. Gallipolis, Ohio. He was elected delegate from Ohio to Republican National Convention in Philadelphia (1872). A close associate of abolitionist John Brown, he was a noted antislavery orator. His poetry, collected in *Poetical Works*, includes "The Dawn of Freedom," "The Day and the War," and "The Triumph of Liberty."

Bell, John, American statesman T 86
Bell, Joseph, English doctor, model for Sherlock Holmes
    D 288

Bell, Margaret Elizabeth (1898–   ), American author of children's books, b. Prince of Wales Island, Alaska. She is best known for novels set in Alaska, including *Watch for a Tall White Sail* and *The Totem Casts a Shadow*.

Belladonna, drug, from the plant, the deadly nightshade
    D 323; P 322
    plants, medicinal P 314; picture P 315
Bellamy, Edward, American novelist A 206
    Looking Backward U 256
Bellay (bel-LAY), Joachim du, French poet F 434, 436
Belle Isle, Strait of, north of Newfoundland, Canada
    N 141
    Cartier's explorations C 124d
Bellerophon (bell-ER-o-phon), hero in Greek myth G 364
Belleville Breviary, illuminated manuscript, picture
    B 319
Bellevue, Nebraska N 82

Bellingshausen (BELL-ings-how-zen) Sea, part of the South Pacific off Antarctic, between Palmer Peninsula to the east and Thurston Peninsula to the west. It was named for Fabian Gottlieb von Bellingshausen, the leader of a Russian Antarctic expedition (1819–21).
    arm of the Antarctic Ocean O 45

Bellingrath Gardens, Alabama, picture A 123
Bellini (bel-LI-ni), Giovanni, Venetian painter P 21
    Bellini family B 136
    Renaissance art R 169
    Titian, pupil of Bellini T 199

Bellini, Vincenzo (1801–1835), Italian composer, b. Catania, Sicily. Known chiefly for his operas, he is noted for elegance of his melodic style, which has been compared to Chopin's. His best-known operas are *I Puritani, La Sonnambula*, and *Norma*.
    Italian styles in opera O 135
    Norma, opera O 149

Bellini family, Jacopo, Gentile, and Giovanni, Italian
    painters B 136
Bell Island, Newfoundland, Canada
    iron mines at Wabana N 143
Bellman, Carl Michael, Swedish poet S 52

Bello (BAY-o), Andrés (1781–1865), South American educator, statesman, and author, b. Caracas, Venezuela. He accompanied Simón Bolívar to London and served on Colombian, Venezuelan, and Chilean legations (1810–29). As Chilean secretary of state (1834), he wrote Chilean code of civil law. His works include *Silva a la agricultura de la zona tórrida*. L 71
    Chile, history of C 255

Belloc, Hilaire (Joseph Hilary Pierre Belloc) (1870–1953), English writer, b. St. Cloud, France. He was a Liberal member of Parliament (1906–10). With G. K. Chesterton and C. Chesterton he founded *New Witness*, a review designed to attack political abuses (1912). He was leader

of intellectual Catholicism in England. Among Belloc's numerous works are *The Bad Child's Book of Beasts*, a four-volume *History of England*, and a travel journal, *The Path to Rome*.
    The Yak, nonsense rhyme N 274

Bellow, Saul, American novelist A 213; N 349
Bellows, for making fires hotter F 143
Bellows, George Wesley, American artist U 122
    Anne in White, painting U 118
Bells B 136–37
    bronze B 409
    Christmas customs C 290
    communication, use in C 437
    Liberty Bell L 169
    orchestra, use in P 153
Bell-shaped curve, or normal curve, in probability
    P 472

Bell-Smith, Frederic Marlett (1846–1923), Canadian painter, b. London, England. Noted for landscapes and street scenes, he was one of the founders of Society of Canadian Artists (1867). Works include *Lights of a City Street* and *Tower Bridge, London*.

Bell Telephone Company
    library in Holmdel, New Jersey, picture L 178
    public utilities P 513
Bell towers see Campaniles
Belmont Stakes, horse race H 232
Belmopán, capital of Belize B 132
Belorussia (byel-o-RU-sia) (Belorussian Soviet Socialist
    Republic) B 138; U 27, 37
    flag F 239

Belshazzar (bel-SHAZZ-ar), in Old Testament (Daniel 5), son of Nabonidus, last Chaldean king of Babylonia. During a feast at which he allowed his court to drink from vessels taken from temple, mysterious handwriting appeared on wall. Daniel interpreted it as end of Chaldean kingdom, and that night Belshazzar was killed and Babylonia conquered (539 B.C.). The phrase "handwriting on the wall" now refers to impending calamity.

Belt conveyors H 145
Belt loaders, construction equipment B 446
Beltsville Small White, turkeys P 423
Beltways, or ringroads, around cities
    Baltimore and Washington, D.C. M 121
Belugas, whales W 147; picture W 149
Bely, Andrei, Russian author U 62

Belyayev, Pavel I. (1925–70), Russian cosmonaut, b. Chelishchevo. A fighter pilot during World War II, he later served in the Far East and Black Sea areas before joining the cosmonaut program (1960). He commanded space craft Voskhod II (1965) when Aleksei Leonov made first walk in space. Both are heroes in the Soviet Union.
    space flight data S 344

Bemelmans (BEM-el-mans), Ludwig (1898–1962), American author and illustrator, b. Merano, Austria (now in Italy). He went to United States (1914) and became a citizen (1918). He wrote and illustrated books for children and adults. He is known for his humor and whimsical charm of his stories and paintings. His books for children include *Parsley, Quito Express,* and *Madeline's Rescue,* which won Caldecott Medal in 1954. Some of his adult books are *How to Travel Incognito* and *Best of Times.*
    Madeline's Rescue, picture from B 309
    picture books for children C 243

Ben, meaning in names   **N** 5
Benares, India see Banaras
Benavente (bay-na-VEN-tay), **Jacinto,** Spanish writer
  S 371

Ben Bella, Ahmed (1919–), former premier of Algeria, b. Marnia. One of the "nine fathers of Algerian independence," he helped found Secret Organization (1947) and took part in other nationalist activities; he was captured and ·jailed by the French (1956–61). He was named vice-premier in provisional government (1958), and premier when Algeria won independence (1962). He was president of the Republic of Algeria (1963–65) until ousted by a military coup.
  Algeria, history of   **A** 163

Benchley, Robert Charles (1889–1945), American humorist, writer, and actor, b. Worcester, Mass. He was drama critic for *Life* (1920–29) and *The New Yorker* (1929–40). He wrote, directed, and acted in many screen shorts. He appeared in supporting roles in several motion pictures and participated in many radio programs. His books include *The Early Worm,* and *Inside Benchley.*

Bendick, Jeanne (1919–), American author and illustrator of children's books, b. New York City. She writes non-fiction books for elementary school-age children and has written about 60 and illustrated over 100. Among her books are *The Human Senses* (1968) and *The First Book of Names, Sets, and Numbers* (1971).
  Books: From Author to Library   **B** 329–34

Bends, knots   **K** 291
Bends, the, or caisson disease   **U** 15
  deep-sea divers victims of   **D** 81, 82
  helium mixture helps prevent   **H** 108
  problem for oceanographic research   **O** 42
  tunnels   **T** 318

Benedict XV (Giacomo della Chiesa) (1854–1922), Italian pope (1914–22), b. Pelgi, near Genoa. He became archbishop of Bologna (1907), then cardinal (1914), and he succeeded Pius X as pope. He made repeated statements advocating world peace. The *Code of Canon Law* was issued (1918) during his reign.
  Roman Catholic Church, history of   **R** 298

Benedict, Ruth Fulton (1887–1948), American anthropologist, b. New York, N.Y. She taught at Columbia University (1923–48). While with the U.S. Office of War Information (1943–46), she studied contemporary cultures. Her book about Japan, *The Chrysanthemum and the Sword,* was helpful in shaping U.S. policy there. She believed anthropologists should participate in solving social problems. In *Race: Science and Politics* she tried to disprove theories of racial superiority. She was author of *Patterns of Culture.*

Benedict of Nursia, Saint (480?–543?), Italian monk, called Patriarch of Western Monasticism, b. Nursia, Umbria. He was educated in Rome, where he became disillusioned by the corrupt life around him. He retreated to a cave in Subiaco (500?), and a community of monks grew up around him. He established a monastery (529?) on Monte Cassino that became center of Benedictine Order. He wrote *Regula Monachorum,* a set of strict rules that govern monks of this order.

Benedictines, or Rule of Saint Benedict, religious order
  Christianity and the monasteries   **C** 283;   **M** 294;
  R 291
Benefice (BEN-e-fis) **system,** in Catholic Church   **R** 293

Beneficiaries (ben-e-FI-ci-aries), persons receiving money from insurance, wills, or trusts   **I** 295

Benelux, economic union of Belgium, the Netherlands, and Luxembourg. The original agreement, signed in 1944, was put into effect in 1948. Its primary goal of removing tariff barriers was achieved (1950), but other aims, such as uniform taxes, wages, and prices, have yet to be realized. An example of prosperity through cooperation, it was a precursor of European Common Market.

Beneš (BEN-esh), **Eduard** (1884–1948), Czechoslovakian statesman, b. Kožlany, Bohemia. He worked with Tomáš Masaryk for a Czechoslovak national state (formed 1918). A delegate to Versailles peace conference (1919–20) and to League of Nations (1923–27), he was elected Czechoslovak president (1935). He resigned when Germans invaded (1938) and became head of Czech government-in-exile (1939–45). He was re-elected president after war (1946) but resigned (1948) rather than co-operate with Communists in the government. His writings include *My War Memories* and *Democracy: Today and Tomorrow.*

Benét (ben-AY), **Laura** (1884?–), American poet and author of books for children, b. Fort Hamilton, N.Y. The sister of William Rose and Stephen Vincent Benét, she has written biographies, such as *The Boy Shelley* and *Enchanting Jenny Lind,* and novels *The Hidden Valley* and *Goods and Chattels.*

Benét, Stephen Vincent, American poet   **A** 210

Benét, William Rose (1886–1950), American writer, b. Fort Hamilton, N.Y. Brother of Stephen Vincent Benét, he was on staff of *Century Magazine* (1911–18), N.Y. *Evening Post Literary Review* (1920–24), and *Saturday Review of Literature* (from 1924). His volumes of poetry include *Merchants from Cathay* and *The Falconer of God.* He wrote an autobiography in verse, *The Dust Which Is God,* for which he was awarded the Pulitzer prize (1942). His novels include *The First Person Singular.*

Benevolent and Protective Order of Elks see Elks, Benevolent and Protective Order of (BPOE)
Bengal, Bay of, arm of the Indian Ocean   **O** 47
Bengali, language   **B** 44c
Bengalis, people of Bangladesh   **B** 44, 44c; picture
  B 44a
Bengal tigers   **T** 186;   **C** 136
Benghazi (ben-GHA-zi), Libya, dual capital with Tripoli
  L 203–04
Benguela (beng-EL-a), Angola   **A** 260
Ben-Gurion (ben-GU-ri-on), **David,** first prime minister ·of
  Israel   **B** 138; picture   **P** 456a
Ben Hur, a Story of the Christ, motion picture   **M** 474
Benign tumors, of the body   **C** 89;   **D** 194
Benin (ben-ENE), ancient kingdom in Africa   **N** 256
  early art achievements   **A** 71–72
  ivory carvings, pictures   **A** 73, **I** 488
Benin, modern African country   **B** 139–40
  flag   **F** 235
Benin City, Nigeria   **N** 255

Benjamin, in Old Testament (Genesis 35:16–18), founder of tribe of Benjamin, one of 12 tribes of Israel, and youngest son of Jacob and Rachel. His tribe occupied an area in center of Palestine between Judah on the south and Ephraim on the north.   **J** 140

Benjamin, Judah Philip, British-born American lawyer and statesman   **L** 361

Bennett, Arnold, English novelist   **E** 266

Bennett, Floyd (1890–1928), American aviator, b. Warrensburg, N.Y. Aide to Admiral R. E. Byrd, he accompanied him on expedition to Greenland (1925) and on flight over North Pole (1926). He was awarded Congressional Medal of Honor for first polar flight.

Byrd and Bennett   **B** 481

Bennett, James Gordon (1795–1872), American newspaper publisher, b. Keith, Banffshire, Scotland. He emigrated to Halifax, Nova Scotia, and then to United States (1819). He became Washington correspondent of New York *Enquirer* (1826), and when that paper merged with *Morning Courier* (1829), he served as associate editor (until 1832). He started New York *Herald* (1835), which acquired a tremendous circulation because of Bennett's innovations: accurate, detailed, and often sensational reporting of news events; personal interviews; use of the telegraph in reporting; and distribution by carriers.

Bennett, John, American writer   **C** 241

Bennett, Lerone, Jr. (1928–   ), American author and lecturer, Negro, b. Clarksdale, Miss. A staff member of the Johnson Publishing Company, Inc. (since 1953), he was associate editor of *Jet* magazine and has been senior editor of *Ebony* magazine (since 1960). In addition to short stories and articles for periodicals, he has written *Before the Mayflower: A History of the Negro in America 1619–1964,* and *Black Power, USA.*

Bennett, Richard Bedford, Viscount Bennett (1870–1947), Canadian statesman, b. Hopewell Hill, New Brunswick. Conservative member of Canadian House of Commons (1911–17, 1925–39), he was minister of justice and attorney general (1921), minister of finance (1926), leader of Conservative Party (1927–38), and prime minister (1930–35). During his administration Bank of Canada and Canadian Broadcasting Commission were established. He retired to England (1938) and was made viscount (1941).

New Brunswick, people associated with   **N** 138c

Ben Nevis, highest mountain in Great Britain   **S** 86
Bennington flag, 1777   **F** 229

Benny, Jack (Benjamin Kubelsky) (1894–1974), American comedian, b. Waukegan, Ill. He started his career as a violinist in 1912. The Jack Benny Show, first heard on radio in 1932, was on TV from 1950 to 1964. Benny, perpetually 39, was given a special award (1957) by the National Academy of Television Arts and Sciences for the best continued performance by a male entertainer. Pictures   **R** 58;   **T** 301.

Benson, Benny, designed Alaska's flag   **A** 128
Benteen, Frederick, American army officer   **I** 214

Bentham, Jeremy (1748–1832), English reformer and philosopher, b. London. He was a leading advocate of utilitarianism, a system of ethics defining highest good as "greatest good for the greatest number." He gave up his law practice in order to devote himself entirely to social criticism and reform. His works include *Introduction to the Principles of Morals and Legislation.*

Bentley, E. C., English author of detective stories   **M** 555
Benton, Thomas Hart (1782–1858), American statesman **M** 379
Benton, Thomas Hart (1889–1975), American artist **M** 379

teacher of Jackson Pollock   **P** 387

Bent's Fort, Colorado   **C** 410;   **F** 376
Benue (BEN-oo-ay) **River,** west Africa   **N** 255
Benz, automobile   **A** 545

Benz (BENTS), **Karl** (1844–1929), German engineer and automobile manufacturer, b. Karlsruhe. He is often credited with constructing first practical motorcar (1885), essentially a three-wheeled carriage propelled by a gasoline engine. He established a firm in Mannheim, Germany, for manufacture of motorcars, which merged (1926) with firm of engineer Gottlieb Daimler to manufacture the Mercedes-Benz auto.

Benzene (C_6H_6), a colorless, highly inflammable liquid made by distilling coal tar, also obtainable from petroleum. It has the structure of a six-sided ring with a carbon atom at each corner. Discovered (1825) by Michael Faraday, it is a basic raw material in manufacture of many important chemicals. It is also used as a solvent for paints and varnishes, and in aircraft and auto fuels. It is classed scientifically as an aromatic hydrocarbon.

Faraday's discoveries   **F** 44

Benzine, commercial name for a highly volatile and inflammable mixture of carbon-hydrogen compounds derived from petroleum. It is also referred to as petroleum ether and cleaner's naphtha, since it is used as a solvent. It is not to be confused with the single substance benzene.

Ben-Zvi (ben-tz-VE), **Isaac,** or **Itzhak** (1884–1963), Israeli statesman, b. Poltava, Russia. He organized Zionist movement in Russia. He fled to Palestine (1907) and helped organize Jewish army that later became rebel underground Haganah. As head of governing Council of Palestine, he was spokesman for Israeli independence under British mandate. As head of Mapai (Labor) Party, he was elected second president of Israel (1952). A noted Oriental scholar, he wrote on archeology, ethnology, and history of Near East. His works include *Eretz Israel in Past and Present,* written with former Israeli prime minister David Ben-Gurion.

Beograd, Yugoslavia see Belgrade
Beowulf (BAY-o-wulf), epic poem   **B** 141–42
Old English literature   **E** 245
Be Prepared, Scout motto   **B** 360
Berbera, Somalia   **S** 255

Berbers, peoples of the Berber Hamitic language group of Libya, Tunisia, Algeria, and Morocco. Majority are farmers or herdsmen and reside in self-governing villages loosely united in confederations. The Tuareg Berbers are nomadic camel herdsmen organized into clans, which are united into groups, each headed by a chief. They profess Islam. Berber culture is depicted on tomb paintings of ancient Egypt.

Berceo, Gonzalo de see Gonzalo de Berceo
Berceuse, a musical form   **M** 535
Berea (ber-E-a) **College,** Berea, Kentucky   **K** 220
Beregovoi, Georgi T., Soviet cosmonaut   **S** 344

Berenson, Bernard (1865–1959), American art critic, collector, and writer, b. Vilna, Lithuania. He was an authority on Italian Renaissance art. His works include *The Venetian Painters of the Renaissance.*

Berg (BAIRK), **Alban** (1885–1935), Austrian composer, b. Vienna. He was one of leading composers of early 20th century. A pupil and disciple of Arnold Schoenberg, he

Berg, Alban (continued)
wrote songs, chamber music, and orchestral works, but
he is chiefly known for his operas *Wozzeck* and *Lulu*
(incomplete) and his Violin Concerto.
  Wozzeck, opera **O** 155

Berg (BERG), **Patty** (Patricia Jane Berg) (1918–),
American golfer, b. Minneapolis, Minn. She won most
major golf tournaments, both amateur and professional,
including U.S. Women's Amateur (1938) and U.S.
Women's Titleholders (seven times between 1937 and
1957). She was chosen three times as outstanding
woman athlete of the year by Associated Press.

Bergelson, David, Yiddish author **Y** 351
Bergen, Edgar, American ventriloquist **V** 301
Bergen, Norway **N** 344
Bergerac, Cyrano de see Cyrano de Bergerac

Bergh, Henry (1811–1888), American philanthropist, b.
New York, N.Y. Son of New York shipping magnate
Christian Bergh, he was founder (1866) and first
president of American Society for the Prevention of
Cruelty to Animals (ASPCA). He helped found Society for
the Prevention of Cruelty to Children (1875).

Bergman, Ingmar, Swedish motion–picture director
  M 488, 488c

Bergman, Ingrid (1915–), Swedish stage and screen
actress, b. Stockholm. She gained international fame
from her first American film, *Intermezzo*, with Leslie
Howard (1939). She won Antoinette Perry (Tony) award
for Broadway performance of *Joan of Lorraine* (1947) and
Academy Awards for *Gaslight* (1944) and *Anastasia*
(1956). Her other films include *For Whom the Bell Tolls,
The Inn of the Sixth Happiness, Cactus Flower,* and *A
Walk in the Spring Rain.*

Beriberi, disease caused by lack of thiamine, or vitamin
B_1. It can be prevented by diet containing whole grains.
It is most common in parts of Far East where main food
is rice from which thiamine-rich outside coating is
removed. It affects nerves, especially those that control
muscles.
  vitamins, discovery of **V** 370a, 370c–370d
  vitamins in control of disease **D** 216

Bering (BARING), **Vitus,** Danish explorer **B** 142
Bering Sea **O** 46
  early Eskimo called Bering Sea people **E** 284
Bering Strait, separating Asia and North America
  B 142; **O** 46
  Alaska's distance from Asia **A** 128
Berkeley, Sir William, English colonial governor **B** 8–9
Berkelium (BER-kli-um), element **E** 154, 159
Berkner, Lloyd, American physicist **I** 310–11
Berkshire Hills, Massachusetts **M** 137; picture **M** 140

Berkshire Music Festival, series of outdoor summer concerts begun by Henry K. Hadley at Interlaken, Mass.
(1934). Series is located (since 1936) at Tanglewood in
Lenox, Mass., where the Boston Symphony Orchestra
performs a 6-week concert series in July and August.
  music festivals in the United States **M** 551

Berlanga (ber-LON-ga), **Tomás de,** discovered Galápagos
  Islands **E** 56

Berlin, Congress of (1878), assembly in Berlin of
delegates from Germany, Austria-Hungary, France, Britain, Italy, Russia, and Turkey. It met in response to
Britain's and Austria-Hungary's disapproval of the Treaty
of San Stefano (1878), which had increased Russian influence in Middle East. Congress resulted in Treaty of
Berlin, which gave independence to Montenegro, Serbia,
and Rumania and divided Bulgaria into three parts.
  Bismarck, Otto von **B** 250
  Cyprus, transfer of **C** 558

Berlin, Germany **B** 143–45; **G** 157
  "Cold War," start of, between East and West **G** 164
  Hansa quarter, picture **E** 332
  made an enclave at end of World War II **W** 306
  main street in East Berlin, picture **G** 163
  main street in West Berlin, picture **G** 164
  Truman orders Berlin airlift **T** 302

Berlin, Irving (Israel Baline) (1888–), American
songwriter, b. Temum, Russia. He went to United States
in 1893. He wrote scores for Broadway shows and
movies. His approximately 1,000 songs include "White
Christmas" and "Alexander's Ragtime Band." He received a gold medal from Congress (1954) for "composing many popular songs, including 'God Bless America.'"

Berlin airlift **I** 325
  United States Air Force, role in **U** 160

Berliner, Emile (1851–1929), American inventor, b. Hanover, Germany. Among his many inventions were microphone; Gramophone, forerunner of modern phonograph
that first used discs; and a way of making discs in
quantity.
  records or discs for the phonograph **P** 197; **R** 123

Berliner Ensemble, theater, East Berlin **T** 160
Berlin-to-Baghdad Railroad **I** 381
Berlioz (BAIR-li-ose), **Hector,** French composer **B** 145
  band music **B** 39
  choral music **C** 279
  French music **F** 445
  La Damnation de Faust **F** 73
  opera **O** 137
  romantic orchestral music **R** 311
Bermuda (ber-MU-da), British crown colony of islands
  in the Atlantic Ocean **B** 146–48
  limestone quarry, picture **Q** 5
Bermuda chub, fish, picture **A** 280
Bermuda grass **G** 317
Bermuda onions **O** 118

Bermuda Triangle, a part of North Atlantic Ocean in
which over 50 ships and 20 planes have disappeared with
no survivors. The area is enclosed roughly by an imaginary line from Bermuda to Florida, to Puerto Rico, back
to Bermuda. In 1945 five U.S. planes on a training
mission disappeared at the same time, as did a search
plane sent later. In 1968, U.S. submarine *Scorpion* was
another unexplained disappearance.

Bermúdez (ber-MU-deth), **Juan de,** Spanish navigator
  B 148
Bern, capital of Switzerland **S** 498

Bernadette of Lourdes (Maria Bernarde Soubirous),
Saint (1844–1879), French peasant girl said to have had
visions of Virgin Mary at Lourdes (1858), b. Lourdes,
Hautes-Pyrénées. Through her, waters at Lourdes with
miraculous power became known. She joined Sisters of
Charity at Nevers (1866). She was canonized in 1933.

Bernadotte (BER-na-dot), **Count Folke** (1895–1948), Swedish diplomat and humanitarian, b. Stockholm. A member

of Swedish royal family, he was vice-chairman of Swedish Red Cross during World War II. He helped speed exchange of war prisoners and acted as peace emissary at end of war. He was assassinated in Palestine by terrorists while trying, on behalf of United Nations, to stop fighting between Arabs and Jews. He wrote *The Curtain Falls, Instead of Arms,* and *People I Have Met.*

distinguished Swedish statesmen **S** 487

Bernadotte, Jean Baptiste *see* Charles XIV John, king of Sweden and Norway
Bernard (bair-NAR), **Claude,** French psysiologist **D** 325; **M** 207
studies of the animal body **B** 195
Berne Convention, 1886 **T** 245
Bernese Alps, Switzerland **A** 174; picture **S** 497

Bernhardt, Sarah (Henriette Rosine Bernard) (1844–1923), French actress, b. Paris. Called Divine Sarah, she was known for her *voix d'or* ("golden voice"). She performed with Comédie Française (1874–80), touring Europe and United States with great success. She was noted for her performances in plays by Hugo, Sardou, Rostand, and Racine. Despite a leg amputation (1915), she continued her acting career. She wrote a volume of memoirs and several plays. She was made member of Legion of Honor (1914).

Bernini (ber-NI-ni), **Giovanni Lorenzo,** Italian sculptor, painter, and architect **B** 148
baroque architecture **B** 57, 59
Italian architecture **I** 472
place in the history of sculpture **S** 101
statue of David **D** 44; **S** 100
Vision of Saint Theresa, picture **B** 56
Bernoulli (bair-NOOL-li), **Daniel,** Swiss scientist and mathematician **A** 36
Bernoulli's principle, law in physics **A** 36, 40

Bernstein, Leonard (1918–), American conductor, pianist, and composer, b. Lawrence, Mass. Associated with New York Philharmonic from 1943 and musical director 1958–69, he was the first man born and trained in the United States to hold that position. His compositions, ranging from classical to popular, include symphonies *The Age of Anxiety* and *Jeremiah,* a ballet, *Fancy Free,* the theatrical rock *Mass,* and scores of several musical shows, such as *Wonderful Town* and *West Side Story.*
musical comedy, history of **M** 543

Berra, Yogi (Lawrence Peter Berra) (1925–), American baseball player, b. St. Louis, Mo. He was catcher for New York Yankees (1947–63) and was chosen to play in the All-Star game 14 times. He was the American League's Most Valuable Player (1951, 1954, 1955). Berra was field manager for the Yankees (1964). He was a coach for the New York Mets and manager from 1972 to 1975.

Berries
garden fruits **G** 52
poisonous plants **P** 322–23

Berrigan, Daniel J. (1921–), American Jesuit priest, writer and peace activist, b. Virginia, Minn. He became active in the peace movement and was a member of a peace group that went to North Vietnam (1968) to arrange the release of 3 captured U.S. airmen. He and his brother, **Philip F.** (1923–), also a Jesuit priest, became nationally known when they destroyed draft files in Catonsville, Md. (1968). Tried and convicted for this act, they served sentences in federal prisons. Books by Daniel Berrigan include *False Gods, Real Men; Trial of the*

Catonsville Nine. Philip Berrigan has written *Prison Journals of a Priest Revolutionary.*

Berruguete (bair-ru-GAY-tay), **Alonso,** Spanish artist **S** 364
Berry, Chuck, American rock music performer **R** 262c

Berry, Martha McChesney (1866–1942), American educator and philanthropist, b. near Rome, Ga. She was founder (1902) of Berry schools for underprivileged children from the mountain areas of Georgia. This self-supporting school system now includes three schools and a college at Mt. Berry, Ga. She was awarded Roosevelt Memorial Medal for service to the nation (1925) and in a national poll (1931) was voted one of 12 greatest American women.

Bertelli (ber-TEL-li), **Luigi,** Italian writer **I** 480
Bertha, or **Berthrada,** mother of Charlemagne **C** 188
believed to be original Mother Goose **N** 402

Berthon, George Theodore (1806–1892), Canadian painter, b. Vienna, Austria. Known for his portraits, he was an honorary life member of Ontario Society of Artists. A portrait of Sir John Beverly Robinson, considered his masterpiece, hangs in Osgoode Hall, Toronto.

Berthrada *see* Bertha
Beryl, gem mineral **G** 71
Beryllium (ber-ILL-ium), element **E** 154, 159–60
used in space ships and nuclear equipment **M** 313
Berzelius (ber-ZE-lius), **Jöns,** Swedish chemist **C** 212–13
Beschady (be-yesh-CHA-dy) **Mountains,** Europe **P** 359
Bessarabia (bess-a-RAY-bia), Union of Soviet Socialist Republics **R** 358
the Moldavian Republic **U** 44
Bessemer (BESS-em-er), **Sir Henry,** English Inventor of Bessemer steel process **B** 149
Bessemer process, for producing steel **B** 149
iron and steel **I** 398
Bessette, Alfred *see* André, Brother
Best, Charles H., Canadian physiologist **B** 52; picture **D** 216
Best Dog in Show, award **D** 261
Best Friend of Charleston, locomotive **L** 328
early transportation in South Carolina **S** 301–02
railroads, early history **R** 89
Best of Breed, dog show award **D** 261
Betancourt (bate-an-COOR), **Rómulo,** Venezuelan statesman **V** 300
Beta (BAY-ta) **particles,** of radioactive atoms **A** 488; **R** 67
ions and ionization **I** 353
radioactive radiation **R** 45
Beta rays, streams of beta particles of radioactive elements **R** 67
radiations emitted by nuclei **N** 359
Betelgeuse (BET-el-geuse), star **S** 407, 408
constellations **C** 491

Bethesda, in New Testament (John 5:2–9), pool in Jerusalem possessed of miraculous healing powers. It is the place where Jesus is said to have cured a man who had been an invalid for 38 years.
Christian shrines in Old City of Jerusalem **J** 80

Bethlehem, Jordan **J** 139
birthplace of Jesus Christ **J** 82
Israeli occupation, 1967 **J** 139

Bethune, Mary McLeod, American educator **B** 149
Negro political leaders **N** 100
Beti, Mongo, Cameroonian novelist **A** 76c

Bidault (be-DO), **Georges** (1899–   ), French statesman, b. Moulins, Allier. A leader in French underground during World War II, he was president of National Council of the Resistance (CNR) (1943–44). He was twice premier and several times foreign minister (between 1944 and 1954). He split with Charles de Gaulle over Algeria and lived in exile 1962–68.

Bidding, in game of bridge C 107

Biddle, Francis (1886–1968), American lawyer, jurist, and cabinet member, b. Paris, France. Private secretary to Supreme Court Justice Oliver Wendell Holmes (1911–12), he was also special assistant U.S. attorney (1922–26), U.S. Circuit Court of Appeals judge (1939–40), U.S. attorney general (1941–45), and U.S. representative to Nuremberg war-crimes trials (1945–46). His writings include *Mr. Justice Holmes* and *The Fear of Freedom.*

Biddle, Nicholas, American financier   **J** 7
Biddy basketball   **B** 90
Bidpai (BID-pie), **Fables of**   **F** 4, 6
Bidwell, John, American pioneer and rancher   **O** 263–64
Biennials (by-EN-ni-als), plants   **P** 303
  gardens and gardening   **G** 29–30, 46
Bienville (bi-EN-vill), **Jean Baptiste Lemoyne, Sieur de,**
  French founder of New Orleans   **L** 361, 362
Bierce, Ambrose, American writer and journalist   **H** 280
Bifocal glasses   **O** 166
Bifrost, bridge to Asgard, home of the Norse gods
  N 277
Big bang theory, of the universe   **U** 204
Big Bear, constellation *see* Ursa Major
Big Ben, clock bell, London   **L** 335; pictures **L** 338,
  U 70
Big Bend National Park, Texas   **T** 132–33
Big Bertha, giant German cannon   **G** 425
Big Black River, Mississippi   **M** 352
Big business, in United States   **U** 130–31
Big Dipper, star group   **C** 491, 492
  direction finder   **D** 183
Big Dog, constellation *see* Canis Major
Big Ear, the National Radio Astronomy Observatory,
  West Virginia   **W** 137; picture **R** 69
Bigelow (BIG-elow), **Erastus,** American inventor   **R** 352
Bigelow Papers, The, by James Russell Lowell   **L** 369

Bigfoot, a creature named for its huge footprints and
said to live in mountains of northwestern United States
and British Columbia, Canada. It is also known by the
Indian name Sasquatch. In reported sightings, it is
described as a shy apelike creature 2 to 3 m, or 7 to
10 ft, tall. Footprints supposedly made by Bigfoot have
been photographed and cast in plaster. Except for their
size (about 41 cm, or 16 in, long), they are like human
footprints. Still, Bigfoot remains a mystery.

Big Four, term originally designating Great Britain,
France, Italy, and United States, or their leaders at Paris
Peace Conference (1919). Since World War II, Soviet
Union has replaced Italy in their conferences.

Big-game hunting   **H** 290–91
Big Hole National Battlefield, Montana   **M** 438
Bighorn Mountains, Wyoming   **W** 325
Bighorns, or Rocky Mountain sheep   **S** 145; picture
  H 218
  hoofed mammals   **H** 221
Big Muddy, Missouri River   **M** 383
Big Sky Country, name given to Montana   **M** 428
Big stick, foreign policy of Theodore Roosevelt   **R** 329
Big Thicket National Preserve, Texas   **T** 133
Big Thompson River, Colorado   **C** 405
Big top, circus tent   **C** 302
Big Trees, sequoias   **P** 316
  giants of nature   **G** 200, 202–03
  Yosemite National Park   **Y** 352
Big Wave, The, book by Pearl Buck, excerpt   **B** 421–22
Bikila, Abebe, Ethiopian athlete   **E** 299

Bikini, a coral atoll in the Marshall Islands, west central
Pacific. The people were relocated because of U.S. nuclear
testing (1946–58). They returned (1968) but were relocated
again (1978) because of dangerous radioactivity.

Bilateral (by-LAT-er-al) **agreements,** between two nations
  I 323
Bilateral treaties   **T** 270–71
Bile, secretion of the liver as aid to digestion   **B** 275
Bilingual World, The, or Monde Bilingue, Le, French
  movement for joint use of French and English   **U** 195

Billboards, used for outdoor advertising   **A** 28–29
  Ogden Nash, poem against   **H** 280
  See also Signs and billboards
Bill Haley and the Comets, American rock music group
  R 262c
Billiard balls   **P** 324
Billiards   **B** 174–76
Billings, Montana   **M** 440
Billings, John Shaw, American surgeon and librarian
  L 188–89
Billings, Josh *see* Shaw, Henry Wheeler
Billings, William, American hymn composer   **H** 313
  songs of the Revolutionary War   **N** 23
Billingsgate, London   **L** 339

Bill of lading, a contract between a shipper and a carrier
in which carrier acknowledges receipt of goods to be
shipped and promises to deliver them at a certain time.

Bill of Rights, American   **B** 177–80
  civil rights, historical origins   **C** 314
  freedom of religion, speech, and press   **F** 457
  The Federalist, position of   **F** 78
  jury, trial by   **J** 159–60
  Madison, principal author   **M** 8
  ten original amendments to the U.S. Constitution
    U 146, 155
  See also Civil liberties and civil rights; United States
    Constitution
Bill of Rights, Canadian   **B** 180; **C** 78
Bill of Rights, English   **B** 180
  civil rights, historical origins   **C** 314
  England, 1689   **E** 224; **J** 159
  English Bill of Rights and taxation   **T** 26
Bill of Rights, French
  French Declaration of the Rights of Man   **B** 180; **C** 314
Bill of Rights, Universal
  Universal Declaration of Human Rights   **B** 180; **C** 314
Bill of Rights Day   **B** 180
Bills, suggested laws   **U** 140–41
Billy goats   **G** 244

Billy the Kid (William H. Bonney) (1859–1881), American
outlaw, b. New York, N.Y. He worked for cattleman in
Pecos Valley (1877) until employer's death at outbreak of
Lincoln County cattle conflict (1878). The Kid became
leader of a war faction in 1878. A notorious outlaw, he
became heavily involved in cattle theft. Captured by
sheriff Pat Garrett in 1880, he escaped but was later
fatally shot by Garrett. He killed a total of 21 persons.

Biloxi (bil-OX-i), Mississippi   **M** 360
  shrimp boats, picture   **M** 357
Bimetallism (by-MET-al-lism), monetary system   **M** 409
Bimini Islands, Bahamas   **B** 17
  Ponce de León's search for Fountain of Youth
    P 391
Binary form, a basic design used in writing music
  M 535
Binary (BY-nary) **stars**   **S** 409
  study of revolving stars   **A** 475
Binary numeration system   **N** 401
  automation   **A** 530
  computers   **C** 453, 456
Binchois, Gilles, Flemish composer   **D** 363; **F** 443
  Renaissance music   **R** 172
Binding knots   **K** 290
Binding of books *see* Bookbinding
Bindweed   **W** 104

Binet (bi-NAY), **Alfred** (1857–1911), French psychologist,
b. Nice. He was director of the laboratory of physiologi-

Binet, Alfred (continued)
cal psychology at the Sorbonne in Paris. Together with Théodore Simon he developed the Binet-Simon test for measuring intelligence.
  tests and testing **T** 117

Bingham, Hiram, American missionary in Hawaii **H** 70
Binoculars O 167
  prism binoculars **L** 147, 265; diagram **L** 264
Binocular (two-eyed) **vision P** 490–91
Bionominal, name of two terms to show genus and species **K** 252
Binomial (by-NO-mial) **theorem,** mathematical formula worked out by Newton **N** 206
Binturongs, mammals related to mongooses **G** 89, 91
Bío-Bío River, Chile **C** 254
Biocells, batteries **B** 99
  bacterial fermentation produces electricity **F** 91
Biochemistry, study of the composition of living things **B** 181–84; **C** 214
  advances in, as branch of biology **B** 195
  body chemistry **B** 289–97
  medical laboratory tests **M** 201, 209
  Pasteur, Louis **P** 95
  viruses **V** 361–70a
  See also Body chemistry; Genetics; Photosynthesis
Biodegradable materials
  problems for water supplies **W** 59

Biofeedback. Certain bodily activities, such as the heartbeat and blood pressure, are involuntary—that is, they are not usually controllable by the individual. But experiments have shown that some patients with a dangerously irregular heartbeat can be trained to regulate the rate. The key to this training is feedback—information from instruments that let the patient know when the heart beats faster or slower. Some patients learn to control the beat well enough to get along even after the instrument is removed. Similarly, patients have learned to control their blood pressure. There is hope that biofeedback may become a method of treating disorders connected with involuntary activities.

Biogenesis (by-o-GEN-e-sis), **Pasteur's theory of B** 194
Biogeography (by-o-ge-OG-raphy), study of geography of plants and animals **G** 107–08
  life, distribution of plant and animal **L** 233
Biographical (by-o-GRAPH-ic-al) **dictionaries R** 129–30
Biographical novel B 186
Biography (by-OG-raphy), author's account of a person's life **B** 185–86
  American literature **A** 196, 214–15
  Boswell's *Life of Samuel Johnson* **E** 258
  creative writing **W** 321
  library arrangement **L** 183
  list of books of, for children **C** 248a
  Pulitzer prizes **P** 526–27
Biological clocks L 247–50
Biologicals (by-o-LOJ-ic-als), drugs **D** 326–27
Biological warfare see Bacteriological warfare
Biology (by-OL-ogy) **B** 187–96
  biochemistry **B** 181–84
  genetics **G** 77–88
  life, rhythms and clocks **L** 243–50
  medicine, history of **M** 203–208c
  Mendel's experiments in genetics **M** 219
  science, advances in **S** 76
  science and society **S** 79
  taxonomy **T** 28–32
  See also Evolution
Bioluminescence (by-o-lu-min-ES-cence), light emitted by living organisms **B** 197–98

centipedes and millipedes **C** 168
natural sources of light **L** 288

Biome, in ecology, a major grouping of plants and animals as, for example, tundra. It is based chiefly on climate factors. The word comes from Greek words meaning "life" and "group."

Biometrics, or **biometry,** use of statistical methods in biology. By testing only a small part, one can estimate the results that one can obtain in testing the whole.

Biophysics P 238
Biopsy, examination of a living tissue **M** 209
Biosatellite, picture **S** 42

Biosphere, the entire realm of living organisms on earth, as well as the air, soil, and water in which they live. The biosphere does not include those parts of the earth that are not inhabited by living things.

Biotic patterns, in geography **G** 99
Biotin, a B-complex vitamin **V** 370d
Biplanes, early types of airplanes **A** 572
Birch, tree, picture **P** 292
  shapes of leaves, picture **L** 116
  state tree of New Hampshire **N** 149
  uses of the wood and its grain, picture **W** 223
Birdbanding B 229
  migrating ducks, picture **H** 187
Bird Came Down the Walk, A, poem by Emily Dickinson, **D** 164
Bird Day see Arbor Day
Birdhouses B 248–49
  how to attract birds **B** 243
Birdie, golf score **G** 255
Bird in Space, sculpture by Brancusi, picture **F** 431
  Brancusi's style **B** 370

Bird of paradise, member of a family of birds in which the adult males are brilliantly colored and decorated. The birds are found chiefly in the forests of Australia, New Guinea, and neighboring islands.
  birds of the equatorial rain forests **B** 225

Birds B 199–249
  adaptations to other organisms **L** 221
  adaptive radiation **B** 209–10, 221
  aging process **A** 83
  animal communication **A** 276–77, 278–80
  animal problem-box tests **A** 284–85
  Audubon's paintings **A** 490–491
  banding **B** 229
  beaks, or bills **B** 221, 222, 223
  biological clocks and compasses **L** 249–50
  birdbaths **B** 243
  birdhouses, how to build **B** 248–49
  bird watching **B** 233–44
  caring for the young **B** 215–16
  carry diseases **I** 286
  courtship and mating **B** 212
  devices to attract birds **B** 243
  distribution by vegetation belts **B** 223, 224
  egg and embryo, diagram **E** 89
  eggs and incubation **B** 213–14
  evolution of **B** 206–10
  extinct and threatened species **B** 229–32
  feeders and food **B** 243
  feeding their young **B** 215–16
  feet **F** 83–84
  finches showing adaptations supporting Darwin's theory of natural selection, picture **E** 345

flash patterns of color **B** 237
flight patterns **B** 237
flyways of North America, map-diagram **B** 217
fossil **B** 206–07, 209–10
four-chambered heart **M** 72
giants of nature **G** 200, 204
habitats and haunts **B** 219–28, 237, 243
history and evolution of **B** 206–10
homing and migration **H** 186–88
identifying **B** 233, 237
largest **A** 263
life lists, records of bird watching **B** 244
locomotion **A** 294–96
migration **B** 211, 216–17; **H** 186–88
myths about **M** 559–60
nest building **B** 212–13
nest identification **B** 244
nests, where located **B** 220; pictures **B** 218
New Zealand birdlife **N** 239–40
of prey **B** 222
pets **B** 245–49; **P** 180–81
pollination of flowers **F** 279
poultry **P** 420–23
prehistoric animals, development of **P** 438
protection of birds **B** 232
protective coloration **B** 200, 225
provincial see Canadian province articles
refuges, pictures **B** 211, 230
reproduction **R** 179
songs and other sounds **B** 212, 237
state **U** 90–93; for pictures see state articles
"talking" birds **P** 83–86
territory songs **A** 278; picture **A** 279
through the year with birds **B** 211–17
wading birds **B** 223
warm-blooded **B** 259
web-footed **B** 223
where birds live **B** 218–28, 238
Birds, fossil B 206–07, 209–10
Birds as pets B 245–49; **P** 180–81
Birdseye, Clarence, American inventor **I** 346–47
food preservation and processing **F** 346
Bird's Eye View of the Mandan Village, A, painting by
Catlin **U** 119
Birds fly, line game **G** 23
Bird snakes S 207
Bird's-nest fungi F 500
Birds of prey B 222
eagles **E** 2
Birdsongs B 212, 237
Bird watching B 233–44
Bird Woman see Sacajawea
Biremes (BY-remes), ships **T** 261
Birmingham, Alabama **A** 112–13, 122, 124
Birmingham, England **U** 71
Birney (BER-ni), **Alice McLellan,** American educator **P** 67
Birney, James G., American abolitionist **N** 94; **P** 385
Birr Castle, Ireland, gardens, picture **G** 32
Birth control see Family planning
Birthday cards, how to make **G** 374
Birthday parties P 87–89
Birthdays, of famous people
arranged by the month see articles on individual
months
holidays honoring **H** 147–50
Birthday stones see Birthstones
Birth defects
causes of mental retardation **R** 190–91
Birthmark, The, story by Nathaniel Hawthorne **S** 166
Birth of a Nation, The, motion picture **M** 472
Birth of Venus, painting by Botticelli **I** 466
Birthrate, number of births per thousand persons **P** 394

Birthstones G 72
See also names of stones and articles on individual
months
Biscuits, manufacture and packaging of **B** 389
Bishop, Barry C., American scientist **E** 337

Bishop, Billy (William Avery Bishop) (1894–1956), Canadian aviator, b. Owen Sound, Ontario. He is credited with
shooting down 72 enemy aircraft during World War I and
was awarded many medals, including Victoria Cross
(1917), Britain's highest award for bravery. As member
of British Air Ministry, he established separate Canadian
Air Force (1918). He was co-founder of one of the first
commercial aviation companies in Canada. He was honorary air vice-marshal and director of air force recruiting.
Canadian Air Force, history of **C** 82

Bishop, Charles Reed, American banker in Hawaii **H** 70

Bishop, Claire Huchet (?–), American author, b.
Brittany, France. She headed first French public library
for children (1924), L'Heure Joyeuse, begun by Americans in Paris. Her books for children include *Pancakes-
Paris, Augustus,* and *The Five Chinese Brothers.*

Bishops, of the church **C** 281
cathedral, principal church of a bishopric **C** 131
conflicts between bishops of east and west led to
break in the church **R** 289
Bishops' schools, or Cathedral schools **M** 295
Bishop's University, Lennoxville, Quebec **Q** 10b
Bismarck, capital of North Dakota **N** 334
Bismarck, Otto von, the "Iron Chancellor", German
statesman **B** 250; pictures **B** 250, **P** 456a
Germany, history of **G** 161
Bismarck Archipelago, Pacific Islands **P** 5
Bismarck Sea O 46
Bismuth, element **E** 154, 160; **M** 227
Bison (BY-son) hoofed mammals **B** 250a; pictures
B 250a, **H** 216
Bison Area Indians of North America **I** 164–69
National Bison Range, Montana **M** 439
Old Bison Hunters, Indians of North America **I** 163
slaughter in Kansas **K** 176
Wood Buffalo National Park, Alberta, Canada **C** 57
Bisque (BISK), unglazed china
dolls made of **D** 265
Bissau, capital of Guinea-Bissau **G** 406b
Bissell, George, American lawyer **P** 177
Bisymmetrical (by-sim-MET-ric-al) **balance,** in design
D 133
Bitonality, in music **M** 400–01
Bitter, a sense of taste **B** 286

Bittern, small to medium-size bird of the heron family.
Bitterns live in swamps and marshy ponds, where their
yellowish-brown coloring blends with the reeds and
grasses. They have long legs, long necks, and long,
sharp bills with which they spear fish. When alarmed,
bitterns remain motionless, their bills pointing upward.
The American bittern is known for its croaking call.
nest, picture **B** 244

Bitterroot, flower
state flower of Montana **M** 428

Bittersweet, vine or shrub that grows in most of North
America. Up to 30 ft. long, it bears clusters of small
green flowers. Its yellow fruit shows red seeds. "Bittersweet" is also a popular name for nightshade, a woody
climbing shrub with purple flowers and poisonous red
berries, found in North America, Europe, and Asia.

Bituminous (bit-TU-min-ous) **coal,** soft coal   C 362, 363
  fuels   F 487
Bivalves, mollusks with two shells   O 271–74;   S 148
Bizerte (bi-ZERT), Tunisia   T 310

Bizet (bi-ZAY), **Georges** (Alexandre César Léopold Bizet) (1838–1875), French composer, b. Paris. He is best known for opera *Carmen.* Bizet greatly influenced French dramatic music. Besides *Carmen,* his operas include *The Pearl-Fishers* and *The Fair Maid of Perth.* He also wrote the suite *Children's Games,* and a symphony in C.   F 446
  Carmen, opera   O 142

Bjerknes (BYURK-nes), **Jakob Aall Bonnevie** (1897–   ), Norwegian-American meteorologist, b. Stockholm, Sweden. He has proposed the theory that cyclonic storms are created when cold polar air moves in under warm air masses. He won the National Medal of Science in 1966.

Bjørnson (BYERN-son), **Bjørnstjerne,** Norwegian author
  S 51
Blab schools   L 292
Black, color   D 139
  funeral custom   F 494

Black, Hugo La Fayette (1886–1971), American jurist, b. Harlan, Ala. Black received his law degree from the University of Alabama (1906). He practiced law in Birmingham and was active in local Democratic politics. In 1926, and again in 1932, he was elected U.S. Senator. He was a strong supporter of President Franklin D. Roosevelt's New Deal policies, and in 1937 Roosevelt appointed him to fill a vacancy as Associate Justice of the U.S. Supreme Court. Black was a strong advocate of individual liberties and civil rights. He retired in 1971.

Black, Joseph, Scottish scientist   M 23;   S 70–71, 72

Black, Shirley Temple (Mrs. Charles Black) (1928–   ), American .movie star and political figure, b. Santa Monica, Cal. Her movie career began when she was 3½, and she starred in such films as *The Littlest Rebel* and *Rebecca of Sunnybrook Farm.* She ran for Congress from California (1967), but lost. She was a member of U.S. delegation to United Nations in 1969. In 1974 she was named U.S. ambassador to Ghana. Picture   M 475.

Black Americans   N 89–105
  Abolitionist movement   N 94–95
  Black Regiment, Revolutionary War   R 222
  civil rights movements   C 316
  Civil War, United States   C 318, 320–21, 327–28
  Confederate States   C 458, 459
  Dred Scott Decision   D 310–11
  Emancipation Proclamation   E 185–86;   N 95
  Hall of Fame for baseball   B 81
  literature   A 213;   N 101
  Negro hymns and spirituals   H 313;   N 105–07
  newspapers   N 198
  Reconstruction Period   R 117–20
  rock music   R 262a, 262b, 262d
  segregation   S 113–15
  slavery   S 197–20
  Uncle Tom's Cabin by Harriet Beecher Stowe   S 436
  Underground Railroad   U 11–12
  United States   U 132–33, 155–58
Black Angus cattle, picture   C 149
Blackball, to vote against   B 21

Blackbeard (Edward Teach, or Thatch) (?–1718), British pirate. He was privateer for British in West Indies during War of Spanish Succession (1701–13) who turned to piracy, plundering coasts of North Carolina and Virginia (1713–18). He was killed during attack by ships sent out by planters and governor of Virginia.
  piracy and buried treasure   N 308;   P 264

Black bears   B 106; picture B 107
  Yellowstone National Park   Y 346
Black Belt, or Black Prairie, United States landform
  Alabama   A 115
  Mississippi   M 352
Blackberries   G 298, 301

Blackbirds, any of several varieties of birds mostly black in color and feeding mainly on seeds, grains, and insects. North American blackbirds belong to a family that includes the orioles, cowbirds, and grackles. Perhaps best known is the red-winged blackbird. Males are black with a flash of red at the upper part of each wing. Females are brownish and lack shoulder markings. The European blackbird, found in Europe and Asia, belongs to the thrush family and is not related to the North American. Pictures   B 216, 240.

Black cats   S 475
Black Codes, laws passed by Southern states just after Civil War   N 95;   R 117
  Johnson, Andrew   J 125
Black death see Bubonic plague
Black-eyed Susans, flowers, picture   W 170
  Maryland, state flower of   M 115
Black-figure pottery, ancient Greece   P 414
Blackfoot, Indians of North America   I 166; picture I 167
Black Forest, Germany   G 153; picture G 105
Blackfriars, London theater   S 132
Black Hawk, Indian chief   I 84

Black Hawk War, war between United States and faction of Fox and Sauk (Sac) Indians led by Chief Black Hawk. War was caused by Black Hawk's refusal to recognize cession of 50,000,000 acres of land in Illinois, Wisconsin, and Missouri to U.S. Government by representative of the two tribes in 1804. When squatters laid claim to Black Hawk's village near Rock Island, Ill. (1831), Black Hawk began the war, which ended with his defeat (1832) at Bad Axe River in Wisconsin.
  Indian wars against westward expansion   I 213;   W 207

Blackheads   D 190
Black Hills, South Dakota, Wyoming   S 312, 315;   W 323; picture S 319
Black Hills National Forest, South Dakota, picture   N 35

Black hole, according to theory, an extremely small object formed from the atoms of a very large star that has run out of nuclear fuel, cooled, and collapsed quickly. The body formed is so dense that a marble-size piece of it would weigh many billions of tons. The enormous gravitational attraction of the body prevents the escape of all matter and energy, including light energy. As no light can radiate from the object, it cannot be seen in the sky, and hence is called a "black hole."   S 411

Black Hole of Calcutta, dungeon in Fort William, 18th-century British fort in Calcutta, India. When the fort was taken by the Nawab (governor) of Bengal (1756), a number of people were imprisoned in the Black Hole, a small, poorly ventilated cell, and some died.

Blackjack oak, tree, shapes of leaves, picture   L 116

Black Kettle (1803?–1868), Cheyenne Indian chief, b. in what is now S. Dak. He offered peace and friendship to U.S. troops in Colorado but was refused. He obeyed orders to move his village to Sand Creek but was betrayed and attacked by militia (1864). In spite of treaty and reparations made to the Indians, their new village in Washita Valley was attacked by General Custer's troops, and Black Kettle was killed.

Black lady, card game **C** 112
Black letter, typeface design **T** 345

Black market, illegal market where goods are bought and sold in violation of government regulations. Black markets may develop where and when commodities are scarce and people are willing to pay higher prices. Term may also apply to trading of currency.

Blackmun, Harry Andrew (1908–   ), American jurist b. Nashville, Ill. Graduated from Harvard Law School, he was in private practice in Minneapolis (1934–50), and was resident counsel at Mayo Clinic (1950–59). He was appointed to U.S. Court of Appeals by President Eisenhower (1959). Blackmun was unanimously confirmed by the Senate as 99th Justice of the U.S. Supreme Court (1970) following its refusal to confirm two Southern nominees.

Black Muslims (Nation of Islam) **N** 104a–104b
  See also Elijah Muhammad

Blackout, covering or putting out of all lights to hide an area or object as protective measure against air attack. Blackouts were used especially as defense against Nazi air attacks during World War II. Unplanned blackouts sometimes occur due to electrical power failures.

Black Panthers (Black Panther Party) **N** 105
Black Peter, servant of Sinter Klaas, picture **C** 293
Black powder, or gunpowder, explosive **E** 389–90, 391
  guns and ammunition **G** 414

Black Power, slogan, first popularized in 1966, that has come to represent a political and economic movement on the part of Negroes to become independent of the white community. It expresses also the desire of many Negroes to relate to their African background and to be known as Blacks. Many define the term as the power of Black peoples to control their own destiny. Some militants see Black Power as a dream of a separate state. The term was used by Stokely Carmichael in a call for removal of whites from leadership and policy-making positions in civil rights organizations. By 1968 Black Power in its non-separatist sense had been accepted by less militant leaders, such as Whitney Young of the Urban League.
  continuing struggle in Negro history **N** 104b

Black racer, snake, picture **S** 205
Black Regiment or **First Rhode Island Regiment,**
  Revolutionary War **R** 222
Black Renaissance (ren-nais-SONCE) **N** 98
Blacks **N** 89–105
  See also Black Americans; Negroes; names of African countries, Negro leaders and organizations
Black Sea **O** 46

Black September Organization, a Palestinian guerrilla group that takes its name from the month in 1970 when the government of Jordan opened its campaign to crush Arab terrorist groups. The organization, which deals in occasional random terrorism directed against the State

of Israel, was responsible for the murder of eleven Israeli athletes at the 1972 Olympic Games in Munich, Germany.

Blackshirts, fascist parties
  British **F** 64
  Italian fascists and Mussolini **F** 63; **M** 552
Black snake, picture **S** 205
Black Stone of Mecca *see* Kaaba
Blackstrap molasses **S** 453
Black Tea **T** 38
Blacktop, asphalt for roads **R** 252
Black walnuts **N** 423
Black Warrior River, Alabama **A** 115, 120
Blackwater River, Ireland **I** 386

Blackwell, Elizabeth (1821–1910), first woman physician in United States, b. Bristol, England. She went to United States in 1832. After graduating from medical school, she found that because she was a woman, no hospital would permit her to practice, so she opened New York Infirmary for Indigent Women and Children (1854), and first women's medical college (1868). She helped found London School of Medicine for Women (1869).

Black widow spiders **I** 284; **S** 388; pictures **I** 282,
  S 387
Bladder **B** 278
Blades, of airplane propellers **A** 558
Blades, of broad leaves **L** 114
Blade tools, prehistoric man **P** 444
Blaeu (BLA-u), **William,** Dutch geographer **M** 94
Blaiberg, Philip *see* Barnard, Christiaan
Blaine, James Gillespie, American statesman **M** 45
  Garfield and Blaine **G** 55
Blair, Eric *see* Orwell, George

Blair House, historic mansion in Washington, D.C. Built in 1824 by Joseph Lovell, first surgeon general of the U.S. Army, and bought in 1836 by Francis Preston Blair, Sr., a member of Andrew Jackson's "kitchen cabinet," it has been owned by the U.S. Government since 1942 and is used to house distinguished guests. It is joined to Lee Mansion and sometimes called Blair-Lee House.

Blake, Nicholas *see* Lewis, Cecil Day
Blake, William, English poet and artist **B** 250b
  children's literature **C** 237
  English literature **E** 259
  God Creates the World, drawing **E** 259
  illustration of books **I** 90
  water-color painting **E** 240
Blanc (BLON), **Mont,** France **A** 174; pictures **A** 175,
  F 409, **G** 94
  first successful ascent **M** 489
  Mer de Glace, glacier, picture **G** 224

Blanchard, Doc (Felix Anthony Blanchard) (1924–   ), American football star, b. McColl, S.C. He was an outstanding fullback for U.S. Military Academy (1944–46) and winner of over 20 national football awards.

Blanchard (blon-SHAR), **Jean-Pierre François** (1753–1809), French balloonist, b. Les Andelys. He made his first balloon ascent in 1784. With American physician Dr. John Jeffries, he piloted first air trip across English Channel (1785). Blanchard made numerous first ascents in Europe and United States (1785–96).
  balloon and parachute experiments **B** 31; **P** 60

Bland, James Allen (1854–1911), American self-trained songwriter and minstrel performer, b. Flushing, N.Y. He

Bland, James Allen (continued)
wrote Virginia's official state song, "Carry Me Back to Old Virginia," in addition to "Oh Dem Golden Slippers," "In the Evening by the Moonlight," and "Climbing up the Golden Stairs."

Bland Bill, 1877 **H** 81
Blankets, electric **E** 118
Blanket stitch, in embroidery **E** 188
Blank verse, unrhymed verse **P** 353
 quotations from Shakespeare's plays **S** 133–37
Blantyre, Malawi **M** 51

Blarney stone, an inscribed stone supposed to impart gift of words, especially of flattery, persuasion, or deception, to any one who kisses it. It is located in 15th-century Blarney Castle in County Cork, Ireland, where tourists or pilgrims lean over backward to reach it.

Blasco-Ibáñez (BLAS-co-e-BON-yeth), **Vicente**, Spanish author **S** 371
Blast furnaces **I** 397; pictures **M** 319
 fuel **F** 488
 refining of metals **M** 228
Blasting, in mining, pictures **M** 315–16, 434
 quarrying method **Q** 5
Blasting caps **E** 392; picture **E** 391
Blasting gelatin, picture **E** 390
Blaze, horse marking, picture **H** 238
Blazoning, describing arms in heraldry **H** 117–18; pictures **H** 115
Bleaching
 beauty culture of the hair **B** 111
 chlorine **I** 349
 furniture **F** 504
 of fats and oils **O** 77
 paper making **P** 52
Bledsoe, Jules, American singer **N** 107
Bleeding
 first aid **F** 157–58
Bleeding Kansas **K** 191, 192
Blegen (BLAIG-en), **Carl W.**, American archeologist **T** 293
Blenheim (BLEN-im), **battle of**, 1704 **B** 101
Blenheim Palace, Oxfordshire, England, picture **U** 69
Blennerhassett Island, West Virginia **W** 136

Blennies (name means "slimy"), large group of small, slender, slimy fish with few or no scales. This group includes rock eel, Molly Miller, and rock skipper. Most live in shallow waters of Atlantic and Pacific, but some live in deep waters of these oceans and in Arctic Ocean.

Blessings, prayers **P** 434–35
Blériot (blay-ri-O), **Louis**, French engineer **A** 572
Blessed Virgin Mary see Mary, Virgin

Bligh (BLY), **William** (1754–1817), English naval officer, b. Tynten, Cornwall. Captain of the ship *Bounty*, he was set adrift in an open boat with 18 of his men by a mutinous crew and finally reached the East Indies after a 4,000-mile voyage (1789). (*Mutiny on the Bounty*, by James Norman Hall and Charles B. Nordhoff, is based on this incident.) He later became governor of New South Wales, Australia (1805–08), where his soldiers mutinied and imprisoned him (1808–10). He returned to England in 1810 and was made a vice-admiral (1814).
 breadfruit introduced to Jamaica **J** 18

Blight, general name for many plant diseases and symptoms such as spots, wilting, and death of plant or its parts, when these are caused by fungi or bacteria.

Blind **B** 251–54
 Keller, Helen **K** 201
 library service **L** 172
 public assistance **W** 120
Blindfish **C** 157; picture **C** 158
Blind Man's Buff, painting by Goya **G** 279
Blind Men and the Elephant, The, fable by John Godfrey Saxe **F** 7
Blindness **B** 251–52
 electric eels injure their own eyes **E** 86–87
 night blindness **V** 370b
Blindness of Tobit, The, etching by Rembrandt **G** 304
Blind salamanders **C** 157; picture **C** 158
Blind snakes **S** 207
Bliss, Mary Elizabeth ("Betty") Taylor, acting first lady in Taylor's administration **F** 170; picture **F** 171
Blitz, bombing of England, 1940 **W** 290
 London raids **L** 340

Blitzkrieg (BLITZ-kreeg) (German for "lightning war"), sudden military attack launched by combined air and ground forces with overwhelming speed and force, designed to cause an enemy's rapid surrender. It was first used by Germans during invasion of Poland (1939).

Blixen, Baroness Karen see Dinesen, Isak

Bloch (BLOCK), **Ernest** (1880–1959), American composer, b. Geneva, Switzerland. He went to United States (1916) and became citizen (1926). He was director of Cleveland Institute of Music (1920–25) and San Francisco Conservatory (1925–30). Much of his music, such as *Trois Poèmes Juifs, Schelomo,* and *Suite hebraique,* was the result of his Jewish heritage. He also wrote an opera, *Macbeth,* and a rhapsody, *America.*

Block, Adriaen, Dutch explorer of North America. He made voyages up Hudson River (1610 and 1614); navigated Long Island Sound, Connecticut River, and Buzzards' and Nahant bays in Massachusetts; and discovered Block Island, R.I., which bears his name. He provided valuable information for first detailed map (1616) of southern New England coast.

Block, Conrad (Konrad Bloch) (1912–), American biochemist, b. Neisse, Germany. Higgins professor of biochemistry at Harvard University (since 1954), he won Nobel prize in physiology and medicine (1964) for studies that showed how cholesterol is made and used.

Blockade, blocking of a coastline or harbor by enemy warships, or of a frontier by enemy troops, to prevent anyone or anything from entering or leaving. A blockade is an act of war intended to isolate an enemy by cutting off his means of trade, supplies, and communications.

Blockhouses, forts **F** 377
Block Island, Rhode Island **R** 220
Block mountains **M** 496
Block printing
 Chinese, ancient **C** 433; picture **C** 432
 history of printing **P** 457
 woodcut printing **W** 228–29
Block-signal system, of railroads **R** 85
Bloemfontein (BLOOM-fon-tain), judicial capital of South Africa **S** 271
Blois (BLWA), France
 château, Renaissance style **F** 421; picture **F** 422
Blood **B** 255–59
 anemia **D** 192–93
 blood counts in blood tests **B** 257; **M** 201, 209
 blood derivatives, medical techniques with **M** 211

cells, picture **C** 160
circulation, studies of **B** 188, 189; **M** 205–06
circulatory system of human body **B** 275–77
genes determine types **G** 87
Harvey's contribution to studies of circulation **H** 52
heart **H** 86–86c
hemophilia **D** 188
insect's blood system **I** 271
stain removal **L** 84
transfusion **T** 251
vitamin K aids clotting **V** 371
warm- and cold-blooded animals **B** 259
Blood, diseases of
anemia **D** 192–93
leukemia **D** 200
Blood, Sweat and Tears, American rock music group **R** 262d
Blood banks M 201, 211
blood transfusions **T** 251
Blood counts B 257; **M** 201, 209
Blood groups or blood types **B** 257–58
reactions to blood transfusions **T** 251
study of races of man **R** 29
Bloodhound, tracking dog **D** 262
Blood pressure M 208f–208g
high blood pressure **D** 198–99
Blood tests B 257; **M** 201, 209
Blood transfusion T 251
blood groups **B** 258
medicine, techniques of **M** 210–11
Blood vessels B 275–76
heart, function of **H** 86–86c
smoking and blood vessel disease **S** 203
Bloodworms W 310
Bloody Mary see Mary I, queen of England

Bloomer, Amelia Jenks (1818–1894), American reformer, b. Homer, N.Y. She wrote and lectured on temperance and women's rights and popularized new style in women's dress designed by Elizabeth Smith Miller. Consisting of a short-skirted dress over trousers, it became known as bloomer costume, and pants as bloomers.
bicycle changed women's fashions **B** 173

Blooms, rapid growth of algae **P** 279–80

Blount, Winton Malcolm (1921–   ), American businessman and administrator, b. Union Springs, Ala. He was founder and president of a large construction firm, and served as president of U.S. Chamber of Commerce. He was postmaster general (1969–71).

Blow, Henry Taylor (1817–1875), American businessman and politician, b. South Hampton Co., Va. He played an important role in industrial development of St. Louis, Mo. A strong opponent of spread of slavery, he joined the Free-Soil Party, and helped establish the state Republican Party. He served in U.S. House of Representatives (1863–67).
Dred Scott case **D** 310

Blow, Susan, American educator **K** 244
Blowflies, picture **I** 282
Blowfish see Puffer
Blowguns G 424; pictures **A** 301
Blowouts, or gushers, oil wells **P** 172–73
Blowpipes, glassmaking **G** 226, 230; picture **G** 231
bottle making **B** 341
Blowtorch, oxacetylene **G** 60–61
Blubber, fatty tissue **W** 151
Eskimo food **E** 290
extracting whale oil **W** 153

Blue babies, children born with defective hearts **H** 86b
Blue-Backed Speller, by Noah Webster **P** 193–94
early textbooks **T** 138
spelling words from **S** 379
Blueberries G 301; picture **G** 299
Bluebirds B 220; picture **B** 239
Idaho, mountain bluebird state bird of **I** 54
Missouri, state bird of **M** 367
Nevada, mountain bluebird state bird of **N** 123
New York, state bird of **N** 210
Blue Birds, Camp Fire Girls **C** 37; picture **C** 39
Bluebonnet, state flower of Texas **T** 123
Bluebottle flies, pictures **I** 276
Blue Boy, The, painting by Thomas Gainsborough **G** 4
Blue cheese D 13
Blue-collar workers L 8
Bluefin, fish
habitat, feeding habits, uses **F** 215
Bluefish F 188
Bluegill, fish, picture **F** 209
Bluegrass Basin, of Kentucky **K** 215
Bluegrass State, nickname for Kentucky **K** 212
Blue Grotto, Capri, Italy **C** 156; **I** 428
Blueground, or kimberlite, diamond-bearing rock **G** 70
Blue hen chicken
state bird of Delaware; picture **D** 87
Blue Hen State, nickname for Delaware **D** 86, 87
Blue jays, birds, pictures **B** 245, 247

Blue laws, legislation that seeks to regulate matters of individual conscience or conduct, such as laws prohibiting drinking or Sunday labor. The term originated during colonial days in New Haven, Conn., where such laws were bound in blue paper.

Blue Nile River, Africa **N** 260; **E** 299; **S** 448
Blue ox, Babe, belonging to Paul Bunyan **F** 312
Blue Plate, Legend of the L 133

Blueprint, photographic print on bright-blue background, made by process invented (1842) by Sir John Herschel. Process is used mainly for copying architects' plans and mechanical drawings. The name has come to be used for any plan or design.
airplane models, top secret **A** 105–06
plumbing systems **P** 343

Blue Riband, award for Atlantic crossing **O** 21–22
Blue Rider, The, modern art group in Germany **M** 391
German art **G** 171
Kandisky, Wassily **K** 166
Klee, Paul **K** 271
Blue Ridge mountain range, eastern United states **G** 135
Maryland **M** 116
North Carolina **N** 309
South Carolina **S** 298
Tennessee **T** 76
Virginia **V** 346; picture **V** 355
Blue Ridge National Parkway N 315–16; picture **N** 308
Blues, the, music **J** 57–58
folk songs **F** 304
gospel song **N** 106
Handy, W. C., father of the blues **H** 34
Negro folklore **F** 313
Blue spruce, tree
state tree of Colorado, picture **C** 401
state tree of Utah, picture **U** 241

Bluestocking, term used to mock literary or pedantic woman, often implying that she has only affected or

Bluestocking (continued)
superficial interest in intellectual matters. Term derived
from women's literary discussion group in 18th-century
London, called Bluestocking Club because of informal
blue stockings worn by a guest.

Blue whales W 149
  giants of nature G 202
  largest mammal M 61
  ocean life O 40–41
Blum (BLOOM), **Léon,** French statesman F 419
Blunderbuss, smooth-bore gun G 420
Blunger (BLUN-ger), a clay-mixing machine, used in ceramics C 178
Blurb, form of advertising on book jacket B 317

Bly, Nellie (Elizabeth Cochrane Seaman) (1867–1922),
American journalist, b. Cochran Mills, Pa. She wrote for
Pittsburgh *Dispatch,* New York *World,* and New York
Journal. She pretended insanity to get into mental ward
at Blackwell's Island, New York, in order to write about
conditions there. She made round-the-world trip (1889) to
beat fictional record in Jules Verne's *Around the World
in 80 Days.* Traveling by ship, train, and horse, she
completed trip in 72 days, 6 hours, 11 minutes, then a
record time. She wrote *10 Days in a Madhouse, Around
the World in 72 days,* and *Nellie Bly's Book.*

Blytheville, Arkansas A 430
BMEWS (Ballistic Missile Early Warning System) U 161

B'nai B'rith, Independent Order of (from Hebrew, meaning "sons of the covenant"), Jewish fraternal organization founded in 1843 to promote charity and brotherly
love by uniting Jews in cultural, social, civic, and
philanthropic activities. There are over 2,500 lodges in
33 countries, whose activities include Hillel chapters on
college campuses, the B'nai B'rith Youth Organization,
Anti-Defamation League, UN Liaison Office, and vocational and armed services programs. The organization
publishes the *National Jewish Monthly* and *Jewish Heritage.*

Bo, Sierra Leone S 175

Board of trade, organization for development and
protection of business interests. Term also refers to
organization of merchants and manufacturers of a city,
working to promote civic enterprises of a community.

Boars, male pigs H 209; P 248
  wild boar, picture H 212
Boar's Head, The, English carol C 122
Boas, snakes S 206–07; picture S 212
Boat racing B 264
  rowing competition R 338–39
Boats and boating B 260–64
  ancient water craft S 155
  balsas, pictures A 252, B 304, L 50
  Bangladesh B 44; picture B 44b
  canal boats E 278–80
  canoes and canoeing C 99–100a
  catamaran, picture T 262
  Chinese dwellings C 263
  early transportation T 257
  felucca, on the Nile, pictures N 260, R 240
  gondolas on the canals, Venice, pictures B 55,
    H 179, I 456
  houseboats H 176–77
  hydrofoils H 304–05
  iceboating I 28–29
  inventions in water transportation I 337
  johnboats for float fishing M 366
  junks, picture R 249
  kayaks C 99; E 289; picture G 370
  Mississippi riverboats, pictures I 358, M 352
  murkab on the Nile, picture S 449
  rowing R 338–39
  safety measures S 6
  sailboats, types of, pictures S 9
  sailing S 9–15
  sightseeing on Lake Xochimilco, picture L 30
  weather warning flags F 246
  Why do boats float? F 251
  See also Canoes and canoeing; Rowing; Sailing; Water
    sports
Bobber, for pole and line fishing F 205
Bobbies, English policemen P 373; picture P 372
  London L 338
Bobbin, spool for holding thread I 234
  cotton yarn on spools C 525
Bobbin lace L 19
Bobcats C 139; picture C 140
Bobko, Karol J., American astronaut S 347
Bobo Dioulasso (BO-bo diu-LA-so), Upper Volta U 228
Bobolinks, birds B 220; picture B 233
Bobsledding B 264–66
  Olympic event O 109
Bobwhites, or quail, birds B 220; picture B 233
  See also Quail
Bocachee see Tomochichi
Boccaccio (bo-CA-chi-o), **Giovanni,** Italian writer I 476–77
  short stories S 165
Boccherini (bo-car-E-ni), **Luigi,** Italian composer C 186;
  I 485
Boccioni (bo-CHO-ni), **Umberto,** Italian painter I 473
  modern art M 391
  space shapes in sculpture S 105
Bock beer B 117
Böcklin (BUK-lene), **Arnold,** Swiss artist G 171
Bode (BO-da), **Johannes,** German astronomer S 242–43
Bode's law S 242
Bodhisattvas (bo-dis-AT-vas), Buddhist deities B 424
Bodleian (bod-LE-ian) **Library,** Oxford University L 197
Bodmer, Johann, Swiss professor G 175
Bodoni (bo-DO-ni), **Giambattista,** Italian printer T 345
Body, human B 267–83
  adolescence, changes during A 22
  aging A 81
  air pollution, effect on A 108–09, 110
  anthropological studies A 306–07
  antibodies and antigens A 317
  blood B 255–59
  body's senses B 283–88
  brain B 363–69
  cancer and cancer research C 89–95
  cells C 159–64
  chemistry see Body chemistry
  control of parasite diseases D 188
  dreaming, effects of D 306
  drugs affect D 326–27
  energy, source of E 201
  feet and hands, basic pattern of F 79–80, 83
  G-forces and weightlessness S 340j–340 L
  hair H 2–3
  health H 82–85
  heart H 86–86c
  immunology I 104–07
  mental health M 220–22
  osmosis O 234–35
  physical examination by a doctor M 208e–208h
  reproductive organs R 179–80
  senses, guards on the alert B 280–82, 283–88
  smoking, effects of S 203

teeth T 47–49
  voice apparatus V 375
  water percentage in W 51
Body chemistry B 289–97
  biochemistry B 183–84
  body catalysts C 199
  cancer research C 94–95
  drugs supply hormones D 326
  food chain processes L 239–40
  living matter, chemical makeup of L 211–12
  viruses, chemical makeup of V 363
Body-drop, automobile assembling A 550

Body language, a term used to describe some forms of nonverbal communication. Generally, it refers to facial expressions and gestures that reveal emotions and attitudes. For example, certain facial expressions and body gestures signify pain among people everywhere. In this way body language can communicate a message that might not be easily conveyed through speech. Used with verbal communication, it can express attitudes that words alone cannot.

Body lice I 283–84
Body's senses B 283–88
  guards on the alert B 280–82
  nervous system, biological studies of B 195
Body temperature B 279
  anesthesia produced by lowering A 259
  hibernation H 122–24
  how a nurse takes temperature N 414
  medical examination, techniques of M 208e
  sleep lowers S 200
  studies of Alakaluf Indians A 306–07
Boerhaave (BOOR-ha-va), **Hermann,** Dutch doctor M 206
Boers, Dutch settlers in South Africa A 68; S 273
  Boer War B 298
Boer War, 1899–1902 B 298–99; E 228; S 273
  Africa, struggle for A 68

Bogart, Humphrey DeForest (1899–1957), American actor, b. New York, N.Y. His portrayals of hardened and cynical characters, starting with stage and screen versions of *The Petrified Forest* (1935–36), made him one of Hollywood's greatest box-office attractions. Appearing in over 50 motion pictures, he won the 1951 Academy Award for best actor for his performance in *The African Queen*.

Bogalusa, Louisiana L 361
Bogey (BOAG-y), golf score G 255
Bog iron I 406
  New Jersey's Pine Barrens N 171
Bogotá (bo-go-TA), capital of Colombia C 383; pictures C 379, 383
  University of the Andes, picture S 285
Bogs
  cranberry bog, picture G 300
  Okefenokee Swamp, Georgia G 132; picture G 143
Bohème (bo-EM), **La,** opera by Giacomo Puccini O 140

Bohemia (bo-HE-mia), territory of Czechoslovakia bounded by the countries of Austria, Germany, and Poland and the regions of Moravia and Silesia. Rich in mineral, agricultural, and industrial resources, it is especially famous for its hops and glass and ceramics industry. Principal cities are Prague and Pilsen, and noted resorts include Carlsbad and Marienbad. Attaining the height of its political power during the Luxemburg dynasty (1310–1437), it became part of Austrian Empire (1526–1918). Incorporated as a province of Czechoslovakia (1918), it now is linked with Moravia and Silesia to form a state (since 1949). Picture C 563.

Böhl de Faber (BURL day FA-ber), **Cecilia,** Spanish writer S 370
Bohr, Niels, Danish atomic physicist B 300; C 216; picture C 215; P 232
Boiardo (bo-YAR-do), **Matteo Maria,** Italian poet I 477
Boileau-Despréaux (bwa-LO-day-pray-O), **Nicholas,** French poet F 438
Boilers
  heating systems H 98–99
  steam engines S 421
Boiling point H 92–93
  liquids, properties of L 310
  water W 54
  why a geyser plays G 193
Boise (BOI-se), capital of Idaho I 65–66
Boise National Forest, Idaho I 64
Boise River, Idaho I 57; picture I 58
Bok, Edward, Netherlands-born American writer A 215
Bokassa I, formerly Jean Bedel Bokassa, emperor of Central African Empire C 173
Bok Singing Tower, Florida F 269
Bolas, hunting devices I 211
Bolas spiders S 386
Boleyn (BULL-in), **Anne,** 2nd queen of Henry VIII of England E 220; H 109
  Reformation in England C 286
Bolívar (bo-LI-var), **Simón,** South American liberator and patriot B 301, 306
  Colombian independence leader C 384
  flags F 227
  present Organization of American States outgrowth of his ideal O 210
  San Martín, José de, meeting with S 35
  Simón Bolívar's birthday holiday H 149
Bolivia (bo-LIV-ia) B 302–06
  corn harvest, picture S 290
  flag F 242
  life in Latin America L 47–61
  national anthem N 21
Bollée (bo-LAY), **Amédée,** French Inventor A 544
Boll weevil C 523
  Alabama's monument to cotton pest A 119
Bolmarcich, Francisco Orlich see Orlich, Francisco Bolmarcich

Bologna (bol-ON-yah), **Giovanni da** (Jean Bologne) (1529?–1608), Flemish sculptor, b. Douai, France. He became court sculptor to Medici family in Italy (1558). His statues include Fountain of Neptune in Bologna and equestrian statue of Cosimo I de' Medici.

Bolsheviks, Communist supporters of Lenin L 138
  Stalin, an organizer for S 395
Bolt, Robert, English playwright E 268
Bolt-action, of guns and rifles G 418–19
Bolton, Guy, English-born American dramatist M 542

Bolton, Sarah Knowles (1841–1916), American author and reformer, b. Farmington, Conn. She wrote such biographies as *Poor Boys Who Became Famous, Girls Who Became Famous,* and *Famous Men of Science.*

Bolts, fasteners N 3
Bolyai, Johann, Hungarian mathematician M 159

Bomarc, U.S. Air Force surface-to-air missile armed with a nuclear warhead. The Bomarc finds its target by means of radar signals. It has two sections, or stages. The upper stage is powered by ramjet engines. The lower stage is a solid-fuel booster rocket (some Bomarcs still

Bomarc (continued)
have liquid-fuel boosters, however).
  Canadian bases C 82

Bombardier, Joseph-Armand, Canadian inventor of the
    snowmobile S 215
Bombay, India B 307–08
  commercial center of India I 122; pictures I 124
  nuclear power plant, picture P 427
  one of the great cities of the world, picture C 310
Bombs
  atomic N 362–63
  hydrogen H 306; N 364–65

Bonaire (bo-NAIRE), or Buen Aire, or Buen Ayre, tropical
island of the Netherlands Antilles in the Caribbean Sea.
Its main products—sisal, divi-divi, and goat manure—
are exported from Kralendijk, the chief city.
  Caribbean Sea and islands C 116–19

Bonanza farms, large wheat farms N 328
Bonaparte, Napoleon see Napoleon I

Bonaparte family (Buonaparte in Italian), Corsican
family of Italian descent, brought to prominence in
Europe by French emperor Napoleon I (1769–1821).
Joseph (1768–1844), brother of Napoleon I, was king of
Naples (1806–08) and king of Spain (1808–13). Louis
(1778–1846), brother of Napoleon I, was king of the
Netherlands (1806–10). Jérôme (1784–1860), brother of
Napoleon I, was king of Westphalia (1807–13). François
Charles Joseph, or Napoleon II (1811–32), son of Napo-
leon I, was titular king of Rome. Charles Louis Napoleon,
or Napoleon III (1808–73), son of Louis and nephew of
Napoleon I, was emperor of France (1852–70).

Bonar Law, Andrew see Law, Andrew Bonar

Bond, Carrie Jacobs (1862–1946), American songwriter,
b. Janesville, Wis. Her most famous and popular songs
were "A Perfect Day" and "I Love You Truly."

Bond, George, American naval officer U 19

Bond, Julian (1940–), American politician and civil
rights leader, Negro, b. Nashville, Tenn. Elected a member
of the Georgia House of Representatives (1965), he was
barred from taking his seat because of his anti-Vietnam
War stand, but the U.S. Supreme Court ruled (1966) his
constitutional rights had been violated. He was the first
Negro nominated for vice-president (1968 Democratic
convention)—a symbolic nomination, since he was not
old enough to serve. Picture N 104a

Bond, Shadrach, American statesman and pioneer I 84
Bonding, of adhesives G 242
Bondmen, peasants bound to the land S 197
Bondone, Giotto di see Giotto di Bondone
Bonds, certificates of loans S 428
Bonds, chemical C 200, 218
Bône, Algeria see Annaba
Bone china, ceramic work C 173
  English porcelain P 418
Bones, of animals
  birds B 199, 200–01
  body, human B 270; diagram B 271
  feet F 80–82
  hands F 83
  marrow of B 273
  What is a backbone? K 251
Bongo drums D 336
Bongos, hoofed mammals H 221; picture H 217

Bonheur (bon-ER), Rosa (Marie Rosalie Bonheur)
(1822–1899), French painter, b. Bordeaux. She is known
for spirited animal paintings, as Horse Fair.

Bonhoeffer, Dietrich (1906–45), German Protestant theologian and pastor, b. Breslau, Germany. Barred from
teaching because of his early opposition to Nazism, he
was active in international activities of his church. He
joined in underground German resistance to Hitler, was
arrested in 1943, and hanged in 1945. In Letters and
Papers from Prison published in 1951, he stressed the
need for religion to involve itself in worldly activities.
He is an important voice in Protestant radical theology.

Bonhomme Richard, ship commanded by John Paul
    Jones J 134
  battle scene R 206
Boniface (BON-i-face) VIII, pope
  dispute with King Philip The Fair of France
    R 293
Boniface, Saint, English missionary C 284; R 290

Bonin Islands, volcanic islands in the Pacific Ocean. The
three main groups are the Bailey Islands, the Beechey
Islands, and the Parry Islands.
  Pacific Ocean and islands P 5

Bonito (bon-E-to), fish F 188
Bon Marché (bon mar-SHAY), Paris, first department
    store D 118
Bonn, capital of West Germany G 158
  Christmas in, picture C 291
Bonneville (BON-nev-ille), Benjamin L. E. de, French-born
    American explorer O 260
Bonneville, Lake, Utah L 31
  prehistoric geological formation U 244
Bonneville Dam, Oregon and Washington D 19–20
Bonneville Salt Flats, Utah U 243
  automobile racing A 540; S 22
Bonney, William H. see Billy the Kid
Bonspiel, curling tournament C 555

Bontemps (BON-tomp), Arna Wendell (1902–73), American author, b. Alexandria, La. He was a distinguished
member of a group of black writers and poets known
as the Harlem Renaissance group. His books include
The Story of the Negro and Black Thunder.

Booby, seabird with long pointed wings, wedge-shaped
tail, and straight beak. They dive for their food with
great force, and sleep on the water's surface. The bird
was named "booby" (which means "fool" or "dunce")
because it does not attempt to escape or defend itself
when in danger.

Book, Shrine of the, Jerusalem J 81
  picture M 513
Book awards
  children's literature, awards for B 309–10b
  influence on children's literature C 242
  Nobel prizes N 265–66
  Pulitzer prizes P 524–28
  See also National Book Awards
Bookbinding B 327–29
  how medieval books were made B 320–21, 322
Book catalogs, in libraries L 185
Book clubs P 514
  paperbacks for young people P 58a
Book design B 323–26, 331
  choice of typefaces T 345–46
  medieval books B 319–21
Booker T. Washington National Monument V 353

Book fair, exhibition of children's books held by school, library, or professional or other group to interest children and their parents in good books for youngsters. Very often books may be purchased as well as examined at the fair. Book fairs are sometimes held during National Children's Book Week in November or during Children's Spring Book Festival in May.

Frankfurt Book Fair in West Germany for general publishing **P** 515

Bookkeeping and accounting B 311–14
  checking accounts in banks **B** 49
  See also Calculators; Computers
Bookkeeping machines O 57
Book matches M 153
Bookmobiles, libraries **L** 173
Book of Common Prayer see Prayer, Book of Common
Book of Kells see Kells, Book of
Book of Mormon M 457
Book of Psalms (SALMS), or Psalter **H** 309

Book of the Dead, collection of Egyptian hymns, prayers, and magic chants that made up funeral rites of ancient Egypt. It was based on the Osirian religion and remained in use from about 1500 B.C. to the early centuries of the Christian era. Only fragments written centuries apart exist today. Writings have been found on pyramid walls, on mummy cases, and on papyri in sarcophagi (coffins).

Book of the Year for Children Medal B 309
Book reports B 314–17
Book reviews B 317
  literary criticism **L** 313
  news of books **B** 331, 334
Books B 318–34
  awards and medals for children's literature
    B 309–10b
  bibliography for a composition **B** 170
  binding see Bookbinding
  blind, books for the **B** 252–53
  bookmaking **B** 329–34
  care of **B** 329; **L** 180
  children's literature **C** 236–48b
  classics in literature **C** 334
  collecting autographed books **A** 526–27
  comic books **C** 422–23
  copyright, notice of **T** 244–45
  design see Book design
  easy-to-read books **C** 243
  education, history of **E** 65–66
  encyclopedias **E** 193–97
  Frankfurt Book Fair **P** 515
  from author to library **B** 329–34
  front matter **B** 322, 331; **L** 180–82
  history of bookmaking **B** 318–22
  How can books be kept from coming apart? **B** 329
  illuminated see Illuminated manuscripts
  illustration and illustrators **I** 89–97
  indexes see Indexes and indexing
  invention of **I** 338
  Islamic illustrations **I** 421; picture **I** 418
  largest and smallest at Library of Congress **W** 32
  layout **B** 322
  Leipzig book fair **F** 11
  Newbery, John **N** 137
  novels **N** 345–49
  on storytelling **S** 435
  paper **P** 51–57
  paperback books **P** 58–58a, 514
  parts of a book **L** 180–81
  picture books for children **C** 242–43
  pocket editions invented by Manutius **B** 322

  prayer books **P** 434
  printers and publishers famous for design **B** 324, 326
  printing **P** 457–67
  programed instruction **P** 475–477
  publishing **P** 513–15
  reference books **R** 129–31
  reports and reviews **B** 314–17
  talking books **B** 253
  textbooks **T** 138–39
  typefaces **T** 343–46
  word origins **W** 241
  See also Illuminated manuscripts; Libraries
Book Week C 242
  exhibits for **B** 316
Boomers, land seekers **O** 95
Boomers, red kangaroos **K** 170; picture **K** 168
Boomslangs, snakes **S** 207

Boomtown, town that grows suddenly because of industrial activity or the discovery of a valuable natural resource. Boomtowns, such as San Francisco, Calif., and Tombstone, Ariz., developed in the United States during the 19th century when the discovery of gold or silver brought an influx of people to the town. Rochester, N.Y., became a boomtown with the opening of the Erie Canal.
  Denver **D** 116

Boondoggle, to engage in unimportant or insignificant work or to waste time. Name became popular when it was applied to federal relief projects during the New Deal. Term originally was used by cowboys to describe activity of making saddle trappings out of scraps of leather, which they did to kill time.

Boone, Daniel, American pioneer **B** 335
  birthplace, Daniel Boone Homestead **P** 139
  Horn in the West, outdoor drama at Boone, N.C. **N** 315
  settlement of Kentucky **K** 225, 226
  westward movement **W** 145
  Wilderness Road **O** 255
Boonesborough, frontier fort **F** 376
Boone's Lick Trail, early road **M** 374
Boone's Trace, pioneer road **P** 260
Boongaries, tree kangaroos **K** 170
Booster shots, of vaccines or toxoids **V** 261
  medicine, techniques of **M** 210
Booster stage, of multistage rockets **R** 259
Boot camps, for recruits
  United States Marine Corps **U** 180
  United States Navy **U** 189–90
Boötes (bo-O-tese), constellation **C** 492

Booth, Edwin Thomas (1833–1893), American actor, b. Bel Air, Md. He was brother of John Wilkes Booth, Lincoln's assassin. The greatest tragedian of his day, known especially for Shakespearean roles, he set a record when he appeared in 100 consecutive performancies of *Hamlet.* He built Booth Theater in New York, N.Y. (1869), and founded the Players Club there (1888). He was elected to the Hall of Fame (1925).

Booth, John Wilkes (1838–1865), American actor and assassin of President Abraham Lincoln, b. Bel Air, Md. Sympathetic to Confederate cause in Civil War, he plotted with group of men to kidnap President Lincoln but then decided upon assassination. He shot Lincoln at a performance in Ford's Theater (April 14, 1865) in Washington, D.C., and shouted "Sic semper tyrannis! [Thus ever to tyrants], the South is avenged!" He broke his leg in escaping but managed to reach Virginia, where he either was killed or committed suicide.
  bitter aftermath of Civil War **C** 327; **L** 297

Boothe, Clare see Luce, Clare Boothe

Booth family, English family of evangelists associated with Salvation Army. Salvation Army was started by **General William** (1829–1912) as Christian Mission in Whitechapel district of London (1865). It later became Salvation Army (1878), with chapters around the world; **William Bramwell** (1856–1929) succeeded his father as general, and another son, **Ballington** (1859–1940), withdrew to found Volunteers of America; other descendants have continued in Salvation Army affairs.

Boothia Peninsula, in Arctic Circle, picture **C** 53
Bootleggers, in the Roaring Twenties **C** 496
Boots and shoes see Shoes
Bora (BO-ra), wind of Adriatic region **M** 213
   Albania **A** 145
Borah, William Edgar, American statesman **I** 67
Borax, mineral **C** 22
Bordeaux, France **F** 406
Borden, P. E. I., Canada **P** 456b, 456e

Borden, Gail (1801–1874), American inventor and surveyor, b. Norwich, N.Y. He invented meat biscuit, condensed milk, and method of concentrating juices. He opened first condensing plant in Wassaic, N.Y. (1861), and introduced dairy sanitation methods that are now compulsory. Borden took charge of survey of Texas and made first topographical map of Republic of Texas.

Borden, Sir Robert Laird (1854–1937), Canadian lawyer and statesman, b. Grand Pré, Nova Scotia. He was elected to Canadian House of Commons (1896), where he became leader of Conservative Party (1901). As prime minister (1911–20) he led Canada through World War I and afterward served as delegate to Paris Peace Conference and as representative to League of Nations. He was knighted in 1914.
   Canada, history of **C** 75, 81

Border states, American Civil War **C** 458
Borecole see Kale
Borers, insects **P** 289
Bores, of guns **G** 414–15
Bores, tidal waves **T** 185
   Amazon River **A** 179
   Bay of Fundy, Canada **N** 138
Borescopes, optical instruments **O** 168

Borges (BOR-hace), **Jorge Luis** (1899–   ), Argentine author and university professor, b. Buenos Aires. A member of Argentine Academy of Letters, he is a writer of essays, poems, and novels, including *El Idioma de los Argentinos* and *Ficciones.* **L** 72

Borghese Gallery, Rome, picture **M** 510

Borgia (BOR-ja) **family,** noble Italian family of Spanish origin, powerful during 15th and 16th centuries. **Alfonso** (1378–1458) became Pope Calixtus III (1455), and **Rodrigo** (1431?–1503) became Pope Alexander VI (1492). Rodrigo's son **Cesare** (1475?–1507) was a cardinal who left his office and tried to conquer a kingdom in central Italy. Cesare was known for his cruelty and treachery. His methods are praised in Machiavelli's *Il Principe.* Rodrigo's daughter **Lucrezia** (1480–1519) was a great patron of the arts. She was reputed to have been cruel and villainous, but probably did not commit many of the crimes of which she has been accused.

Borglum, Gutzon (John Gutzon de la Mothe Borglum) (1871–1941), American sculptor, b. Idaho. He is best known for national memorial at Mt. Rushmore, S.D., with its heads of Washington, Jefferson, Lincoln, and Theodore Roosevelt. His other works include large head of Lincoln at the Capitol in Washington, D.C., and *The Mares of Diomedes,* in the Metropolitan Museum of Art.

Borgo Maggiore (ma-JO-ray), San Marino **S** 34
Boris I (BO-ris), czar of Bulgaria **B** 444
Boris III, king of Bulgaria **B** 444
Boris Godunov (BOR-is goo-du-NOF), dramatic poem by Pushkin **D** 298; **U** 60
Boris Godunov, opera by Mussorgsky **O** 140–41
Borlaug, Norman, American agronomist **F** 343
Borman, Frank, American astronaut **S** 344, 346

Bormann (BOR-monn), **Martin Ludwig** (1900–   ), German Nazi leader, b. Halberstadt. Chief of staff of Nazi Party (1933–41), he was appointed Hitler's third deputy (1941). He was sentenced in absentia at Nuremberg Trials (1946) to die as war criminal, but it is not known whether he is dead or alive and in hiding.

Borneo **B** 336–38; **I** 218–19
   See also Malaysia
Bornholm (BORN-holm) **Island,** Denmark **D** 108
Bornu (BOR-nu), ancient African empire **C** 183
Borodin (BO-ro-din), **Alexander,** Russian scientist and composer **U** 63
   opera **O** 136
Boron, element **E** 154, 160
   control rods for nuclear reactors **N** 363
Borough (BUR-o), unit of municipal government **M** 503
Borromini, Francesco, Italian architect **I** 473
Bosch, Hieronymus, Flemish painter **D** 352; **P** 23
   Temptation of Saint Anthony, painting **D** 355

Bosch (BOSH), **Juan** (1909–   ), Dominican statesman and writer, b. La Vega. He founded Dominican Revolutionary Party (1939). During his political exile (1942–61) he traveled in Latin America. Elected president of Dominican Republic in first free general elections (1962), he served until overthrown and exiled (1963). An attempt in 1965 to restore him to power failed because of American intervention, and he lost his bid for re-election in 1966.
   Dominican Republic, history of **D** 283

Bosnia and Herzegovina (HER-tze-go-vi-na), Yugoslav state **Y** 358
Bosporus, strait, Turkey **T** 324, 326
Boston, capital of Massachusetts **B** 339–40; **M** 141
   Boston Metropolitan Area **M** 146
   colonial newspapers **N** 198
   first high school, 1820 **E** 72
   Hub of the Universe, origin of the term **M** 134
   museums and libraries **M** 143–44
   police strike, Coolidge's stand **C** 495–96
   skyline view, picture **M** 139
   urban landscape of New England **N** 138h

Boston, Ralph (1939–   ), American long jumper, Negro, b. Laurel, Miss. He won long jump at 1960 Olympic Games. In 1961 he became first man to jump more than 27 feet, leaping 27 feet, 3¼ inches, to break Jesse Owens' 25-year-old record.

Boston Light, Boston Harbor, Massachusetts **L** 278
Boston Massacre, 1770 **R** 196
   Adams, John **A** 8
   Adams, Samuel, protests **A** 17
   events leading to Declaration of Independence **D** 60
Boston Mountains, Arkansas **A** 421
Boston News-Letter, newspaper **M** 141

Boston Port Bill, 1774 R 197
Boston Public Latin School B 340; C 394
Boston's City Hall A 387; picture B 340
Boston Symphony Orchestra
Berkshire Festival M 551
Boston Tea Party, 1773 R 196
Adams, Samuel, organizes A 17
described in *Johnny Tremain* R 209–10
events leading to Declaration of Independence D 60
Revere, Paul, participates in R 192–93
Boston terrier, dog D 261; picture D 256
Boswell, James, Scottish biographer E 258–59
Samuel Johnson's Club J 131
Botanical (bo-TAN-ic-al) **gardens** Z 379; pictures Z 378
Botany, study of plants B 340, 190; P 290–304
archeological studies A 359–60
Carver, George W., new uses of plants C 128–29
cell structure C 159–64
classification of plants (taxonomy) T 28–32
experiments and projects E 356–59
food plants P 305–10
fossils F 378
fruit defined F 280
genetics G 77–88
kingdoms of living things K 249–59
leaves L 114–20
life L 208–14
Linnaeus invented classification system L 304
medicinal plants P 310–15
Mendel's experiments G 80–82; M 219
odd and interesting plants P 316–20
photosynthesis P 221–23
poisonous plants P 321–23
reproduction R 176–77
taxonomy T 28–32
See also Plants
Botany Bay, Australia A 516
Botha (BO-ta), **Louis,** Afrikaner leader S 273

Botha (BO-ta), **Pieter Willem** (1916–), prime minister of South Africa, b. Paul Roux district, Orange Free State. After a long career in South African politics and government, he was elected prime minister in 1978, succeeding B. John Vorster. As defense minister (1965–78), Botha established a modern South African defense force and developed a domestic armaments industry to supply it.

Bothnia, Gulf of, an arm of the Baltic Sea O 45
Bothwell, James Hepburn, 4th earl of, husband of Mary Queen of Scots M 130
Bo Tree, sacred to Buddhists B 423

Botsford, Amos (1744–1812), Canadian statesman, b. Newtown, Conn. He fought for British in American Revolution and represented British Government in settling Loyalists in Nova Scotia (1782). He was the first speaker of New Brunswick's House of Assembly.

Botswana (bot-SWA-na) B 340a
children, picture A 54
flag F 235
poetry of the Tswana A 76a
Botswana and Swaziland, University of, at Kwaluseni, Swaziland S 480b
Böttger (BERT-ker), **Johann,** German potter, first porcelain maker in Europe C 176–77
Botticelli (bo-ti-CHEL-li), **Sandro,** Italian painter B 340b; I 469
Adoration of the Magi, painting N 41
Birth of Venus, painting I 466
Florentine painting P 20
Primavera, painting B 340b

Renaissance art R 162, 166
Saint Augustine of Hippo, painting C 282
Bottled gas F 489
Bottlenose dolphins D 270–73, 274, 276
Bottlenose whales W 147, 149
Bottles and bottling B 341–43
antique bottles A 320
vacuum, or thermos, bottles V 265
Bottle trees, or baobab trees P 283
famous trees in the Sudan S 447
Botulism (BOT-ul-ism), poisoning B 11; F 354

Boucher (bu-SHAY), **François** (1703–70), French painter, b. Paris. He was appointed first court painter to Louis XV (1765) and director of the Royal Academy of Painting and Sculpture (1765). A protégé of Madame de Pompadour (from 1745), he painted portraits, genre pictures, landscapes, and designs for tapestries in decorative, rococo style. His works include *Diana and Callisto.*
French art, history of F 425
rococo style in painting P 24

Boudinot (BU-din-o), **Elias** (1740–1821), American political leader, b. Philadelphia, Pa. He joined Committee of Correspondence in New Jersey (1774) and was then elected to the Continental Congress (1777). As president of Congress, he signed peace treaty with Great Britain (1782) ending Revolutionary War. He was elected to House of Representatives (1789–95) and served as director of U.S. Mint in Philadelphia (1795–1805). He organized (1816) and was first president (1816–21) of American Bible Society.

Bouffant (bou-FONT), shape in fashion design F 65

Bougainville (BOU-gan-vil), volcanic island in southwestern Pacific, largest of the Solomon Islands and part of Papua New Guinea. Bougainville contains two densely forested mountain ranges and rich volcanic soil. It was the last major Japanese stronghold in Solomon Islands during World War II. P 59

Bought Me a Cat, folk song F 322
Boulder, Colorado C 414
Boulder caves C 156–57
Boulder clay, soil deposited by glaciers S 234
Boulle (BOOL), **André,** French cabinetmaker D 77; F 508

Boulton (BOLT-on), **Matthew** (1728–1809), English manufacturer and engineer, b. Birmingham. He became a partner of James Watt (1775) and supplied capital, factory, and know-how for producing Watt's steam engines. He also invented a steam-powered press for making coins, used in Britain until 1882. He was prominent in British scientific circles and was a friend of Benjamin Franklin, Priestley, and Darwin. I 239

Boumedienne, Houari, Algerian political leader A 163
Boundaries
defined by rivers R 241
territorial expansion of the United States T 105–15
Bounties
government aid to agriculture A 94
military service encouraged by bounties D 289
See also Subsidies
Bounty, Mutiny on the *see* Bligh, William
Bourassa (BOO-ras-sa), **Henri,** Canadian journalist Q 13

Bourbon, House of, French royal family, descended from 9th-century baron Aimar (or Adhemar), whose seat was Castle of Bourbon. The dynasty, founded (1589) in France by Henry IV, lasted until 1793 and continued dur-

Bourbon, House of (continued)
ing restoration (1814–30) under Louis XVIII and Charles X and under Louis Philippe (1830–48) of Bourbon-Orléans line. The grandson of Louis XIV, Duke of Anjou, founded Bourbon royal line in Spain (1700–1931) as Philip V of Spain. Philip's son Charles founded royal family (1735–1861) in Naples and Sicily. The house is remembered for extravagances of Louis XIV and Louis XV of France.
 France, history of F 415–16

Bourgeoisie (BOORJ-wah-zi), people of the middle class
 power and economic influence increased by Age of
 Exploration E 387
Bourguiba (boor-GHE-ba), Habib, president of Tunisia
 T 312
Bournonville, Auguste, father of Danish ballet B 28
Bourse, a money exchange S 428
Bouts, Dierik, Dutch painter D 351
 Last Supper, painting D 354
Bovidae (BO-vi-de), cattle family C 147
 hoofed mammals H 220
Bovines (BO-vines), cattlelike hoofed mammals H 220;
 pictures H 216
Bow and arrow see Bows and arrows

Bowditch (BOWD-itch), Nathaniel (1773–1838), American mathematician and astronomer, b. Salem, Mass. A self-educated man, he went to sea in 1795 as a clerk and became a ship's master in 1802. His revision of J. H. Moore's The Practical Navigator, which appeared as The New American Practical Navigator in 1802, was made the standard authority of the United States Navy Department. Bowditch worked on astronomical problems in his leisure time and wrote articles on the subject.

Bowdoin (BO-din), James (1726–1790), American states-man, b. Boston, Mass. He was a member of Massa-chusetts General Court (1753–56) and Council (1757–69) and of the Constitutional Convention (1779). As governor of state (1785–87) he put down Shays' Rebellion. He was a delegate to national constitutional convention and first president of American Academy of Arts and Sciences (1780–90). Bowdoin College in Maine is named for him.

Bowdoin College, Maine M 40
Bow drill, tool T 210b–211
Bowed instruments M 545–46
Bowell (BO-well), Sir Mackenzie, Canadian statesman
 O 125
Bowen, Elizabeth, English writer E 267
Bowerbirds, picture A 273
Bowes-Lyon, Elizabeth see Elizabeth, queen consort of
 George VI
Bow hunters, archers A 366
Bowie (BOO-ie), James, American soldier and frontiers-man B 344
 Travis succeeds him as commander of Alamo T 135
Bowie knife, origin of B 344
Bow kite K 270
Bowknots K 290
Bowler hats, picture L 335

Bowles, Chester Bliss (1901–), American diplomat, b. Springfield, Mass. He established advertising firm of Benton and Bowles (1929) and was special assistant to secretary-general of UN (1946–48), governor of Connecti-cut (1949–51), ambassador to India and Nepal (1951–53), congressman (1959–60), undersecretary of state (1961), and president's special advisor on African, Asian, and Latin-American affairs (1961 to 1963). He was again ambassador to India (1963 to 1969). He is author of several books, including Ambassador's Report and The Conscience of a Liberal.

Bowl games, in football F 365
Bowlines, knots K 290
Bowling B 345–49
 See also Cricket
Bowling, pitching in cricket C 531–32
Bowl of Plums, painting by Chardin F 424
Bowls, or lawn bowling B 349

Bowne, John (1627?–1695), American Quaker leader, b. Matlock, England. He arrived in Boston in 1649 and settled in Flushing in 1653. In his home Bowne held Quaker meetings, for which he was imprisoned and later banished. Harsh treatment of him helped bring religious freedom to citizens of New Netherland in 1663.

Bows and arrows A 366–68
 famous inventions I 335
Bow-steerers, iceboats I 29; picture I 30
Box cameras P 202–03
 photography as a hobby P 215
Boxcars, of railroads R 82
Boxer, dog, picture D 254
Boxer Rebellion, 1900, revolt in China against foreigners
 B 350; C 272
 Open-Door policy M 189–90
 Peking's Legation Quarter P 118
Boxing B 351–53
 related to fencing F 84
 Olympic Games, combative sports O 109
Boxing Day H 152
Box kites K 268–69
 invention of K 267
Box office, where theater tickets are sold T 156
Box turtles T 332
 pets P 181
Box wrenches, tools T 215
Boy Blue, nursery rhyme N 406
Boyce, William D., American publisher, organized Boy
 Scouts of America B 357

Boycott, refusal of business or social group to deal with an individual, organization, or country to show disap-proval or to force acceptance of demands. Boycotts are used by organized labor against employers whom they consider to be unfair and sometimes by nations for political purposes. Term originated in Ireland when Captain Charles Cunningham Boycott (1832–97) treated tenants on his estate so unjustly that it resulted in their refusal to deal with him.
 Martin Luther King's bus boycott K 248

Boyd, Belle, American Civil War spy S 389
Boyden, Seth, American inventor and manufacturer
 N 178
Boyer, Jean Pierre, Haiti president H 10
Boy Jesus, Bible story B 168–69
Boyle, Robert, English scientist B 354
 chemistry, history of C 209
Boyle's law B 354
 chemistry, history of C 209
 gases G 57
Boyne, battle of the, 1690 I 390; U 73
Boyne River, Ireland I 386
Boy Prisoners in the Tower, legend P 470
 England, history of E 220
Boys' camps see Camping, organized
Boys' clubs
 Junior Achievement, Inc., a student business
 J 157–58

Boys' Clubs of America B 355
Boy Scouts B 356–60
 bugle, use of B 429
 Burmese, picture A 459
 sending messages with signal flags, picture F 247
Boy Scouts of Canada B 357, 360
Boysenberries G 301
Boy's Life, magazine M 16

Boys' State, convention, sponsored by American Legion, of high school boys, usually juniors, chosen for leadership, character, scholarship, and service. It has been held annually (since 1935), usually at a college or university. Its object is to show members how government operates. Headquarters is in Indianapolis, Ind.

Boys Town, Nebraska N 82
Boz, pen name used by Charles Dickens D 158–63

Bozeman Trail, frontier trail to Montana goldfields. It ran from Julesburg, Colorado, to Virginia City, Montana, and was named for John M. Bozeman (1835–67), who opened it (1863). The trail ran through Sioux hunting territory and was scene of many Indian attacks during next decade until all posts were finally abandoned.
 Wyoming W 330, 337

BPOE see Elks, Benevolent and Protective Order of
Brace-and-bit, tool T 214
Bracelets, jewelry J 99, 100
 Danish, picture D 71
Brachiosaurs (BRAC-ki-o-saurs), dinosaurs D 177
 giants of nature G 200
Brackenbridge, Hugh Henry, American novelist A 198
Bracket fungi F 500
Bracts, of plants P 295
Braddock, General Edward, British soldier F 460
 Washington, George, on his staff W 37
Bradford, William, governor of Plymouth Colony P 346
 American colonies, history of A 187
 American literature A 195

Bradley, Omar Nelson (1893–   ), American army officer, b. Clark, Mo. During World War II he led U.S. First Army in Normandy invasion on D Day (June 6, 1944). As commander of Twelfth Army Group (1945) he commanded largest American force ever to serve under one field leader. He became general in 1945 and was promoted to general of the Army in 1950. He served as head of Veterans Administration (1945–48), chief of staff of the Army (1948–49), first chairman of Joint Chiefs of Staff (1949–53), and chairman of military committee of NATO (1949–53). He has been chairman of the board of Bulova Watch Co. since 1958.

Bradley, Thomas (1917–   ), American politician, b. Calvert, Texas. A former police officer, he was elected to the Los Angeles City Council in 1963. In 1973 he won election as the first black mayor of Los Angeles.

Bradstreet, Anne, American poet A 196

Brady, Diamond Jim (James Buchanan Brady) (1856–1917), American financier, b. New York, N.Y. A longtime employee of New York Central Railroad, he made his fortune as promoter and executive for companies manufacturing railroad equipment. His nickname comes from his love of valuable jewels. He used part of his money for producing Broadway shows and for charity.

Brady, Mathew B. American photographer C 434
Braga (BRA-ga), Portugal P 401

Bragg, Braxton, American Civil War general C 326
 Mexican War M 239
Bragi (BROG-i), Norse god N 280
Brahe (BRA), **Tycho,** Danish astronomer B 361
 astronomy, history of A 472
Brahman see Atman, Hindu spiritual principle
Brahmans, a caste in Hindu society H 130
 education of ancient times E 62
Brahmaputra (brah-ma-PU-tra) **River,** Asia R 242
 joins the Ganges G 25
 rivers of India I 125
Brahms, Johannes, German composer B 362
 choral music C 279
 First Symphony O 189
 German music G 188
 symphonies M 541
Braided rug R 354
Braille (BRAIL), alphabet of the blind B 252–53
 Braille typewriter, picture T 347
Braille, Louis, French teacher and musician B 252–53
Brain B 363–69
 aging process A 85
 birds B 203
 body controls and guards B 280, 282–83
 body's senses B 283–88
 damage caused by alcoholism A 148
 damage caused by a stroke D 208
 Does a larger brain mean greater intelligence? B 366
 dreaming experiments D 305–06
 electroencephalograms show "brain waves"
  M 208h–209
 epilepsy D 196
 hypnosis H 314–16
 in fishes, size of regions related to senses F 190
 insects I 269
 learning L 98–106
 mammals M 61
 medical and surgical techniques M 208h, 209, 210
 operations in hyperbaric chambers M 210
 primates M 418
 psychology P 488–501
 ultrasonoscope, to detect abnormal conditions M 209
Brain coral, picture J 74

Brain drain, migration of specialists and technicians from one country to another. The term was originally used with special reference to the immigration of British engineers, doctors, and scientists to the United States and to countries of the Commonwealth. However, the brain drain is now becoming an international problem. It is particularly serious when underdeveloped countries lose their highly-trained people. In 1967 the United Nations was asked to undertake a study of the international migration of talent and skills.

Brainstorming, method used to solve problems through unstructured group discussion. Method is based on idea that more effective solutions can be reached through interplay of several minds than by one individual alone.

Brainteasers, puzzles T 289
Braintree (now Quincy), Massachusetts, home of Adams family A 8, 12

Braithwaite, William Stanley Beaumont (1878–1962), American poet and anthologist, Negro, b. Boston, Mass. He published annually (1913–29) Anthology of Magazine Verse and Year Book of American Poetry. His writings include The House of Falling Leaves, anthologies The Book of Elizabethan Verse and The Book of Modern British Verse, and autobiography The House Under Arcturus. He was recipient of Spingarn medal (1918).

Brakemen, on trains R 86
Brakes
  airbrake, invention of the R 88
  hydraulic H 303
  Westinghouse, George, and air brakes W 125
Bramah (BRA-mah), **Joseph,** English engineer L 324
Bramante (brom-ON-tay), **Donato,** Italian architect
    I 467
  Renaissance architecture R 167
  Tempietto of San Pietro Church, Rome, picture I 464
Bran, of grain G 282
  flour and flour milling F 275
Branca (BRON-ca), **Giovanni,** Italian architect
    E 209
  showed principle of steam turbine T 320
Brancusi, Constantin, Rumanian-French sculptor B 370
  Adam and Eve, sculpture S 104
  Bird in Space F 431
  French school of art F 432
  place in the history of sculpture S 104
Brand, Hennig, German alchemist
  phosphorus discovered by C 212; M 152
Brand, Vance D., American astronaut S 345–46
Brandeis (BRAND-ice), **Louis,** American jurist B 370
Brandeis University, Waltham, Massachusetts B 370
Brandenburg Gate, East Berlin, Germany, map G 151
Branding, of cattle R 104–05
Brand names *see* Trademarks

Brando, Marlon (1924–), American actor, b. Omaha, Neb. He appeared on Broadway in *I Remember Mama, Candida,* and *A Streetcar Named Desire.* Hollywood introduced him to the film public in 1950 in *The Men.* He then did the film version of *A Streetcar Named Desire* and followed it with memorable performances in *On the Waterfront* (for which he won an Academy Award in 1954), *The Young Lions, Burn,* and *The Godfather.* He directed and starred in *One-Eyed Jacks.*

Brandon, Manitoba, Canada M 81

Brandt (BRONT), **Willy** (Herbert Frahm) (1913–), German political leader, b. Lübeck. A member of the Social Democratic Party, he fled Germany when Nazis gained power. He was a journalist in Norway and Sweden (1933–45) and correspondent for Scandinavian newspapers in Berlin, Germany (1945–47). He returned to Germany and regained German citizenship in 1948. He was member of Bundestag (1949–57), president of Berlin House of Representatives (1955–57), and governing mayor of West Berlin (1957–66). He was vice-chancellor and foreign minister of West Germany (1966–69), and became chancellor in 1969. He resigned in 1974. He was awarded the Nobel peace prize in 1971.

Brandy, a distilled beverage W 159
Branford Trolley Museum, East Haven, Conn. C 476

Branley, Franklyn M. (1915–), American science writer, b. New Rochelle, N.Y. A graduate of New York and Columbia Universities, he has taught high school science and has written about 50 books on all phases of science for young people from beginning readers up. Among his books are *Air Is All Around You, The Big Dipper,* and *Man in Space to the Moon.*

Brant, Joseph (Thayendanegea), Mohawk Indian B 371
  hostilities during Revolutionary War R 205
  Indian Wars I 212
Braque (BROC), **Georges,** French painter B 371; P 30
  Clarinet, collage, picture C 376
  modern art M 390

Picasso and Braque P 243
  Still Life: The Table, painting B 371
Brasilia (bra-ZI-lia), capital of Brazil B 380; pictures
    S 295; C 308
Brass B 410
  alloys A 168
  antiques A 321
  major Connecticut industry C 473
  zinc Z 370
Brass band B 38
Brass instruments M 549; pictures M 547
  bugle B 429
  orchestra O 183; picture O 187
  orchestra seating plan O 186
  wind instruments W 182–83
Bratislava (BRA-ti-sla-va), Czechoslovakia C 562
Bratsk (BROTSK), U.S.S.R.
  hydroelectric power plant, picture P 425
Brattain, Walter H., American physicist T 252; picture
    E 147
Braun, Wernher von *see* Von Braun, Wernher
Brave New World, novel by Huxley E 267

Braxton, Carter (1736–1797), American statesman, b. Newington, Va. He was a member of the Virginia House of Burgesses between 1761 and 1775 and then served at the Continental Congress (1775–76, 1777–83, 1785), where he signed the Declaration of Independence.

Brazil B 372–84
  Amazon River A 178–79
  coffee C 371–72
  coffee beans drying, picture S 289
  flag F 242
  immigration I 103
  landforms of South America S 276
  Latin-American art and architecture L 64
  Latin-American politics L 52
  life in Latin America L 47–61
  literature L 72–73
  national anthem N 21
  origin of name D 369
  Portugal, history of P 403
  Rio de Janeiro R 236–37
  roads near Santos, picture G 102
  rubber trees R 342
  São Paulo S 36
Brazil Current, of Atlantic Ocean A 478; S 279
Brazilein (bra-ZIL-le-in), dye D 369
Brazil nuts N 421
Brazilwood B 372
Brazing and soldering S 249–50
Brazos (BRA-zos) **River,** Texas T 125

Brazza (BRA-tza), **Count Pierre Paul François Camille Savorgnan de** (1852–1905), French explorer of Africa, b. Rio de Janeiro, Brazil. A brother of explorer Giacomo de Brazza, he made several expeditions to West Africa, where he founded Franceville and Brazzaville and claimed the territory for France (1879). He was governor of French Congo (later French Equatorial Africa) from 1886 to 1897. C 464; G 4

Brazzaville, capital of the Congo C 461–464
Bread B 385–89
  ancient millstones for grinding flour, picture A 355
  black or rye bread R 364
  bread wheats W 154, 156
  Cyprus, ancient baking methods, picture C 558
  Egyptian statuette, bread making, picture A 350
  experiments: growing bread molds A 316; E 351
  flour from different kinds of wheat F 274

food regulations and laws **F** 350
 mold **F** 496, 497
 unleavened and leavened compared **F** 88
 wheat **W** 154, 156
 See also Flour and flour milling
Bread-and-butter notes **L** 158–59
Breadfruit, a tropical fruit **M** 74
 introduced into Jamaica by Captain Bligh **J** 18
Bread Loaf Mountain, Vermont
 Bread Loaf School of English, Middlebury College
 V 316
Bread mold **F** 496, 497; picture **P** 292
 experiments **A** 316; **E** 351
Breakbone fever see Dengue
Breakers, giant waves **S** 478
Breakers, hard-coal preparation plants **C** 367
Breakfast cereals **G** 285
Breaking a mirror, superstition **S** 475
Breaking a wishbone, superstition **S** 475

Breakwater, a structure built out into the sea or a lake
to break the force of the waves and so protect the
harbor or beach; differs from jetty which has the function of directing the course of water to make it carry
sediment farther out.

Breast cancer **C** 92
Breastplates
 armor, picture **A** 434
 diving equipment **D** 79
Breaststroke, in swimming **S** 492; picture **S** 489
Breastworks, field fortifications **F** 377
Breathing **B** 277–78
 artificial respiration **F** 159–61
 birds **B** 203
 crocodilian adaptations for staying underwater
 C 535
 dolphins and porpoises **D** 273
 emphysema (disease) affects **D** 196
 first aid for stoppage of breathing **F** 159–61
 narcotics cause interruption of breathing and death
 results **N** 13
 oxygen and oxidation **O** 269
 plants, respiration of **P** 294
 respiratory system of fishes **F** 186–87
 ventriloquism **V** 301–03
 voice training and singing **V** 375–76

Brébeuf (bray-BUF), **Jean de, Saint** (1593–1649), French
Jesuit missionary, b. Bayeux. He went to Canada (1625)
and worked among the Huron Indians. He established
first mission on Georgian Bay (1626) and translated
catechism into Huron language. He was captured and
killed by Iroquois. He was canonized in 1930.

Brecht (BRECKT), **Bertolt,** German playwright **G** 179
Breckinridge, John Cabell, vice-president, United States
 K 225; **V** 330; picture **V** 327
 Confederate general in Civil War **C** 321
Breda, Treaty of, 1667 **S** 478b
Breech-loaders, guns **G** 418
Breeder reactors, for producing plutonium **U** 231
Breeds, of animals
 cats, pedigreed **C** 141
 cattle **C** 147
 dairy cattle **D** 4; pictures **D** 5
 dogs **D** 252–62
 fur colors, by mutation **F** 514
 horses **H** 237–38, 241, 244; pictures **H** 239–40
 pigs **C** 151
Breed's Hill, Boston, near Bunker Hill **M** 146;
 R 199–200

Breezes, sea see Sea breezes
Breitinger, Johann, Swiss professor **G** 175
Bremen (BREM-en), Germany **G** 158

Brendan, or **Brenainn, Saint** (484–577), Irish saint, b.
Tralee, County Kerry. He is the hero of medieval legend
The Navigation of St. Brendan, which tells of his journey
in search of the "isles of the blessed." The legend has
become exaggerated but is probably based on two short
voyages that he did make. He founded several monasteries in Ireland, including Clonfert (559), of which he was
abbot. His feast day is celebrated May 16th in Ireland.

Brennan, William Joseph (1906–), American jurist,
b. Newark, N.J. After graduation from the University
of Pennsylvania (1928), he earned his law degree from
Harvard (1931). He practiced law in Newark until 1949
(except for military service during World War II). From
1949 to 1956 he served successively as judge of the
New Jersey Supreme Court, Appelate Division; and the
State Supreme Court. In 1956 Eisenhower appointed
Brennan associate justice of the U.S. Supreme Court.
Justice Brennan has been identified with the more liberal
element in his opinions dealing with civil rights.

Brenner Pass, through the Alps **A** 174
Breslau, now Wroclaw, Poland **P** 361

Brest-Litovsk, Treaty of, peace agreement between
Russia and the Central Powers, signed (Mar., 1918)
during World War I. Bolsheviks took control of Russian
government (Nov., 1917), surrendered to Germany (Dec.,
1917). Russia lost Poland, Lithuania, and southern Latvia
to Germany, and parts of Transcaucasia to Turkey. Fin-
land, Estonia, northern Latvia, and the Ukraine became
independent after defeat of Central Powers. Russia declared treaty invalid (Nov., 1918).

Breton, André, French poet and surrealist **F** 442;
 M 394
Bretons, people of Brittany, France **F** 403
Brett, John, English engineer **T** 52
Bretton Woods, New Hampshire **N** 160
Bretton Woods Conference, 1944 **B** 50–51
Breuer (BROI-er), **Marcel,** Hungarian furniture designer
 and architect **F** 510
 use of concrete in architecture **A** 386
Brewis, colonial American dish **C** 390

Brewster, Sir David (1781–1868), Scottish physicist, b.
Jedburgh. He made important studies of light and lenses,
discovering law, named for him, that deals with reflected
light. His theories led him to invent such instruments as
the kaleidoscope and a lens used in lighthouses.

Brewster, William, Pilgrim father **P** 344

Brezhnev (BRAYGE-nef), **Leonid Ilyich** (1906–), Soviet
political leader, b. Dneprodzerzhinsk, Ukraine. A member
of the Communist Party since 1931, he was a political
commissar in the Army (1941–45). He became a member
of the Central Committee of the Communist Party (1952),
chairman of the Presidium (1960–64), and first secretary of the Central Committee (1964). He became the
general secretary of the Communist Party (1966), the
first to hold that title since Stalin. He shares leadership
of the U.S.S.R. with Premier Kosygin. **U** 51
 Communism **C** 443

Brian Boru, king of Ireland **I** 390
Briand (bri-ON), **Aristide,** French statesman **P** 105
Briand-Kellogg Pact, 1928 see Kellogg-Briand Pact, 1928

Brices Cross Roads National Battlefield Site, Mississippi **M** 358
Bricklaying B 391–93
  building a house, picture **B** 43
Bricks B 390–94
  building construction **B** 430
  houses **H** 174–75
Bridal rings J 98
Bridal Veil, waterfall **N** 243
Bridal veils W 100
Bride-price, or lobola **S** 268
Bridewell, a prison **P** 469
Bridge, card game **C** 107–12
Bridge, The, modern art group in Germany **M** 391
Bridgeport, Connecticut **C** 476–77
Bridger, Jim, American scout and mountain man **F** 523
  overland trails **O** 260
  Wyoming, settlement of **W** 335
  Yellowstone National Park **Y** 345
Bridges B 395–401
  Chesapeake Bay Bridge-Tunnel **B** 399; **M** 117; **T** 318
  Galata Bridge, Golden Horn, Turkey, picture **T** 327
  Jefferson Street Bridge, Indiana **I** 147
  Kaibab Suspension Bridge, picture **G** 292
  New York City **N** 230
  reinforced concrete used in **C** 166; picture **C** 165
  swinging bridge, picture **J** 155
  Tower Bridge, London, picture **E** 305
  twin bridge, Delaware Memorial, picture **D** 94
  Verrazano-Narrows Bridge, New York, picture **W** 220
  See also Covered bridges
Bridges, of ships **O** 23
Bridges, Robert, English poet **E** 265
Bridgetown, capital of Barbados **B** 53; picture **C** 117

Bridgman, Laura (1829–1889), American teacher of the handicapped, b. Hanover, N.H. Blind, deaf, and mute, she was educated by means of a newly devised raised letter alphabet. Her achievements led to modern methods of teaching the disabled.

Brigade system, for fur trading **F** 524
Briggs, Austin, American illustrator **I** 95
Brigham Young University, Provo, Utah **U** 248–49
Bright, Charles, English engineer **T** 52
Brightness, or magnitude, of stars **S** 406–07
Brighton, England, picture **U** 68
Bright's disease D 201–02
Brimstone see Sulfur
Brine, salt and water solution **S** 20; **W** 56
  leather process for preserving hides **L** 108
  processing of fish **F** 212, 222
  use in preserving food **F** 347
Brine shrimp S 171

Brink, Carol Ryrie (1895–   ), American writer of children's books, b. Moscow, Idaho. Her most popular book, *Caddie Woodlawn,* based on incidents out of her grandmother's frontier childhood, won the Newbery Medal in 1936. Other titles include *All Over Town* and *Anything Can Happen on the River.*

Brisbane, capital of Queensland, Australia **A** 514

Briscoe, Robert (1894–1969), Irish statesman, b. Dublin. As a member of Sinn Fein movement and the Irish Republican Army, he worked for Ireland's independence from Britain (1922). He served in the Irish parliament (1927–65) and was twice lord mayor of Dublin (1956–57; 1961–62), the first Jew to hold the post.

Bristlecone pine, tree **P** 317; **T** 274

Bristle worms, or polychaetes **W** 310
Bristol Clock Museum, Bristol, Conn. **C** 476
Britain, ancient name of England, Scotland, Wales
  early history of England **E** 214–17
  Hadrian's Wall, picture **A** 353
Britain, battle of, 1940 **W** 289–90
Britannia metal K 288
British Columbia, Canada **B** 402–07
  Canada's Cordillera **C** 51
  Salmon Area Indians **I** 180
  taiga region, agriculture in **T** 11
  valley formed by a glacier, picture **I** 16
  Vancouver **V** 276
British Columbia, University of B 405
British Commonwealth of Nations see Commonwealth of Nations
British East India Company E 43
  early monopoly of trade **T** 305
  Ganges valley controlled by **I** 133
British Empire E 225–32
  extent of, 1939 **E** 229
  United Kingdom of Great Britain and Northern Ireland **U** 65, 66
  See also Commonwealth of Nations
British Expeditionary Force (B.E.F.)
  World War I **W** 273
  World War II **W** 288
British Guiana see Guyana
British Honduras see Belize

British Indian Ocean Territory, British dependency consisting of Chagos Archipelago (former dependency of Mauritius), and Aldabra, Des Roches, and Farquhar islands (former dependencies of Seychelles). The territory was formed in 1965 by agreement with Mauritius and Seychelles.

British International (Harmsworth) **Cup Race,** boating **B** 264
British Isles, group that includes Great Britain, Ireland, and many smaller islands **E** 212; **U** 66
  geographic makeup (land areas) of the United Kingdom **U** 68
British Museum, London **M** 511, 514; picture **M** 515
  library **L** 177, 197–98; picture **L** 179
British North America Act, 1867 **M** 3
  Canada **C** 73
  Quebec **Q** 16
British Patent Office P 97
British Society for the Promotion of Permanent and Universal Peace P 104
British Solomon Islands Protectorate
  Guadalcanal **P** 6
British Somaliland, now Somalia **S** 255
British South Africa Company Z 368
British thermal units, or Btu's, measure of heat **H** 91
British Togoland see Togo
British Union, historic flag **F** 227
Britons, early people of England **E** 214–15
Brittany, region of France, pictures **F** 410, 413
Britten, Benjamin, English composer **E** 271
  opera **O** 138
  Peter Grimes, opera **O** 151
Brno (BER-no), Czechoslovakia **C** 562
Broadcast, a way of sowing seed **F** 58
  early agriculture **A** 96
Broadcasting, radio and television **R** 53–58; **T** 70–71
Broadheads, tips of archery arrows **A** 367
Broad jump, now called Long jump, field event **T** 240
Broadsides, newssheets
  ballads **B** 22
  political songs **N** 22

Broadtail, fur F 518
Broadway theater district, New York City T 161
    theaters in New York City N 233–34
Broadwood, John, English piano builder P 242
Broccoli, vegetable V 289
    flowers we eat P 307–08; picture P 309
Broch, Hermann, German writer G 180
Brock, Sir Isaac, British soldier O 125
    Canadian forces in War of 1812 W 11
Broilers, chickens P 420
Brokers, or agents, negotiators of sales and purchases
    S 116–17
    real estate R 113
    stocks and bonds, dealers in S 430–32
Bromine (BRO-mene), element E 154, 160
    iodine and other halogens I 349
Bronchial (BRONC-ial) **tubes,** respiratory system B 277
Bronchitis (bron-KY-tis), inflammation of bronchial tubes
    D 193–94
    smoking, effects of S 203
Bronchoscopes (BRONC-ho-scopes), optical instruments
    O 168

Bronck, or **Bronk, Jonas** (?–1643?), Danish pioneer in
America. He was the first settler (1639) in area of New
York above the Harlem River, now lower Westchester
County and the Bronx, which is named after him.

Broncos, untamed horses
    rodeo riding R 281
    See also Mustangs
Brontë (BRON-te), **Anne,** English novelist B 408; E 261
Brontë, Branwell, English writer B 408
Brontë, Charlotte, English novelist B 408; E 261
    themes of her novels N 346
Brontë, Emily, English novelist B 408; E 261
    themes of her novels N 346
Brontë family B 408
Brontosaurs, dinosaurs D 176–77; P 436–38
    giants of nature G 200
Bronx, New York City N 228–29
    Bronx Community College, picture N 234
    Hall of Fame for Great Americans H 12–14
Bronx Zoo, New York City, picture Z 375
Bronze B 408–10
    alloys A 168
    ancient art A 236
    armor A 433
    bell casting B 137
    chemistry, history of C 205
    China's early use of C 268–69
    decorative arts D 68, 75
    tin T 195
Bronze Age B 408–09
    metals and metallurgy M 233
    prehistoric man P 446
    time of the Trojan War T 294
Bronze Star, American award, picture M 199
Brooches (BROACH-es), jewelry J 99
Brooke, Alan Francis see Alanbrooke, 1st Viscount

Brooke, Edward William (1919–), U.S. senator from
Massachusetts, Negro, b. Washington, D.C. He headed
the Boston finance commission (1961–62) and served as
attorney general of Massachusetts (1962–66). He was
elected to the U.S. Senate in 1966. Picture N 101.

Brooke, Sir James, British ruler (White Rajah) of
    Sarawak M 56
Brooke, Rupert, English poet E 265
Brook Farm, utopian community, Massachusetts U 256
  in American literature A 202

Brooklyn, New York City N 228
Brooklyn Botanical Garden, New York, picture Z 375
Brooklyn Bridge, New York City B 398; N 230

Brooks, Angie Elizabeth (Mrs. Isaac Randolph) (1928–
    ), b. Virginia, Liberia. Liberian assistant secretary
of state, she has been a delegate to the U.N. since
1954 and was 2nd woman president of the General Assembly (1969–70).

Brooks, Gwendolyn (1917–), American poet, b. Topeka,
Kans. She was the first Negro woman to win a Pulitzer
prize (1950), which was given to her for her collection of
poems *Annie Allen.* Her other collections include *A Street
in Bronzeville* and *Bean Eaters.*
    Negro artists and writers N 102

Brooks, Phillips, American Episcopal bishop, author of
    "O Little Town of Bethlehem" C 122
Brooks, Van Wyck, American writer A 214
Brooks Range, Alaska A 132, 135
Brook trout, fish, picture F 210
Broomcorn, a sorghum K 182
Brooms, poem by Dorothy Aldis F 120

Brotherhood Week, observance dedicated to increasing understanding among people of different ethnic and
religious backgrounds. Established in 1946 by the National Conference of Christians and Jews, it is celebrated during the week of Washington's birthday.

Brothers Karamazov, The, novel by Dostoevski D 287
Brothers of the Bridge, early order of bridge builders
    B 395
Brotherton, now Indian Mills, New Jersey
    first Indian reservation in United States N 178
Brotulids (bro-TU-lids), deep-sea fishes F 197
Broughton, Jack, English boxing champion B 353

Browder, Earl Russell (1891–1973), American Communist
Party leader, b. Wichita, Kans. He was general secretary
of the American Communist Party (1930–45) and Communist candidate for president (1936, 1940). He was
removed from post (1945) and expelled from party
(1946) for advocating co-operation with capitalism, then
officially vindicated by party (1956).

Brown, Charles Brockden, American novelist A 198

Brown, Claude (1937–), American author, Negro, b.
New York, N.Y. His autobiography, *Manchild in the Promised Land* (1965), is a description of life in the ghetto.

Brown, Father, fictional character created by Gilbert
    Keith Chesterton M 555
Brown, Ford Madox, English artist E 241
Brown, George, Canadian statesman B 411
    Brown and Macdonald M 3
Brown, H. Rap, American black power advocate N 104b
Brown, James, American singer R 262d

Brown, Jimmy (James Nathaniel Brown) (1936–),
American football player, Negro, b. St. Simons Island, Ga.
After starring at Syracuse University, he played pro
football as a fullback with the Cleveland Browns
(1957–66). He set several records and was named National Football League Player of the Year (1958, 1963)
and Athlete of the Year (1965). After retiring from football
he became a movie actor.

Brown, John, American abolitionist B 411–12
    abolitionist movement in Negro history N 94

Dutch and Flemish art   D 352
Children's Games, painting   D 354
Harvesters, The, painting   R 170
Wedding Dance, The, painting   B 415
Bruges (BRUGE), old Flemish town in Belgium   S 428
Brulé (bru-LAY), **Étienne,** French explorer   G 326, 329; M 272

Brumel, Valery (1942–   ), Russian athlete, b. Tolbuzino, Siberia. He jumped 7 feet 5¾ inches, setting new world high-jump record in Moscow (1963). He was named Master of Sport of U.S.S.R., highest honor awarded to athlete by Soviet Union, in 1961. He won a gold medal in 1964 Olympics. A motorcycle accident the next year ended his career. Picture   O 114.

Brumidi (bru-MI-di), **Constantino,** Italian artist   W 30

Brummell, Beau (George Byron Brummell) (1778–1840), English dandy, b. London. A close friend of Prince of Wales, later George IV, who made him an officer in King's regiment (1794), he became noted for excellent taste in dress, and established standards of fashion. After losing his fortune by gambling, he fled to Calais, France, to escape creditors (1816). He was British consul in Caen (1830–32) and died in insane asylum in Caen.

Brunei (BRUNE-i), **sultanate of,** British protectorate on Borneo   B 336, 338
   flag   F 237
   Malaysia   M 56
   Southeast Asia   S 328
Brunel (bru-NEL), **Isambard,** English engineer   O 24
Brunelleschi (bru-nel-LESC-i), **Filippo,** Italian architect   A 380–81
   Florence Cathedral, Italy, picture   I 462
   Foundling Hospital, Florence   R 163; picture   R 165
   Italian architecture   I 465
   perspective rules established   P 158
   Renaissance architecture   R 161, 163

Brunhoff, Jean de (1899–1937), French author and illustrator of children's books, b. Paris. He exhibited with group of artists at Galérie Champigny in Paris. His stories about an elephant who leaves the jungle to lead life in Paris were based on bedtime stories told to his children. His books include *The Story of Babar, the Little Elephant* and *The Travels of Babar*.
   Babar, the King, picture from   C 246

Brünnhilde see Brynhild
Brushes
   paintbrushes, how to care for   P 34
Brushes, of electric generators and motors   E 121, 131
   electric motors   E 137
Brusilov (bru-SI-lof), **Aleksei,** Russian general   W 278
Brussels, capital of Belgium   B 129
   City Hall, picture   B 131
   German troops, 1914, picture   W 272
Brussels sprouts, vegetable related to cabbage   V 287
   leaves we eat   P 307; picture   P 306
Brussels Universal and International Exhibition, 1958   F 17
Brutus, Marcus Junius, Roman statesman   C 6
Bryan, John Neely, first settler in Dallas, Texas   D 14
Bryan, William Jennings, American statesman   B 415–16
   famous Nebraskan   N 84
   McKinley and Bryan   M 188
   oratory   O 181
Bryant, William Cullen, American poet and editor   B 416
   American literature   A 200
Bryce Canyon National Park, Utah   U 249; picture   U 106

Bryde's whales   W 149–50
Brynhild (BRURN-hilt), in Norse mythology   N 281
   in Wagner's operas called Brünnhilde   O 152
Bryophyllum, or **life plant,** picture   P 300
   leaves, special kinds of, picture   L 120
Btu's see British thermal units
Buada, main center of Nauru   N 61
Bubble chambers
   ions and ionization   I 353
Bubble sextants, instruments for air navigation   N 67

Buber (BU-ber), **Martin** (1878–1965), Jewish religious philosopher, b. Vienna, Austria. A professor of comparative religion at the University of Frankfurt (1923–33), he was forced by Nazis to leave Germany. He went to Israel and became professor of social philosophy at Hebrew University in Jerusalem (1938–51). He played an important role in Zionist movement and in reviving literature and culture of Chasidic sect.

Bubi, a people of Africa   E 273
Bubonic plague, disease   I 287
   disaster at the end of the Middle Ages   M 295
   medieval England   E 219
   Norway   N 344
   Roman Catholic Church damaged by   R 293
Buccaneers (buc-ca-NEERS), pirates of the Spanish Main   P 263
   Henry Morgan, lieutenant governor of Jamaica   J 18
Bucephalus (bue-CEPH-a-lus), favorite horse of Alexander the Great   A 151, 153
Buchanan, James, 15th president of United States   B 417–20
   pre-Civil War days   C 321, 322
Bucharest (bu-ca-REST), capital of Rumania   R 357; pictures   R 358, 359

Bucher, Lloyd (1927–   ), American naval officer, b. Pocatello, Idaho. He commanded the U.S.S. *Pueblo*, an electronic intelligence ship that was seized by North Korea in the Sea of Japan on January 23, 1968. Bucher and his crew were held as spies for nearly a year. After lengthy negotiations and a United States government apology, the North Koreans released Bucher and his men. A U.S. Navy court of inquiry later recommended that Bucher be court-martialed for failing to defend his ship properly, but the Secretary of the Navy set aside the court's ruling.

Buchmanism (BOOK-man-ism) (also called the Oxford Group Movement), international program organized (1921) at Oxford University by American evangelist **Frank Nathan Daniel Buchman** (1878–1961). Its program of spiritual restoration advocated "world-changing through life-changing." It held that path to ideal society lay in character improvement, especially development of such traits as honesty and selflessness. The movement spread to 60 countries and was later called Moral Re-Armament.

Buck, Pearl, American author   B 421
   American literature   A 212
   Big Wave, The, excerpt   B 421–22
Bucket brigades, for fire fighting   F 146
Buckeye, tree
   state tree of Ohio   O 61
Buckeye State, nickname for Ohio   O 61, 64
Buckingham, James, English traveler and author   U 256
Buckingham Palace, of Britain's royal family   L 336
Buckskin, leather from deer   L 107
Buckwheat, grain   G 285
   seeds, pictures   G 284
Bucolic (bue-COL-ic) **poetry,** about country life   E 151

Bucrania (bu-CRAY-nia), sculptured ornament **D** 70
Budapest (BU-da-pest), capital of Hungary **H** 286; picture **H** 287
  bookmobile, picture **L** 199
Buddha (BU-dha), **Prince Siddhartha Gautama,** founder of Buddhism **B** 422–25
  statue in Kamakura, Japan, picture **R** 147
Buddhism, religion founded by Buddha **B** 423–25
  Asia, chief religions of **A** 460
  Burma **B** 454
  China **C** 261
  fables and folk tales **F** 3
  food taboos **F** 334
  funeral customs **F** 492
  Great Buddha of Kamakura, Japan, picture **J** 47
  Indian literature **O** 220e
  Japan **J** 24–25, 31, 46
  Lamaism in Tibet **T** 175
  Laos **L** 41
  marriage rites **W** 102–03
  oriental sculpture **O** 212–13, 216
  originated in India **I** 131
  religions of the world **R** 147
  religious holidays **R** 154
  Southeast Asia **S** 330
  Thai monks, picture **A** 447
Budding, a type of reproduction **R** 176
  hydra **J** 73
Budding, plant propagation by grafting **N** 420
  apple trees **A** 335, 337
  orange trees **O** 178

Budge, Don (John Donald Budge) (1915–), American tennis player, b. Oakland, Calif. He was first to achieve tennis "Grand Slam," winning U.S., British, Australian, and French singles championships in same year (1938). He became professional player (1939) and thereafter won several professional championships. He wrote *How Lawn Tennis Is Played* and *Budge on Tennis.*

Budgerigars (BUDGE-eri-gars), "talking" birds **P** 83; pictures **P** 84
  budgies as pets **B** 245
Budget, United States Bureau of the **I** 253
Budgets, family **B** 425–26
  installment buying **I** 288–89
  See *also* Consumer education
Budgies see Budgerigars
Buds, of plants
  trees **T** 282–83
Bud scales, of plants **P** 295
Buen Aire see Bonaire, island
Buena Vista (BUANE-a VE-sta), **battle of,** 1847 **M** 239
  Taylor, Zachary **T** 35

Bueno (bu-A-no), **Maria Esther** (1940–), Brazilian tennis player, b. Rio de Janeiro. She won Brazilian National Championship (1954), U.S. Women's Singles Championship (1959, 1963, 1964, 1966), British Women's Singles (Wimbledon) (1959, 1960, 1964).

Buenos Aires (BUANE-os I-res), capital of Argentina **B** 426–28
  cities of Argentina **A** 394, 395
  Plaza de Mayo, picture **A** 391
  port, picture **S** 293

Buff, Conrad (1886–), American artist and author, b. Speichen, Switzerland, is noted for lithographs (in the Metropolitan and British museums) as well as for murals. His wife, **Mary Buff** (1890–), has been an art teacher, critic, and assistant art curator of Los Angeles Museum. They have written and illustrated books for children, including *Dancing Cloud,* and *Forest Folk.*

Buffalo, American see Bison
Buffalo, hoofed mammals **B** 250a; pictures **B** 250a, **H** 216
  Asian work animal **A** 451
  buffalo wolves **D** 245
  plowing a rice paddy, picture **B** 456
Buffalo, New York **N** 222–23
Buffalo Bill (William F. Cody), American scout **B** 428
  Pony Express rider **P** 392
Buffalo National River, Arkansas **A** 428

Buffer state, small independent country situated between larger rival powers and serving, it is hoped, to reduce conflict between them or absorb military clashes. Belgium and Luxembourg were buffer states between France and Germany before World War II.

Buffet (buf-FAY) meals **T** 2–3
Bugaku, Japanese drama **T** 164
Buganda (bu-GAN-da), former kingdom, now a region in Uganda **U** 6, 7

Bugging, or electronic eavesdropping, is the practice of using supersensitive listening devices for the purpose of intercepting private conversations. The propriety of government use of these devices for law enforcement became a controversial topic during the late 1960's.

Bugle, musical instrument **B** 429; **M** 549
  See *also* Trumpet
Bugle calls **B** 429
Bug River, Europe **P** 359
Bugs see Insects
Buhlwork, decorative art **D** 77
Building construction **B** 430–38
  air conditioning **A** 101–03
  bricks and masonry **B** 390–94
  bridges **B** 395–401
  bulldozers and other equipment **B** 445–48
  construction engineers **E** 205, 207
  elevators and escalators **E** 172–75
  explosives in construction **E** 394
  fireproofing **B** 438
  heating **H** 96–99
  hoisting and loading machinery **H** 143–45
  insulation and insulating materials **I** 290–92
  invention of tools for **I** 348
  lighting **L** 279–90
  masonry **B** 391–94
  mechanical drawing **M** 197
  plumbing **P** 341–43
  stone masonry **B** 392–94
  Why don't tall buildings blow down in a strong wind? **B** 438
Building materials **B** 430–31
  adobe houses **H** 173
  bricks and brick masonry **B** 390–94
  cement and concrete **C** 167–68
  fireproofing **B** 438
  glass, as a structural material **G** 237
  homes **H** 171–77
  influenced architecture **A** 384, 385, 386, 387
  insulating materials **I** 290–92
  iron and steel **I** 396–408
  lumber and lumbering **L** 372–77
  stone **S** 433
  stone masonry **B** 393–94
  wood and wood products **W** 222–28

Bujumbura, capital of Burundi   **B** 463, 464
Bukovina (bu-ko-VI-na), Rumania   **R** 355–56
Bulawayo, Rhodesia   **R** 229
Bulbs, underground stems   **P** 300
  gardens and gardening   **G** 40; picture **G** 41
  garden selection   **G** 29
  leaves, special kinds   **L** 120

Bulganin (bull-GAN-yin), **Nikolai Aleksandrovich** (1895–1975), Russian political leader, b. Nizhni-Novgorod (now Gorki). He joined Communist Party in 1917 and served with secret police (1918–22). He held various Party offices, including membership on Central Committee (1939–61), Politburo (1948–52), and Party Presidium (1952–59). He was minister of defense (1953–55), member of Supreme Soviet (1937–58), and premier (chairman of Council of Ministers) of Soviet Union (1955–58) until removed from office on charge of conspiring against Party.

Bulgaria (bul-GAIR-ia)   **B** 439–44
  Balkan wars   **B** 19
  flag   **F** 239
  World War I   **W** 275, 281
Bulge, battle of the, 1944–45   **W** 304
  Belgium   **B** 131
  Eisenhower, Dwight D.   **E** 109–10
Bulkheads, protecting partitions   **T** 318
Bull, constellation see Taurus
Bull, John, English composer   **N** 16
Bull, Ole, Norwegian violinist   **G** 376
  founded Norwegian Theater, Bergen   **I** 2
Bullboats, made of buffalo hide   **M** 383;   **N** 329
Bull dancing, of ancient Crete   **B** 449
Bulldog, picture   **D** 256
Bulldozers   **B** 445–46
  clear land for farming   **F** 57
  roads and highways   **R** 251
  shaping a yard, picture   **B** 437
  See also Hoisting and loading machinery
Bulletproof vests, of fiber glass   **A** 435
Bullets, ammunition for guns   **G** 414, 417
Bullfighting   **B** 449–51
  arenas, pictures   **A** 212, **E** 304
  How did bullfighting begin?   **B** 449
  Mexico   **M** 241
  South America, picture   **S** 285
  Spain   **S** 352; picture **S** 350
Bullfrogs   **F** 470, 472, 473
Bullheads, fish
  baits and lures   **F** 206
  habitat, feeding habits, uses   **F** 216
Bull-horn acacia, tree   **A** 328;   **P** 283
Bull in the ring, circle game   **G** 13
Bullion, gold bars   **G** 247
  money   **M** 409
Bull-leaping, sport of ancient Crete   **A** 227
Bull Moose Party, or **Progressive Party,** United States **P** 381
  Roosevelt, Theodore   **R** 330
  symbol   **P** 379
  Taft, William Howard   **T** 9
Bull Run, battles of, 1861, 1862, Civil War   **C** 322, 323
  Jackson, Thomas J., gets nickname "Stonewall"   **J** 8
Bulls
  Apis, sacred bull of Egypt   **C** 145
  Assyrian art   **A** 240; picture **A** 241
  dairy cattle   **D** 4
  elephants   **E** 167
  moose, picture   **H** 215
  rodeo riding   **R** 281
Bulls and bears, in stock exchanges   **S** 432

Bully, starting play in field hockey   **F** 115
Bulnes (BOOL-nase), **Manuel,** president of Chile
  C 255
Bulwer-Lytton, Edward see Lytton, E.G.E.L. Bulwer-
Bumblebees   **B** 124; pictures **B** 123, 124

Bumbry, Grace (1937–   ), American soprano, b. St. Louis, Mo. She sang with the State Opera in Basel, Switzerland (1960–63), and was the first Negro to sing at the Bayreuth Festival in Germany. Her Metropolitan Opera debut (1965) was as Princess Eboli in *Don Carlos.*

Bumppo, Natty, hero of Cooper's Leatherstocking
  Tales   **C** 498
  American literature, classics in   **A** 200
Bunche, Ralph, American educator and United Nations mediator   **B** 452
  Negro educators and public officials   **N** 99

Bund (from German, meaning "league" or "union"), pro-Nazi organization formed in United States (1930's) mainly by German-Americans who supported Adolf Hitler. It pursued a policy of anti-Semitism and was headed by Fritz Kuhn, who was jailed in 1941. It was disbanded after United States entered World War II.

Bund, The, avenue in Shanghai, People's Republic of China   **S** 138
Bundestag, West German parliament, lower house   **G** 158
Bunin (BOON-yin), **Ivan,** Russian author   **U** 61
Bunker Hill, battle of, 1775   **M** 146;   **R** 199
Bunker Hill flag   **F** 244; picture **F** 229
Bunker Hill Monument, site of battle   **A** 12
Bunraku, Japanese puppet play   **J** 32;   **P** 535

Bunsen burner, gas burner used in laboratories to provide a very hot, clean flame. It was named for Robert Bunsen, German chemist.

Bunt, in baseball   **B** 72
Buntline, Ned see Judson, Edward
Buntline Special, Colt revolver   **G** 422
Buñuel, Luis, Spanish motion-picture director   **M** 488a
Bunyan, John, English writer and preacher   **E** 256
Bunyan, Paul, American folk hero   **F** 312
  children's literature   **C** 236
  statue in Bangor, Maine   **M** 44
Bunyoro (bun-YO-ro), former kingdom, Uganda   **U** 6
Buonaparte see Bonaparte
Buonarroti, Michelangelo see Michelangelo
Buoninsegna, Duccio de see Duccio de Buoninsegna
Buoyancy (BOY-an-cy), upward push on a floating object   **F** 250
  giants of nature   **G** 204
Buoys
  ocean currents measured with   **O** 32–33
Buraimi oasis, Arabia   **U** 64a
Burbage, James, English actor   **D** 295
Burbage, Richard, English actor   **S** 131
Burbank, Luther, American horticulturalist   **B** 453
Burdock, weed, picture   **W** 105

Bureaucracy, a term generally used to refer to the administrative machinery of a government. It is sometimes applied to any large organization divided into many departments or bureaus with a hierarchy of employees each responsible to a superior. It is often used as a term of disparagement.
  See also Civil service

Bureaus, of the United States Government see by name, as Alcohol, Tobacco and Firearms, Bureau of

Burger, Warren Earl (1907–), American lawyer and jurist, b. St. Paul, Minn. He entered private practice after graduating from law school (1931) and was later named (1955) a judge on the U.S. Court of Appeals for the District of Columbia, where he became known for his strong stand on law and order. He was named (1969) by Nixon to succeed Warren as chief justice of the U.S. Supreme Court.

Burgess, Gelett (Frank Gelett Burgess) (1866–1951), American humorist, writer, and illustrator, b. Boston, Mass. Known for writing nonsense jingles, such as "The Purple Cow," he also coined many new words—such as "blurb," meaning the writing on a book jacket. He illustrated many of his own books, including *Why Men Hate Women* and *Look 11 Years Younger.*
"I Wish That My Room Had a Floor," nonsense rhyme **N** 274

Burgess, Thornton Waldo (1874–1965), American writer, b. Sandwich, Mass. Associate editor of *Good Housekeeping* (1904–11), he is best known for nature and animal stories written for children, including Old Mother West Wind series, *Burgess Bedtime Stories,* and *Burgess Bird Book for Children.*

Burgesses, House of, Virginia **V** 358
Jefferson, Thomas **J** 64
Burghers of Calais, statues by Rodin **S** 103
Burghley, Lord see Cecil, William
Burgoyne, John, English military commander **R** 203–04
Washington and Burgoyne **W** 40
Burgtheater, Vienna, Austria, picture **A** 519
Burgundian (bur-GUN-dian) **period,** in Dutch and Flemish music **D** 363
Burgundy wine W 189
Buri, Norse god **N** 277
Burial customs see Funeral and burial customs
Buried treasure P 264
Burins, cutting tools **D** 75
engraving and graphic arts **E** 272; **G** 303
woodworking **W** 229
Burke, Edmund, English statesman **E** 259; **O** 181
Burke, John, American statesman **N** 335
Burkitt's tumor, type of cancer **C** 93–94

Burleigh (BUR-li), **Henry Thacker** (1866–1949), American singer and composer, Negro. b. Erie, Pa. He introduced Negro spirituals on concert stage in United States and abroad, and he preserved, in writing, folk songs of the Negro race, which were previously handed down orally. Burleigh sang command performances before King Edward VII of England and other heads of state. His best-known works include songs "Little Mother of Mine," "Deep River," and "Just You."
Negro spirituals **N** 107

Burlesque, a form of humor **H** 280
Burlington, Vermont **V** 318
Burma B 454–59
Boy Scout, picture **A** 459
bride and groom, picture **F** 41
dance **D** 31
flag **F** 237
gemstones found in **G** 70
monks at mealtime, picture **F** 339
Thant, U **T** 154
World War II **W** 294, 302, 306
Burma Road B 459
Burmese cats C 142; picture **C** 143

Burne-Jones, Sir Edward Coley (1833–1898), English painter, b. Birmingham. He was associated with pre-Raphaelite artists Dante Gabriel Rossetti and William Morris. His paintings are characterized by dreamlike, romantic idealism. They include *The Golden Stairs, The Depths of the Sea,* and *King Cophetua and the Beggar Maid.* He also designed tapestries and stained-glass windows for firm of William Morris.
Praising Angels, tapestry **T** 23

Burnett, Frances Hodgson, American novelist
children's literature **C** 240
Burnett, Peter H., American pioneer **O** 261
Burney, Charles, English music scholar **G** 183; **M** 524

Burnford, Sheila (1918–), Canadian author, b. Scotland. She was author of popular animal story *The Incredible Journey* and *Field of Noon,* as well as articles for *Punch,* the Glasgow *Herald,* and *Canadian Poetry.*

Burnham, Forbes (1923–), (Linden Forbes Burnham), prime minister of Guyana (formerly British Guiana). The son of a village schoolmaster, Burnham was a brilliant student. He completed his education in England, where he earned his law degree. He entered politics on his return to British Guiana, and at the age of 36 was elected mayor of Georgetown, the capital city. In 1964 he was elected prime minister. He continued to hold that post when the colony became independent Guyana in 1966. Burnham holds moderate political views in a country where political and racial tension between East Indian and Negro populations is a problem.

Burning, combustion **F** 137
Burnoose, Arab dress **C** 351

Burns, E. L. M. (Eedson Louis Millard Burns) (1897–), Canadian general, b. Westmount, Quebec. He held various commands during World Wars I and II and was chief of staff of UN Truce Supervision Organization in Palestine (1954–56) and commander of UN Emergency Force in Middle East (1956–59). He was Canadian representative to disarmament conferences in Geneva (1960, 1962–67); and was adviser to Canadian government on disarmament (1960–68).

Burns, John Horne, American novelist **A** 213
Burns, Robert, Scottish poet **B** 460; **E** 259
quotation from "To a Louse" **Q** 20
"Red, Red Rose, A" **B** 460
Robert Burns's Birthday, holiday **H** 147
"Sweet Afton" **B** 460

Burns, Tommy (Noah Bursso) (1881–1955), Canadian boxer, b. Hanover, Ontario. He won heavyweight title (1906) in 20-round decision over Marvin Hart but lost title (1908) to Jack Johnson in a fight so brutal police had to stop it in 14th round.

Burns and scalds
first aid **F** 162
safety measures **S** 3
Burnside, Ambrose, American soldier and statesman **R** 225
Civil War campaigns **C** 325
Bur oak
state tree of Illinois **I** 70
Burr, Aaron, American political leader **B** 461–62
as vice-president, picture **V** 325
Blennerhassett Island, West Virginia **W** 136
duels and dueling **D** 341
Hamilton and Burr **H** 20
Jefferson and Burr **J** 68

Butterfly stroke, swimming   S 492–93

Butterfly valves, diagram   V 269

Buttermilk, liquid left over from making butter   B 467
  dairy products   D 10–11

Butterwort, plant, picture   P 316

Butting, contest among Eskimo   E 289

Button, Sir Thomas, British explorer-trader in Canada
  M 82

Buttonholes, how to make   E 188

Buttons and button collecting   B 478–80
  abacus made of buttons, picture   A 2

Buttonwood Tree Agreement, 1792   S 430

Buttress, in architecture   A 378
  Gothic flying buttress   G 265
  Middle Ages, architecture of the   M 296–97

Butyl (BU-til), synthetic rubber   R 346

Butyl alcohol   F 90

Buxtehude (boox-teh-HU-de), **Dietrich,** German composer   B 64

Buyers, for stores   F 70

Buying on margin, a stock purchase in which only a
  part of price is paid   S 432

Buys Ballot's law, of winds and pressure   W·186

Buzzards, soaring hawks, worldwide in distribution.
Closely related to eagles, buzzards have hooked bills
and broad, rounded wings. They feed on a variety of
small mammals and reptiles. In America these birds
are commonly called hawks.

Buzzards Bay, Massachusetts
  light tower, picture   L 277

Byblos (BIB-los), site of ancient Phoenician city, Lebanon
  invention of alphabet   A 170

Byelorussia see Belorussia

Bykovsky, Valery Fyodorvich (1934–   ), Russian cosmonaut, b. Pavlovo-Pasad. He orbited earth (June, 1963)
simultaneously with Valentina Vladimirovna Tereshkova
(first woman astronaut), although in different space capsule. He orbited 81 times and covered 2,046,000 miles
in 4 days, 23 hours, and 6 minutes—setting new records.
  space flight data   S 344

Bylaws, laws or rules by which a city, corporation, or
other organization governs its affairs and members. In
the case of a municipality a bylaw has the force of law,
whereas in other organizations it is merely an agreement among members. Term also refers to a secondary
rule subordinate to a constitution.
  parliamentary procedure   P 79

Bypass engines   J 86

Byrd, Harry F., U.S. senator   V 360

Byrd (BIRD), **Richard Evelyn,** American explorer   B 481
  polar exploration by air   P 365
  polar regions   P 368

Byrd, William, English composer   E 269
  chamber music   C 185
  Renaissance music   R 173

Byrd, William, II, Virginia diarist   A 196–97

Byrnes, James Francis, American statesman   S 309

Byron, George Gordon, Lord, English poet   B 481–82
  place in English literature   E 260–61
  Childe Harold's Pilgrimage, excerpt   B 482
  Prisoner of Chillon, The, excerpt   B 482

Byssus (BISS-us), filaments of mussels   O 272

Byzantine (BIZ-an-tene) **architecture**   B 483–90
  art as a record   A 438b
  cathedrals   C 131
  early architecture   A 377
  Russian architecture   U 52

Byzantine art   B 483–90
  art as a record   A 438b
  early Christian art in Italy   I 458
  enameling   E 191; picture E 192
  Harbaville Triptych, picture   S 97
  illuminated manuscripts   I 87–88
  influence on medieval art   M 296, 297
  jewelry designs   J 94
  mosaics, painting   P 17–18; picture P 16

Byzantine Empire, or Eastern Roman Empire   B 491–92
  art and architecture   B 483–90
  Constantine the Great   C 489
  Crusades   C 538–40
  decline of the Roman Empire in the west   R 308
  decorative arts   D 70
  Turkey, history of   T 327

Byzantium (bi-ZAN-tium), later Constantinople (now Is-
  tanbul), Turkey   B 491; T 326
  one of the world's great cities   C 305

ILLUSTRATION CREDITS

The following list credits, by page, the sources of illustrations used in Volume B of THE NEW BOOK OF KNOWLEDGE. Credits are listed illustration by illustration—left to right, top to bottom. Wherever appropriate, the name of the photographer or artist has been listed with the source, the two being separated by a dash. When two or more illustrations appear on one page, their credits are separated by semicolons.

234 Harry & Ruth Crockett; John H. Gerard; courtesy picture; John H. Gerard; John H. Gerard.
235 Karl Maslowski—Photo Researchers; Camera Clix; Arthur A. Allan—Bird Photographs; National Audubon Society; Karl Maslowski—Photo Researchers.
236 Camera Clix; John H. Gerard; Arthur A. Allan—Bird Photographs; courtesy picture; courtesy picture.
238 Gaetano Di Palma
239 Leonard Lee Rue—Annan; John H. Gerard; courtesy picture; John H. Gerard; Karl Maslowski—Photo Researchers.
240 George Systrand—Annan; Bird Photographs; John H. Gerard; Photo Researchers; Bird Photographs; Louis Ruhe & David Roth—National Audubon Society.
241 John Markham—Annan; John H. Gerard; John H. Gerard; N. D. Searcy; John H. Gerard.
242 John H. Gerard; Karl Maslowski—Photo Researchers; S. A. Grimes; Hal H. Harrison—Camera Clix.
243 Gaetano Di Palma
244 Gaetano Di Palma
245 Charles E. Mohr—National Audubon Society
246 Bradley Smith—Photo Researchers
247 FPG; John H. Gerard; H. V. Lacey—Annan.
249 George Bakacs
249a Culver Pictures
250 Rae McIntyre—Annan; Bern Keating—Black Star.
252 Sally Di Martini—American Foundation for the Blind.
253 American Foundation for the Blind, Inc.
255 Donald Johnson and Caspar Henselmann
256 Donald Johnson and Caspar Henselmann
257 Chas. Pfizer & Co., Inc.; Dr. Keith R. Porter—Biological Laboratories, Harvard University.
258 Donald Johnson and Caspar Henselmann
259 Donald Johnson and Caspar Henselmann
260 DPI; Horst Schafer—Photo Trends.
261– George Bakacs
263
265 Myles Adler
267– Donald Johnson and Caspar Henselmann
285
286 Donald Johnson and Caspar Henselmann; Nancy Grossman.
289 Donald Johnson and Caspar Henselmann
290 Donald Johnson and Caspar Henselmann
291 Donald Johnson and Caspar Henselmann
292 Donald Johnson and Caspar Henselmann
294 Donald Johnson and Caspar Henselmann
295 Donald Johnson and Caspar Henselmann
298 George Buctel
300 I. Fat—Black Star
301 Robert Conlan
303 George Buctel
304 Eric Ergenbright—Lenstour; Jacques Jangoux
305 Charles Perry Wiemer; Foto Linares.
307 George Buctel; FPG.
308 E. Boubat—*Réalités;* Joseph Breitenbach.
309 Copyright 1953 by Ludwig Bemelmans, permission of the Viking Press
310a From *Up the Road Slowly* by Irene Hunt, Follett Publishing Co., 1966; Copyright 1970 by Maurice Sendak. Harper & Row, Publishers.
310b Copyright 1962 by Brian Wildsmith—Permission of Franklin Watts, Inc.
311 Ezra Stoller Associates

318 Courtesy of Oriental Institute, University of Chicago; Howard Koslow
319 Bibliothèque Nationale
320 The Pierpont Morgan Library
321 From *A History of Book Illustration* by David Bland, published by Harcourt, Brace & World.
323 Reprinted with permission of The Macmillan Co. from *Ronnie and the Chief's Son* by Elizabeth Coatsworth, illustrated by Stefan Martin, Copyright 1962.
324 From *Gunnar's Daughter* by Sigrid Undset, reprinted with permission of Alfred A. Knopf, Inc.
328 James Caraway
330 Robert Bendick
333 Gerald McConnell
334 Suzanne Szasz
335 Robert Frankenberg
336 Christa Armstrong—Nancy Palmer
337 George Buctel
338 Lowber Tiers—Monkmeyer; Horace Bristol, Jr.—Photo Researchers; Lowber Tiers—Monkmeyer; UPI.
339 George Buctel
340 Elliot Erwitt—Magnum
340a George Buctel
341 Glass Container Manufacturers Institute Inc.
343 Ewing Galloway
344 Robert Frankenberg
345 Edward Vebell; Edward Vebell; George Bakacs.
346 Edward Vebell; George Bakacs.
347 George Bakacs
351 Marvin E. Newman
354 The National Portrait Gallery, London
355 Boys' Clubs of America
356 Boy Scouts of America
358 Don Spaulding
359 Boy Scouts of America; William Hillcourt—Boy Scouts of America; Greater New York Councils, Boy Scouts of America.
361 Culver
362 Bettmann Archive
363 Donald Johnson and Caspar Henselmann
364 Donald Johnson and Caspar Henselmann
367 Caspar Henselmann
368 Donald Johnson and Caspar Henselmann
371 National Gallery of Art, Washington, D.C., Chester Dale Collection
372 Martin Swithinbank—PIP
373 George Buctel
374 Jerry Frank—Alpha
376 Dan Page—Photo Researchers
377 Harrison Forman
379 Ed Drews—Photo Researchers; Scheier—Monkmeyer.
380 Joe Barnell—Shostal
381 David Pratt—Rapho Guillumette; Dan Page—Photo Researchers.
382 Raymond Nania—Photo Researchers; John Moss—Photo Researchers.
385 David Sousa
386 George Sottung
387 George Sottung
390 Marc & Evelyne Bernheim-Rapho
392 Herbert Lanks—A. Devaney; George Bakacs.
394 Scofield—Ewing Galloway; James Sawders—Cushing.
395 Sabine Weiss—Rapho Guillumette
396 Charles Rotkin—PFI
397 Howard Koslow
398 Fred Lyon—Rapho Guillumette
399 Manugian Studio—Cyr Agency; Ben Feder; Camera Press Ltd.—Illustration Research Service.

400 Barnaby's Picture Library—Illustration Research Service
401 Allen J. Herman—Alpha
403 George Hunter—Shostal
404 George Hunter; Bob & Ira Spring.
405 George Buctel
406 Esther Henderson—Rapho Guillumette; Bob & Ira Spring; George Hunter.
406b British Columbia Government Photo
406c Diversified Map Corp.
406d Annan Photo Features
409 Olin Mathieson Chemical Corp.
413 W. T. Mars
415 The Detroit Institute of Arts
417 James Cooper
418 Mercersberg Academy; The James Buchanan Foundation for the Preservation of Wheatland, Lancaster, Pa.
419 Bettmann Archive
420 Bettmann Archive
423 William Froelich
424 Henri Cartier-Bresson—Magnum; Lawrence L. Smith—Photo Researchers.
426 George Buctel
427 Bildarchiv H. Von Irmer; Bildarchiv H. Von Irmer; Carl Frank.
428 Robert Frankenberg
429 Shostal
432 Chase Manhattan Bank; Chase Manhattan Bank; Chase Manhattan Bank.
433 Henry Brennan; Chase Manhattan Bank; J. Alex Langley—Pan American.
436 A. Devaney; A. Devaney; National Association of Home Builders; National Association of Home Builders; Henry Brennan; A. Devaney.
437 National Association of Home Builders; Ray Jacobs' Studio; Henry Brennan.
439 George Buctel
440 Camera Press Ltd.—Pix
441 PIP; Shostal.
442 Peter Schmid—Pix
443 Dennis Stock—Magnum
445 ANI
446 Caterpillar Tractor Co.; Alpha.
447 ANI; Ted Speigel—Rapho Guillumette.
451 Vincent J-R Kehoe
452 United Nations
453 UPI
455 George Buctel
456 Pictorial Parade; United Nations.
457 Stockpile
458 Fujihira—Monkmeyer; Harrison Forman.
461 Robert Conlan
463 George Buctel
464 Kay Honkanen—Ostman; Diafrica (Belgium).
465 Greyhound Corp.
467 USDA Photo
468 Annan; Hugh Spencer; Lynwood M. Chace.
469 Gaetano Di Palma
470 Ross E. Hutchins
471 T. Shaw—Annan
472– Gaetano Di Palma
475
476 George Bakacs
478 Robert Crandall Associates
484 Scala; Shostal.
485 Hirmer; George R. Hann.
486 Hirmer
487 Art Reference Bureau
488 Jane Latta—Photo Researchers
489 Hirmer; Josephine Powell.
490 Hirmer
491 W. T. Mars